Electron Microscopy in Human Medicine

Volume 5

Cardiovascular System,
Lymphoreticular and Hematopoietic System

Electron Microscopy in Human Medicine

Volume 5

Cardiovascular System, Lymphoreticular and Hematopoietic System

Edited by

Jan Vincents Johannessen

Departments of Pathology,
The Norwegian Radium Hospital
and Norsk Hydro's Institute for Cancer Research,
Oslo, Norway
and
Columbia University College of Physicians and Surgeons,
New York

McGRAW-HILL International Book Company

New York · St Louis · San Francisco · Auckland · Bogotá · Guatemala
Hamburg · Johannesburg · Lisbon · London · Madrid · Mexico
Montreal · New Delhi · Panama · Paris · San Juan · São Paulo
Singapore · Sydney · Tokyo · Toronto

This book was set in Times New Roman 327 and Univers

British Library Cataloguing in Publication Data

Electron microscopy in human medicine.
  Vol. 5: Cardiovascular system, lymphoreticular
  and hematopoietic system
    1. Diagnosis, Electron microscopic
    I. Johannessen, Jan Vincents
    616.07'58   RB43.5   80–40859
    ISBN 0–07–032505–7

**Electron Microscopy in Human Medicine
Volume 5**

1234 WC&S 83210

Printed and bound in Great Britain.

Contents of Volume Five

Part One
The Heart

Part Three
Lymphatic Vessels

Part Four
The Thymus

Part Five
Blood and Bone Marrow

The Contributors

Robert M. Bearman received his medical education at the University of North Dakota at Grand Forks and Tufts University in Boston and his pathology training at the Stanford University Medical Center in Stanford, California, and the University of California in San Diego. From 1976 to the present he has been a Fellow in Hematopathology at the City of Hope National Medical Center in Duarte, California.

One of Dr. Bearman's main interests is the study of thymic disorders at the ultrastructural level.

Richard D. Brunning obtained his B.S. degree in medicine at the University of North Dakota, Grand Forks and his M.D. at McGill University in Montreal. After internship at St. Paul Ramsey County Hospital in St. Paul, Minnesota, and Fellowship in pathology at University of Minnesota in Minneapolis, in 1965 he joined the Faculty of the Department of Laboratory Medicine and Pathology at the University of Minnesota College of Medical Sciences where he is Professor and Director of the Hematology Laboratories.

His numerous articles include standard reference works on his special fields of interest: electron microscopy of hematopoietic malignances and cytochemical characterization of acute leukemias.

Victor J. Ferrans, M.D., Ph.D. is a graduate of the Tulane University School of Medicine in New Orleans. He is Chief of the Ultrastructure Section in the Pathology Branch of the National Heart, Lung, and Blood Institute in the National Institutes of Health, Bethesda, Maryland. The world's leading expert on ultrastructural heart pathology, Dr. Ferrans has also contributed standard reference papers on vascular, pulmonary, and metabolic diseases.

Harry L. Ioachim graduated from the Faculty of Medicine, University of Bucharest, Romania. After having served as Assistant Professor in the Department of Pathology at that faculty, he went to the Institut du Cancer, Villejuif, France as Chargé de Recherches; thereafter he went to the Department of Pathology, College of Physicians and Surgeons of Columbia University where he became Assistant, Associate and finally full Professor of Pathology. Since 1968 he has been Staff Attending Pathologist at the Lenox Hill Hospital in New York and is still affiliated to Columbia University as Clinical Professor of Pathology.

Dr. Ioachim, who is also Editor of the well-known *Pathobiology Annual* series, has published more than a hundred papers on experimental and clinical pathology. Most of these are standard reference papers and reflect his special fields of interest: hematopathology, cancer immunology, experimental leukemia, and lymphoma.

Lee V. Leak completed his Ph.D. on experimental cell biology at the Michigan State University before going to Harvard University in Boston as a research fellow. He later became director of the Laboratory of Cellular Biology at the Shiners Burns Hospital in Boston and a faculty member of the Harvard Medical School's Department of Anatomy and is now professor and chairman of the Department of Anatomy and Director of the Ernest Everett Just Laboratory of Cellular Biology, College of Medicine, Howard University, Washington, D.C.

He has contributed important papers and chapters in books on ultrastructure and function of the lymphatic vascular system in health and disease, including works on the ultrastructural basis of lymphatic capillary permeability (with Dr. John F. Burke) and the function of lymphatics in early inflammation.

Gerald David Levine attended the Medical School of the University of Cape Town where he obtained the degree of M.B. Ch.B. Following internship at Groote Schuur Hospital in Cape Town and residency at the same hospital's Department of Pathology, he became Master of Medicine (M.Med. Pathol.) in 1966. After two years as Senior Principal Pathologist at the Frere Hospital in East London, South Africa, he came to Washington University School of Medicine, St. Louis, Missouri, as Fellow in Surgical Pathology. He later went to Stanford University School of Medicine in California where he was Assistant Professor of Pathology and Associate Director of the Division of Surgical Pathology when he left in 1978 to become Director of Surgical Pathology at the Children's Hospital in San Francisco.

Dr. Levine has won several awards and contributed standard works which mainly reflect his special field of interest: the pathology of thymic lesions and tumors of the anterior mediastinum. Dr. Levine, together with Juan Rosai, is the author of the Armed Forces Institute of Pathology fascicle on tumors of the thymus.

Jorge E. Maldonado, M.D., Ph.D. was Professor of Medicine and Director of the Laboratory of Hematologic Electron Microscopy of the Mayo Clinic and Mayo Medical School in Rochester, Minnesota until appointed Director of the Hematology and Oncology Unit, Ministry of Health and Centro Médico Docente La Trinidad in Caracas, Venezuela.

His important work on ultrastructural hematology has established him as one of the world's leading hematologists.

Preface to series

The electron microscope has made its way from the research laboratories into almost all fields of human medicine. In some disciplines, such as nephrology and virology, it has already become an established and indispensable tool. In others, such as oncology, it is rapidly becoming one.

The rapid expansion of electron microscopy in human medicine represents a challenge to most medical institutions. Their electron microscopy laboratories are often run by people without training in human pathology while most pathologists lack ultrastructural experience.

The present series is the first comprehensive attempt to bridge this gap by letting leading experts present the current state of the art in one all-embracing endeavour. This kind of information has previously been scattered as numerous papers in medical and nonmedical journals or books dealing with limited fields only.

Electron Microscopy in Human Medicine should provide a solid foundation for those who are in the process of building up experience in ultrastructural pathology, and also broaden the horizon of those with experience in one narrow area of human electron microscopy. The series, furthermore, should present the clinicians with a dynamic ultrastructural view of the diseases they deal with and help them to decide when to save material for electron microscopical investigation.

Without the enthusiastic and idealistic support of all the authors of this series and the excellent cooperation provided by the publishers and my hospital, the editing of this venture would have been at best troublesome and at worst impossible.

Oslo, 1977. Jan Vincents Johannessen

Preface

Blood and bone marrow presented themselves early as ideal targets for outstanding investigative electron microscopists such as Bessis, Bernhard and Zucker-Franklin. Two of today's leading ultrastructural hematologists, Richard D. Brunning and Jorge E. Maldonado keep up the fine tradition with their chapters on blood and bone marrow in this volume.

Our knowledge of the lymphoreticular system in health and disease has increased tremendously during the last decades. This has resulted in what seems to be a never-ending flow of functional and diagnostic concepts, particularly with regard to tumors, which continue to bewilder those of us who are not occupied full-time with these matters. Dr. Harry Ioachim, a leading cell biologist and pathologist, who has made significant contributions to the pathology of the lymphoreticular system, has provided the chapters on lymph nodes and spleen for this book, while Gerald D. Levine, who ranks with Juan Rosai as the top authority on the pathology of the thymus, has together with his associate Robert M. Bearman contributed the chapter on this organ.

As a result of recent developments in biopsy techniques the disorders of the heart have been extensively studied by electron microscopy. The unchallenged leader in this field, Victor J. Ferrans, has contributed the chapter on the heart, while another top authority, Lee V. Leak, contributed the chapters on the lymphatics and blood vessels.

This volume of the series *Electron Microscopy in Human Medicine* should be of inestimable value to morphologists, biochemists, physiologists, pharmacologists, and clinicians studying these organs in health and disease, and to those studying them in experimental animals and *in vitro*.

Oslo, 1980.   Jan Vincents Johannessen

Acknowledgements to Part One

The editorial assistance of Mrs. Dorothy Veigle and the technical assistance of Mrs. Esther Wilhoite are gratefully acknowledged.

Acknowledgements to Part Two

The author is indebted to the Allergy and Infectious Disease Institute (Al-10639) and the Heart and Lung and Blood Institute (HL-13901) of the National Institutes of Health for support of the personal research cited in this part. The technical assistance of Mr. Willie J. Mayfield and Miss Angelia Vasquez is gratefully acknowledged. Gratitude is expressed to Miss Olivia O'Neal and Miss L. Jenkins for typing the manuscript.

The following micrographs are reproduced with the authorization of the publishers or authors: Figure 13.15 from M. Simionescu *et al.*, *J. Cell Biol.*, **68**, 705, 1976; Figure 13.16 from M. Simionescu *et al.*, *Thrombosis Res.*, suppl. II, **8**, 247, 1976; Figure 13.19(b) from W. S. Beacham, A. Konishi, and C. C. Hunt, *Am. J. Anat.*, **146**, 385, 1976; Figure 13.20(a), (b) from J. A. G. Rhodin, *J. Ultrastruct. Res.*, **18**, 667, 1967; Figure 13.24 from M. W. Brightman and T. S. Reese, *J. Cell Biol.*, **40**, 648, 1969; Figure 13.27 from L. V. Leak, *J. Ultrastruct. Res.*, **35**, 127, 1971; Figures 13.28(a), (b) from M. Simionescu *et al.*, *J. Cell Biol.*, **67**, 863, 1975; Figure 13.30 from M. W. Brightman and T. S. Reese, *J. Cell Biol.*, **40**, 648, 1969; Figure 13.35(e) from W. S. Beacham, A. Konishi, and C. C. Hunt, *Am. J. Anat.*, **146**, 385, 1976; Figure 13.36 from J. A. G. Rhodin, in R. Wells (ed.), *Microcirculation in Clinical Medicine*, Academic Press, London, 1973; Figure 13.37(b) from M. Simionescu *et al.*, *J. Cell Biol.*, **67**, 863, 1975; Figures 14.1 and 14.2(a), (b) from M. Karnovsky, *J. Cell Biol.*, **35**, 213, 1967; Figures 14.3 and 14.4 from N. Simionescu *et al.*, *Thrombosis Res.*, Suppl. II, **8**, 257, 1976; Figure 14.5 from N. Simionescu *et al.*, *J. Cell Biol.*, **64**, 586–607, 1975.

Acknowledgements to Part Three

The author is indebted to the Allergy and Infectious Disease Institute (Al-10639) and the Heart and Lung and Blood Institute (HL-13901) of the National Institutes of Health for support of the personal research cited in this part. The technical assistance of Mr. Willie J. Mayfield is gratefully acknowledged. Gratitude is expressed to Miss Olivia O'Neal and Miss L. Jenkins for typing the manuscript.

The following micrographs are reproduced with the authorization of the publishers and authors: Figures 17.5(b), 17.6(a), 17.9(b), and 17.11 from L. V. Leak, "The Fine Structure and Function of the Lymphatic Vascular System," in H. Meessen (ed.), *Handbuch der Allgemeinen Pathologie*, vol. III, Springer-Verlag, Berlin, 1972; Figures 17.9(a) and 18.6(a), (b) from L. V. Leake, "Pulmonary lymphatic and interstitial fluid," in J. Brain, D. Proctor, and L. Reid (eds.), *Respiratory Defense Mechanisms*, vol. II, Marcel Dekker, New York, 1977; Figure 18.1 from L. V. Leak and J. F. Burke, *J. Cell Biol.*, **36**, 129, 1968; Figure 18.2(a) from L. V. Leak and J. F. Burke, *Am. J. Anat.*, **118**, 785, 1966; Figure 18.2(b) from L. V. Leak, *Microvasc. Res.*, **2**, 361, 1970; Figure 18.4(a), (b) from L. V. Leak, *Fed. Proc.*, **35**, 1863, 1976; Figure 18.7(a), (b) from L. V. Leak, *J. Cell Biol.*, **50**, 300, 1971; Figure 19.1(b), (c) from L. V. Leak, *J. Ultrastruct. Res.*, **39**, 24, 1972; Figure 19.2(a) from L. V. Leak and J. F. Burke, "Early events of tissue injury and the role of the lymphatic system in early inflammation," in B. J, Zweifach *et al.* (eds.), *The Inflammatory Process*, vol. III, Academic Press, New York, 1974; Figure 19.4 from L. V. Leak, *J. Cell Biol.*, **50**, 300, 1971.

Acknowledgements to Part Four

The following micrographs are reproduced with the authorization of the publishers and authors: Figures 22.8, 22.9(b) inset, and 22.13 from G. D. Levine *et al.*, *Am. J. Path.*, **81**, 49, 1975; Figure 22.10(b) from G. D. Levine and K. G. Bensch, *Cancer*, **30**, 500, 1972.

Acknowledgements to Part Five

The following micrographs are reproduced with the authorization of the publishers and authors: Figure 24.1 from A. Polliack and E. Rachmilewitz, *Br. J. Haemat.*, **24**, 319, 1973 (Blackwell Scientific, Oxford); Figure 24.2 from A. Polliack, X. Yataganas, B. Thorell, and E. A. Rachmilewitz, *Br. J. Haemat.*, **26**, 201, 1974 (Blackwell Scientific, Oxford); Figure 24.6 from J. E. Maldonado and H. F. Taswell, *Blood*, **44**, 495, 1974 (Grune and Stratton, New York); Figure 24.7(a) from P. Kerkhoven, H. R. Marti, and G. Hug, *Virchows Arch. A. path.*, Anat. Hist., **363**, 1, 1974 (Springer-Verlag, Heidelberg); Figure 24.7(b) from G. Hug, Kwan Yuen Wong, and B. Lampkin, *Lab. Invest.*, **26**, 11, 1972 (Williams and Wilkins, Baltimore); Figures 24.8 and 24.9 from J. G. White, *Arch. intern. Med.*, **133**, 545, 1974; Figures 24.10 and 24.11 from B. Frisch, S. M. Lewis, D. Sherman, J. M. White, and E. C. Gordon-Smith, *Br. J. Haemat.*, **28**, 109, 1974 (Blackwell Scientific, Oxford); Figures 25.5 (a) and (b) from R. W. McKenna, C. O. Bloomfield, F. Dick, M. Nesbit, and R. D. Brunning, *Blood*, **46**, 481, 1975 (Grune and Stratton, New York); Figure 25.9 from J. E. Maldonado, J. Maigne, and D. Lecoq, *Blood Cells*, **2**, 167, 1976 (Springer-Verlag, Heidelberg);

Figure 25.12 from J. L. Ulloyt and D. Bainton, *Blood*, **44**, 469, 1974 (Grune and Stratton, New York); Figure 25.13 from L. C. Peterson, C. D. Bloomfield, and R. D. Brunning, *Am. J. Med.*, **60**, 209, 1976 (Dun-Donnelly, New York); Figure 25.14(a) from J. E. Maldonado and T. Pintado in M. G. Baldini and S. Ebbe (eds.), *Platelet Production, Function, Transfusion, and Storage*, Grune and Stratton, New York, 1974; Figures 25.19(a) and (b) from L. C. Peterson, C. D. Bloomfield, R. D. Sundberg, K. J. Gajl-Peczalska, and R. D. Brunning, *Am. J. Med.*, **59**, 315, 1975 (Dun-Donnelly, New York); Figures 25.23(a) and (b) from R. W. McKenna, C. D. Bloomfield, and R. D. Brunning, *Cancer*, **36**, 428, 1975; Figures 26.3(a) and (d) from R. D. Brunning and J. Parkin, *Am. J. clin. Path.*, **66**, 10, 1976 (Lippincott, Philadelphia); Figure 26.5(b) from R. D. Brunning and J. Parkin, *Am. J. Path.*, **79**, 565, 1975; Figures 30.1(b) to 30.3 from J. G. White, *Am. J. Path.*, **69**, 225, 1972 (Harper and Row, New York); Figure 30.5 from M. Djaldetti, S. Weiss, and U. Gafter, *Am. J. clin. Path.*, **65**, 942, 1976 (Lippincott, Philadelphia).

Acknowledgements to Part Six

The skillful work of Elena C. Schmidt, Ph.D., Anita Feddick, electron microscopy technician, and Tove Bamberger, secretary, is gratefully acknowledged.

The following micrographs are reproduced with the authorization of the publishers and authors: Figure 31.1 from I. Olah, P. Röhlich, and I. Törö, *Ultrastructure of Lymphoid Organs*, Lippincott, Philadelphia, 1975; Figure 32.5 from M. Bessis, *Living Blood Cells and Their Ultrastructure*, Springer-Verlag, New York, 1973; Figure 32.2 from S. C. Luk, C. Nopajaroonsri, and G. T. Simon, *Lab. Invest.*, **29**, 258, 1973; Figure 32.21 from J. L. Ziegler and I. T. Magrath, "Burkitt's lymphoma," in H. L. Ioachim (ed.), *Pathobiology Annual*, Appleton-Century-Crofts, New York, 1974, p. 130; Figure 32.22: embedded tissues obtained by courtesy of Dr. B. Mackay, Anderson Hospital and Tumor Institute, Houston, Texas; Figure 32.32 from R. C. Braylan, E. S. Jaffe, and C. W. Berard, "Malignant lymphomas: current classification and new observations," in S. C. Sommers (ed.), *Pathology Annual*, Appleton-Century-Crofts, New York, 1975, p. 258.

Acknowledgements to Part Seven

The skillful work of Elena C. Schmidt, Ph.D., Anita Feddick, electron microscopy technician, and Tove Bamberger, secretary, is gratefully acknowledged.

The following illustrations are reproduced with the authorization of the publishers and authors: Figure 33.1 from I. Olah, P. Röhlich, and I. Törö, *Ultrastructure of Lymphoid Organs*, Lippincott, Philadelphia, 1975; Figure 34.9: embedded tissues obtained by courtesy of Dr. B. Mackay, Anderson Hospital and Tumor Institute, Houston, Texas.

Part One

The Heart

Victor J. Ferrans

1. Introduction to Part One

Detailed, systematic studies of ultrastructural aspects of cardiac pathology have been made possible by the advent of open heart surgery and intraoperative biopsies, and by the development of catheter techniques for obtaining endomyocardial biopsies with a high degree of safety. Nevertheless, many gaps remain in our knowledge of myocardial ultrastructural pathology. It is hoped that the account which follows will be regarded as a progress report, rather than a definitive description, and that it will serve as a stimulus for other researchers to continue investigation in this field.

2. Normal Myocardial Ultrastructure

Normal myocardium[31] is composed of the following cells and elements.

1. Cardiac muscle cells, which are connected end-to-end and side-to-side to one another by specialized intercellular junctions.
2. Vascular elements with a particularly rich network of capillaries but also including arterial, venous, and lymphatic vessels.
3. Connective tissue cells, among which are pericytes, fibroblasts, mast cells, primitive mesenchymal cells, and histiocytes.
4. Neural elements.
5. Extracellular elements of connective tissue, including collagen fibrils, elastic fibers, connective tissue microfibrils, and proteoglycans.

The basic design of a cardiac muscle cell is that of an irregularly shaped cylinder measuring from 60 to 100 μm in length and from 10 to nearly 20 μm in diameter. Structural components of the cardiac muscle cell include the sarcolemma, the intercellular junctions, the nucleus, the myofibrils, the mitochondria, the sarcoplasmic reticulum, the transverse tubular system (T-system), ribosomes, cytoskeletal filaments, glycogen particles, Golgi complexes, lysosomes, and residual bodies. The sarcolemma consists of the plasma membrane and the basal lamina (also known as external lamina, glycocalyx, basement membrane); it is composed of a finely fibrillar form of collagen and collagen-associated proteins.[38] These structures are illustrated in Figures 2.1, 2.2, 2.3.

The contractile proteins are arranged into sarcomeres, which constitute the functional units of contraction and are attached end-to-end, thus forming myofibrils. The myofibrils are arranged parallel to the longitudinal axis of the cell and have a characteristic pattern of bands or striations which reflect the organization of the sarcomeres. The following three bands compose the sarcomeres.

1. The A-bands, which contain myosin in the form of "thick" filaments (120–160 Å in diameter).
2. The I-bands, which contain actin in the form of "thin" filaments (50–80 Å in diameter).
3. The Z-bands, which contain α-actinin and other, incompletely characterized, proteins.

The thick and thin filaments interdigitate so that each thick filament is surrounded by six thin filaments, thus providing the basis for the sliding filament mechanism of muscle contraction. The substructure of the Z-bands remains controversial. Nevertheless, it is clear that they have a tetragonal substructure, apparently because of the presence of periodic filamentous projections that connect the thin filaments in the

4

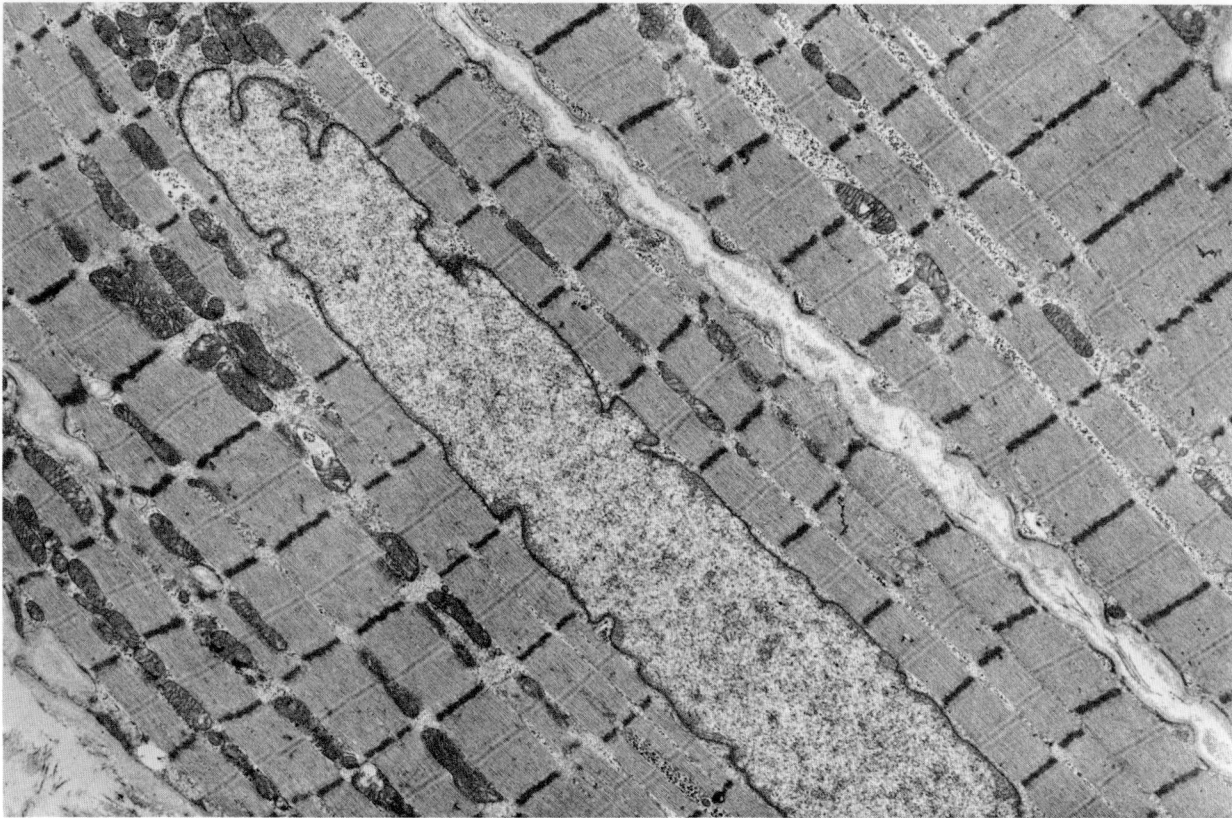

Figure 2.1. Normal myocardium.
Longitudinal section through normal sized human cardiac muscle cell, showing nucleus, myofibrils, and mitochondria. ($\times$ 11,000)

areas of Z-bands.[67] The Z-bands of adjacent myofibrils normally are aligned in lateral registration, and this registration is maintained by transversely oriented cytoskeletal filaments that interconnect the Z-bands.[58] In certain compact cardiac muscle cells the individual myofibrils are not clearly evident because contractile elements tend to form a continuum rather than to be separated into discrete bundles.

The intercellular junctions[100] have the following structural components.

1. Undifferentiated regions in which the apposed membranes bear no specialized structures and are separated by a space of 200 Å.
2. Desmosomes, which resemble those of other cell types and reinforce intercellular adhesion.
3. Myofibrillar insertion sites, in which the terminal set of thin filaments of a given myofibril inserts into a mass of material that resembles Z-band material and is attached to the inner or cytoplasmic aspect of the plasma membrane.
4. Nexuses, which are points of low electrical resistance for transmission of the activating impulse from one cell to another and are characterized by a typical narrowing of the space between the apposed plasma membranes to 30–40 Å.

The mitochondria are ovoid or elongated and appear structurally similar to those of

5

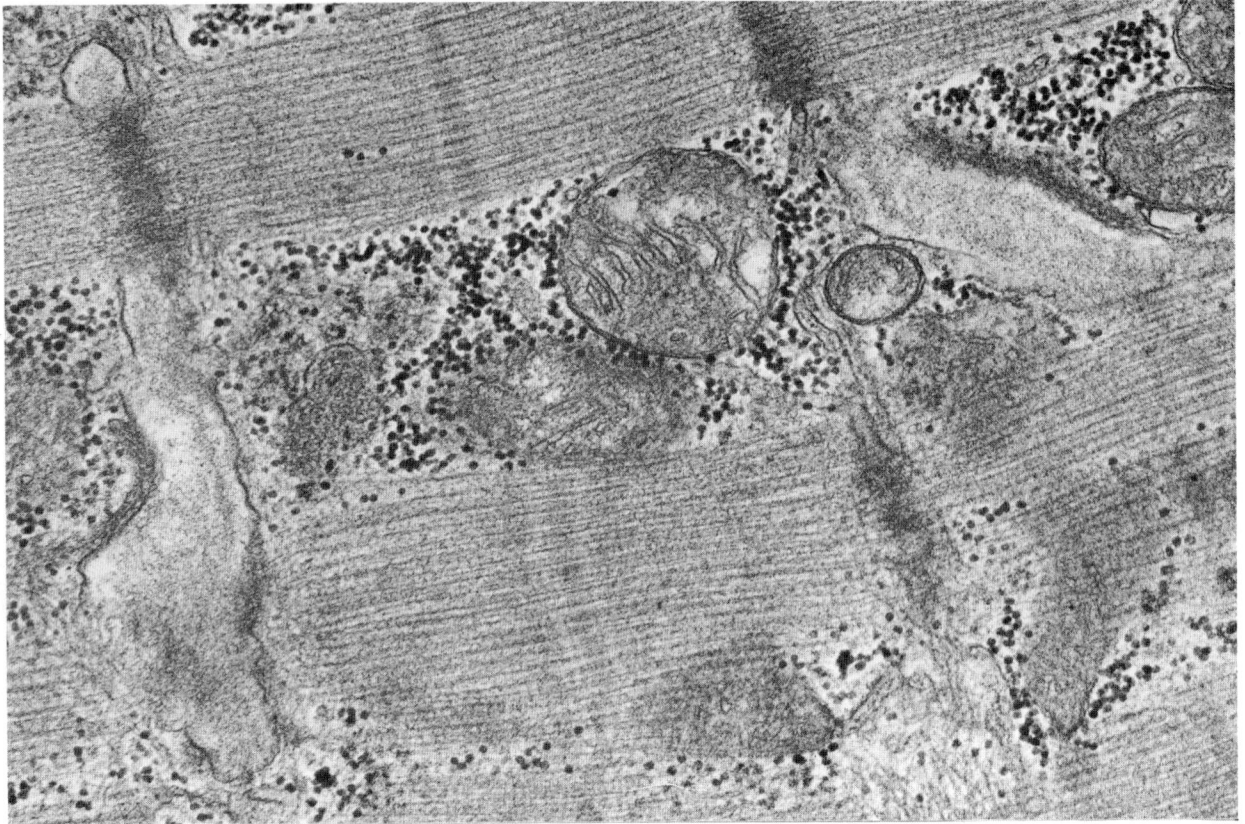

Figure 2.2. Sarcoplasmic reticulum and T-tubules.
Two T-tubules, lined by basal lamina, course transversely across the cytoplasm of human cardiac muscle cell. Elements of junctional SR (lower left and upper right) are closely apposed to the T-tubules. The dark particles are glycogen. Cytoskeletal filaments course transversely at the levels of the Z-bands (upper left and lower right). (× 49,000)

other tissues. The cristae are closely packed; dense granules, considered to be binding sites for divalent cations, are prominent in the mitochondrial matrix. The mitochondria are scattered between the myofibrils, and usually form clusters in the myofibril-free areas at the nuclear poles, where the Golgi complexes, lysosomes, residual bodies (lipofuscin granules), and glycogen particles also are located.

The nucleus is composed of the inner and the outer nuclear membranes, the nuclear chromatin, and the nucleolus. Nuclear pore complexes are present throughout the nuclear membranes and provide direct routes for nucleocytoplasmic exchanges. The shape of the nucleus varies according to the stage of contraction or relaxation of the cell. The nuclear membranes become partially folded during contraction and smooth during relaxation.[16] They are connected directly to the tubules of the sarcoplasmic reticulum; in addition, cytoskeletal filaments extend from the nuclear membranes to adjacent Z-bands, and nuclei also are surrounded by a basketlike array of cytoplasmic microtubules. Thus, these structures maintain the nuclei in their position.[58]

T-tubules are cylindrical invaginations of the plasma membrane. They course at the levels of the Z-bands, extending deeply into the cell and forming specialized

6

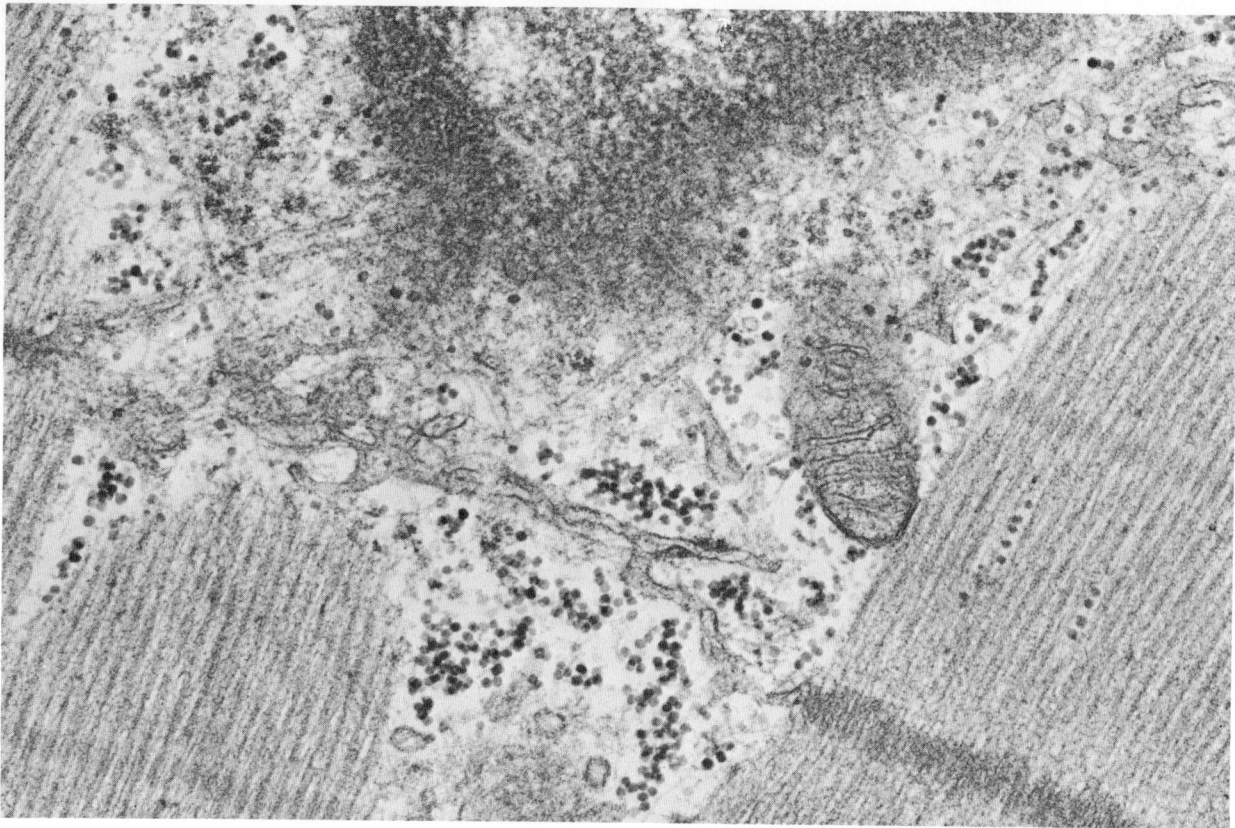

Figure 2.3. Microtubules and cytoskeletal filaments.
End of nucleus of human cardiac muscle cell surrounded by numerous microtubules, a network of tubules of free SR, and scattered cytoskeletal filaments. (× 69,000)

structures (dyads and triads) with the junctional sarcoplasmic reticulum. Thus, they participate in the rapid activation of myofibrils located away from the cell surfaces.

The sarcoplasmic reticulum (SR) consists of a network of intracellular tubules that are not open to the extracellular space.[134] In addition to associated coated and uncoated vesicles, the SR has at least three distinct components: free SR, junctional SR, and extended junctional SR. The SR forms a network of branching and anastomosing tubules that have a clear content and surround the myofibrils. The junctional SR is composed of saccular dilatations (terminal cisternae) that are connected to the free SR, have a dense content (junctional granules), and are closely approximated to the sarcolemma either at the free surface of the cell or at the level of the T-tubules.

The extended junctional SR is composed of structures that, although similar to those of junctional SR, are not closely approximated to the sarcolemma. Extended junctional SR is relatively abundant in atrial myocardium, in which T-tubules are absent in some cells and poorly developed in others (many species differences exist in this regard). T-tubules are absent from cells in the sinoatrial node, the atrioventricular node and the bundle of His and its ramifications. Atrial muscle cells contain specific granules of unknown function (atrial granules); these are not present in ventricular myocardium or specialized conducting tissues.[31]

7

3. Myocardial Hypertrophy

Myocardial hypertrophy is defined as an increase in the mass of the heart muscle beyond the limits of normal for age, sex, and body weight. Up to a certain limit, known as the critical heart weight (500 g), hypertrophy is thought to be mediated by an increase in the size of the individual cardiac muscle cells. Evidence presented by Linzbach[97] and more recently by Astorri *et al.*[8] suggests that an increase in cardiac mass beyond the critical heart weight is associated with the formation of additional cardiac muscle cells. How new cardiac muscle cells form under these circumstances is not known, for which reason this concept remains controversial. It is known that the rate of mitosis of cardiac muscle cells falls to negligible levels within a short period of time after birth,[144] and evidence of new cell division in greatly hypertrophied hearts has not been observed.

Cardiac hypertrophy can be classified as being concentric (pressure overload, characterized by thick chamber walls and normal or smaller than normal chamber volumes) or eccentric (volume overload, characterized by large chamber volumes and by walls of variable thickness). Hypertrophy also can be classified as being symmetric or asymmetric. In most types of heart disease the degree of hypertrophy is similar in the various regions of a given cardiac chamber (symmetric hypertrophy). The exception to this is hypertrophic cardiomyopathy,[123] in which the ventricular septum becomes thickened to a greater extent than the posterolateral free wall of the left ventricle at the level of the inferior border of the posterior leaflet of the mitral valve. In hypertrophic cardiomyopathy, the ratio of the thickness of ventricular septum and left ventricular posterolateral free wall usually exceeds 1·3, whereas in normal individuals and in those with other types of cardiac hypertrophy it is usually 1·0.

Cardiac hypertrophy also can be regarded as existing in the following three stages.[111]

1. Developing hypertrophy.
2. Stable hyperfunction (compensated hypertrophy).
3. Cellular exhaustion in which cardiac function deteriorates and degenerative changes become prominent in the muscle cells.

The morphometric changes associated with the various types and stages of hypertrophy have not been fully elucidated yet. It is clear that most of the increment in muscle mass that occurs in hypertrophy is mediated through increases in mitochondrial and myofibrillar components. However, the quantitative relations between these two components can vary considerably. In the pressure overload type of hypertrophy, the fractional volume of mitochondria increases at first, then normalizes, and in the late stages of hypertrophy it decreases to well below normal.[4, 14, 68, 73, 116, 133, 143] Very pronounced increases in the fractional volume of mitochondria occur in the hypertrophy that is associated with deficiency of copper,[69] iron,[69] or thiamine.[19] Other quantitative studies have shown that the dimensions of the sarcomeres and myofilaments do not differ in normal and in hypertrophied hearts.[121] A detailed review of morphometric changes in cardiac hypertrophy is beyond the scope of this chapter, and the reader is referred to the accounts of Page and collaborators[116, 133] for additional information on cardiac morphometry. For a number of technical reasons, including the stringent requirements for fixation of high quality and for the avoidance of contraction band artifacts (which occur unavoidably in muscle tissues that are cut and allowed to retract before fixation), morphometric studies have been largely limited to tissues fixed by perfusion. This, of course, excludes human material obtained by biopsy.

3.1. Hypertrophy without degeneration

Hypertrophied, nondegenerated cardiac muscle cells (Figure 3.1) may be qualitatively normal in every respect except for their size, which may be increased to over 50 μm in transverse diameter.[46, 108] Considerable variation in cell diameter can exist in myocardium of any given patient, even among immediately adjacent muscle cells. Variations in the size of mitochondria also occur: giant mitochondria (Figure 3.2) can be encountered, especially in hypertrophied atrial muscle;[138] in contrast, abnormally small mitochondria, which often give the appearance of being budding forms, are very common in patients with cardiac failure, particularly in those with congestive cardiomyopathies.[54] Other alterations in myocardial hypertrophy include enlargement of the nuclei and Golgi complexes. The nuclear membranes show marked increases in the irregularity of their contours. Intranuclear tubules[51] may develop as the most extreme form of irregularity of contour of the nuclear surfaces (Figure 3.3). Ribosomes, both free and membrane-bound (rough surfaced endoplasmic reticulum), are increased in number; the latter structures may form large whorls or stacks of cisterns of reticulum in the vicinity of the nuclear pores. T-tubules become dilated and tortuous. The degree of tortuosity of the membranes in intercellular junctions also increases markedly. Cell shapes become more irregular and "multiple intercalated discs" are found more frequently than in normal hearts.[92] Multiple intercalated discs is a term used to describe the intercellular junctions associated with interlocking segments of the cytoplasm of two adjacent cardiac muscle cells that are connected side-to-side.[92, 103] These interlocking segments reinforce the structural connections between adjacent layers of muscle cells and tend to prevent "slippage" of such layers.

Other changes occur that are indicative of formation of new sarcomeres in hypertrophied muscle cells. Currently available evidence suggests that the contractile proteins are synthesized by the ribosomes, after which they become aggregated into filaments and assembled into sarcomeres. Such aggregation and assembly appear to occur very rapidly in normal hearts, and little or no evidence of this process is usually evident on morphologic study. It has been suggested that accumulations of Z-band material play a critical role in the process of sarcomerogenesis by serving as loci for the aggregation of other contractile proteins.[94] For this reason, considerable attention has been given to the focal accumulations of Z-band-like material that occur in hypertrophied cardiac muscle cells.[13, 94, 108] These accumulations (Figures 3.4, 3.5,

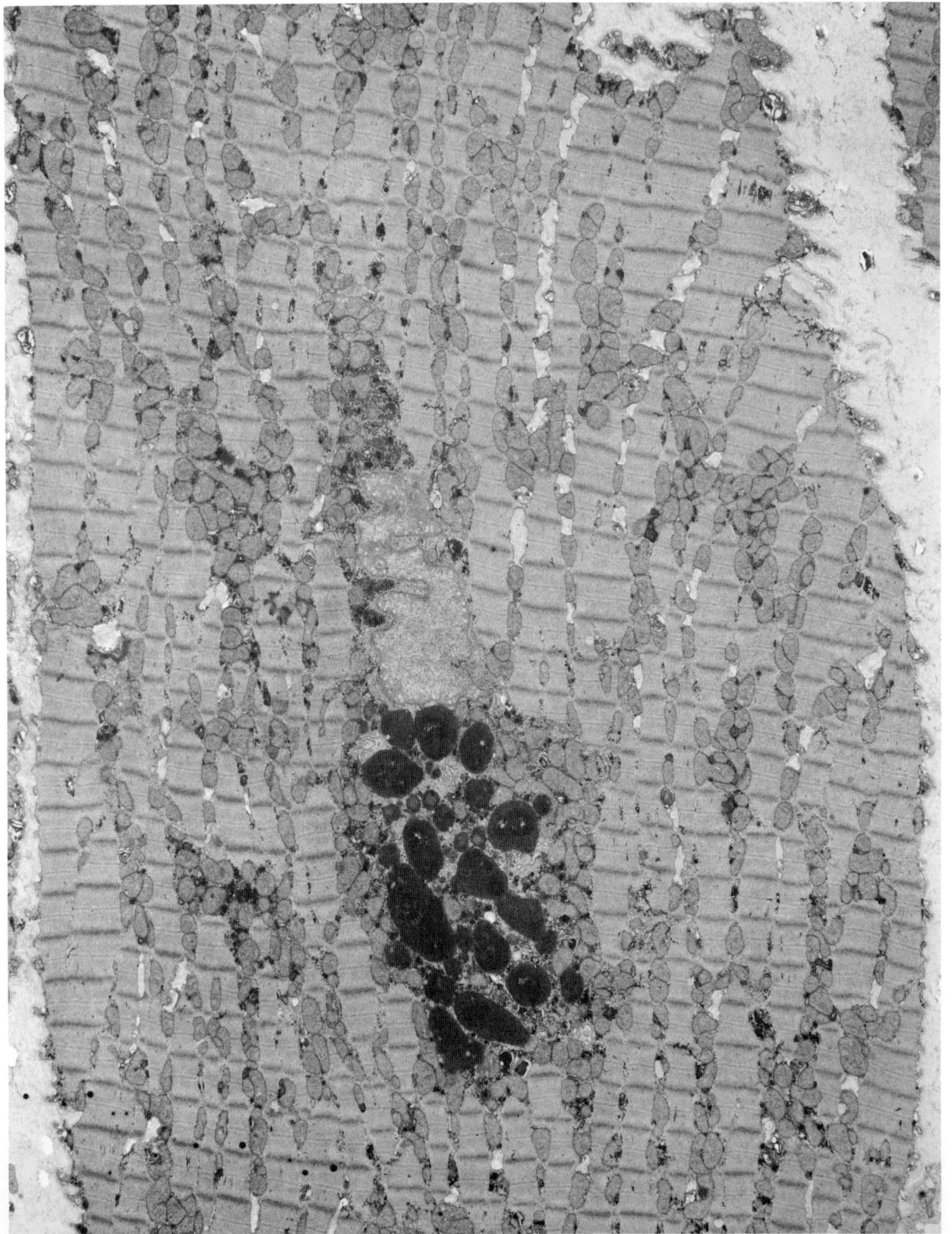

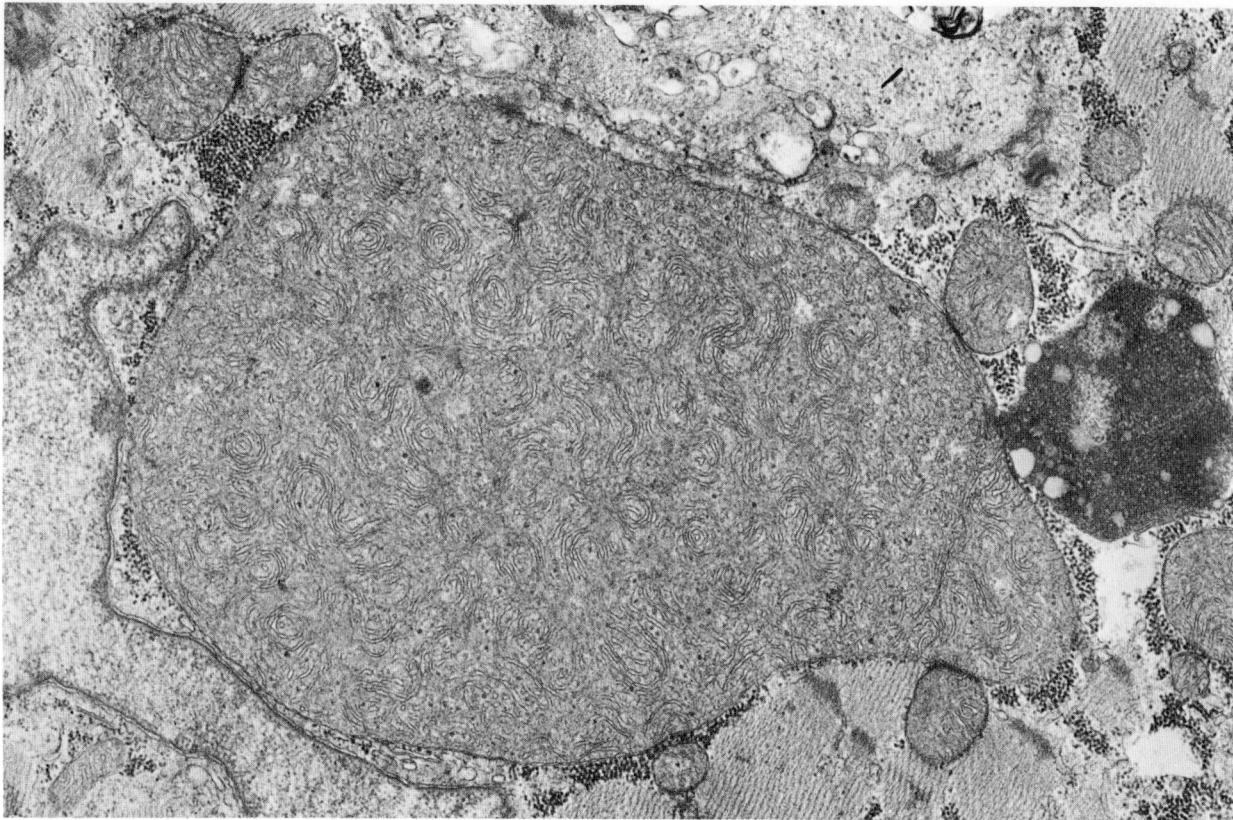

Figure 3.2. Giant mitochondrion.
Giant mitochondrion, adjacent to small or normal sized mitochondria, is present in left atrial muscle cell of patient with mitral valvular disease. ($\times$ 19,000)

3.6) are composed of electron-dense material associated with fine filaments. In many instances, they show no ordered substructure, while in others they have a highly organized tetragonal lattice (Figure 3.6). The reasons for these differences in substructure are not clear. Nevertheless, it should be pointed out that masses of Z-band material with the organized substructure just described are seen only very rarely in normal hearts. They do not occur in the rapidly growing hearts of newborn animals (at the time when cardiac muscle mass is increasing most rapidly) unless abnormal hemodynamic burdens (i.e., aortic or pulmonary arterial constriction) are imposed on these hearts.[13] Therefore, it is not certain that they represent a mechanism for normal or accelerated sarcomerogenesis. In fact, there is evidence that such masses are indicative, at least in some instances, of arrested sarcomerogenesis.[108] This would account for the finding of these masses in Purkinje fibers and in ventricular myocardium of old but apparently healthy cats. In our experience, masses of highly organized Z-band

Figure 3.1. Myocardial hypertrophy without degeneration.
Enlarged cardiac muscle cell from crista supraventricularis of patient with crista hypertrophy and obstruction to right ventricular outflow. The cell appears qualitatively normal. Note the cluster of lipofuscin granules at the lower nuclear pole. ($\times$ 6,500)

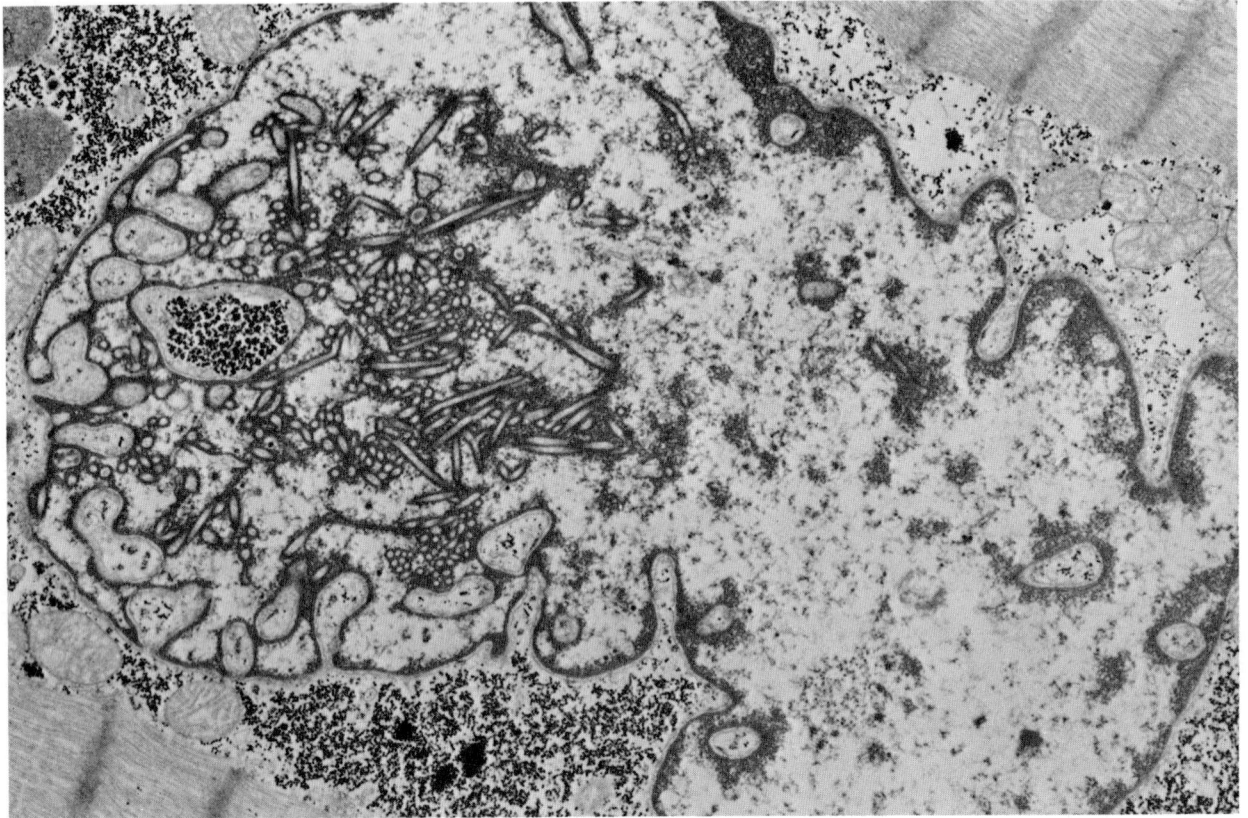

Figure 3.3. Nuclear tubules.
Irregular invaginations of the nuclear membranes and clusters of intranuclear tubules are found in severely hypertrophied muscle cell. (× 15,000)

material are most prevalent in the large, dilated left atria of patients with mitral valvular disease, where they occur in association with a variety of degenerative changes.[138] Studies of skeletal muscle[108] also suggest that many of the large masses of highly organized Z-band material are degenerative in origin.

3.2. Hypertrophy with degeneration

A number of chronic degenerative changes of uncertain cause may develop in cardiac muscle cells after cardiac hypertrophy has existed for a long period of time.[104, 108] These changes include interstitial fibrosis, cellular atrophy (Figure 3.7), cellular and myofibrillar disorganization, Z-band abnormalities, myofibrillar lysis (Figures 3.8, 3.9, 3.10), myelin figures (Figure 3.11), proliferation of SR and formation of

12

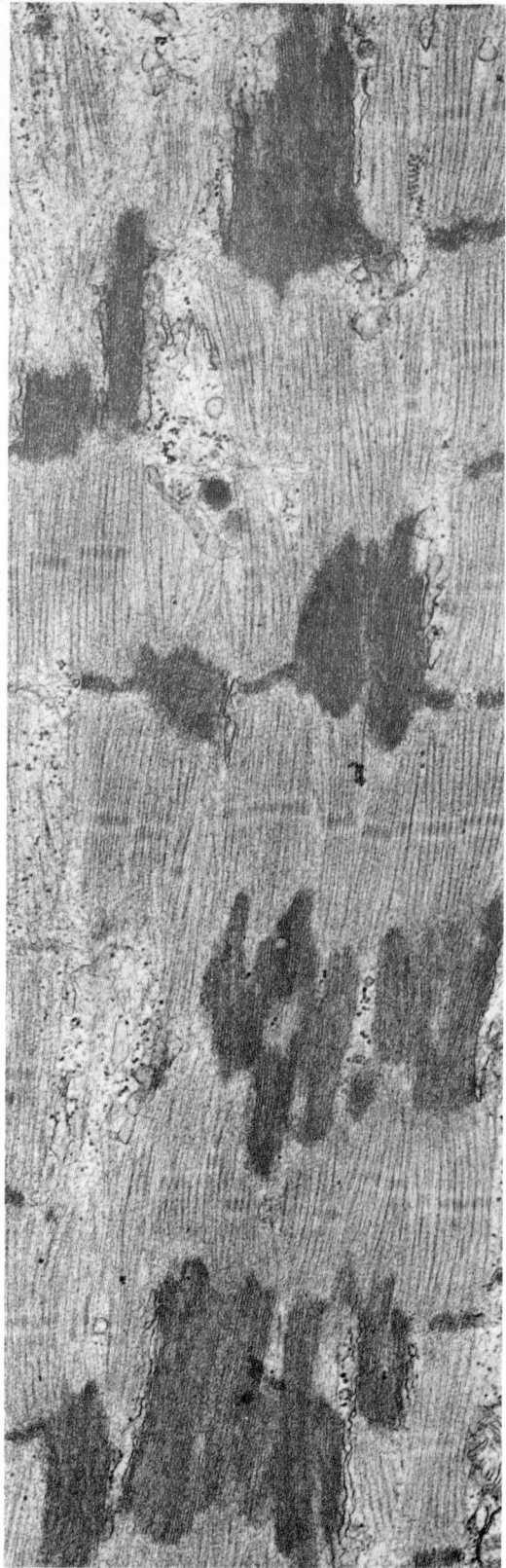

Figure 3.4. Widening of Z-bands.
Greatly widened Z-bands occur in left atrial muscle cell of patient with mitral valvular disease. ($\times$ 25,000)

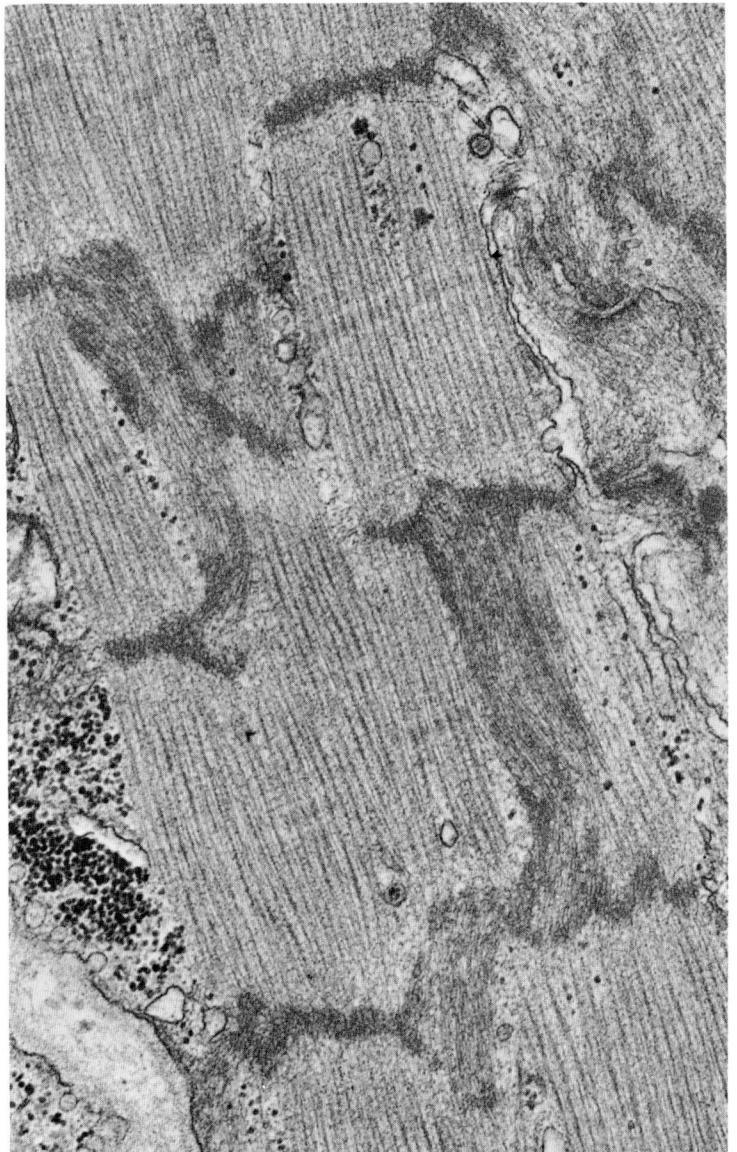

Figure 3.5. Z-band material and sarcomerogenesis.
Expansions of Z-band material are suggestive of various stages in the formation of new sarcomeres in left atrial muscle cell of patient with mitral valvular disease. (× 36,500)

aggregates of SR tubules (Figures 3.12, 3.13, 3.14), lipid accumulation, spherical microparticles associated with the plasma membranes (Figure 3.15), intramitochondrial (Figure 3.16) and intranuclear (Figure 3.17) glycogen, thickened basal laminae (Figure 3.18), intracytoplasmic junctions (Figure 3.19), and partial or complete dissociation of intercellular junctions (Figures 3.18, 3.19). The cardiac muscle cells in areas of interstitial fibrosis become separated from one another by accumulations of collagen fibrils, microfibrils, small elastic fibers, and connective tissue ground

14

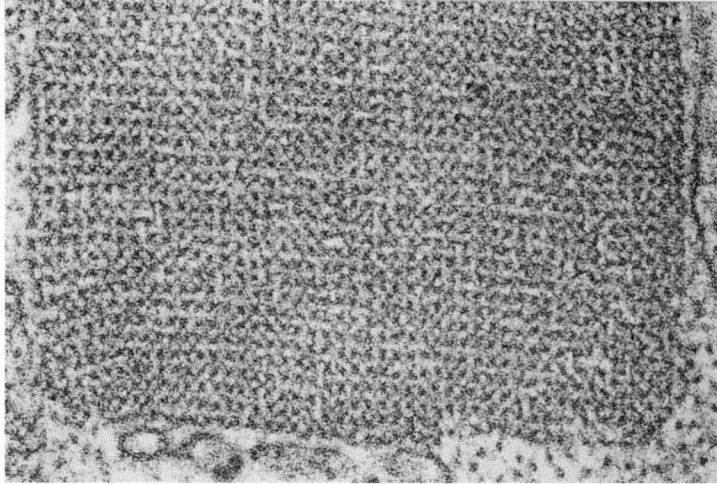

Figure 3.6. Substructure of Z-band material.
Transverse section through mass of Z-band material shows complex tetragonal lattice. (× 123,000)

substance (Figure 3.7). The deposition of collagen alters considerably the structure of the normal connective tissue framework that surrounds the muscle cells and can be responsible, at least in part, for the decreased myocardial compliance that can occur in hypertrophy. The biochemical types of these collagen deposits and their cellular sources remain to be investigated.

Loss of contractile elements may be the most important degenerative change occurring in hypertrophied cardiac muscle cells. This can lead either to atrophic cells recognized by transverse diameters less than 5 μm, or to large cells that appear pale-staining and empty by light microscopy. The loss of contractile elements (Figures 3.8, 3.9, 3.10) involves lysis of both thin and thick filaments; however, the latter often seem to be lost preferentially, leaving disorganized tangles of thin filaments still attached to Z-bands. Increased numbers of 100 Å filaments and masses of Z-band material often are associated with these changes. The Z-band material may be either highly organized or in the form of streaming, elongated clumps with no discernible substructure. Cells with loss of contractile elements are distinguishable from necrotic cells because they show preservation of the structure of the nucleus, mitochondria, and SR, components which are disrupted in cellular necrosis.

Other degenerated cardiac muscle cells, which also appear pale-staining by light microscopy because of their loss of myofibrils, are filled with a network of tubules of SR which have proliferated and occupied most of the sarcoplasm (Figure 3.12). This proliferation can be associated with the formation of aggregates of tubules of free SR.[104] Two types of these aggregates of tubules have been recognized according to whether or not they form orderly arrays associated with Z-band material. Junctional and extended junctional SR also can proliferate and form complex aggregates, particularly in hypertrophied atria (Figures 3.13 and 3.14). Again, two different types of these aggregates are distinguishable according to the size of their components and to their content of junctional granules arranged into a central dense line.[137]

15

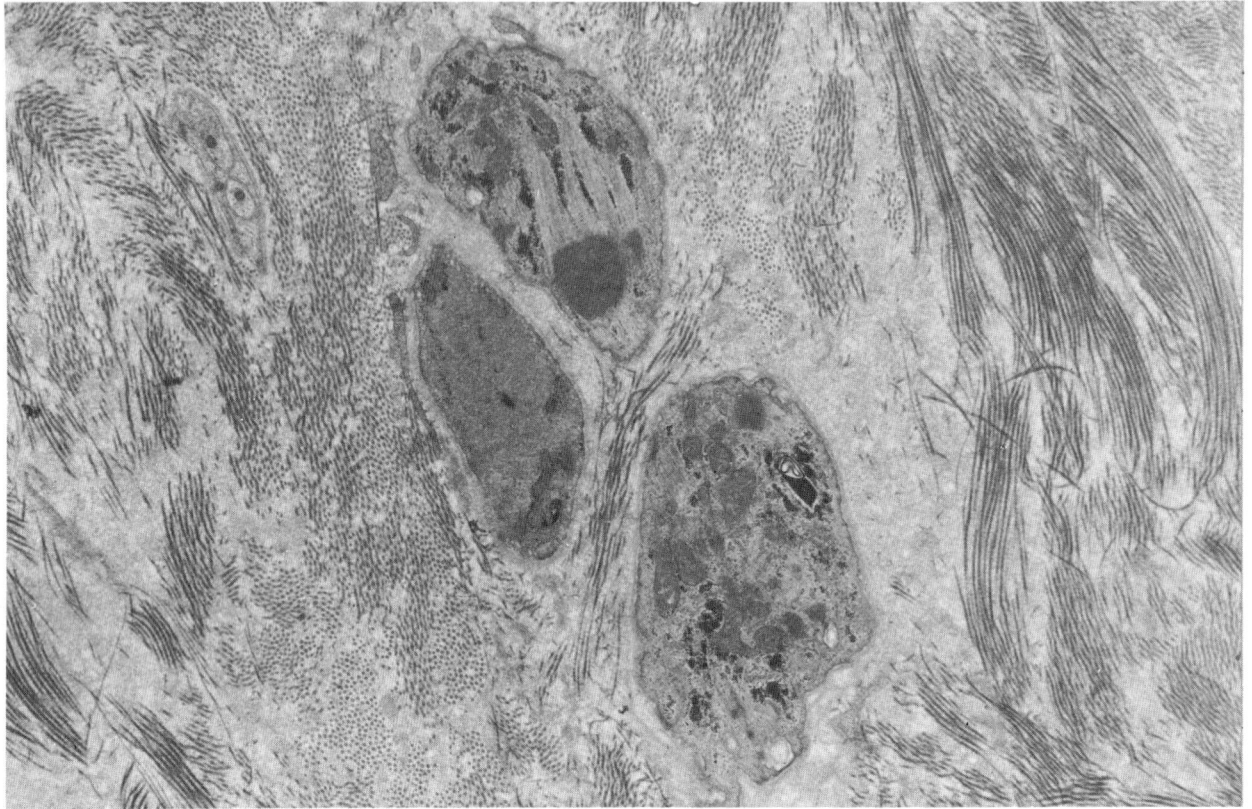

Figure 3.7. Myocardial fibrosis in hypertrophy.
Small, atrophic, isolated muscle cells, one of which contains a mass of Z-band material, surrounded by large numbers of collagen fibrils and by amorphous material in greatly hypertrophied crista supraventricularis of patient with double outlet right ventricle and infundibular pulmonic stenosis. ($\times$ 10,500)

The cytoplasm in certain degenerated cardiac muscle cells can be largely occupied by large numbers of mitochondria, glycogen particles, residual bodies (Figure 3.11), or lipid droplets. A small ($<$ 1 per cent) fraction of the mitochondrial population in hypertrophied cells may contain glycogen deposits (Figure 3.16). This glycogen appears morphologically different from glycogen in the main cytoplasmic compartment.[22, 79, 105] Less frequently, deposits of intranuclear glycogen also occur in hypertrophied cardiac muscle cells (Figure 3.17); however, the presence of such deposits does not correlate with other findings of myocardial degeneration.[53]

Dissociation of cardiac muscle cells (Figure 3.15), with partial or complete loss of specialized intercellular contacts, is a typical feature of severe myocardial degeneration.[80, 108] Cells showing this change have fingerlike projections (Figure 3.18) that extend into the interstitial connective tissue from the ends of the cells (i.e., from the regions where intercellular junctions were previously present). Intracytoplasmic junctions, i.e., junctions formed (Figure 3.19) by the specialized apposition of two areas of the plasma membrane of the same cell (rather than by the apposition of the plasma membranes of two different cells) often are present in the fingerlike projections at the

16

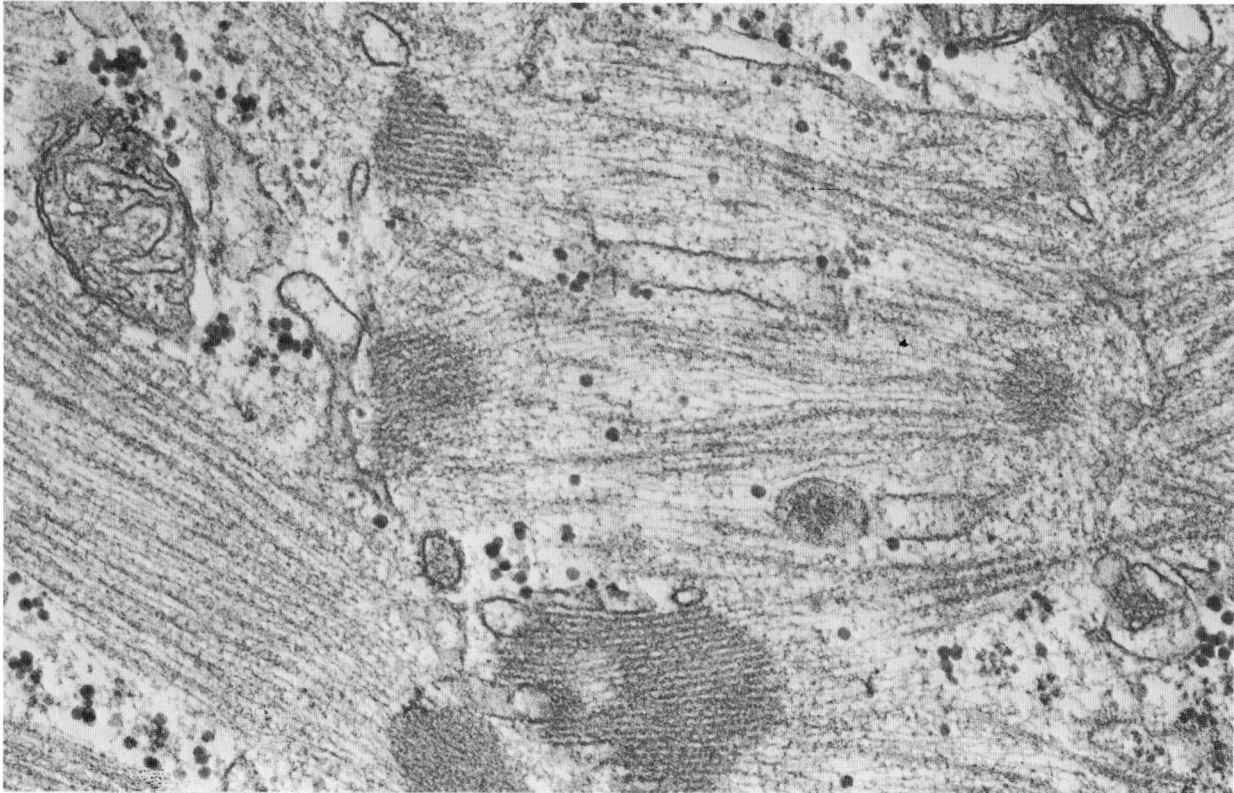

Figure 3.8. Myofibrillar lysis in late hypertrophy.
Hypertrophied, degenerated cardiac muscle cell showing accumulations of Z-band material associated with marked decrease in number of myosin filaments. (× 65,000)

end of muscle cells terminating in fibrous tissue. This suggests[23] that such junctions are formed as the result of rearrangement of preexisting junctional components that previously had been parts of intercellular junctions; however, the possibility of *de novo* synthesis of abnormal junctions cannot be excluded.

Also present in areas of fibrosis and cellular dissociation are spherical microparticles that are composed of central dense cores surrounded by single trilaminar membranes (Figure 3.15). These microparticles usually range from 300 to 1,000 Å in diameter (average 500 Å) and are located either between the plasma membranes and the basal lamina or external to the basal lamina. These particles appear to be formed from the plasma membranes by a process of budding. This process mediates the shedding of certain areas of plasma membranes, particularly those of junctions, in locations where the surfaces of cardiac muscle cells are remodeled. Evidence has been presented to show that this process also occurs in a variety of tissues other than heart, and that spherical microparticles can be phagocytosed by the cardiac muscle cells, giving rise to structures that resemble multivesicular bodies.[62]

The degenerative alterations just described are not specific for any one given type of heart disease. They occur in chronic mitral[138] and aortic[107] valvular disease,

17

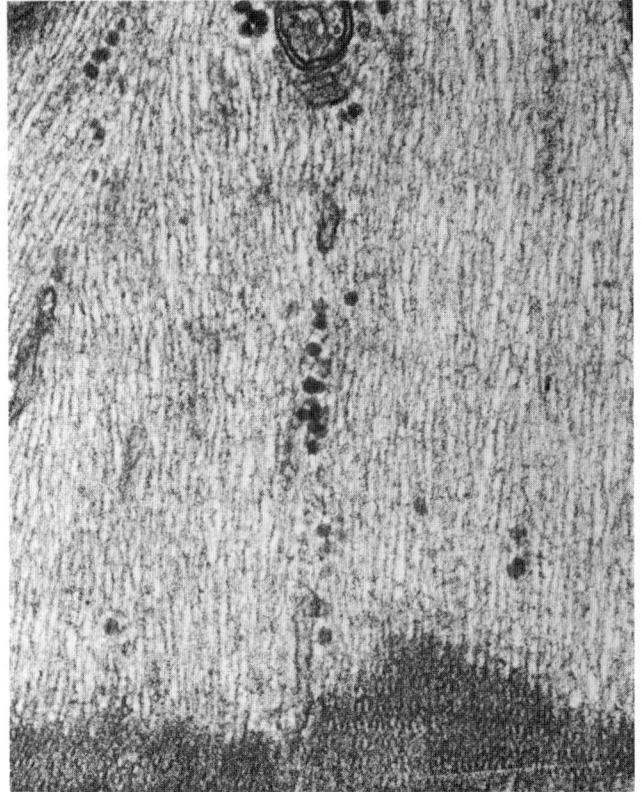

Figure 3.9. Loss of myosin filaments.
Altered myofibril in hypertrophied, degenerated cardiac muscle cell composed of mass of Z-band material (bottom) and actin filaments (coursing vertically); the latter are not associated with myosin filaments. ($\times$ 75,000)

congestive[54, 90, 91] and hypertrophic[54, 80, 108] cardiomyopathy, and several different congenital malformations.[80, 81] Because they show a clear relationship to the duration and severity of the heart disease, the evaluation of these changes constitutes a most important aspect of the ultrastructural pathology of the heart.

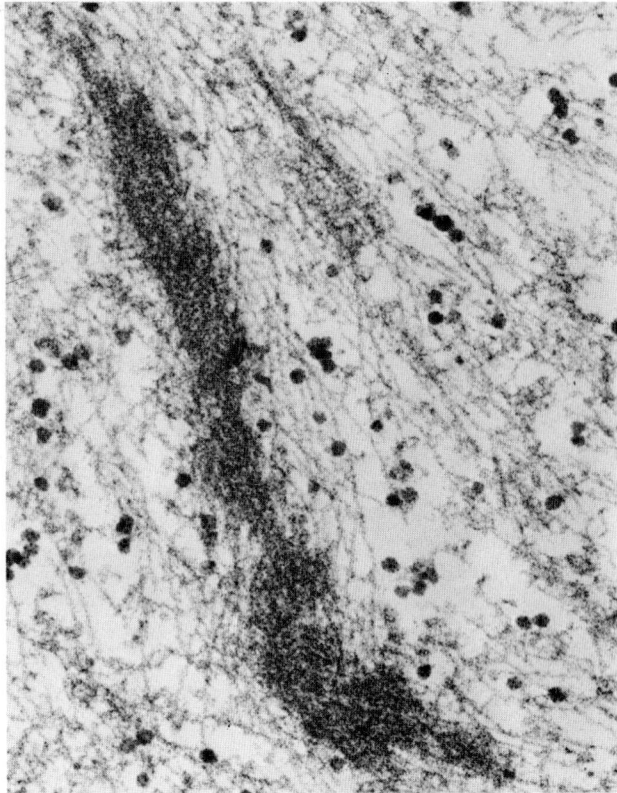

Figure 3.10. Late stage of myofibrillar lysis.
Disorganized, tangled actin filaments associated with mass of
Z-band material with no discernible substructure. (× 90,000)

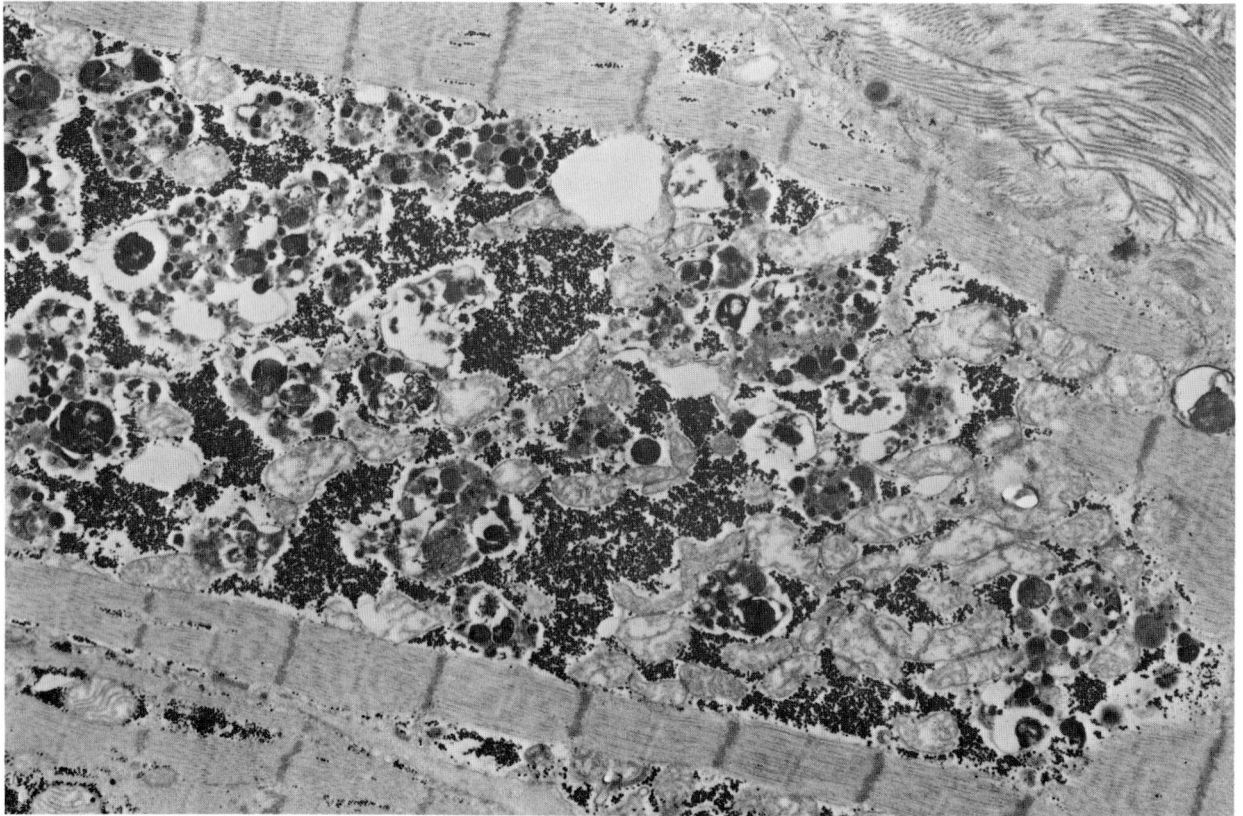

Figure 3.11. Glycogen and residual bodies in degenerated cardiac muscle cell.
Cell in ventricular septum of patient with fibrous ring type of subaortic stenosis and asymmetric septal hypertrophy contains large amounts of glycogen and numerous pleomorphic, electron-dense residual bodies. (× 12,000)

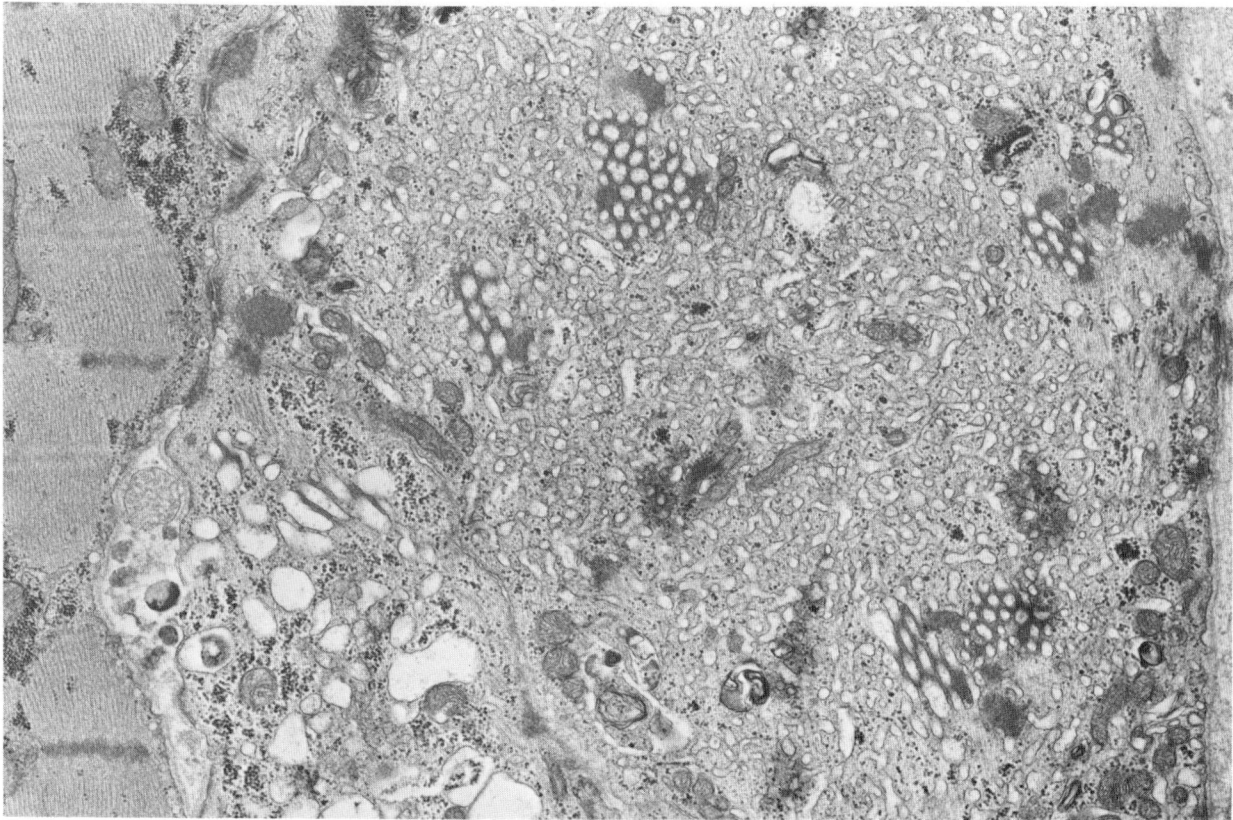

Figure 3.12. SR proliferation and aggregates of SR tubules.
Left atrial muscle cell of patient with mitral valvular disease has lost most of its myofibrils and is filled with tubules of SR. Some of the latter form aggregates associated with Z-band material. (× 18,000)

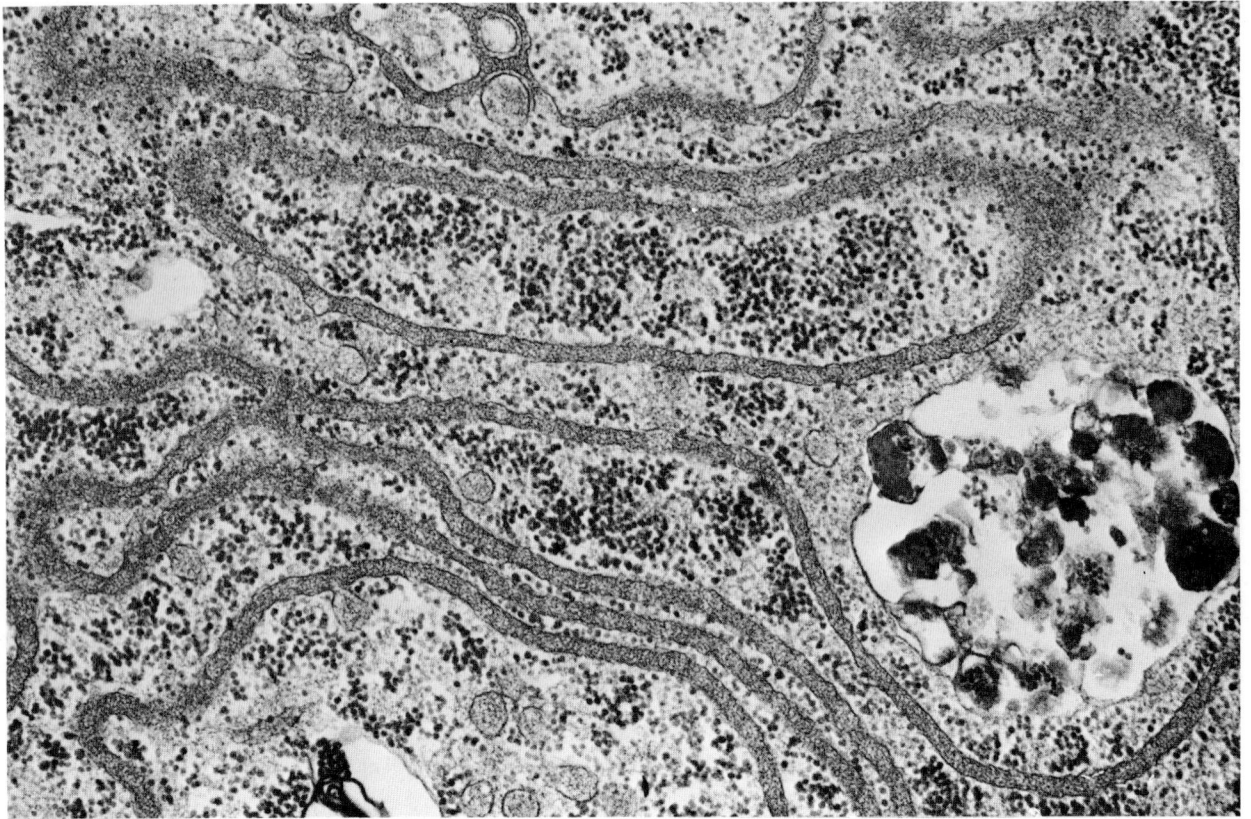

Figure 3.13. Proliferation of type A extended junctional SR.
Stack of cisternae and associated vesicles of type A extended junctional SR (note the finely granular, electron-dense content) in left atrial muscle cell of patient with mitral valvular disease. ($\times$ 44,500)

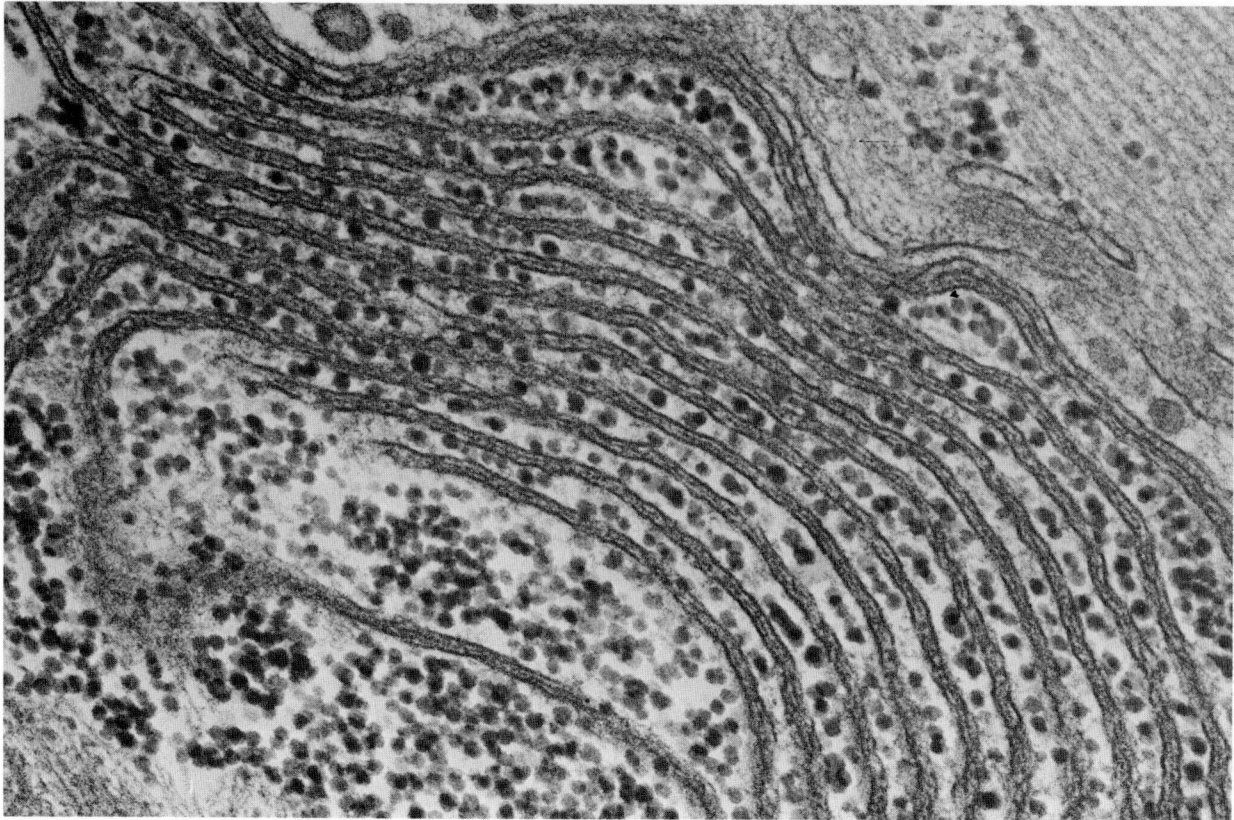

Figure 3.14. Proliferation of type B extended junctional SR.
Parallel array of cisternae of type B extended junctional SR. These cisternae are much smaller than those shown in Figure 3.13, and they are characterized by an electron-dense central line. (×96,000)

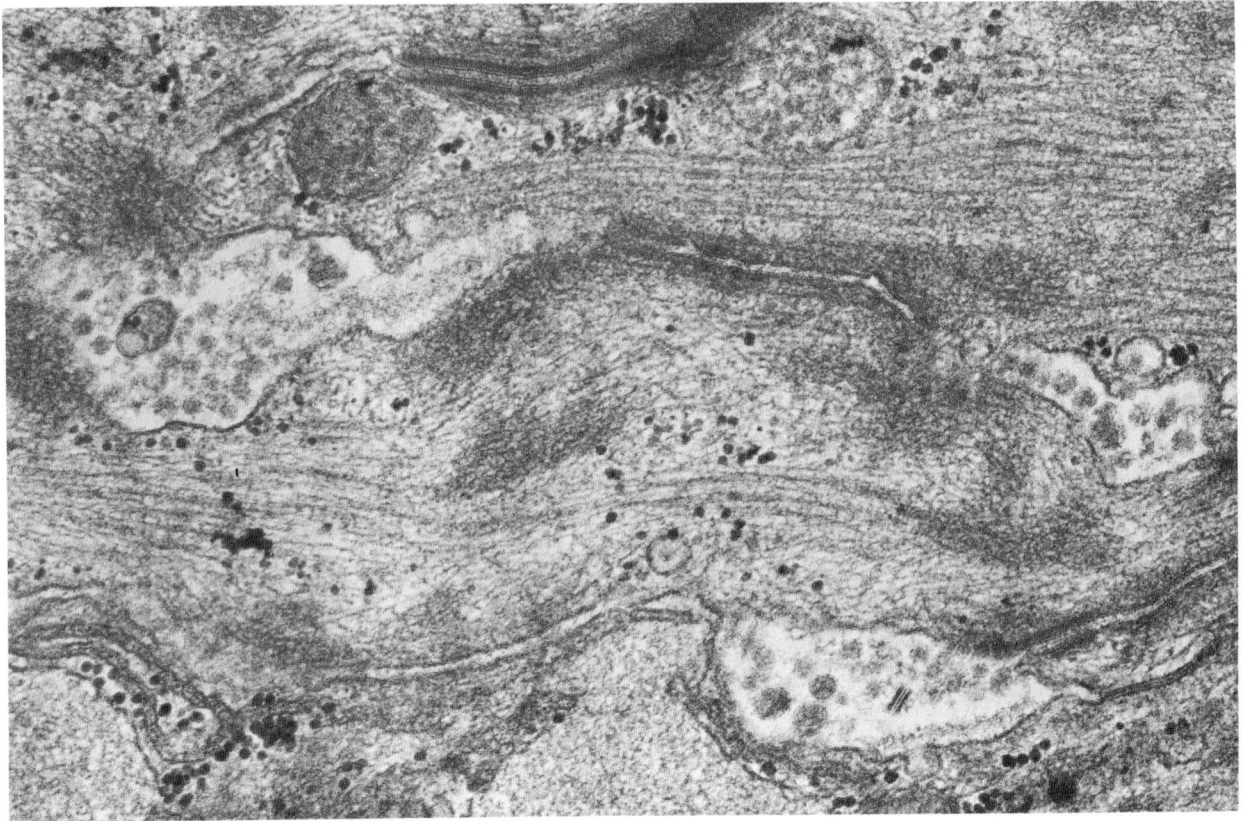

Figure 3.15. Dissociation of intercellular junction.
Junction between two hypertrophied muscle cells shows several areas of widening of the space between the apposed plasma membranes. This space contains clusters of spherical microparticles and a remnant of a nexus (lower right). (×63,500)

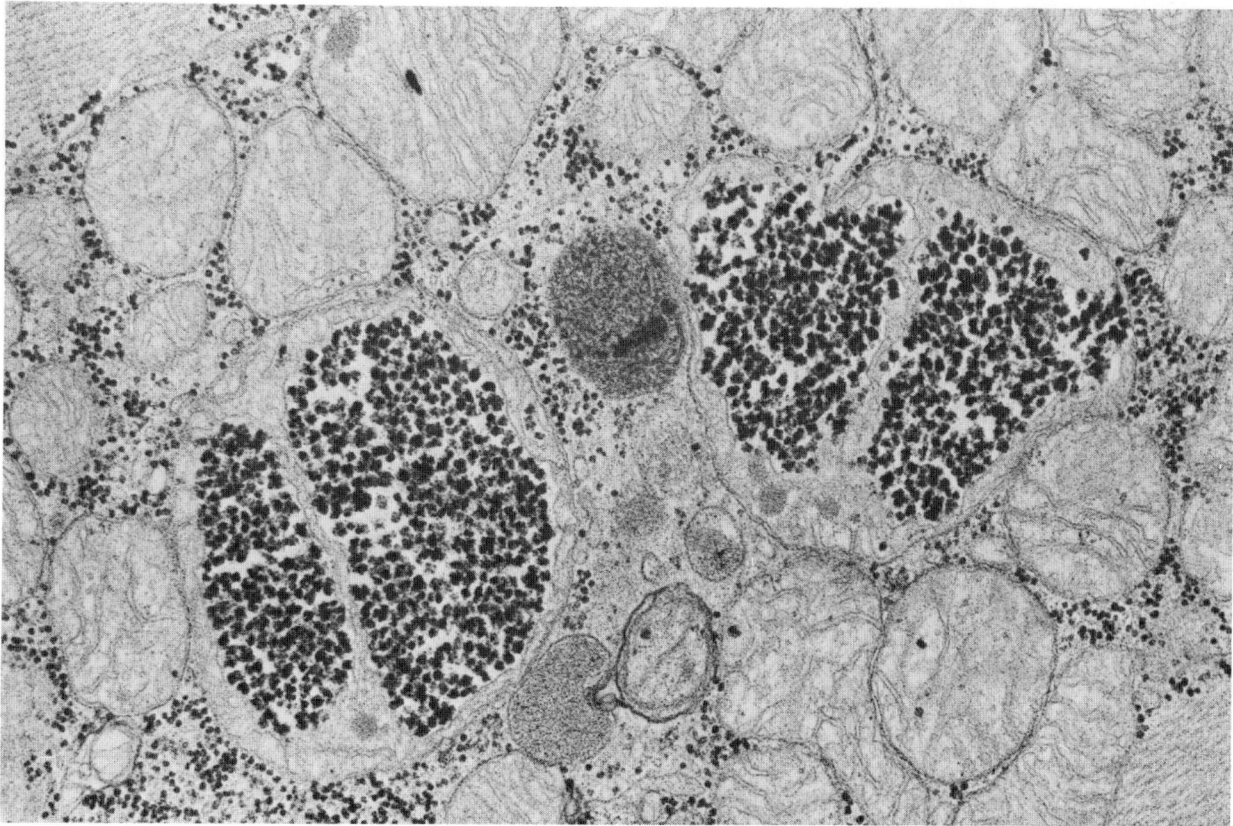

Figure 3.16. Intramitochondrial glycogen.
Large accumulations of intramitochondrial glycogen are present in hypertrophied muscle cell of dog subjected to anoxic cardiac arrest under total cardiopulmonary bypass and then allowed to recover for 4 weeks. Small, rounded, gray inclusions also visible in mitochondria. (× 45,000)

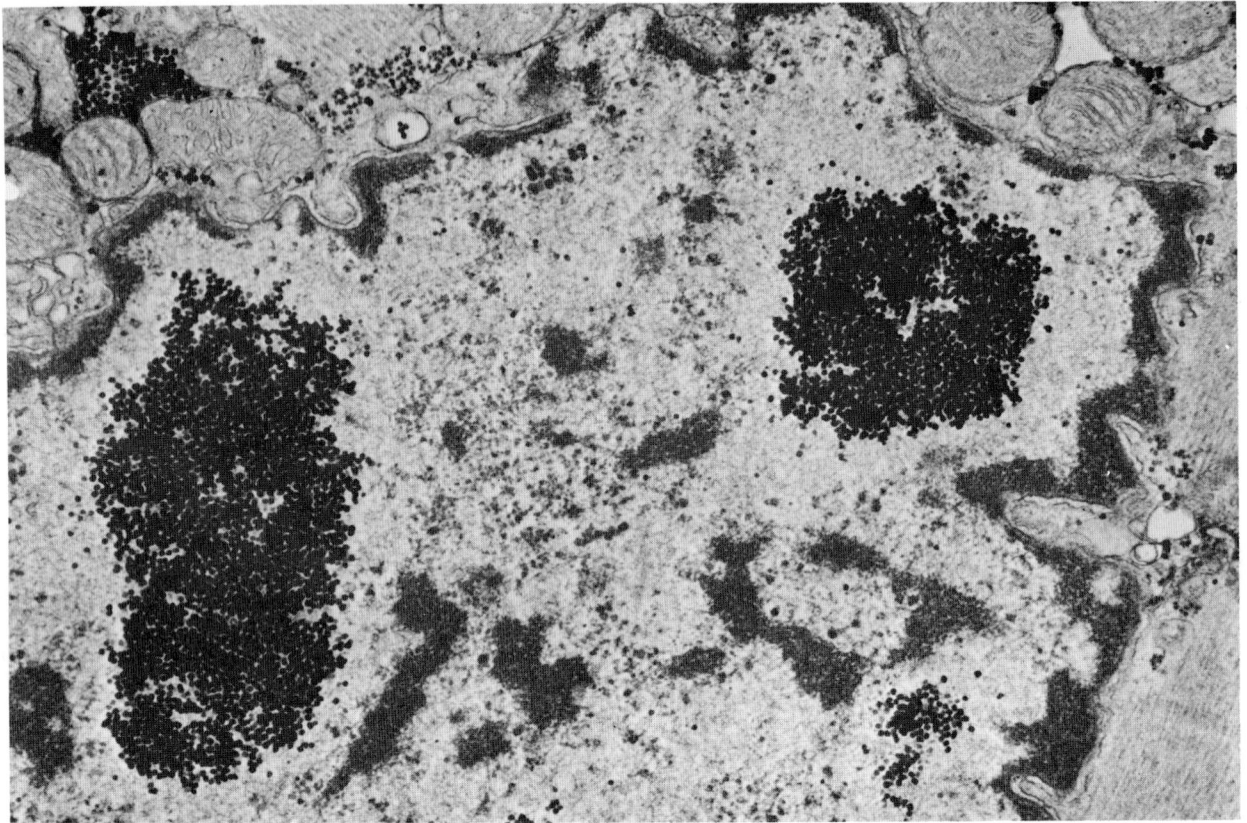

Figure 3.17. Intranuclear glycogen.
Two large accumulations of glycogen particles located within the nucleus of a hypertrophied cardiac muscle cell. (×27,000)

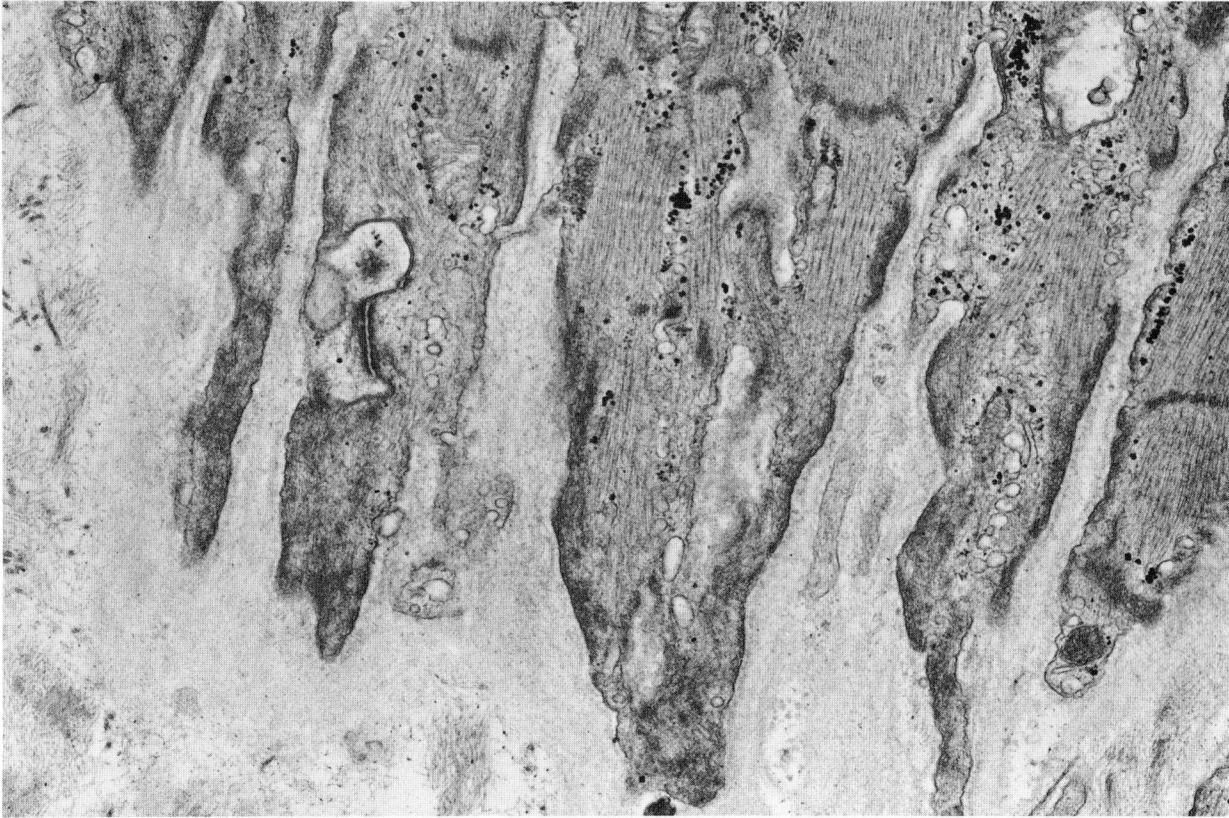

Figure 3.18. Separation of cardiac muscle cells in fibrosis.
Cardiac muscle cell in area of fibrosis has greatly thickened basal lamina and focal subsarco-lemmal accumulations of Z-band material. This cell is connected to an adjacent cell only by a small area of junction (left of center); the remaining areas of the end of this cell terminate in the interstitium without forming junctions. (× 22,000)

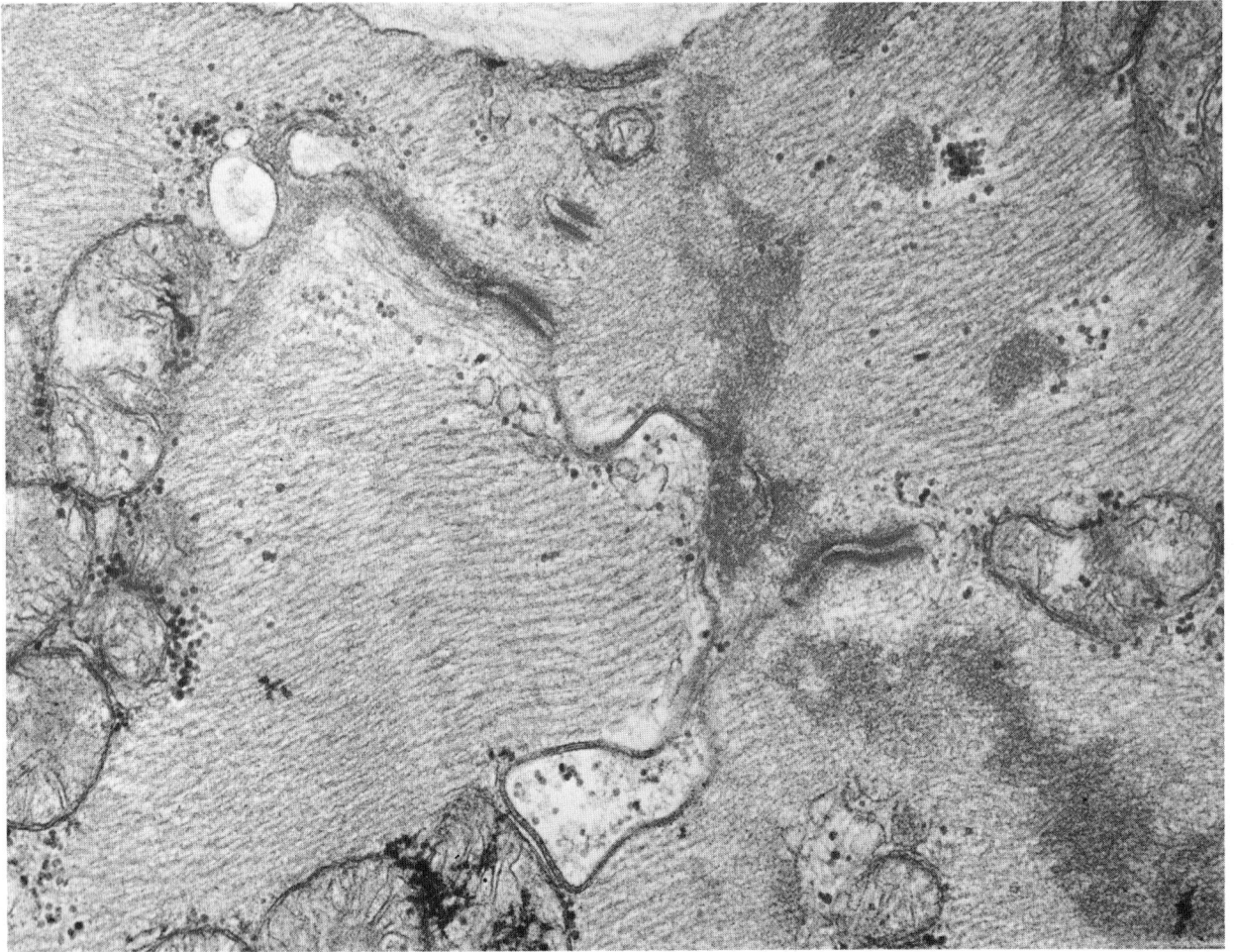

Figure 3.19. Intracytoplasmic junctions.
Several isolated segments of membranes bearing junctional components are present in the cytoplasm of a cardiac muscle cell. One of these segments is quite long and has a nexus; others are shorter and have desmosomes. (×49,500)

4. Cardiomyopathies

In reviewing the morphological features of the cardiomyopathies,[123] it is convenient to classify these diseases into four major types.

1. Hypertrophic.
2. Congestive or ventricular dilated.
3. Endomyocardial diseases with or without eosinophilia.
4. Infiltrative (amyloid, iron, glycogen, calcium, lipids, acid mucopolysaccharides).

4.1. Hypertrophic cardiomyopathy

The asymmetric hypertrophy that occurs in patients with hypertrophic cardiomyopathy is accompanied by disarray of the muscle cells. The disarray of whole groups of cardiac muscle cells, and of myofibrils within individual cells (Figure 4.1), in the ventricular septum is now well recognized as a major anatomic feature of hypertrophic cardiomyopathy.[55] It is also known that the disarray is much more extensive, especially in the free walls, in patients without obstruction to left ventricular outflow.[106]

The distribution of the muscle disarray in hypertrophic cardiomyopathy can be patchy, a finding which leads to uncertainty regarding the role of myocardial biopsy in detecting this abnormality. Furthermore, it is now recognized that muscle cells disarray also occurs, albeit with a much lower incidence and with a much lesser degree of severity, in patients with various other types of heart disease;[109] it is also found in normal embryonic hearts, in hearts of a number of invertebrates and in salamander hearts that are grown in organ culture, in normal AV nodal cells and in Purkinje cells.[55] Thus, this finding is not qualitatively specific for hypertrophic cardiomyopathy. Similarly, the asymmetric septal hypertrophy is not completely specific for hypertrophic cardiomyopathy.[101, 102, 110] Accordingly, the diagnosis of hypertrophic cardiomyopathy must be made on the basis of the combination of clinical, hemodynamic, and morphologic findings.

4.2. Congestive or ventricular-dilated type of cardiomyopathy

The major morphologic feature of idiopathic dilated cardiomyopathy is dilatation of both ventricular cavities.[123] About 75 percent of these patients also have left ventricular thrombi at necropsy. Focal endocardial thickenings often are present near the apices of the ventricles. Grossly evident scarring of the left ventricular free wall

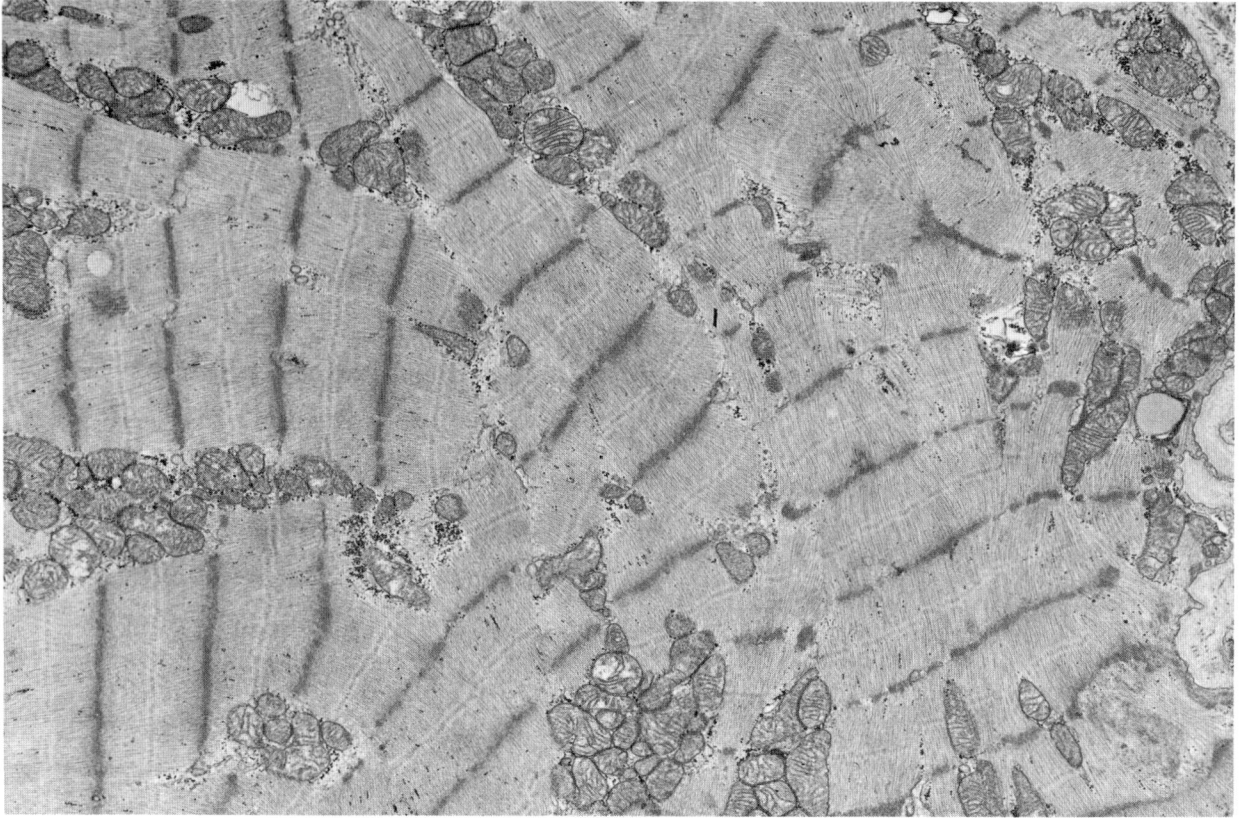

Figure 4.1. Myofibrillar disarray.
Ventricular septal muscle cell from patient with hypertrophic cardiomyopathy showing myofibrils that course in several different directions. (× 10,500)

occurs only in 25 percent of patients; it is usually limited to the papillary muscles and the inner half of the wall. Although usually normal, the margins of the leaflets of the mitral and tricuspid valve may be focally thickened by fibrous tissue. Histologic study of myocardium in these patients has disclosed a variety of nonspecific changes. Many muscle cells are hypertrophied; others are atrophied. The amount of fibrous tissue between muscle cells usually is increased. Inflammatory cells are seldom seen, and the intramural coronary arteries are normal.

Electron microscopic study of several large series of patients has demonstrated changes of hypertrophy with and without myocardial cellular degeneration.[54, 90, 91] Abnormalities of orientation of myofibrils occur only in a small percentage of patients and they are not associated with the extensive disarray of groups of cells (whorl formation) seen in hypertrophic cardiomyopathy. No virus particles have been observed, in spite of intensive searches, and the relationship of viral infections to the dilated type of cardiomyopathy remains to be clarified. The findings in patients with histories of chronic alcoholism have not been clearly distinguishable from those in patients with cardiomyopathy developing without a historical background of alcoholism. There is general agreement that all the morphologic findings in the ventricular-dilated type of cardiomyopathy are nonspecific. Nevertheless, the cardiac ultrastructural changes in patients with idiopathic cardiomyopathy of the ventricular-dilated type are of interest, because the combination of hypertrophy, interstitial fibrosis, and severe degenerative changes in myocardium of these patients correlates with a poor clinical prognosis.

Of the various clinical syndromes associated with congestive cardiomyopathy, the following are of special interest.

1. Alcoholic cardiomyopathy[49] which can occur with or without associated malnutrition and thiamine deficiency and which, in several epidemics, has been complicated by the toxicity of cobalt salts added to beer (cobalt–beer cardiomyopathy).
2. The postpartal or peripartal cardiomyopathy syndrome.[140]
3. The syndrome of infantile cardiomyopathy with histiocytoid change in the cardiac muscle cells.[52]
4. Anthracycline cardiomyopathy.[11, 45]

The first two are well known, although their pathogenesis remains unclear. The third of these syndromes has received very little attention, but probably is much more common than would appear to be the case on the basis of the few patients reported in the literature, and the fourth is becoming increasingly common because of the increasing use of anthracyclines in cancer chemotherapy.

4.3. Infantile cardiomyopathy

We are aware of the existence of 14 patients, ranging in age from 6 to 24 months, presenting with the syndrome of infantile cardiomyopathy and histiocytoid change in the muscle cells.[52] These patients have severe, eventually fatal cardiac arrhythmias, most frequently paroxysmal supraventricular tachycardia. Necropsy discloses increased cardiac weight and nodular areas of yellow-white discoloration of the myocardium. Endocardial thickening, cardiac dilation, and mural thrombi are less frequent. Yellow-white nodules are found on the cardiac valves in approximately 50 percent of the patients. Histologic study reveals large (20 to 40 μm in diameter), rounded or oval-shaped cells with smooth borders, one or two nuclei, and lightly eosinophilic cytoplasm with numerous vacuoles. Some of these cells appear to be isolated in the interstitium, either singly or in clusters; they do not contain any myofibrils and resemble foamy or lipid-filled histiocytes. Other cells, however, are in direct contact with unaltered cardiac muscle cells and with cells that appear to be intermediate forms between normal cardiac muscle cells and the histiocyte-like cells just described.

At the ultrastructural level (Figure 4.2), the histiocyte-like cardiac muscle cells show the following characteristics.

1. Increase in cellular size.
2. Altered cell shape (round or oval).
3. Loss of myofibrils, sarcoplasmic reticulum, and T-system.
4. Marked increase in the fraction of the total cell volume occupied by mitochondria.
5. Accumulation of variable amounts of glycogen and lipids.

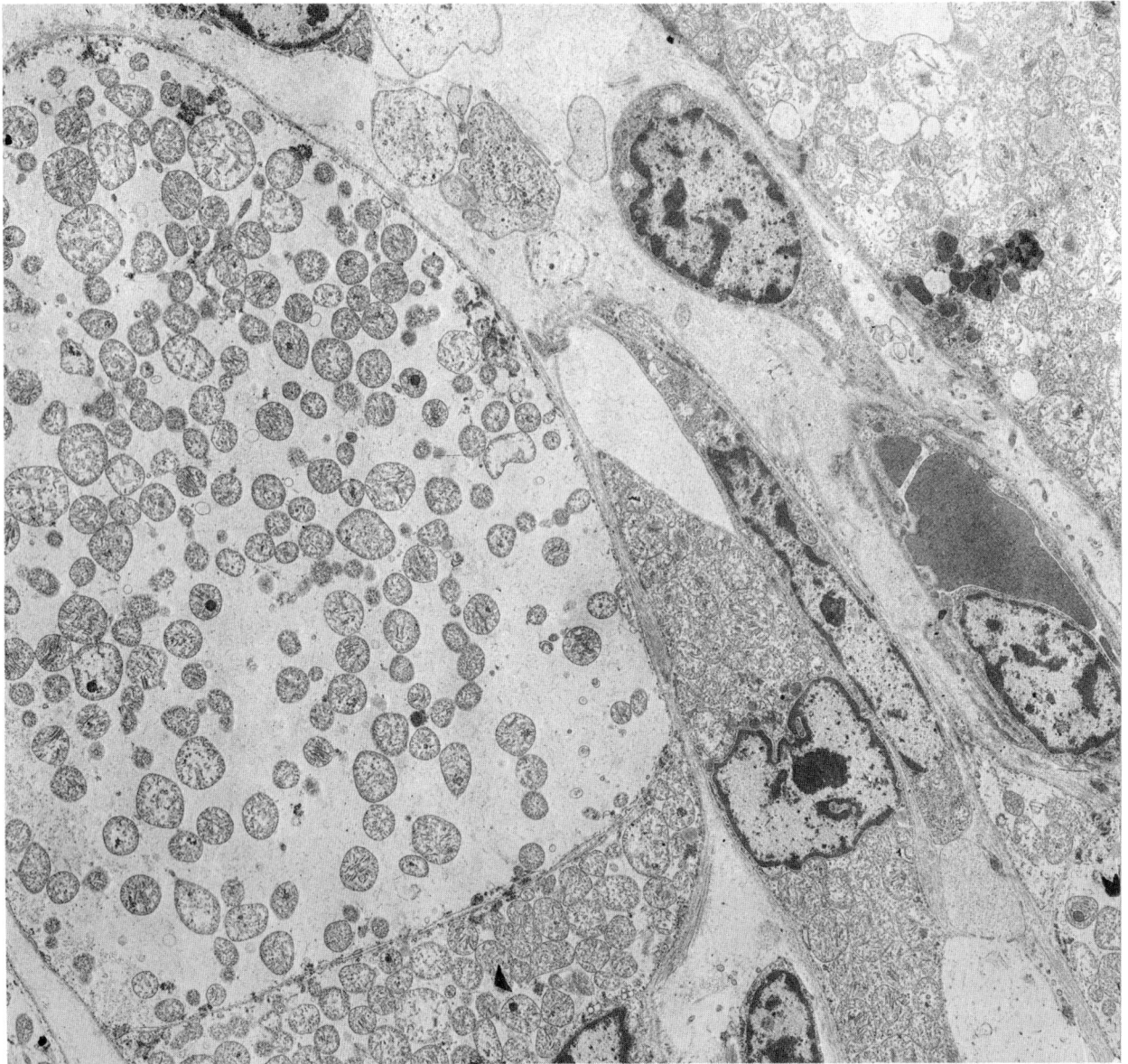

Figure 4.2. Infantile cardiomyopathy.
View of several cardiac muscle cells that have lost their myofibrils and have become enlarged. Remnants of intercellular junctions are still present (lower left); the cytoplasm of these cells appears lucent and contains many mitochondria, some with lipid inclusions. (× 5,000)

6. Partial or complete dissociation of intercellular junctions.
7. Preservation of nuclear structure.

Infantile cardiomyopathy represents a state of myocardial damage or degeneration related either to viral infection or to other unknown agents. Small children are un-usually susceptible to this damage (as they are to damage by viral infections of the heart). The peculiar distribution of the lesions, not only in the myocardium, but also in the valves, reflects the occurrence of multiple foci of involvement by a process that eventually leads to cardiac hypertrophy and focal degeneration of the muscle cells.

4.4. Anthracycline-induced cardiomyopathy

The morphologic features of the cardiac lesions in patients with the ventricular-dilated type of cardiomyopathy suggest the possibility that impairment of protein synthetic processes is a major factor mediating the irreversibility of the late stages of this disorder, and that damage to the genetic material of the muscle cells may be an important determinant of the degenerative changes. Such a hypothesis receives support from the clinical and biochemical findings in the cardiomyopathy induced by antineoplastic agents of the anthracycline group.[45]

Anthracyclines, the most important of which are adriamycin and daunorubicin, are highly effective antineoplastic drugs that produce a high incidence of acute cardiac effects as well as a chronic syndrome characterized by congestive heart failure and cardiomegaly. The acute cardiotoxic effects of anthracyclines consist of hypotension, tachycardia, and various arrhythmias, which develop within minutes after intravenous administration. Chronic toxicity is manifested by the insidious onset of severe, often fatal congestive heart failure; this may develop only after several weeks or months of treatment, sometimes after the course of therapy has been completed. The chronic cardiotoxicity is dose-dependent and generally occurs following a cumulative dose in excess of 500 mg/m^2 of body surface. Nucleolar segregation of the myocytes is the only cardiac morphologic change that has been found to occur within minutes after administration of adriamycin.[112] Nuclear lesions have been observed only in a small percentage of cardiac muscle cells in patients who died from chronic anthracycline toxicity. These lesions consist of various degrees of unraveling of nuclear chromatin fibers into fine fibrils and filaments. Although these changes also occur in conditions other than anthracycline toxicity, they can be reproduced *in vitro* by incubating pieces of myocardium with anthracycline-containing solutions.[25]

The morphologic changes[11, 24, 45] in chronic anthracycline cardiotoxicity are cardiac dilatation and (less frequently) mural thrombosis, degeneration and atrophy of cardiac muscle cells, and interstitial edema and fibrosis. The first two of these changes are similar to those seen in patients with congestive (ventricular-dilated) cardiomyopathy. The degeneration of cardiac muscle cells can assume two forms: the first is characterized by loss of myofibrils, so that by light microscopy the affected cells appear pale-staining but nonvacuolated, and the second is manifested by marked cytoplasmic vacuolization, usually associated with myofibrillar loss. Thus, the degeneration of cardiac muscle cells in chronic anthracycline toxicity (Figures 4.3, 4.4) involves the myofibrils, the nuclei, the T-tubules, the sarcoplasmic reticulum, the intercellular junctions, and the mitochondria. The myofibrils show lysis of the myofilaments. The vacuolization of the cytoplasm is mainly due to pronounced swelling of the SR; accumulation of lipid and dilatation of the transverse tubular system also contribute to the vacuolated appearance. The intercellular junctions undergo dissociation, with formation of hemidesmosomes, intracytoplasmic junctions, and spherical microparticles. The mitochondria show pleomorphism, decrease in size, alterations in

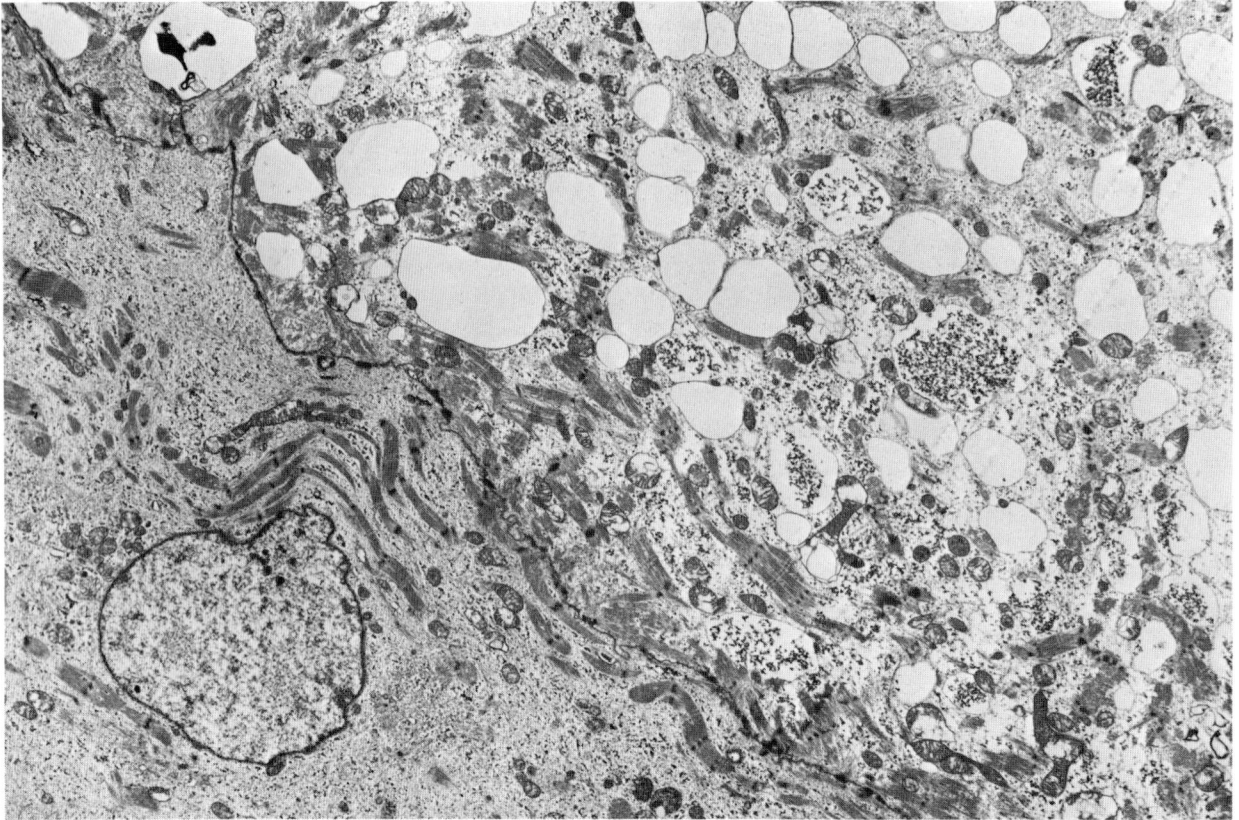

Figure 4.3. Adriamycin-induced cardiomyopathy.
Two Purkinje fibers from pig with adriamycin-induced cardiomyopathy. One (lower left) appears normal; the other (upper right) shows pronounced vacuolization due to dilatation of SR. ($\times$ 6,400)

the density of the matrix, and concentric lamellae (myelin figures) composed of electron-dense material. These changes also occur focally in specialized conducting cells (Figures 4.3, 4.4). Inflammatory reaction usually is absent or minimal and limited to the presence of small numbers of macrophages.

Cyclophosphamide, another antineoplastic agent, produces an acute cardiomyopathy when given in large acute doses. This cardiomyopathy is characterized by sudden cardiac failure, pericarditis, and hypotension. Microthrombi in capillaries are associated with multifocal cardiac necroses.[5]

4.5. Endomyocardial diseases with and without eosinophilia

Löffler's fibroplastic parietal endocarditis, eosinophilic leukemia (without abnormal myelopoiesis), and endomycardial fibrosis appear to be the same disease at different stages in its development. Patients with eosinophilia associated with a transient, benign, febrile illness such as tropical eosinophilia or Löffler's pneumonia represent

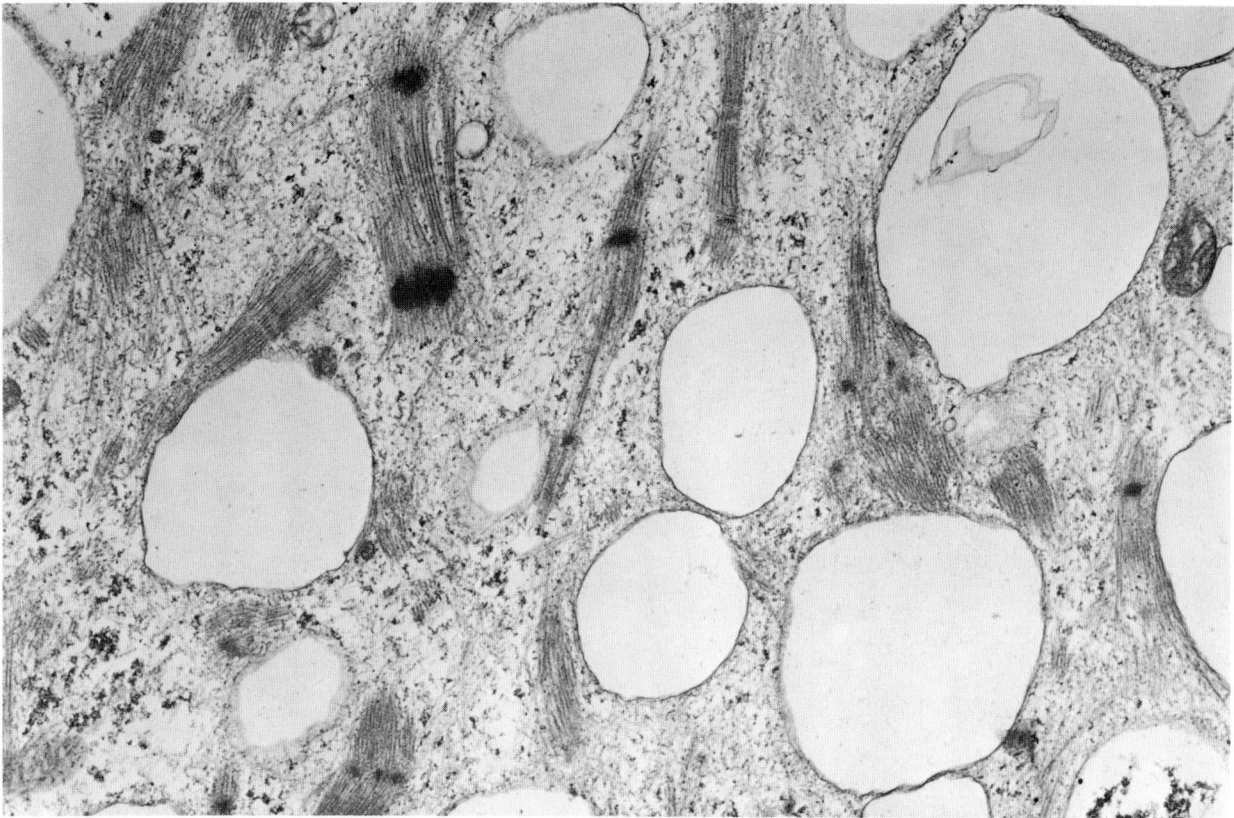

Figure 4.4. SR dilatation in adriamycin-induced cardiomyopathy.
Purkinje cell in same tissue as in Figure 4.3 shows marked dilatation of SR. (× 18,700)

one end of the spectrum of this disease; patients with severe endomyocardial fibrosis and no blood eosinophilia represent the other end. Between these extremes there may be other patients who still have eosinophilia but less extensive endocardial fibrotic scarring. Our current concept of this group of diseases is that invasion of endocardium by eosinophilic leukocytes can produce endocardial damage and eventual fibrosis. As these changes proceed, the eosinophilia may subside, leaving only scar tissue.[122]

In four patients who had eosinophilia associated with the distinctive endocardial lesions and restrictive cardiomyopathy of Löffler's endocarditis and endomyocardial fibrosis, the blood eosinophils were vacuolated, contained reduced numbers of crystalloid granules, and showed evidence of stimulation or activation. Developing eosinophils in bone marrow were not abnormal, suggesting that these abnormalities were acquired after the cells left the marrow.[135] Thus, the restrictive cardiomyopathy of hypereosinophilic states may be the result of prolonged release of products from degranulating eosinophilic leukocytes.

Cardiac biopsies from two patients with endomyocardial fibrosis disclosed myocardial degeneration as well as dense fibrous tissue associated with fibroblastic cells.

35

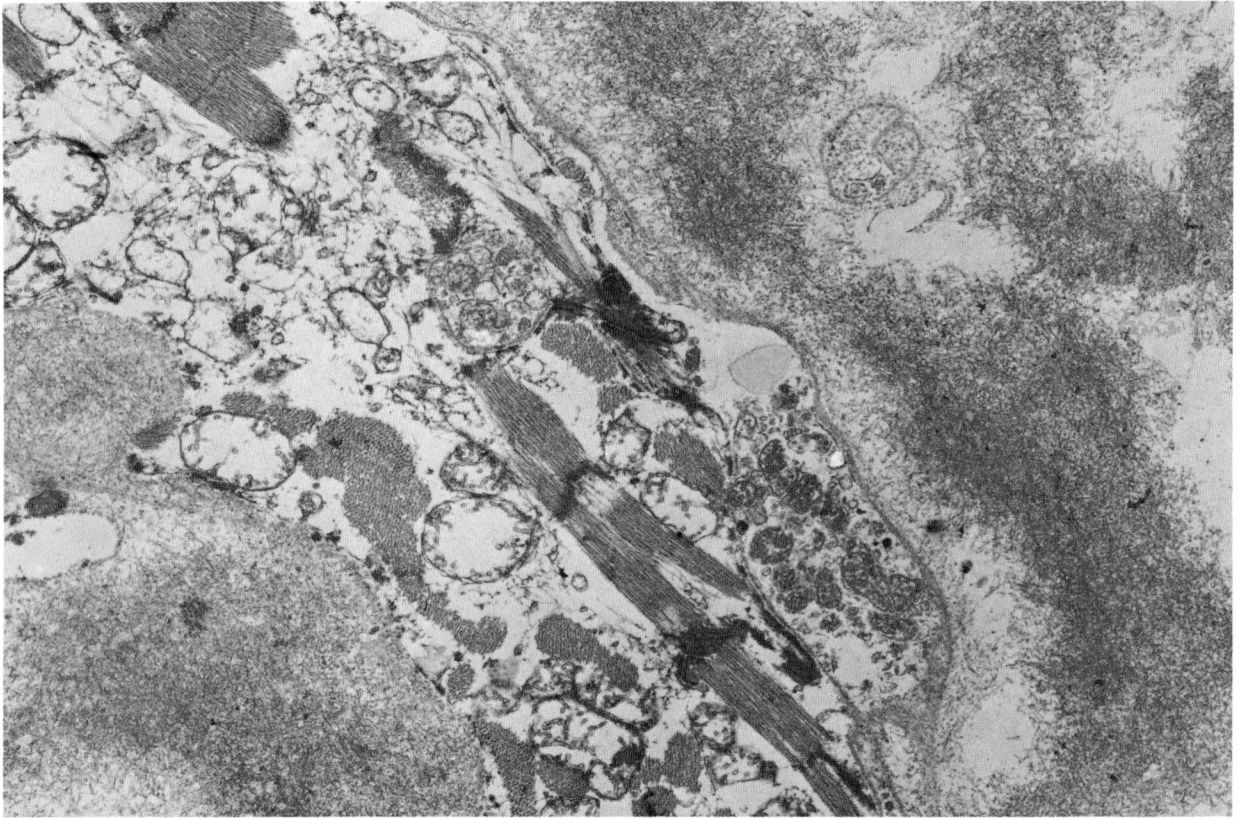

Figure 4.5. Cardiac amyloidosis.
Small, atrophic muscle cell is surrounded by ring of amyloid fibrils. ($\times$ 16,000)

In some areas, the fibrous tissue appeared younger, with cells apparently secreting fibrillar material that was interpreted as a precursor of collagen.[70]

4.6. Infiltrative cardiomyopathies

The infiltrative cardiomyopathies[123] can be classified into two broad categories, according to whether the infiltrates are localised to the myocardial interstitium (amyloid, neoplasms, sarcoid granulomas) or to the interior of the muscle cells (lipids, glycogen, iron).

4.6.1. Amyloid

Amyloid (Figures 4.5, 4.6) may be deposited in any portion of the heart, and the deposits may be large or small. Cardiac dysfunction results from amyloidosis when the amyloid deposits are grossly visible and distributed throughout the ventricular walls, which become firm and rubbery. Amyloid also can be deposited in the walls and lumina of intramural coronary arteries, in mural and valvular endocardium and

36

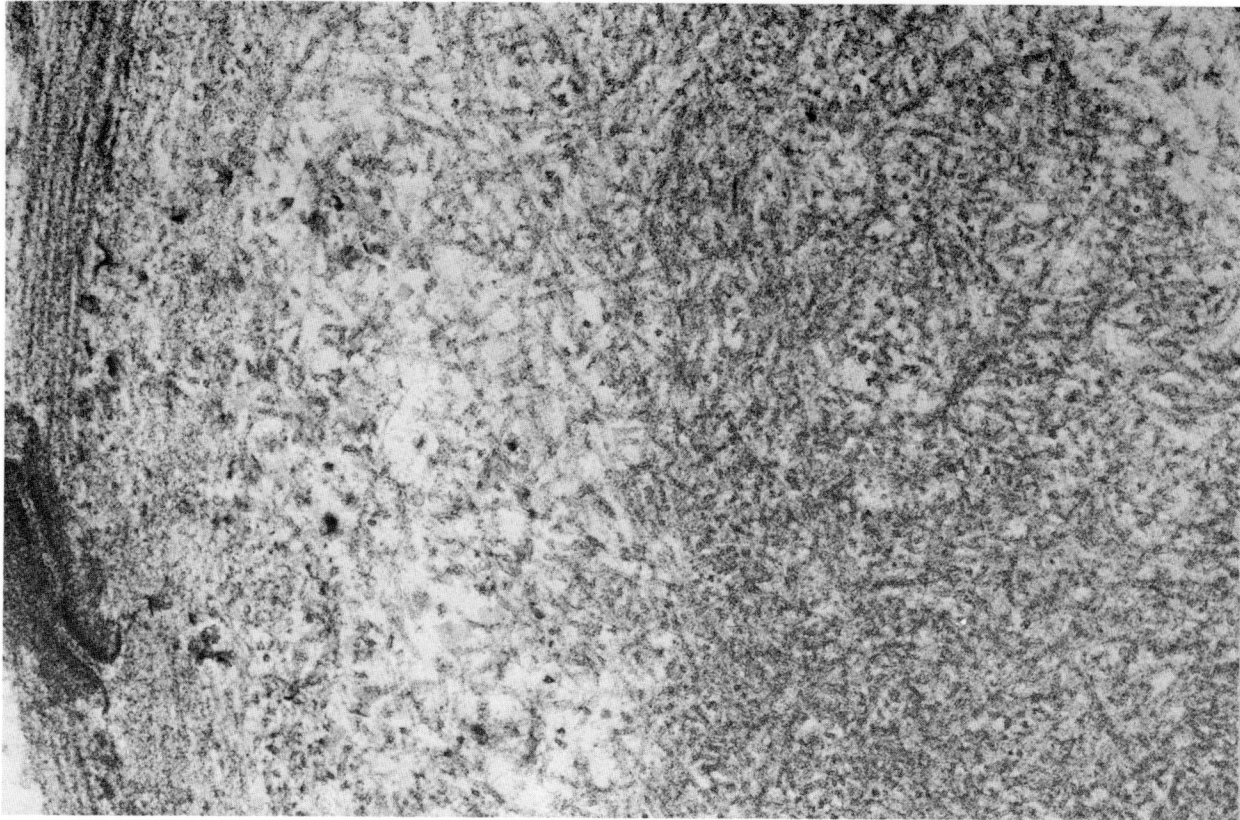

Figure 4.6. Amyloid fibrils.
Layer of typical amyloid fibrils is adjacent to plasma membrane of cardiac muscle cell.
($\times 85{,}000$)

in epicardium, conduction tissue, and cardiac nerves.[26] Amyloid deposits are composed of fine fibrils that measure about 100 Å in diameter and follow straight or gently curving courses. It is important to distinguish between amyloid fibrils and connective tissue microfibrils. The diagnosis of amyloid should be confirmed by the demonstration of the dichroism (green color when viewed with polarized light) that amyloid shows after staining with Congo red.

4.6.2. Lipids

Infiltration of the cytoplasm of cardiac muscle cells by lipid droplets (fatty degeneration) is a common finding in many disorders, including hypoxia and congestive cardiomyopathy associated with alcoholism. The droplets show no substructure, except that at their edges they may have small, thin, electron-dense lamellae. The significance of these lamellae is uncertain.

Fabry's disease may be singled out among the lipid storage diseases as the one in which significant accumulations of glycolipid material occur not only in the cardiac muscle cells (producing cardiomegaly and congestive heart failure) but also in cardiac

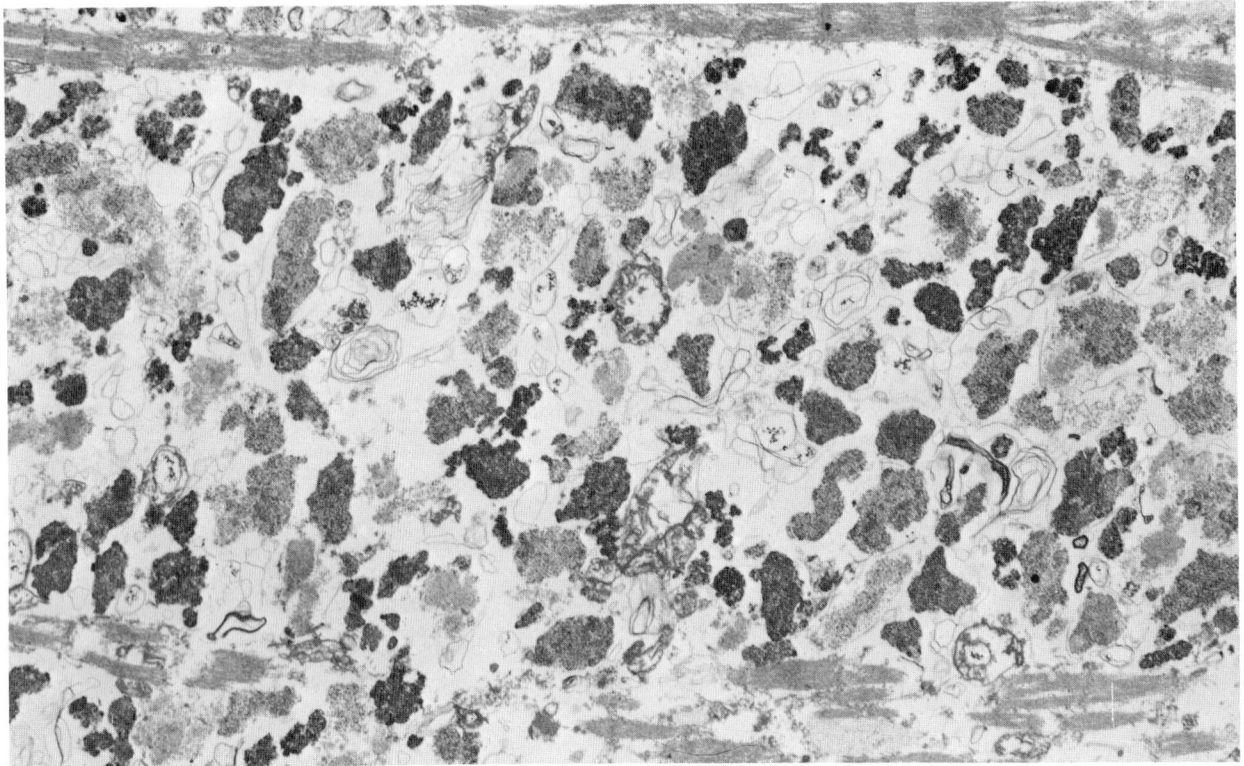

Figure 4.7. Cardiac hemosiderosis.
Deposition of iron particles in cardiac muscle cell of patient with cardiac hemosiderosis is associated with marked myofibrillar loss. ($\times 9{,}250$)

valvular fibroblasts and in endothelial cells and vascular smooth muscle cells in the heart and elsewhere.[10,35,50] This glycolipid accumulates in the form of birefringent granules composed of concentric or parallel lamellae spaced from 40 to 65 Å apart.

Less extensive and less prominent deposits of glycolipid material occur in cardiac muscle cells, vascular smooth muscle, and valvular fibroblasts of patients with the Hurler syndrome.[120] These deposits differ morphologically from those presumed to contain acid mucopolysaccharides, which have a lucent appearance due to lack of preservation of the stored material (Hurler cells). The glycolipid deposits form concentric or parallel lamellae similar to those in Fabry's disease. As in the latter, such deposits are present within lysosomes. Similar electron-lucent deposits are seen in mitral valvular fibroblasts in Hunter syndrome,[114] Sandhoff's disease,[15] Sanfilippo disease type A ,[29] and generalized gangliosidosis.[72] Intracellular collagen deposits also occur in valvular connective tissue in the Hurler syndrome.[119]

4.6.3. Iron

Cardiac dysfunction will occur if the cardiac iron deposits (hemochromatosis or hemosiderosis) are sufficiently large,[27] i.e., dysfunction usually occurs in patients when the iron deposits are grossly visible but not when they are only microscopically visible. These deposits (Figures 4.7, 4.8) are more extensive in ventricular than in

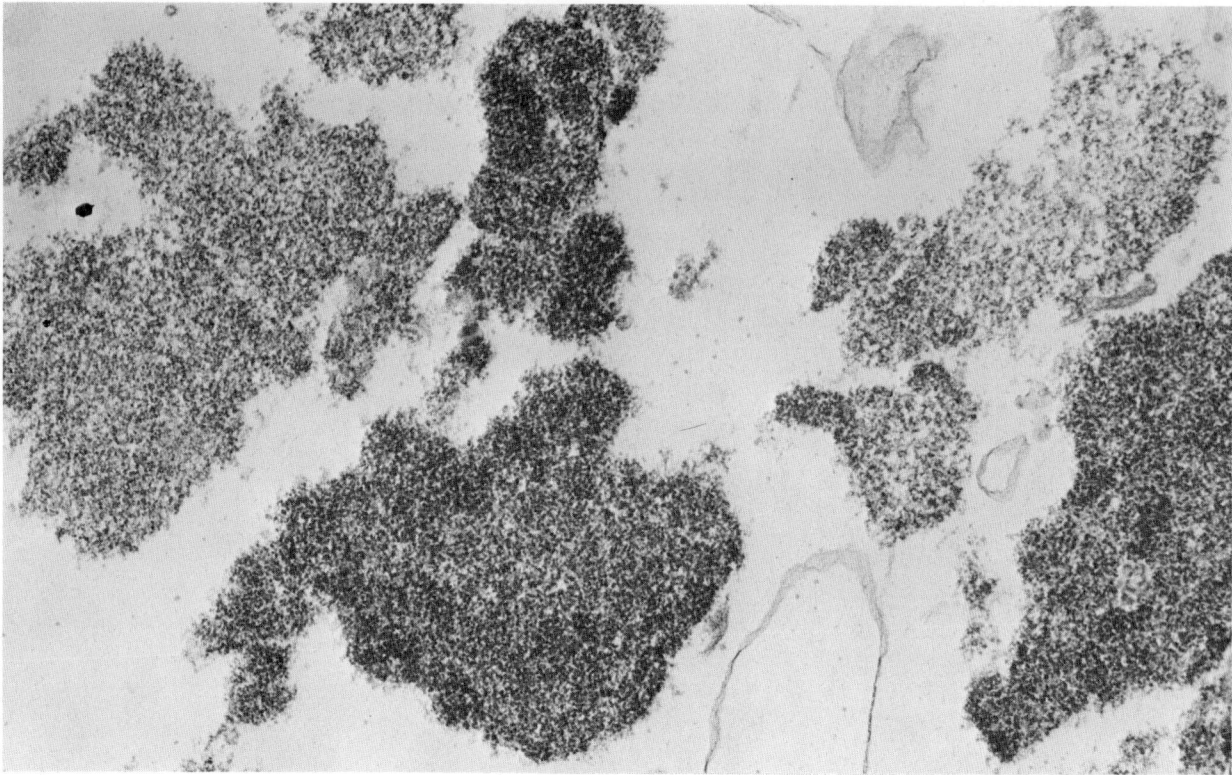

Figure 4.8. Iron deposits in heart.
High magnification view of hemosiderin particles in cardiac muscle cell of same patient as in
Figure 4.7. (×58,000)

atrial myocardium, and least extensive in conduction tissue. They are intracellular in
location, and usually intralysosomal. They can be identified specifically by energy
dispersive X-ray microanalysis.

4.6.4. Carbohydrates

A deficiency of one of the enzymes involved in the synthesis or degradation of glycogen produces glycogen storage disease, of which at least eight types are now recognized.[48] Cardiac involvement is known to occur in types II, III, and IV. Most patients
with glycogen storage disease causing gross cardiomegaly have type II (Pompe's disease), a deficiency of α-1,4-glucosidase, a lysosomal enzyme. Microscopically, the
muscle cells show a characteristic lacework pattern, with large, clear, central spaces
in the cytoplasm and a peripheral rim of compressed cytoplasm. In type II glycoge-
nosis much of the stored glycogen is localized within lysosomes, and the individual
glycogen particles are normal in appearance. In contrast to this, in type IV glycoge-
nosis (deficiency of branching enzyme, which is not a lyosomal enzyme), deposits of
abnormal glycogen are found in the cytoplasm of cardiac muscle cells (and also in
other tissues, especially liver). These deposits of glycogen are basophilic in sections

39

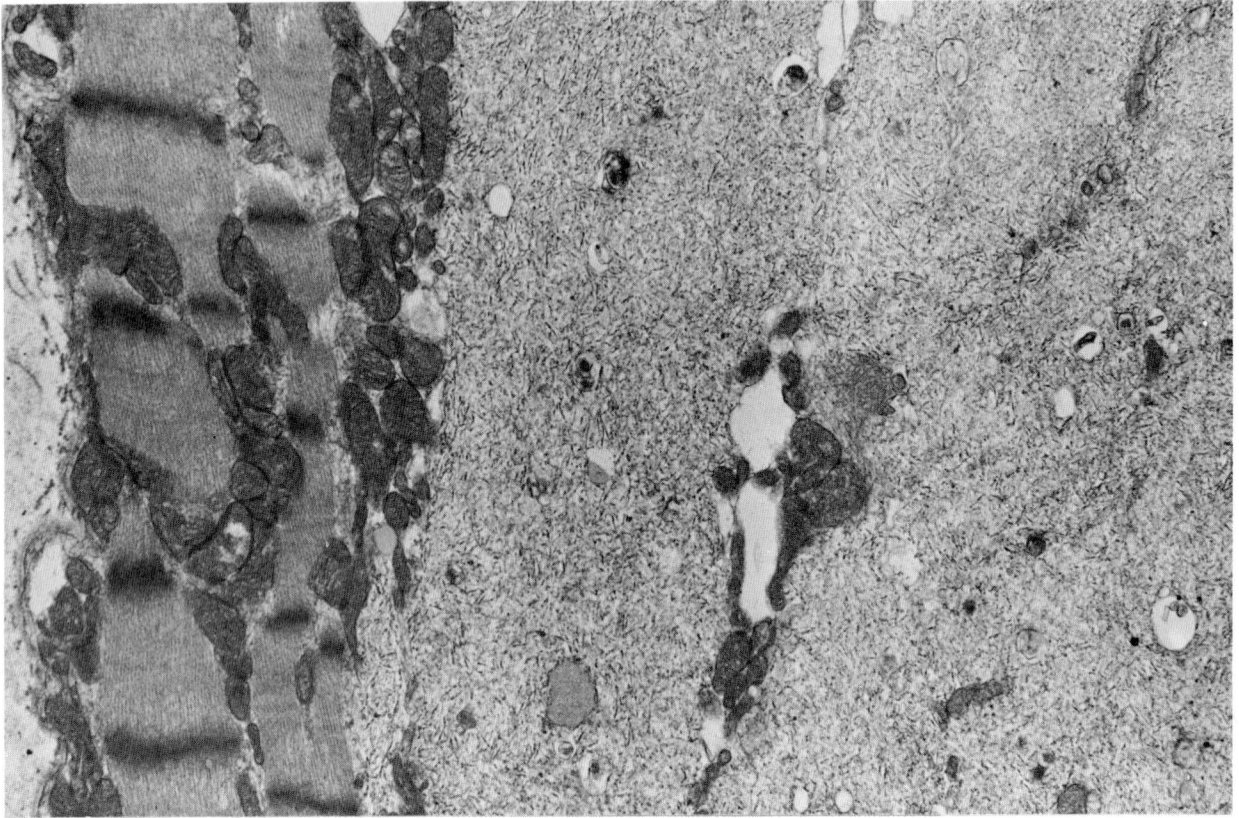

Figure 4.9. Basophilic degeneration of heart.
Cardiac muscle cell contains numerous fibrils of basophilic material; only a thin, peripheral rim of contractile elements and mitochondria remains. (× 16,000)

stained with hematoxylin and eosin, and on ultrastructural study they appear composed of nonbranching fibrils that measure from 40 to 80 Å in diameter and resemble those in the glycogen-related type of basophilic degeneration of the heart (Figures 4.9, 4.10, 4.11). The latter condition is very commonly found in the hearts of older individuals. Its pathogenesis is unknown.

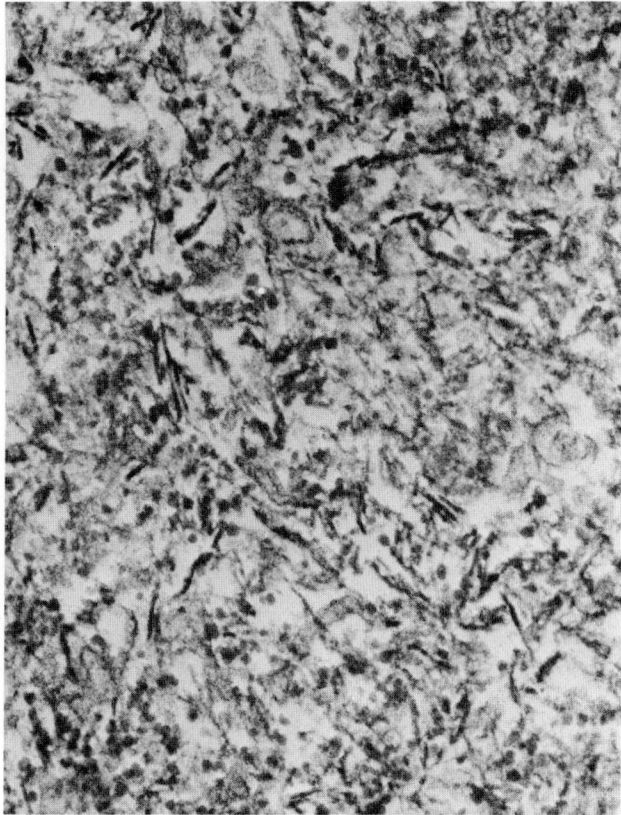

Figure 4.10. Basophilic degeneration of heart.
High magnification view of fibrils of basophilic material. These
fibrils are interspersed with glycogen particles. (× 74,500)

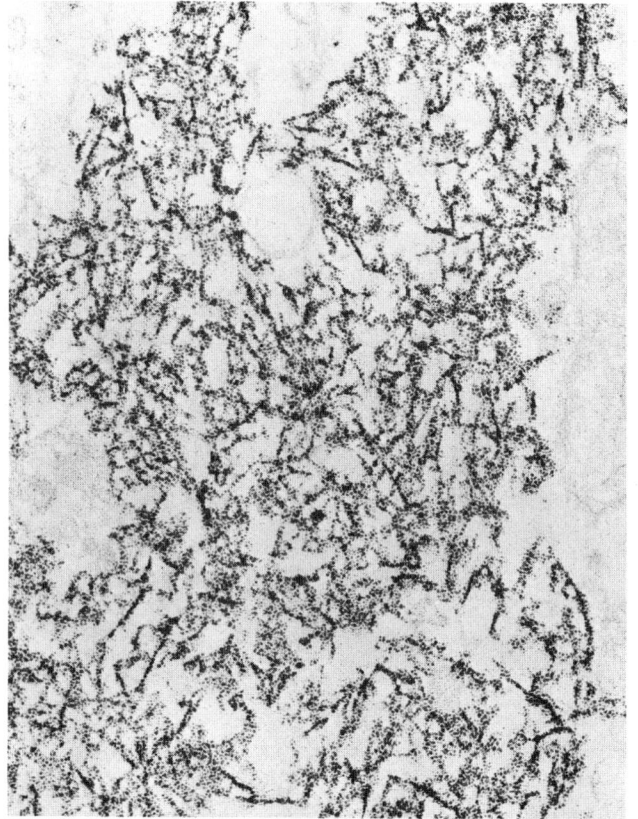

Figure 4.11. Histochemical demonstration of baso-philic degeneration material.
Fibrils of basophilic material are intensely stained by the periodic acid–thiosemicarbazide–silver proteinate method of Thiéry. Compare with Figure 4.10. (×80,000)

5. Myocardial Ischemia

Ischemia of less than 15 minutes' duration produces reversible injury to the muscle cells.[77,78] This injury is characterized by glycogen depletion, mild mitochondrial swelling, and relaxation of sarcomeres (reflecting loss of contractility). Changes of irreversible injury develop when the period of ischemia is prolonged for more than 20 minutes. With increasing duration of ischemia, these changes become more severe and affect a higher percentage of the muscle cells in the ischemic area. These changes[6,7,33,77,78] consist of depletion of glycogen, mitochondrial swelling associated with the formation of intramitochondrial flocculent precipitates that contain abundant lipid but no demonstrable calcium, intracellular swelling, margination of nuclear chromatin, pronounced relaxation and stretching of the myofibrils (wavy fibers), and formation of small defects or holes in the plasma membrane (Figures 5.1, 5.2, 5.3). The intercellular junctions then undergo various degrees of dissociation.[7]

These changes are not useful in the diagnosis of early myocardial infarction in human necropsy material because they bear a close resemblance to early postmortem autolytic alterations.[75] They also resemble the changes produced by poor tissue fixation, and great care is needed in their interpretation.

The changes just described progress to coagulation necrosis, in which the muscle cells appear relaxed and the myofilaments become progressively more indistinct, as is characteristically the case in central areas of myocardial infarcts. In contrast, peripheral areas of infarcts show a different type of necrosis, known as necrosis with contraction bands, which is characterized by hypercontraction of the myofibrils, intramitochondrial electron-dense calcific deposits, and progression to myocytolysis (Figures 5.4, 5.5, 5.6). This type of necrosis is related to the entry of large amounts of calcium ions into cells damaged by ischemia.[74,89,141] The passage of calcium through damaged, abnormally permeable plasma membranes is responsible for the hypercontraction, and this occurs when severely ischemic tissue is reperfused with arterial blood.[74,89,141] Massive intracellular swelling can be associated with reperfusion of severely ischemic myocardium. The presence of calcium in the intramitochondrial deposits has been confirmed by energy dispersive X-ray microanalysis.[21] Thus, the morphologic appearance of irreversibly injured, ischemic cardiac muscle cells differs according to whether or not cell death occurs with or without the ischemic tissue having been reperfused. It should be noted, however, that flow through the ischemic area often cannot be reestablished when attempts are made to reperfuse tissue that has been ischemic for a long time (i.e., in excess of 90 minutes). Under these circumstances, the microcirculation in the ischemic area may have suffered irreversible damage, with severe endothelial cell swelling, capillary disruption, aggregation of platelets, and microthrombosis. These secondary alternations give rise to the "no reflow"

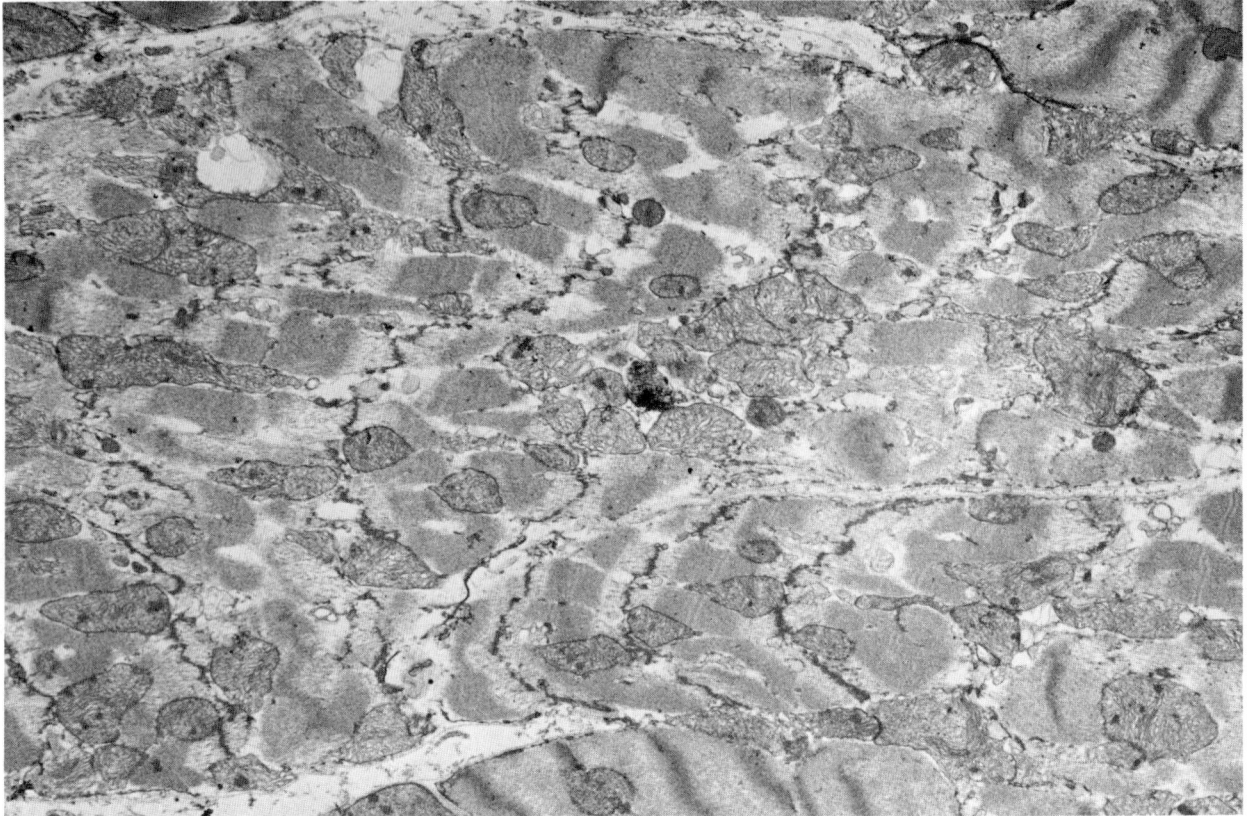

Figure 5.1. Coagulation necrosis.
Area of myocardial coagulation necrosis showing relaxation of myofibrils (which have prominent I-bands), intramitochondrial flocculent precipitates, glycogen loss, and disrupted plasma membranes. (× 10,250)

phenomenon.[88,142] The myocytolysis appears to be mediated through rapid lysis of the myofilaments, a change that results in an empty appearance of the cells.

Two important roles of electron microscopy in studies of myocardial ischemia relate to the evaluation of, firstly, therapeutic interventions designed to reduce the size of myocardial infarcts by providing some sort of protection to myocardium at risk and, secondly, methods for improving myocardial preservation during elective cardiac arrest in open heart operations. Various interventions for reducing infarct size have different hemodynamic and pharmacological effects and these, in turn, have different morphological counterparts. For example, morphometric data suggest that propranolol diminishes mitochondrial swelling[85] and reduces ischemic microvascular changes,[86] while hyaluronidase seems to produce an increase in the quantity of glycogen in ischemic cells.[87] Extensive studies indicate that the ultrastructural changes that develop in hearts arrested electively during the course of cardiac operations resemble in many ways those produced by ischemia.[130] The most extreme of these changes is the massive hypercontraction of muscle cells that occurs in the "stone heart syndrome."[9,96] The extent of ischemic changes in operatively arrested hearts depends

44

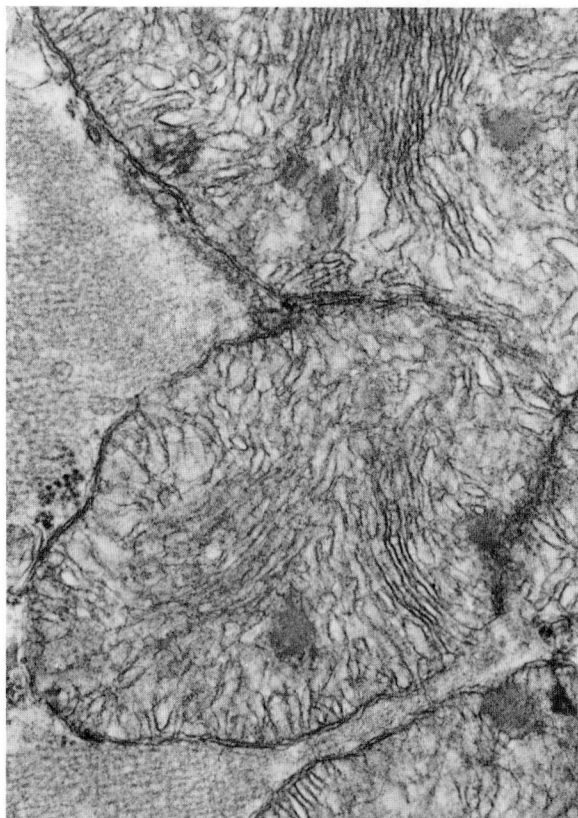

Figure 5.2. Intramitochondrial flocculent precipitates.
High magnification view of mitochondria in same area as shown in Figure 5.1, illustrating flocculent precipitates of moderate electron density. Compare with Figures 5.5 and 5.6. (×43,500)

on the duration of the cardiac arrest, the temperature at which the heart is arrested and maintained, the presence of previous cardiac hypertrophic or degenerative changes, and the specific method (i.e., with or without coronary perfusion using "cardioplegic" or "preserving" solutions) employed to arrest the heart.[130]

In chronic myocardial ischemia, ultrastructural study[84] has disclosed a variety of nonspecific alterations, including intramitochondrial calcific deposits and intramitochondrial inclusions that differ from the calcific and flocculent inclusions described above. The significance of such inclusions is uncertain.

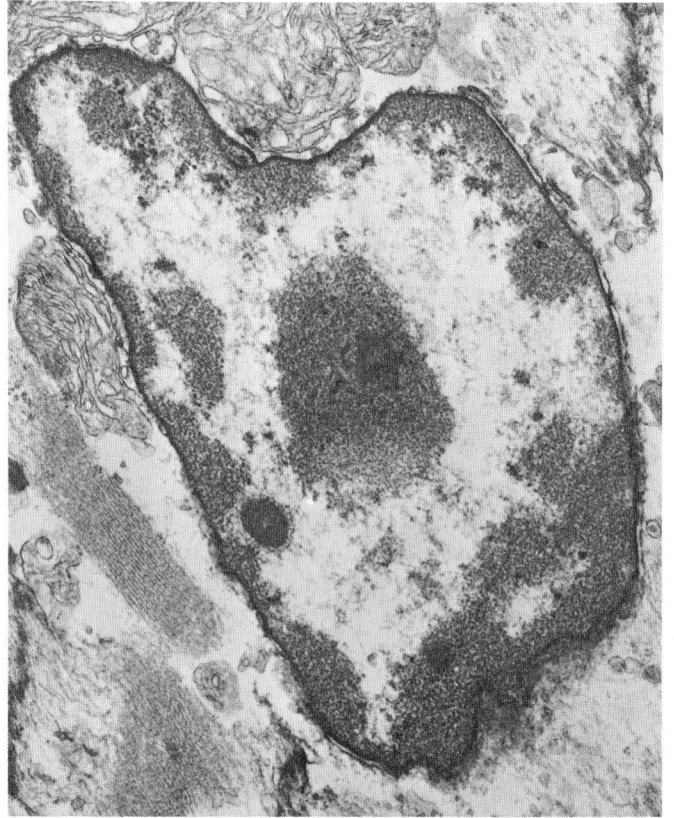

Figure 5.3. Margination of nuclear chromatin.
Coarsely marginated clumps of nuclear chromatin are adjacent to the nuclear membrane in necrotic muscle cell. (×21,500)

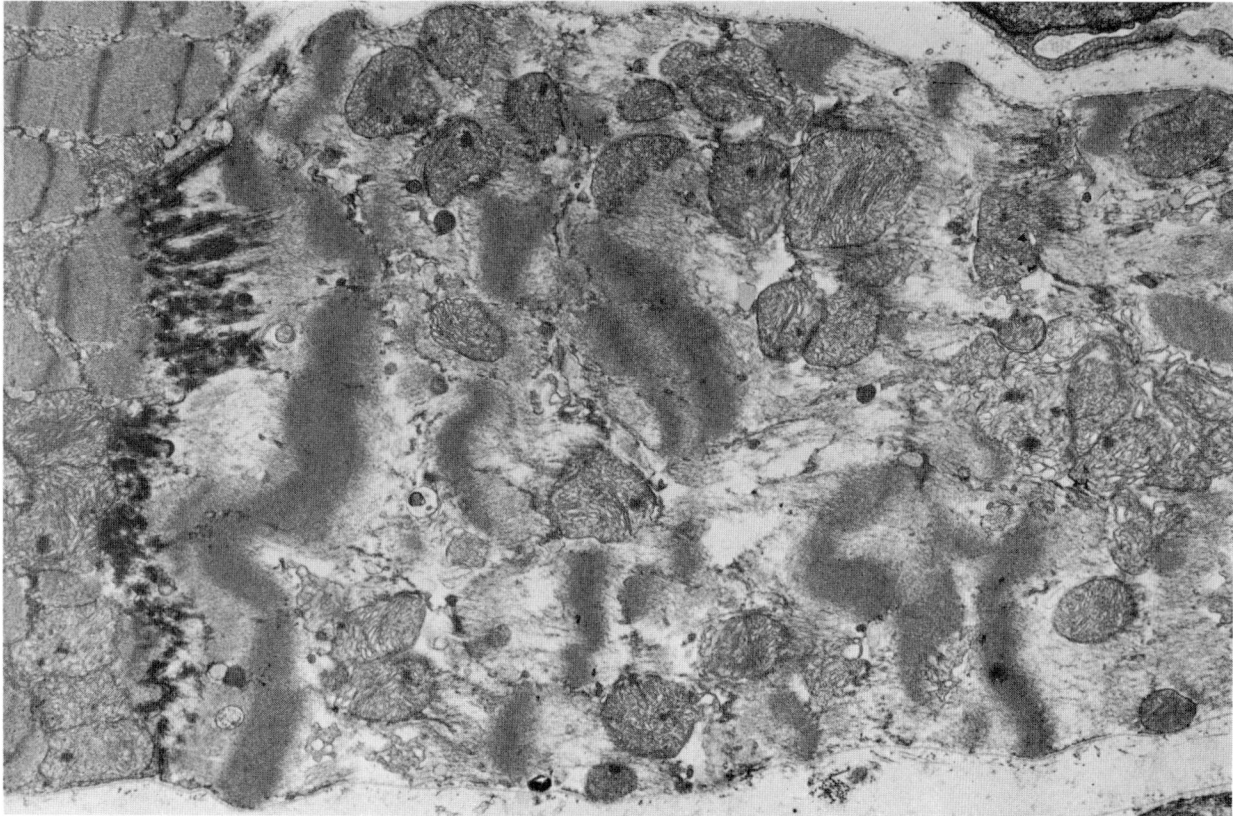

Figure 5.4. Necrosis with contraction bands.
Necrotic cardiac muscle cell shows disruption of plasma membrane, severe hypercontraction bands and dense intramitochondrial inclusions. (× 12,100)

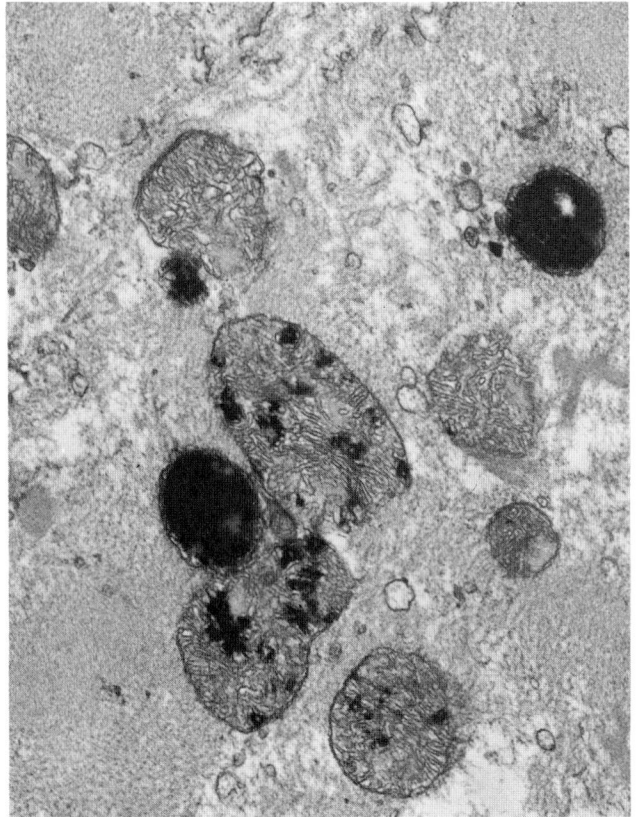

Figure 5.5. Early mitochondrial calcification.
Contraction bands in necrotic muscle cell associated with deposition of dense, calcific material within mitochondria. (×26,500)

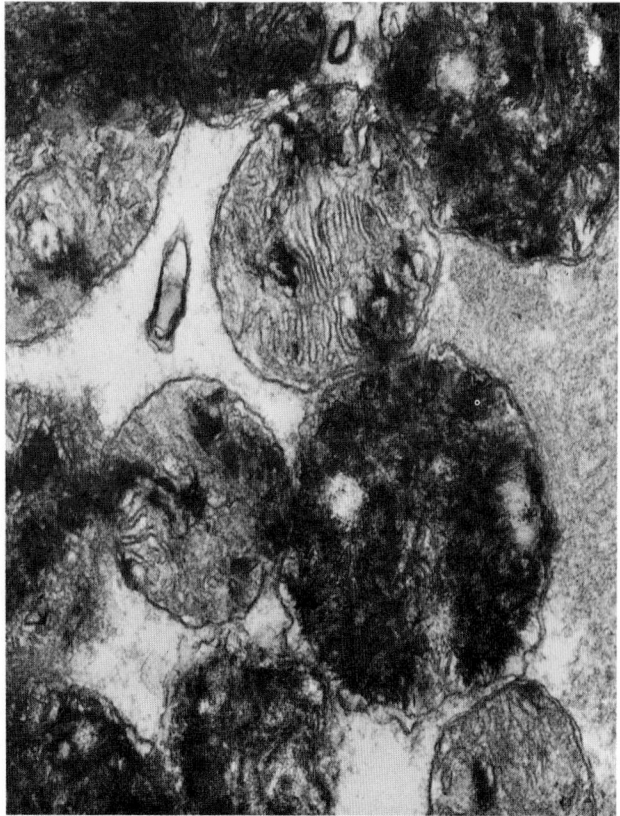

Figure 5.6. Advanced mitochondrial calcification.
Calcific deposits fill most of the mitochondria in this necrotic
muscle cell. ($\times$ 43,000)

6. Myocarditis

Myocarditis can be produced by viruses, bacteria, fungi, parasites, and toxic chemical agents.[1,28,34,83,125] However, little information is available on the features of myocarditis in humans. Myocardial biopsy in patients with the clinical picture of acute myocarditis usually discloses cellular damage and inflammatory cellular infiltrates (Figure 6.1), but no morphologic evidence of a specific agent. The relationship between acute myocarditis and chronic cardiomyopathy remains obscure. The cardiac disease (Chagas disease) produced by *Trypanosoma cruzii* is of great public health importance in many developing countries. In this disease[32,128,129] the infecting organism usually is demonstrable in myocardium only during the early phase, after which a chronic cardiomyopathy develops in association with immunologic phenomena that are incompletely understood at the present time.

Coxsackie viruses are a common cause of myocarditis.[1,28,83] Because of their size and morphology, these viruses are very difficult to distinguish from ribosomes in tissue sections. Under certain circumstances Coxsackie viruses form viral crystals in tissues, and such crystals have been detected in myocardium of one patient with viral myocarditis.[71] Myocardial endothelial cells from this patient also contained tubuloreticular structures of the type known to occur in various other tissues in patients with systemic lupus erythematosus, neoplastic diseases, and other viral infections. We have observed such tubuloreticular structures (Figures 6.2, 6.3) in myocardial endothelium in a variety of congenital and acquired heart diseases in human and animals, and we do not believe that they are of diagnostic significance.[17]

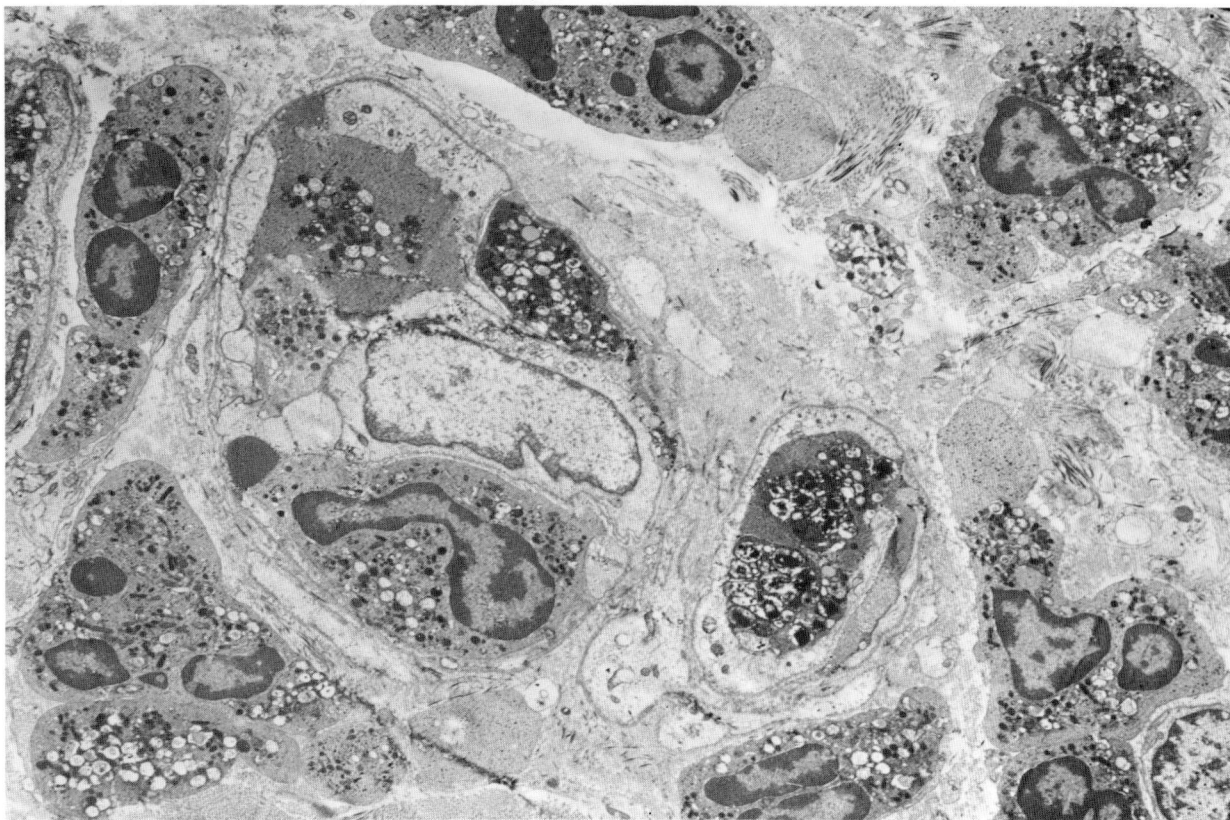

Figure 6.1. Acute myocarditis.
Numerous polymorphonuclear leukocytes are present within and in the vicinity of capillaries in myocardial biopsy specimen from boy with clinical picture of acute myocarditis. (× 6,000)

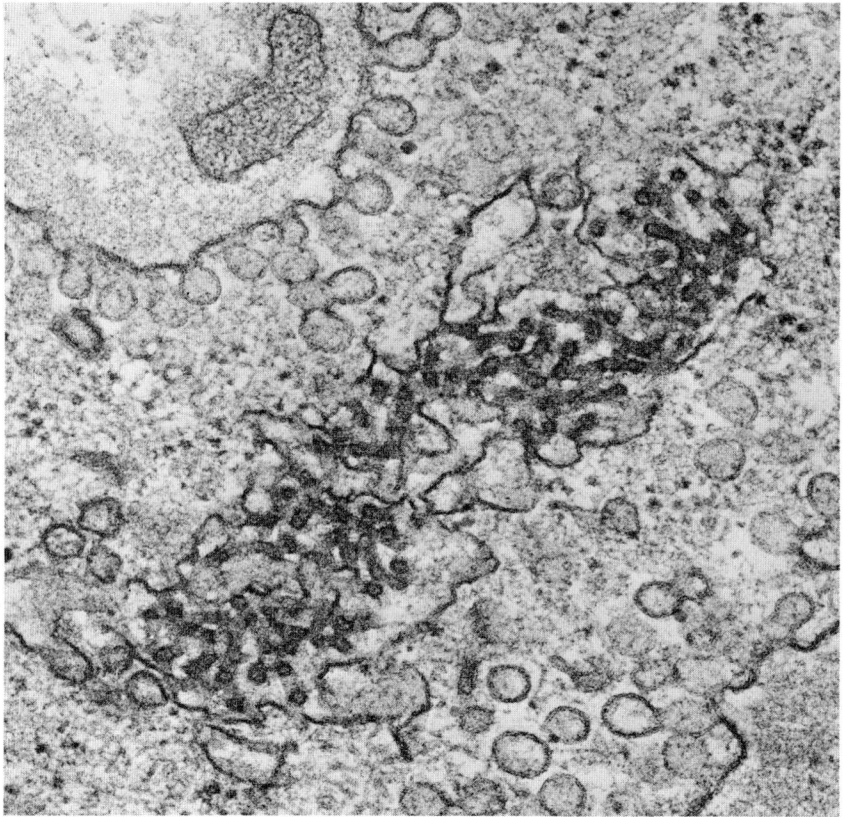

Figure 6.2. Cytoplasmic tubuloreticular structures.
Tubuloreticular structures, derived from tubular invaginations of endoplasmic reticulum membranes into lumina of reticulum cisternae, shown in the cytoplasm of a cardiac capillary endothelial cell from a patient with thyrotoxicosis. (× 90,000)

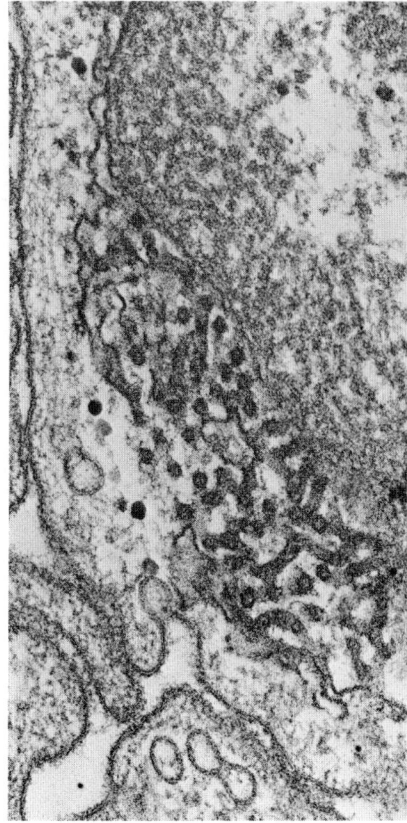

Figure 6.3. Tubuloreticular structures in nuclear cisterna.

Tubuloreticular structures (same tissue as in Figure 6.2) present within nuclear cisterna of capillary endothelial cell. (×90,000)

7. Acute Rheumatic Fever and Chronic Rheumatic Valvular Disease

Cardiac morphologic changes produced by the rheumatic process can be classified into two categories:

1. Lesions directly related to acute rheumatic fever.
2. Lesions occuring in chronic rheumatic valvular disease.

Acute rheumatic fever is manifested by inflammation of the endocardium, myocardium, and pericardium, often in association with extracardiac lesions. The acute rheumatic process appears to be mediated by an unusual type of immune response that is directed against streptococcal components but also involves cross-reactions against heart tissue components.

7.1. Acute rheumatic fever

Microscopic examination of the heart in acute rheumatic fever reveals a specific lesion, the Aschoff nodule, and nonspecific inflammatory lesions.[60,136] Aschoff nodules consist of spindle-shaped collections of Aschoff cells, various other types of cells, and altered connective tissue. They follow a cycle of development and resolution which begins with an exudative–degenerative phase, continues to a stage of maturity (granulomatous phase) characterized by the presence of typical Aschoff cells, and eventually concludes with healing by fibrosis. The components of Aschoff nodules are Aschoff cells, Anitschkow cells, plasma cells, lymphocytes, fibrinoid material, focally swollen hypereosinophilic and fragmented bundles of collagen, and, in relatively early stages of the lesions, neutrophilic and eosinophilic leukocytes. The presence of Aschoff cells constitutes the basis for the identification of Aschoff nodules. These cells (Figure 7.1) are large, ovoid or elongated in shape, have irregular cell borders, abundant, variably basophilic cytoplasm, and from one to five nuclei. In some Aschoff cells, the nuclei have uniformly distributed chromatin, whereas in others the chromatin forms a serrated bar in the middle of the nucleus (Anitschkow-type or caterpillar-type nucleus). The cytoplasm of Aschoff cells contains variable numbers of

Figure 7.1. Aschoff cells.
Two Aschoff cells, one with three nuclei and one with two nuclei, are surrounded by collagen in Aschoff nodule from boy with rheumatic valvular disease who underwent mitral valvular replacement because of intractable cardiac failure. Note the chromatin bar in one of the nuclei at lower right. These cells contain ribosomes, mitochondria, and a few lysosomes, but lack a basal lamina. ($\times$ 14,000)

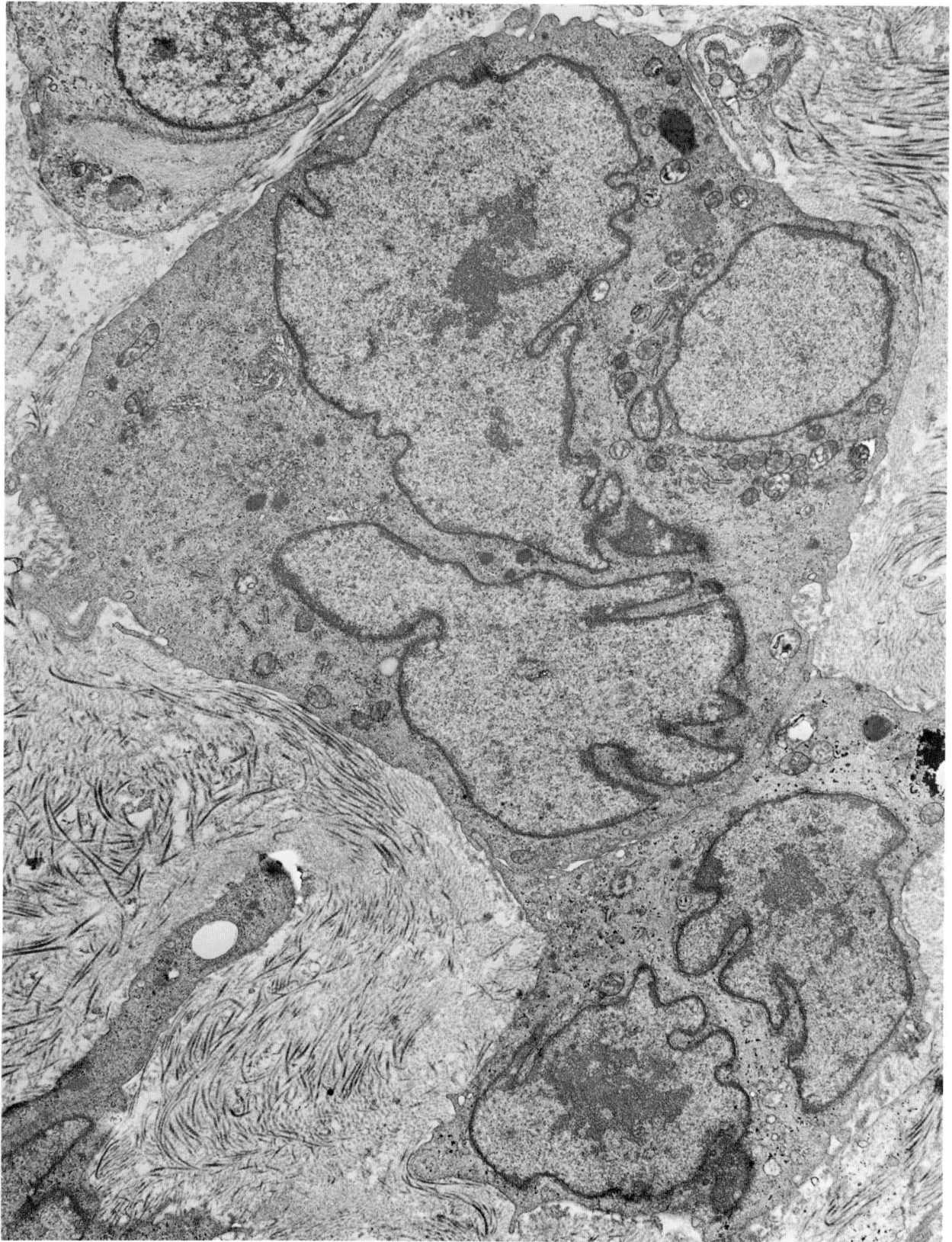

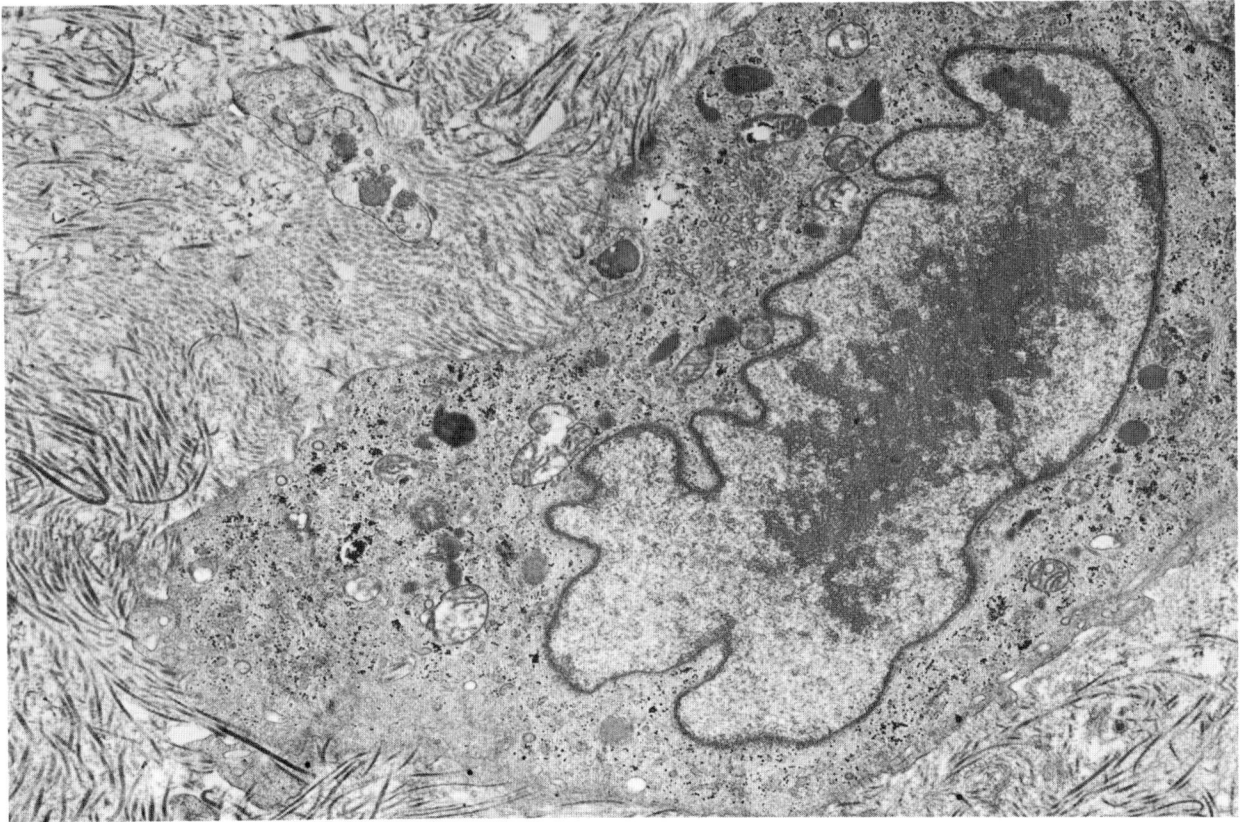

Figure 7.2. Anitschkow cell.
Anitschkow cell in same lesion as in Figure 7.1 has typical nucleus. A centrally located chromatin bar occupies the middle third of the nucleus and has projections that extend toward the nuclear periphery. (× 12,700)

cytoskeletal filaments, actin-like filaments, ribosomes, and cisternae of rough surfaced endoplasmic reticulum; lysosomes and residual bodies are few, and basal laminae and intercellular junctions are not present.[36,60,93,126,127] There is no ultrastructural evidence to suggest that these cells are derived from cardiac muscle cells, and Aschoff cells are in many respects similar to multinucleated giant cells in various types of granulomas.

Anitschkow cells (Figure 7.2) are small, elongated cells that have a scanty cytoplasm and lack basal laminae; they show fewer surface irregularities than do Aschoff cells. Their cytoplasm contains few organelles, and their nuclei typically show the serrated chromatin bar (caterpillar nuclei). Anitschkow cells are present (in small numbers) in normal hearts and in a number of abnormal conditions.[117,139] Thus, they are not specific for acute rheumatic fever. We consider them to be fibroblast-like cells that participate in the process of healing by fibrosis. Anitschkow-type nuclei can be found in cells other than Anitschkow cells, including endothelial cells, cardiac muscle cells, smooth muscle cells, and Schwann cells. The cardiac muscle cells at the

56

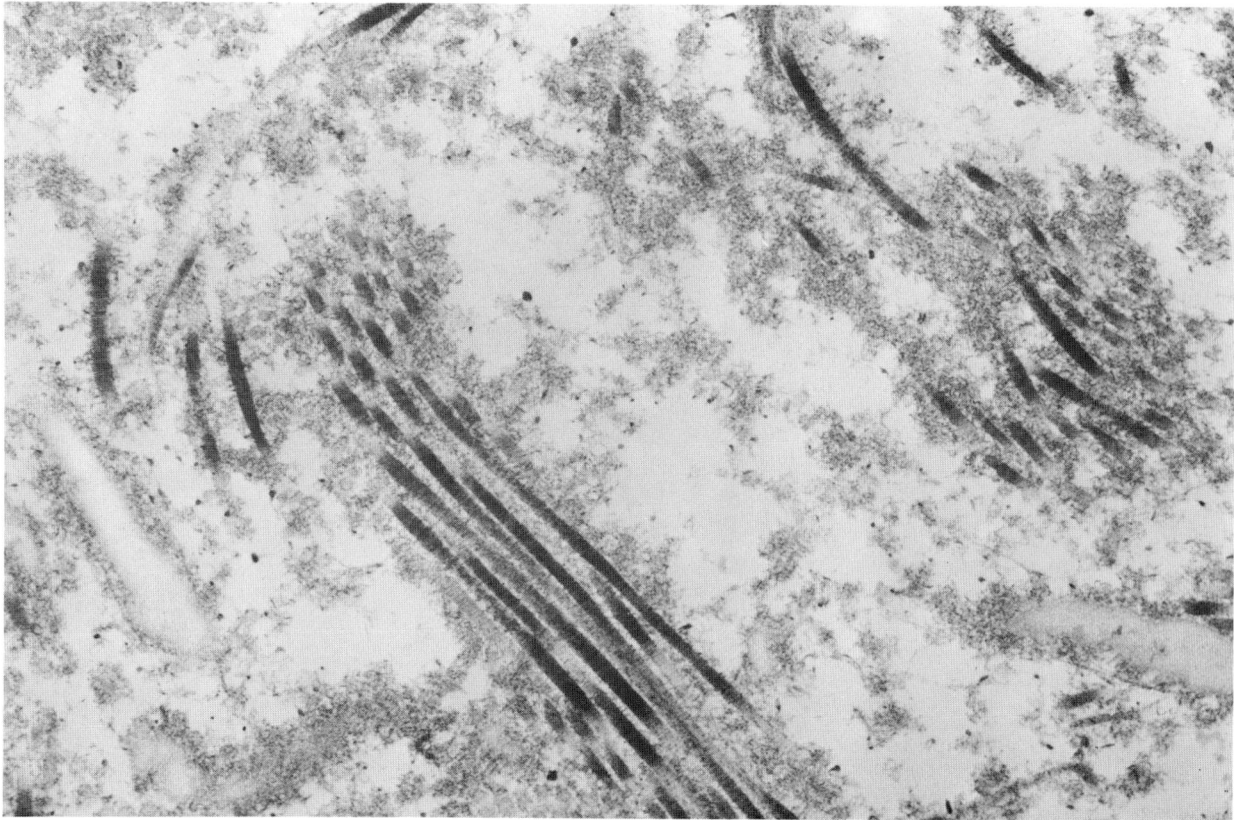

Figure 7.3. Fibrinoid material.
Deposits of fibrinoid material in Aschoff nodule composed of collagen fibrils associated with finely fibrillar and amorphous material of moderate electron density. (×30,000)

edges of Aschoff nodules often show atrophy and various types of damage. Some of these cells lose their contractile elements to the extent that they are hardly recognizable as cardiac muscle cells. The fibrinoid material in Aschoff nodules (Figure 7.3) is composed of damaged collagen combined with fibrin and other plasma proteins. It is possible that some of the collagen damage is produced by collagenase released from polymorphonuclear leukocytes (Figure 7.4) that invade the area of inflammation.

The myocarditis that develops in acute rheumatic fever is manifested not only by the specific lesions (Aschoff nodules) just described, but also by a nonspecific myocarditis and by inflammation of valvular and mural endocardium. The inflammation of valvular endocardium is characterized by valvular edema, leukocytic and lymphocytic infiltrates, and verrucous lesions (Figure 7.5). The verrucae are composed of fibrinoid and thrombotic material together with aggregated and degranulated platelets.[131] The endocardial endothelial cells in these areas are damaged or lost. The healing phase of acute valvulitis is characterized by vascularization and fibrotic thickening of the cusps.

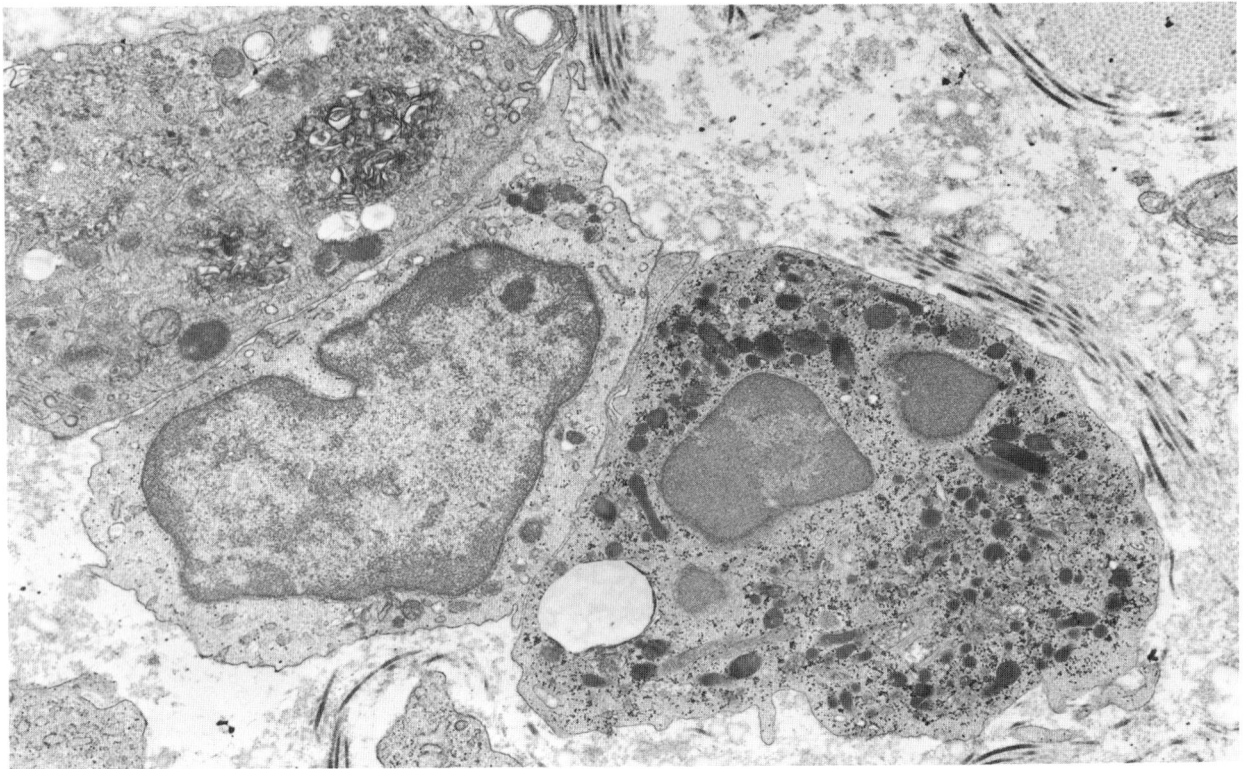

Figure 7.4. Acute rheumatic valvulitis.
A polymorphonuclear leukocyte, a macrophage-like cell, and a mononuclear cell adjacent to altered collagen in aortic valve with acute rheumatic valvulitis. (× 10,500)

7.2. Chronic rheumatic valvular disease

The mechanisms by which acute valvulitis leads to chronic valvular deformity are believed to involve continuing endocardial inflammation, neovascularization of the valve cusps, scarring by deposition of new fibrous connective tissue, and degeneration of preexisting connective tissue that has been altered by the inflammatory process.[136] Relatively little is known of the factors influencing the progression of these changes, although it is clear that there is a correlation between the severity of episodes of carditis and that of subsequent chronic valvular disease. A considerable degree of remodeling of valvular architecture occurs as rheumatic valves become deformed. This remodeling must involve the synthesis of large amounts of new collagen as well as the removal and replacement of old collagen. Although little information is available on the structure of these valves, fragmentation and degeneration of collagen are known to occur in rheumatic valves.[44] Such valves contain mature collagen fibrils, thought to be of type I collagen, as well as finer fibrils that may represent type III collagen.

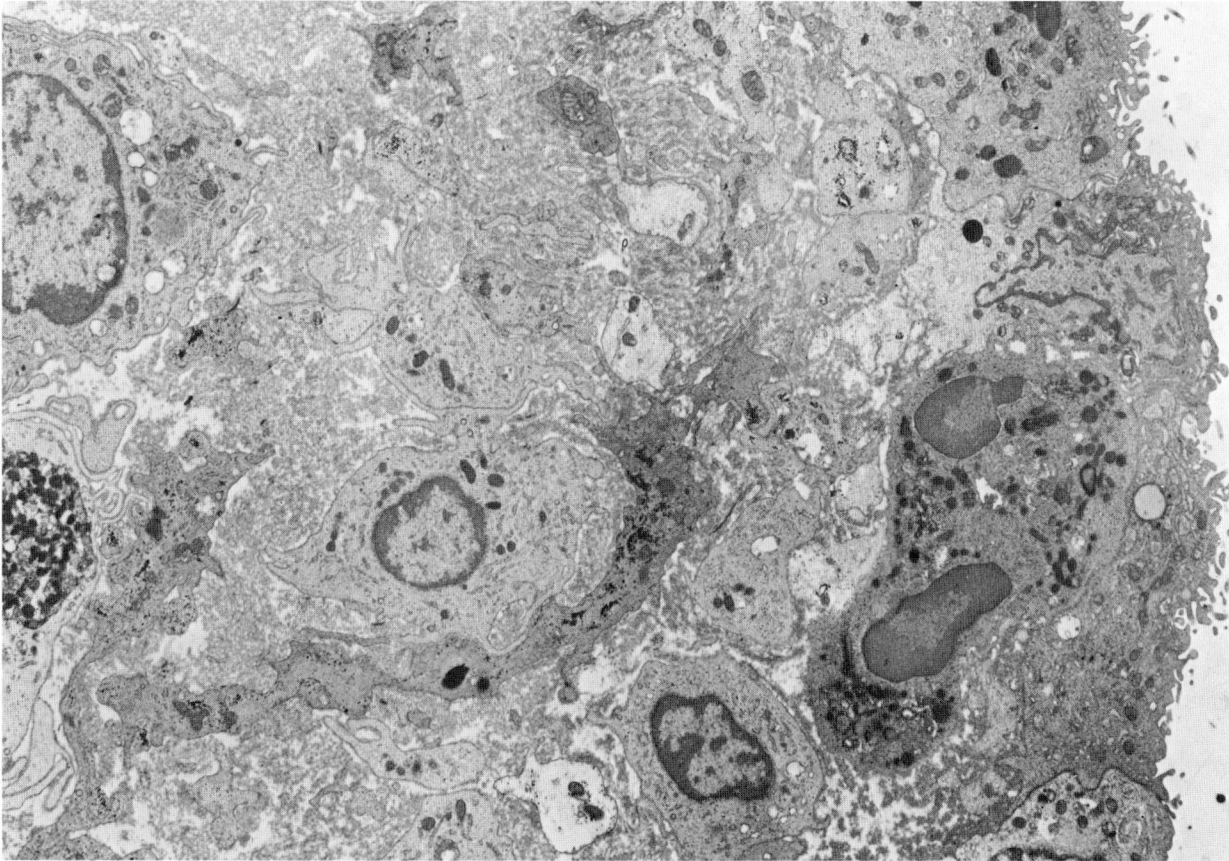

Figure 7.5. Acute rheumatic valvulitis.
Several inflammatory cells of various types are found in edematous interstitium subjacent to valvular endothelial surface. (× 7,500)

8. Other Diseases of Cardiac Valves and Mural Endocardium

8.1. Endocarditis

Ultrastructural studies have been made of the valvular lesions of nonbacterial thrombotic endocarditis[115] and of infective endocarditis produced by bacteria[37,66,113] and fungi.[30] These studies have demonstrated that damage to valvular endothelium predisposes to infective endocarditis by creating areas of endothelial denudation in which platelet-fibrin thrombi can form and serve as the points of initial attachment of the infective agent to the valvular surface. One study has documented the presence of cell wall-deficient organisms in certain infected heart valves,[118] and other studies have detected the infecting organisms in deformed mitral valves from patients with Whipple's disease[95,98] and in human endocarditis caused by psittacosis.[12] Studies of infective endocarditis affecting glutaraldehyde-treated porcine valvular heterografts (Figure 8.1) have shown that fibrin deposits in these valves probably are the first sites of bacterial colonization and that bacterial invasion can lead to considerable destruction of valvular bioprostheses.[47]

8.2. Mitral valvular prolapse

The syndrome of mitral valvular prolapse ("floppy valves") is characterized by a marked increase in the surface area of the valve leaflet(s), which balloon and prolapse into the left atrium during systole. Prolapsed leaflets show a variety of connective tissue changes, and at this time it is uncertain which of these are primary and which are secondary to the mechanical trauma. Fibroelastotic thickening occurs in both the atrialis and the ventricularis layers of the leaflet. Myxoid material accumulates in variable amounts in the spongiosa and in the fibrosa, and evidence of collagen destruction is found. Areas of myxoid change contain poorly differentiated mesenchymal cells and a fine network of filaments and spicules composed of acid mucopolysaccharides. Some of the collagen fibrils show fragmentation, splitting, and increased granularity, and others have a spiraling or twisted appearance. Elastic fibers exhibit cystic spaces, fragmentation, and dissolution. Thus, all types of connective tissue elements are altered in prolapsed mitral valves.[56] These changes resemble those described in spontaneous rupture of chordae tendineae.[43]

60

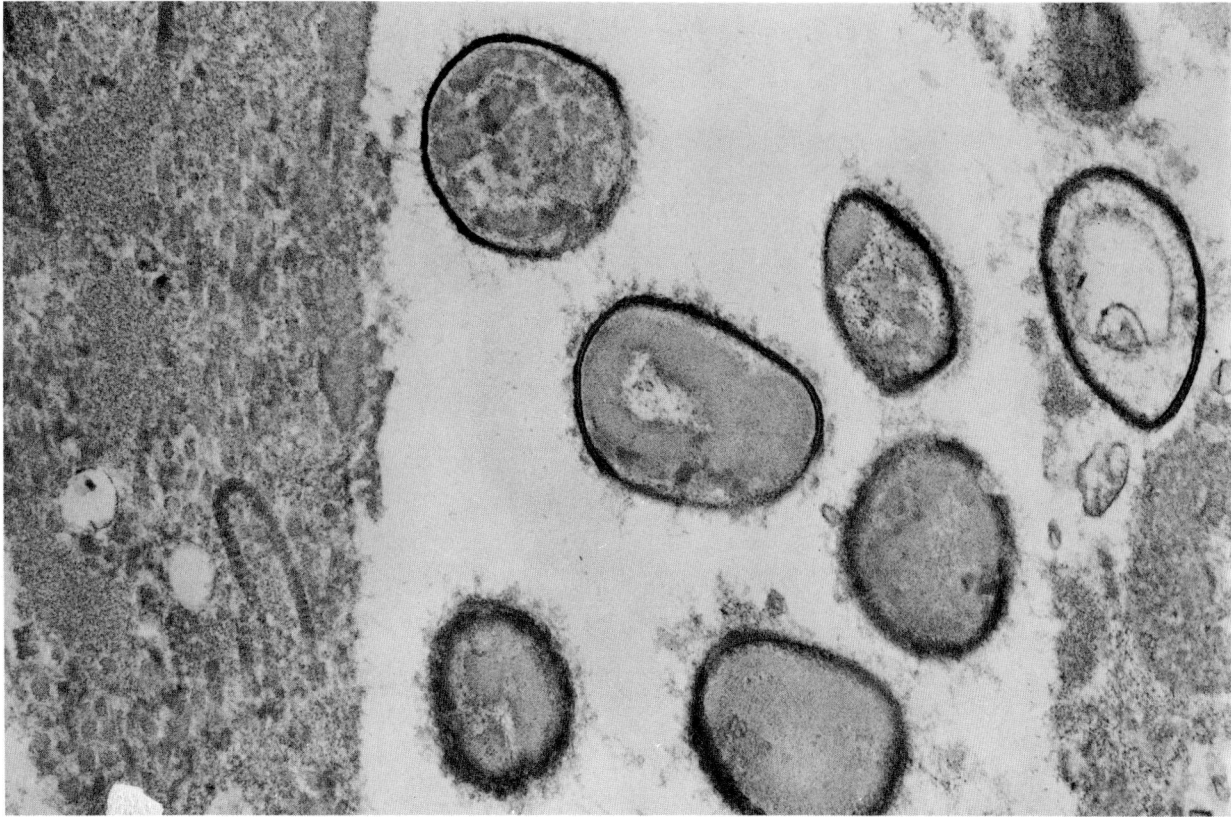

Figure 8.1. Prosthetic valvular infection.
Staphylococci located on surface of porcine valvular heterograft removed because of infection. The organisms are altered and partially lysed as the result of previous therapy with nafcillin and the collagen adjacent to them is necrotic. (× 46,000)

8.3. Valvular dysplasia

A syndrome of valvular stenosis manifested by marked thickening of the leaflets, but without commissural fusion, occurs in small children and is thought to be due to incomplete differentiation of the valvular tissue into its normal multilayered structure.[76] Electron microscopic study in our laboratory (unpublished data) has confirmed the presence of primitive mesenchymal cells, poorly organized bundles of collagen (which is ultrastructurally normal), and large amounts of myxoid tissue in these valves.

8.4. Endocardial fibroelastosis

The pathological reactions of endocardium to injury are not well understood. In general, they lead to a gross anatomic picture of endocardial thickening. The latter involves various types of changes in the cell population as well as in the extracellular

61

elements of connective tissue. The type of endocardial thickening depends primarily on which of these elements shows the greatest quantitative increase.

In congenital fibroelastosis, there is a considerable increase in both collagen and elastic fibers. However, the elastic fibers show a marked increase in diameter (compared to normal) as well as in number, and they impart a characteristic appearance to the thickened endocardium (Figures 8.2 (a), (b)). In contrast to this, the elastic fibers in acquired endocardial fibroelastosis (Figures 8.3 (a), (b)) remain small even though they greatly increase in number; the collagen fibrils also increase in number, and the ratio of collagen to elastic fibers can vary considerably.[65] Several methods can be used for the selective ultrastructural staining of elastic fibers.[2, 20,82] Acquired fibroelastosis can occur either as a disease involving the endocardium diffusely or in localized areas (Figures 8.4, 8.5). In the latter instances, hemodynamic forces are thought to play an important role in the pathogenesis of the endocardial thickening.

8.5. Carcinoid heart disease

A peculiar type of thickening affects mural and valvular endocardium, particularly in the right side of the heart, in patients with the carcinoid syndrome. The secretion of some unidentified material by hepatic metastases of the carcinoid tumor is thought to induce endocardial injury, which heals by fibrous plaque-like thickenings.[18, 59] These contain smooth muscle cells and myofibroblasts embedded in a stroma rich in acid mucopolysaccharides, collagen, and microfibrils, but devoid of elastic fibers (Figures 8.6, 8.7, 8.8). The smooth muscle cells contain variable numbers of myofilaments and cisternae of rough surfaced endoplasmic reticulum; their basement membranes are greatly thickened, reduplicated, and arranged in layers (Figures 8.8, 8.9).

8.6. Prosthetic heart valves

Electron microscopy studies have proven valuable in evaluating prosthetic heart valves and their long-term performance. Rigid-framed, ball-valve types of prostheses[3, 124] as well as bioprostheses[61] have been studied, and scanning electron microscopy has proved to be a useful adjunct in this respect.

Figure 8.2. Congenital endocardial fibroelastosis.
(a) Characteristic large elastic fibers (compare with Figures 8.3 (a), (b)). From preparation stained by silver tetraphenylporphin sulfonate method of Albert.[2] ($\times$ 13,500)
(b) Large elastic fibers from preparation stained with uranyl acetate and lead citrate. ($\times$ 30,000)

Figure 8.3. Acquired endocardial fibroelastosis.
(a), (b) Views of thickened endocardium in patient with acquired endocardial fibroelastosis secondary to insertion of prosthetic aortic valve. Elastic fibers are very small. From preparations stained by silver tetraphenylporphin sulfonate method[2] and uranyl acetate and lead citrate, respectively. ((a) $\times$ 11,250, (b) $\times$ 30,000)

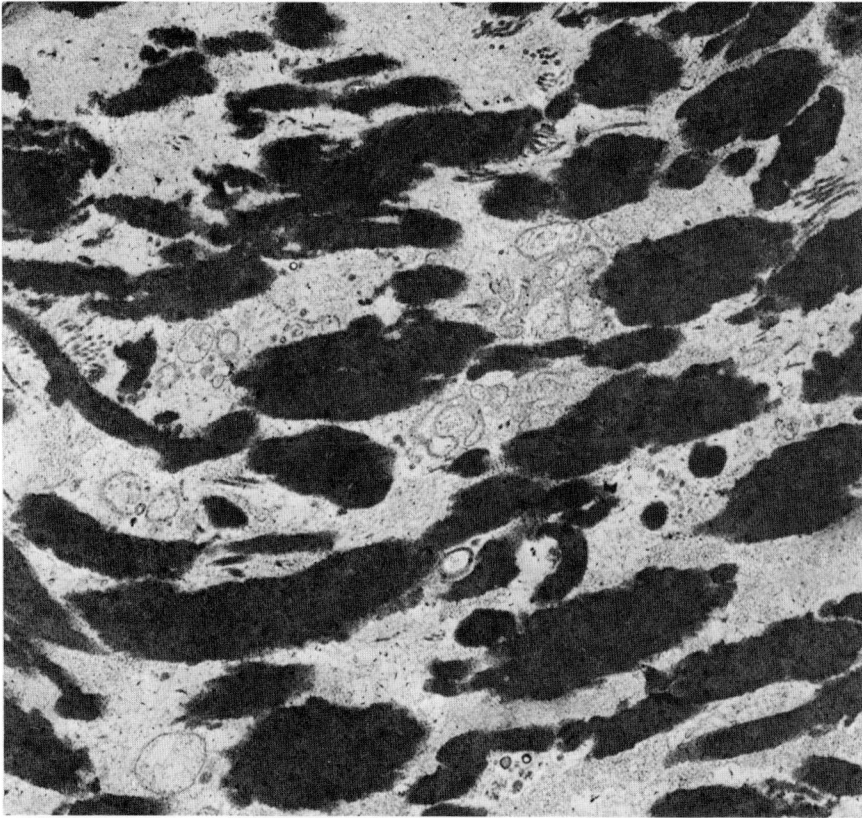

(a)

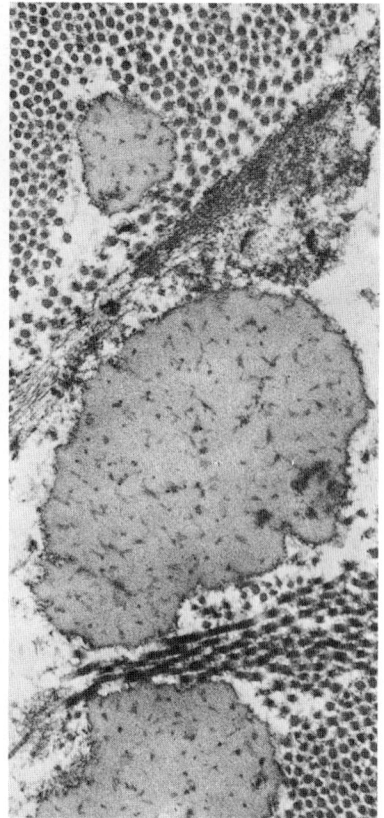

(b)

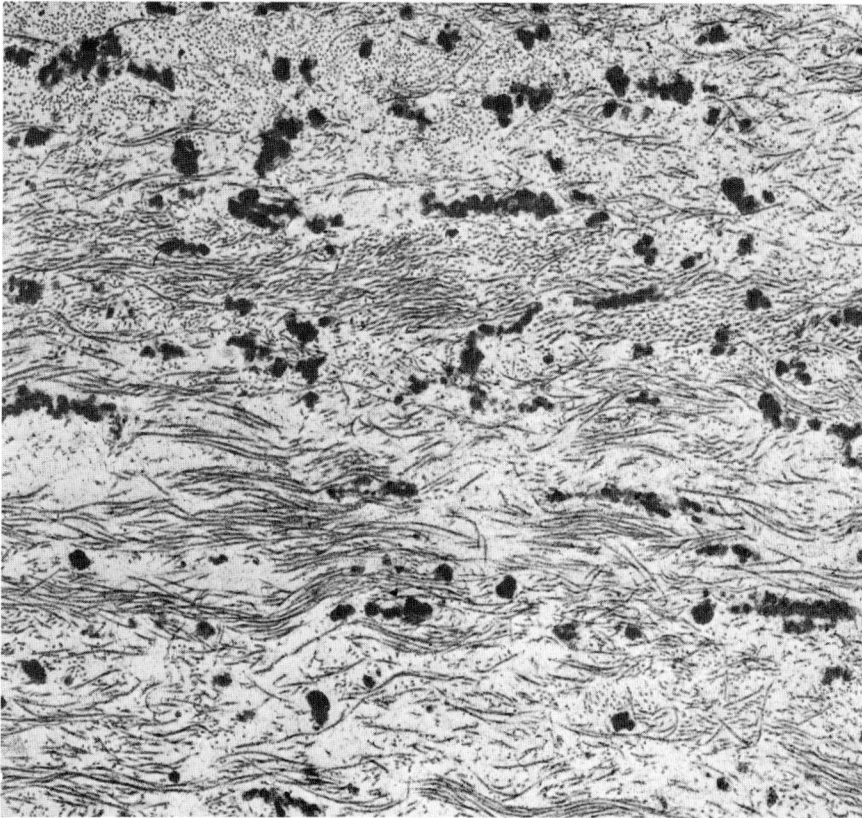

(a)

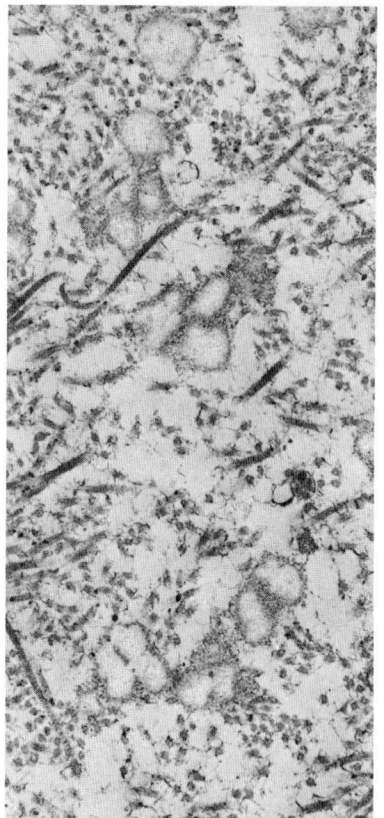

(b)

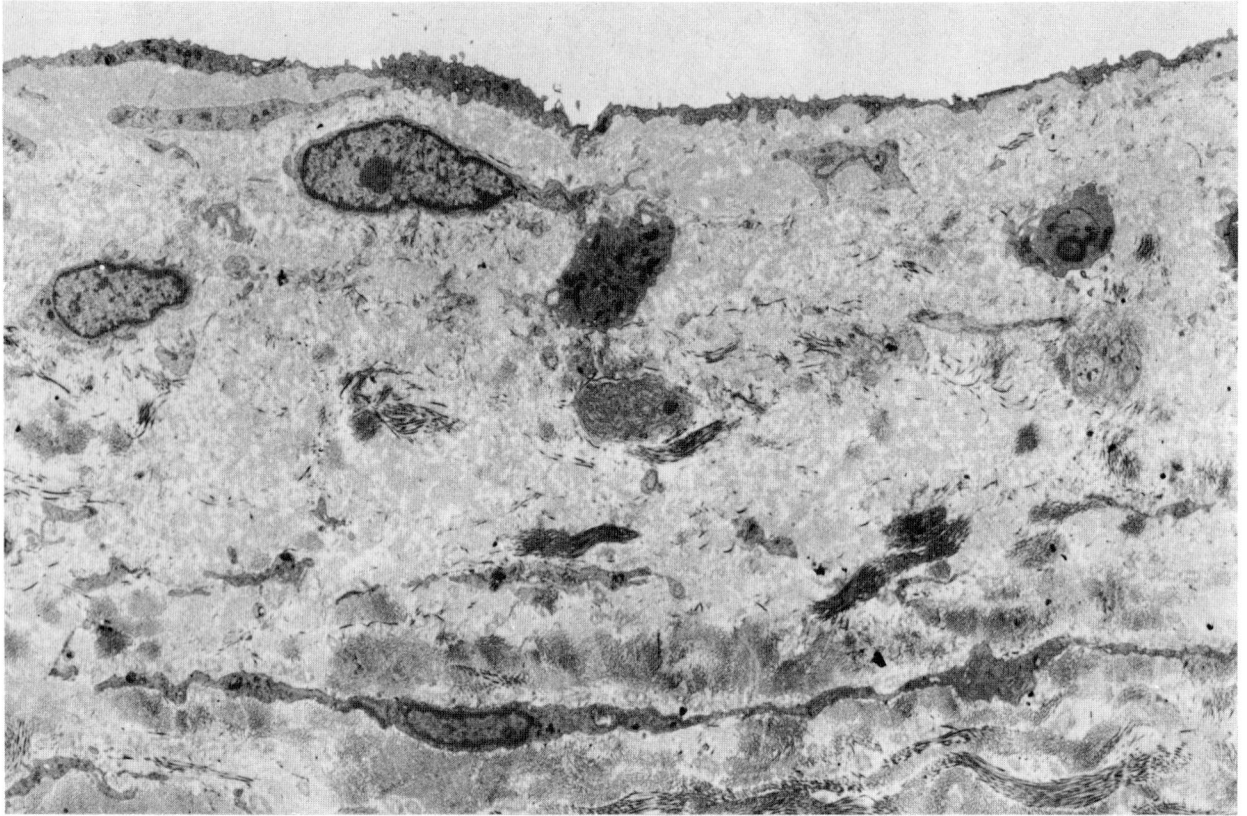

Figure 8.4. Endocardial thickening in pulmonary infundibulum.
Low magnification view of localized area of endocardial fibroelastotic thickening in pulmonary infundibulum of patient with tetralogy of Fallot. Elongated fibroblast-like cells are present in stroma rich in collagen and connective tissue ground substance. (× 4,200)

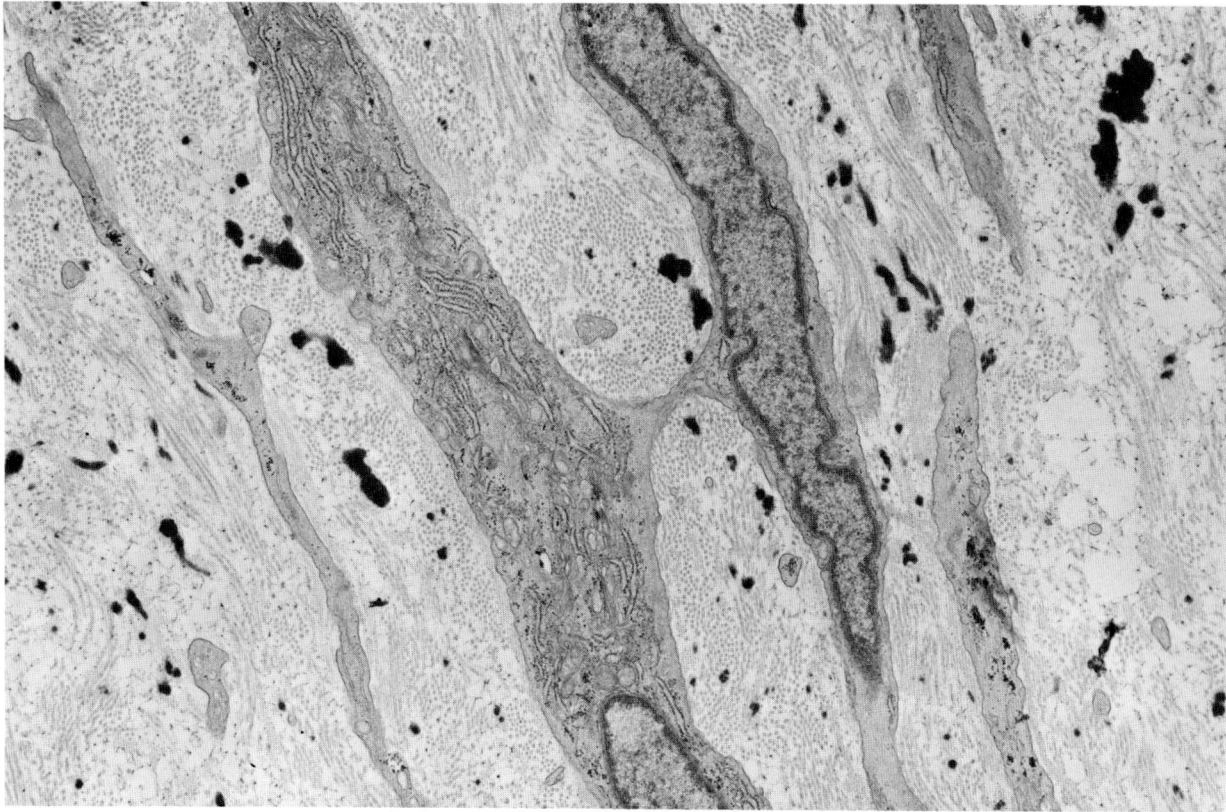

Figure 8.5. Elastic fibers in endocardial thickening.
Fibers in area similar to that shown in Figure 8.4 are small and appear densely stained by the method of Brissie et al.[20] Fibroblasts with abundant rough surfaced endoplasmic reticulum are present in this area. (×10,800)

Figure 8.6. Carcinoid endocardial plaque.
Smooth muscle cell and myofibroblast-like cells with abundant rough surfaced endoplasmic reticulum are surrounded by multilayered basal laminae. (× 7,900)

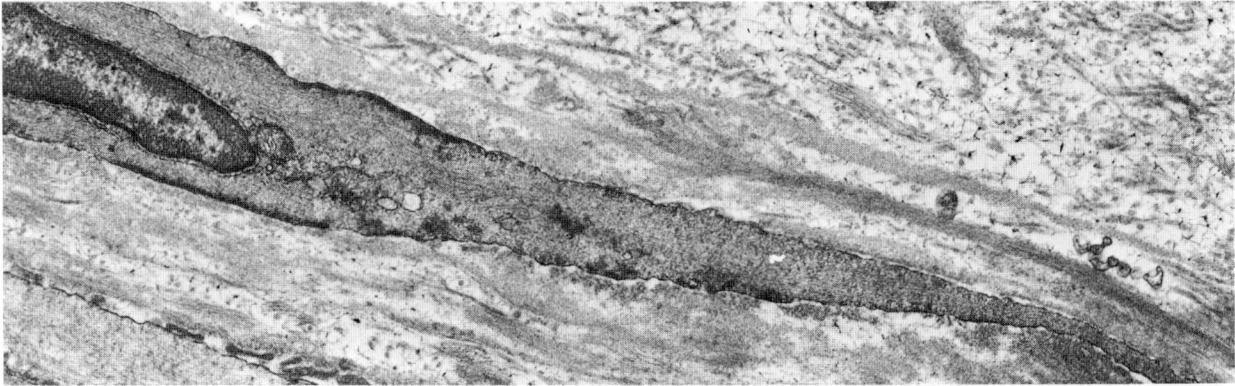

Figure 8.7. Smooth muscle cell in carcinoid endocardial plaque.
Mature smooth muscle cell surrounded by thickened basal lamina and by collagen fibrils associated with small spicules of acid mucopolysaccharide material. (× 20,100)

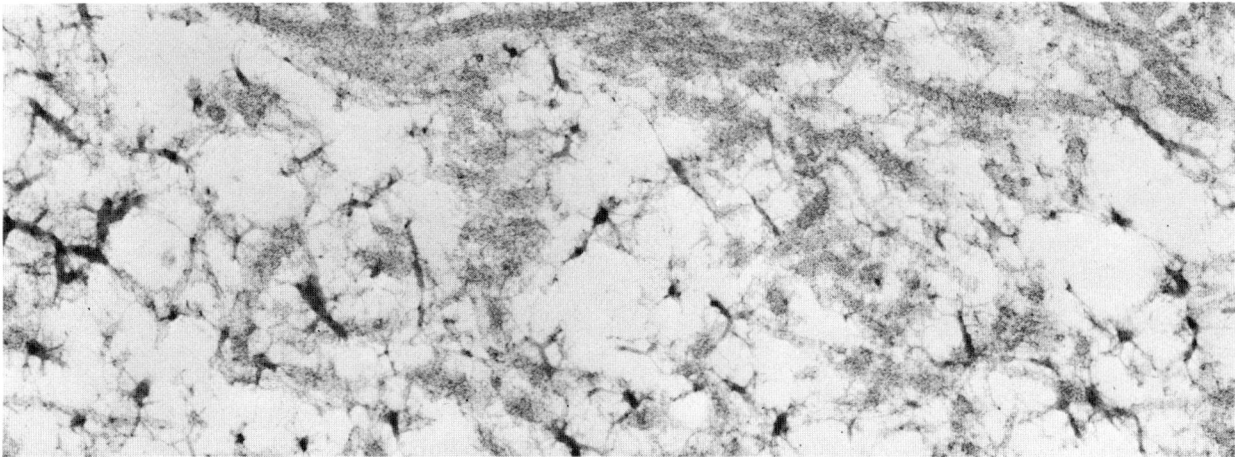

Figure 8.8. Acid mucopolysaccharide material in carcinoid plaque.
High magnification view of spicules of acid mucopolysaccharide material. (× 87,000)

9. Cardiac Tumors

Primary tumors of the heart are extremely rare. The most common of these is the myxoma, which accounts for 25 per cent of all tumors and cysts of the heart and pericardium. In adults, almost half of the benign tumors of the heart are myxomas. In infants and children, the most common cardiac tumor is the rhabdomyoma.

9.1. Cardiac myxoma

Myxoma is the cardiac tumor that has been most extensively investigated by electron microscopy.[57,63,99] Myxomas arise from the endocardium as polypoid, often pedunculated masses that project into the lumen of a cardiac chamber. Their most common site of origin is the fossa ovalis region of the left (less often, the right) atrium. They frequently extend into the area of the mitral orifice, thereby mimicking signs and symptoms of mitral valvular disease; their other frequent mode of clinical presentation is by producing systemic (or pulmonary) emboli caused by fragments of tumor, which is friable and gelatinous. Microscopically, myxomas are characterized by a myxoid stroma, rich in acid mucopolysaccharides. Scattered within this stroma are cells (myxoma cells) that exhibit several different types of arrangements: cords, capillary-like structures, networks of stellate-shaped cells, and more complex, multilayered structures resembling primitive blood vessels (Figures 9.1, 9.2, 9.3). Other cells observed are endothelial cells, fibroblast-like cells, macrophages, and mature and immature smooth muscle cells. Derivation of these four types of cells from myxoma cells is suggested by the finding of variously differentiated intermediate cell types. The cytoplasm of myxoma cells contains large numbers of 100 Å filaments, small numbers of 60 to 80 Å filaments, and patches of electron-dense material into which both types of filaments insert. The thin cytoplasmic filaments correspond in size to actin filaments and the thicker (100 Å) filaments to the "intermediate" or cytoskeletal filaments of other cells; the electron-dense patches appear analogous to the peripherally located dense areas of smooth muscle cells. Cardiac myxomas arise from multipotential mesenchymal cells.

9.2. Cardiac rhabdomyoma

Ninety percent of cardiac rhabdomyomas are multiple. They occur with equal frequency in the right and left ventricles, and involve one or both atria in 30 percent of

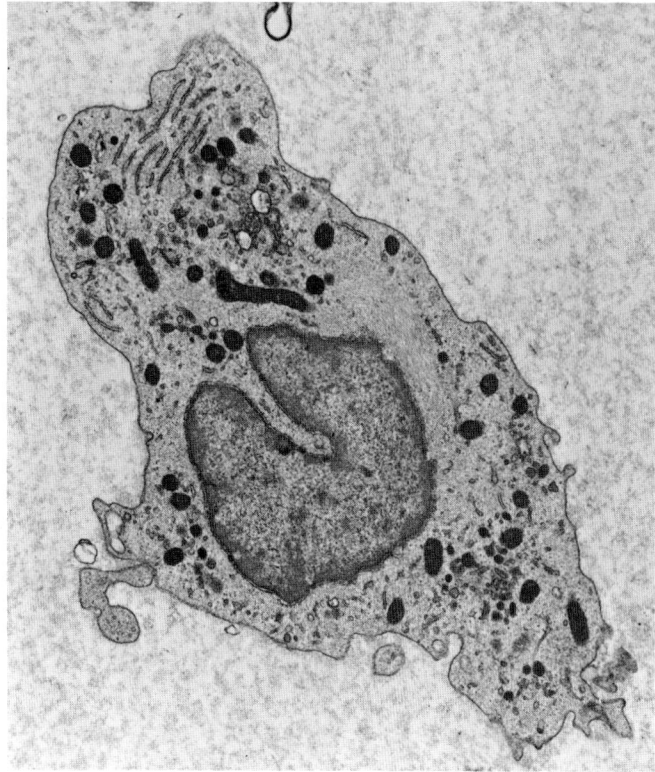

Figure 9.1. Cardiac myxoma cell.
Myxoma cell in finely fibrillar myxoid stroma. The cell contains a few cisternae of rough surfaced endoplasmic reticulum, mitochondria, and numerous cytoplasmic filaments and dense bodies. (×9,000)

patients. In at least 50 percent of patients, one or more of the tumor masses is intracavitary and obstructs intracardiac blood flow. Rhabdomyomas of the heart[39,42,132] are composed of "spider cells" (Figures 9.4, 9.5 (a), (b), (c)) which have central cytoplasmic masses containing the nucleus, clusters of mitochondria, and disorganized contractile elements (including masses of Z-band material). Scattered bundles of myofibrils radiate from the central mass toward the periphery of the cell. Large amounts of glycogen are present in these cells, usually surrounding the central mass, and the empty appearance of the rhabdomyoma cells is due to their glycogen, which remains unstained in ordinary histologic preparations. Typical components of sarcoplasmic reticulum are associated with the myofibrils of rhabdomyoma cells. Peripheral areas of these cells also contain structures resembling rudimentary T-tubules (Figure 9.5 (b)). The rhabdomyoma cells have distinct intercellular junctions that resemble intercalated discs, with well-defined desmosomes and nexuses (Figure 9.5 (c)). Many of these cells also contain leptofibrils (Figure 9.4), arranged either peripherally or in spiraling clusters in the central areas. Rhabdomyomas are derived from cardiac muscle cells and appear to represent hamartomas rather than true tumors.

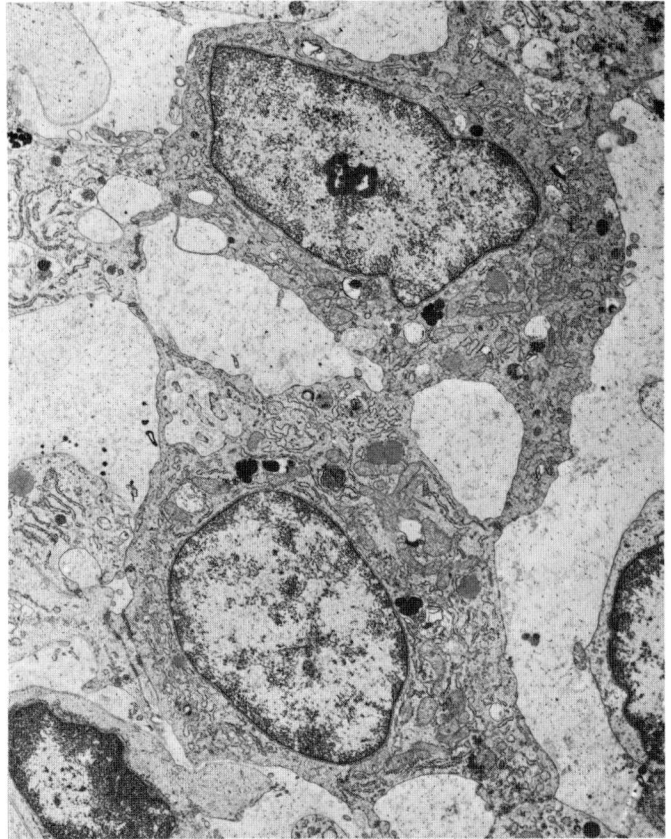

Figure 9.2. Network of stellate-shaped cardiac myxoma cells.
Polygonal or stellate-shaped myxoma cells connected to one another by small intercellular junctions of the zonula adherens type, forming a discrete network in the myxoid stroma. (×7,500)

9.3. Endocardial papillary elastofibroma

Endocardial papillary elastofibromas[64, 99] are composed of multiple papillary fronds that are attached to the endocardium by a pedicle and most frequently arise from valvular (rather than mural) endocardium. Each papillary frond consists of:

1. A central core of dense, often hyalinized collagen.
2. A peripheral zone of loose connective tissue containing collagen, small elastic fibers, and acid mucopolysaccharides.
3. A surface layer of hyperplastic endothelial cells.

Endocardial papillary elastofibromas are benign and probably are hamartomas.

70

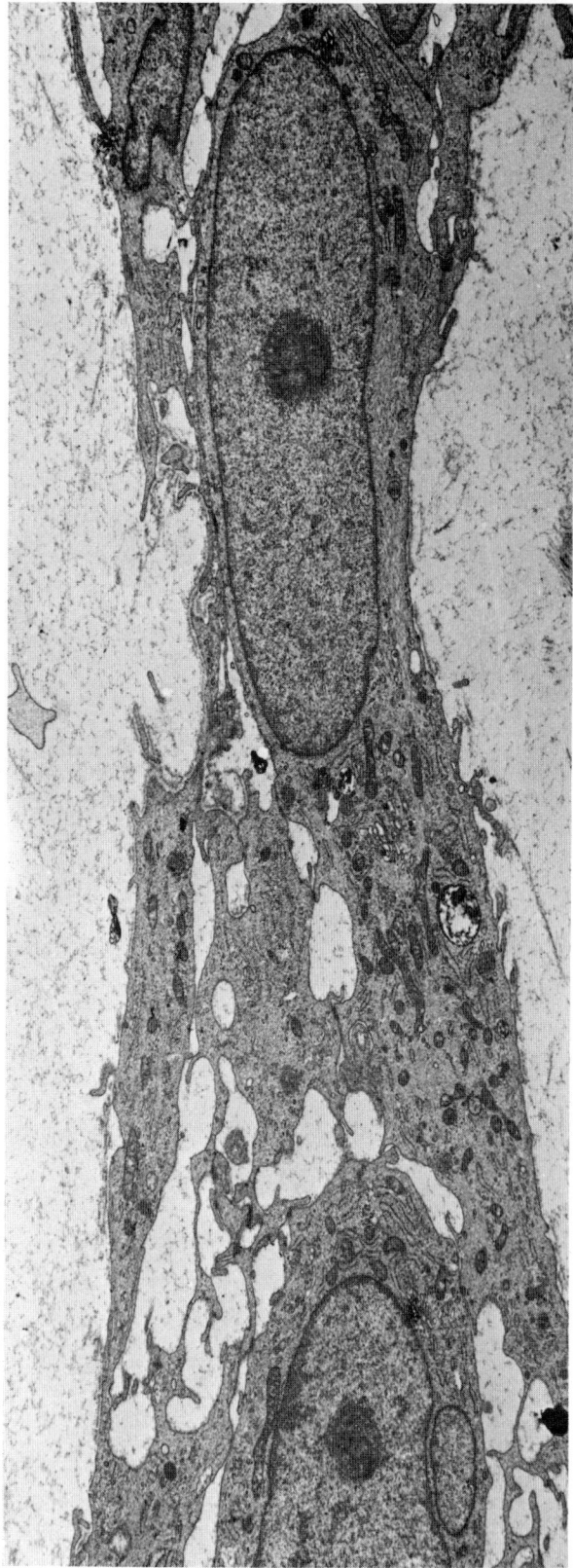

Figure 9.3. Cord-like arrangement of myxoma cells.
Several myxoma cells, morphologically similar to those shown in Figures 9.1 and 9.2, connected by small intercellular junctions to form a cord-like structure. (× 7,400)

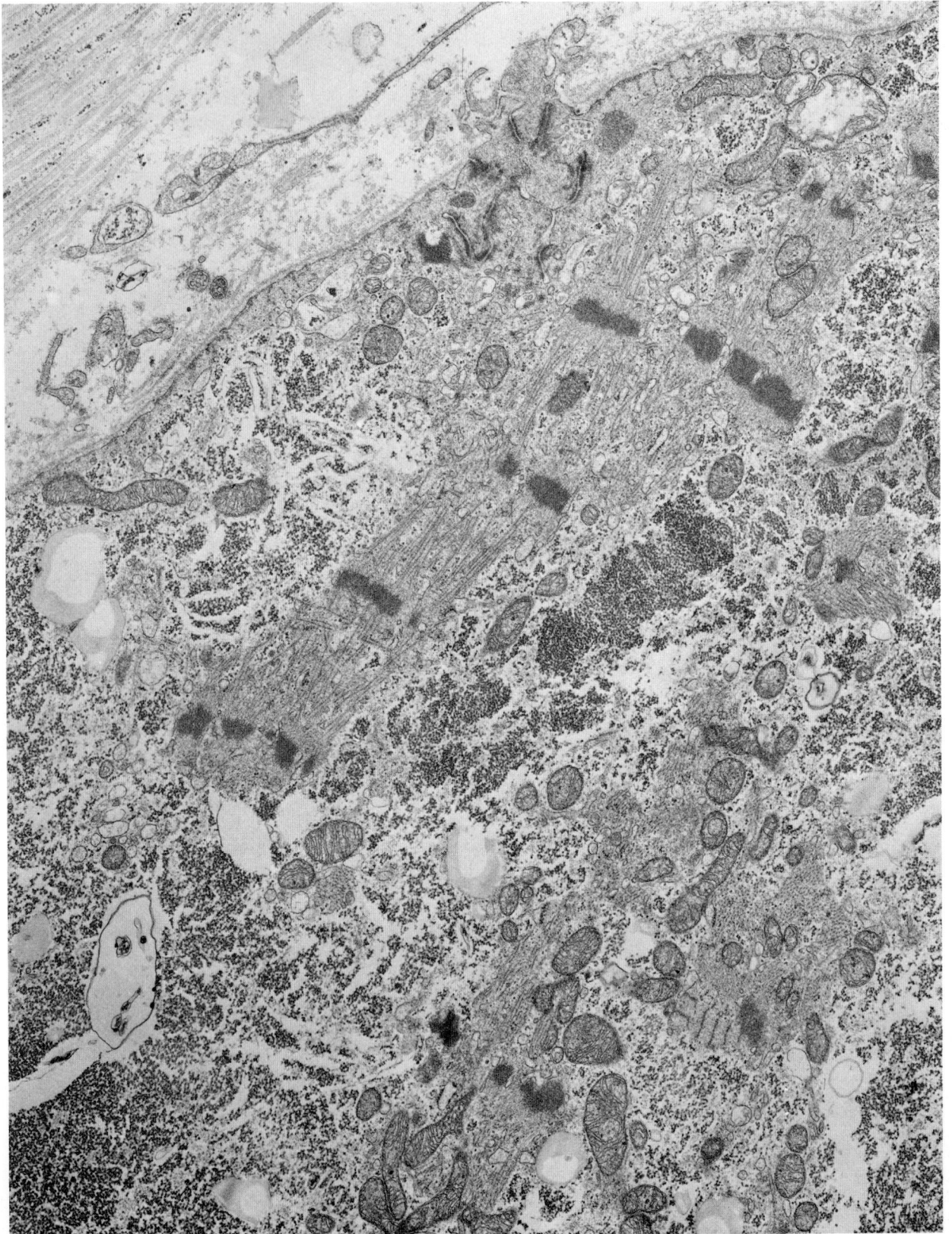

9.4. Other cardiac tumors

Limited ultrastructural study has been applied to other cardiac tumors including granular cell tumor[41] (showing cells filled with membrane-bound dense bodies, some of which contain packets of microtubules (angulate bodies)), mesothelioma of the atrioventricular node,[40] rhabdomyosarcoma,[99] and angiosarcoma.[99]

Figure 9.4. Cardiac rhabdomyoma.
Peripheral portion of cardiac rhabdomyoma cell (spider cell), showing myofibrils, mitochondria, large amounts of glycogen, a few lipid droplets and leptofibrils, and a small intracytoplasmic junction (top). (× 20,000)

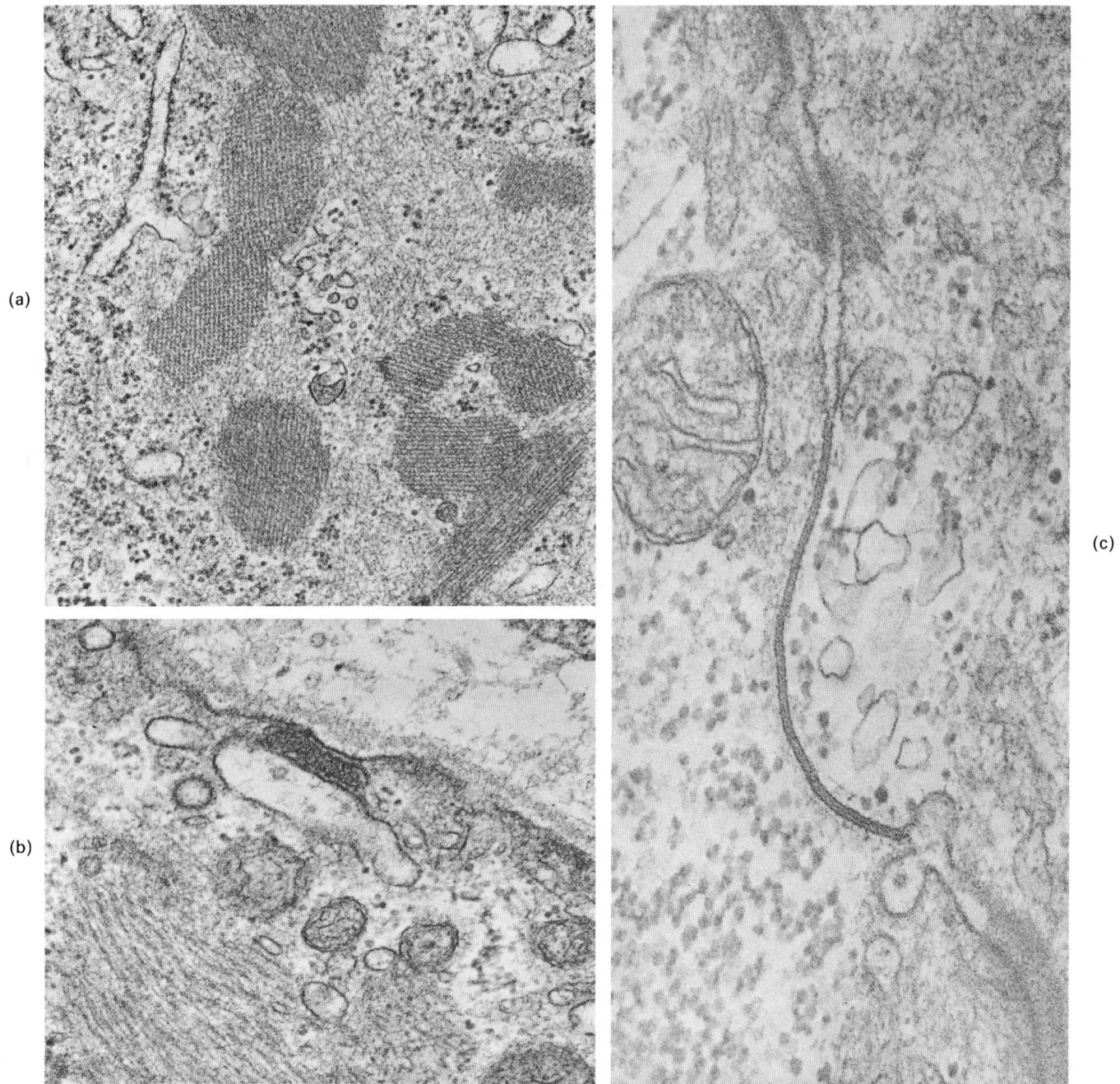

Figure 9.5. Cardiac rhabdomyomas.

(a) Masses of Z-band material in rhabdomyoma cell. These cells often contain masses of highly organized Z-band material similar to those seen in cardiac muscle cells in a variety of conditions (compare with Figure 3.6). ($\times$ 45,000)

(b) SR in cardiac rhabdomyoma cell. Small cisterna of junctional SR has dark content and lies between plasma membrane at cell surface and invagination of plasma membrane deeper in the cell. Note coated vesicle adjacent to plasma membrane invagination. ($\times$ 62,500)

(c) Intercellular junction in cardiac rhabdomyoma. One nexus and several desmosomes connect two rhabdomyoma cells. ($\times$ 84,000)

References to Part One

1. Abelmann, W. H., "Viral myocarditis and its sequelae," *Ann. Rev. Med.*, **24**, 145, 1973.
2. Albert, E. N. and Fleischer, E., "A new electron-dense stain for elastic tissue," *J. Histochem. Cytochem.*, **18**, 697, 1970.
3. Allwork, S. P. and Norton, R., "Surface ultrastructure of silicone rubber aortic valve poppets after long-term implantation. A scanning electron microscope study of four poppets," *Thorax*, **31**, 742, 1976.
4. Anversa, P., Vitali-Mazza, L., Visioli, O., and Marchetti, G., "Experimental cardiac hypertrophy: A quantitative ultrastructural study in the compensatory stage," *J. Mol. Cell. Cardiol.*, **3**, 213, 1971.
5. Appelbaum, F. R., Strauchen, J. A., Graw, R. G., Jr., Savage, D. D., Kent, K. M., Ferrans, V. J., and Herzig, G. P., "Acute lethal carditis caused by high-dose combination chemotherapy. A unique clinical and pathological entity," *Lancet*, **1**, 58, 1976.
6. Ashraf, M. and Halverson, C. A., "Structural changes in the freeze-fractured sarcolemma of ischemic myocardium," *Am. J. Path.*, **88**, 583, 1977.
7. ——— and ———, "Ultrastructural modifications of nexuses (gap junctions) during early myocardial ischemia," *J. Mol. Cell. Cardiol.*, **10**, 263, 1978.
8. Astorri, E., Bolognesi, R. Colla, B., Chizzola, A., and Visioli, O., "Left ventricular hypertrophy: a cytometric study on 42 human hearts," *J. Mol. Cell. Cardiol.*, **9**, 763, 1977.
9. Baroldi, G., Milam, J. D., Wukasch, D. C., Sandiford, F. M., Romagnoli, A., and Cooley, D. A., "Myocardial cell damage in 'stone hearts'," *J. Mol. Cell. Cardiol.*, **6**, 395, 1974.
10. Becker, A. E., Schoorl, R., Balk, A. G., and Van der Heide, R. M., "Cardiac manifestations of Fabry's disease: Report of a case with mitral insufficiency and electrocardiographic evidence of myocardial infarction," *Am. J. Cardiol.*, **36**, 829, 1975.
11. Billingham, M. E., Mason, J. W., Bristow, M. R., and Daniels, J. R., "Anthracycline cardiomyopathy monitored by morphologic changes," *Cancer Treat. Rep.*, **62**, 865, 1978.
12. Birkhead, J. S. and Apostolov, K., "Endocarditis caused by a psittacosis agent," *Br. med. J.*, **36**, 728, 1974.
13. Bishop, S. P., "Effect of aortic stenosis on myocardial cell growth, hyperplasia, and ultrastructure in neonatal dogs," in *Recent Advances in Studies on Cardiac Structure and Metabolism*, vol. III, N. S. Dhalla (ed.), *Myocardial Metabolism*, University Park Press, Baltimore, 1973, pp. 637–656.

75

14. ——— and Cole, C. R., "Ultrastructural changes in the canine myocardium with right ventricular hypertrophy and congestive heart failure," *Lab. Invest.*, **20**, 219, 1969.

15. Blieden, L. C., Desnick, R. J., Carter, J. B., Krivit, W., Moller, J. H., and Sharp, H. L., "Cardiac involvement in Sandhoff's disease: inborn error of glycosphingolipid metabolism," *Am. J. Cardiol.*, **34**, 83, 1974.

16. Bloom, S., "Structural changes in nuclear envelopes during elongation of heart muscle cells," *J. Cell Biol.*, **44**, 218, 1970.

17. Boor, P. J., Ferrans, V. J., Jones, M., Kawanami, O., Thiedemann, K.-U., Herman, E. H., and Roberts, W. C., "Tubuloreticular structures in myocardium. An ultrastructural study," *J. Mol. Cell. Cardiol.*, **11**, 967, 1979.

18. Boutet, M., Lagacé, R., and Delage, C., "Les lésions du coeur droit dans le syndrome carcinoïdien. Étude histochimique et ultrastructurale," *Un. méd. Can.*, **103**, 844, 1974.

19. Bózner, A., Knieriem, H. J., Meeson, H., and Reinauer, H., "Die Ultrastruktur und Biochemie des Herzmuskels der Ratte im Thiaminmangel und nach einer Gabe von Thiamin," *Virchows Arch. Cell Path.*, **2**, 125, 1969.

20. Brissie, R. M., Spicer, S. S., and Thompson, N. T., "The variable fine structure of elastin visualized with Verhoeff's iron hematoxylin," *Anat. Rec.*, **181**, 83, 1975.

21. Buja, L. M., Dees, J. H., Harling, D. F., and Willerson, J. T., "Analytical electron microscopic study of mitochondrial inclusions in canine myocardial infarcts," *J. Histochem. Cytochem.*, **24**, 508, 1976.

22. ———, Ferrans, V. J., and Levitsky, S., "Occurrence of intramitochondrial glycogen in canine myocardium after prolonged anoxic cardiac arrest," *J. Mol. Cell. Cardiol.*, **4**, 237, 1972.

23. ———, ———, and Maron, B. J., "Intracytoplasmic junctions in cardiac muscle cells," *Am. J. Path.*, **74**, 613, 1974.

24. ———, ———, Mayer, R. J., Roberts, W. C., and Henderson, E. S., "Cardiac ultrastructural changes induced by daunorubicin therapy," *Cancer*, **32**, 771, 1973.

25. ———, ———, and Rabson, A. S., "Unusual nuclear alterations," *Lancet*, **1**, 402, 1974.

26. ———, Khoi, N. B., and Roberts, W. C., "Clinically significant cardiac amyloidosis. Clinicopathologic findings in 15 patients," *Am. J. Cardiol.*, **26**, 394, 1970.

27. ——— and Roberts, W. C., "Iron in the heart. Etiology and clinical significance," *Am. J. Med.*, **51**, 209, 1971.

28. Burch, G. E., "Ultrastructural myocardial changes produced by viruses," in *Recent Advances in Studies on Cardiac Structure and Metabolism*, vol. VI, A. Fleckenstein and G. Rona (eds.), *Pathophysiology and Morphology of Myocardial Cell Alterations,* University Park Press, Baltimore, 1975, pp. 501–523.

29. Cain, H., Egner, E., and Kresse, H., "Mucopolysaccharidosis III A (Sanfilippo disease type A). Histochemical, electron microscopical and biochemical findings," *Beitr. path. Anat.*, **160**, 58, 1977.

30. Calderone, R. A., Rotondo, M. F., and Sande, M. A., "*Candida albicans* endocarditis: Ultrastructural studies of vegetation formation," *Infec. Immunity*, **20**, 279, 1978.

31. Challice, C. E. and Virágh, S., *Ultrastructure of the Mammalian Heart*, Academic Press, New York, 1973.

32. Cossio, P. M., Laguens, R. P., Diez, C., Szarfman, A., Segal, A., and Arana, R. M., "Chagasic cardiopathy. Antibodies reacting with plasma membrane of striated muscle and endothelial cells," *Circulation,* **50**, 1252, 1974.

33. Crozatier, B., Ashraf, M., Franklin, D., Ross, J., Jr., Nimmo, L., and McKown, D., "Sarcomere length in experimental myocardial infarction: Evidence for sarcomere overstretch in dyskinetic ventricular regions," *J. Mol. Cell. Cardiol.*, **9**, 785, 1977.

34. Davies, M. J., "Myocarditis," in A. Pomerance and M. J. Davies (eds.), *The Pathology of the Heart*, Blackwell Scientific Publications, Oxford, 1975, pp. 193–210.

35. Desnick, R. J., Bleiden, L. D., Sharp, H. L., and Moller, J. H., "Cardiac valvular anomalies in Fabry's disease: Clinical, morphologic and biochemical studies," *Circulation*, **54**, 818, 1976.

36. Dreier, E. O. and Serochkin, G. G., "[Ultrastructure of the cells of rheumatic granuloma]", *Vopr. Revm.*, **10**, 37, 1970.

37. Durack, D., "Experimental bacterial endocarditis. IV. Structure and evolution of very early lesions," *J. Path.*, **115**, 81, 1975.

38. Fawcett, D. W. and McNutt, N. S., "The ultrastructure of the cat myocardium. I. Ventricular papillary muscle," *J. Cell Biol.*, **42**, 1, 1969.

39. Fenoglio, J. J., Jr., Diana, D. J., Bowen, T. E., McAllister, H. A., Jr., and Ferrans, V. J., "Ultrastructure of a cardiac rhabdomyoma," *Human Pathol.*, **8**, 700, 1977.

40. ———, Jacobs, D. W., and McAllister, H. A., Jr., "Ultrastructure of the mesothelioma of the atrioventricular node," *Cancer*, **40**, 721, 1977.

41. ——— and McAllister, H. A., Jr., "Granular cell tumors of the heart," *Archs Path.*, **100**, 276, 1976.

42. ———, McAllister, H. A., Jr., and Ferrans, V. J., "Cardiac rhabdomyoma: A clinicopathologic and electron microscopic study," *Am. J. Cardiol.*, **38**, 241, 1976.

43. ——— and Pham, T. D., "Ruptured chordae tendineae: An electron microscopic study," *Human Pathol.*, **3**, 415, 1972.

44. ——— and Wagner, B. M., "Studies in rheumatic fever. VI. Ultrastructure of chronic rheumatic heart disease," *Am. J. Path.*, **73**, 623, 1973.

45. Ferrans, V. J., "Overview of cardiac pathology in relation to anthracycline cardiotoxicity," *Cancer Treat. Rep.*, **62**, 955, 1978.

46. ———, "Myocardial ultrastructure in human cardiac hypertrophy," in M. Kaltenbach, F. Loogen, and E. G. J. Olsen (eds.), *Cardiomyopathy and Myocardial Biopsy*, Springer-Verlag, Berlin, Heidelberg, New York, 1978, pp. 100–120.

47. ———, Boyce, S. W., Billingham, M. E., Spray, T. L., and Roberts, W. C., "Infection of glutaraldehyde-preserved porcine valve heterografts," *Am. J. Cardiol.*, **43**, 1123, 1979.

48. ———, Buja, L. M., and Jones, M., "Ultrastructure and cytochemistry of glycogen in cardiac diseases," in *Recent Advances in Studies on Cardiac Structure and Metabolism*, vol. III, N. S. Dhalla (ed.), *Myocardial Metabolism*, University Park Press, Baltimore, 1973, pp. 97–144.

49. ———, ———, and Roberts, W. C., "Cardiac morphologic changes produced by ethanol," in M. A. Rothschild, M. Oratz, and S. Schreiber (eds.), *Alcohol and Abnormal Protein Biosynthesis*, Pergamon Press, New York, 1974, pp. 139–185.

50. ———, Hibbs, R. G., and Burda, C. D., "The heart in Fabry's disease. A histochemical and electron microscopic study," *Am. J. Cardiol.*, **24**, 95, 1969.

51. ———, Jones, M., Maron, B. J., and Roberts, W. C., "The nuclear membranes in hypertrophied human cardiac muscle cells," *Am. J. Path.*, **78**, 427, 1975.

52. ———, McAllister, H. A., Jr., and Haese, W. H., "Infantile cardiomyopathy with histiocytoid change in cardiac muscle cells. Report of six patients," *Circulation*, **53**, 708, 1976.

53. ———, Maron, B. J., Buja, L. M., Ali, N., and Roberts, W. C., "Intranuclear glycogen deposits in human cardiac muscle cells: ultrastructure and cytochemistry," *J. Mol. Cell. Cardiol.*, **7**, 373, 1975.

54. ———, Massumi, R. A., Shugoll, G. I., Ali, N., and Roberts, W. C., "Ultrastructural studies of myocardial biopsies in 45 patients with obstructive or congestive cardiomyopathy," in *Recent Advances in Studies on Cardiac Structure and Metabolism*, vol. II, E. Bajusz, G. Rona, A. J. Brink, and A. Lochner (eds.), *The Cardiomyopathies*, University Park Press, Baltimore, 1973, pp. 231–272.

55. ———, Morrow, A. G., and Roberts, W. C., "Myocardial ultrastructure in idiopathic hypertrophic subaortic stenosis. A study of operatively excised left ventricular outflow tract muscle in 14 patients," *Circulation*, **45**, 769, 1972.

56. ———, Rentería, V. G., Jones, M., Knight, P. O., and Roberts, W. C., "Ultrastructure of prolapsed (floppy) mitral valves," *J. Mol. Cell. Cardiol.*, **9**, suppl. 1, 22, 1977.

57. ——— and Roberts, W. C., "Structural features of cardiac myxomas. Histology, histochemistry and electron microscopy," *Human Pathol.*, **4**, 111, 1973.

58. ——— and ———, "Intermyofibrillar and nuclear-myofibrillar connections in hyman and canine myocardium. An ultrastructural study." *J. Mol. Cell. Cardiol.*, **5**, 247, 1973.

59. ——— and ———, "The carcinoid endocardial plaque. An ultrastructural study," *Human Pathol.*, **7**, 387, 1976.

60. ——— and ———, "Pathology of rheumatic heart disease," *Israel J. Med. Sci.*, (in press).

61. ———, Spray, T. L., Billingham, M. E., and Roberts, W. C., "Structural changes in glutaraldehyde-treated porcine heterografts used as substitute cardiac valves. Transmission and scanning electron microscopic observations in 12 patients," *Am. J. Cardiol.*, **41**, 1159, 1978.

62. ———, Thiedemann, K.-U., Maron, B. J., Jones, M., and Roberts, W. C., "Spherical microparticles in human myocardium. An ultrastructural study," *Lab. Invest.*, **35**, 349, 1976.

63. Fine, G., Morales, A., and Horn, R. C., Jr., "Cardiac myxoma. A morphologic and histogenetic appraisal," *Cancer*, **22**, 1156, 1968.

64. Fishbein, M. C., Ferrans, V. J., and Roberts, W. C., "Endocardial papillary elastofibromas. Histologic, histochemical, and electron microscopic findings," *Archs Path.*, **99**, 335, 1975.

65. ———, ———, and ———, "Histologic and ultrastructural features of primary and secondary endocardial fibroelastosis," *Archs Path. Lab. Med.*, **101**, 49, 1977.

66. Geissinger, H., Miniats, O., Ruhnke, H., and Djurickovic, D., "Experimental staphylococcal endocarditis in pigs," *J. Comp. Pathol.*, **83**, 323, 1973.

67. Goldstein, M. A., Schroeter, J. P., and Sass, R. L., "Optical diffraction of the Z lattice in canine cardiac muscle," *J. Cell Biol.*, **75**, 818, 1977.

68. ———, Sordahl, L. A., and Schwartz, A., "Ultrastructural analysis of left ventricular hypertrophy in rabbits," *J. Mol. Cell. Cardiol.*, **6**, 265, 1974.

69. Goodman, J. R., Warshaw, J. B., and Dallman, P. R., "Cardiac hypertrophy in rats with iron and copper deficiency: quantitative contribution of mitochondrial enlargement," *Pediat. Res.*, **4**, 244, 1970.

70, Grosgogeat, Y. and Nicholas, G., "La biopsie endomyocardique: son intérêt en pathologie tropicale. A propos de 3 nouveaux cas," *Archs Mal. Coeur*, **70**, 179, 1977.

71. Haas, J. E. and Yunis, E. J., "Viral crystalline arrays in human Coxsackie myocarditis," *Lab. Invest.*, **23**, 442, 1970.

72. Hadley, R. N. and Hagstrom, J. W. C., "Cardiac lesions in a patient with familial neurovisceral lipidosis (generalized gangliosidosis)," *Am. J. clin. Path.*, **55**, 237, 1971.

73. Hatt, P. Y., Berjal, G., Moravec, J., and Swynghedauw, B., "Heart failure: an electron microscopic study of the left ventricular papillary muscle in aortic insufficiency in the rabbit," *J. Mol. Cell. Cardiol.*, **1**, 235, 1970.

74. Hearse, D. J., "Reperfusion of the ischemic myocardium," *J. Mol. Cell. Cardiol.*, **9**, 605, 1977.

75. Herdson, P. B., Kaltenbach, J. P., and Jennings, R. B., "Fine structural and biochemical changes in dog myocardium during autolysis," *Am. J. Path.*, **57**, 539, 1969.

76. Hyams, V. J. and Manion, W. C., "Incomplete differentiation of the cardiac valves," *Am. Heart J.*, **76**, 173, 1968.

77. Jennings, R. B., Baum, J. H., and Herdson, P. B., "Fine structural changes in myocardial ischemia," *Archs Path.*, **79**, 135, 1965.

78. ——— and Ganote, C. E., "Structural changes in myocardium during acute ischemia," *Circulation Res.*, **34** and **35**, suppl. III, 111–156, 1974.

79. Jones, M. and Ferrans, V. J., "Intramitochondrial glycogen in hypertrophied infundibular muscle of patients with congenital heart diseases," *Am. J. Path.*, **70**, 69, 1973.

80. ——— and ———, "Myocardial ultrastructure in children and adults with congenital heart disease," in W. C. Roberts (ed.), *Congenital Heart Disease in Adults*, Davis, Philadelphia, 1979, pp. 501–530.

81. ———, ———, Morrow, A. G., and Roberts, W. C., "Ultrastructure of crista supraventricularis muscle in patients with congenital heart diseases associated with right ventricular outflow tract obstruction," *Circulation*, **51**, 39, 1975.

82. Kajikawa, K., Yamaguchi, T., Katsuda, S., and Miwa, A., "An improved electron stain for elastic fibers using tannic acid," *J. Electron Microsc., Tokyo*, **24**, 287, 1975.

83. Kawai, C., Matsumori, A., Kitaura, Y., and Takatsu, T., "Viruses and the heart: Viral myocarditis and cardiomyopathy," *Prog. Cardiol.*, **7**, 141, 1978

84. Kawamura, K., Cowley, M. J., Karp, R. B., Mantle, J. A., Logic, J. R., Rogers, W. J., Russell, R. O., Jr., Rackley, C. E., and James, T. N., "Intramitochondrial inclusions in the myocardial cells of human hearts with coronary disease," *J. Mol. Cell. Cardiol.*, **10**, 797, 1978.

85. Kloner, R. A., Fishbein, M. C., Braunwald, E., and Maroko, P. R., "Effect of propranolol on mitochondrial morphology during acute myocardial ischemia," *Am. J. Cardiol.*, **41**, 880, 1978.

86. ———, ———, Cotran, R. S., Braunwald, E., and Maroko, P. R., "The effect of propranolol on microvascular injury in acute myocardial ischemia," *Circulation*, **55**, 872, 1977.

87. ———, ———, Maclean, D., Braunwald, E., and Maroko, P. R., "Effect of hyaluronidase during the early phase of acute myocardial ischemia: An ultrastructural and morphometric analysis," *Am. J. Cardiol.*, **40**, 43, 1978.

88. ———, Ganote, C. E., and Jennings, R. B., "The 'no reflow' phenomenon after temporary coronary occlusion in the dog," *J. clin. Invest.*, **54**, 1496, 1974.

89. ———, ———, Whalen, D. A., Jr., and Jennings, R. B., "Effect of a transient period of ischemia on myocardial cells. II. Fine structure during the first few minutes of reflow," *Am. J. Path.*, **74**, 399, 1974.

90. Knieriem, H.-J., "Electron microscopic findings in congestive cardiomyopathy," in M. Kaltenbach, F. Loogen, and E. G. J. Olsen (eds.), *Cardiomyopathy and Myocardial Biopsy*, Springer-Verlag, Berlin, Heidelberg, New York, 1978, pp. 71–86.

91. Kunkel, B., Lapp, H., Kober, G., and Kaltenbach, M., "Ultrastructural evaluations in early and advanced congestive cardiomyopathies," in M. Kaltenbach, F. Loogen, and E. G. J. Olsen (eds.), *Cardiomyopathy and Myocardial Biopsy*, Springer-Verlag, Berlin, Heidelberg, New York, 1978, pp. 87–99.

92. Laks, M. M., Morady, F., Adomian, G. E., and Swan, H. J. C., "Presence of widened and multiple intercalated discs in the hypertrophied canine heart," *Circulation Res.*, **27**, 391, 1970.

93. Lannigan, R. and Zaki, S., "Electron microscopic appearances of rheumatic lesions in the left auricular appendage in mitral stenosis," *Nature*, **198**, 898, 1963.

94. Legato, M. J., "Sarcomerogenesis in human myocardium," *J. Mol. Cell. Cardiol.*, **1**, 425, 1970.

95. Lie, J. T. and Davis, J. S., "Pancarditis in Whipple's disease: Electron-microscopic demonstration of intracardiac bacillary bodies," *Am. J. clin. Path.*, **66**, 22, 1976.

96. ——— and Sun, S. C., "Ultrastructure of ischemic contracture of the left ventricle ('stone heart')", *Mayo Clin. Proc.*, **51**, 785, 1976.

97. Linzbach, A. J., "Heart failure from the point of view of quantitative anatomy," *Am. J. Cardiol.*, **5**, 370, 1960.

98. McAllister, H. A. and Fenoglio, J. J., Jr., "Cardiac involvement in Whipple's disease," *Circulation*, **52**, 152, 1975.

99. McAllister, H. A., Jr. and Fenoglio, J. J., Jr., *Tumors of the Cardiovascular System*, Armed Forces Institute of Pathology, Washington, 1978.

100. McNutt, N. S., "Ultrastructure of intercellular junctions in adult and developing cardiac muscle," *Am. J. Cardiol.*, **25**, 169, 1970.

101. Maron, B. J., Clark, C. E., Henry, W. L., Fukuda, T., Edwards, J. E., Matthews, E. C., Jr., Redwood, D. R., and Epstein, S. E., "Prevalence and characteristics of disproportionate ventricular septal thickening in patients with acquired or congenital heart diseases. Echocardiographic and morphologic findings," *Circulation*, **55**, 489, 1977.

102. ———, Edwards, J. E., and Epstein, S. E., "Disproportionate ventricular septal thickening in patients with systemic hypertension," *Chest*, **73**, 466, 1978.

103. ——— and Ferrans, V. J., "Significance of multiple intercalated discs in hypertrophied human myocardium," *Am. J. Path.*, **73**, 81, 1973.

104. ——— and ———, "Aggregates of tubules in human cardiac muscle cells," *J. Mol. Cell. Cardiol.*, **6**, 249, 1974.

105. ——— and ———, "Intramitochondrial glycogen deposits in hypertrophied human myocardium," *J. Mol. Cell. Cardiol.*, **7**, 697, 1975.

106. ———, ———, Henry, W. L., Clark, C. E., Redwood, D. R., Roberts, W. C., Morrow, A. G., and Epstein, S. E., "Differences in distribution of myocardial abnormalities in patients with obstructive and non-obstructive asymmetric septal hypertrophy (ASH): Light and electron microscopic findings," *Circulation*, **50**, 436, 1974.

107. ———, ———, and Roberts, W. C., "Myocardial ultrastructure in patients with chronic aortic valve disease," *Am. J. Cardiol.*, **35**, 725, 1975.

108. ———, ———, and ———, "Ultrastructural features of degenerated cardiac muscle cells in patients with cardiac hypertrophy," *Am. J. Path.*, **79**, 387, 1975.

109. ——— and Roberts, W. C., "Quantitative analysis of cardiac muscle cell disorganization in the ventricular septum of patients with hypertrophic cardiomyopathy," *Circulation*, **59**, 689, 1979.

110. ———, Savage, D. D., Clark, C. E., Henry, W. L., Vlodaver, Z., Edwards, J. E., and Epstein, S. E., "Prevalence and characteristics of disproportionate ventricular septal thickening in patients with coronary artery disease," *Circulation*, **57**, 250, 1978.

111. Meerson, F. Z., Zaletayeva, T. A., Lagutchev, S. S., and Pshennikova, M. G., "Structure and mass of mitochondria in the process of compensatory hyperfunction and hypertrophy of the heart," *Expl Cell Res.*, **36**, 568, 1964.

112. Merski, J. A., Daskal, I., and Busch, H., "Effects of adriamycin on ultrastructure of nucleoli in the heart and liver cells of the rat," Cancer Res., **36**, 1580, 1976.

113. Mitomo, Y., "Ultrastructural changes in the bacterial vegetative endocarditis," *Bull. Tokyo med. dent. Univ.*, **21**, 79, 1974.

114. Nagashima, K., Endo, H., Sakakibara, K., Konishi, Y., Miyachi, K., Wey, J. J., Suzuki, Y., and Onisawa, J., "Morphological and biochemical studies of a case of mucopolysaccharidosis II (Hunter's syndrome)," *Acta path. jap.*, **26**, 115, 1976.

115. Nakao, K. and Angrist, A. A., "Electron microscopy of nonbacterial valvular vegetations in rats with arteriovenous shunts," *Br. J. exp. Path.*, **48**, 494, 1967.

116. Page, E. and McCallister, L. P., "Quantitative electron microscopic description of heart muscle cells: Application to normal, hypertrophied, and thyroxin-stimulated hearts," *Am. J. Cardiol.*, **31**, 172, 1973.

117. Pienaar, J. G. and Price, H. M., "Ultrastructure and origin of the Anitschkow cell," *Am. J. Path.*, **51**, 1063, 1967.

118. Piepkorn, M. W. and Reichenbach, D. D., "Infective endocarditis associated with cell wall-deficient bacteria. Electron microscopic findings in four cases," *Human Pathol.*, **9**, 163, 1978.

119. Rentería, V. G. and Ferrans, V. J., "Intracellular collagen fibrils in cardiac valves of patients with the Hurler syndrome," *Lab. Invest.*, **34**, 263, 1976.

120. ———, ———, and Roberts, W. C., "The heart in the Hurler syndrome. Gross, histologic and ultrastructural observations in five necropsy cases," *Am. J. Cardiol.*, **38**, 487, 1976.

121. Richter, G. W. and Kellner, A., "Hypertrophy of the human heart at the level of fine structure. An analysis and two postulates," *J. Cell Biol.*, **18**, 195, 1963.

122. Roberts, W. C., Buja, L. M., and Ferrans, V. J., "Löffler's fibroplastic parietal endocarditis, eosinophilic leukemia and Davies' endomyocardial fibrosis. The same disease at different stages?" *Pathologia Microbiol.*, **35**, 90, 1970.

123. ——— and Ferrans, V. J., "Pathologic anatomy of the cardiomyopathies. Idiopathic dilated and hypertrophic types, infiltrative types, and endo-myocardial disease with and without eosinophilia," *Human Pathol.*, **6**, 287, 1975.

124. Rodman, N. F., Doty, D. B., and Caughey, R. C., "Surface ultrastructural studies of mitral valve prosthetic devices," in *Scanning Electron Microscopy 1974*, part III, *Proceedings of the Workshop on Advances in Biomedical Applications of the SEM*, IIT Research Institute, Chicago, 1974, pp. 729–736.

125. Rona, G., Hüttner, I., and Boutet, M., "Microcirculatory changes in myocardium with particular reference to catecholamine-induced cardiac muscle cell injury," in *Handbuch der allgemeinen Pathologie III*, vol. 7, H. Meessen (ed.), *Microcirculation*, Springer-Verlag, Berlin, Heidelberg, New York, 1977, pp. 791–888.

126. Roy, P. E., "Nodule d'Aschoff: Etude ultrastructurale," *Archs Mal. Coeur*, **67**, 199, 1974.

127. ———, "De la participation des histiocytes et des fibres musculaires lisses dans la formation des nodules d'Aschoff," *Un. méd. Can.*, **103**, 913, 1974.

128. Sanabria, A., "[Ultrastructure of *Trypanosoma cruzi* in the rat myocardium. I. Trypanosoma stage]," *Acta cient. venez.*, **16**, 163, 1965.

129. ———, "[Ultrastructure of *Trypanosoma cruzi* in the rat myocardium. II. Crithidia and leishmania stages,]" *Acta cient. venez.*, **16**, 174, 1965.

130. Schaper, J., Hehrlein, F., Schlepper, M., and Thiedemann, K.-U., "Ultrastructural alterations during ischemia and reperfusion in human hearts during cardiac surgery," *J. Mol. Cell. Cardiol.*, **9**, 175, 1977.

131. Siew, S., "Scanning electron microscopy of acute rheumatic valvulitis," in R. P. Becker and O. Johari (eds.), *Scanning Electron Microscopy*, AMF, O'Hare, Illinois, 1978, pp. 341–348.

132. Silverman, J. F., Kay, S., McCue, C. M, Lower, R. R., Brough, A. J. and

Chang, C. H., "Rhabdomyoma of the heart. Ultrastructural study of three cases," *Lab. Invest.*, **35**, 596, 1976.

133. Smith, H. E. and Page, E., "Morphometry of mitochondrial ultrastructure during myocardial cell hypertrophy and atrophy," *Anat. Rec.*, **181**, 483, 1975.

134. Sommer, J. R. and Waugh, R. A., "Ultrastructure of heart muscle," *Environ. Health Perspect.*, **26**, 159, 1978.

135. Spry, C. J. F. and Tai, P. C., "Studies on blood eosinophils. II. Patients with Löffler's cardiomyopathy," *Clin. Exp. Immunol.*, **24**, 423, 1976.

136. Stollerman, G. H., *Rheumatic Fever and Streptococcal Infection*, Grune and Stratton, New York, 1975.

137. Thiedemann, K.-U. and Ferrans, V. J., "Ultrastructure of sarcoplasmic reticulum in atrial myocardium of patients with mitral valvular disease," *Am. J. Path.*, **83**, 1, 1976.

138. ——— and ———, "Left atrial ultrastructure in mitral valvular disease," *Am. J. Path.*, **89**, 575, 1977.

139. Wagner, B. M. and Siew, S., "Studies in rheumatic fever. V. Significance of the human Anitschkow cell," *Human Pathol.*, **1**, 45, 1970.

140. Walsh, J. J., Burch, G. E., Black, W. C., Ferrans, V. J., and Hibbs, R. G., "Idiopathic myocardiopathy of the puerperium (post-partal heart disease)," *Circulation*, **32**, 19, 1965.

141. Whalen, D. A., Jr., Hamilton, D. G., Ganote, C. E., and Jennings, R. B., "Effect of a transient period of ischemia on myocardial cells. I. Effects on cell volume regulation," *Am. J. Path*, , 381, 1974.

142. Willerson, J. T., Watson, J. T., Hutton, I., Templeton, G. H., and Fixler, D. E., "Reduced myocardial reflow and increased coronary vascular resistance following prolonged myocardial ischemia in the dog," *Circulation Res.*, **36**, 771, 1975.

143. Wollenberger, A. and Schulze, W., "Über das Volumenverhältnis von Mitochondrien zu Myofibrillen im chronisch überlasteten, hypertrophierten Herzen," *Naturwissenschaften*, **49**, 161, 1962.

144. Zak, R., "Development and proliferative capacity of cardiac muscle cells," *Circulation Res.*, **35**, suppl. 2, 17, 1974.

Part Two

Blood Vessels

Lee V. Leak

10. Introduction to Part Two

The first living creatures were unicellular organisms, existing as isolated cells or clusters of cells organized into colonies. With such an arrangement, nutritional molecules and waste metabolites could readily diffuse through intercellular spaces and into the external environment. However, with the evolution of multicellular forms, there arose a need for greater specializations of various cellular and tissue types, greatly increasing the number, size, and activities. As a result the shear mass of the organism was increased to a point where the majority of its cellular components were no longer in physical contact with the external environment, thus rendering the process of diffusion inefficient. With increased morphological complexity in the phylogenetic scale, there was also an increase in the specialized structures that were needed to serve the various cellular and tissue activities of the organism, requiring the supply of gases and nutrients to cellular components. Likewise, the products of metabolism had to be removed in order to create a stable environment, permitting these specialized cells and tissues to function efficiently. To this end, a tubular system (cardiovascular) which carries fluids and pigments capable of transporting oxygen was developed out of the need to provide a stable environment for cells to maintain their existence.[55]

In certain invertebrates the blood vascular system is open so that its contents (i.e., hemolymph) pass freely from the arteries into the extracellular spaces to invade the major organs and tissues, providing a medium in which gases, metabolites, and nutrients are carried to the individual cells. From these tissue spaces the fluids slowly diffuse into veins and back into the heart.[8]

With tissue diversity, the development of a complex pumping organ (heart) facilitated the circulation of large quantities of fluids which included plasma proteins and cells throughout the body. In higher animals, including man, components of the circulatory system include the heart and blood vessels, with the lymphatic system serving to drain the extracellular component of fluids and cells from the interstitium for return to the blood vascular system. Each component of the cardiovascular system is characterized as an element within a fluid-filled dynamic system, all of which are lined by a single layer of squamous epithelium (endothelium). Oxygenated blood is continuously supplied to the systemic circulation by repeated contractions and relaxation of the heart muscles. This tubular unit consists of a pair of hollow-valved muscular pumps which drives the blood through a vascular system to reach the various tissue components of the body. Blood leaving the heart at a high pressure and velocity is received by the arteries whose walls are highly elastic. This muscular pump provides the power for propelling blood to the lungs for oxygenation (pulmonary circulation) and subsequently returning it to the heart for redistribution to the systemic circulation. This distribution takes place through a series of arteries beginning with the vessels which have walls rich in elastic tissue and smooth muscle cells. Blood continues through the arterial tree, through vessels of a decreasing caliber until a diameter of 4·7 mm is reached. The arterial tree terminates in short, narrow, muscular arteries (arterioles) from which blood enters the capillary bed. This segment is composed of an extensive network of microscopic vessels with extremely attenuated walls. The microvascular bed is the site of action for the transfer of gases, nutrients, metabolites, and hormones. In addition, it is here that the movement of fluid and crystalloids occurs across the blood–tissue interface.[22,38,85] From the capillaries the blood, now reduced in oxygen and containing products of metabolism, moves slowly under low pressure into the venules and veins. These vessels are generally larger with thinner walls than the corresponding arteries. From the large veins blood enters the right atrium and is pumped into the lungs to be oxygenated for recirculation throughout the body.

As indicated in Part One concerning the structure and function of the heart, this muscular pump along with the blood vessels are referred to as the cardiovascular system. The wall of the heart can be divided into three tunics or layers, epicardium, myocardium, and endocardium. The epicardium consists of a continuous layer of mesothelial cells and an underlying connective tissue component containing blood vessels, lymphatics, and nerves. The myocardium forms the middle tunic of the heart and provides the greater mass of this muscular pump. It contains muscle fibers that are arranged in layers and compact bundles surrounded by connective tissue components. The myocardium is supplied with numerous blood capillaries in addition to a plexus of lymphatic vessels which serve to drain this region of the heart. It also contains specialized fibers that form the impulse conducting system of the heart. The innermost tunic or layer, the endocardium, lines the chambers of the heart and is continuous with the blood vessels leaving and entering the heart. It consists of a continuous layer of endothelium which rests on a basal lamina. The subendocardial layer contains a layer of loose connective tissue with collagen fibers that are continuous with the interstitial areas of the myocardium.

The recognition of capillaries as the ultimate subdivision of the vascular tree through which blood flows en route from arteries to veins confirmed William Harvey's concept of a closed circulation for the cardiovascular system.[65] Although subsequent light microscopic studies[12] provided a good knowledge of the general structural layout of the vascular wall, there was no information regarding the fine structural details of the varied components of the vascular wall that could be correlated or compared with the physiologic aspects of vascular permeability along various segments of the vascular tree.

The advent of the electron microscope and the improvements in techniques for processing tissues for electron microscopy[76,90,98,106,111,112,120] provided a turning point for reinvestigating the structural aspects of the cardiovascular system. Since its application to the problem in 1952, electron microscopic studies on the cardiovascular system have provided a large body of information which established the multilayered structure of the vascular wall and the existence of significant ultrastructural differences that can be related to the varied segmental permeability along the vascular tree. This report will review briefly the ultrastructural aspects of the various segments of the vascular wall and present some recent findings put forward by a number of investigators that relate to the structural basis of exchange across the capillary and venular walls.

11. General Survey of the Blood Vascular System

Generally, the wall of all blood vessels follows a common plan of organization. In most cases (except some segments of the microvasculature, e.g., capillaries, venules, sinusoids) the wall is composed of three layers, a tunica intima, the innermost layer, a tunica media, the middle layer, and a tunica adventitia, the outermost layer. In some vessels certain features of this common plan are emphasized while in others they may be reduced or completely omitted.

11.1. Tunica intima

The tunica intima, which is present in all vessels, consists of a specialized, simple, squamous epithelial tissue, the endothelium, which lines the chambers of the heart as well as all blood vessels. This endothelial lining also shows structural variability which can be related to the function of vessels in various tissues and organ systems of the body. The endothelial cells rest on a basal lamina which overlies a subendothelial layer composed of fibroelastic tissue. In arteries this layer is in the form of an internal elastic lamina consisting of narrow bands of elastic fibers and some collagen fibers. In veins very few elastic fibers are observed, instead there are many collagen fibers within the subendothelial layer.

11.2. Tunica media

This layer occurs between the intima and tunica adventitia and is usually circularly or spirally organized. In the conducting or elastic arteries there are large amounts of elastic fibers arranged in sheetlike plates with fenestrae. They alternate with smooth muscle cells in addition to collagen fibers. In the distributing and muscular arteries, smooth muscle cells predominate.

11.3. Tunica adventitia

The tunica adventitia is longitudinally arranged. Immediately adjacent to the tunica media the elastic tissue may often be concentrated into an elastic layer (prominent in the larger conducting and distributing arteries). The remainder of the adventitial coat is composed of moderately compact fibroelastic tissue which blends into the surrounding loose connective tissue. In large and medium sized veins this layer is very prominent and contains fibroblast, collagen, and elastic fibers. The outer fibroelastic tissue of the tunica adventitia acts to restrain the expanding media and intima. In larger vessels (arteries and veins) this layer contains small blood vessels, *vasa vasorum*, lymphatics, and nerves which may merge with the adjacent loose connective tissue common to the vascular tree.

12. Classification of Blood Vessels

In addition to the size and morphological differences that are related to the segmental specializations along the cardiovascular system, there are also specific functional features that are differentially related to the various segments of the vasculature. Such morphological and physiological differences permit a classification of the various transitional forms exhibited along the entire vascular tree. Those vessels seen with the unaided eye (i.e., vessels larger than 100 μm) fall within the realm of the macrovasculature. However, vessels with a diameter of less than 100 μm can only be visualized with the light optical microscope and form a rich network of vessels termed the microvasculature.

The arterial side of the cardiovascular system not only serves as a conducting system, but also provides a major elastic buffering system. Using size, structural features, and functional activities, the arterial blood vessels have been classified into three major groups.

1. Large elastic or conducting arteries.
2. Muscular arteries, also termed distributing arteries.
3. Arterioles, the smallest sized, predominantly muscular vessels.

There is a repeated branching which gives rise to arterioles and vessels of progressively diminishing caliber and wall structure. This repeated dichotomous branching also provides a vast increase in the cross sectional area for the arterial tree.[3]

12.1. Elastic arteries

The conducting arteries contain large amounts of elastic tissue within their wall. They are of a large caliber and include the aorta and its major branches such as the innominate, subclavian, common carotid, femoral, and pulmonary arteries. The elastic arteries are considered as shock absorbers since they are able to withstand rapid and large changes in the pulse pressure by rapidly dilating with each systole. The recoil of the large amounts of elastic membranes within the vessel wall causes a contraction of the vessel, which narrows its lumen, thus propelling the blood onward during diastole. The recoil of the elastic membranes and subsequent contraction of the vessel wall is greatly facilitated by the contraction of smooth muscle cells within the tunica media.[3] The arrangement of components within the wall of elastic arteries (i.e., elastic membranes, smooth muscle cells), their activities, and properties provide a relatively smooth and continuous flow of blood toward the distributing arteries.

91

12.2. Muscular arteries

The distributing or muscular arteries are responsible for bringing blood to specific muscles and organ systems (i.e., femoral, testicular, etc.). In the larger muscular arteries, there is a relatively thick layer of collagenous and reticular fibrils interposed between the internal elastic membrane and the endothelial lining. There may also be longitudinally oriented smooth muscle cells in the connective tissue layer. For the smaller arteries, there is also a well-developed internal elastic lamina beneath the endothelium consisting of a single layer of elastic fibers in contrast to the fenestrated platelike layers found in the much larger arteries.[12]

The internal elastic membrane is prominent in all muscular arteries except in the umbilical artery, where it is missing. It appears as a refractive narrow zone with a wavy outline when collapsed muscular arteries are viewed in histological sections and a smooth circular band in the dilated vessel.

Muscular arteries are also characterized by prominent layers of smooth muscle cells within the tunica media. Smooth muscle cells are circumferentially arranged with strands of intervening elastic and collagen fibers. This area is bounded by an external elastic lamina which is much thinner than the internal elastic membrane. The external elastic lamina marks the inner margin of the tunica adventitia, forming a distinct border in the larger muscular arteries. However, it is indistinct or absent in the small muscular arteries.

The adventitia is relatively thick, consisting of dense fibrous connective tissue in which collagenous and elastic fibers are longitudinally or spirally arranged. This layer blends with the adjacent connective tissue without the observation of a clearly defined line of demarcation between the two. It contains a network of smaller blood vessels (*vasa vasorum*) as well as nerves and lymphatic vessels.

12.3. Arterioles

The transition from muscular arteries to arterioles is a gradual one and includes the smallest vessels along the arterial tree which measure 30–100 μm in diameter. The wall is thicker relative to the luminal diameter than in other blood vessels and contains one or two layers of spirally arranged smooth muscle cells within the tunica media. There is also a prominent internal elastic lamina in the tunica intima of the arteriole.

12.4. Microvasculature

As the microvascular bed is approached, the caliber and elastic properties of the wall of the arteriole gradually decrease. This network of microscopic vessels lying between the smallest recognizable arteries and veins represents the terminal portion of the cardiovascular system that is charged with the role of providing the transfer of gases and nutrients and metabolic waste products. It includes the fine ramifications of arterioles, capillaries, and postcapillary venules.[46, 130] The capillary bed is drained by vessels of an increasingly large diameter, the venules. Immediately connected to the capillary is the postcapillary venule which measures 10–30 μm in diameter. Collecting venules (30–50 μm in diameter) connect postcapillary venules to the muscular venules. These vessels are 50–100 μm in diameter and traditionally were referred to as venules. In light microscopic preparations, they are recognized as microvessels with thin walls which accompany arterioles which have slightly thicker walls. These venules serve to collect blood from the capillary bed for return to the heart via the medium and large size veins.[130]

12.5. Muscular veins

In contrast to the muscular arteries, the veins are extremely variable in wall structure with a larger percentage of collagen fibers and fewer elastic fibers than is found in the arterial tree. They are thin walled and collapsible, serving a capacitance rather than a resistance function.[3] Veins also differ from arteries in that they possess valves and are more firmly embedded in the adjacent connective tissue.[7,69]

13. Electron Microscopic Structure of the Mammalian Vascular Wall

Prior to the application of electron microscopy to studies of the cardiovascular system, combined histological and histochemical studies demonstrated that the vascular wall was generally organized into a repeating pattern of concentric lamellae. However, no sharp line of demarcation could be made between the types of cells or connective tissue components within the walls of the larger vessels.[12]

When the techniques of electron microscopy were brought to bear on the problem of the structure of the cardiovascular system, it was recognized that the endothelial cells lining the vascular wall formed a continuous layer[16,17,63,91,96,98,101] while in other segments of the vascular tree the endothelial lining was extremely attenuated, having fenestrae[52,95,96,97,127] or there were discontinuities within its wall.[34,54,124]

13.1. Ultrastructure of the arterial wall

Although in the early ultrastructural studies of the larger elastic muscular arteries it proved difficult to obtain meaningful information relative to the precise morphological and topographical arrangement of the cellular and connective tissue components within the arterial wall, some measure of success was achieved by a number of investigators[16,17,63,96,98,101] in distinguishing the regular alternating pattern of connective tissue and cellular layers throughout the arterial wall. Since these early studies, the application of improved techniques of tissue preservation by a number of investigators has yielded more precise information on the multilayered structure of the arterial wall.

13.1.1. Tunica intima

In the elastic and muscular arteries the innermost layer of the vascular wall is composed of a continuous cellular layer, the endothelial lining, and a subendothelial layer of loose connective tissue which may also contain fibroblasts and smooth muscle cells. The electron microscope has revealed that a certain structural uniformity exists throughout the arteries of different sizes.

Endothelium

The luminal surface of the arterial wall is lined by a continuous sheet of squamous

94

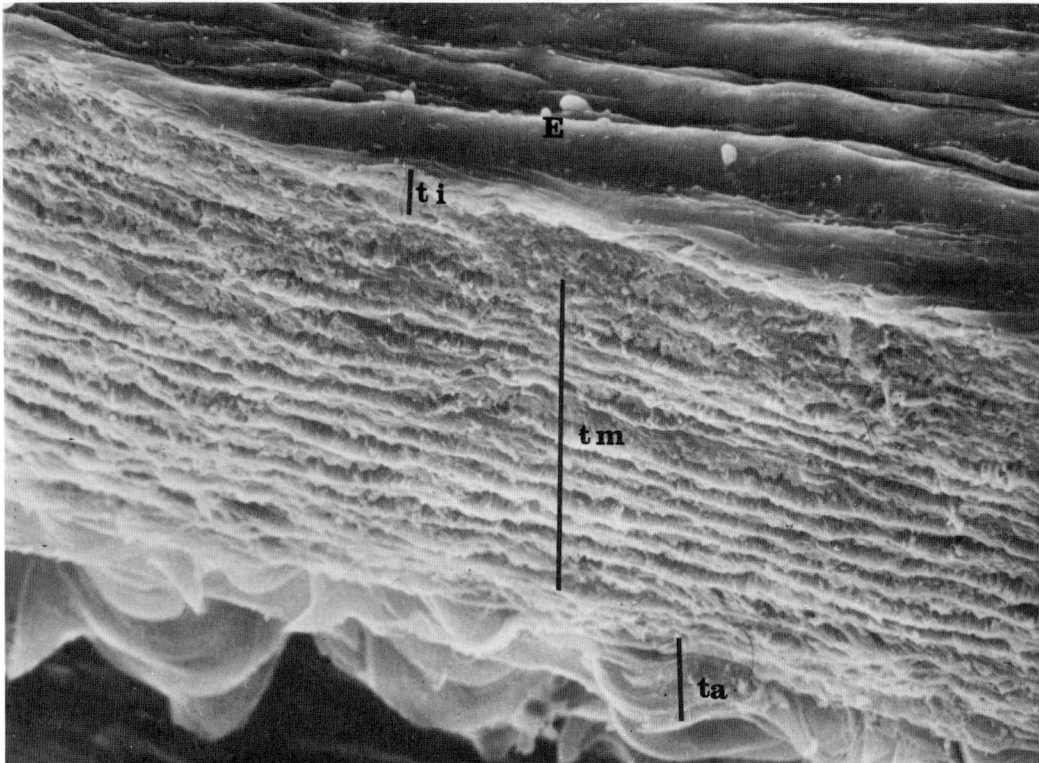

Figure 13.1. Luminal surface of arterial wall.
Rabbit aorta showing luminal surface lined by endothelial cells (E). The aorta was sectioned to demonstrate the thickness of the vessel wall and shows the tunica intima (ti), tunica media (tm), and tunica adventitia (ta). The lamellar arrangement of smooth muscle cells and the intervening plates of elastic fibers can be appreciated in this survey SEM. (× 950)

endothelial cells. The thickness varies from 5 μm in the nuclear region to less than 1 μm in the more peripheral cell margins.[35]

In scanning images of the luminal surface of large arteries, the cells lining its surface appear squamous or oblong with prominent nuclear bulges within the central part of the cells. These dome-shaped bulges are relatively uniform throughout the luminal surface (Figure 13.1).

When the pressure close to that of systole is maintained during perfusion fixation, very few longitudinal folds are observed[1] in contrast to their appearance when the tissue is processed by immersion fixation[28,49,117,122]

The surface of the endothelial cell appears generally smooth with only occasional microprojection (Figure 13.2). The intercellular junctions are recognized by the slightly elevated ridges produced by the overlapping of adjacent cell margins (Figure 13.2). These marginal appendages are similar to the marginal folds observed in thin sections.[35,36] In thin sections of the arterial wall it is evident that the endothelial cells are closely apposed at their margins by intercellular junctions to form a continuous layer throughout the length of the vessel (Figures 13.3, 13.4). However, variations of its thickness can be detected depending on the degree of distension of the arterial wall

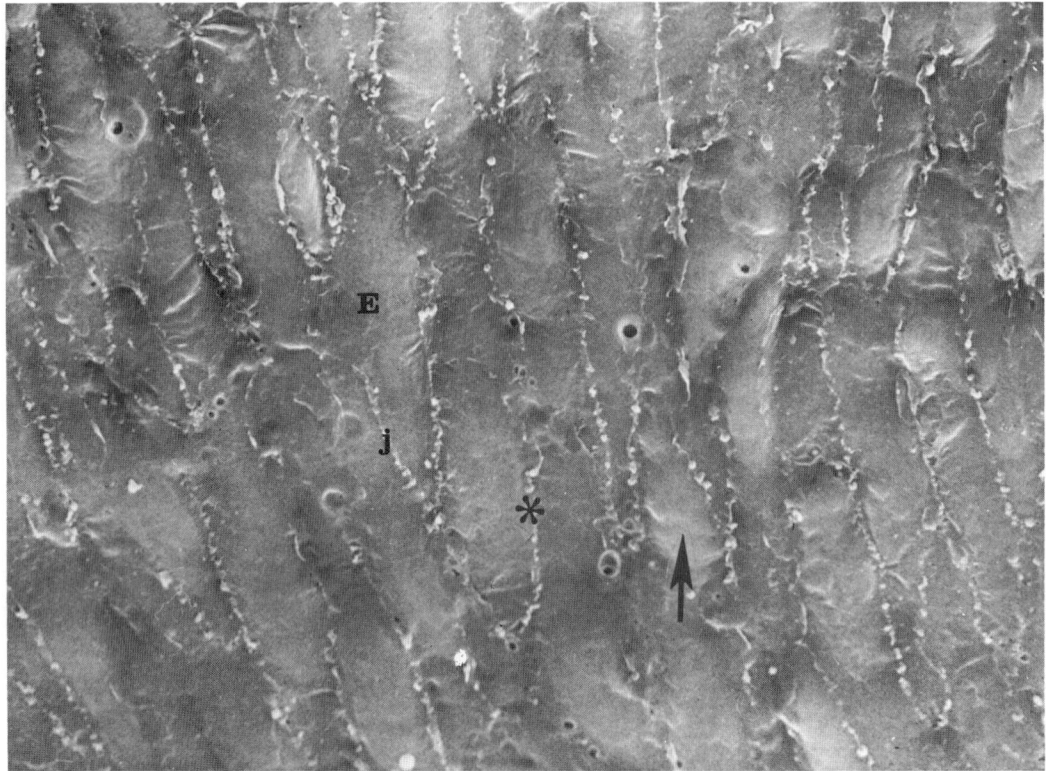

Figure 13.2. Endothelial cells of luminal surface.
SEM of aorta showing the topography of the endothelial cells (E) which form plate-like sheets closely applied at intercellular junctions (j), indicated by ridge-like borders (*) between the adjacent cells. The centrally located nucleus (arrow) creates dome-like structures along the luminal surface. (× 2,040)

(Figures 13.3, 13.5). The endothelial cell contains a prominent elongated nucleus which is located in the central cytoplasm (Figure 13.4). The long axis of the cell and its nucleus are arranged in the longitudinal plane of the vessel (Figure 13.4). The cytoplasm is surrounded by a plasmalemma which is invaginated to form numerous plasmalemmal (micropinocytotic) vesicles (Figure 13.5).

The peripherally located plasmalemmal vesicles are open to both the luminal and tissue fronts while those in the central part of the cell lie free in the cytoplasm (Figure 13.5). Florey and Sheppard[42] observed that when the protein horseradish peroxidase was intravenously injected there was rapid passage into the wall of arteries via plasmalemma vesicles (caveolae) as well as through the clefts of intercellular junction.

Closely applied to the plasmalemma on its luminal surface is a thin surface coat, the endocapillary or endothelial layer.[77] Other cytoplasmic organelles common to the

Figure 13.3. Arterial wall.
Rabbit aorta showing the tunica intima (ti) consisting of endothelial cells (E) and an underlying subendothelial layer (*) and the tunica media (tm) consisting of alternating layers of smooth muscle cells (sm) and elastic fibers (el) embedded in a homogeneous ground substance. Survey EM. (× 2,700)

96

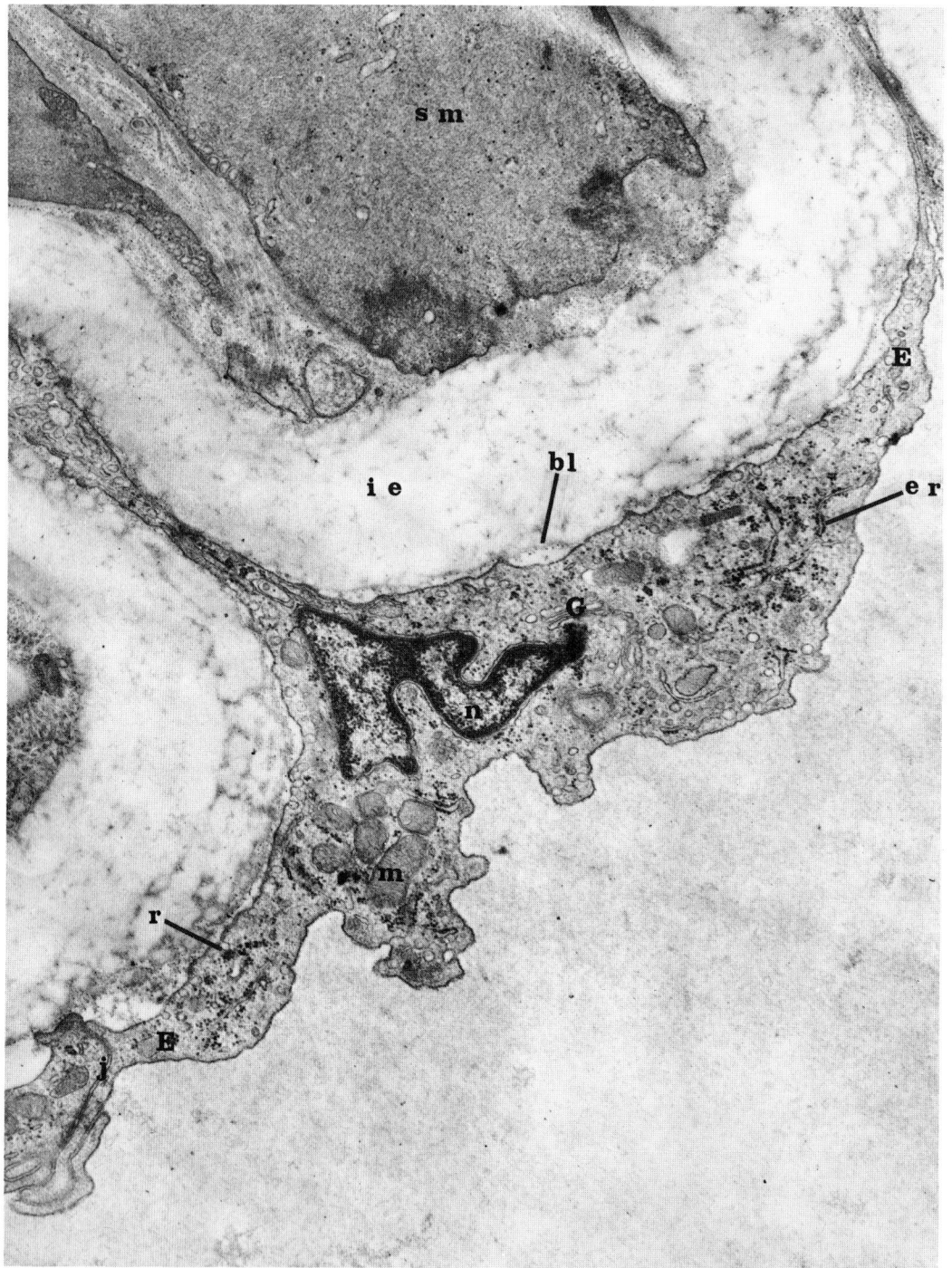

Figure 13.4. Endothelial cells of muscular artery.
The nucleus is centrally located (n) and is surrounded by cytoplasmic organelles consisting of a Golgi complex (G), mitochondria (m), ribosomes (r), and a sparse distribution of endoplasmic reticulum (er) of the rough variety. The endothelial cells (E) rest on a basal lamina (bl) which adjoins the internal elastic lamina (ie). Portions of smooth muscle cells (sm) are shown in the upper portion of the micrograph. The endothelial cells are held together by intercellular junctions (j) where the cell margins often interdigitate with each other. (×22,500)

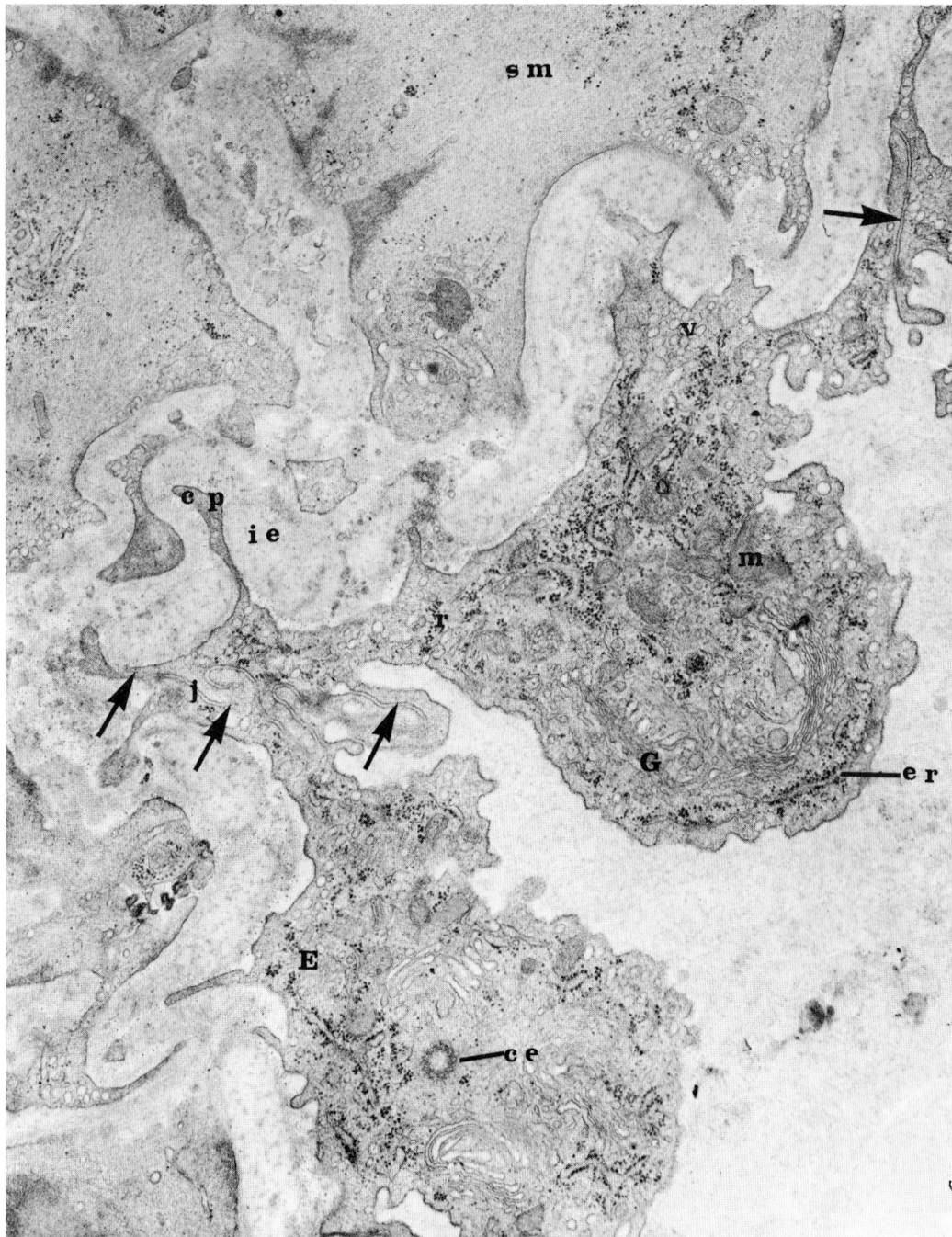

Figure 13.5. Perinuclear region of endothelial cells.
Arterial wall endothelial cells (E) contain extensive cytoplasmic projections (cp) on their basal surfaces which extend into the underlying subendothelial layer (internal elastic lamina, ie). The area within the perinuclear region of the endothelial cell shows an accumulation of cytoplasmic organelles consisting of a centriole (ce), Golgi complex (G), ribosomes (r), mitochondria (m), and rough endoplasmic reticulum (er). Also visible are numerous plasmalemmal invaginations (v) at the periphery of the cell and parts of smooth muscle cells (sm) of the tunica media. Intercellular clefts of the intercellular junctions (j) between adjacent endothelial cells can be quite extensive as indicated by the arrows. (×24,300)

endothelial cell include a Golgi complex and centriole, located in the perinuclear region of the cell (Figures 13.4, 13.5). The endoplasmic reticulum is of the rough variety and occurs in the perinuclear cytoplasm and in the attenuated regions of the cytoplasm. Ribosomes are free in the cytoplasm as well as attached to the endoplasmic reticulum (Figures 13.4, 13.5). In addition to the micropinocytotic vesicles, larger vesicles and lysosomes may also appear in close proximity to the Golgi complex. Elongated granules containing an electron-dense matrix were also observed in the endothelial cells by Weibel and Palade.[123] Microtubules are found in close association with centrioles and throughout the cytoplasm. The endothelial cells contain cytoplasmic filaments (approximately 60 Å in diameter). These filamentous structures are similar to the cytoplasmic filaments found in an increasingly large number of non-muscle cells. There is an increasing body of information which provides both morphological and biochemical evidence that actin filaments occur in non-muscle cells.[102, 103] There is also indirect evidence, such as cell and nuclear shortening, which suggests that endothelial cells may respond to various stimuli by contracting.[82] The actin-like filaments within the cytoplasm would provide a mechanism for effecting this structural change.

Combined transmission electron microscopy and freeze-fracture replication studies suggest that the endothelial cells are held in close apposition by occluding (tight) and gap (communicating) junctions (Figure 13.15).[57, 114] The term communicating junction (*macula communicans*) was proposed by Simionescu[113] to describe the structural and functional relationships of this intercellular junction. Therefore, the communicating junction represents the structure which permits two adjacent cells to communicate with each other by allowing small molecules to pass between neighboring cells.[75]

Internal elastic lamina

In addition to a basal lamina (Figure 13.4), a subendoethelial layer underlies the endothelial cells of the arterial wall. It contains a prominent internal elastic lamina and collagen fibers which are organized into longitudinal bundles parallel with the long axis of the vessel and smooth muscle cells (Figures 13.3, 13.5, 13.6). The width of the subendothelial layer is bridged by a series of basal endothelial projections as well as projections from smooth muscle cells which penetrate the internal elastic membrane to make intimate contact with each other to form myoendothelial junctions (Figures 13.3, 13.7, 13.9).

13.1.2. Tunica media

The smooth muscle cell comprises the main component of the tunica media in the vascular wall and is found in the wall of all vessels (arteries and veins) except capillaries and those venules in which pericytes are found.[108, 114] The muscle cells are arranged in a helical fashion around the vascular walls.[101] Each muscle cell is surrounded by a basal lamina, bundles of collagen fibers, and elastic fibers (Figures 13.3, 13.8). Adjacent smooth muscle cells are held in close apposition by communicating (gap or nexus) junctions (Figures 13.9, 13.10) which may provide a means for the conduction of impulses and the transmission of low molecular weight molecules

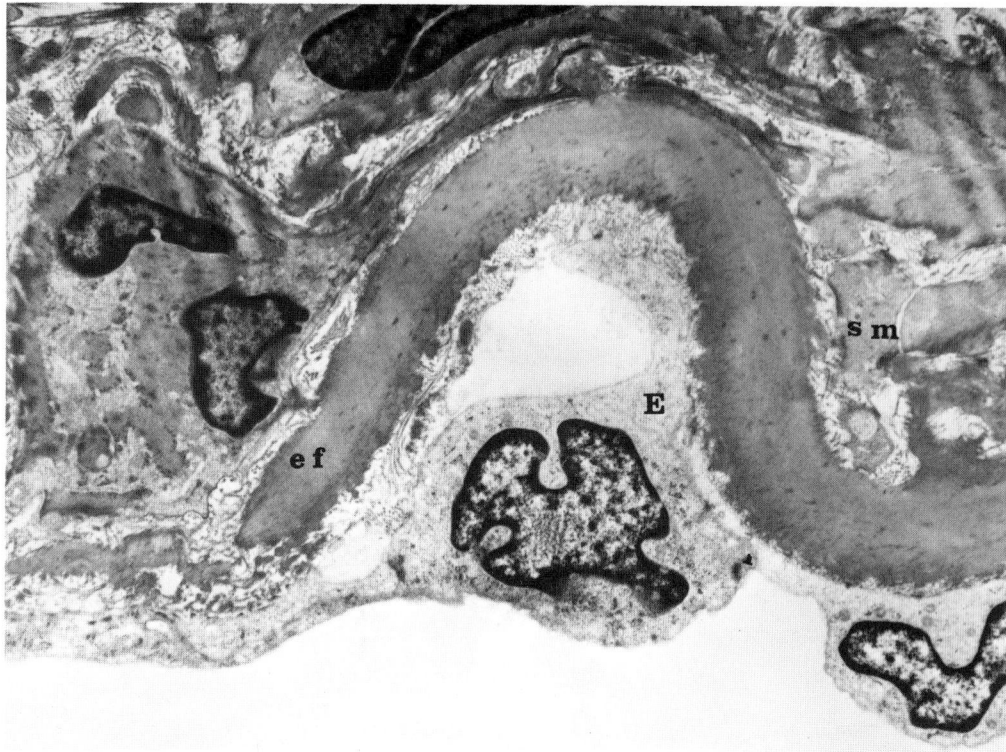

Figure 13.6. Internal elastic lamina.
The subendothelial layer of large vessels such as the aorta contains extensive plaques of elastin (ef) as indicated in this electron micrograph. The plaques of elastin fibers are closely applied to the basal surface of the endothelial cells (E) and smooth muscle cells (sm) of the tunica media. (× 10,000)

between adjacent cells.[29, 75, 113] The sarcoplasm is surrounded by a sarcolemma which contains numerous sarcolemmal vesicles or caveolae (Figures 13.8, 13.9, 13.10). Freeze-fracture replications of the sarcolemma indicate that these caveolae can be quite numerous over the surface of the cell. In addition to providing an increased surface area for the smooth muscle cells, the sarcolemmal invaginations bring the membrane in close contact with the peripherally located myofilamentous components of the sarcoplasm. The nucleus occupies a central position within the cell and is surrounded by the sarcoplasmic organelles (Figures 13.8, 13.9). These include a Golgi complex which is surrounded by vesicles and closely associated centrioles. The rough endoplasmic reticulum is located in the perinuclear sarcoplasm and within the subsarcolemma at various regions along the length of the cell (Figures 13.8, 13.9).

The mitochondria of smooth muscle cells are spherical or elongated structures. Their internal membrane organization and structure are similar to that for mitochondria in other cell systems. They are most numerous in the juxtanuclear areas, but are also found throughout the sarcoplasm between myofilaments and in the peripheral regions of the cell beneath the sarcolemma (Figures 13.8, 13.9).

The major part of the smooth muscle cell is occupied by myofilaments. They are arranged with their long axes coinciding with the long axis of the cell. The myofila-

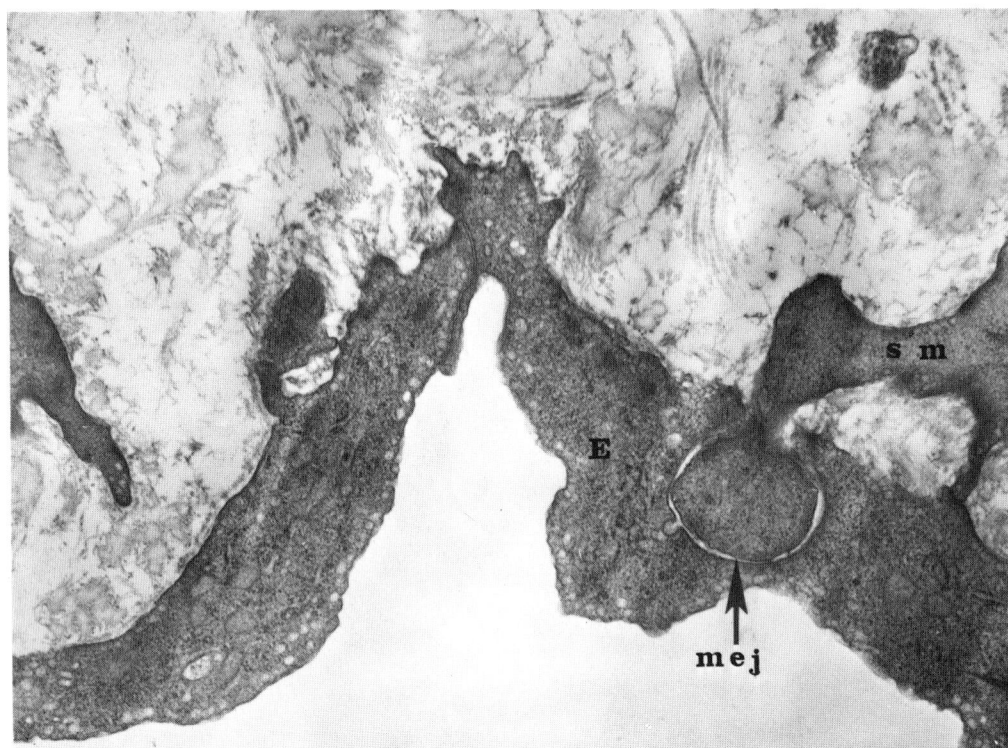

Figure 13.7. Myoendothelial junctions.
Smooth muscle cells (sm) of the tunica media often make intimate contact with the endothelial cells (E) of the tunica intima to form myoendothelial junctions (mej). Here a lateral projection of smooth muscle makes intimate contact in a tongue and groove fashion (arrow). (× 21,000)

ments measure from 60–80 Å in width and usually occupy areas of the sarcoplasm which are devoid of other cell organelles (Figures 13.8, 13.9). Dense plaques or dense segments of myofilaments are often observed in the periphery of the cell beneath the sarcolemma (Figures 13.8, 13.10). It has been suggested that these structures serve to attach the myofilaments to the sarcolemma.[63,68,100,106,107] The concept which suggests that two types of myofilaments exist in smooth muscle comes from morphological[37,88,99] and biochemical[104] studies which have demonstrated the presence of acto-myosin in the smooth muscle cell. Although intervening layers of elastic and collagen fibers are found between adjacent layers of smooth muscle cells, numerous points of contact are made along the lateral surfaces between adjacent cells via cytoplasmic processes and at the terminal ends of cells (Figures 13.3, 13.9, 13.10).

Figure 13.8. Smooth muscle cell of tunica media.
Portion of smooth muscle cell (sm) in a section cut parallel to the longitudinal axis of the cell showing the centrally located nucleus (n) with an accumulation of cytoplasmic organelles in the perinuclear region. Golgi complex (G), mitochondria (m), rough endoplasmic reticulum (er), and ribosomes (r) are aggregated in the perinuclear sarcoplasm. The periphery of the cell contains numerous small filaments (f) and electron-dense plaques (dp) that are interdispersed throughout various regions of the sarcoplasm and in the subsarcolemmal regions of the cell. Endothelial cells (E) with cytoplasmic projections (cp) at the basal surface which bridge the internal elastic lamina are also visible. (× 18,000)

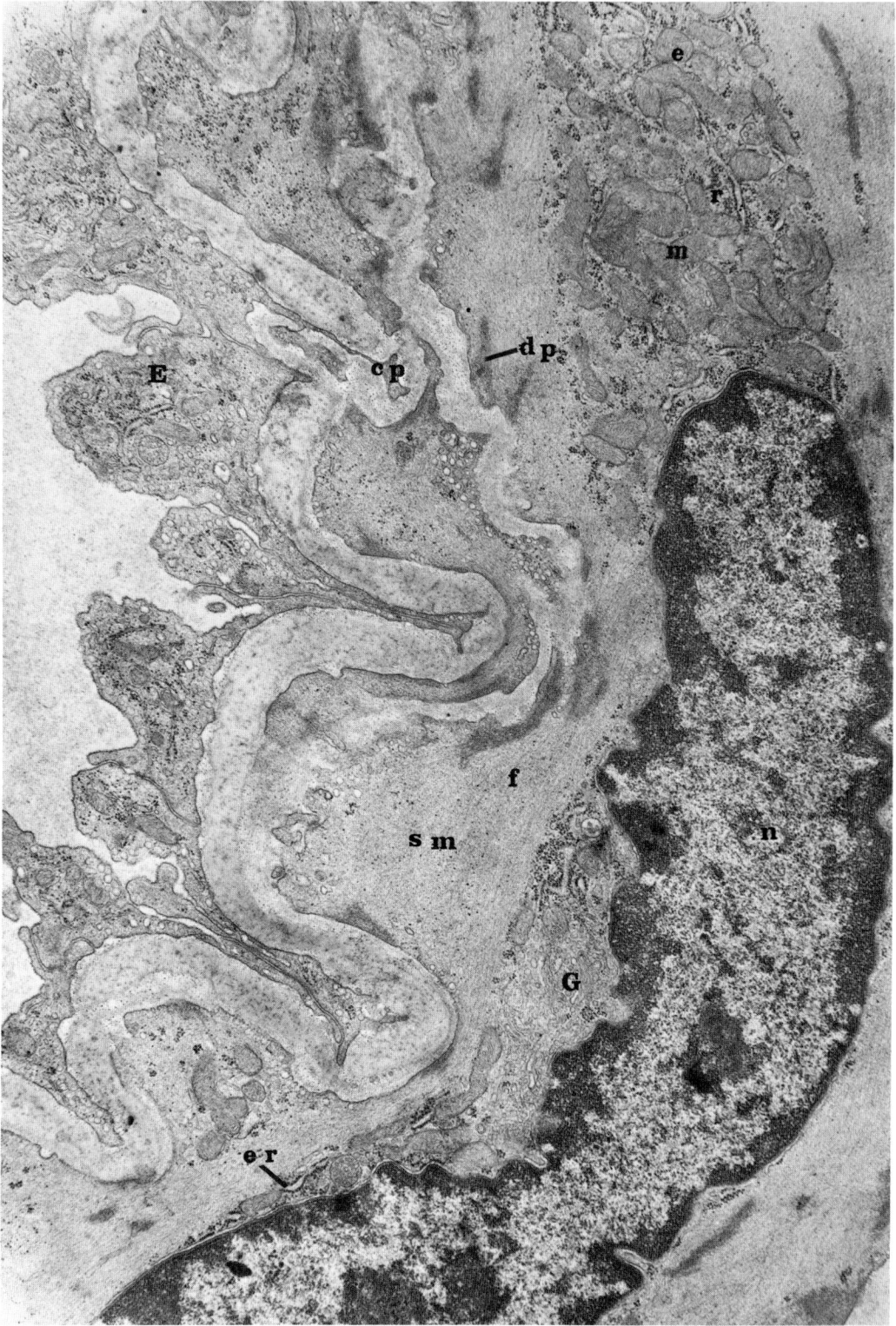

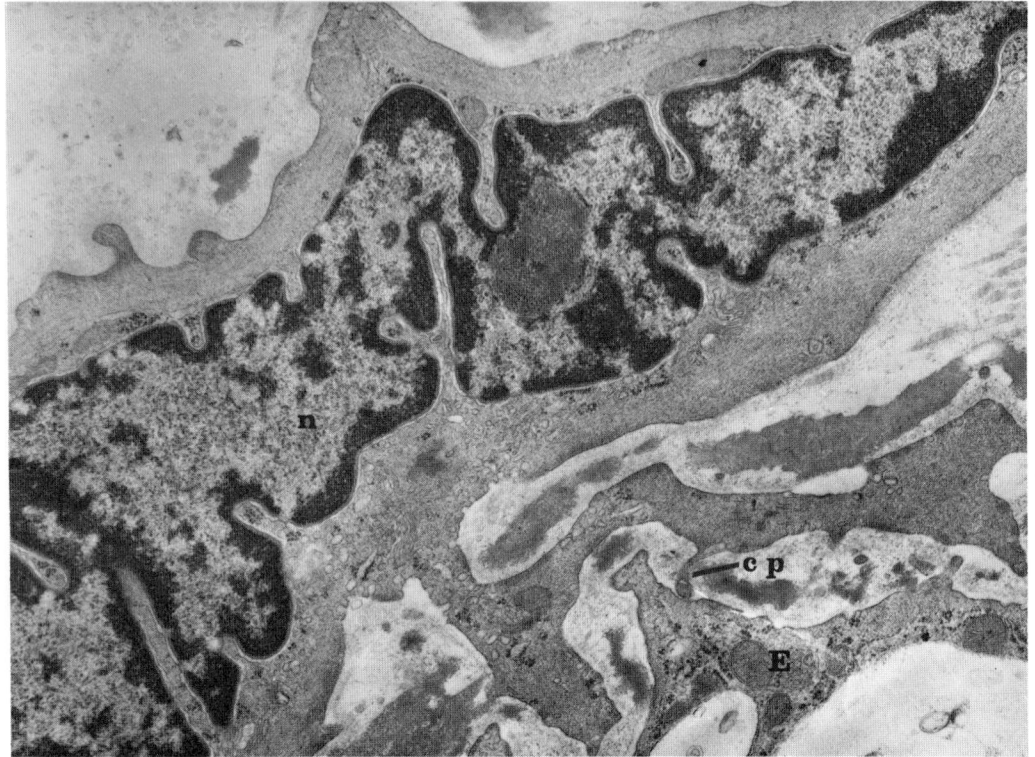

Figure 13.9. Smooth muscle cell of tunica media.
The nucleus (n) has a cork screw appearance indicating that the cell was in a contracted state during fixation. Lateral cell processes (cp) extend from the smooth muscle cell to make intimate contact with adjacent endothelial cells (E) of the tunica intima. (× 20,000)

It is generally agreed that only a portion of the smooth muscle cells are innervated[107] and that the communicating (gap) junctions provide the rapid spread of excitation or proprogation of contraction impulses between adjacent cells.[29,114]

13.1.3. Adventitial layer and connective tissue

The adventitial layer consists of spindle-shaped fibroblasts and loosely arranged bundles of collagen fibrils (Figure 13.11). The fibroblasts are circumferentially arranged with their attenuated cytoplasmic strands separated by collagen fibrils. Mast cells are often observed in close proximity to blood vessels within the adventitial layer of the large muscular arteries and veins. Nerve axons completely or partially surrounded by Schwann cells are also found in the adventitial layer (Figures 13.11, 13.12). Fibroblasts with extremely flattened cytoplasmic processes are observed near the outer boundary of the adventitia (Figures 13.11, 13.12). These have been termed veil cells by Majno[79] and are observed in the walls of arteries and veins[107,108] and lymphatic vessels.[72]

104

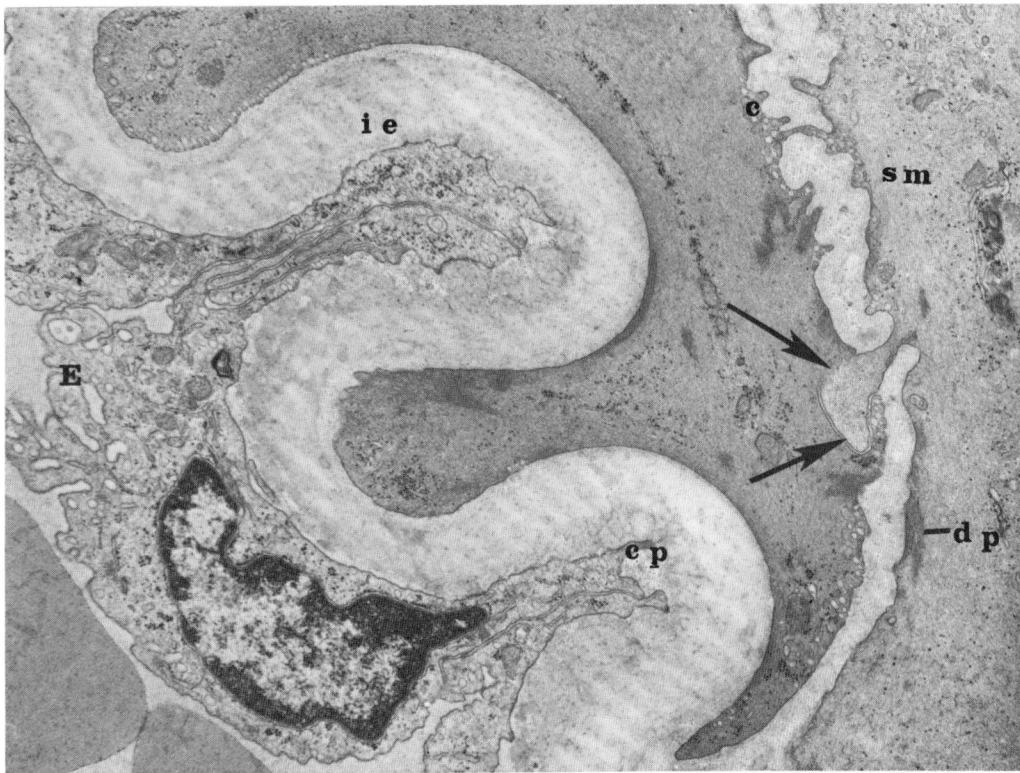

Figure 13.10. Communicating junctions between smooth muscle cells.
Adjacent smooth muscle cells of the tunica media make contact by lateral cell projections which form close contact with adjacent cells (arrows). Dense plaques (dp) are also seen in the periphery of the smooth cells (sm). The sarcolemma is invaginated to form numerous caveolae (c) along the periphery of the cell. Cytoplasmic projections (cp) extend from the base of the endothelial cells (E) into the internal elastic lamina (ie). ($\times$ 14,500)

13.2. Ultrastructure of the microvascular wall

The microvasculature consists of those vessels located between the arterial and venous components of the blood vascular system.[19,46,130] Some components of the microvasculature serve a regulatory function while others provide for the nutritional needs of the surrounding tissues.[18,64,119] Direct observation of the microvessels in living animals and the subsequent observation of the same vessels after fixation and staining have provided an organizational framework for defining the different physiological and structural components of the microcirculatory system.[18,19,64,65,74,121] More recent studies utilizing improved microinjection techniques[4,5,32,51,58,81] and computer assisted analysis of video images[59] have made it possible to observe and analyze specific segments of the microvasculature in the living animal. These studies have provided information which makes it possible to more clearly define the structural and functional features which are characteristic for a given microvascular region. Although the microvasculature is organized to meet the specific functional needs of a given system, it is generally agreed that most microcirculatory beds share certain

105

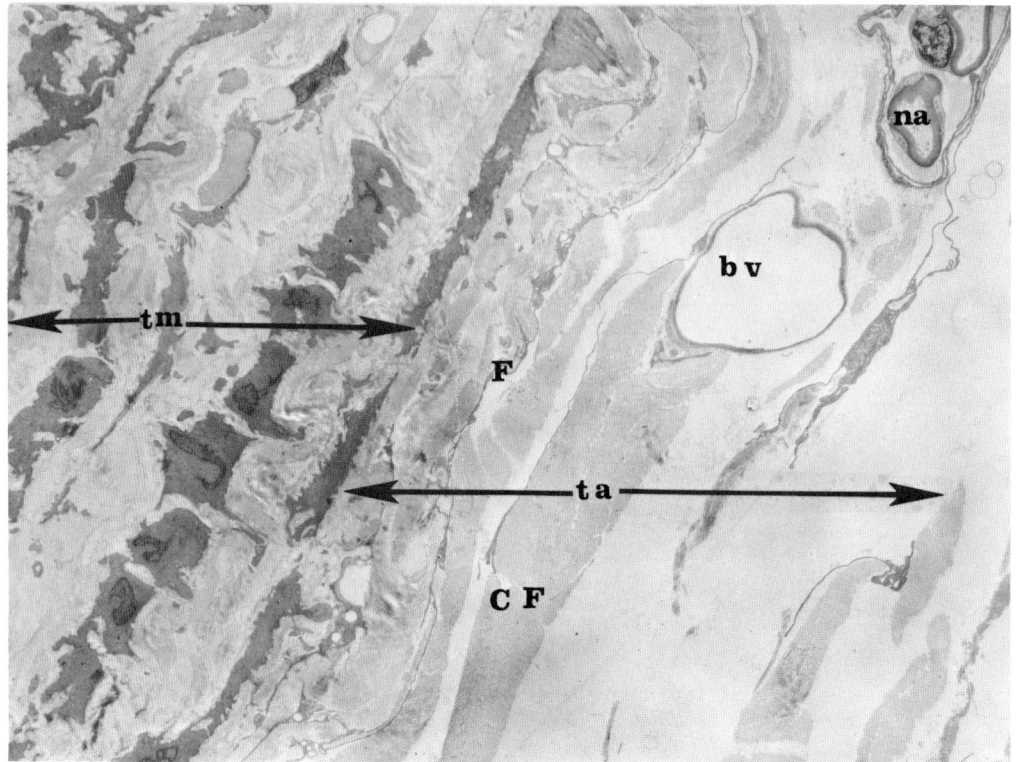

Figure 13.11. Junction between tunica media and tunica adventitia.
The tunica adventitia (ta) contains blood vessels (bv) (vasa vasorum) and myelinated nerve axon (na). Bundles of collagen fibers (CF) are separated by thin strands of cell processes extending from fibroblast (F). tm: tunica media. Survey EM. ($\times$ 1,800)

fundamental, structural, and functional features which meet the regulatory and nutritional needs of the surrounding cells and tissues of each system.[130, 131]

The central framework of the terminal vascular bed consists of the arteriolar stem which subdivides several times while giving off numerous side branches along its course. The distal portion of the anteriolar stem is progressively thinned out into extremely fine terminal arterioles approximately 10–12 μm, which are of capillary dimensions. However, they are recognized as arterioles by the high velocity of the blood flow and the scalloped configuration imparted by the thin layer of smooth muscle cells within the tunica media of these vessels when in the contracted state. Zweifach[130] suggested that the terminal arteriole be used to designate the segment of the arteriolar stem from which capillary side branches are distributed. Due to the presence of numerous precapillary side branches, a number of workers refer to this segment as precapillary arterioles. For arterioles of 100 μm diameter range, there are usually two or more layers of smooth muscle cells. As the arteriole becomes progressively reduced in diameter, there is a corresponding decrease in the thickness of its three tunics, i.e., intima, media, and adventitia so that in the terminal arteriole the media contains only a single layer of smooth muscle cells.

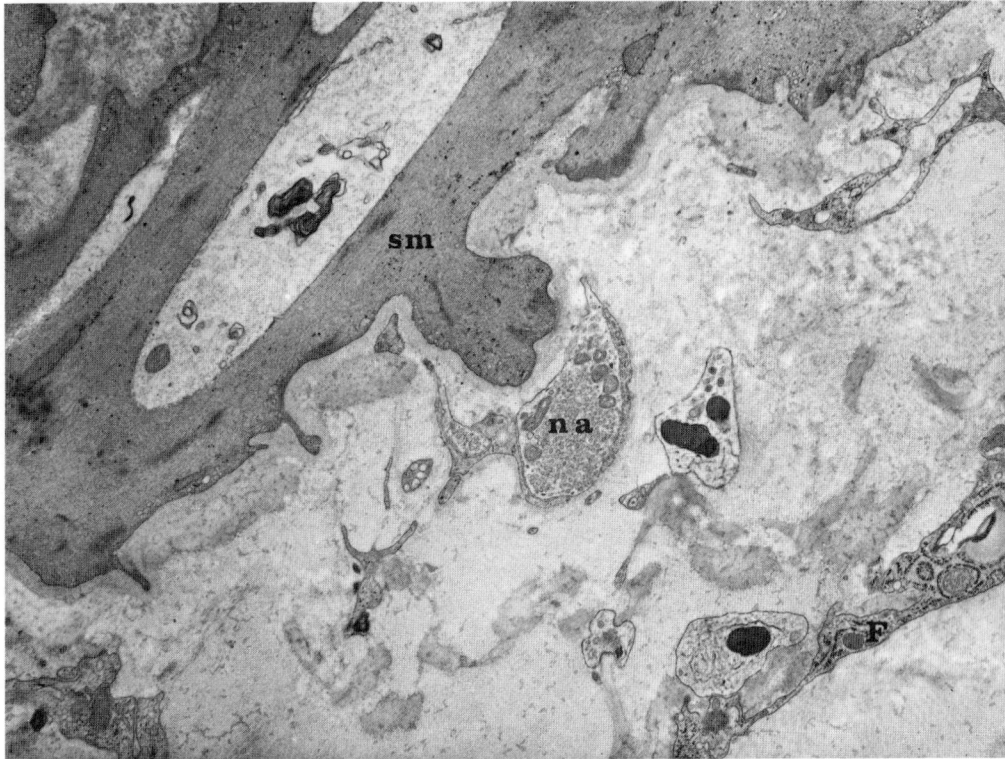

Figure 13.12. Nerve axons in adventitial layer.
Unmyelinated nerve axons (na) occur in the tunica adventitia and are often seen in close apposition to the peripheral layer of smooth muscle cells (sm) of the tunica media. Part of a fibroblast (F) is visible at lower right. (× 11,000)

13.2.1. Arteriole

The endothelial cells lining the arteriole are extremely flat with heights of up to 2 μm in areas occupied by the nucleus while the more attenuated areas measure 0·1 to 0·5 μm in thickness (Figures 13.13, 13.14). In longitudinal sections of the vessel, the endothelial cells overlap for varying distances and are held in close contact by a combination of tight (occluding) and communicating (gap) junctions (Figure 13.15). This combination of occluding junctions, occupying several layers of gap junctions which are intercalated between the ridges, not only insures strong cell to cell adhesion but both types of junctions provide a sealing of the intercellular spaces on one hand and the establishment of cell-to-cell communication on the other. There is no consistent pattern of overlapping between adjacent endothelial cells. Instead, overlapping occurs against and toward the direction of blood flow.[9, 107] The endothelial cells also contain numerous plasmalemmal vesicles. Organelles of the endothelial cells and their ultrastructure are similar to those of the larger arteries. Cytoplasmic filaments and microtubules also occur in the endothelial cells of normal arterioles of the myometrium,[109] and in cerebral arteries and arterioles during hypertension.[48]

107

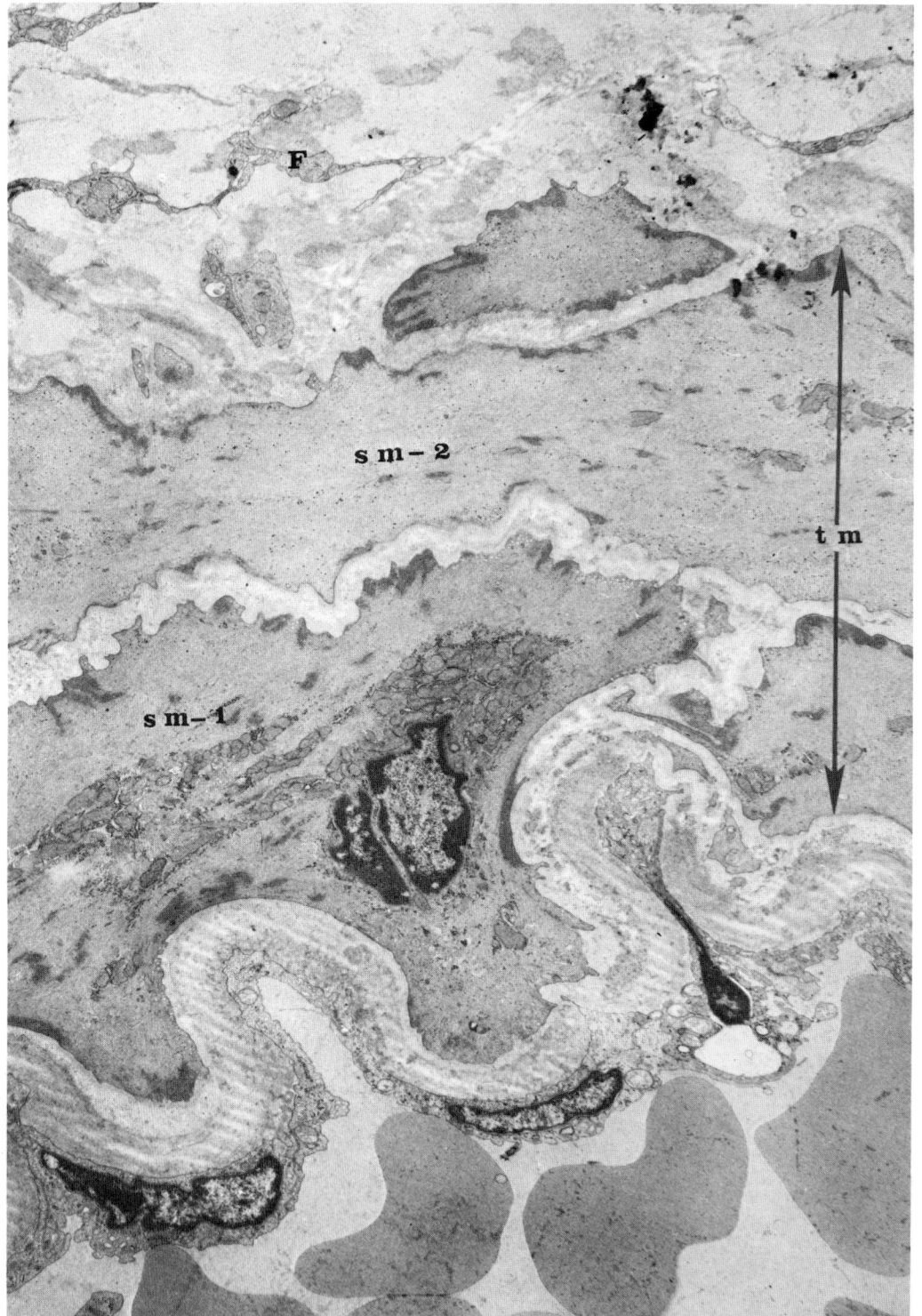

Figure 13.13. Wall of arteriole.
Section through the wall of a medium size artery showing two complete layers of smooth muscle cells (sm-1, sm-2) which make up the tunica media (tm). The outer boundary of the tunica adventitia is indicated by thin cytoplasmic processes from fibroblast (F). (×6,200)

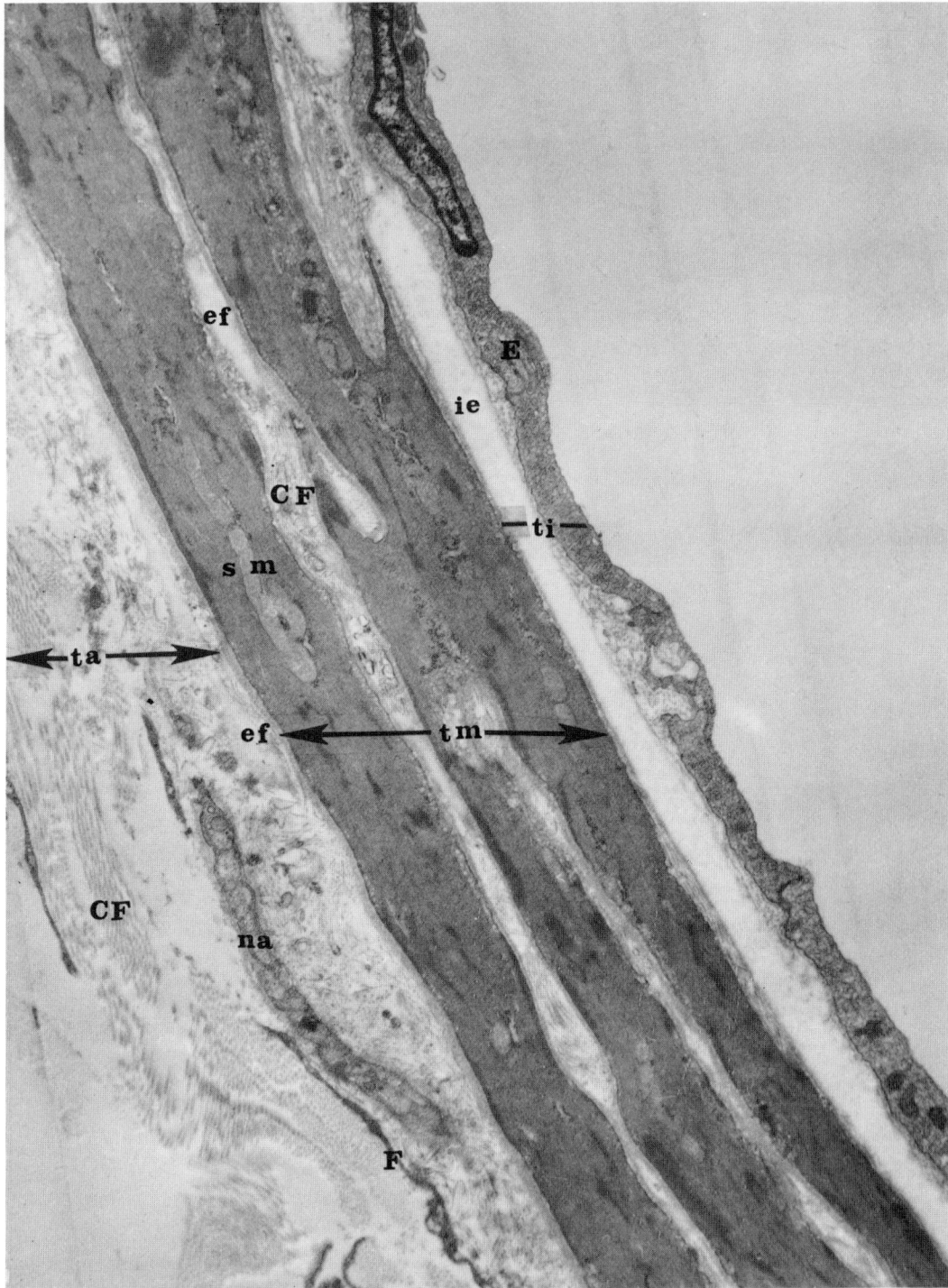

Figure 13.14. Wall of arteriole.
Section of arterial wall showing endothelial cells (E) of the tunica intima (ti) with its internal elastic lamina (ie). The tunica media (tm) consists of two continuous layers of smooth muscle cells (sm) separated by strands of elastic fibers (ef) and collagen fibers (CF). The tunica adventitia (ta) contains thin processes from fibroblast (F), collagen (CF) and elastic fibers (ef), and unmyelinated nerve axons (na). (× 12,000)

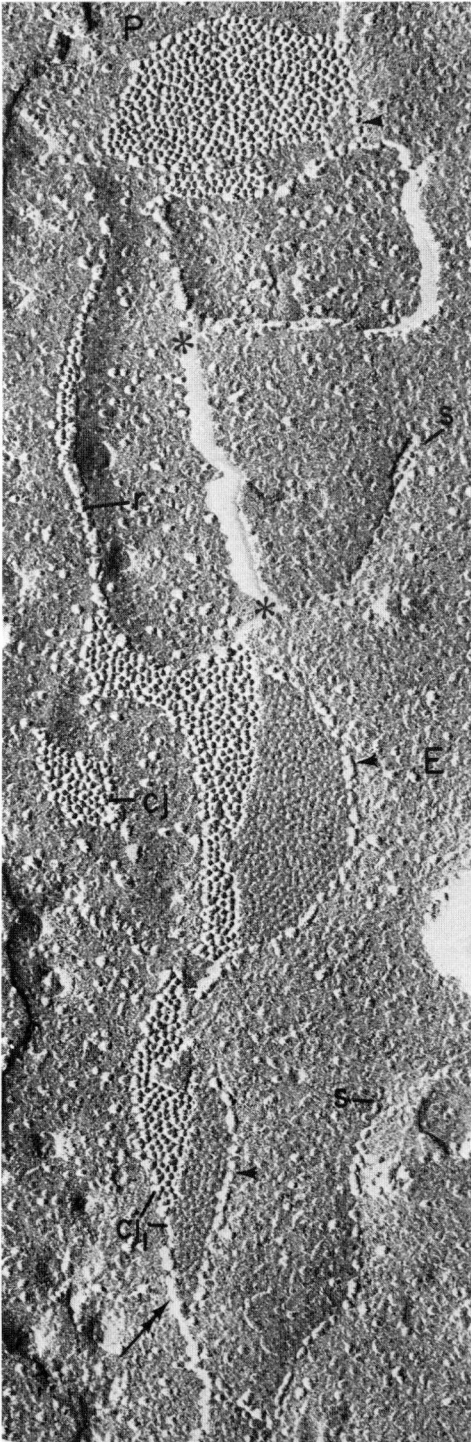

The endothelial cells rest on a basal lamina and are separated from the adjacent smooth muscle cells by elastic and collagenous fibers (Figures 13.13, 13.14). Like the large arteries, there are also basal protrusions from the endothelium which extend across the subendothelial layer to make contact with the adjoining layer of smooth muscle cells.

The tunica media in arterioles of 100 μm in diameter are characterized by two to three layers of smooth muscle cells that are generally circumferentially arranged (Figures 13.13, 13.14). With a decrease in the diameter of the arteriole, the media contains only one layer of smooth muscle cells (Figures 13.17, 13.18). Here the smooth muscles are usually spindle-shaped with a relatively uniform length of approximately 35 μm and 5 μm wide in the regions occupied by the nucleus. They are completely surrounded by a basal lamina except for junctions formed with adjoining smooth muscle cells and the endothelial cells. Each layer of smooth muscle is separated by a narrow band consisting of small patches of elastic and collagen fibers.

The adventitial layer of the arteriole contains an occasional fibroblast and a loosely arranged network of collagenous fibers. The fibroblasts, which are located at or near the outer boundary of the adventitia, have extensive cytoplasmic processes which are extremely flattened and often give the impression of forming a barrier between the adventitia and the surrounding connective tissue (Figures 13.14, 13.17, 13.18). These represent the veil cells described by Majno[79] and Rhodin.[107] The adventitia also contains nonmyelineated nerves that are surrounded by Schwann cells. Small blood vessels within the adventitia are accompanied by macrophages and an occasional mast cell.

13.2.2. Terminal arteriole

This segment of the arteriolar stem represents the final arteriolar ramification (Figure 13.19(a), (b). It measures 30–35 μm in diameter and contains a continuous single layer of smooth muscle cells and a scant supporting connective tissue layer.[19,132] The size and shape of the endothelial cells of the terminal arterioles are similar to those in the larger arterioles, the intercellular junctional arrangement between the adjacent cells is also generally the same as those of the larger arterioles. There are numerous micropinocytotic vesicles at both luminal and connective tissue surfaces and the cytoplasm contains more filaments than those observed in the larger arterioles.[9,107] The endothelial cells are separated from the single layer of smooth muscle cells by a basal lamina which in many areas is shared by the two cell types. In some regions, the smooth muscle cells are arranged in a spiral while in others they have a more circular

Figure 13.15. Composite junction in endothelial cells of rat mesenteric artery (M. Simionescu et al.).
Communicating plaques intercalated within the meshes of an occluding junction (arrowheads). The continuity of the occluding junction between the two asterisks is uncertain. A small independent communicating junction appears at cj and a linear extension of an intercalated plaque is seen at r on the P face. The occluding junction shows two free spurs (s) on the E face. There are few or no occluding junction particles along the perimeter of communicating plaques on the P face. The E face of cj_1 is outlined by occluding junctional particles on both sides. The boundary particles project a longer shadow on the P face (double arrow) than on the E face. ($\times$ 100,000)

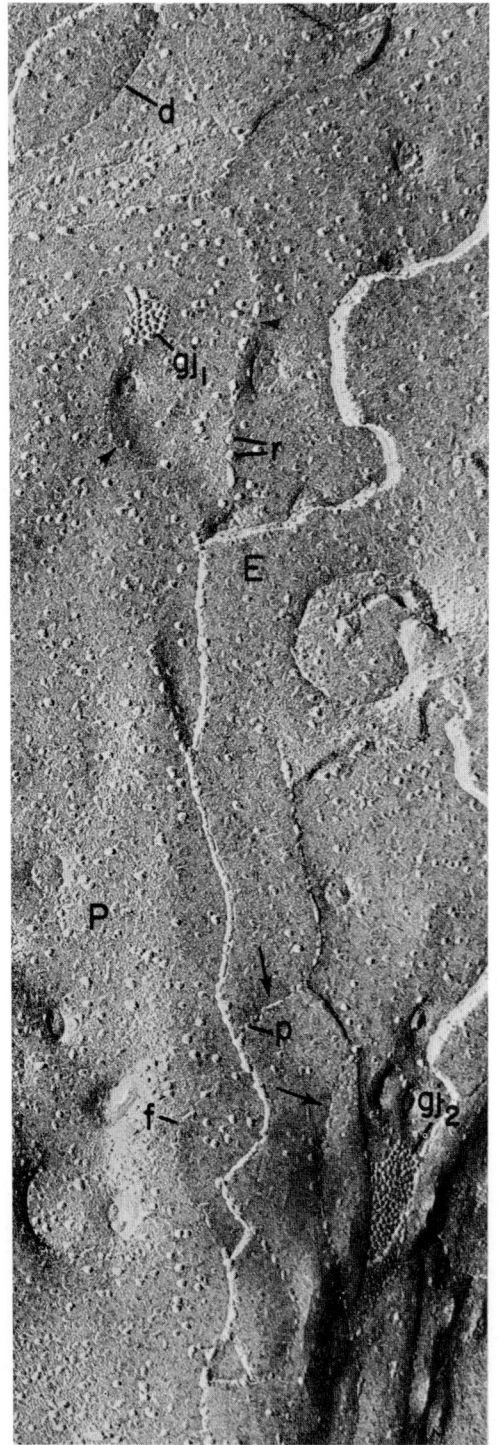

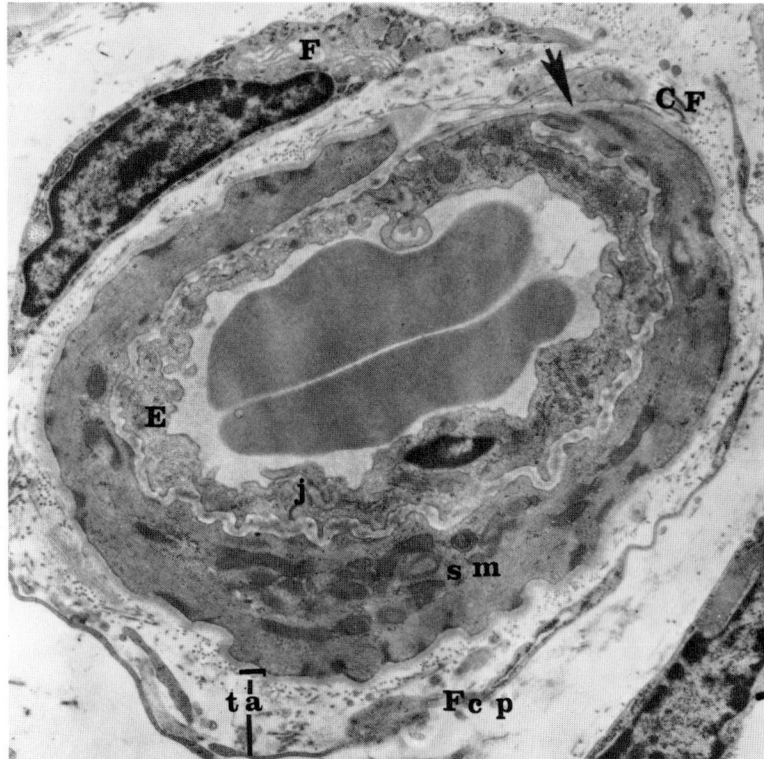

Figure 13.17. Wall structure of small arteriole.
Cross section through an arteriole containing parts of two erythrocytes in the lumen. The endothelial cells (E) contain the usual complement of organelles. Adjacent endothelial cells are held in close apposition by intercellular junctions (j). A single layer of smooth muscle cells (sm) makes intimate contact with the endothelial cells (arrow). The tunica adventitia (ta) contains fibroblast (F) with extremely attenuated cytoplasmic processes (Fcp) which surround the outer boundary of the vessel wall and are separated from the smooth muscle by collagen fibrils (CF). ($\times$ 10,200)

arrangement. There is also membrane-to-membrane contact between smooth muscle cells and endothelial cells. The adventitial layer of the terminal arteriole contains an occasional fibroblast and small bundles of collagen fibers. Nonmyelinated nerves run just external to the smooth muscle layer with occasional contacts being formed between free axons and smooth muscle cells.[107]

13.2.3. Precapillary sphincter

The junctional segment from which smaller branches come off the terminal arterioles was designated as the precapillary sphincter by Chambers and Zweifach[19] which

---

Figure 13.16. Occluding junction in endothelial cells of rat mesenteric vein (M. Simionescu et al.).
The occluding junction consists of a rather loose meshwork of ridges on the P face (arrowheads) and grooves on the E face (arrows). The P face ridges are either marked by discontinuous rows of particles (r) or by narrow furrows (f). The E face grooves appear either marked by particles (p) or are particle-free (d); gj_1 and gj_2 indicate two small gap junctions. P:P face, E:E face. ($\times$ 100,000)

113

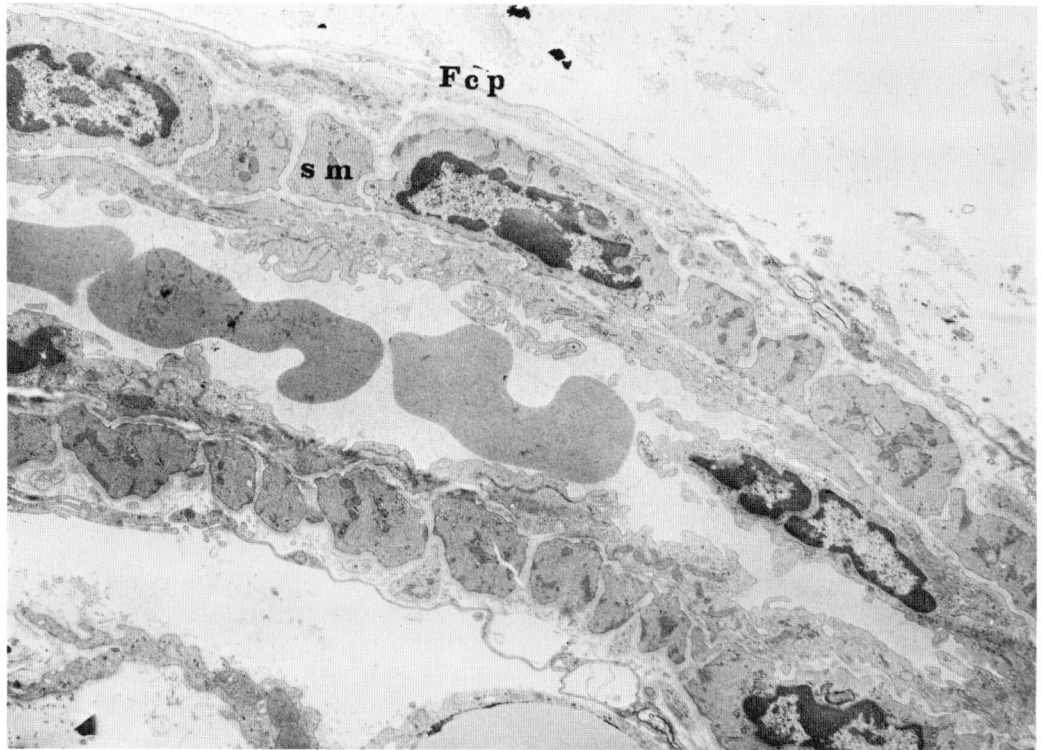

Figure 13.18. Longitudinal section through small arteriole.
The wall consists of a single layer of smooth muscle cells (sm). The extent of the thin cytoplasmic processes (Fcp) of fibroblast which forms the outer boundary is seen to good advantage in this longitudinal section. (× 9,000)

described the muscular arrangement around the region of bifurcation. The abrupt angle of the branching pattern and the muscular arrangement around the orifice enables these structures to regulate the amount of blood entering the capillary vessels. In ultrastructural studies of this region, Rhodin[107] proposed the term precapillary sphincter for the muscular arrangement around the orifice of the smaller side branches which come off the terminal arteriole. The small side branches come off the terminal arteriole at a right angle and may range from 40 to 10 μm in diameter. At the site of branching the smooth muscle cells surround the narrow orifice in a circular

Figure 13.19. Terminal arteriole (W. S. Beacham, A. Konishi, and C. C. Hunt 13.19(b)).

(a) Photograph of fixed and embedded microcirculatory bed of rat mesocecum taken by Normarski optics. The terminal arteriolar segment originates in the lower left corner, arches to the right, crossing three venules, and empties into a collecting venule at D.

(b) Low power micrograph of bifurcation in Figure 13.19(a), rectangle A. The channel just prior to bifurcation had an inside diameter of 28 μm and features of a terminal arteriole. The smaller branch vessel was 14 μm in diameter and the larger 20 μm. One layer of smooth muscle cells (sm) covers endothelial cells (E). The adventitial layer is composed of fibroblasts and sparse collagen bundles. Long arrows indicate direction of blood flow.

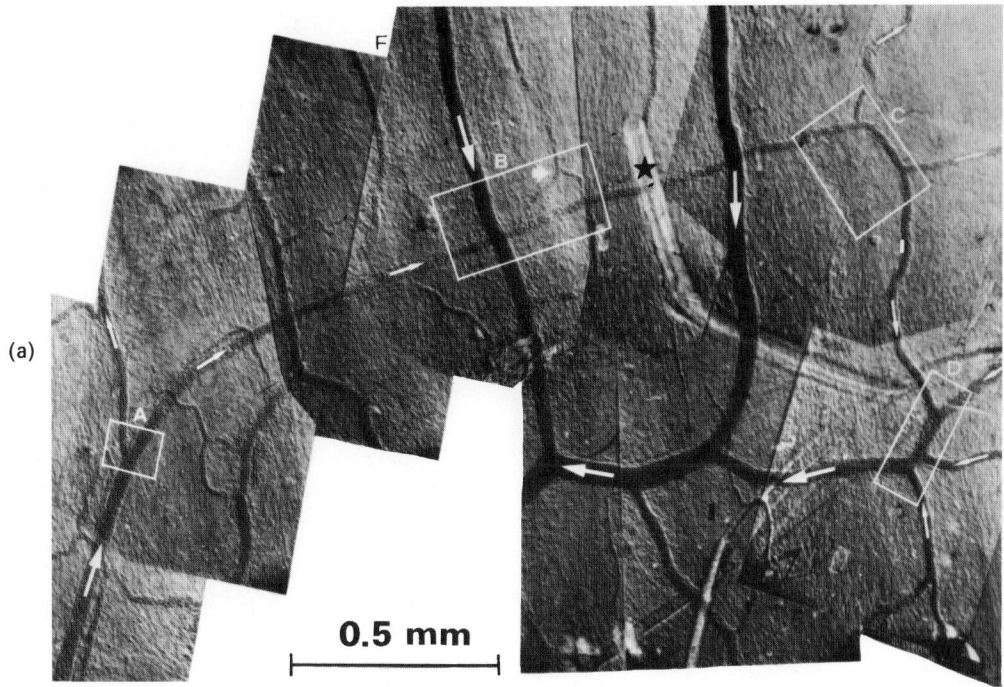

(a)

0.5 mm

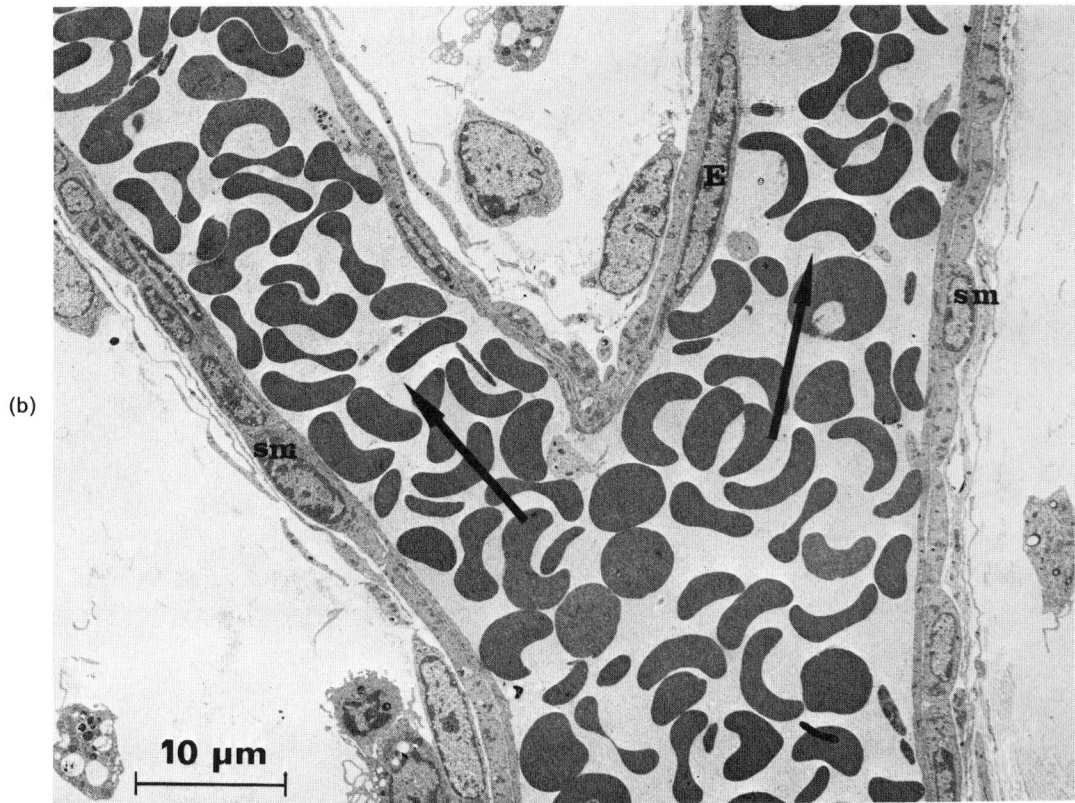

(b)

10 µm

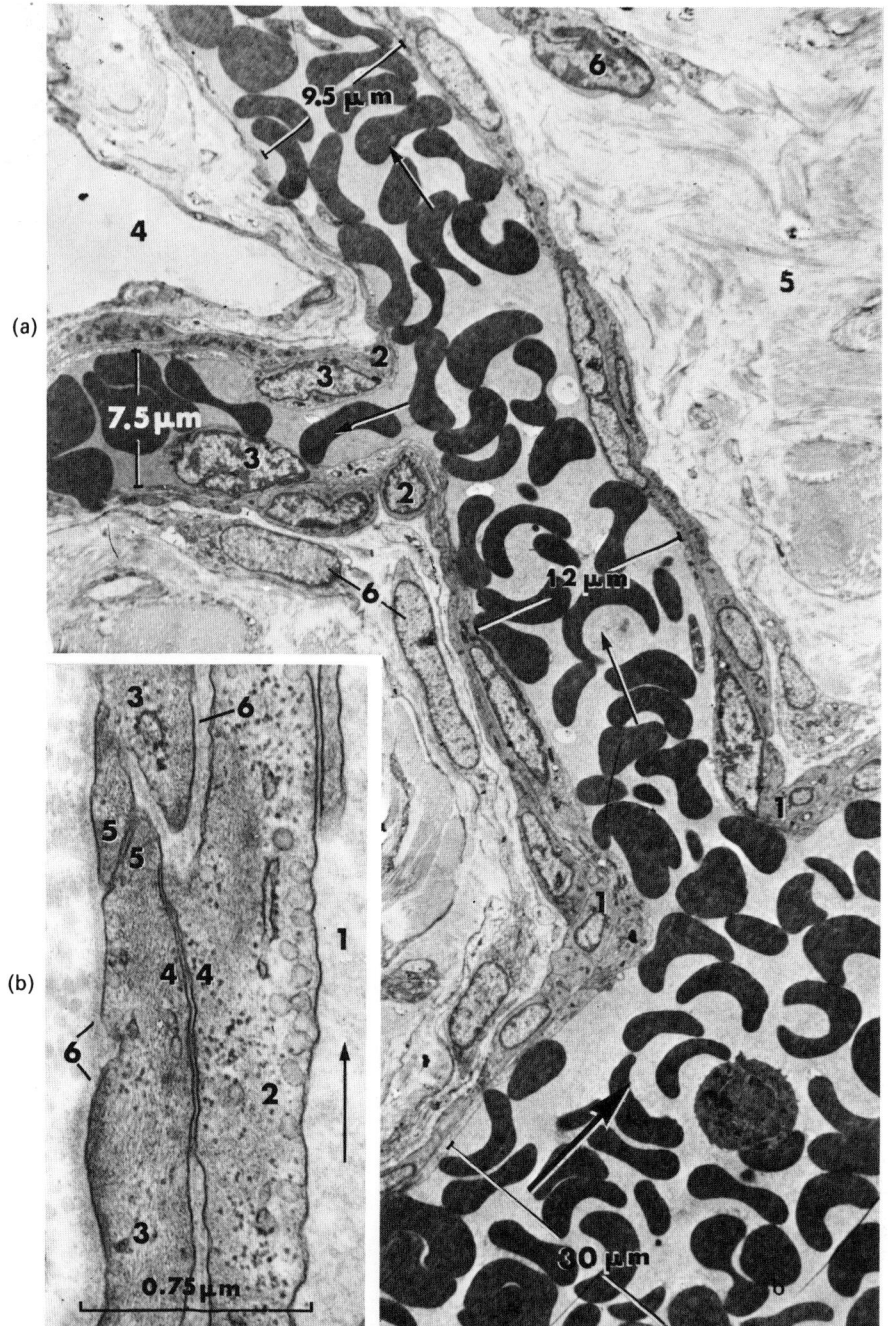

Figure 13.20. Precapillary sphincters (J. A. G. Rhodin).

(a) Longitudinal section of precapillary sphincter area from dermis of rabbit. Arrows indicate direction of blood flow. 1: Smooth muscle cells surround the arteriole and the area where a 12 μm arteriole branches off from the 30 μm arteriole. 2: The point at which the smooth muscle cells form a final sphincter-like arrangement as the capillary emerges with a luminal diameter of 7.5 μm. 3: Endothelial cell nuclei, 4: lymphatic capillary, 5: collagen fibrils, 6: fibroblasts. (×2,200)

(b) Detail of wall of arteriole. 1: Lumen, 2: endothelium, 3: smooth muscle cells, 4: myoendothelial junction, 5: myo-myo junction, 6: basal lamina. (×44,000)

116

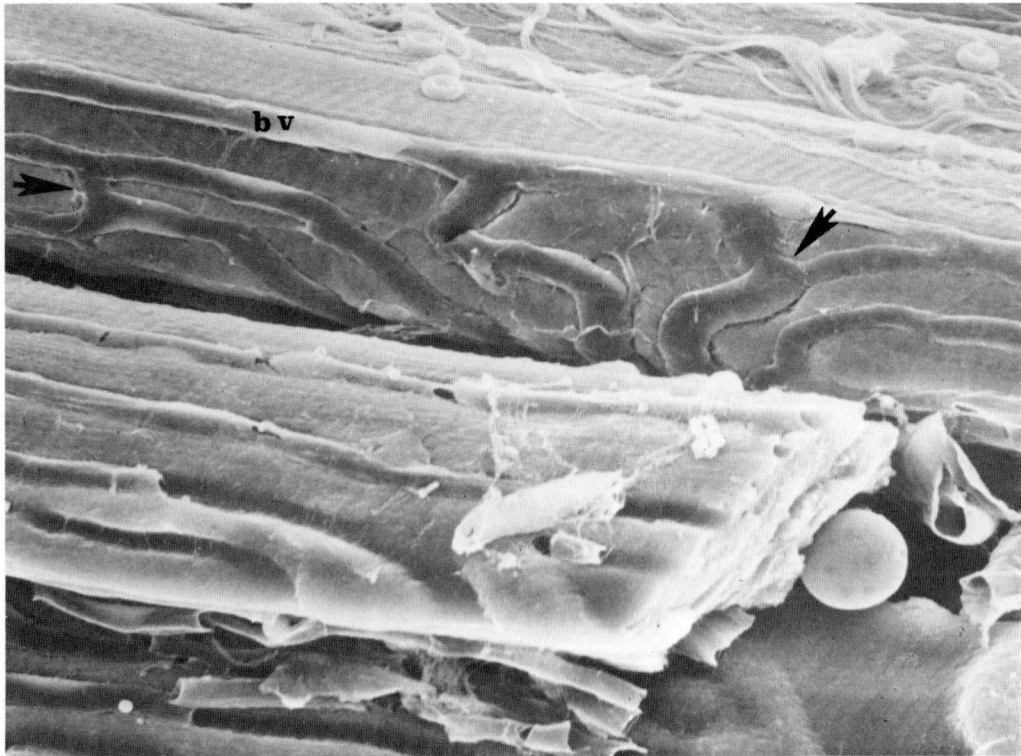

Figure 13.21. Capillary network.
SEM showing the ramifications of small blood vessels (bv) in close contact with myofibers of the rabbit diaphragm. Branching of the microvasculature is indicated at arrows. (× 7,600)

fashion (Figure 13.20(a)). The endothelial cells which line the precapillary sphincter are generally shorter than those in the terminal arteriole. The nucleus is also shorter and thicker, bulging into the lumen to reduce the luminal diameter of the precapillary sphincter (Figure 13.20(a)). The contacts between the endothelial and smooth muscle cells are noticeably increased in this region, as indicated by numerous processes which bridge the basal lamina to make membrane-to-membrane contacts between endothelium and smooth muscle cells (Figure 13.20(b)). The number of unmyelinated nerves accompanied by Schwann cells are also numerous in the precapillary sphincter.[9,107]

The adventitia of the precapillary sphincter also contains fibroblasts and a sparse distribution of collagen fibers. In their earlier studies Chambers and Zweifach[19] envisaged local control of blood flow by chemical mediators. The demonstration by Rhodin[107] and Beacham et al.[9] of the annular arrangement of smooth muscle cells around the junctional precapillary sphincter, the presence of numerous unmyelinated nerves, and the numerous myoendothelial junctions provides structural evidence that this segment represents a determinant of blood flow to the capillary network beyond the terminal arteriole, thus confirming the precapillary sphincter concept as originally formulated by Chambers and Zweifach.[19] This terminal part of the arteriolar system could control the flow of blood to the capillary bed by increasing or reducing

117

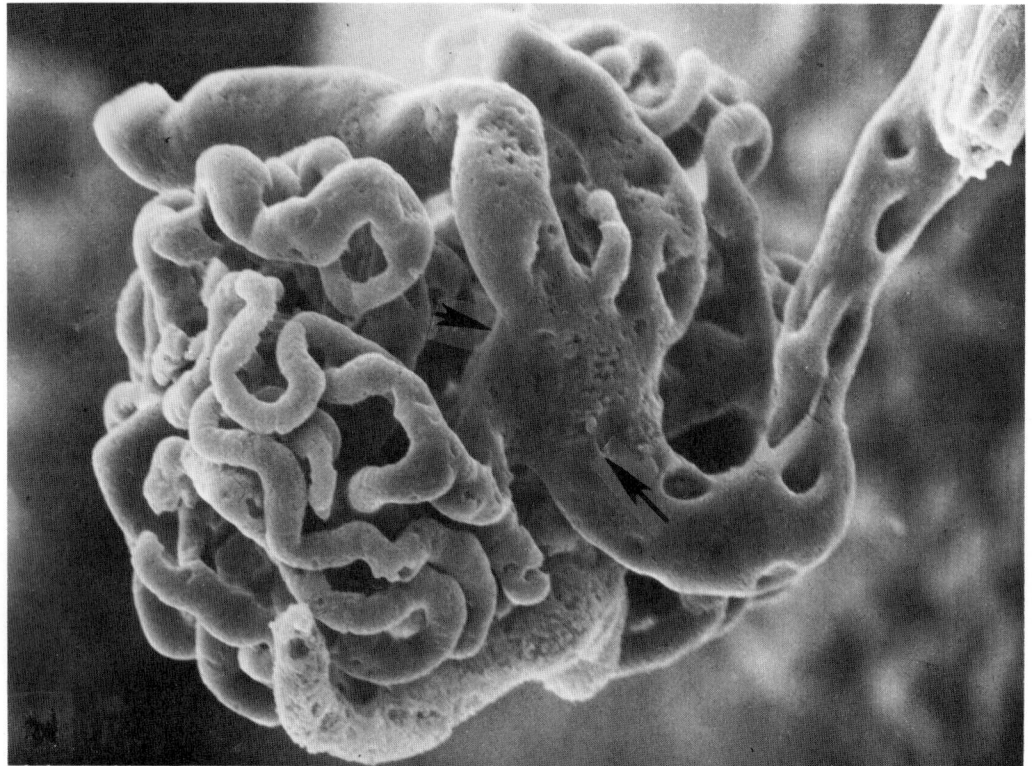

Figure 13.22. Glomerular capillaries.
SEM of latex cast of glomerular capillaries. The rich plexus of vessels extending from the afferent arteriole (arrows) is seen to good advantage in three dimensional relief. (× 11,000)

the luminal diameter or by completely obliterating the lumen, shunting blood to other parts of the microvascular bed or bypassing it completely.

As smaller side branches of the terminal arteriole continue toward the capillaries, they exhibit discontinuous contractile smooth muscle cells in their walls.[19,46,89] Chambers and Zweifach[19] designated the segment of the microcirculation in which muscle cells are spread at irregular intervals as "metarteriole". Subsequently, Zweifach[130] defined this segment of the arteriolar tree as a primary structural unit which serves as a framework for the distribution of capillaries. In its distal continuation, the metarteriole is cone-shaped in its longitudinal configuration with a tapering diameter toward the capillaries. Beyond this, the capillary network consists of endothelial tubes which lack smooth muscle cells in their walls. These thin-walled vessels intercommunicate to form a capillary network of variable organization, depending on the type of tissue involved (Figures 13.19(a), (b), 13.20(a), (b), 13.21, 13.22).

Prior to the application of electron microscopy to the study of the blood vascular system, blood capillaries were classified into two varieties: small blood vessels, barely wider than the red blood cell (6 to 12 μm in diameter), and large capillary channels found in specialized areas such as the liver, spleen, adrenals, and bone marrow. The larger vessels were more irregular in shape and lined by a discontinuous wall. How-

118

ever, electron microscopy has revealed marked variations in the ultrastructure of capillaries in various tissues.[11, 35, 41, 105]

13.2.4. The capillaries

Capillaries consist of thin-walled tubes lined by a single layer of extremely flattened polygonal endothelial cells which display differences in their ultrastructure and intercellular junctions. The tube is surrounded on its tissue front by a glycoprotein basal lamina which also surrounds perivascular cells or pericytes. The outer or adventitial layer consists of connective tissue fibers with irregularly spaced connective tissue cells. Variations in the fine structural features and their arrangement in the capillary wall have provided the basis for a variety of classifications which have been designated for different capillaries. Bennett et al.[11] proposed a classification based on the degree of completeness of the endothelium, basement membrane, and pericapillary cells. However, the classification in general use distinguishes capillaries according to the degree of completeness of the endothelial layer.[53, 62, 79, 94, 105, 106, 118]

Continuous capillaries

The continuous capillary is found in many tissues including muscle, skin, lung, and connective tissues throughout the body and the central nervous system (Figures 13.23, 13.24). The endothelial layer is thin except in areas occupied by an oval nucleus. The cytoplasm in the perinuclear region contains the major cell organelles, i.e., mitochondria, Golgi apparatus, a pair of centrioles, and sparse elements of the endoplasmic reticulum studded with ribosomes (Figure 13.23). Vesicles of various sizes appear in the perinuclear region and may contain an electron-dense flocculent material. The more attenuated portion of the cytoplasm contains a sparse distribution of mitochondria, free ribosomes, and short segments of endoplasmic reticulum (Figure 13.24). Microtubules and cytoplasmic filaments are also found in the capillary endothelium.[14, 15, 82] The plasma membrane is a typical unit membrane. By using the dye ruthenium red, Luft[77] observed a densely staining layer along the luminal surface of the endothelial cells which compared to the endocapillary layer of Chambers and Zweifach.[20, 21] This layer is believed to be rich in mucopolysaccharides since the ruthenium red reaction is selective for acidic mucopolysaccharides.[78]

The capillary endothelium is characterized by the presence of numerous small vesicular invaginations (caveolae) along its blood and tissue fronts (Figures 13.23, 13.25). They measure approximately 500–700 Å in diameter and also occur within the endothelial cell cytoplasm (Palade, 1953). The subsequent observation of similar structures in a variety of tissues prompted the suggestion that these vesicles may account for the bulk movement of fluids from one side of the cell to the other.[2, 10, 39, 41, 86, 91, 116] Capillary endothelial cells are connected to each other by occluding junctions. In freeze-cleaved preparations (Figures 13.26(a), (b), 13.28(a), (b) the junctions consist of two to five ridges or shallow grooves which form a continuous network or they appear like a maze in which the grooves are staggered in parallel fashion.[114] The endothelial cells rest on a basal lamina and underlying collagen fibers which are produced by the surrounding endothelial cells as well as by smooth muscle cells.[6, 79]

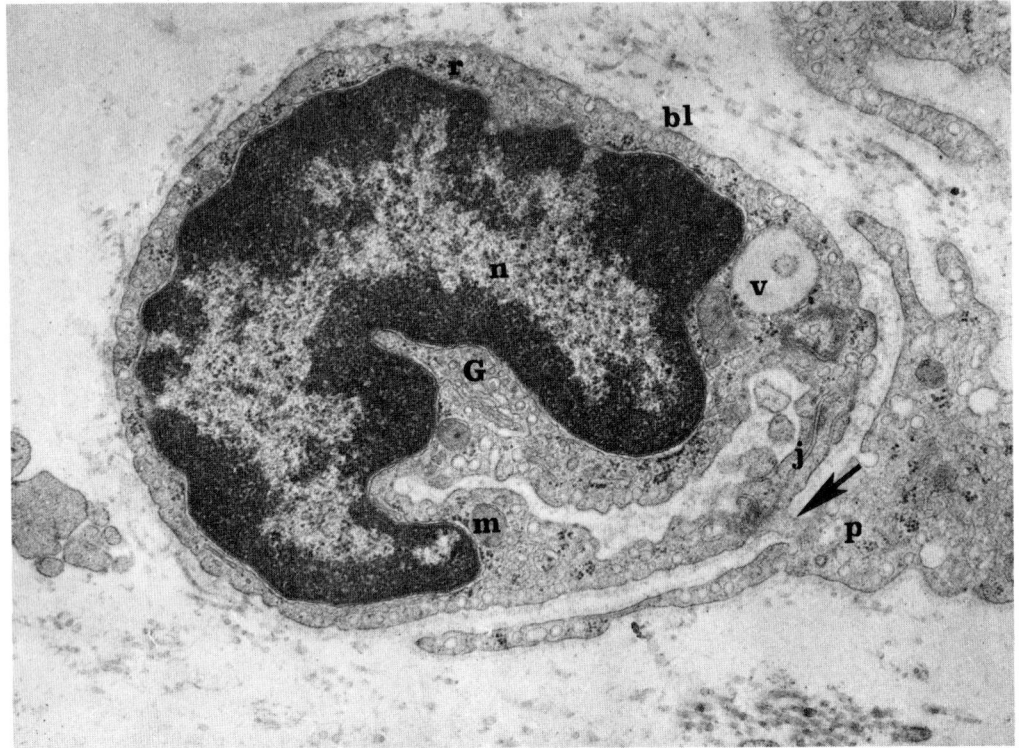

Figure 13.23. Continuous capillary.
The capillary lumen is very narrow and contains a flocculent material of precipitated plasma protein. The thickest part of the endothelial cells occurs in regions occupied by a centrally situated nucleus (n) which is surrounded by a thin rim of cytoplasm containing ribosomes (r), mitochondria (m), Golgi complex (G), and a vesicle (v) with an electron-dense material presumed to be lipid. Terminal margins of the endothelial cells are held in close apposition to form intercellular junctions (j). The capillary basal lamina (bl) surrounds the basal surface of the endothelial cells and is jointly shared by a portion of the pericyte (p) which comes in close contact with the basal surface of the endothelial cell (arrow). (× 30,700)

Since its observation as a component of the capillary wall[91] the basement membrane has been regarded as playing an important role in providing a filterable bearer to large molecules.[14, 15, 33, 35, 81] In the smallest lymphatic vessels (lymphatic capillaries) this structure appears as an irregular or discontinuous band, therefore the lymphatic endothelial cells are directly exposed to the surrounding fluids and large molecules of the interstitium.[43, 44, 70, 73] An irregular basal lamina is observed in regenerating blood vessels which are also very permeable to large molecules.[24]

Intimately associated with the tissue surface of the endothelium are *pericytes* which are irregularly scattered along the capillary wall (Figures 13.23, 13.25, 13.27). This pericapillary cell is surrounded by a basal lamina which is jointly shared by the endothelium at points of close apposition of the two cells. Since their observation by earlier workers[66, 110, 129] there has been much controversy concerning their role in vasoconstriction on the capillary wall. In the transitional segment between postcapillary venules and collecting venule the pericytes are highly branched and much longer

120

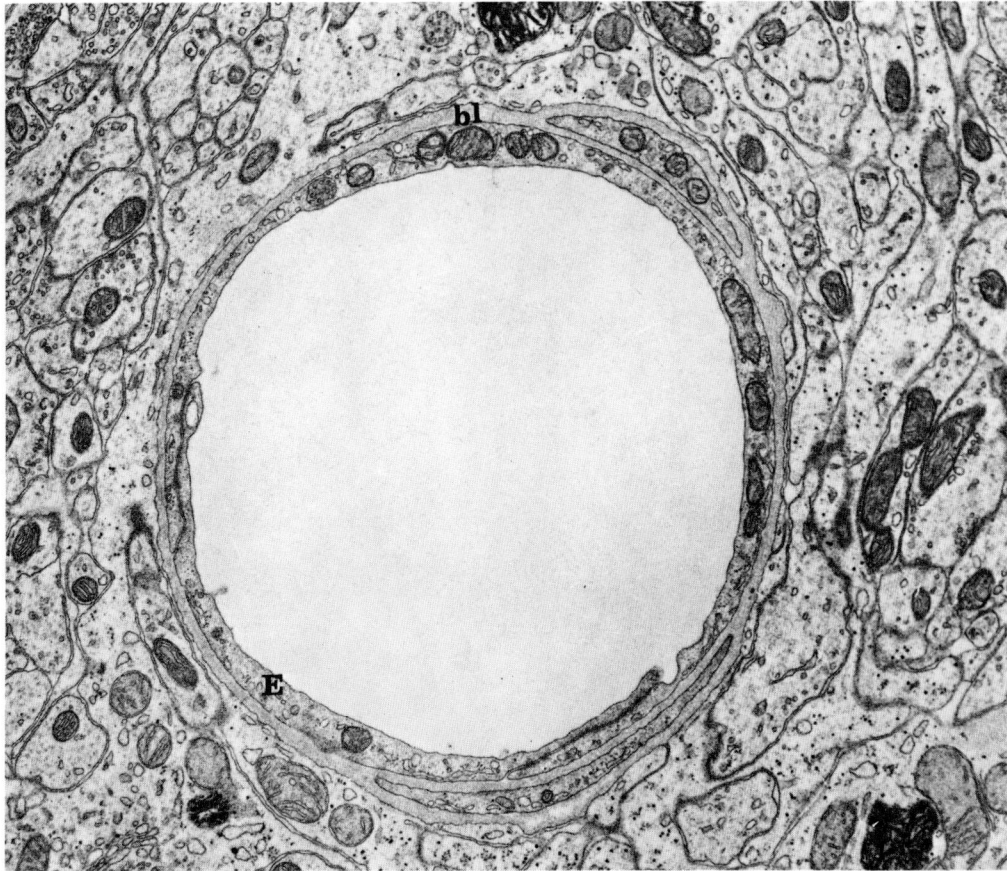

Figure 13.24. Capillary cross section (M. W. Brightman and T. S. Reese).
Blood capillary in rat olfactory bulb. The endothelial cells (E) are extremely thin and are separated from the neurophil by a relatively thick basal lamina (bl). (× 16,000)

with frequent contacts between the pericytes and the endothelium; however, their ultrastructure is similar to capillary pericytes and the cytoplasm lacks filaments characteristic of smooth muscle cells.[108] The outermost layer (adventitia) of the continuous capillary is reduced to the neighboring collagen and elastic fibrils and an occasional fibroblast, macrophage, mast cell, and connective tissue ground substance.[71,92]

Fenestrated capillaries

Although similar to the continuous capillaries in their general structure, the endothelial cells of fenestrated capillaries are extremely attenuated (0·05–0·1 μm in width) and are punctated with rounded windows or fenestrae as shown in Figures 13.29(a), (b), (c), 13.30.[30,31,39,105,128] The fenestrae are approximately 700 Å in diameter and are bridged by a diaphragm (Figures 13.29(b), 13.30). The diaphragm has an average

Figure 13.25. Capillary endothelium.
Freeze-fracture replica showing a muscle capillary and its association with surrounding myofibers (mf) in cardiac tissue. Areas of close apposition between adjacent endothelial cells (E) are shown by a suture-like structure indicating the intercellular junction (j) where cell processes from adjacent cells interdigitate with each other. Parts of a pericyte (p) with cytoplasmic processes is also appreciated at the periphery of the capillary. The numerous surface indentations (arrows) give an appreciation of the extent of plasmalemmal invaginations on the surface of the endothelial cells. ($\times$ 9,500)

thickness of approximately 60 Å and covers the entire circumference of the fenestration. In the center of each fenestrum there is a dense pointlike structure or knob which measures 100–150 Å.[105] In freeze-fracture preparations large surface areas of the endothelium are exposed providing *en face* views of the numerous fenestrations covering the surface of the endothelium (Figure 13.31(a), (b)). In such preparations the fenestrae are arranged in densely packed areas as well as randomly distributed over the endothelial surface. Fenestrated capillaries are observed in endocrine glands, structures engaged in the absorption or production of fluids such as the renal glomerulus, and peritubular capillaries of the kidney, in the choroid plexus and the lamina propria of the small intestine as well as in loose connective tissue and various regions throughout the body. The densely packed fenestrae are surrounded and separated by branching strands of thicker cytoplasm which contain a random distribution of organelles (Figures 13.31(b), 13.32). The strands often extend for long distances as if providing structural rigidity for the wide areas of attenuated cytoplasm.[45,126] Like the continuous capillaries, the endothelial cells of fenestrated vessels rest on a continuous basal lamina.

122

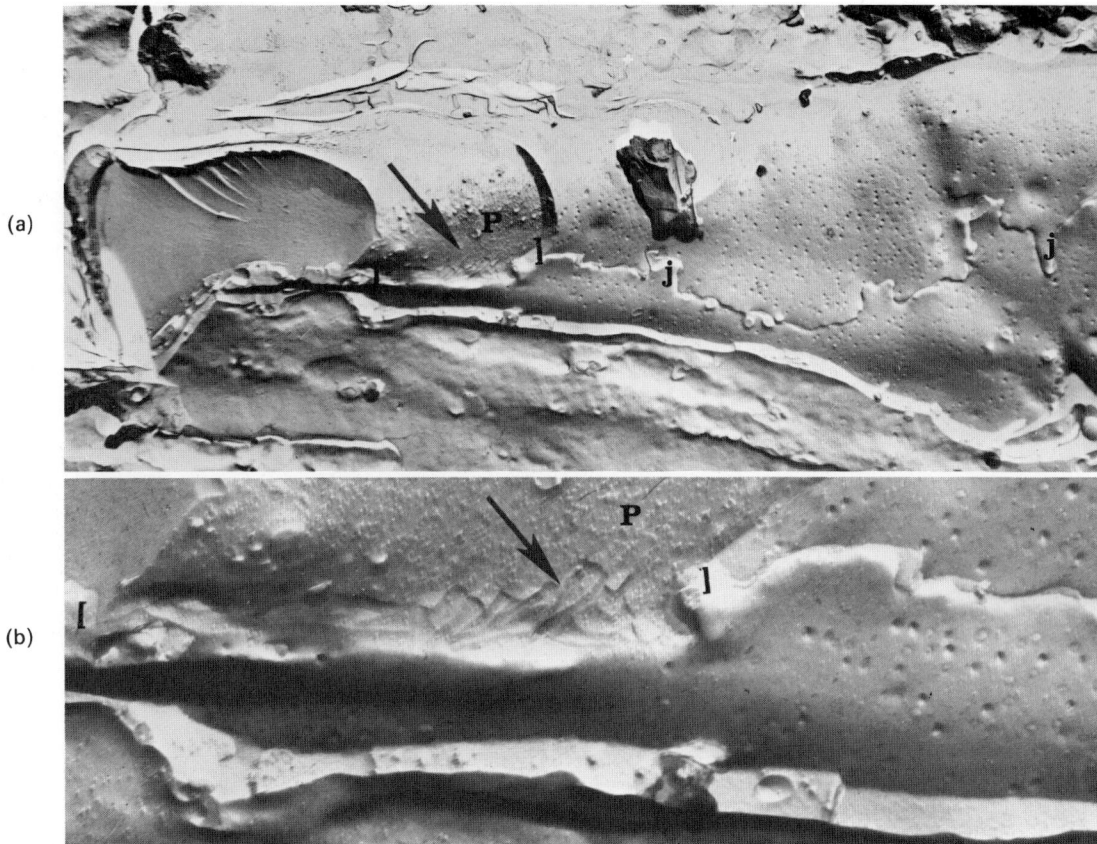

Figure 13.26. Occluding junctions in capillary endothelium.

(a) Freeze-fracture replica showing the three dimensional arrangement of blood capillary in mouse heart tissue. The extent of the intercellular junctions with overlapping endothelial cell processes is indicated (j). The fracture plane has passed along the P face showing the occluding junctions as a lattice work of ridges (arrow). (× 8,300)

(b) Ridges (occluding junctions, arrow) at higher magnification. (× 85,050)

Capillaries with a discontinuous endothelium (sinusoids)

The larger capillary channels which exist in specialized organs such as the liver (Figure 13.33), spleen, bone marrow, and lymph node (Figure 13.34) are larger and more irregular in shape. The endothelial wall is extremely thin with an irregular basal lamina and connective tissue layer separating it from the surrounding parenchymal cells. Except in the perinuclear area, the cytoplasm of endothelial cells is expanded into a very thin sheet abundantly perforated with small and large fenestrations which often produce large gaps in the cytoplasm, exposing the surrounding parenchyma and connective tissue.[87] Adjacent cell margins overlap to form intercellular junctions in some areas, but in other areas neighboring cells are separated by large gaps between the cell margins.

Venous capillaries and postcapillary venules

The terminal segment of true capillaries merges with the venous capillaries and post-capillary venules (pericytic capillaries)[12, 20] whose functions are more sensitive to

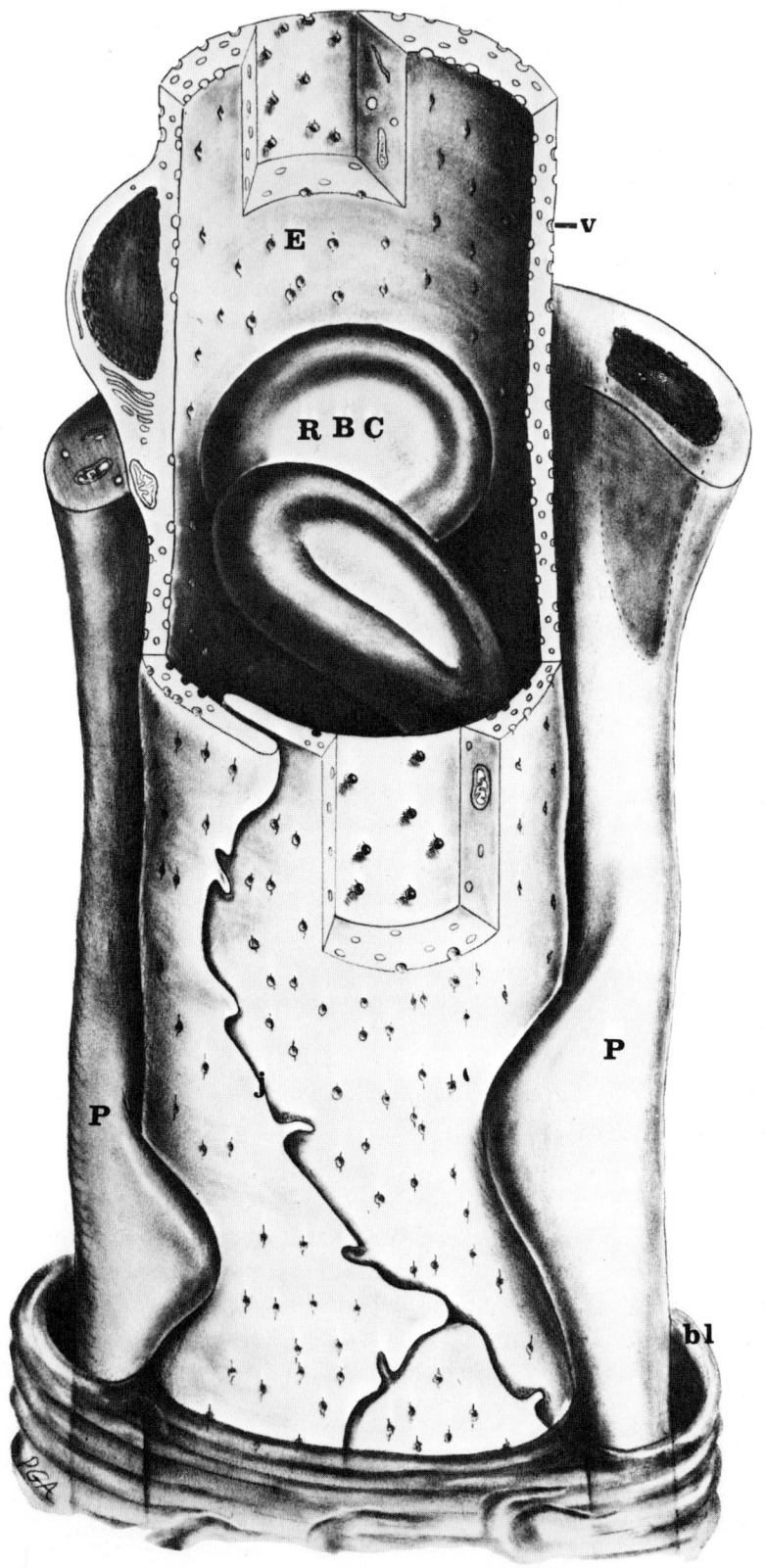

chemical, mechanical, and thermal influences than the arteriole component of the microcirculatory bed.[80,81] Subtle differences in vascular diameter and changes in the number of cell layers along short segments of the capillary bed make it very difficult to determine the transition from true capillaries to postcapillary venules. However, due to the sensitivity of venules to histamine, serotonin, and other vasoactive substances, it is possible to label this segment of the microvascular bed by injecting tracer particles such as colloidal carbon following the production of an inflammatory response.[25,26,80,81] Leakage of carbon particles from undamaged small venules has also been observed in small intestinal mucosa and in muscles (cremaster) by Hurley.[56] On the other hand, improved phase and Normarski optical methods combined with cinephotographic techniques make it possible to observe blood flow within the capillary bed and subsequently study the same vessels with the electron microscope (Figures 13.19, 13.35). From such studies, various segments of the venous capillaries and postcapillary venules (pericytic venules) have been identified as demonstrated in Figures 13.35, 13.36.[9,108] In common with the true capillaries (arteriolar capillaries), venous capillaries consist of flattened endothelial cells folded to form a very thin tube which is surrounded by a continuous basal lamina. Pericytes with numerous cytoplasmic processes are widely scattered along the connective tissue side of the endothelium (Figures 13.35, 13.36). A basal lamina also surrounds the pericytes except at sites where the plasmalemma of the pericyte is in close contact with the endothelial plasmalemma. The endothelial cells of venous capillaries are generally flattened except for segments occupied by the nucleus. The thickness of the endothelial cytoplasm measures $0.2–0.4$ μm. Occasionally, clusters of fenestrations are observed in the attenuated segments of the endothelium. The fenestrations are similar to those in other fenestrated capillaries and are closed by a diaphragm.[108] The intercellular junctions between endothelial cells are loosely organized. Studies of the intercellular junctions using freeze-fracture methods revealed discontinuous low profile ridges and grooves (Figure 13.37) which suggest that the intercellular junctions are loosely organized.[114] This loose arrangement of the endothelial cell junctions facilitates the separation of adjacent cells of the venous capillaries which are sensitive to vasoactive substances such as histamine, serotonin, and bradykinin.[81,125]

As the venous side of the terminal microvascular bed is approached the postcapillary venules gradually become covered by a complete layer of pericytes which are irregularly scattered along their length (Figure 13.38). The cytoplasm displays features that are very similar to smooth muscle cells, i.e., many areas of the cytoplasm contain bundles of filaments in common with those observed in smooth muscle cells.[108] With increasing vessel diameter (approximately 50 μm) additional cells are

Figure 13.27. Heart muscle capillary (L. V. Leak).
The three dimensional architecture of the heart muscle capillary with its luminal content of red blood cells (RBC) and wall of endothelium (E), basement lamina (bl), and pericyte (P). The diagram was constructed from three dimensional relief images obtained from replicas of heart capillaries of both fixed and unfixed frozen etched preparations. Both luminal and connective tissues surfaces of the endothelium are populated by plasmalemmal invaginations (micropinocytotic vesicles). Cut away segments of the endothelium depict the appearance of these vesicles (v) over the cytoplasmic surface. The topographical association between apposing cell margins to form intercellular junctions (j) is depicted in both surface and cross views. The basement lamina (bl) is continuous over the endothelial surface as well as the adjacent pericyte (P).

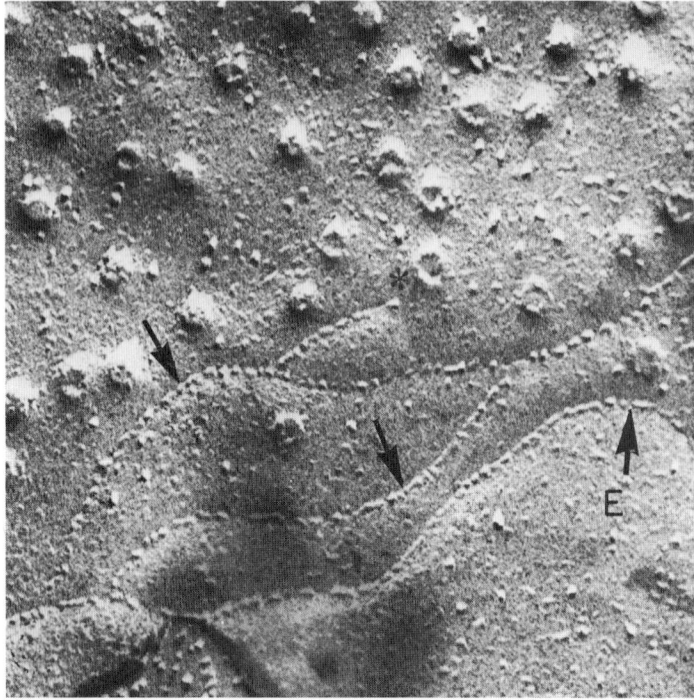

(a)

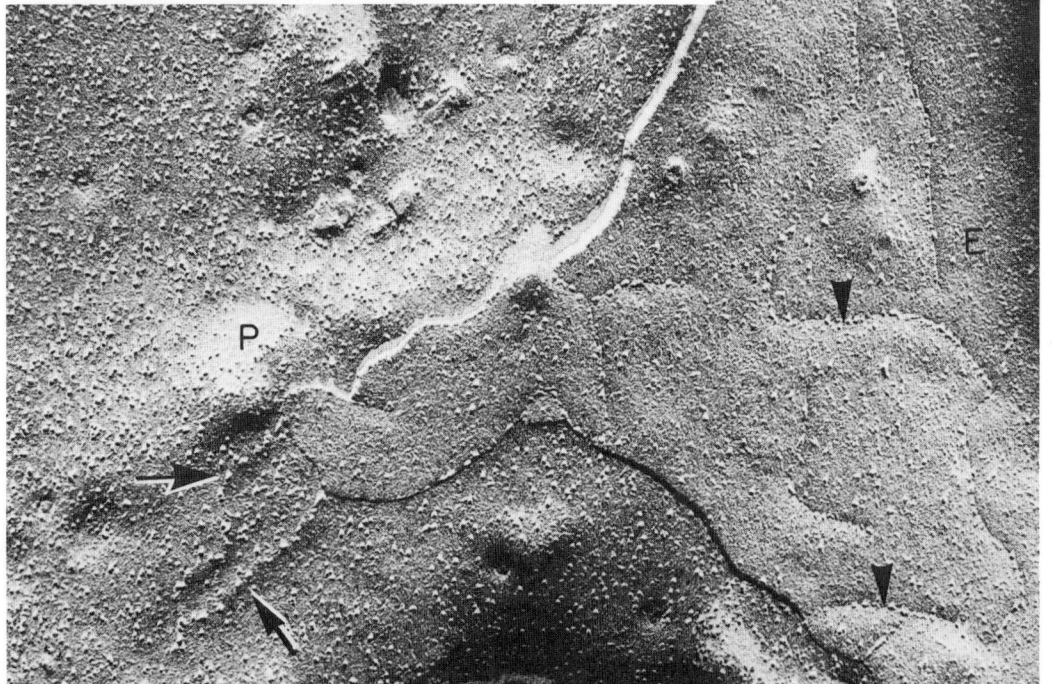

(b)

added to the periendothelial layer with ultrastructural features that are characteristic of smooth muscle cells (Figure 13.39).

13.3. Ultrastructure of the venular wall

Like the arterial wall, the wall of veins also contains three basic tunicas (Figure 13.40), intima, media, and adventitia. Ultrastructural studies of the venular wall revealed that the intima is formed by a continuous layer of polygonal endothelial cells which rests on a thin basal lamina. Adjacent cells are held together by occluding junctions and gap junctions (Fig. 13.16). Extending from the basal surface are short cytoplasmic projections which form myoepithelial junctions with the innermost layer of smooth muscle cells. The subendothelial layer consists of a loose meshwork of collagen fibers and short segments of elastic fibers comprising the internal elastic lamina, which is more prominent in veins of the lower extremities.[3] In veins with valves, the endothelial cells project into the lumen with an intervening band of collagenous and elastic fibers. The valve is composed of leaflets with free edges that are closely apposed to prevent the backward flow of blood.

The middle layer of veins is much thinner than the media in arteries of comparable sizes (Figure 13.39). The media consist of one to several layers of smooth muscle cells that are separated by bundles of collagen fibers that are longitudinally arranged with small bundles of elastic fibers. The layers of smooth muscle cells are helically arranged and form complete layers by means of communicating (gap) junctions between the terminal margins of adjacent cells. Communicating junctions are also formed along the lateral surfaces of adjacent layers of smooth muscle cells by means of short projections from neighboring cells. Therefore, conduction of impulses from cell to cell within each layer in addition to those of adjacent layers is achieved via the communicating junctions.[29,75] The smooth muscle cells of veins contain organelles in common with the smooth muscle cells within the media of arteries. There is no well-defined external elastic lamina in the walls of medium and large size veins.

The adventitia comprises the largest component in the wall of veins. There are large bundles of collagen fibers arranged with their long axes parallel with the long axis of the vessel. The elastic fibers are sparse, occurring between bundles of collagen fibers and fibroblast. Small blood vessels (*vasa vasorum*) and lymphatics which may also penetrate the media are observed in the adventitia. Myelinated and unmyelinated nerves are also observed.

Figure 13.28. Occluding junctions in blood capillary (M. Simionescu, N. Simionescu, and G. E. Palade).

(a) Small vessel, probably blood capillary in rat diaphragm. The fracture plane exhibits an E face of the endothelial plasmalemma on which the tight junction is seen as a maze of branching and staggered grooves marked by discontinuous rows of particles (arrows). ($\times$ 120,000)

(b) Isolated blood capillary from rat omentum. The cleavage plane reveals the E and P faces of the cell membrane of two adjacent endothelial cells and exposes over a long distance (3 μm) a tight junction which consists of a maze of branching and staggered grooves (arrowheads) on the E face and ridges (arrows) on the P face. Most of them form a continuous network: a few appear disconnected. Grooves as well as ridges are marked by discontinuous rows of particles. Note the tendency of the membrane leaflets to fracture along the grooves or ridges of the junction (double arrow). ($\times$ 68,000)

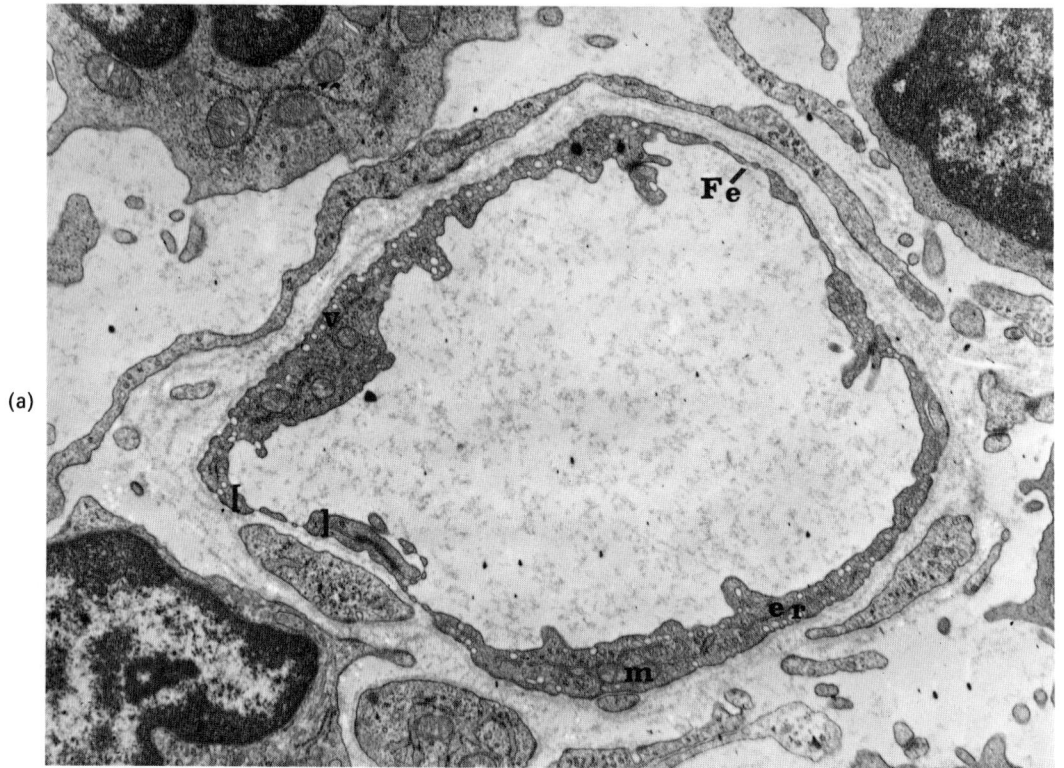

(a)

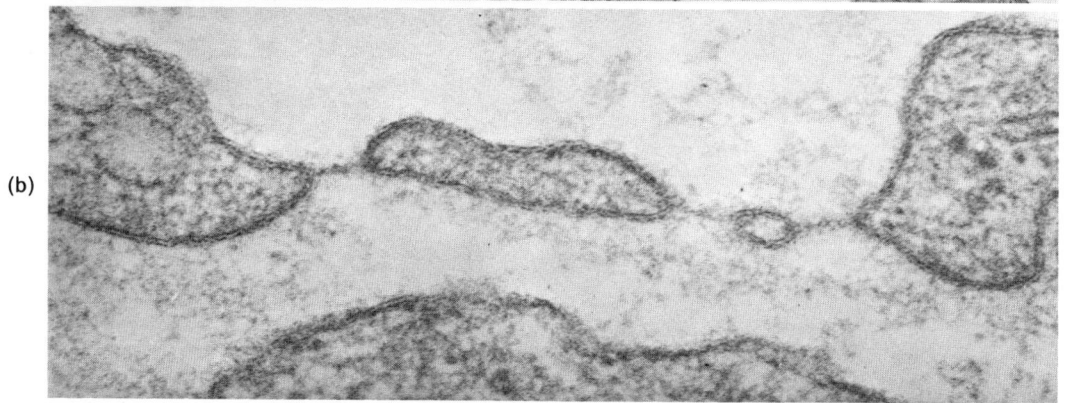

(b)

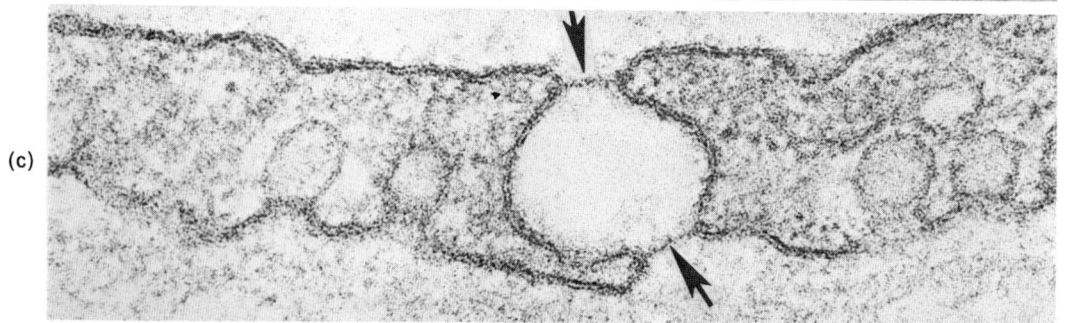

(c)

Figure 13.29. Fenestrated capillary in the lymph node.

(a) Cross section of fenestrated blood capillary in rat popliteal lymph node. Fenestrae (Fe) occur at various regions of the capillary wall and are bridged by diaphragms of a single plasmalemma whose width is thinner than the usual unit plasma membrane. In the thicker regions of this endothelial cell the usual organelles are distributed throughout the cytoplasm, including mitochondria (m), rough endoplasmic reticulum (er). Plasmalemmal invaginations occur on both luminal and connective tissue fronts to form micropinocytotic vesicles (v). ($\times$ 13,000)

(b) Enlargement of fenestrated areas of the endothelium indicating the plasma membrane which extends the width of the fenestrae. ($\times$ 128,500)

(c) Large vesicle bordered on its luminal and connective tissue fronts by thin plasma membranes (arrows). ($\times$ 128,500)

129

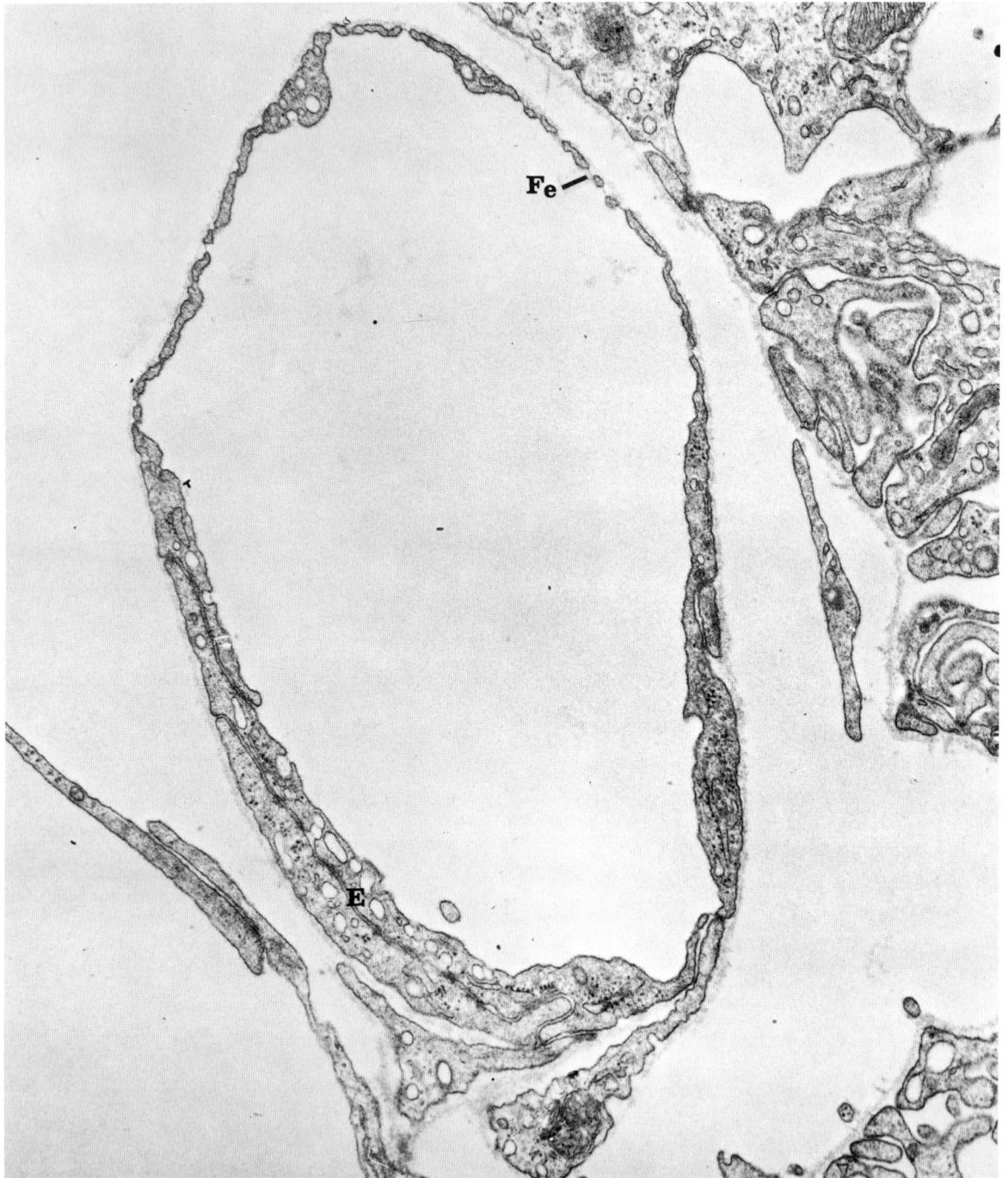

Figure 13.30. Fenestrated capillary in choroid plexus (M. W. Brightman and T. S. Reese).

Cross section of fenestrated capillary in mouse choroid plexus stroma. Fenestrae (Fe) occur along the endothelial (E) wall between the thicker regions of the cytoplasm which contain the usual complement of cytoplasm organelles. (× 18,000)

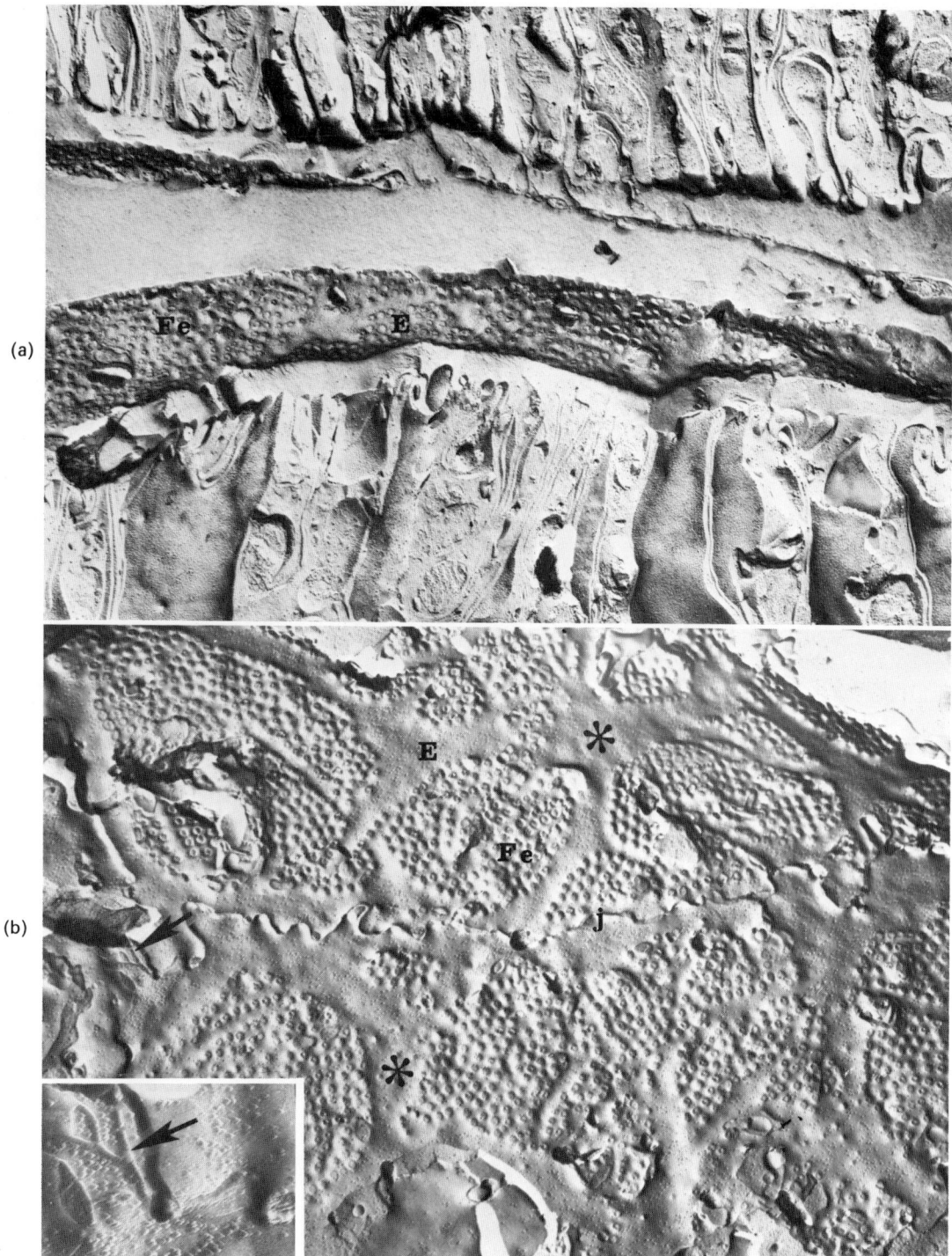

Figure 13.31. Fenestrated capillaries in kidney.

(a), (b) Freeze-fracture replicas showing fenestrated capillaries in peritubular region of kidney. Large areas of the endothelial (E) wall are populated with accumulations of fenestrae (Fe) which are surrounded by thicker regions of the cytoplasm and are indicated by riblike structures (*) ramifying throughout the endothelial wall. The cells are held together by intercellular junctions (j) which contain occluding junctions as indicated by the ridges (arrow). ((a) ×14,150, (b) ×23,750)

Inset: Occluding junctions indicated by ridges (arrow) at higher magnification. (×46,500)

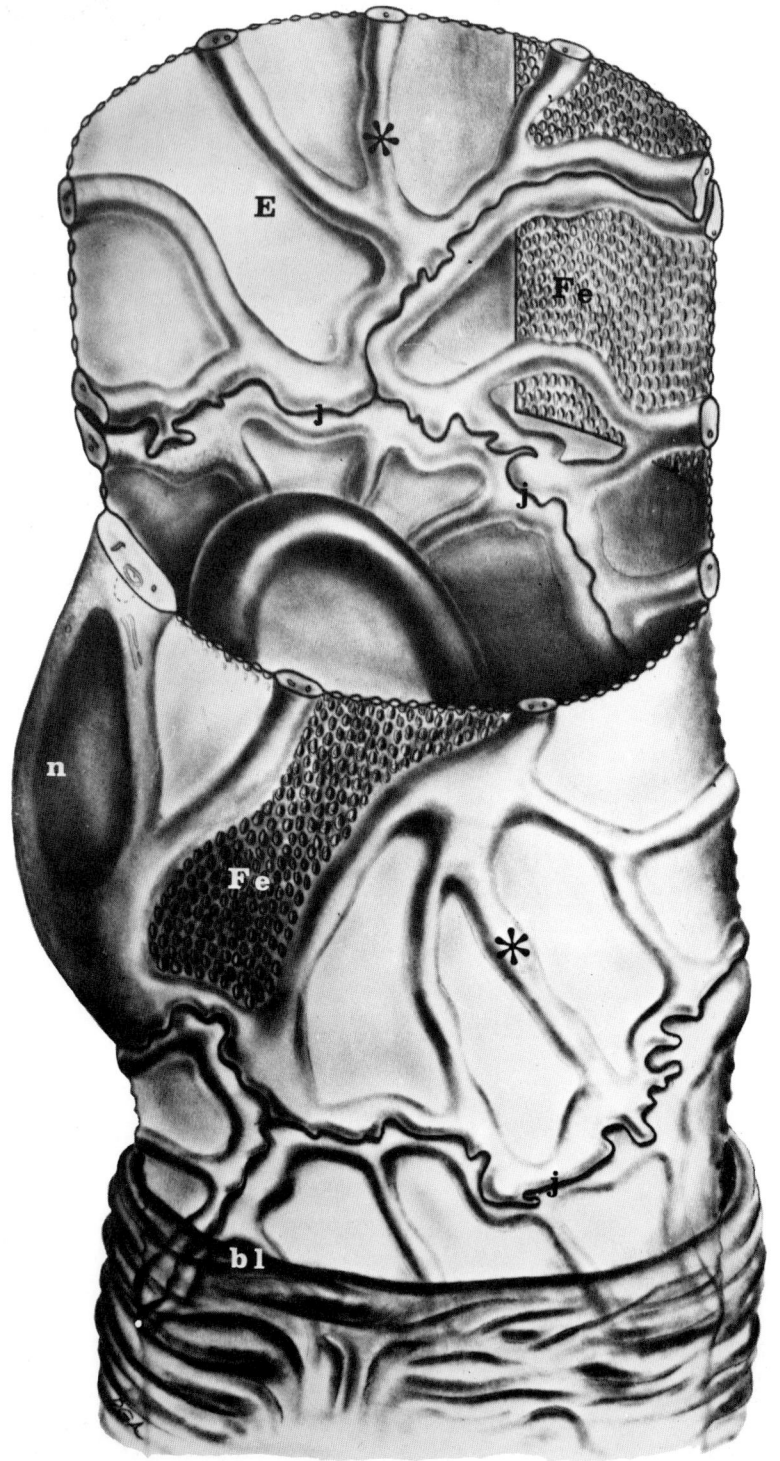

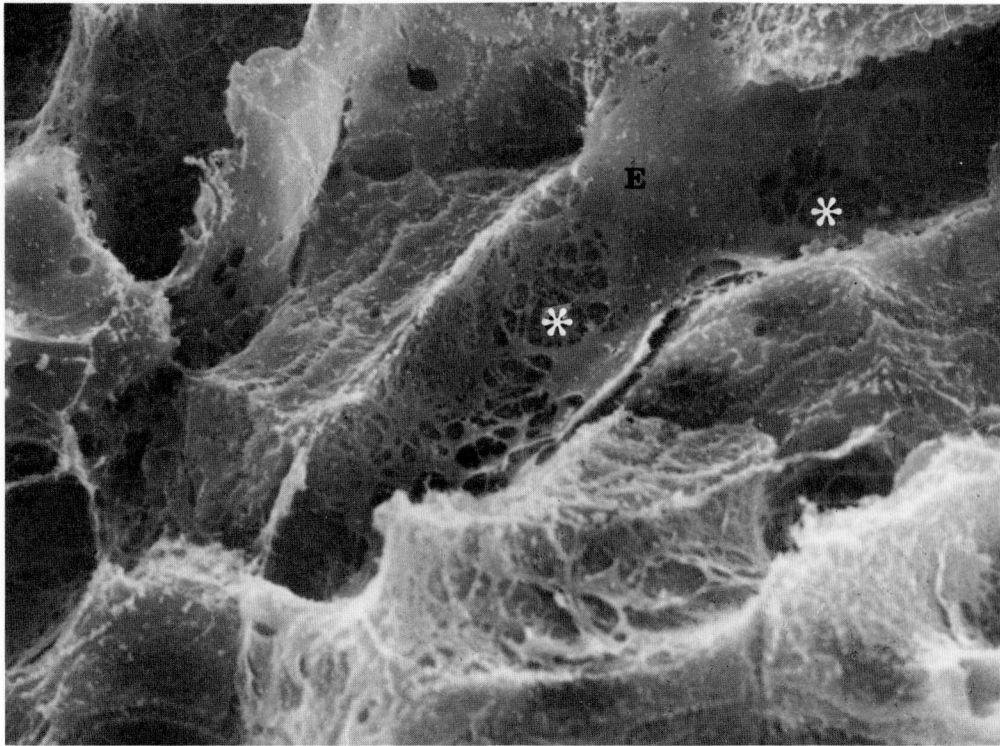

Figure 13.33. Sinusoid in the liver.
SEM showing the endothelial cells (E) extremely attenuated in many regions with the cytoplasm branching to form many discontinuities in the vessel wall. (× 4,000)

Figure 13.32. Three dimensional appearance of fenestrated blood capillary.
Diagram constructed from three dimensional images obtained from freeze-fracture replica and two dimensional images seen in ultrathin sections. The endothelial cells (E) contain wide areas of attenuated cytoplasm punctuated with fenestrae (Fe). These are separated by thick rims of cytoplasm (*) which contain cytoplasmic organelles. The nucleus (n) occupies the thickest region of the cell. The three dimensional appearance of adjacent cell margin to form intercellular junctions (j) is shown in surface and cross-sectional views. Freeze fracture studies have shown that adjacent cells are held together by occluding junctions (see Figure 13.31(b)). Basal lamina (bl) surrounds the connective tissue surface of the endothelial cells.

133

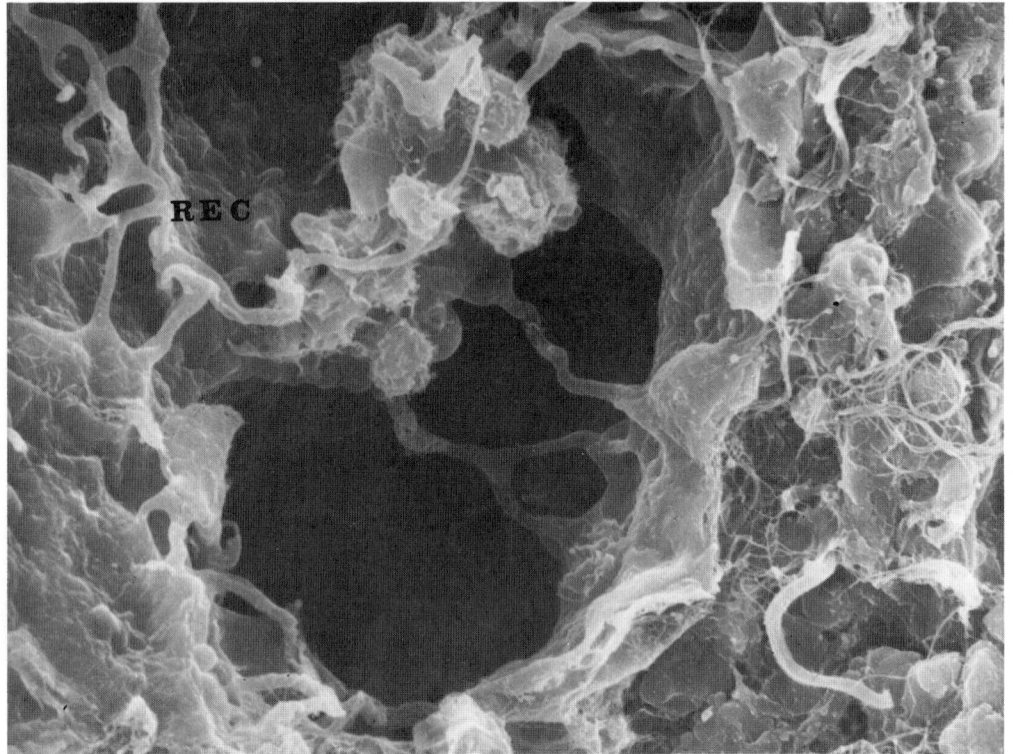

Figure 13.34. Sinusoid in lymph node.
The reticular endothelial cell (REC) lining of sinusoid is also extremely attenuated with discontinuities being observed in the endothelial wall. (× 18,000)

Figure 13.35. Venous capillaries (W. S. Beacham, A. Konishi, and C. C. Hunt 13.35(e)).

(a) Light micrograph from a frame of cine film taken with Nomarski optics *in vivo*. The end of the distal segment of the preferential channel is indicated by the thick solid arrow. White arrows show direction of blood flow.

(b) Low power EM of area shown in (a). Thick solid arrow indicates ends of preferential channel. Areas shown by arrows a, b, and c are illustrated at higher magnification in Figures 13.35(c), (d), (e).

(c) EM of area indicated by arrow a in (b). The periendothelial cell (PE) has the characteristics of a pericyte. The thin process of this cell extending toward the bottom shows endoplasmic reticulum with ribosomes in an orderly arrangement, as seen in fibroblasts. Endothelial cells (E) show two endo-endothelial junctions (j). Arrow shows direction of blood flow.

(d) EM of area shown by arrow b in (b). A single thin endothelial cell process containing ribosomes, pinocytotic vesicles, and very few filaments extends the full length of the figure. Throughout the preferential channel no fenestrations were observed. Arrow indicates direction of blood flow.

(e) EM of area indicated by arrow c in (b). A fibroblast (F) containing phagocytic vesicles is seen in the adventitia. Arrow shows direction of blood flow. PE: periendothelial cell, E: endothelial cell.

134

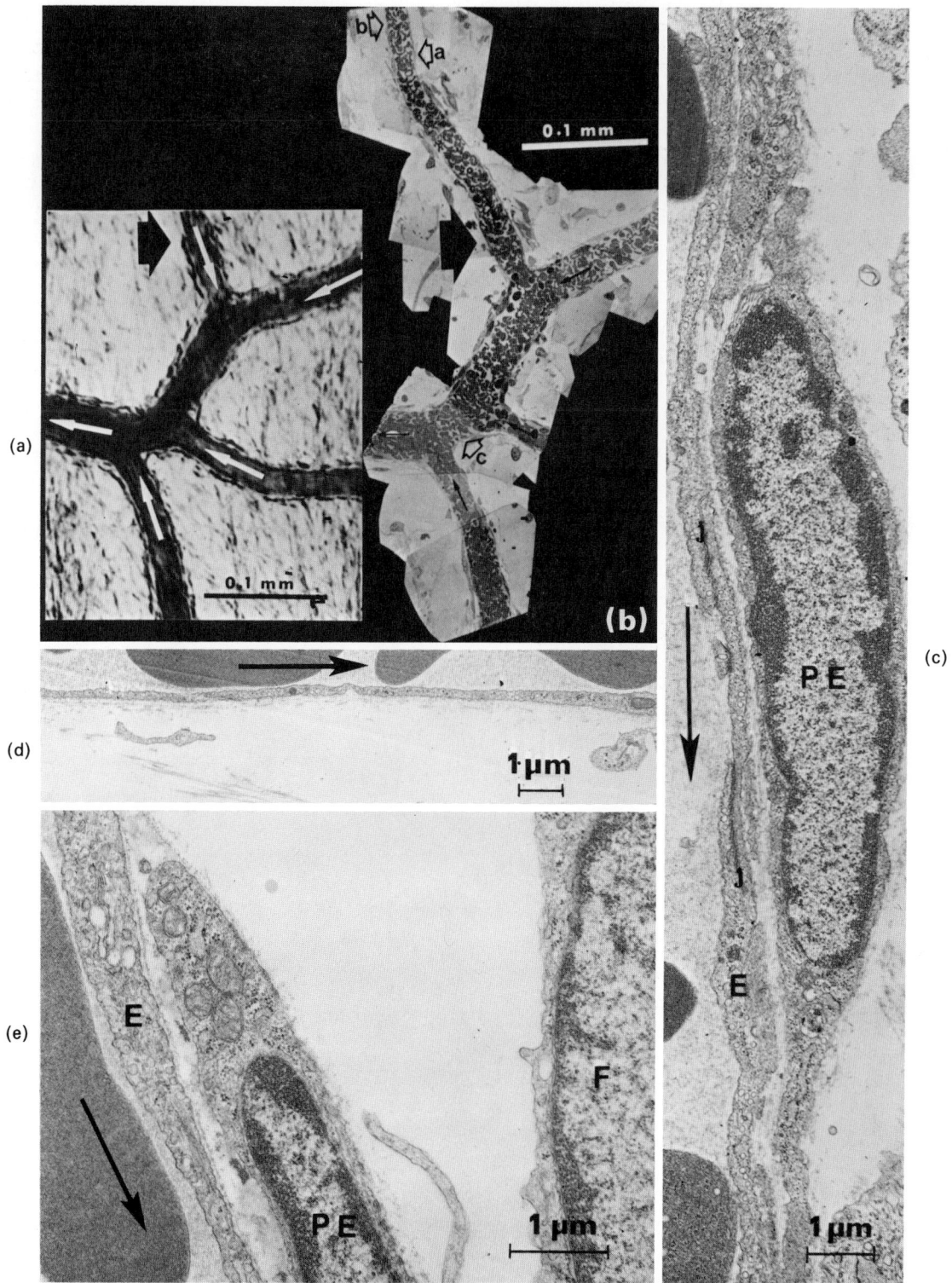

(a)

(b)

(c)

(d)

(e)

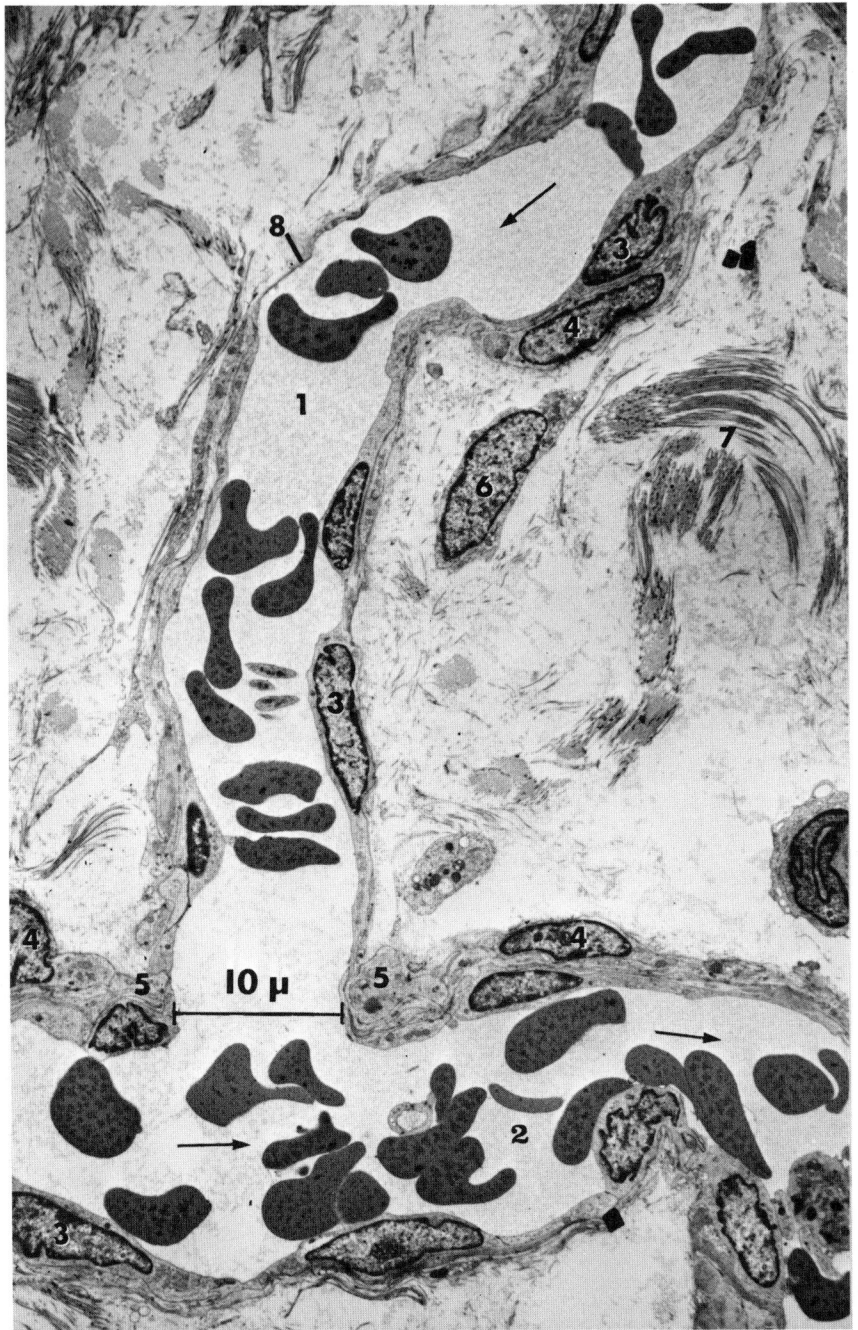

Figure 13.36. Connection between venous capillary and postcapillary venule (J. A. G. Rhodin).

Longitudinal section of connection between venous capillary and postcapillary venule in the dermis of the rabbit. Arrows indicate direction of blood flow. 1: venous capillary, 2: postcapillary venule, 3: endothelial nuclei, 4: nuclei of pericytes, 5: absence of smooth muscle cells at junction of capillary and postcapillary venule, processes of pericytic cytoplasm surround the capillary at this point; 6: fibroblast, 7: collagen fibrils, 8: fenestrations occur in some parts of the endothelium of a venous capillary in the dermis. (× 2,200)

Figure 13.37. Endothelial junctions in pericytic venule (M. Simionescu, N. Simionescu, and G. E. Palade 13.37(b)).

(a) Small vessel (probably pericytic venule) from rat diaphragm. On this P face of the endothelial plasmalemma the tight junction appears as a series of discontinuous low-profile ridges (arrows) which on most of their length are free of associated particles. (×60,000)

(b) Isolated pericytic venule of rat omentum. The endothelial junction appears on the E face (E) as discontinuous shallow grooves free of particles (arrows). Some of these grooves are oriented almost perpendicularly to the general direction of the junction. (×60,000)

137

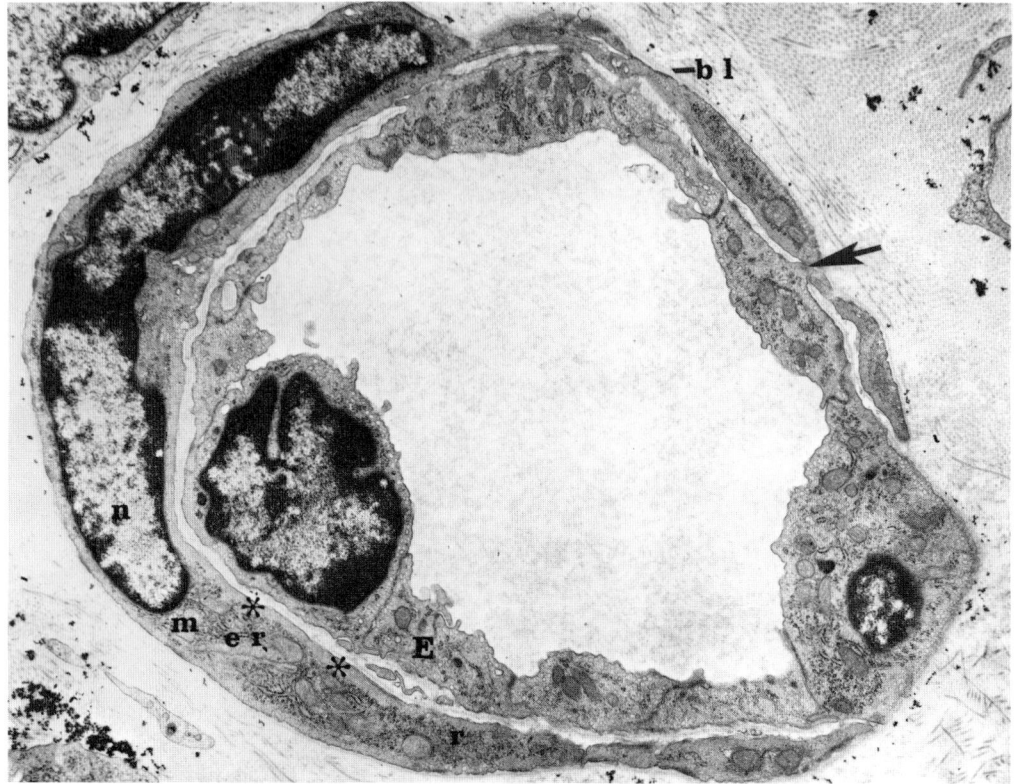

Figure 13.38. Pericytic venule.
Cross section showing the relationships of a pericyte (p) to the endothelium (E). The pericyte has a large nucleus (n) which occupies the widest regions of the cell. The perinuclear cytoplasm contains mitochondria (m), endoplasmic reticulum (er), and numerous free ribosomes (r). The pericyte is surrounded by a basal lamina (bl) on its connective tissue side and is separated from the endothelial cell by a basal lamina (bl) except at points interrupted by projections from the endothelial cells to make intimate contact with the pericyte (arrow). The peripheral portion of the cytoplasm (*) is free of cytoplasmic organelles and contains a filamentous component. (× 7,850)

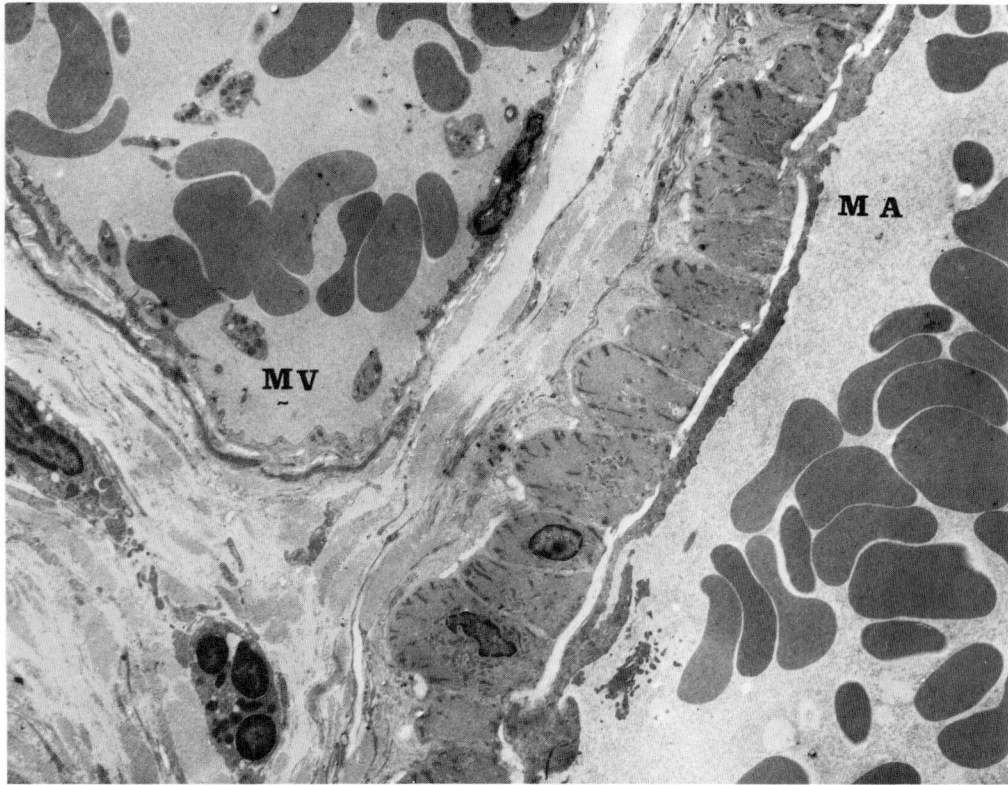

Figure 13.39. Comparison of venular and arterial walls.
Section of muscular vein (MV) with its accompanying muscular artery (MA). (×3,500)

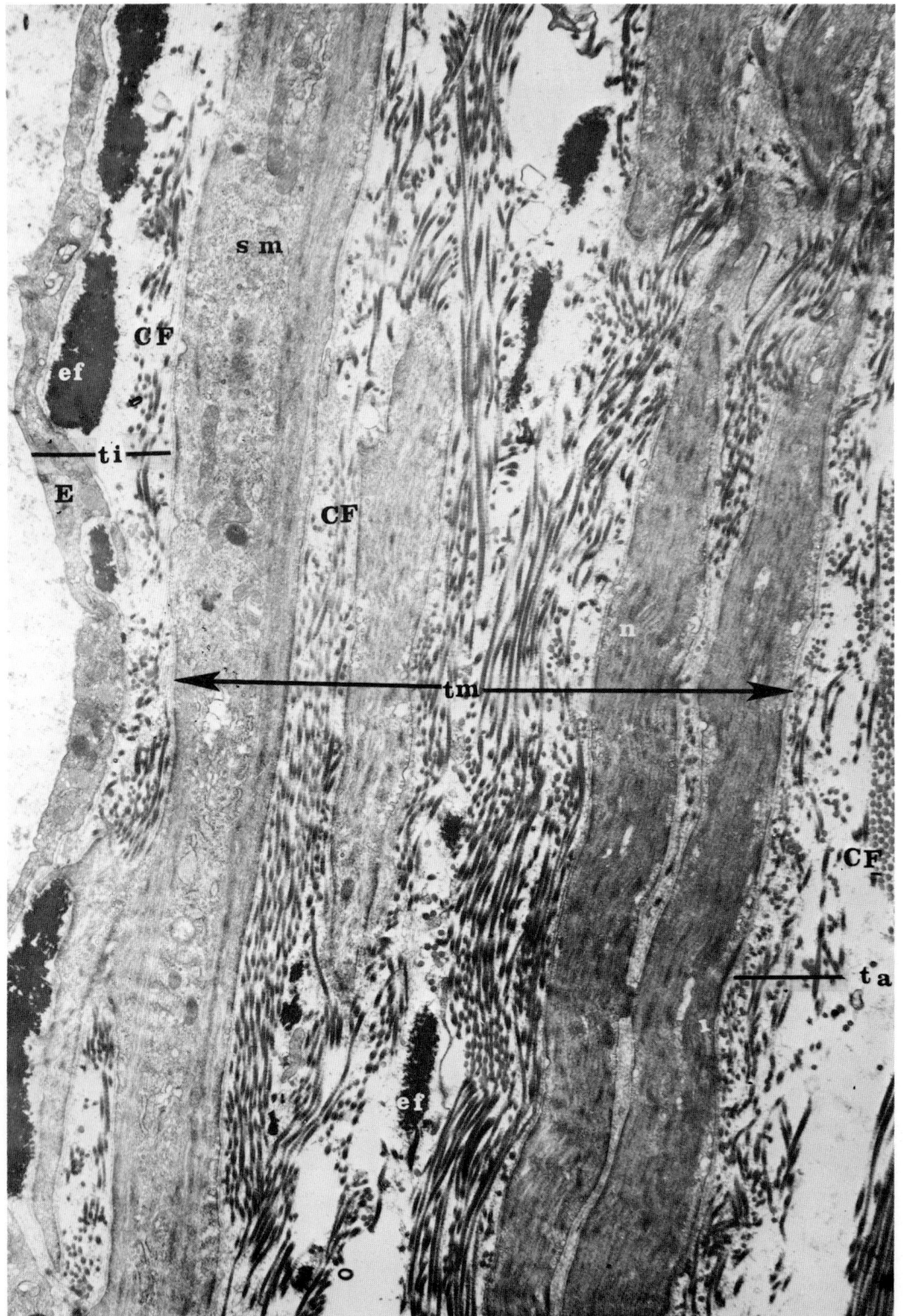

Figure 13.40. Venular wall.
Rat femoral vein. The tunica intima (ti) contains a continuous endothelial (E) layer of cells and a subendothelial layer of elastic fibers (ef) and collagen fibrils (CF). The tunica media (tm) contains layers of smooth muscle cells (sm) separated by collagen bundles (CF) and elastic fibers (ef). The tunica adventitia (ta) contains collagen fibers which blend into the adjoining connective tissue area. (× 10,000)

14. Structural and Functional Relationships of the Vascular Wall

Although filtration occurs to some degree along the total length of the cardiovascular system, the greatest rates of exchange between blood vessels and the surrounding tissues occurs mainly in the capillary segments (arterial and venous) of the microvascular bed. Structurally, the extreme thinness of the capillary endothelium is considered as an important factor in facilitating the exchange of material between the blood and surrounding tissues. In addition, other influences which contribute to the transfer across the vascular wall include pressure regulating mechanisms which are functional within the microvascular bed to ensure a constant fractional flow and distribution of the extracellular fluid.[27,84] In experiments with large molecular weight substances, physiologists have been able to selectively demonstrate the passage of molecules having different molecular weights (40,000 up to 300,000) across the vascular wall. The differential passage of these molecules from the blood stream in various tissues indicated that there existed separate routes for the passage of small and large molecules and thus the concept of small and large pore systems within the capillary endothelial wall.[47,50,67,83,93] With the early ultrastructural observations of numerous vesicles (caveolae) along the blood and tissue fronts of the capillary endothelium, it was suggested that these vesicles may provide a mode of transport across the endothelium.[91] In efforts to establish the structural counterpart of the small and large pore systems, there have been numerous studies which have utilized electron-dense tracer substances in an attempt to monitor the movement of these substances across the endothelium at the ultrastructural level.[23]

Results obtained when horseradish peroxidase was used as a protein tracer of relatively low molecular weight (40,000) indicated that passage across the capillary wall occurred via the clefts of intercellular junction[61] as indicated in Figure 14.1. These studies suggested that the cell junction could be considered as the morphological equivalent of the small pore system. The micropinocytotic (plasmalemmal) vessels (Figure 14.1) were also indicated as additional modes of transport for peroxidase.[161] In studies using larger tracer molecules (ferritin with a diameter of 110Å) the particles were found in micropinocytotic vesicles (Figure 14.2) but not in the endothelial cell junction or the intercellular cleft.[14,15,23,40,60,61] In the capillary endothelium of the central nervous system, there are very few micropinocytotic vesicles and the endothelial junctions are sealed by tight junctions.[13] This is in agreement with the concept of a blood–brain barrier which prevents proteins from passing into the brain interstitial fluid. Since larger particles such as ferritin are transported via micropinocytotic vesicles, it was suggested that the vesicles be considered as the structural equivalent of

141

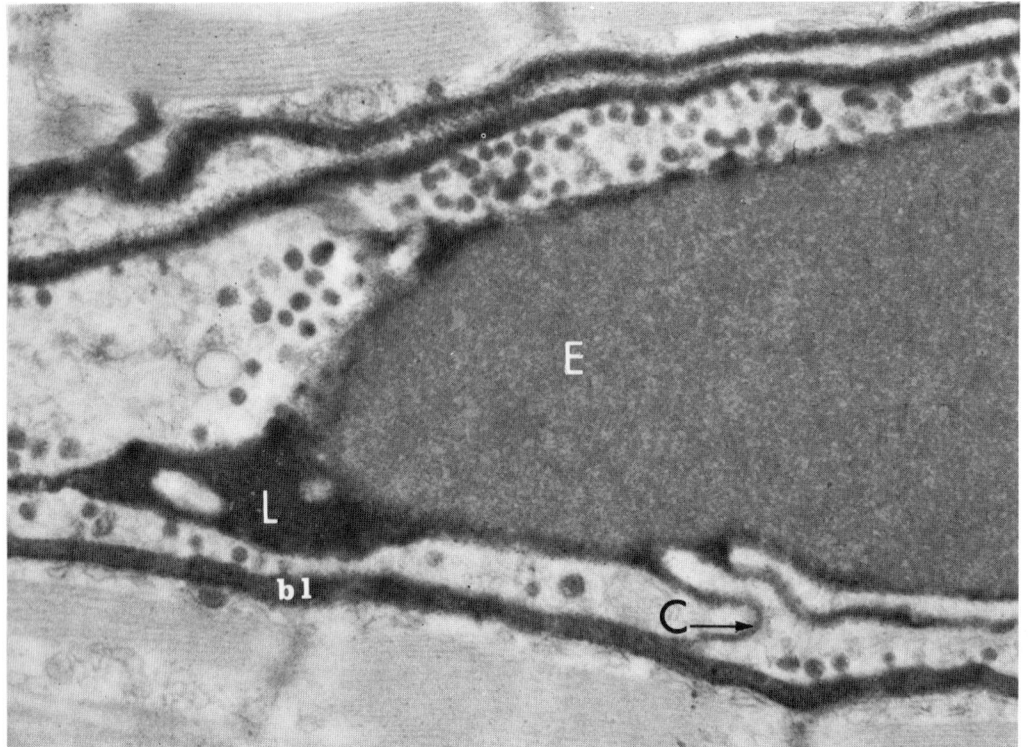

Figure 14.1. Passage of protein tracer via clefts of intercellular junction (M. Karnovsky).

Capillary in heart of mouse sacrificed 10 min after injection of horseradish peroxidase. Peroxidase is present in the lumen (L) around erythrocyte (E). Micropinocytotic vesicles at both the luminal and basal surfaces, as well as those apparently lying free in the cytoplasm, are stained. The intercellular cleft (C) is stained throughout its length, from the lumen to the basal lamina. The basal lamina (bl) is also stained. ($\times$ 32,000)

the large pores that would open to the luminal (loading) and tissue (discharging) fronts of the capillary.

In studies with other large probe molecules such as dextrans and glycogen,[115,116] it has been shown that the tracers are able to cross the capillary wall only via plasmalemmal vesicles (Figure 14.3). For the fenestrated capillaries, tracer molecules injected intravenously are able to penetrate the fenestrae, as indicated by a significant accumulation of the tracers at the tissue front of the capillary against the basal lamina immediately opposite the fenestrae (Figure 14.4).

Results obtained with smaller tracer molecules (myoglobin: mol. wt. 17,800, diameter $25 \times 34 \times 42$Å; hemopeptide: mol. wt. 1,550, diameter ~ 17–20Å) suggested that passage of the tracer was via plasmalemmal vesicles rather than the clefts of intercellular junctions (Figure 14.5). Simionescu et al.[115,116] also found patent transendothelial channels that were made by a series of connecting vesicles (Figure 14.6).

For the discontinuous capillaries, such as sinusoids in the liver, bone marrow, and lymph nodes, there is free passage of large molecules and cells across wide fenestrae within the attenuated endothelium and also through wide gaps between adjacent cell margins.

142

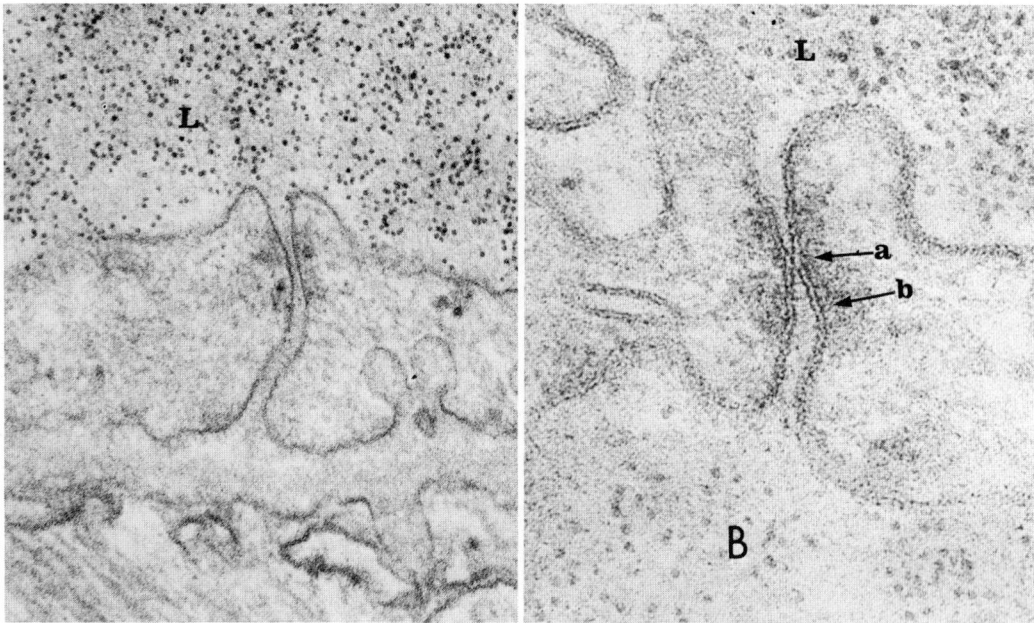

(a)   (b)

Figure 14.2. Passage of ferritin via micropinocytic vesicles (M. Karnovsky).

(a) Capillary in heart of mouse injected with ferritin 10 min and peroxidase 5 min before sacrifice. The lumen (L) shows a high concentration of ferritin but there is none in the intercellular cleft. (× 110,000)

(b) Capillary in heart of mouse injected with ferritin 30 min and peroxidase 20 min before sacrifice. Tissue stained with uranyl en bloc. Ferritin is visible in both the lumen (L) and basal lamina (B) but not in the intercellular cleft. The cell junction shows touching or fusion of the external leaflets of the adjacent plasma membranes, with complete obliteration of the extracellular space. The width of the unit membrane (a) is 65Å, and of the cell junction (b) is 125 Å. The ratio of b:a is 2·0. The arrows show the levels at which the measurements were made. The radial depth of the intermediate line is 100 Å. (× 200,000)

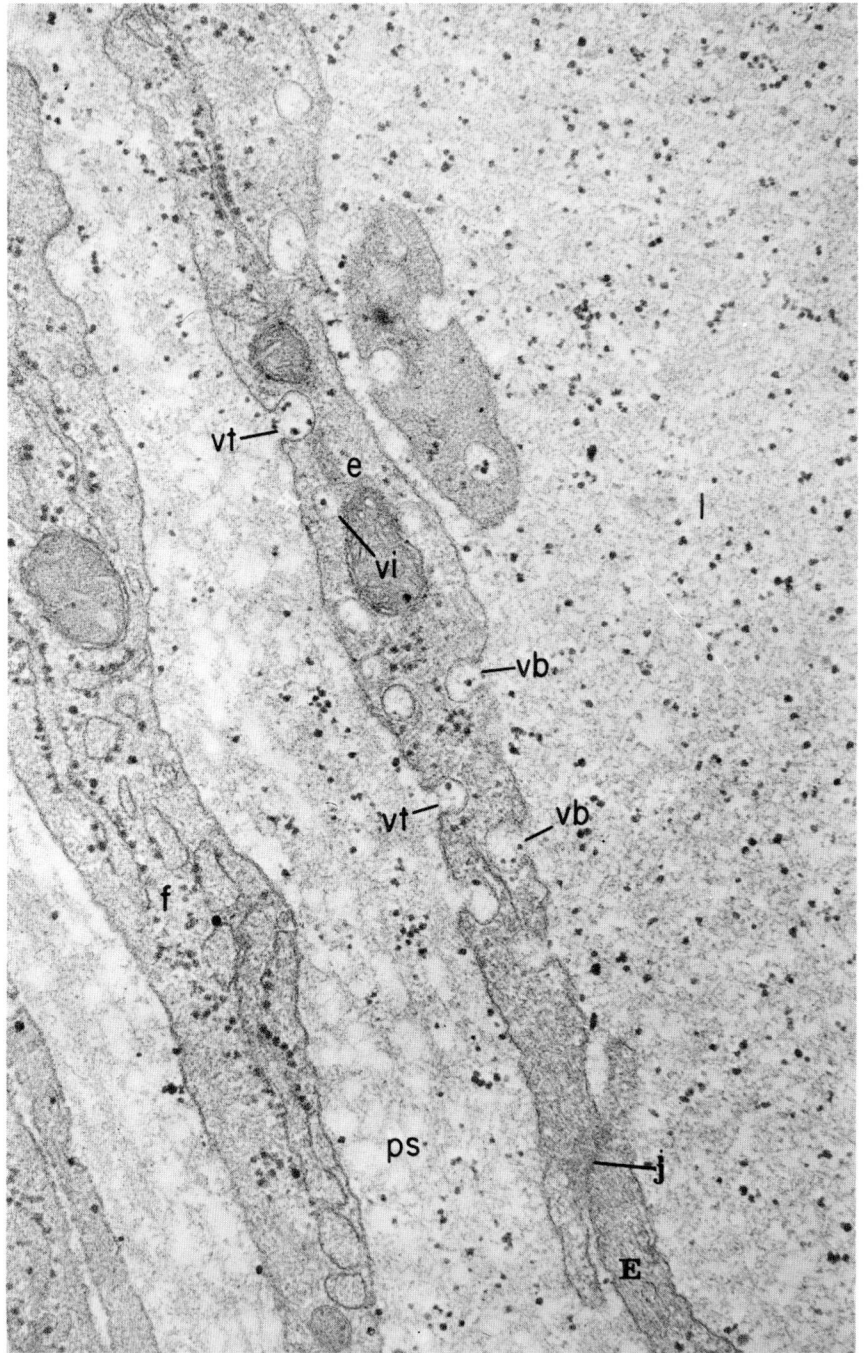

Figure 14.3. Movement of glycogen via plasmalemmal vesicles (N. Simionescu *et al.* **).**

Capillary in rat diaphragm 10 min after intravenous injection of tracer solution of shellfish glycogen. The particles have marked the plasmalemmal vesicles open on the blood front (vb), isolated in the endothelial cytoplasm (vi) or communicating with the subendothelial space (vt). l: capillary lumen, E: endothelium, j: intercellular junction, ps: pericapillary space, f: fibroblast. (×64,000)

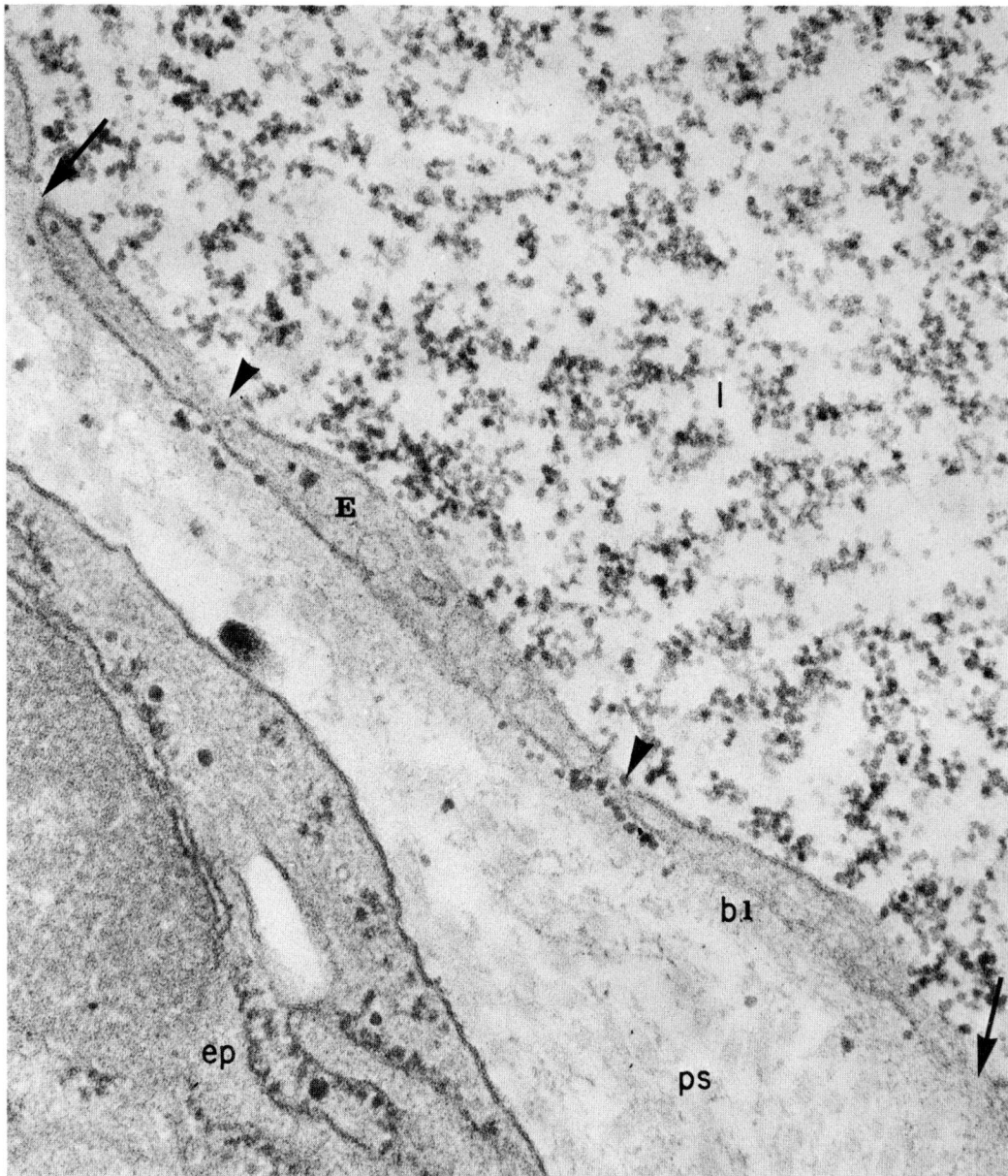

Figure 14.4. Penetration of fenestrae by glycogen tracer (N. Simionescu *et al.*).
Capillary in rat jejunal mucosa 4 min after intravenous injection of tracer solution of shellfish glycogen. Tracer particles are present in high concentration and relatively even distribution in the capillary lumen (l) and have penetrated some fenestrae (arrowheads) while others (arrows) do not present particles at the level of this section. Note a certain accumulation of glycogen particles against the basal lamina (bl). E: endothelium, ps: pericapillary space, ep: epithelial cell. (× 96,000)

145

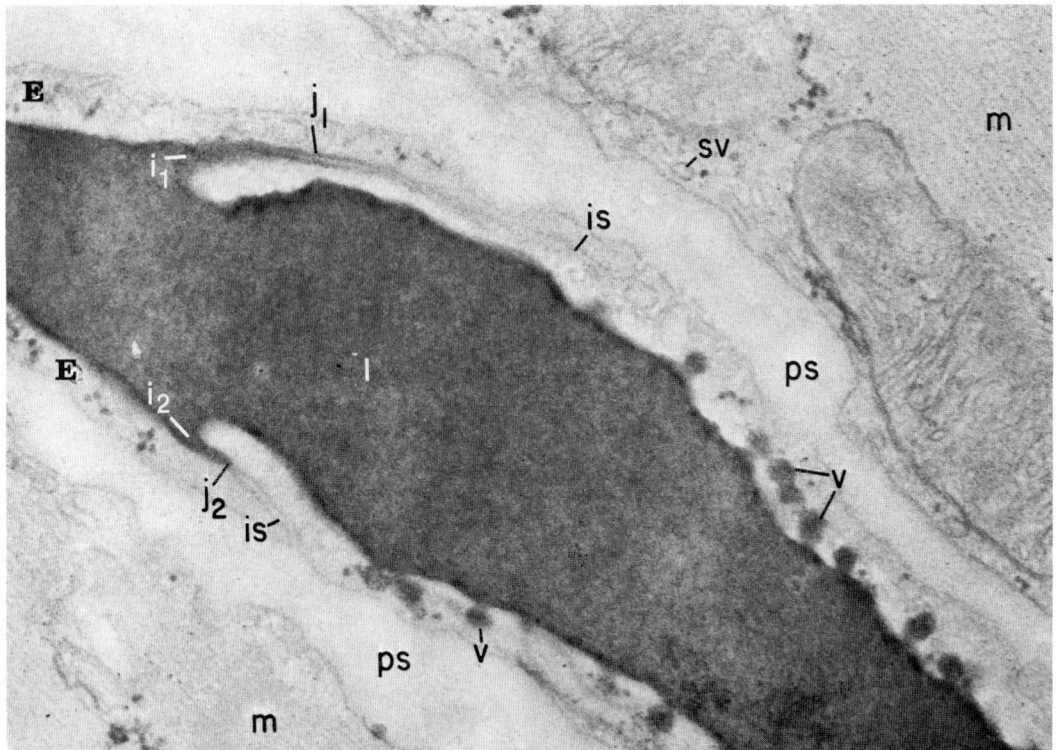

Figure 14.5. Passage of hemopeptide via plasmalemmal vesicles (N. Simionescu, M. Simionescu, and G. E. Palade).

Capillaries in rat diaphragm 35 s after an intravenous injection of a tracer solution of hemopeptide. The reaction product filled the vascular lumen (l) and marked the plasmalemmal vesicles open on the blood front (v) and the infundibula (i_1 and i_2) leading to the junctions (j_1 and j_2).The intercellular spaces (is) beyond the junctions are free of reaction product. E: endothelium, m: muscle cell, ps: pericapillary space, sv: sarcolemmal vesicles. ($\times$ 35,000)

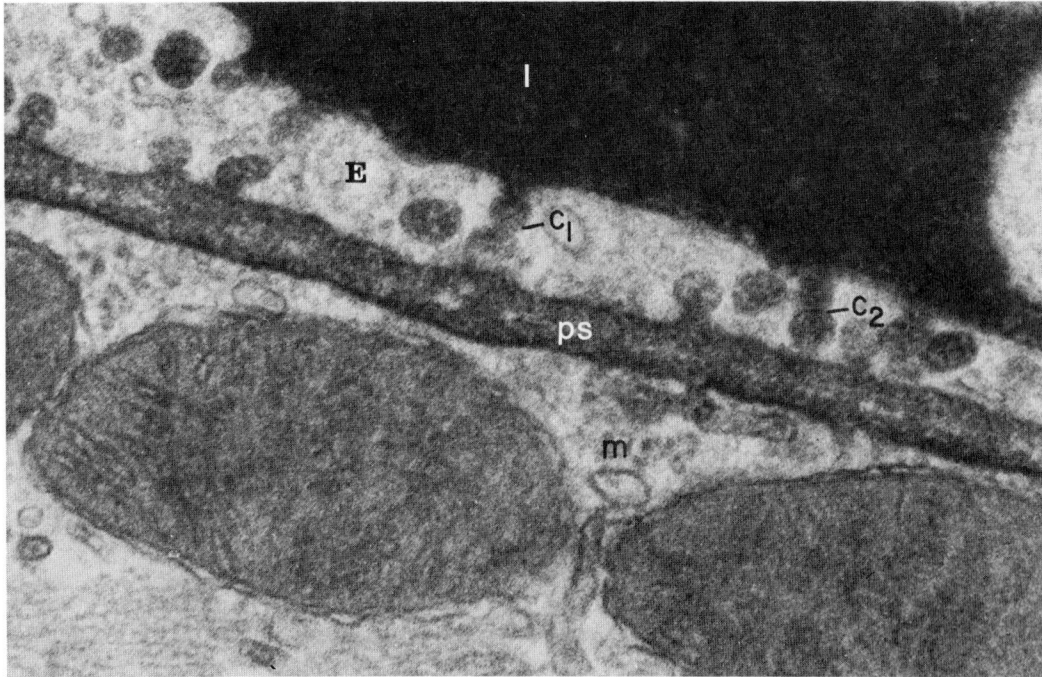

Figure 14.6. Passage of hemopeptide via transendothelial channels.
Capillary in rat diaphragm 45 s after intravenous injection of tracer solution of hemopeptide. C_1 and C_2 show the presence of two images of patent transendothelial channels. After tilting the specimen by $\pm$ 23° in two perpendicular directions, the channel marked C_2 was resolved in two separate vesicles, while the channel C_1 retained its continuity in all positions. I: capillary lumen, E: endothelium, ps: pericapillary space, m: muscle cell. ($\times$ 102,000)

References to Part Two

1. Albert, E. N. and Nayak, R. K., "Surface morphology of human aorta as revealed by the scanning electron microscope," *Anat. Rec.*, **185**, 223, 1976.
2. Alksne, J. F., "The passage of colloidal particles across the dermal capillary wall under the influence of histamine," *Q. Jl exp. Physiol.*, **44**, 51, 1959.
3. Bader, H., "The anatomy and physiology of the vascular wall," in W. F. Hamilton and P. Dow (eds.), *Handbook of Physiology*, section 2, *Circulation*, American Physiological Society, Washington, 1965.
4. Baez, S., "Vascular smooth muscle quantitation of cell thickness in the wall of arterioles in the living animal *in situ*," *Science*, **159**, 536, 1968.
5. ——— and Orkin, L. R., "Microcirculation reactions to chemical denervation in the anesthetized rat. 4th Conference for Microcirculation," *Biblphy. Anat.*, **9**, 61, 1967.
6. Bar, T. H. and Wolff, J. R., "The formation of capillary basement membranes during internal vascularization of the rat's cerebral cortex," *Z. Zellforsch. mikrosk. Anat.*, **133**, 231, 1972.
7. Bardeleben, K., "Das Klapperngesita," *Jena Z. Naturw.*, **14**, 147, 1880.
8. Barnes, R., *Invertebrate Zoology*, Saunders, Philadelphia, 1964, p. 345.
9. Beacham, W. S., Konishi, A., and Hunt, C. C., "Observations on the microcirculatory bed in rat mesocecum using differential interference contrast microscopy *in vitro* and electron microscopy," *Am. J. Anat.*, **146**, 385, 1976.
10. Bennett, H. S., "The concepts of membrane flow and membrane vesiculation as mechanisms for active transport and ion pumping," *J. biophys. biochem. Cytol.*, **2**, 99, 1956.
11. ———, Luft, J. H., and Hampton, J. C., "Morphological classification of vertebrate blood capillaries," *Am. J. Physiol.*, **96**, 381, 1959.
12. Benninghoff, A., "Blutgefässe und Herz," in W. von Moolendorff (ed.), *Handbuch der mikroskopischen Anatomie des Menschen*, vol. VI, part I, Springer, Berlin, 1930.
13. Brightman, M. W. and Reese, T. S., "Junctions between intimately apposed cell membranes in the vertebrate brain," *J. Cell Biol.*, **40**, 648, 1969.
14. Bruns, R. R. and Palade, G. E., "Studies on blood capillaries. I. General organization of blood capillaries in muscle," *J. Cell Biol.*, **37**, 244, 1968.
15. ——— and ———, "Studies on blood capillaries II. Transport of ferritin molecules across the wall of muscle capillaries," *J. Cell Biol.*, **37**, 277, 1968.
16. Buck, R. C., "The fine structure of endothelium of large arteries," *J. biophys. biochem. Cytol.*, **4**, 187, 1958.
17. ———, "The fine structure of the aortic endothelial lesions in experimental cholesterol atherosclerosis of rabbits," *Am. J. Path.*, **34**, 897, 1959.

18. Cannon, W. B., "Organization for physiological homeostasis," *Physiol. Rev.*, **9**, 399, 1929.
19. Chambers, R. and Zweifach, B. W., "Topography and functions of the mesenteric capillary circulation," *Am. J. Anat.*, **75**, 173, 1944.
20. ——— and ———, "Functional activity of the blood capillary bed, with special reference to visceral tissue," *Ann. N.Y. Acad. Sci.*, **46**, 683, 1946.
21. ——— and ———, "Intercellular cement and capillary permeability," *Physiol. Rev.*, **27**, 431, 1947.
22. Chinard, F. P., Vosburgh, G. J., and Enns, T., "Transcapillary exchange of water and of other substances in certain organs of the dog," *Am. J. Physiol.*, **183**, 221, 1955.
23. Clementi, F. and Palade, G. E., "Intestinal capillaries. I. Permeability to peroxidase and ferritin," *J. Cell Biol.*, **41**, 33, 1969.
24. Cliff, W. J., "Observations on healing tissue: a combined light and electron microscope investigation," *Phil. Trans. R. Soc. B*, **246**, 305, 1963.
25. Cotran, R., "The delayed and prolonged vascular leakage in inflammation. II. An electron microscopic study of the vascular response after thermal injury," *Am. J. Path.*, **46**, 589, 1965.
26. ——— and Majno, G., "A light and electron microscopic analysis of vascular injury," *Ann. N.Y. Acad. Sci.*, **116**, 750, 1964.
27. Crone, C., "Capillary permeability II physiological consideration," in B. W. Zweifach, L. Grant, and R. T. McCluskey (eds.), *The Inflammatory Process*, vol. II, chap. 3, Academic Press, New York, 1973, p. 95.
28. Davies, P. F. and Bowyer, D. E., "Scanning electron microscopy: arterial endothelial integrity after fixation at physiological pressure," *Atherosclerosis*, **21**, 465, 1975.
29. Dewey, M. M. and Barr, L., "A study of structure and distribution of nexus," *J. Cell Biol.*, **23**, 553, 1964.
30. Ekholm, R., "The ultrastructure of blood capillaries in the mouse thyroid gland," *Z. Zellforsch. mikrosk. Anat.*, **46**, 139, 1959.
31. ——— and Sjostrand, R. S., "The ultrastructural organization of the mouse thyroid gland," *J. Ultrastruct. Res.*, **1**, 178, 1957.
32. Eriksson, E. and Zarem, H. A., "Growth and differentiation of blood vessels," in G. Kaley and B. M. Altrua (eds.), *Microcirculation*, vol. I, chap. 18, University Park Press, Baltimore, 1977, p. 393.
33. Farquhar, M. G., Wissig, S. L., and Palade, G. E., "Glomerular permeability. I. Ferritin transfer across the normal glomerular capillary wall," *J. exp. Med.*, **43**, 113, 1961.
34. Fawcett, D. W., "Observations on the cytology and electron microscopy of hepatic cells," *J. natn. Cancer Inst.*, **15**, 1475, 1955.
35. ———, "Comparative observations on the fine structure of blood capillaries," in J. L. Orbison and D. Smith (eds.), *The Peripheral Blood Vessels*, Williams and Wilkins, Baltimore, 1963, pp. 17–44.
36. ——— and Wittenberg, J., "Structural specialization of endothelial cell functions," *Anat. Rec.*, **142**, 231, 1962.
37. Fay, F. S. and Cooke, P. H., "Reversible disaggregation of myofilaments in vertebrate smooth muscle," *J. Cell Biol.*, **56**, 299, 1973.

38. Flexner, L. B., Glehorn, A., and Merrell, M., "Studies on rates of exchange of substances between blood and extravascular fluids, exchange of water in guinea pig," *J. biol. Chem.*, **144**, 35, 1942.

39. Florey (Lord), H. W., "The structure of normal and inflamed small blood vessels of the mouse colon," *Q. Jl exp. Physiol.*, **46**, 119, 1961.

40. ———, "The transport of materials across the capillary wall," *Q. Jl exp. Physiol.*, **49**, 117, 1964.

41. ———, "The endothelial cell," *Br. med. J.*, **2**/2512, 487, 1966.

42. ——— and Sheppard, B. L., "The permeability of arterial endothelium to horseradish peroxidase," *Proc. R. Soc. B*, **174**, 435, 1970.

43. Fraley, E. E. and Weiss, L., "An electron microscopic study of the lymphatic vessels in the penile skin of the rat," *Am. J. Anat.*, **109**, 85, 1961.

44. French, J. E., Florey, H. W., and Morris, B., "The absorption of particles by the lymphatics of the diaphragm," *Q. Jl exp. Physiol.*, **45**, 88, 1960.

45. Friederici, H. H., "The three dimensional ultrastructure of fenestrated capillaries," *J. Ultrastruct. Res.*, **23**, 444, 1968.

46. Fulton, G. P., "Microcirculatory terminology," *Angiology*, **8**, 102, 1957.

47. Garlick, D. G. and Renkin, E. M., "Transport of large molecules from plasma to interstitial fluid and lymph," *Am. J. Physiol.*, **219**, 1595, 1970.

48. Giacomelli, F., Wiener, J., and Spiro, D., "Cross-striated arrays of filaments in endothelium," *J. Cell Biol.*, **45**, 1970.

49. Groniowski, J. W., Biezyskowa, W., and Walski, M., "Scanning electron microscopic observations on the surface of vascular endothelium," *Folia Histochem. Cytochem.*, **9**, 243, 1971.

50. Grotte, G., "Passage of dextran molecules across the blood lymph barrier," *Acta chir. scand., suppl.*, **211**, 84, 1956.

51. Guth, P. H. and Rosenburg, A., "*In vivo* microscopy of the gastric micro-circulation," *J. dig. Dis.*, **17**, 391, 1972.

52. Hall, B. V., "Studies of normal glomerular structure by electron microscopy," in *Proceedings of Fifth Annual Conference on the Nephrotic Syndrome*, New York National Nephrosis Fund, 1953, pp. 1–39.

53. Hammerson, F., "Poren- und Fenesterendothelien der Kapillaren in der Skelettmuskulatur der Ratte," *Z. Zellforsch. mikrosk. Anat.*, **69**, 296, 1966.

54. Hampton, J. C., "An electron microscopic study of the hepatic uptake and excretion of submicroscopic particles injected into the blood stream and into the bile duct," *Acta Anat.*, **32**, 262, 1958.

55. Harvey, W., *Exercitatio anatomica de motu cordis sanguinis in animalibus*, Fitzer, Frankfurt, 1628.

56. Hurley, J. V., in *Acute Inflammation*, Williams and Wilkins, Baltimore, 1972, pp. 15–20.

57. Huttner, I., Boutet, M., Rona, G., and More, R. H., "Studies on protein passage through arterial endothelium. III. Effect of blood pressure levels on the passage of fine structural protein tracers through rat arterial endothelium," *Lab. Invest.*, **29**, 536, 1973.

58. Intaglietta, M. R., Pawula, F., and Tompkins, W. R., "Pressure measurements in the mammalian microvasculature," *Microvasc. Res.*, **2**, 212, 1970.

59. ———, Tompkins, W. R., and Richardson, D. R., "Velocity measurements in

the microvasculature of the cat omentum by on-line method," *Microvasc. Res.,* **2**, 462, 1970.

60. Jennings, M. A., Marchesi, V. T., and Florey, H., "The transport of particles across the walls of small blood vessels," *Proc. R. Soc. B,* **156**, 14, 1962.

61. Karnovsky, M., "The ultrastructural basis of capillary permeability studies with peroxidase as a tracer," *J. Cell Biol.,* **35**, 213, 1967.

62. Karrer, H. E. and Cox, J., "The striated musculature of blood vessels. II. Cell interconnections and cell surface," *J. biophy. biochem. Cytol.,* **8**, 135, 1960.

63. Keech, M. K., "Electron microscope study of the normal rat aorta," *J. biophys. biochem. Cytol.,* **7**, 533, 1960.

64. Knisely, M. H., "The histopathology of peripheral vascular beds," in F. R. Moulton (ed.), *Blood, Heart and Circulation,* The Science Press, Lancaster, Pennsylvania, 1940, pp. 303–307.

65. Krogh, A., *The Anatomy and Physiology of Capillaries,* Hafner, New York, 1959, p. 422.

66. ———— and Vimtrup, B., in E. V. Cowdry (ed.), *Special Cytology,* 2nd ed., vol. I., section XII, Harpner (Hoeber), New York, 1932, pp. 475–502.

67. Landis, E. M. and Pappenheimer, J. R., "Exchange of substances through the capillary walls," in W. F. Hamilton and P. Dow (eds.), *Handbook of Physiology Circulation,* section 2, vol. II, American Physiological Society, Washington, 1963, p. 961.

68. Lane, B. P. and Rhodin, J. A. G., "Cellular interrelationships and electrical activity in two types of smooth muscle," *J. Ultrastruct. Res.,* **10**, 470, 1964.

69. Lang, J., "Über die Vascularisation der Wand und des Einbaugewebes mittelgrosser Gefässe des Unterschenkels," *Z. Anat. EntwGesch.,* **122**, 482, 1961.

70. ————, "Studies on the permeability of lymphatic capillaries," *J. Cell Biol.,* **50**, 300, 1971.

71. ————, "Frozen-fractured images of blood capillaries in heart tissue," *J. Ultrastruct. Res.,* **35**, 127, 1971.

72. ————, "The fine structure of the lymphatic system," in H. Meesen (ed.), *Handbuch der allgemeinen Pathologie,* Band III, Springer-Verlag, Berlin, 1972, pp. 149–196.

73. ———— and Burke, J. F., "Fine structure of the lymphatic capillary and the adjoining connective tissue area," *Am. J. Anat.,* **118**, 785, 1966.

74. Lewis, T., *Blood Vessels of the Human Skin and their Responses,* Shaw and Sons, London, 1927.

75. Loewenstein, W., "Permeability of the junctional membrane channel," in B. R. Brinkley and K. R. Porter (eds.), *International Cell Biology,* Rockefeller University Press, New York, 1976–77, pp. 70–82.

76. Luft, J. H., "Improvements in epoxy resin embedding methods," *J. biophys. biochem. Cytol.,* **9**, 409, 1961.

77. ————, "Fine structure of the diaphragm across capillary pores in mouse intestine," *Anat. Rec.,* **148**, 307, 1964.

78. ————, "Ruthenium red and violet. II: Fine structural localization in animal tissues," *Anat. Rec.,* **171**, 396, 1971.

79. Majno, G., "Ultrastructure of the vascular membrane," in W. F. Hamilton and

P. Dow (eds.), *Handbook of Physiology*, section 2, vol. III, *Circulation*, American Physiological Society, Washington, 1965, p. 2293.

80. —— and Palade, G. E., "Studies on inflammation. 1. The effect of histamine and serotonin on vascular permeability: an electron microscopic study," *J. biophys. biochem. Cytol.*, **11**, 571, 1961.

81. ——, ——, and Schoefl, G. I., "Studies on inflammation. II. The site of action of histamine and serotonin along the vascular tree. A topographic study," *J. biophys. biochem. Cytol.*, **11**, 607, 1961.

82. ——, Shea, S. M., and Leventhal, M., "Endothelial contraction induced by histamine type mediators," *J. Cell Biol.*, **42**, 647, 1969.

83. Mayerson, H. S., "The physiologic importance of lymph," in *Handbook of Physiology*, section 2, vol. II, *Circulation*, American Physiological Society, Washington, 1963, pp. 1035–1073.

84. Mellander, S. and Folkow, B., "Aspects of nervous control of precapillary sphincter with regard to capillary exchange," *Acta physiol. scand.*, **175**, 50, 1960.

85. Merrell, M., Gellhorn, A., and Flexner, L. B., "Studies on rates of exchange of substances between the blood and extravascular fluid," *J. biol. Chem.*, **153**, 83, 1944.

86. Moore, D. H. and Ruska, H., "Fine structure of capillaries and small arteries," *J. biophys. biochem. Cytol.*, **3**, 457–462, 1957.

87. Motta, P., Muto, M., and Frijita, T., *The Liver: An Atlas of Scanning Electron Microscopy*, Igaku-Shoin, Tokyo, 1978.

88. Namura, Y., "Myofilaments in smooth muscle of guinea pig *Taenia coli*," *J. Cell Biol.*, **39**, 741, 1968.

89. Nicoll, P. A. and Webb, R. L., "Vascular patterns and active vasomotion as determiners of flow through minute vessels," *Angrology*, **6**, 291, 1955.

90. Palade, G. E., "A study of fixation for electron microscopy," *J. exp. Med.*, **95**, 285, 1952.

91. ——, "Fine structure of blood capillaries," *J. appl. Phys.*, **24**, 1424, 1953.

92. —— and Bruns, R. R., "Structure and function in normal muscle capillaries," *Small Blood Involvement in Diabetes Mellitus*, American Institute of Biological Sciences, no. 39, 1964.

93. Pappenheimer, J. R., "Passage of molecules through capillary walls," *Physiol. Rev.*, **33**, 387, 1953.

94. Parakkal, P. F., "The fine structure of the dermal papilla of the guinea pig hair follicle," *J. Ultrastruct. Res.*, **14**, 133, 1966.

95. Parker, F., "An electron microscope study of coronary arteries," *Am. J. Anat.*, **103**, 247, 1958.

96. Pease, D. C., "Electron microscopy of the vascular bed of the kidney cortex," *Anat. Rec.*, **121**, 701, 1955.

97. ——, "An electron microscopic study of red bone marrow," *Blood*, **11**, 501, 1956.

98. ——, *Histological Techniques for Electron Microscopy*, Academic Press, New York, 1960.

99. ——, "Structural features of unfixed mammalian smooth and striated muscle prepared by glycol dehydration," *J. Ultrastruct. Res.*, **23**, 280, 1968.

152

100. —— and Molenari, S., "Electron microscopy of muscular arteries, pial vessels of the cat and monkey," *J. Ultrastruct. Res.*, **3**, 447, 1960.

101. —— and Paule, W. J., Electron microscopy of elastic arteries; the thoracic aorta of the rat," *J. Ultrastruct. Res.*, **3**, 469, 1960.

102. Pollard T. D., Shelton, E., Weihing, R., and Korn, E. D., "Ultrastructural characterization of F. Actin isolated from *Acanthamoeba castellanii* and identification of cytoplasmic filaments as F. Actin by reaction with heavy meromyosin," *J. Molec. Biol.*, **50**, 91, 1970.

103. —— and Weihing, R. R., "Actin and myosin and cell movement," *CRC Crit. Rev. Biochem.*, **2**, 1, 1974.

104. Prosser, C. L., Burnstock, G., and Kahn, J., "Conduction in smooth muscles. Comparative electrical properties," *Am. J. Physiol.*, **199**, 553, 1960.

105. Rhodin, J. A. G., "The diaphragm of capillary endothelial fenestrations," *J. Ultrastruct. Res.*, **6**, 171, 1962.

106. ——, "Fine structure of vascular walls in mammals with special reference to smooth muscle components," *Physiol. Rev.*, **42**, 48, 1962.

107. ——, "The ultrastructure of mammalian arterioles and precapillary sphincters," *J. Ultrastruct. Res.*, **18**, 181, 1967.

108. ——, "Ultrastructure of mammalian venous capillaries, venules and small collecting veins," *J. Ultrastruct. Res.*, **25**, 452, 1968.

109. Rohlich, P. and Olah, J., "Cross-striated fibrils in the endothelium of the rat myometral and arterioles," *J. Ultrastruct. Res.*, **18**, 667, 1967.

110. Rouget, C., "Sur la contractilite des capillaires sanguins," *C. r. hebd. Séanc. Acad. Sci., Paris*, **88**, 916, 1879.

111. Sabatini, D. D., Bensch, K., and Barnett, R. J., "New means of fixation for electron microscopy," *Anat. Rec.*, **142**, 274, 1962.

112. ——, ——, and ——, "Cytochemistry and electron microscopy. The preservation of cellular ultrastructure and enzymatic activity by aldehyde fixation," *J. Cell Biol.*, **17**, 19, 1963.

113. Simionescu, M., "The organization of cell junctions in the peritoneal meso-thelium," *Anat. Rec.*, **187**, 713, 1977.

114. ——, Simionescu, N., and Palade, G. E., "Segmental differentiations of cell junctions in the vascular endothelium. The microvasculature," *J. Cell Biol.*, **67**, 863, 1975.

115. Simionescu, N., Simionescu, M., and Palade, G. E., "Permeability of intestinal capillaries, pathway followed by dextran and glycogens," *J. Cell Biol.*, **53**, 365, 1972.

116. ——, ——, and ——, "Permeability of muscle capillaries to small heme-peptides, evidence for the existence of patent transendothelial channels," *J. Cell Biol.*, **64**, 586, 1975.

117. Shimamoto, T. Y., Yamashito, O. O., and Sunaga, T., "Scanning electron microscopic observation of endothelial surface of heart and blood vessels," *Proc. jap. Acad.*, **45**, 507, 1969.

118. Simon, G., "Ultrastruktur des Kapillaren. Kap II," *Angiologica*, **2**, 370–434, 1965.

119. Sobin, S. S., "The architecture and function of the microvasculature," in Y. C.

Fund (ed.), *Biomechanics Symposium*, American Society of Mechanical Engineers, New York, 1966, pp. 132–150.

120. Watson, M. L., "Staining of tissue sections for electron microscopy with heavy metals," *J. biophys. biochem. Cytol.*, **4**, 475, 1958.

121. Webb, R. L. and Nicoll, P. A., "The bat wing as a subject for studies in homeostasis of capillary beds," *Anat. Rec.*, **120**, 253, 1954.

122. Weber, G., and Tosi, P., "Observations with scanning electron microscope on the development of cholesterol aortic atherosclerosis in the guinea pig," *Virchows Arch. Path. Anat.*, **353**, 325, 1971.

123. Weibel, E. R. and Palade, G. E., "New cytoplasmic components in arterial endothelial," *J. Cell Biol.*, **23**, 101–112, 1964.

124. Weiss, L., "An electron microscopic study of the vascular sinuses of the bone marrow of the rabbit," *Bull. Johns Hopkins Hosp.*, **108**, 171, 1961.

125. Wilhelm, D. L., "Chemical mediators," in B. W. Zweifach, L. Grant, and R. I. McCluskey (eds.), *The Inflammatory Process*, 2nd ed., vol. II, chap. 8, Academic Press, New York, 1973, pp. 251–301.

126. Wolff, J. and Merker, H. J., "Ultrastruktur und Bildung von Poren im Endothel von porosen und geschlossenen Kapillaren," *Z. Zellforsch. mikrosk. Anat.*, **73**, 174, 1966.

127. Yamada, E., "The fine structure of the renal glomerulus of the mouse. *J. biophys. biochem. Cytol.*, **1**, 551, 1955.

128. Zelander, T., "The ultrastructure of the adrenal cortex of the mouse," *Z. Zellforsch. mikrosk. Anat.*, **46**, 710, 1957.

129. Zimmerman, K. W., "Der feinere Bau der Blutkapillaren," *Z. Anat. EntwGesch.*, **68**, 29, 1923.

130. Zweifach, B. W., "General principles governing behavior of the micro-circulation," *Am. J. Med.*, **23**, 684, 1957.

131. ———, "Introduction: Perspectives in microcirculation," in G. Kaley and B. Altura (eds.), *Microcirculation*, vol. I, University Park Press, Baltimore, 1977, p. 1.

132. ——— and Metz, D. B., "Rat mesoappendix; procedure for bioassay of humoral substances acting on peripheral blood vessels," *Ergebn. Anat. EntwGesch.*, **35**, 176, 1956.

Part Three

Lymphatic Vessels

Lee V. Leak

15. Introduction to Part Three

Physiologists have long realized the importance of the lymphatic vascular system in the removal of fluids, proteins, particulate components, and cells that are not reabsorbed at the venular limb of the blood vascular system. Information obtained from a number of studies has established that the lymphatic system serves primarily as a transport system, designed to maintain homeostasis of the interstitial environment by draining excess fluids and protein from the interstitium for return to the blood stream.[1, 26, 43, 87] The importance of the lymphatic system lies in the fact that normal blood capillaries are permeable to macromolecules in proportion to their molecular size and that these macromolecules, particularly proteins, disturb the normal Starling pattern of exchange between capillaries and tissue spaces and, if left to accumulate, would lead to edema formation within the interstitial spaces.[87]

Although much information has been obtained regarding the overall contribution of the lymphatics to the maintenance of fluid homeostasis for various tissues throughout the body, it is only recently that attention has been focused on problems relating to the underlying structural components and the mechanisms which regulate and control the function of the lymphatic vascular system.[12, 13, 35, 38, 68, 69, 71, 95]

The vasculature comprising the lymphatic system is similar to blood vessels in that the lymphatic vessels form a system of endothelial lined tubes of varying diameter which transport cellular and noncellular components within a liquid medium (i.e., the lymph). However, unlike the blood vascular system, there is no lymphatic circulation. Instead, it is a one-way drainage system. Under physiological conditions this unidirectional flow process begins at the tissue–lymph interface where fluids, proteins, and cells are taken up by the smaller and more permeable lymphatic vessels (the lymphatic capillaries) that extend into the connective tissue spaces where they anastomose to form a rich plexus of blind-end tubes and channels.[49] From the capillaries, the lymph is propelled into an extensive system of collecting vessels whose continuity is frequently interrupted with lymph nodes that serve as a filtering system for selectively removing antigens and other foreign substances from the lymph, thus playing an important role in the overall host defense system.[28, 40, 46]

The collecting vessels usually follow the overall distribution of the arteries and veins, and the lymph that is drained from these channels enters the main lymphatic vessels of the body which are represented by the thoracic duct on the left side and one to several lymphatic trunks on the right side. These open into the venous system near or at the union of the internal jugular and subclavian veins.

In serving as a drainage system, the lymphatics provide a return mechanism for interstitial fluids and proteins without participating in the delivery of those interstitial components. In addition to restoring extravascular proteins to the blood

157

stream,[121] the lymphatics are also important in the response of the organism to infection and the spread of disease,[88] including cancer, to various tissues of the body.

Electron microscopic studies since the early 1960s have revealed much information concerning the structural arrangement of the lymphatic vascular wall, from which concepts have developed on how fluids and large molecules enter the lymphatic vascular system. Likewise, concepts have been advanced to explain how materials are retained within the lymphatic lumen. Such information provides a framework for understanding the contribution of the lymphatic system in normal as well as inflamed tissues.[8, 12, 73]

Although revealing many similarities between the walls of blood and lymphatic vessels, the results from electron microscopic studies have also revealed some unexpected diversities in the structural make-up of lymphatic capillaries, providing morphological evidence for a wide range of divergent activities on the part of the lymphatic capillaries in various regions of the body. In some tissues the primary function of lymphatic capillaries appears to be that of removing fluids and proteins, while in others they play an important role in the removal of hormones.[76, 121]

In outlining the framework of the lymphatic vascular system some of the available data on the ultrastructure and function of the lymphatic vessels will be presented along with recent findings obtained from experiments designed to provide information on the role of the lymphatic capillaries in the formation of lymph.

16. Morphological Types of Lymphatic Vessels

The major components of the lymphatic system can be classified according to morphology and function. They consist of lymphatic trunks, lymphatic collecting vessels, lymphatic capillaries, lymphatic sinusoids, and lymphatic spaces.

16.1. Major lymphatic trunks

The thoracic duct, cisterna chyli, cervical and lumbar vessels make up the major lymphatic trunks (Figure 16.1). These vessels have a large diameter (4–6 mm in man) with a thick vascular wall consisting of three distinct tunics. The tunica intima consists of a single layer of endothelial cells surrounded by a complete basal lamina and discrete strands of elastic fibers that are intermixed with collagen fibers. The intima of these vessels also extends into the lumen as reduplicated cells to form valves (vida infra). The second coat, the tunica media, is composed of one to several layers of smooth muscle cells with elastic and collagen fibers interspersed between the cells. The outermost and third layer is the adventitia which is composed of connective tissue cells and fibers, *vasa vasorum*, and bundles of nerve axons (Figure 16.2).

16.2. Lymphatic collecting vessels

These vessels make up the main branches of the lymphatic vascular system. Like the distributing arteries and medium size veins, they serve as the major channels that are responsible for regional drainage, i.e., they serve as the major channels for the egress of lymph that is drained from the various organs and regions of the body. These vessels are characterized by numerous valves along their length and a diameter which is extremely variable (see Figures 17.4, 17.9). The wall of the collecting lymphatics is also composed of three tunics (i.e., tunica intima, media, and adventitia). Although a tunica media is found in the lymphatic collecting vessels, the smooth muscle cells which make up this layer are not always observed as a continuous layer of cells but may be seen as individual smooth muscle cells that are often arranged in a spiral or coiled fashion along the length of the collecting vessels (see Figures 17.3(a), 17.4).

16.3. Lymphatic capillaries

These vessels comprise the initial segment of the lymphatic vascular drainage system. They are extremely thin walled and are located at the site of extracellular exchange

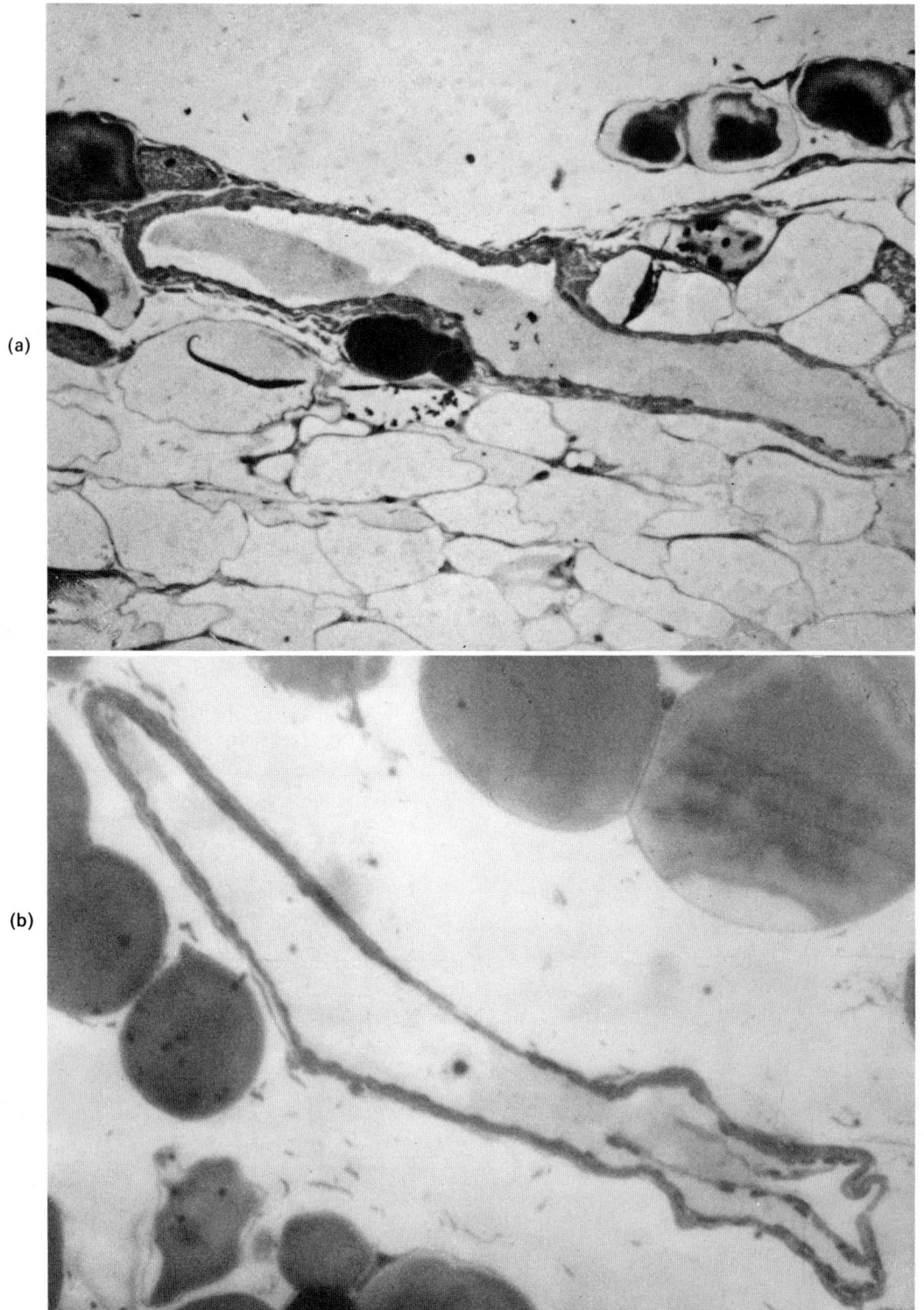

Figure 16.1. Thoracic duct.

(a), (b) Light micrographs of the thoracic duct. In (b) parts of the valve leaflets are shown. ((a) ×900, (b) ×500)

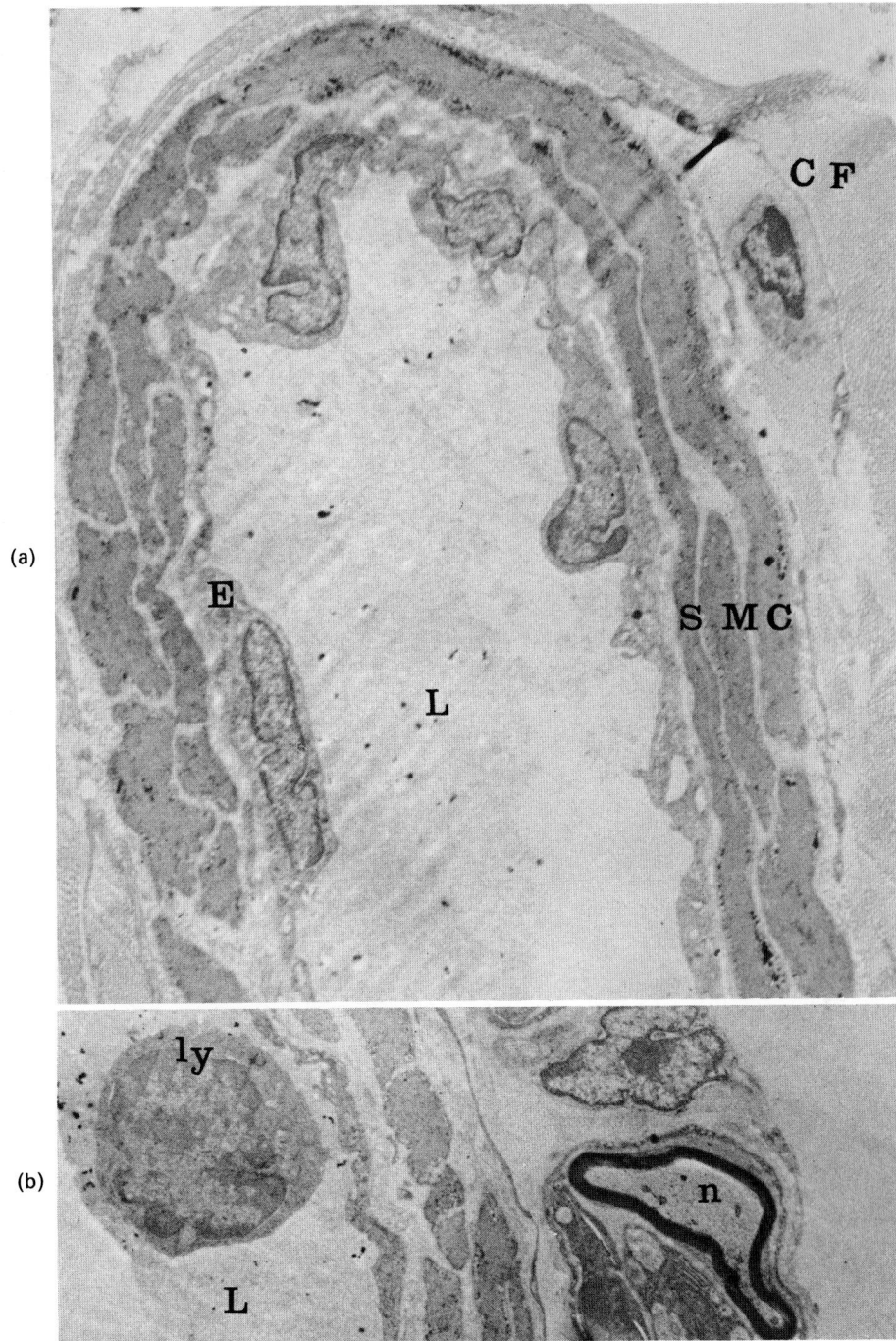

Figure 16.2. Lymphatic ducts.

(a) Portion of a lymphatic duct from the thoracic region. The wall is composed of a continuous endothelial (E) layer, representing the tunica intima, and several layers of smooth muscle cells (SMC), representing the tunica media. Collagen fibers (CF) and fibroblast occupy areas of the adventitia which blends into the surrounding connective tissue. L: lumen (×5,500)

(b) Portion of the thoracic duct showing part of a nerve (n) within the adventitia. The lumen (L) of the lymphatic vessel contain a lymphocyte (ly) and carbon particles. (×4,800)

within the connective tissue areas (see Figure 18.2). Although the walls of these vessels are made up of endothelial cells that form a continuous lining, the intercellular junctions are specialized by having large segments that are free of adhesion devices, thus allowing adjacent cells to be easily separated to accommodate the rapid movement of interstitial fluids and components. The size and shape of the capillaries are extremely variable with diameters ranging from 20 to 60 μm. Occasionally, the lymphatic capillaries appear as bulbous structures as demonstrated in the wings of the bat.[18,117]

16.4. Lymphatic sinusoids

By using improved techniques of intravascular perfusion fixation, Fawcett *et al.*[33] demonstrated lymphatic vessels in the interstitial tissue in the mammalian testis. They observed lymphatic vessels that were labyrinthine and pleomorphic in their three-dimensional configurations. Because of their extremely irregular shape, these vessels were described as lymphatic sinusoids. The wall of the lymphatic sinusoid consists of extremely attenuated cells that form flattened sheets which may be 700–1,000 Å thick in most regions except for those areas of the cytoplasm which are thickened to accommodate an oval nucleus. Like the endothelial cells in the lymphatic capillaries found in the dermis and various viscera of the body, the endothelial cells of the sinusoids also lack a protein polysaccharide basal lamina. These sinusoids form a continuous system of lymphatic channels that are interposed between the seminiferous tubules and perivascular cords and islands of Leydig cells in the testis (as indicated in Figure 16.3). In this system these labyrinthine channels of lymphatic sinusoids serve as the initial drainage site for interstitial fluids and function as well in the removal of hormones secreted by the Leydig cells within the interstitial areas of the testis.[76]

16.5. Lymphatic spaces

In a comparative study of the interstitial compartment in the mammalian testis, Fawcett *et al.*[33] observed very large intercommunicating cavities that were filled with protein rich lymph, but the walls of these cavities were only partially lined by an endothelium. This structural arrangement of endothelial cells provided a situation in which the lumen of the cavity was continuous with the extracellular fluid phase of the surrounding interstitial matrix. The limiting boundary of these lymphatic spaces was very often ill-defined and in many regions, discontinuous. However, in other segments the endothelial wall gradually became continuous so that the lymphatic space was confluent with the lumen of a conventional type of lymphatic vessel. The term discontinuous sinusoids was also suggested as an alternative name for these intercommunicating cavities within the interstitium.[33]

Figure 16.3. Lymphatic sinusoid.
From interstitial tissue of guinea pig testis. The lymphatic sinusoid is surrounded by strands of fibroblast which are separated by collagen fibers (CF). The connective tissue area (CT) and the lumen are filled with fine particles of colloidal ferritin injected into the interstitial area prior to fixation by perfusion. A portion of a blood vessel is located in the upper part of the micrograph. Cross section of a nerve axon (N) is also visible. (× 12,000)

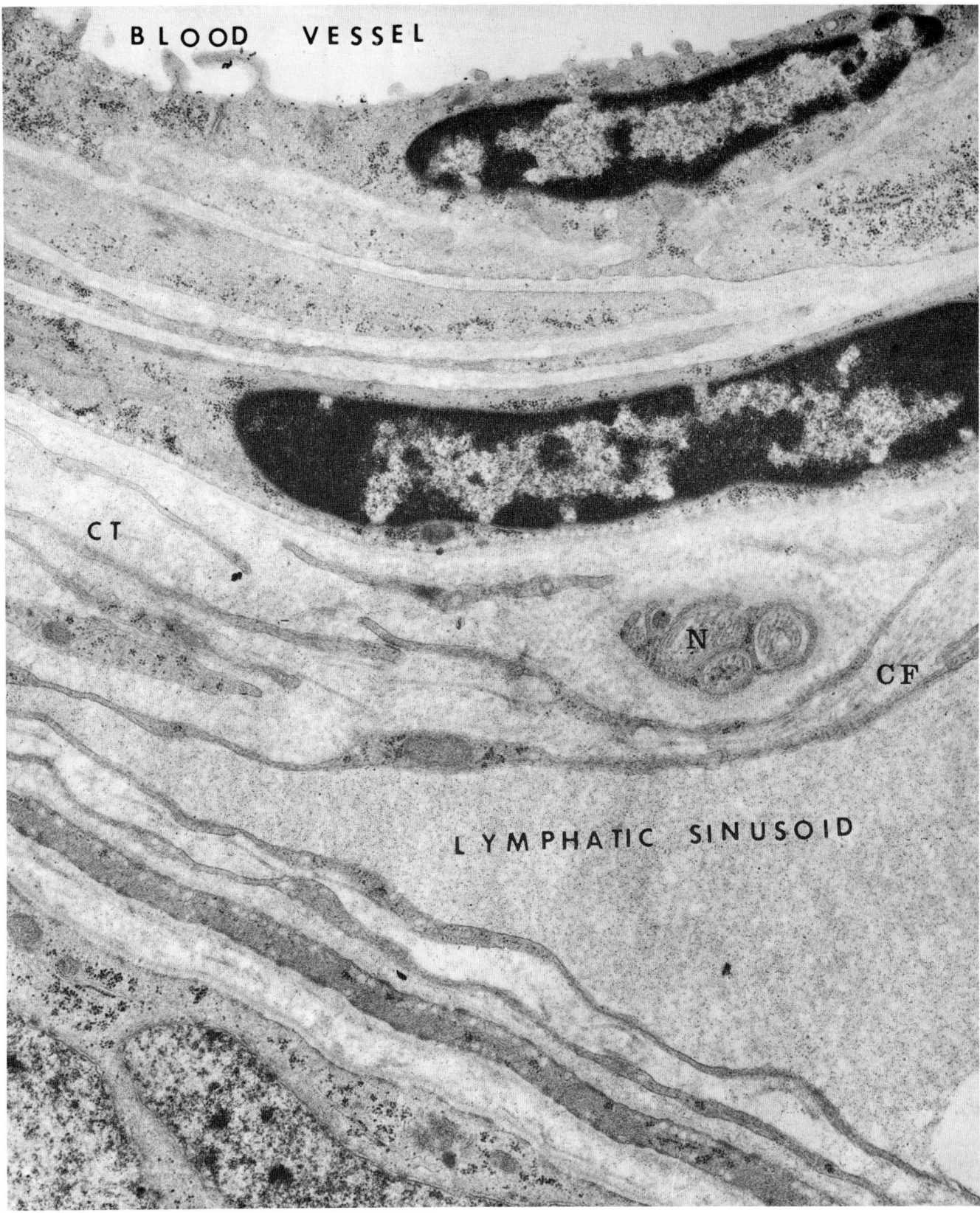

BLOOD VESSEL

CT

N

CF

LYMPHATIC SINUSOID

17. Structural Components of the Major Lymphatic Vascular Wall

Three distinct layers make up the wall of the major lymphatic vessels: the tunica intima, tunica media, and tunica adventitia. The components of the innermost layer are arranged mostly longitudinally. Those of the middle layer are in a spiral or circular arrangement. The components of the outer layer are more loosely arranged and appear to be parallel to the long axis of the vessel wall. The outer layer is continuous with the surrounding connective tissue and adipose tissue in which these lymphatic vessels are usually embedded (see Figures 16.1, 16.2).

17.1. Tunica intima

The luminal surface of the major lymphatic vessels is composed of a single layer of endothelial cells that are closely apposed at the intercellular junctions to form a continuous lining. The cells comprising this innermost layer often appear cuboidal in shape in the contracted vessel, while in the dilated vessel the lining cells become more flattened giving the appearance of squamous cells. The thickness of the endothelial cells varies, measuring 2–4 μm in the perinuclear region while attenuated areas of the cytoplasm may be as thin as 0·1 μm or less (Figures 16.2, 17.1, 17.2).

The protoplasm of the lymphatic endothelial cells is surrounded by a plasmalemma or cell membrane that is similar in structure to the unit membrane described by Robertson.[107] In the electron microscope it appears as two dense leaflets of approximately 35 Å separated by a light intermediate layer measuring 20–25 Å. Numerous invaginations of varying depths occur along the luminal and connective tissue fronts of the endothelium (Figure 17.2). These plasmalemmal invaginations are very similar to the micropinocytotic vesicles observed in blood vessels as well as a variety of cell types in which substances are actively transported into or out of the cell.

Figure 17.1. Major lymphatic vascular wall.

(a) Cross sectional view of a portion of the thoracic duct. Short segments of the endoplasmic reticulum can be seen scattered throughout the cytoplasm of the endothelial (E) cells. The tunica media consists of six to seven layers of smooth muscle cells (SMC) separated from the tunica intima by collagen fibers (CF) and elastic fibers (ef). Thin segments of vial cells (VC) mark the junction between the tunica adventitia and the tunica media. (× 7,500)

(b) A small blood vessel (BV) is located within the tunica media between smooth muscle cells. The endothelium (E) contains rough endoplasmic reticulum (er) and a vesicle (v) with carbon particles. (× 12,600)

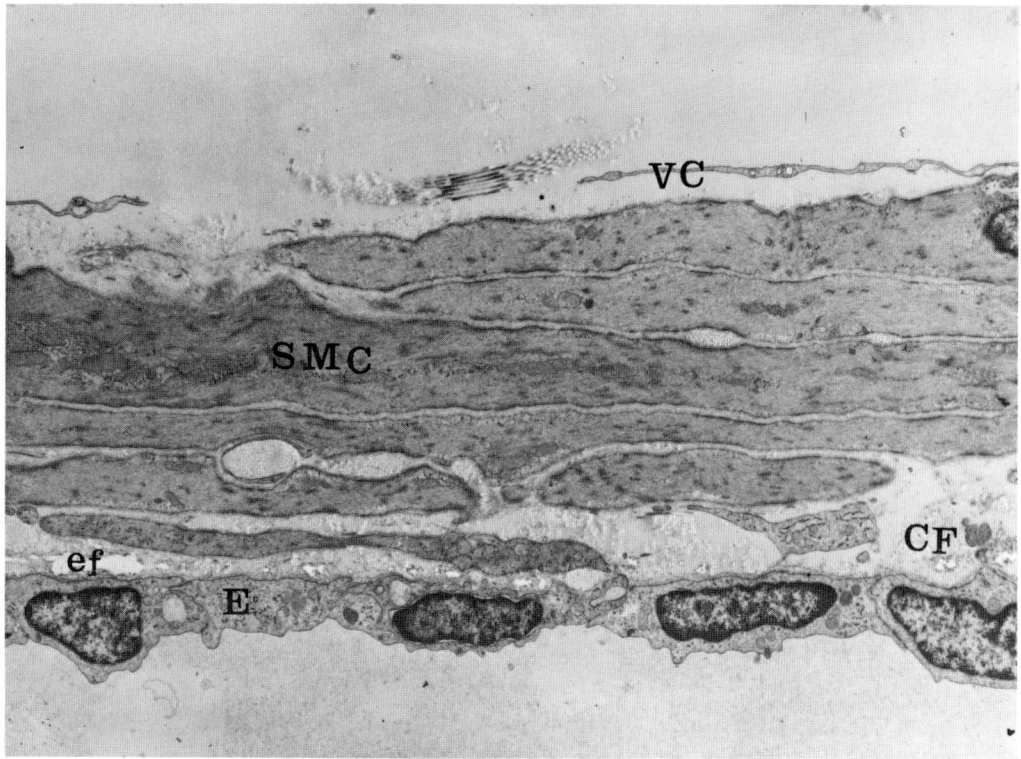

(a)

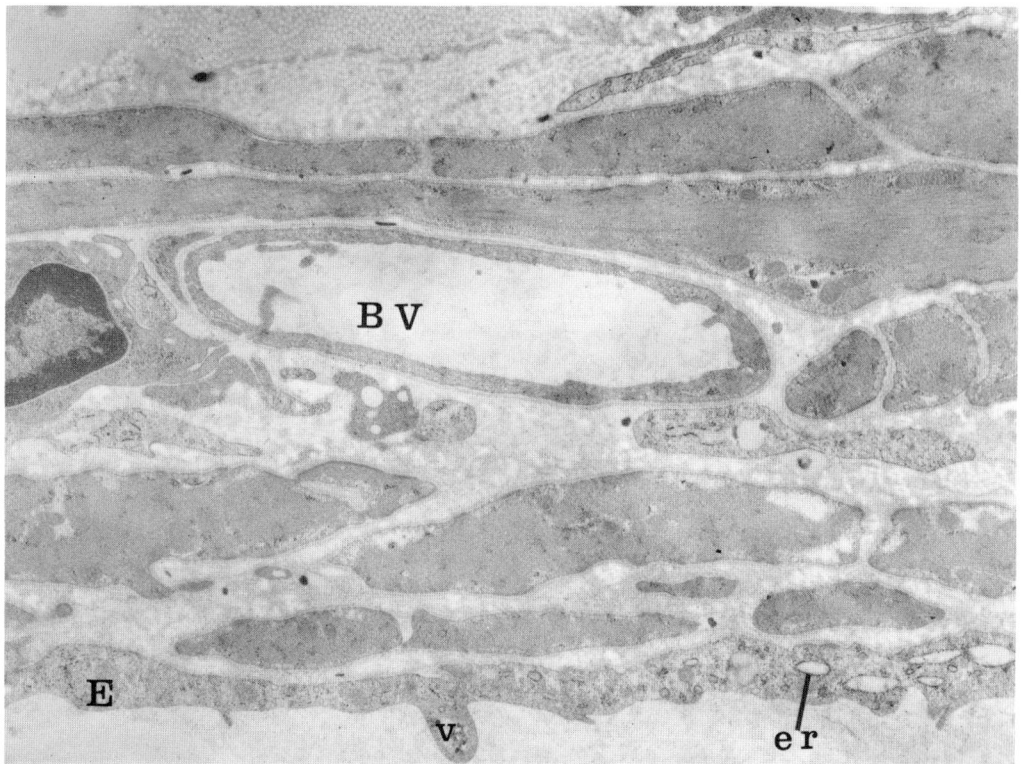

(b)

(a)

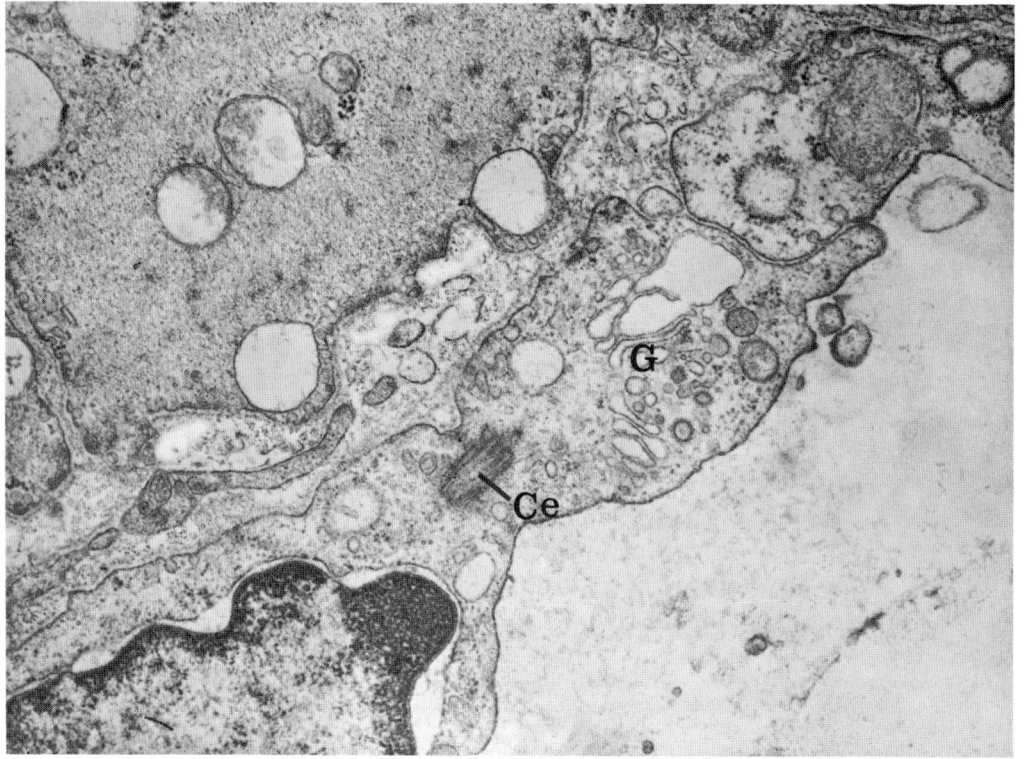

(b)

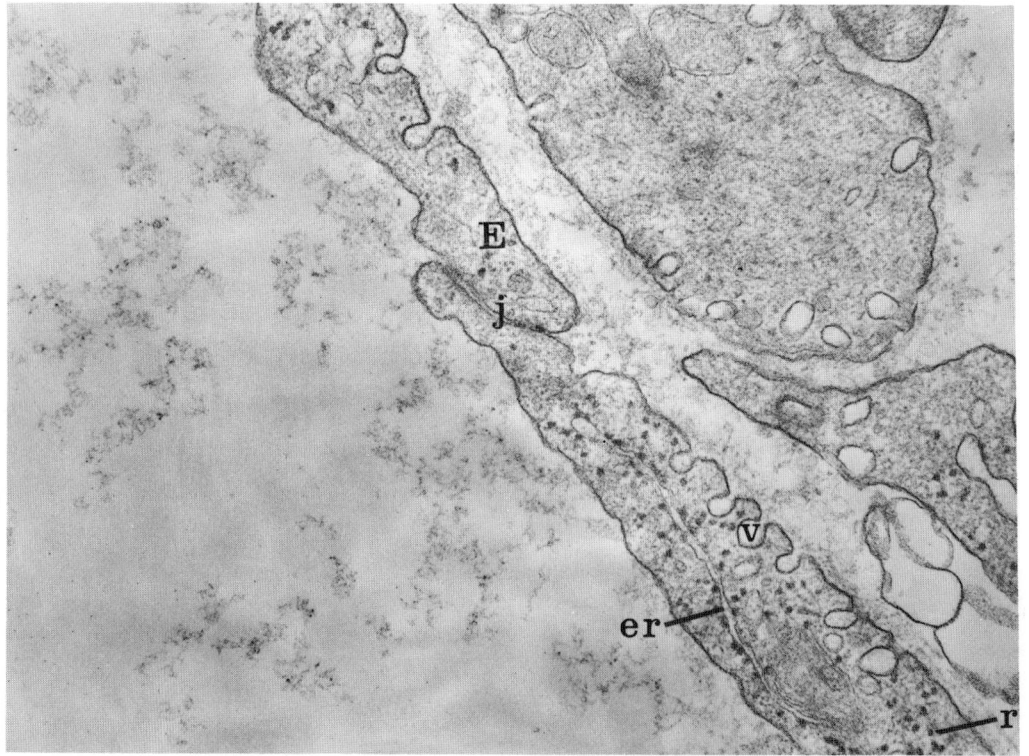

The usual complement of cellular organelles is observed in the endothelial cells of the major lymphatic vessels (Figures 17.1, 17.2). While most of the organelles are localized in the perinuclear region, some are dispersed in the most attenuated areas of the cytoplasm. Although not very extensive, the Golgi complex consists of stacked smooth surface cisterna and clusters of vesicles of varied sizes that are closely associated with its peripheral regions (Figure 17.2(a)). Multivesicular bodies are also observed in the endothelial cells and are very often located near the Golgi region. Complex multivesicular bodies as well as small vacuoles containing electron-dense substances are also seen in other regions of the cytoplasm (Figure 17.4).

The endoplasmic reticulum is sparse and is represented by a randomly disposed cisterna with attached ribosomes. Its lumen contains a fine fibrillar substance of moderate electron density. A large number of free ribosomes are also observed throughout the cytoplasm (Figures 17.1, 17.2). A number of studies have shown that in cells that were actively engaged in the synthesis of proteins for export, the cytoplasm contained large amounts of endoplasmic reticulum of the rough variety.[52,94] The cytological features of the endothelial cells comprising the major lymphatic vessels would suggest that these cells are engaged in a moderate production of protein synthesis, mainly as a part of their own metabolism and that their synthetic apparatus is insufficient for the production of large amounts of proteins to be discharged into the extracellular compartment as is the case for secretory type cells.[51]

Mitochondria are observed in the perinuclear region as well as in other areas of the cytoplasm including the attenuated segments of the endothelium. Spherical and elongated bodies with the usual internal membrane structure and organization typical of mitochondria in the endothelial cells of blood vessels are also observed.

In the distended vessel the luminal surface of the endothelial cells appears relatively smooth with very few cytoplasmic projections. In contrast, in the contracted vessel the luminal surface of the endothelium is thrown into numerous folds which produce fingerlike projections that extend into the lumen of the lymphatic vessel.

Microtubules measuring 250 Å in diameter are routinely observed near the Golgi region and also in close association with centrioles (Figure 17.2). They are also randomly dispersed throughout the perinuclear and attenuated regions of the cytoplasm. There is also a moderate population of cytoplasmic filaments in the endothelial cells of the larger lymphatic vessels (Figure 17.11).

17.1.1. Intercellular junctions

Specializations along the lateral surfaces of the endothelial cells consist of endothelial margins that interdigitate with invaginations of neighboring cells to form imbricating intercellular junctions. Some adjacent cells are held in close apposition at areas where cells overlap each other for short distances (Figure 17.2). Other specializations noted along the lateral surface consist of electron-dense accumulations within the peripheral

Figure 17.2. Lymphatic endothelial cells.
(a) Centriole (Ce) and Golgi apparatus (G) in a juxtanuclear position. (× 7,300)
(b) Numerous vessels (v) visible along the abluminal surface. Note close apposition of adjacent endothelial cells at intercellular junctions (j). Small segments of rough endoplasmic reticulum (er) and free ribosomes (r) appear in the cytoplasm of endothelium cells (E). (× 56,000)

167

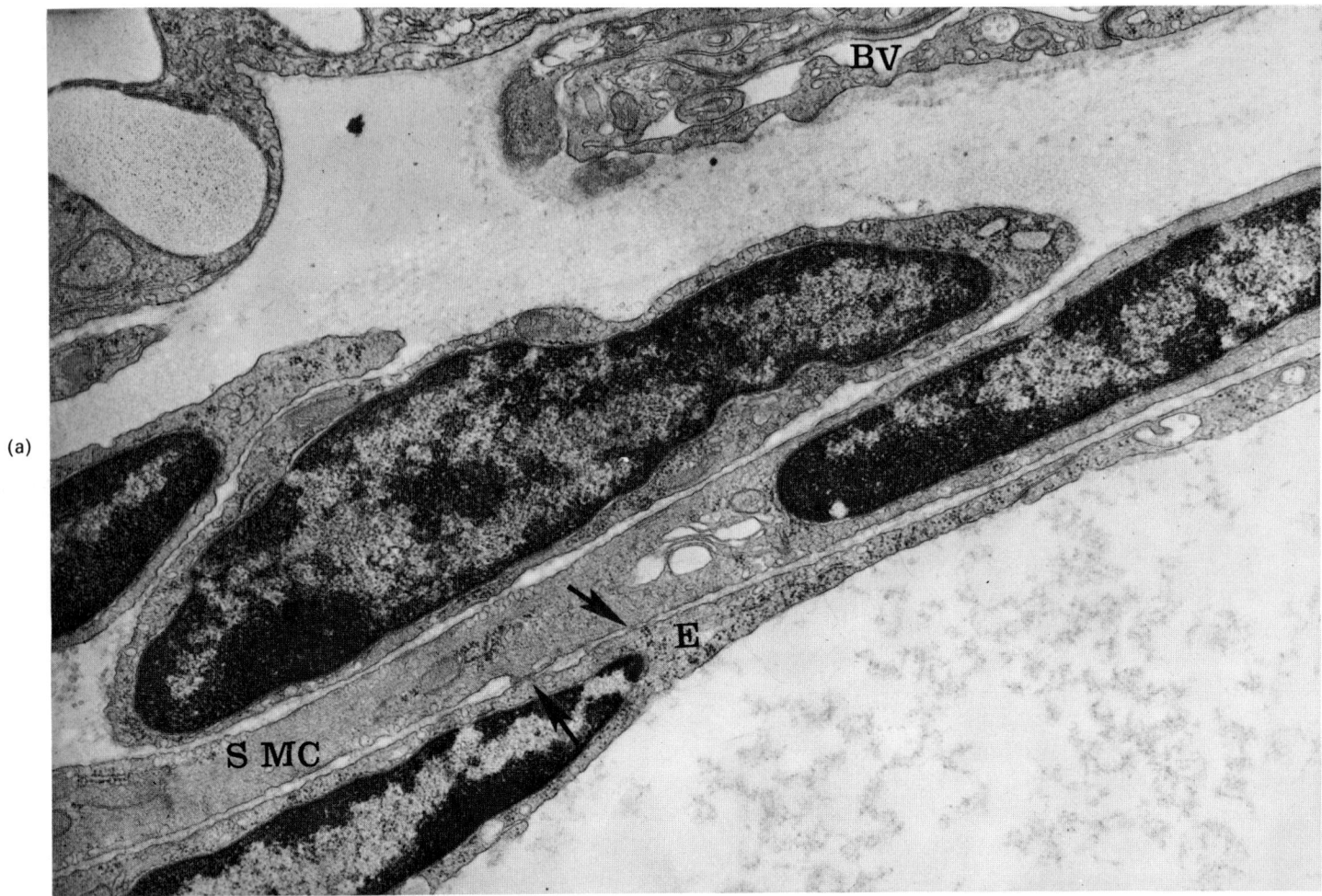

(a)

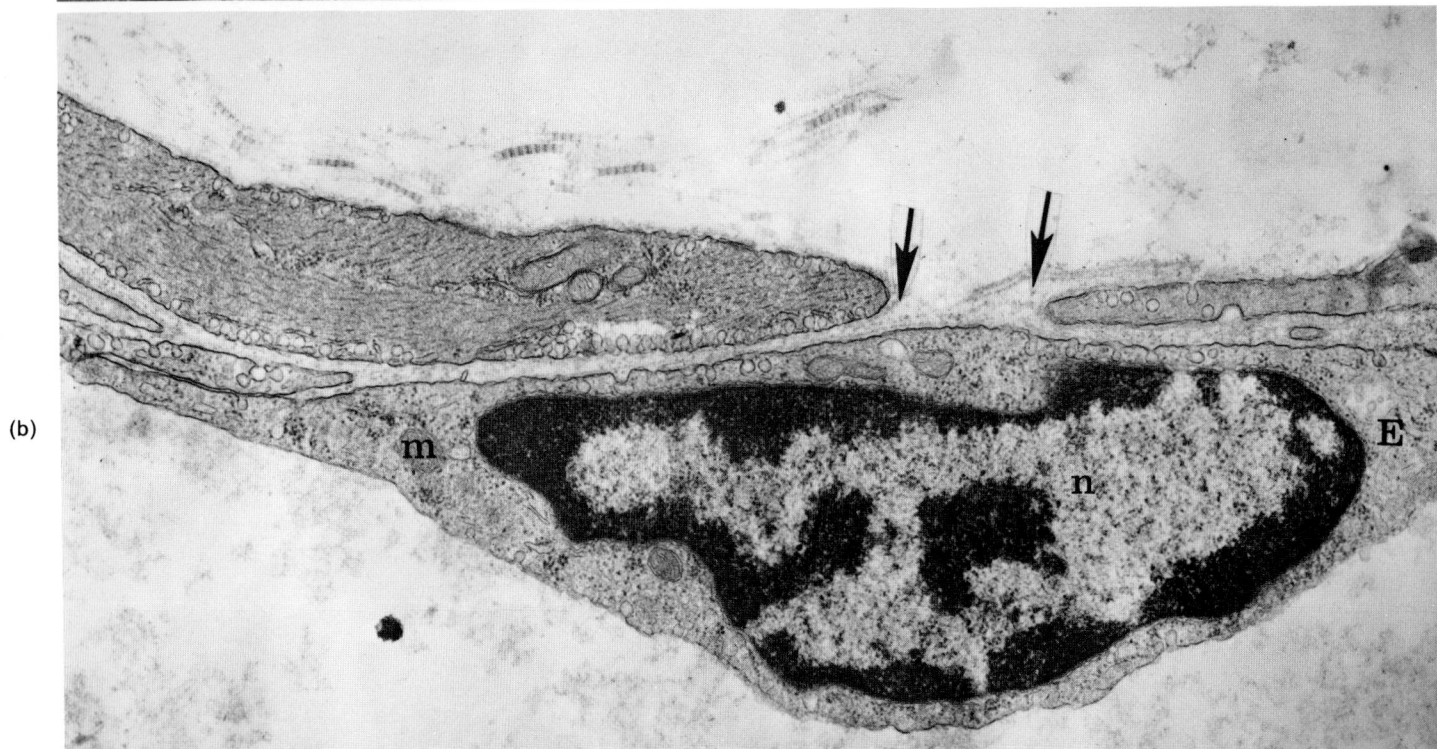

(b)

cytoplasm subjacent to the endothelial plasmalemma. Between the apposing endothelial cells at these areas there is a space of 150–200 Å which may contain electron-dense material. Such areas correspond to desmosomes observed in epithelial cells.[31] In other areas between adjacent endothelial cells, focal sites are observed in which apposing plasma membranes are held in close apposition without an apparent obliteration of the intercellular cleft. Such areas provide for the maintenance of cell-to-cell contact and are similar to maculae adherentes.[30] Occasionally, there are areas in which a small segment of the intercellular cleft is eliminated. This situation occurs when the outer leaflets of adjacent endothelial plasma membranes are fused for a very short distance to form quintuple structures and represent maculae occludentes (tight junctions).

17.1.2. Basal lamina

The endothelial cells of the large trunks are surrounded by a continuous basal lamina. It appears as a fine filamentous network that forms an amorphous band approximately 800–1,000 Å in thickness (Figures 17.1, 17.2).

The basal surface of the endothelial cells is separated from the basal lamina by a translucent space approximately 500 Å in width. In areas where cells of the tunica media come in close contact with the endothelial lining cells, the basal lamina is jointly shared by the two cells.

17.1.3. Elastic fibers

Unlike the media in large size arteries which contains a continuous internal elastic membrane in close apposition to the basal surface of the endothelial cells, the elastic fibers in the thoracic duct are observed in small bundles located between the basal lamina and the innermost layer of cells comprising the tunica media. They appear as discrete bundles which vary from short segments to platelike structures (Figure 17.1(a)). The elastic fibers are composed of longitudinally arranged filaments embedded in an amorphous substance. The filaments occur within the outer mantle of the fiber and are approximately 100 Å in diameter. Cross sections of the filaments reveal a less densely staining center approximately 40 Å in diameter. Differential staining of the filamentous mantle and the central core is obtained when sections of the elastic fibers are stained with phosphotungstic acid, uranyl acetate, and lead. The central core is densely stained with phosphotungstic acid while the individual filaments within the mantle of the elastic fibers are very difficult to differentiate. However, when thin sections of the elastic fibers are stained with uranyl acetate or lead, a reverse staining reaction is obtained in which longitudinally arranged filaments show

Figure 17.3. Wall of lymphatic collecting vessel.

(a) Location of a blood vessel (BV) within the wall of the lympatic collecting vessel. A smooth muscle cell (SMC) of the tunica media lies in close contact with the endothelial cells (E) at several points (arrows). (×23,000)

(b) The incompleteness of the tunica media in collecting vessels is illustrated, where a wide gap is seen between the two adjacent smooth muscle cells (arrows). The nucleus (n) occupies the widest portion of the cell. Mitochondria (m) are observed in the perinuclear area of the endothelial cell (E). (×36,000)

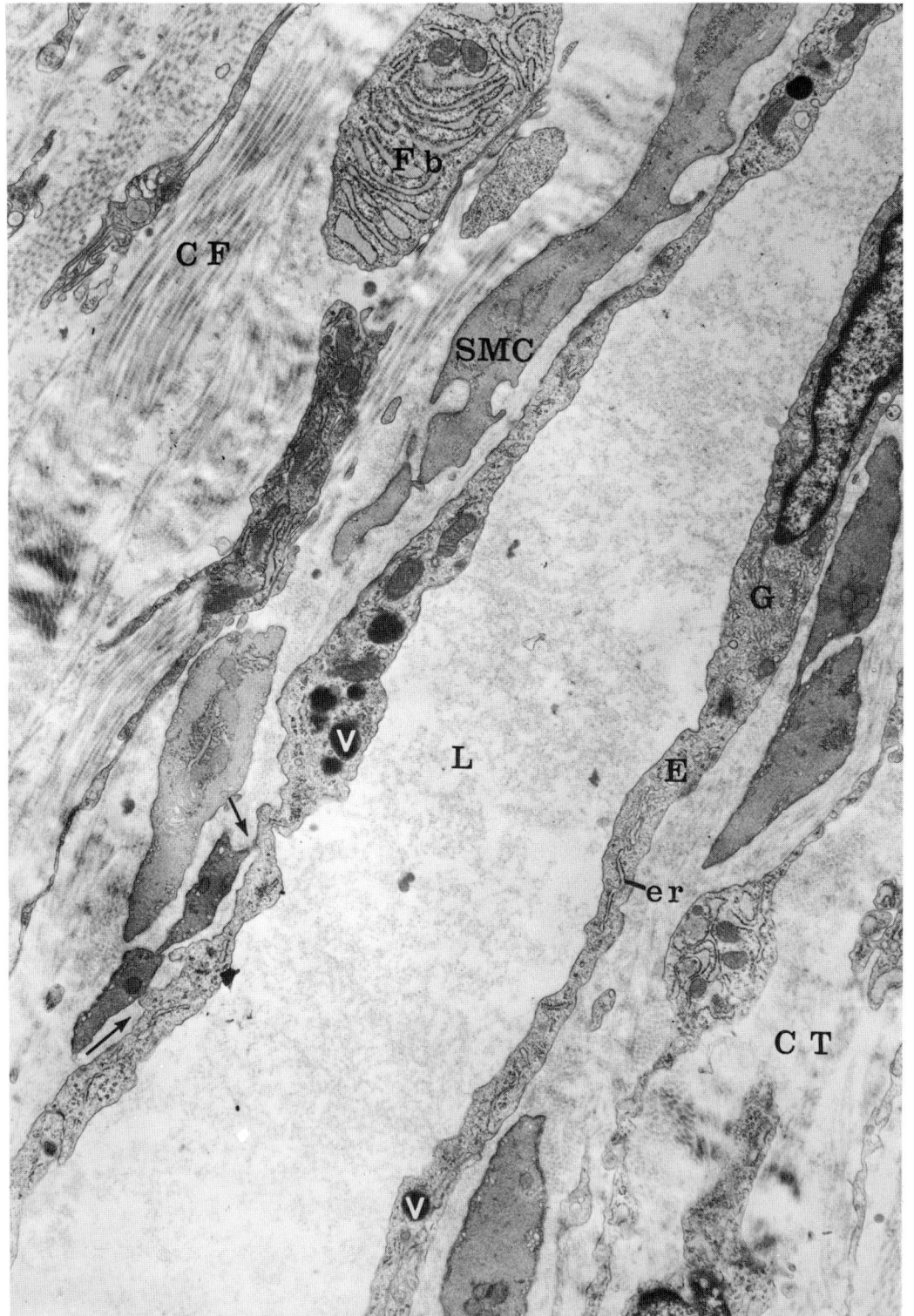

a marked affinity for the uranyl and lead. On the other hand, the central core appears unstained or is only slightly stained with these salts.

Studies of Ross and Bornstein[109] provided information on both the morphologic and chemical make-up of the elastic fibers. The central amorphous component of the elastic fiber was shown to be identical with that previously described for elastin.[15,96,99,111] The longitudinally arranged microfibrils were shown to be rich in polarhydroxy and sulfur-containing amino acids and with less glycine, valine, and proline than the amorphous components of the elastic fibers.[109]

17.2. Tunica media

The middle layer in the walls of the major lymphatic vessels is composed mainly of smooth muscle cells. They are arranged in a circular or spiral fashion around the vessel wall, forming up to eight layers of cells depending on whether the vessel is dilated or in a contracted state (Figures 16.2, 17.1). The smooth muscle cells, like those comprising the media in veins and arteries, are fusiform cylinders with long tapering ends. The nucleus is located in the central part of the cell which is also the region of greatest dimension of the cell. The length of the cell is affected by the state of its contraction making its actual length difficult to determine. In addition, the spiral arrangement of these cells within the wall of the vessel makes it impossible to obtain ultrathin sections through the entire length of a single cell (Figures 17.1, 17.4).

The plasmalemma of the smooth muscle cell is studded with numerous invaginations. They are equally abundant on both surfaces of the cell, and appear at the extreme periphery of the cytoplasm (Figure 17.5). Although some of the vesicles appear to lie free in the cytoplasm, the use of certain electron-dense tracers such as lanthanum in the fixation solutions[103] has revealed that those vesicles within the peripheral cytoplasm are open to the connective tissue areas, as demonstrated by their content of tracer within the lumina of the vesicles. However, some of the vesicles lack the electron-dense tracer and are presumed to represent invaginations that lie free within the cytoplasm. Other tracer studies with ferritin and peroxidase have failed to show that appreciable amounts of the tracer is taken up by these plasmalemmal invaginations for transport into the interior of the cell. The lack of such uptake would suggest that these plasmalemmal invaginations serve a different function to the micropinocytotic vesicles in the endothelial cells of blood and lymphatic vessels. The plasmalemmal invaginations are extremely numerous, occupying large areas of the cell

Figure 17.4. Collecting lymphatic vessel.
Portion of a collecting lymphatic vessel from rat lung. Smooth muscle cells (SMC) comprising the tunica media do not form a continuous sheet but form a spiral arrangement around the lymphatic vessel. Some are in close apposition to the endothelium (arrow). The lumen (L) of the collecting vessels contains a dense precipitate of lymph. The endothelial cells (E) contain the usual complement of organelles including large vesicles (v) containing an electron-dense substance and a Golgi complex (G) situated in the juxtanuclear region. Segments of rough endoplasmic reticulum (er) are visible throughout the thinner cytoplasmic regions of endothelial cells. The adventitia blends with the surrounding connective tissue (CT) area which is rich in collagen fibers (CF) and fibroblasts (Fb). (× 11,500)

171

(a)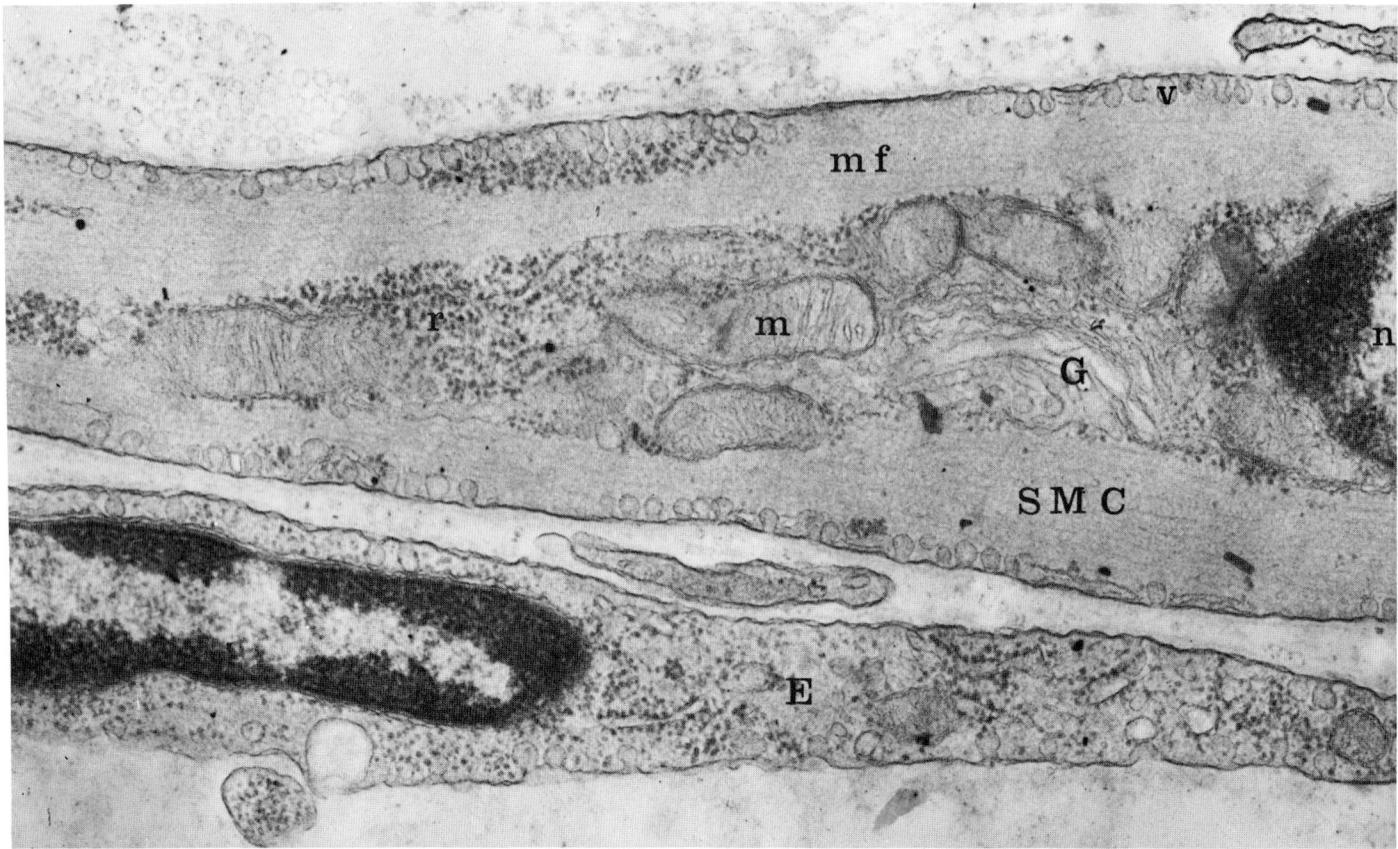

(b)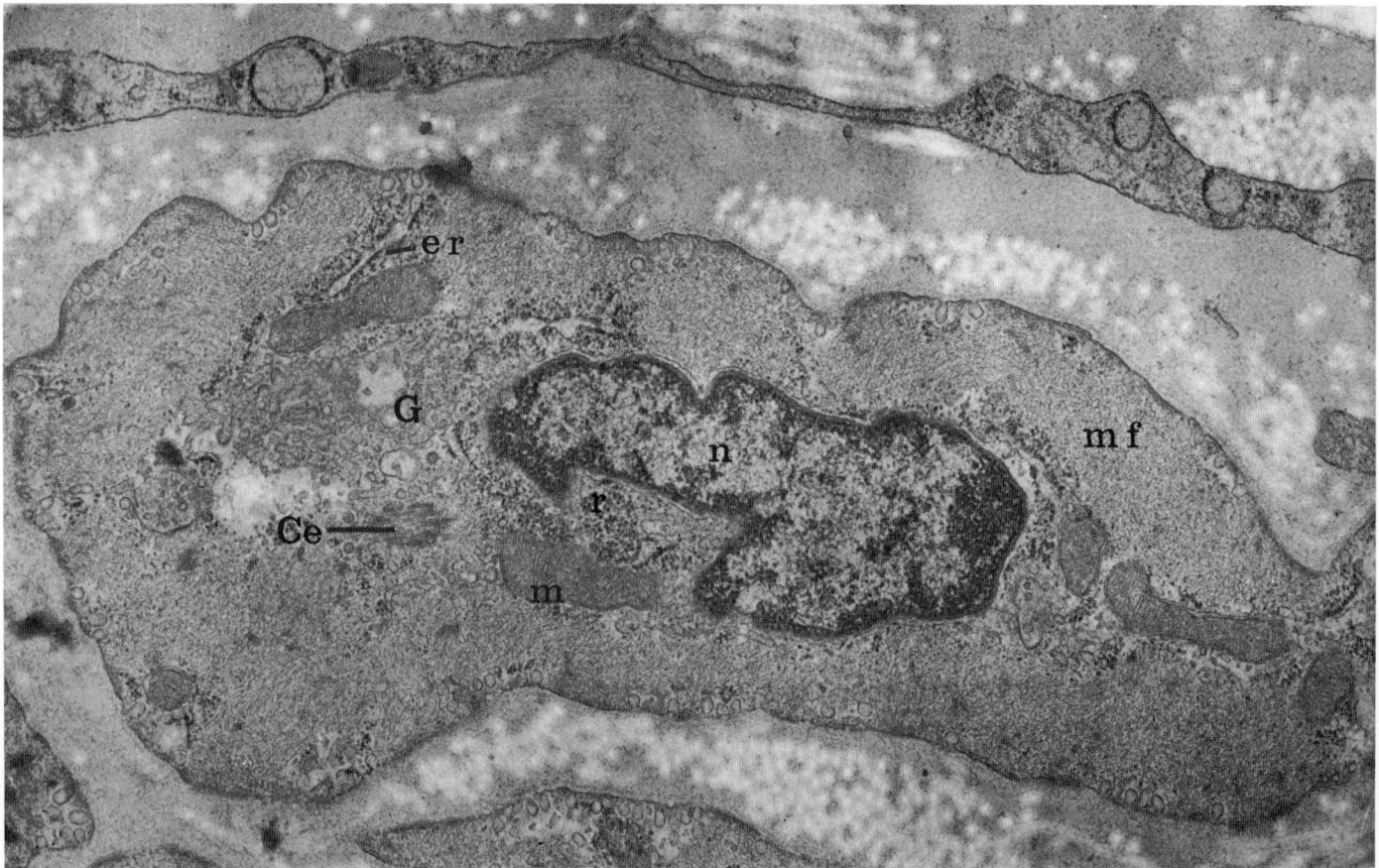

surface (Figures 17.5, 17.6). This cell surface specialization not only increases the total surface area for the muscle cell, but it also provides a reserve of membrane which can be utilized during the extension of the smooth muscle cells. The smooth muscle cells are also surrounded by a basal lamina except at sites of attachment between adjacent cells where communicating junctions (gap junction, nexuses) are formed (Figure 17.7). Gap junctions have a wide distribution, occurring between cells of various tissue types.[23,78,103,108,114] From morphological and physiological studies, it is clear that the gap junction can serve as the pathway for cell to cell communication.[5,25,39,79]

The fine structure of the smooth muscle cell of the lymphatic trunk is characterized by large bundles of filaments approximately 60 Å in diameter (Figures 17.5, 17.6, 17.7). They are arranged with their long axis coinciding with the long axis of the cell. Large numbers of dense bodies or attachment plaques are found in the cytoplasm subjacent to the plasmalemma (Figures 17.5(b), 17.6(b)). The cell is usually filled with the myofilaments in areas devoid of cell organelles. Cytoplasmic organelles are usually found in the perinuclear region (Figure 17.5); however, mitochondria are also dispersed throughout the cell between the myofilaments. A well-developed Golgi complex and numerous vesicles of various sizes are located in a juxtanuclear position (Figure 17.6(b)). Strands of rough endoplasmic reticulum are also seen within the perinuclear region and are sparsely dispersed between myofilaments throughout the cytoplasm (Figures 17.5(b), 17.7(b)). Small segments of sarcoplasmic reticulum are also observed in the perinuclear and peripheral cytoplasm. In earlier studies of the smooth muscle cell, Pease and Molenari[98] suggested that the dense plaques that were located adjacent to the plasma membrane may serve as attachment points for the myofilaments.

In striated muscles two distinct types of filaments are easily recognized with conventional preparative techniques for electron microscopy, but it has been extremely difficult to identify two distinct types of filaments in smooth muscle cells. However, using a variety of preparative techniques to study smooth muscle cells, two types of filaments have been demonstrated. There is a large population of small filaments that range from 40–70 Å in diameter while larger filaments ranging from 120–170 Å are less numerous.[34,91] By applying the method of inert dehydration for studying the structure of smooth muscle, Pease demonstrated a conspicuous system of coarse filaments that were similar to myosin filaments in striated muscle. It was also noted that coarse filaments resembled the system of thick filaments found in certain invertebrate smooth muscle. The demonstration of a system of thick and thin filaments in verte-

Figure 17.5. Smooth muscle cells of tunica media (L. V. Leak).

(a) Portions of the endothelium (E) of a collecting vessel and longitudual view of an adjoining smooth cell (SMC) in the tunica media. In this smooth muscle cell the myofilaments (mf) are distributed in the peripheral cytoplasm of the cell while the Golgi apparatus (G), mitochondria (m), and numerous ribosomes (r) are aggregated in the perinuclear region of the cytoplasm. Part of the nucleus (n) is located to the right. The plasmalemma is distinguished by numerous surface vesicles (v) (caveolae). (× 28,200)

(b) Cross sectional view of smooth muscle cells in the tunica media. The section has passed through part of the nucleus (n) which is centrally located and is immediately surrounded by components of the Golgi apparatus (G) and a centriole (Ce) as well as numerous ribosomes (r) lying free in the cytoplasm, rough endoplasmic reticulum (er), and mitochondria (m). The microfilaments (mf) are distributed in the cell periphery. (× 28,000)

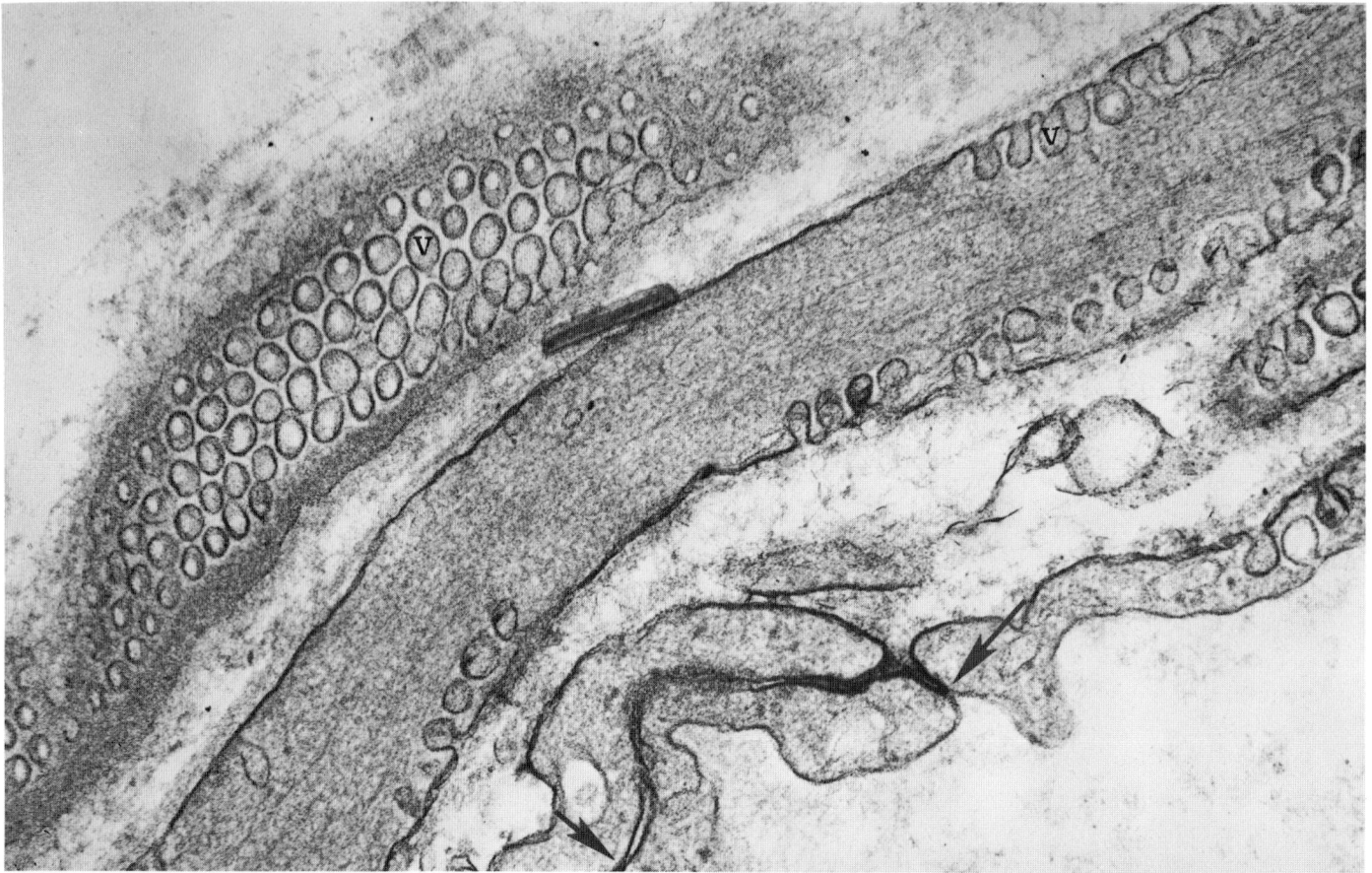

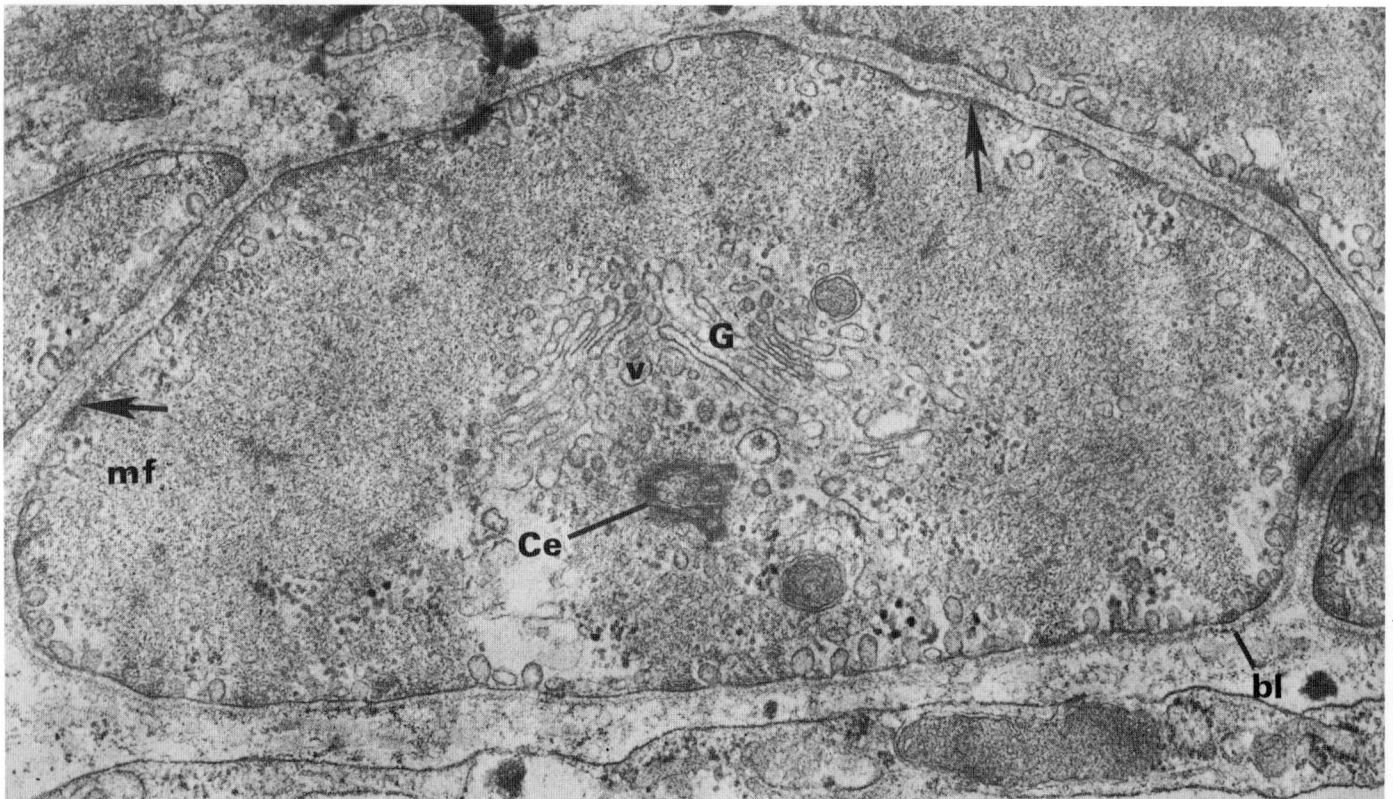

brate smooth muscles[34, 97, 115] would indicate that this muscle may be structured in the same way as the invertebrate smooth muscle and perhaps may operate with a comparable sliding filament mechanism.[80]

17.3. Tunica adventitia

The outermost layer surrounding the lymphatic vessels consists of a connective tissue complex which includes fibroblast, collagen fibers, nerves, and *vasa vasorum*. The boundary of this layer is marked by extremely flattened cells which overlap to form a limiting sheet which separates the wall from the surrounding adipose tissue. The flattened cells that line the outermost boundary are very similar to the vial cells observed by Rhodin[106] in the tunica adventitia of large veins (Figures 16.2, 17.1).

The fibroblasts located in the adventitia are similar to those observed in other connective tissue areas and their cytoplasm contains the usual complement of cellular organelles. The endoplasmic reticulum is extensive and is of the rough variety. The Golgi complex is located in the usual perinuclear region with a moderate number of closely associated vesicles. The mitochondria are evenly dispersed throughout the cytoplasm and numerous ribosomes are scattered singly or as polyribosomes throughout the cytoplasm. The cell is surrounded by a plasma membrane which also possesses numerous inpocketings. As with fibroblasts in other connective tissue areas, there is no basal lamina associated with the boundary of the cell. Numerous axons are present in the adventitia of the large vessels and are often closely associated with the vial cells (Figure 16.2). The axons are often seen extending into the media and may come in close contact with the smooth muscle cells. The *vasa vasorum* consists of small blood vessels which course along the outer regions of the adventitia and may also penetrate the more superficial muscle layers of the media adjacent to the adventitia (Figures 17.1(b), 17.3(a)).

17.4. Lymphatic valves

Both lymphatic trunks and collecting vessels are provided with valves. The valves within the lymphatic vessels appear to be more numerous than those noted for large veins. However, in common with the valves of veins, those in lymphatic vessels also

---

Figure 17.6. Smooth muscle cells of tunica media (L. V. Leak).

(a) The distribution of the surface vesicles (v) (caveolae). Grazing section along surface of a smooth muscle cell of the tunica media from a collecting vessel. The adjacent smooth muscle cell also shows numerous plasmalemmal invaginations. The close proximity of adjacent endothelial cells is appreciated in this micrograph which also demonstrates points of close apposition (arrows) between the endothelial cells. (× 90,000)

(b) Cross section of a smooth muscle cell from the tunica media of a collecting vessel which shows the juxtanuclear area, demonstrating the Golgi apparatus (G) with its numerous closely associated vesicles (v) and a section through a centriole (Ce). The peripheral distribution of myofilaments (mf) can also be appreciated in this electron micrograph. The plasmalemma also contains numerous surface vesicles (caveolae). Dense plaques (arrows) occur subjacent to the plasmalemma. The cell is surrounded by a basal lamina (bl). (× 44,800)

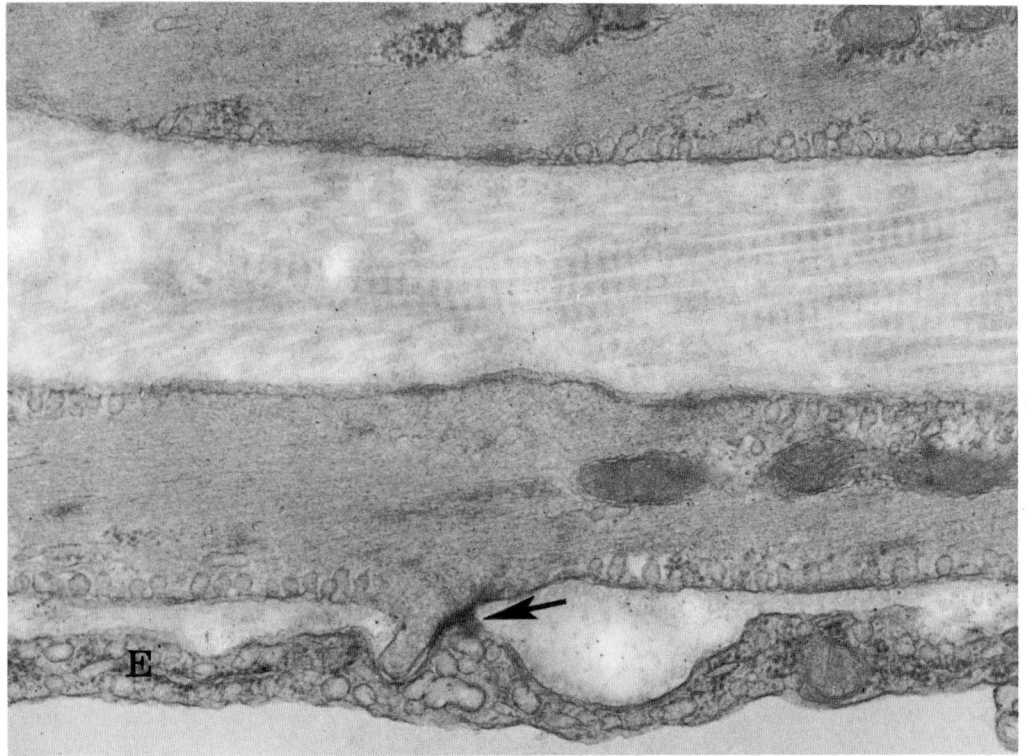

(a)

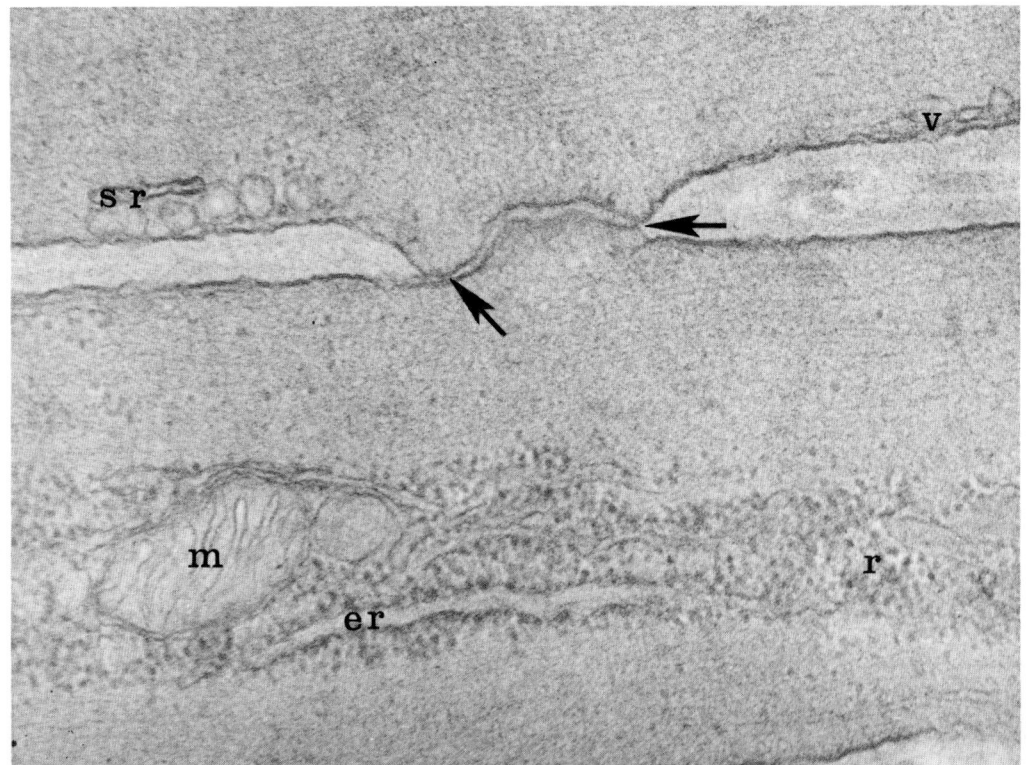

(b)

project into the lumen in the direction of fluid flow. They are arranged in a fashion that allows free and rapid passage of fluids (lymph and cells toward the major lymphatic trunks) in a unidirectional flow so that regurgitation of fluids and cells is prevented.

In thin sections the endothelial folds appear closely apposed with only a narrow band of connective tissue intervening between the two layers of endothelial cells (see Figure 16.1). This band consists of collagen fibers, elastic fibers, and an occasional fibroblast which may cause the apposing endothelial cells to be widely separated (Figure 17.9(b)). Smooth muscle cells are usually excluded from this intervening band of connective tissue.

On close examination of scanning images of the lymphatic valves, it is evident that the lining endothelium is reduplicated as a ring which encircles the lumen of the vessel to form paired leaflets (Figures 17.8(a), 17.9(a)). They consist of two thin cusps whose surfaces are lined with flattened endothelial cells (Figures 17.8(b), 17.9(a)). The lateral border of the adjacent leaflets are fused at their edges for a short distance (Figure 17.8) as they emerge from the vessel wall. The free borders of the leaflets are also covered with endothelial lining cells (Figure 17.10). Both leaflets project into the lumen at an angle, such that their free edges fit together as a miter joint without fusing with each other (Figures 17.8(a), 17.10). Immediately proximal to the base of the paired leaflet, the lymphatic wall is expanded into a sinus or pouch (Figure 17.8(a)). The numerous outpouchings along the length of the vessel account for the vessel's beaded appearance when it is distended or dilated.

Scanning electron microscopic images of the surface of the paired leaflets shows that the endothelial cells are uniformly distributed (Figures 17.8(a), 17.10). A small population of microvillous projections are observed over the apical surface of these cells which line the valve leaflets. A number of cells within the lymph are also observed adhering to the surfaces of the valve leaflets. These free cells contain numerous microvillous projections over their surfaces (Figure 17.10). The shape and surface specializations of the cells are characteristic of lymphocytes. The basal lamina surrounding the vessel wall also continues into the connective tissue septa (Figure 17.11).

The cytoplasm of the endothelial cells which comprise the valve leaflet contains numerous filaments (Figure 17.11) in contrast to the small amounts of filaments noted in the cells of the vessel wall. Both morphological and biochemical data accumulated in recent years suggest that the cytoplasmic filaments observed in a variety of non-muscle cells are indeed actin filaments with properties of contraction.[100, 101]

The presence of numerous cytoplasmic filaments within the endothelial cells of the valve leaflet would provide the contractile properties needed for the leaflet to contract, providing a wider orifice for the passage of fluids and cells while their relaxation would cause an expansion of the paired leaflets to become closely approximated at

---

Figure 17.7. Intercellar junctions in tunica media.
(a) Endothelial cell (E) has made intimate contact with an adjacent smooth muscle cell in the form of an intercellular junction (arrow). ($\times$ 28,800)
(b) Two adjacent smooth muscle cells of the tunica media closely apposed by way of an intercellular junction (arrow). These areas are presumed to represent the nexus or gap junctions. A segment of sarcoplasmic reticulum (sr), surface vesicles (v), mitochondria (m), endoplasmic reticulum (er), and free ribosomes (r) are also visible. ($\times$ 67,000)

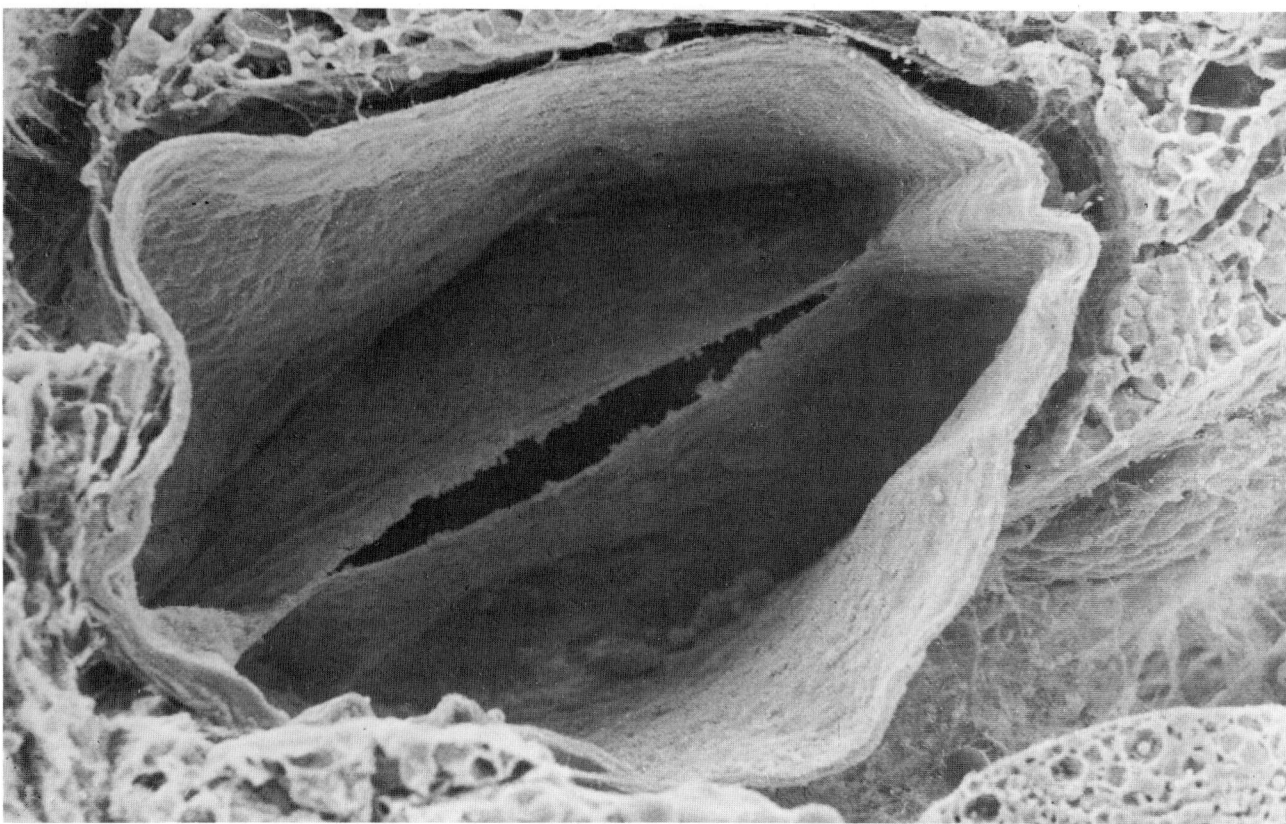

(a)

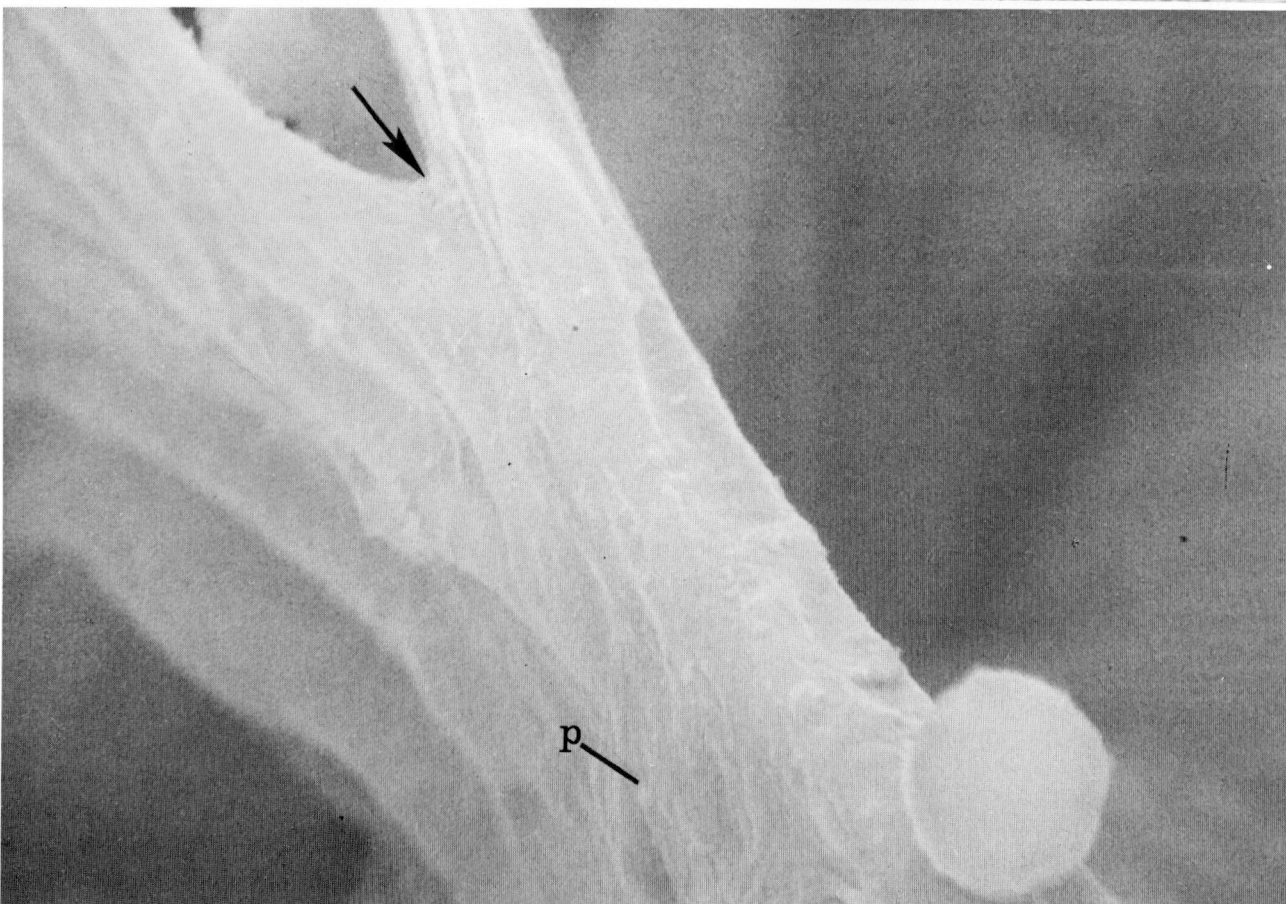

(b)

their free borders, closing the orifice and thus preventing a backflow of fluids and cells. In addition to serving a contractile function for producing movements of the endothelial cells, the cytoplasmic filaments may also be important in stabilizing the endothelial cells of the valve leaflet, allowing them to open for passage of fluids and close to prevent a backward flow of fluids.

Microtubules are also observed in the endothelial cells of the valve leaflet and are presumed to play a role in stabilizing the cells to resist the tensional forces that would be produced by the constant movement of fluids and particulate components over the surfaces of the valve leaflet.

Lauweryns[60] described the lymphatic valve as a simple cone or funnel-like formation which is actually longitudinally suspended in the lymphatic vessel lumen and whose distal or small openings are localized at the deepest point of the funnel. Lauweryns[60] suggested also that this funnel-like architectural arrangement of the valve would maintain the one-way flow of lymph and that it would probably be occluded by a flow against the normal direction. Our scanning electron microscopic observations show that the valves along the lymphatic wall are in the shape of a miter joint which would also present a funneling effect.

17.5. Organization and morphology of lymphatic collecting vessels

The collecting vessels differ from the much larger lymphatic trunks in that the tunica media may be reduced to an incomplete layer of smooth muscle cells. Although they are extremely variable in diameter, the lumina of these vessels are usually smaller than those of the major lymphatic trunks. In receiving the lymph drained from the various regions of the body, the lymphatic collecting vessels contain lymph nodes that are located at various regions along their length. Like the wall of the larger thoracic trunk, the wall of the lymphatic collecting vessel is distinguished by the presence of valves and smooth muscle cells (Figures 17.4, 17.9).

17.5.1. Tunica intima of collecting vessels

The endothelial cells of collecting vessels are extremely attenuated beyond the perinuclear region with adjacent cell margins being held in close apposition by maculae adherentes. Plasmalemmal vesicles occur along both connective tissue and luminal fronts of the endothelial cells. The usual complement of organelles such as mitochondria, Golgi complexes, and endoplasmic reticulum are also observed. There is also a population of filaments and microtubules distributed throughout the cytoplasm (Figures 17.3, 17.4). The basal surfaces of the endothelial cells of the collecting vessels, like those of the larger trunks, also rest on a basal lamina. Occasional elastic fibers are

Figure 17.8. Lymphatic valve.
(a) SEM showing the appearance of a valve in a cross section of the thoracic duct. A pair of leaflets extend from the wall in a circumferential fashion and project into the lumen of the vessel at such an angle that their free edges fit together like a miter joint. (× 400)
(b) Enlarged portion of the valve showing the fused edge attached to the vessel wall (arrow). The endothelial cells comprising the surface of the leaflet are extremely flattened cells with a small number of projections (p) over their free surface. (× 4,700)

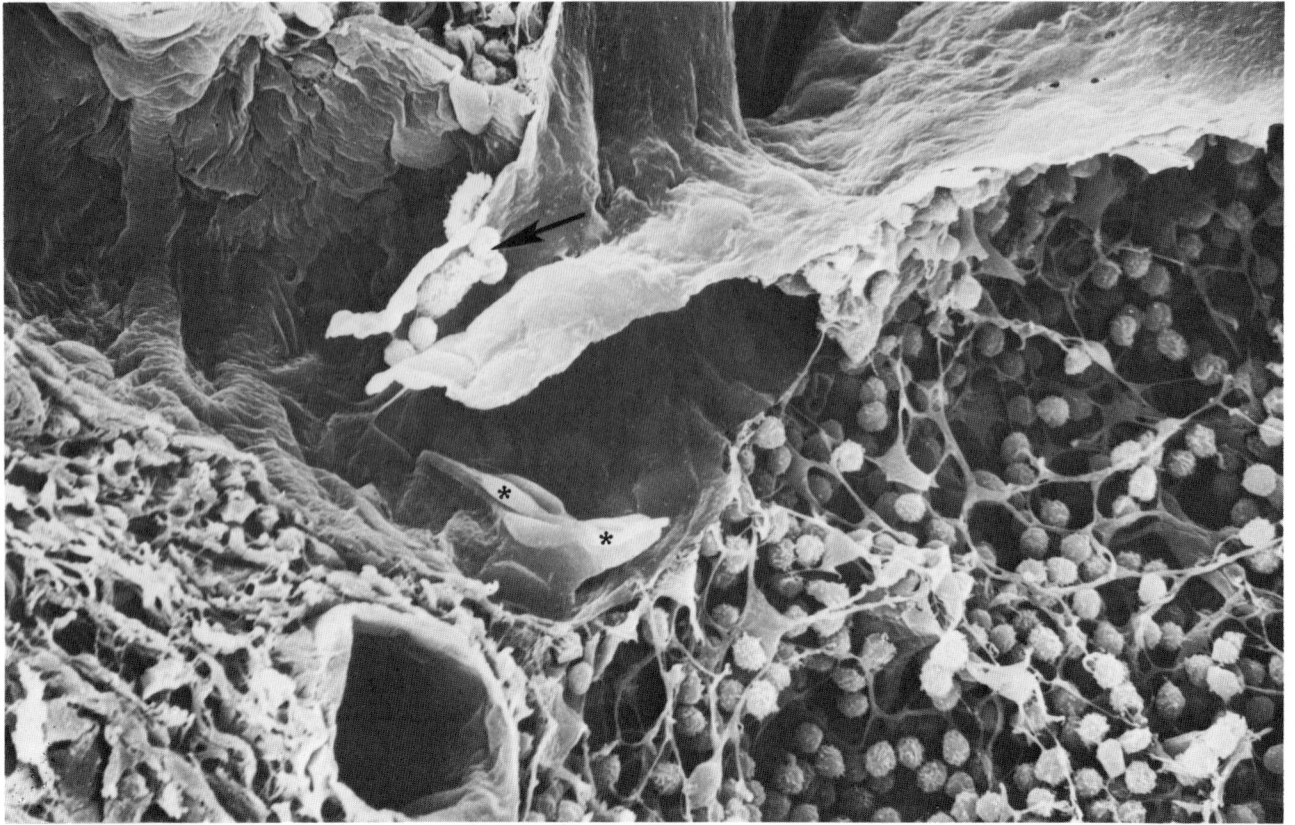

(a)

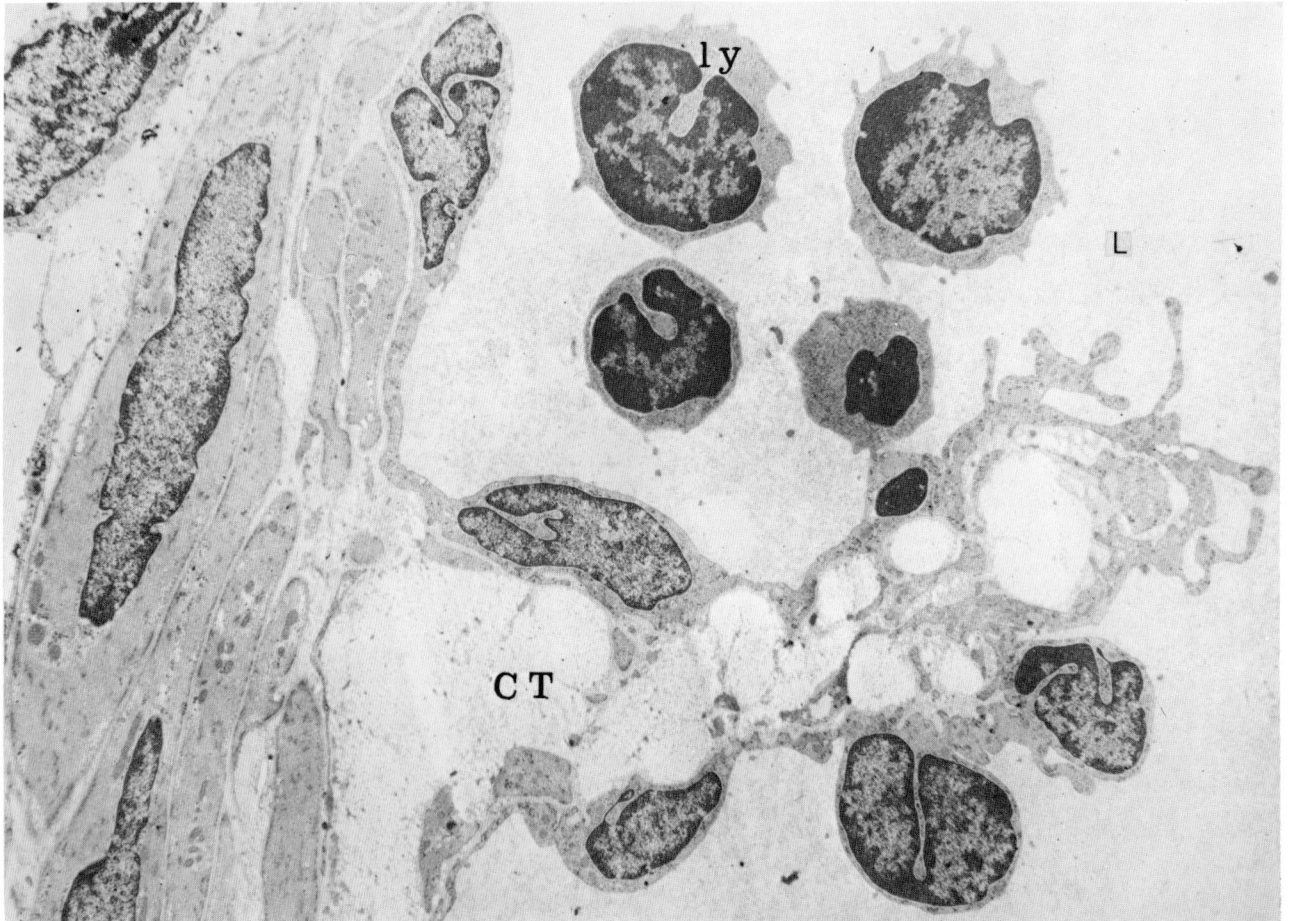

(b)

interspersed between a thin band of collagen fibers that separate the endothelial cells from the adjoining layer of smooth muscle cells comprising the tunica media.

17.5.2. Tunica media of collecting vessels

The smooth muscle cells which make up the tunica media of the collecting vessels may vary from single cells which coil around the vessel to several layers of smooth muscle cells (Figures 17.3, 17.4). The cells are also fusiform cylinders with tapering ends. Cytoplasmic projections extend from the smooth muscle cells to make contact with the endothelial cells of the lymphatic wall (Figures 17.3(a), 17.4). The nucleus occupies a central portion of the cell which is also the area of its greatest dimension (Figure 17.3(b)). The cytocentrum is located in the usual perinuclear position and consists of a pair of centrioles that lie in close proximity to the Golgi complex and its associated vesicles (Figure 17.4).

17.5.3. Tunica adventitia of collecting vessels

The outermost layer of the collecting vessels consists of fibroblasts that appear in close relation to bundles of collagen fibers which surround the smooth muscle cells. Small blood vessels and nonmyelinated axons are also seen in close association with the wall of collecting vessels (Figure 17.3(a)).

Figure 17.9. Lymphatic valves (L. V. Leak).

(a) SEM depicting the arrangement of the valves in collecting vessels from the lung. Lymphoctyes have been trapped in the funnel portion of the valve (arrow). This region also represents a segment of the vessel where several vessels anastomose. The projections (*) in the middle portion of this electron micrograph indicate the entry of a smaller vessel where the opening is guarded by a valve. (× 7,300)

(b) Thin section through the valve of a collecting vessel in which the endothelial cells fold into the lumen (L) and are separated by a corresponding fold of connective tissue (CT) extending from the wall of the vessel. Several lymphocytes (ly) are trapped at the base of the valve. (× 6,400)

Figure 17.10. Lymphatic valve leaflets.
SEM representing an enlargement of free leaflet portion of valve shown in Figure 17.8(a). A number of lymphocytes adhere to the inner surface of the leaflets and along their free edges (arrows). The flattened surfaces of the endothelial cells lining the leaflets can be more clearly appreciated(*). (×3,000)

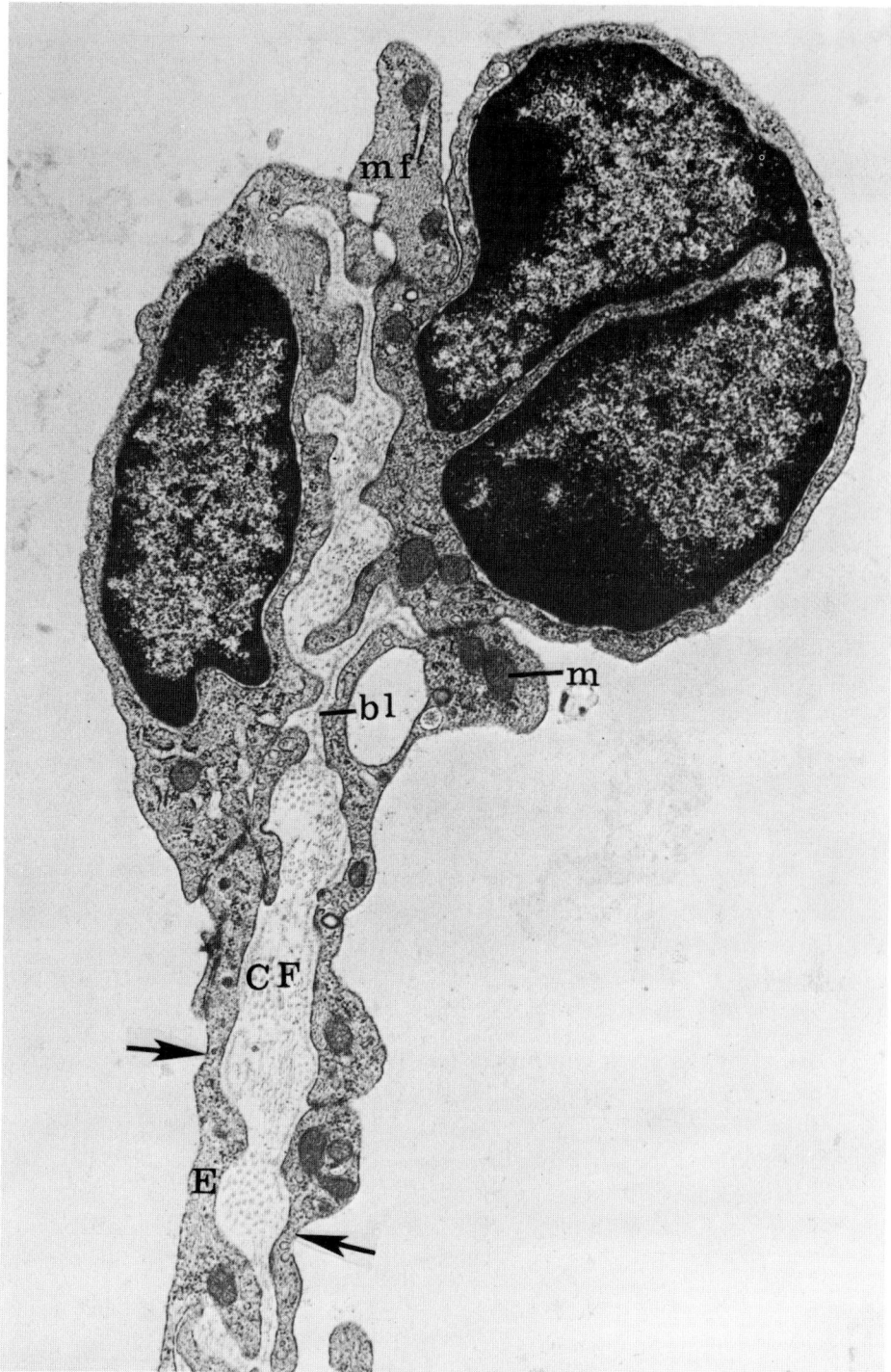

Figure 17.11. Free surface of lymphatic valve (L. V. Leak).
Thin section of the free surface indicating attenuated areas of the endothelial cells (arrows) as well as the thicker regions occupied by the nucleus (n). The cytoplasm contains numerous filaments (mf) and a small population of mitochondria (m). The endothelial cells (E) rest on a basal lamina (bl). The cells are separated from each other by a band of collagen fibers (CF). (×21,200)

18. Organization of the Primary Lymphatic Vessels

In discussing the organization of the lymphatic vascular system, it is important to consider its function as primarily a drainage system developed to accommodate the transduction of fluids and proteins which normally pass across the blood capillary wall and are not reabsorbed into the blood stream. The uptake of these interstitial fluids and proteins is accomplished by extremely thin-walled vessels. Prior to the application of electron microscopic techniques to study the structure and organization of the lymphatic system, the precise classification of the smaller and more delicate vessels which extended into the interstitial spaces still remained unclear.[49,84] Although Hudack and McMaster[49] demonstrated within the connective tissue of the dermis (Figure 18.1) a rich plexus of very small and delicate lymphatics that were highly permeable to colloidal particles injected into the interstitial spaces, there was still very little agreement on the classification of these smaller and more permeable lymphatics found throughout the various tissues of the body.

Just as the morphologist and physiologist used the terms capillary and sinusoids in classifying blood vessels whose walls provided an exchange of fluids and metabolites between the vessel and the surrounding interstitial space,[6,14,58,59,122,123] similar terms have been used to classify the thinnest wall lymphatic vessels. In considering the role of this sytem of vessels from a functional standpoint, the initial site of absorption occurs across the thin-walled lymphatic capillaries. The histologist traditionally described these vessels as having the following characteristics:

1. A variable caliber and large lumen relative to the wall thickness.
2. A more irregular appearance in their cross sectional outline than the blood capillaries.
3. An extremely attenuated endothelial lining.
4. No recognizable adventitia or pericytes.
5. No red blood cells within the lumen of the vessel.

Since these vessels develop secondarily to the major lymphatic trunks and represent the latest and smallest of the hierarchy of lymphatic vessels to be formed during the development of the organism, they are often referred to as terminal lymphatics. These vessels serve as the primary or initial site for the absorption of interstitial fluids, proteins, and cells. It therefore seems more appropriate to use the term lymphatic capillary for the more permeable and thinner walled lymphatic vessels which are located near the site of cellular metabolism and are in close proximity to the blood capillaries and venules. Their strategic location and specific anatomical features provide for a rapid and continuous drainage system for the removal of transit interstitial

184

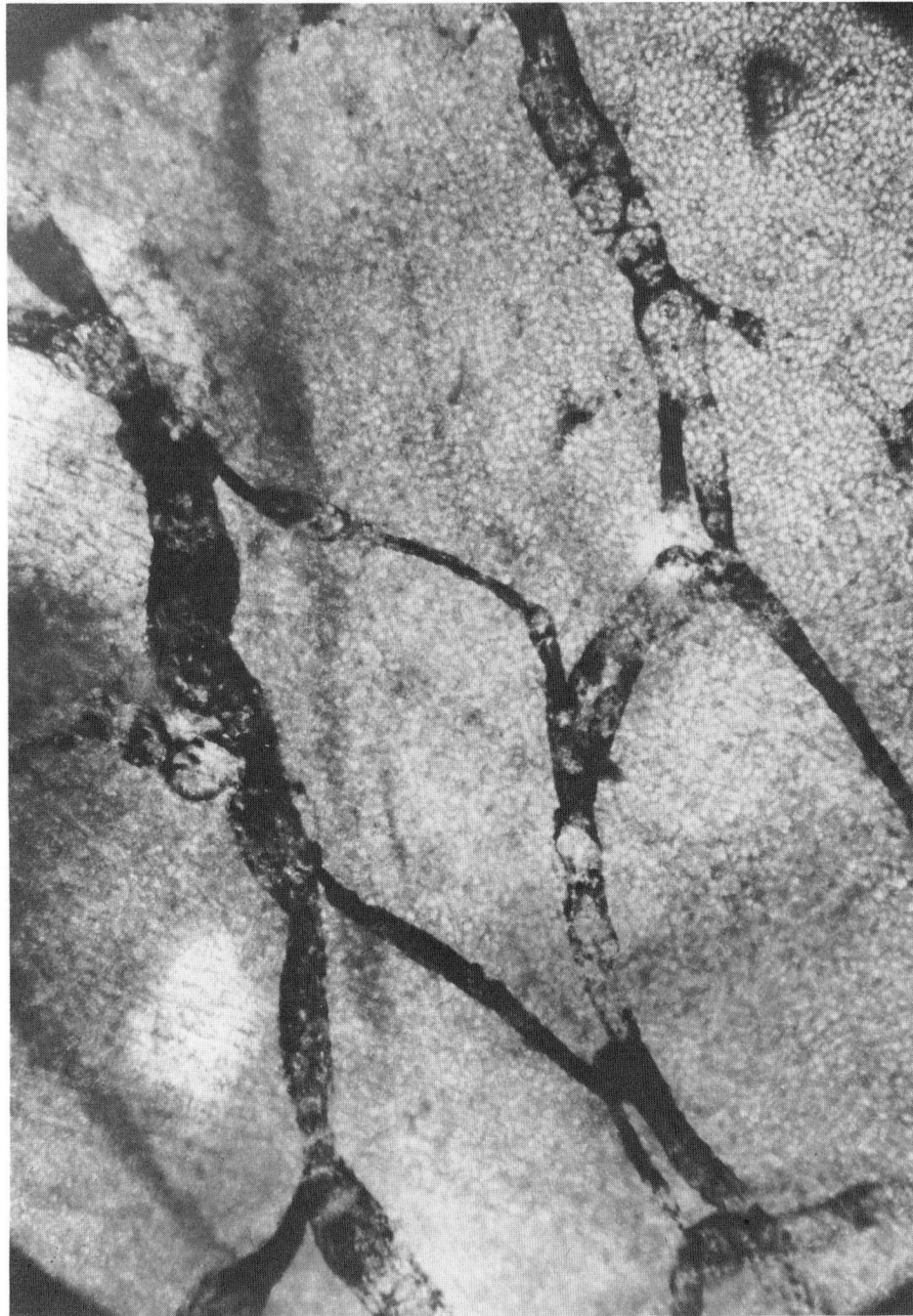

Figure 18.1. Demonstration of rich plexus of lymphatics within the dermis (L. V. Leak and J. F. Burke).
EM of whole mount preparation from guinea pig's ear injected with colloidal carbon to label the rich plexus of lymphatic vessels within the superficial areas of the dermis. (× 100)

fluids, proteins, and cells. With improved preservation techniques, significant advances in our understanding of the structural organization of the lymphatic vessels have come from electron microscopic studies of lymphatic vessels from various regions throughout the body. From such studies various aspects of the lymphatic morphology are revealed that usually escape recognition in the much thicker paraffin embedded specimens. With the higher resolution provided by electron microscopy, additional features have been observed which may now serve as criteria for identifying lymphatic vessels. These include the following:

1. The lining endothelium lacks a continuous basal lamina and cytoplasmic projections extend from both the luminal and abluminal sides giving a very irregular surface contour to the lymphatic endothelium in contrast to the more regular contours observed in blood capillaries and venules.
2. The lymphatic capillary wall is held in close apposition to the surrounding connective tissue by anchoring filaments.
3. Adjacent endothelial cells are extensively overlapping and are loosely adherent with only occasional foci which indicate attachment devices.

While the endothelial cells of collecting vessels are held in close apposition by maculae adherentes, adhesive devices are often absent between apposing endothelial cells of the lymphatic capillaries, making it easy for them to become separated. This feature permits particulate substances to readily pass into the lumen of the more delicate lymphatic vessels.[29,82,83] Therefore, the lymphatic sinusoids and lymphatic spaces (discontinuous lymphatic sinusoids) can be designated as the thin walled vessels of the lymphatic vascular system which are located at the site of the action, i.e., the site of cellular metabolism where there is rapid passage of fluids and cells from the interstitium into the lymphatic lumen.

18.1. Ultrastructure of the lymphatic capillary wall

The earlier electron microscopic studies of the lymphatic capillaries showed their fine structure to be similar to the blood capillary in that the wall of the lymphatic capillary consists of a continuous endothelial lining.[13,37,38,95] The major differences between the two types of vessels revealed at that time were that the lymphatic capillary was irregular in its contour and was not surrounded by a continuous basal lamina. After the use of improved preservation techniques, it became increasingly apparent that the lymphatic capillaries throughout various regions did possess other ultrastructural features that were specific, and different, setting them apart from the blood capillaries. By using various microinjection techniques combined with electron microscopic methods, a number of investigators have examined the lymphatic capillaries in the dermis,[13,18,20,37,71,116] the intestine,[19,24,53,95] the heart,[75,77] the diaphragm,[38,74] the lung,[56,61,63,69] the kidney,[50] the testis,[32,33] and ovary.[89]

18.1.1. Endothelial lining

Although lymphatic capillaries are difficult to recognize in routine histological preparation, the examination of one micrometer epon sections and ultrathin sections

186

reveals that the lymphatic capillary is composed of a continuous endothelial lining and that the cytoplasm is extremely attenuated over large areas of its circumference (Figure 18.2). The nucleus is located in the thicker regions of the cell which characteristically bulges into the lumen of the vessel. The extremely thin regions of the cytoplasm measure from 500 to 1,000 Å in thickness while the thicker areas measure up to 3 μm. The cytoplasm of the endothelial cell is bounded by a plasmalemma which has the appearance of the unit membrane structure described by Robertson[107]. The cytoplasm contains the usual complement of cellular organelles, many of which are restricted to the perinuclear region where the Golgi complex and a pair of centrioles can be observed. The Golgi complex, although not extensive, is observed as a complete unit and consists of stacked smooth surface cisternae and closely associated vesicles of various sizes.

The endoplasmic reticulum within the endothelial cells is of the rough variety and is randomly dispersed throughout the cytoplasm. In addition, ribosomes are scattered throughout the cytoplasm in single units and as polyribosomes.

Large amounts of endoplasmic reticulum of the rough variety are characteristic of cells that have a high rate of protein synthesis for extracellular discharge.[9,52,94] The small amount of rough endoplasmic reticulum in the endothelial cells of lymphatic capillaries perhaps indicates a very slow or very limited turn over of proteins for these cells, i.e., the cell is engaged in protein synthesis only as a part of its own metabolism.

Mitochondria occur throughout the perinuclear area and are also randomly distributed throughout the attenuated rims of the cytoplasm (Figures 17.9, 18.4). They present oval and elongated profiles and display an internal structural arrangement characteristic of mitochondria in other cell types. The outer membrane is continuous while the inner membrane is invaginated into the matrix to form cristae. Profiles of microtubules are observed in the cytoplasm, usually in the vicinity of centrioles as well as throughout other areas of the cytoplasm. They measure approximately 250 Å in diameter and are generally aligned parallel to the long axis of the endothelial cells.

A striking feature of the lymphatic capillary endothelium is the appearance of numerous cytoplasmic filaments which measure 40 to 60 Å in diameter. They are usually arranged parallel to the long axis of the cell and are aggregated into discrete bundles or fascicles within both peripheral and central cytoplasmic areas of the perinuclear region (Figures 18.3, 18.4). In addition, the cytoplasmic filaments are also arranged in irregular patterns. The fascicles of cytoplasmic filaments which appear subjacent to the plasmalemma often give the impression of dense plaques suggestive of possible attachment sites along the plasmalemma. Such areas are reminiscent of dense plaques that are found between the plasma membrane and actin filaments in smooth muscle cells. Although cytoplasmic filaments are observed in endothelial cells of blood capillaries,[85] they are not as abundant as those found in the endothelial cells of lymphatic capillaries. Since the initial studies of Majno and Leventhal[85] and Majno et al.[86] on cytoplasmic filaments in endothelial cells of blood capillaries, numerous morphological and biochemical studies have provided convincing evidence that cytoplasmic filaments in a variety of non-muscle cells are responsible for the contractility of these cells. Cytoplasmic filaments having the properties of actin have been identified in *Physarum*,[90,120] *Acanthamoeba*,[100] and blood platelets.[3] Recent studies of Lauweryns et al.[62] demonstrated that cytoplasmic filaments in lymphatic endothelial cells in the lungs were capable of forming arrowhead complexes with

(a)

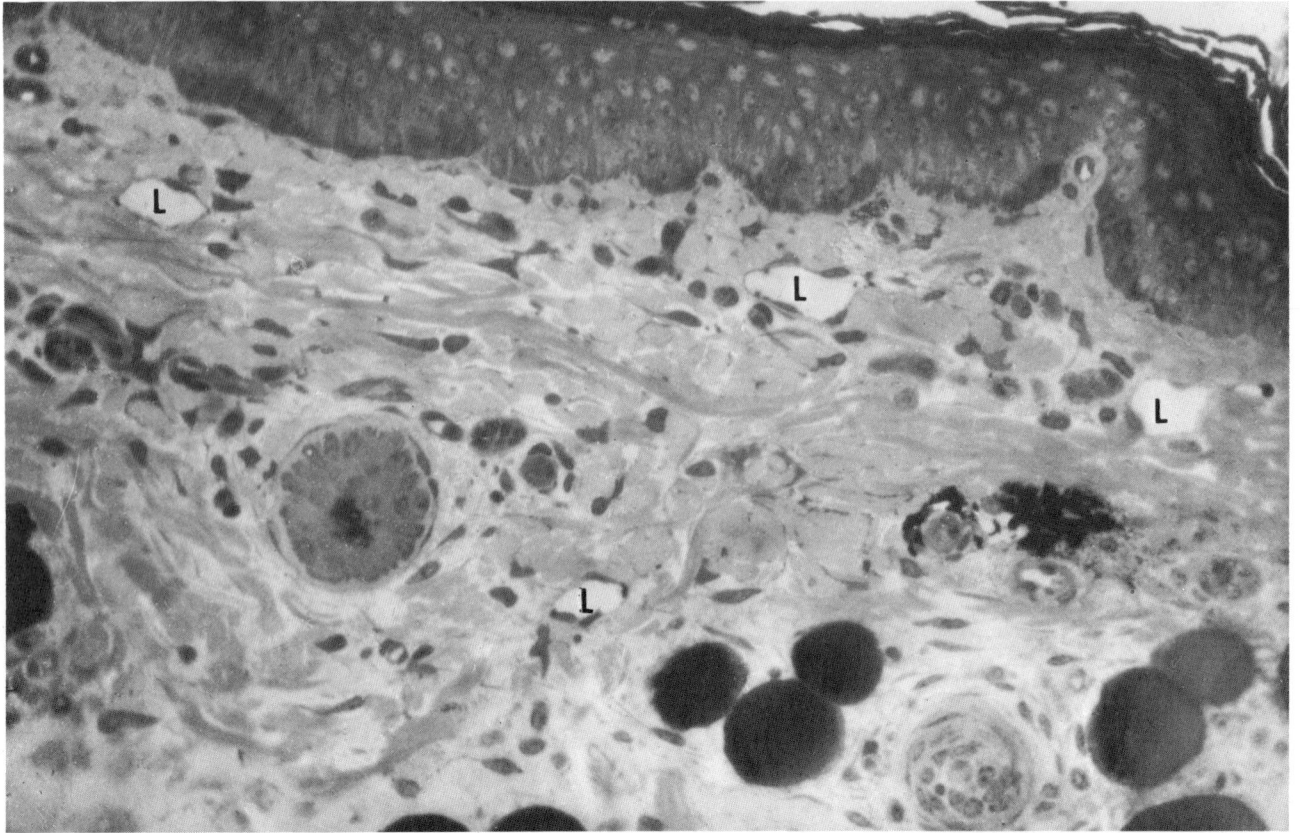

(b)

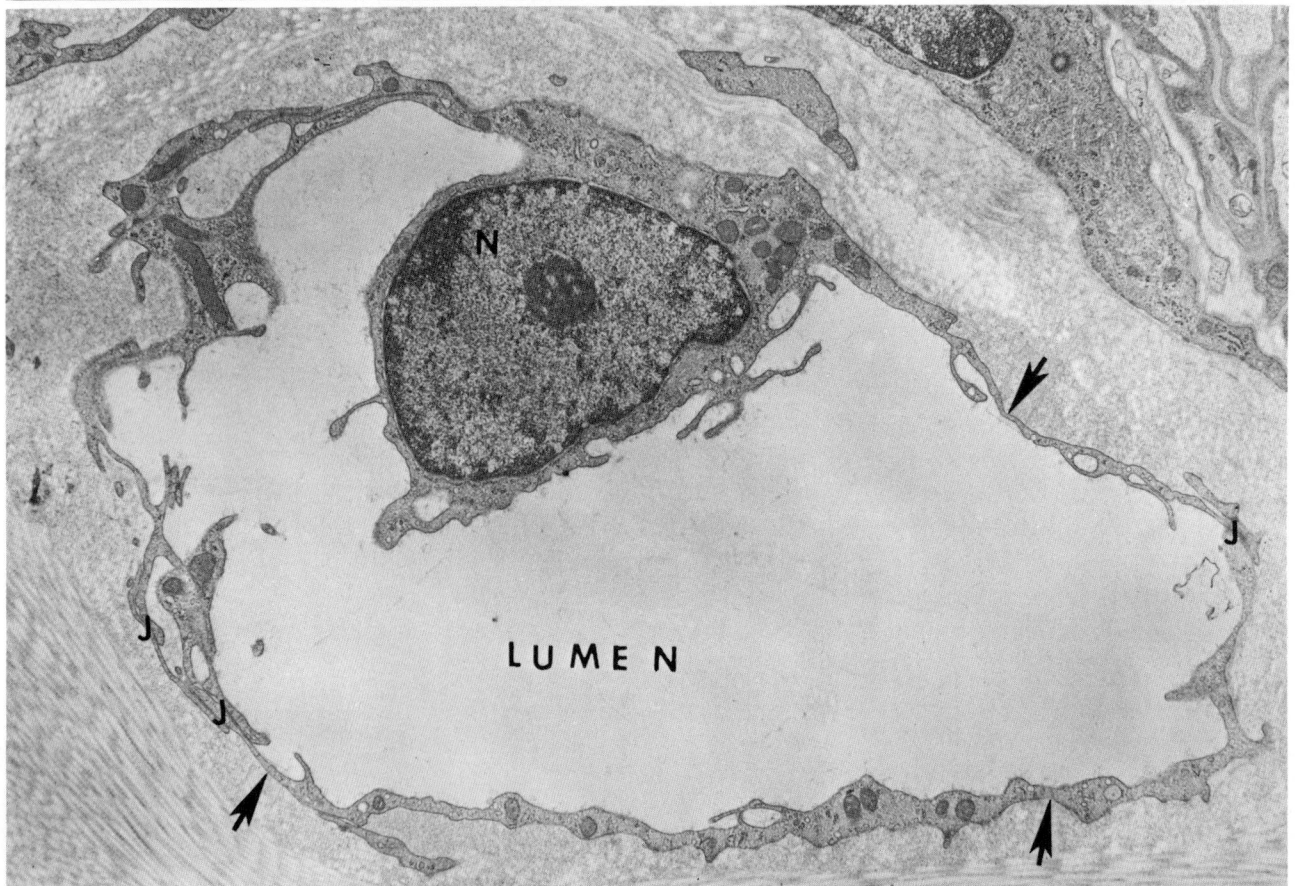

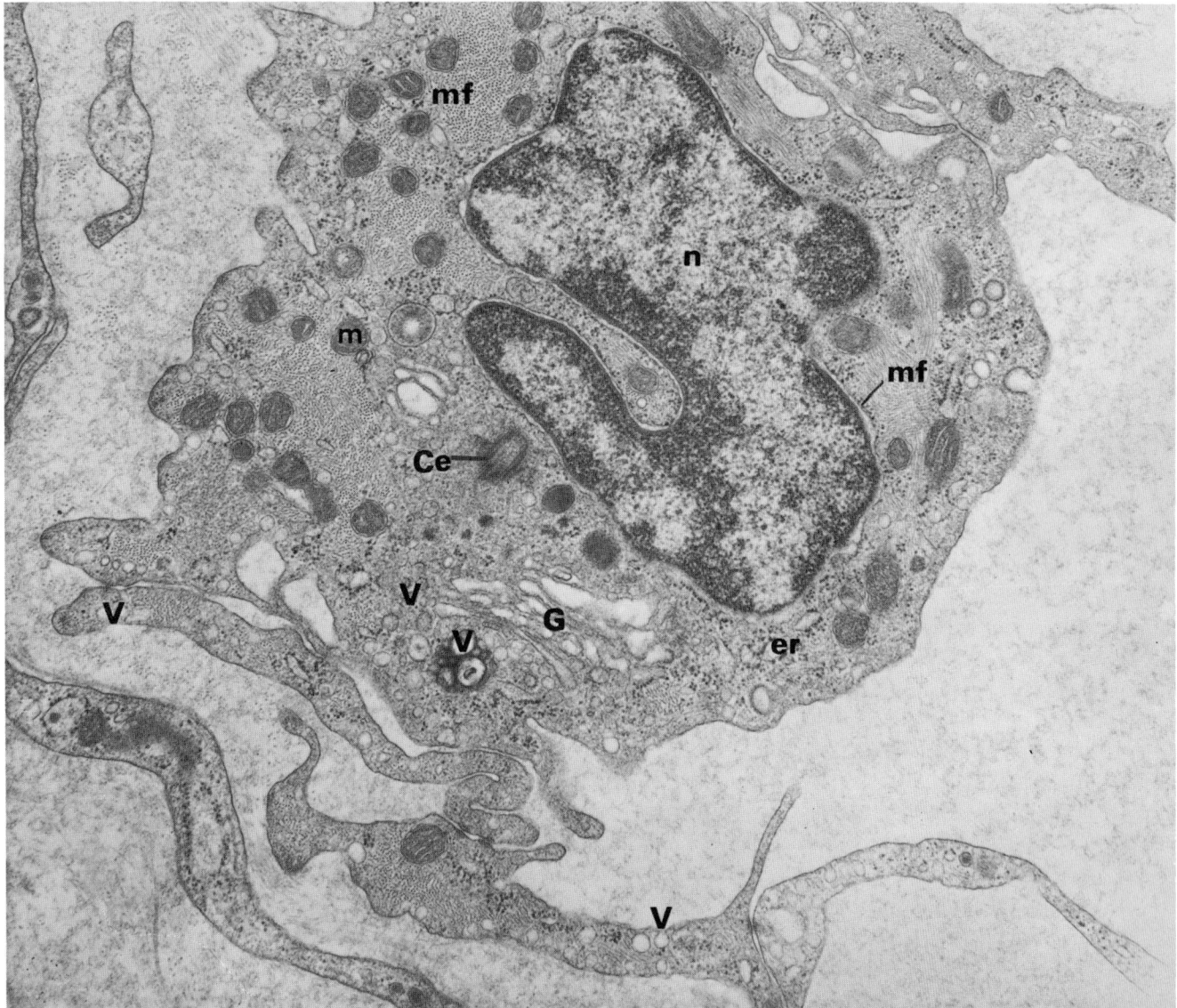

Figure 18.3. Perinuclear region of endothelial cell.
Portion of the endothelial cells of a lymphatic capillary in an area occupied by the nucleus (n).
The cytoplasm surrounding the nucleus contains large numbers of cytoplasmic filaments (mf),
mitochondria (m), a centriole (Ce), a Golgi complex (G), with numerous associated vesicles
(v). er: endoplasmic reticulum. (×25,000)

**Figure 18.2. Lymphatic capillaries (L. V. Leak and J. F. Burke 18.2(a), L. V. Leak
18.2(b)).**

(a) Photomicrograph of an epon embedded section from a guinea pig's ear showing the
distribution of lymphatic capillaries (L) within the dermis. (×450)
(b) Cross section of lymphatic capillary from a guinea pig's ear. The irregular profile and the
close apposition of the capillary to the surrounding connective tissue is evident. Several
areas of the cytoplasm are extremely attenuated (arrows). Adjacent endothelial cells overlap each other as indicated in the intercellular junctions (j). (×11,000)

189

heavy meromyosin which were similar to those formed by actin filaments in muscle cells.

By using the techniques of immunofluorescence, McCuskey[81] demonstrated actomysin in endothelial cells of blood capillaries and sinusoids in the liver, and suggested that the regulation of blood flow through these vessels was controlled by contractile filaments in the cytoplasm of the cells which are responsive to vasoactive substances.

Like the contraction of medium size arteries and veins, the rhythmic contractions noted for the lymphatic collecting vessels can be attributed to the smooth muscle cells within the tunica media of their walls. It is well established that smooth muscle cells provide the motile force for contractions in these vessels.[36,47,48,57,117,118] The smooth muscle cells that are closely applied to the lymphatic endothelium of the collecting vessels are under neurological control as indicated by the number of closely applied axons. In studying lymphatic capillaries in dermal lymphatics with cinephotographic methods, we were able to observe a rhythmic contraction of these delicate lymphatic vessels.[67] Since smooth muscle cells are absent from the walls of lymphatic capillaries, it is suggested that the cytoplasmic filaments represent the intrinsic contractile elements for these vessels.

The endothelial cells of lymphatic capillaries are also distinguished by the presence of numerous plasmalemmal invaginations that extend into the cytoplasm for varying depths along both its luminal and abluminal surfaces (Figures 17.9, 18.4). These invaginations appear in the periphery and also within the deeper regions of the cytoplasm as vesicles that often appear to be in transit across the lymphatic endothelium. They are of a similar dimension to the micropinocytotic vesicles (approximately 750 Å in diameter) that occur in the endothelial cells of blood vessels.[7,92,93,105] When the tracer lanthanum is used in the fixation procedure, this electron-dense substance occurs in the invaginations that were open to the luminal and connective tissue fronts. However, vesicles within the deeper regions of the cytoplasm lack the tracer particles.[66] When colloidal tracers such as ferritin, thorium dioxide, biological carbon as well as the electron-dense protein horseradish perioxidase are injected interstitially and samples taken at various time intervals, these tracers can be observed in the plasmalemmal invaginations and in vesicles within the deeper regions of the cytoplasm where they may lie in close association with the Golgi apparatus (*see below*).

Chemical studies have demonstrated the presence of acid hydrolases within the larger vesicles of endothelial cells. They have an electron-dense central core and represent lysosomes. It is of interest to note that the endothelial cells in lymphatic capillaries in the regressing tail fin of amphibians contain a large number of autographic vacuoles.[64] The presence of these vacuoles coincides with an increase in

---

Figure 18.4. Distribution of organelles in endothelial cell (L. V. Leak)

(a) Numerous cytoplasmic filaments (mf), mitochondria (m), and vesicles (v) of various sizes are visible throughout the cytoplasm as well as near the periphery of the cell. Numerous free ribosomes (r) are also dispersed throughout the cytoplasm. Colloidal ferritin was injected interstitially several minutes before the animal was sacrificed. It is distributed throughout the lumen (L) and plasmalemmal invaginations (v) as well as along the connective tissue (CT) front of the vessel. ($\times$ 53,000)

(b) This segment of the cell shows numerous cytoplasmic filaments (mf) aggregated into fascicles. Many anchoring filaments (af) can be seen along the abluminal surface of the endothelial cell. L: lumen. ($\times$ 34,000)

(a)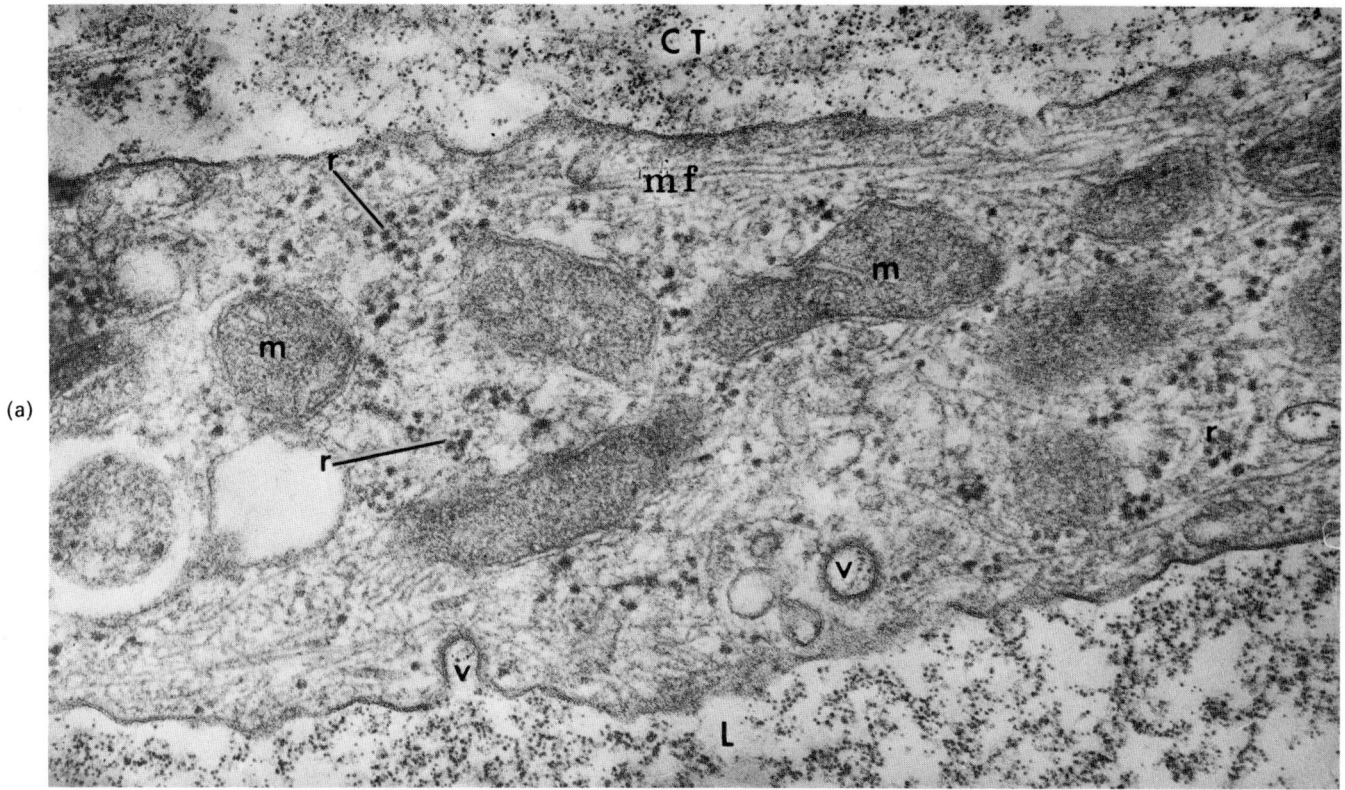

(b)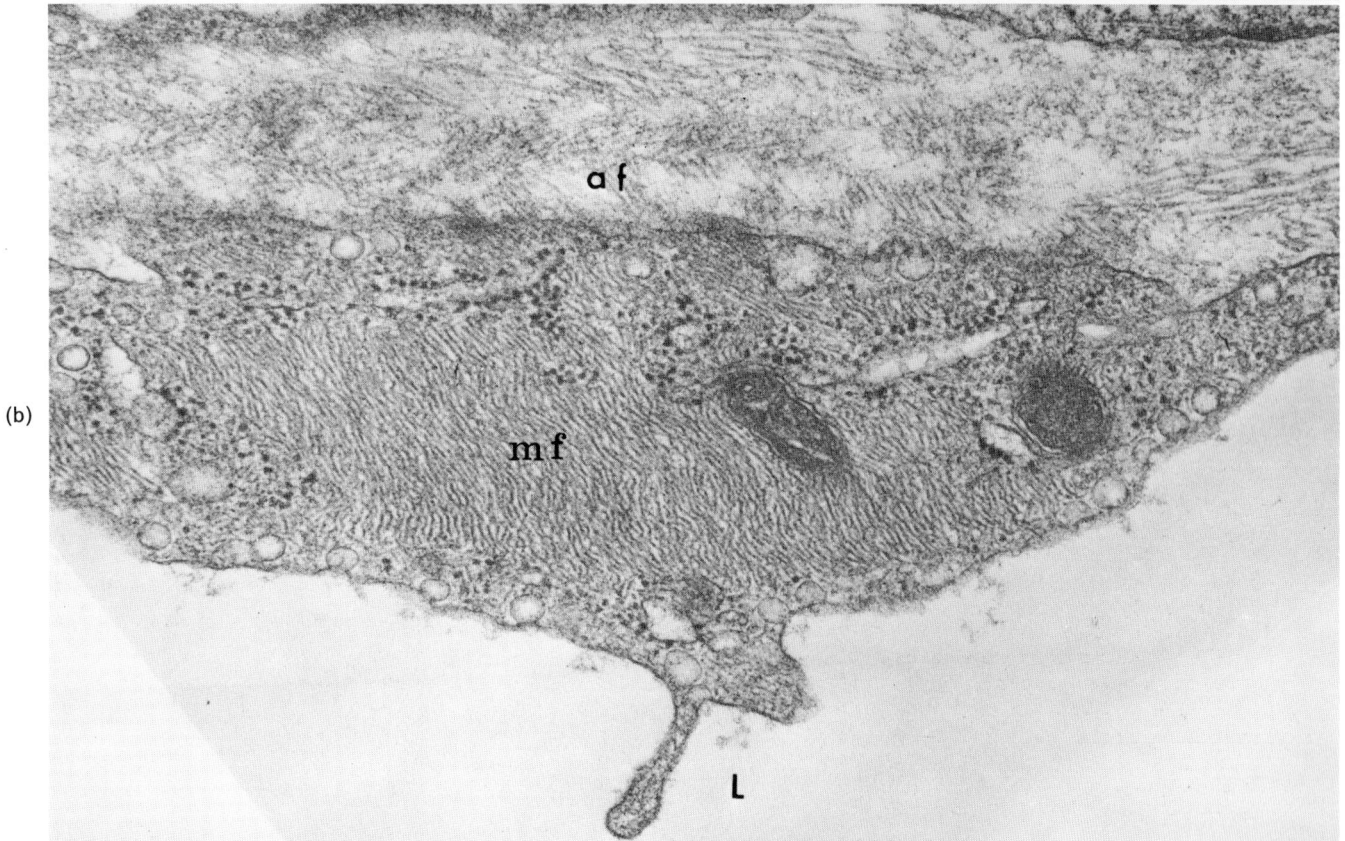

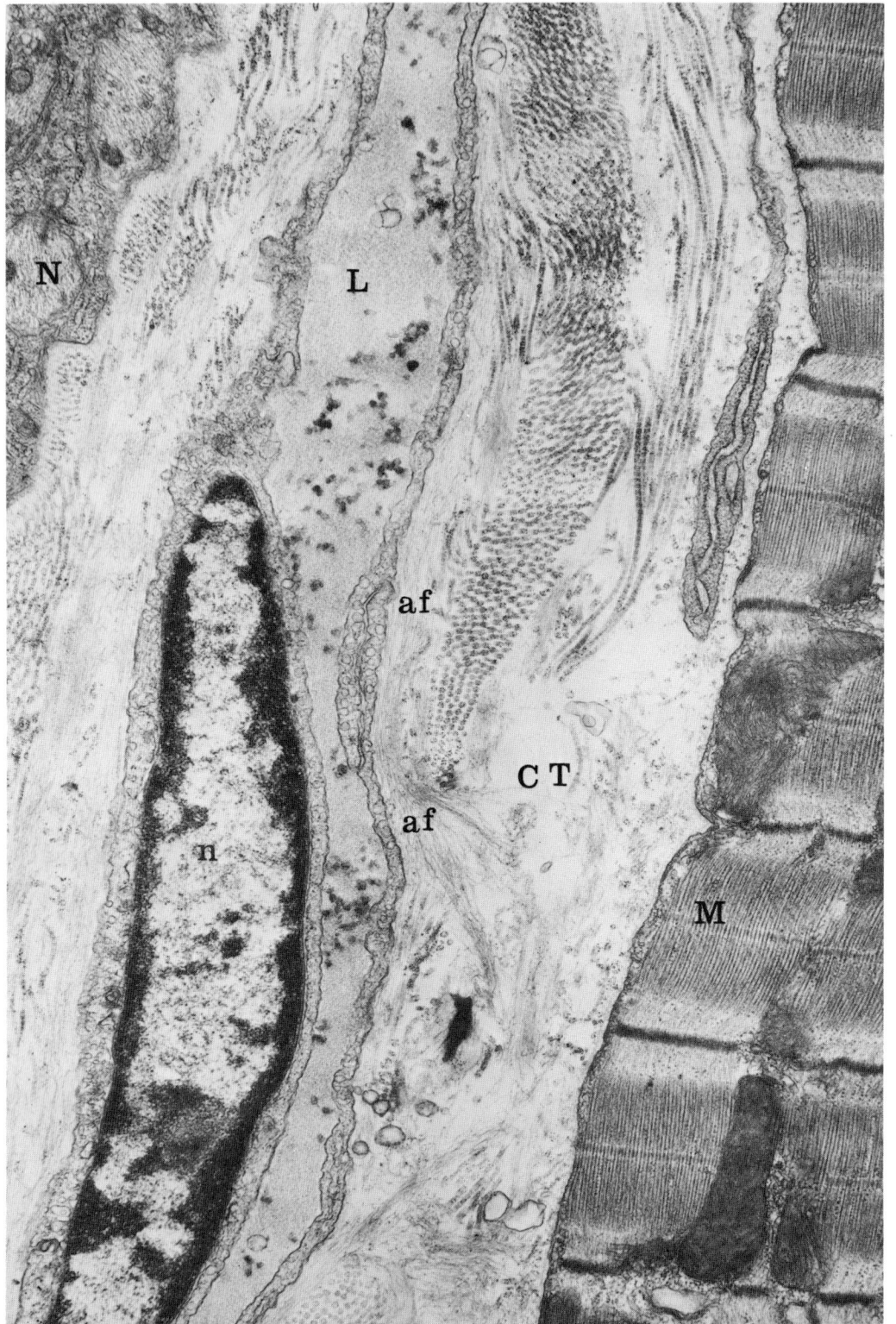

soluble acid hydrolases for the cytoplasmic particles in this tissue[119] and suggests that the lymphatic vessels also play a major role in the intracellular digestion of engulfed substances that are being removed from the surrounding interstitium during tail fin resorption.

18.1.2. Intercellular junctions of lymphatic capillaries

The lymphatic capillary wall is distinguished by a large number of intercellular junctions in which the adjacent cell margins are extensively overlapped (Figure 18.6). The distance between apposing cells may reach several micrometers, extending the total length of the intercellular cleft (see Figure 19.2(a)). They represent patent intercellular junctions which are unique to lymphatic capillaries. It is through such open clefts that large molecules, particulate substances, and cells enter the lymphatic lumen (see Figure 19.2(b)). On the other hand, in some of the overlapping junctions there are regular foci in which the adjacent plasma membranes are closely approximated (Figure 18.6). When such sites are viewed at higher magnifications, it becomes immediately apparent that the apposed membranes are held together by *maculae adherentes* or desmosomes where the distance between apposing cells ranges from 100 to 250 Å in width. Occasionally there are areas of close apposition where short segments of the intercellular cleft are obliterated, and prevent the passage of such molecules as lanthanum and peroxidase (Figure 18.7(a)). These intermittent seals within the intercellular cleft are formed by a fusion between the outer leaflets of adjacent cell membranes and are recognized as quintuple structures which represent *maculae occludentes* (Figure 18.7(b)). These specialized sites serve to maintain cell to cell adhesion without causing a complete obliteration along the total length of the intercellular cleft, providing, instead, a spot-weld effect for maintaining a close continuity between cells along the total length of the lymphatic capillary wall. At the same time, many of the adjacent cell margins remain loosely apposed to each other and are easily separated to form patent channels. These are readily available to accommodate the rapid passage of excessive amounts of interstitial fluids, particulate components, and cells into the lumina of lymphatic capillaries.

18.1.3. Extracellular components of lymphatic capillary wall

Unlike blood capillaries, lymphatic capillaries lack a definitive basal lamina. Its absence provides a feature which serves as a major criterion for differentiating lymphatic capillaries from blood capillaries. In areas where short segments of a basal

---

Figure 18.5. Demonstration of lymphatic anchoring filaments and uptake of colloidal carbon.

Lymphatic capillary within the epicardial region in the heart of a dog. Colloidal carbon was injected into the interstitial areas of the myocardium prior to fixation by perfusion. The lumen (L) of the lymphatic vessel is filled with a gray precipitate of lymph as well as numerous carbon particles which have entered the lymphatic system. The walls of the lymphatic vessel are extremely attenuated except in areas occupied by the nucleus (n). The abluminal surface contains numerous anchoring filaments (af) which extend out into the adjoining connective tissue (CT). A portion of a myofiber (M) is shown to the right and part of a nerve axon (N) is visible at upper left. ($\times 25,300$)

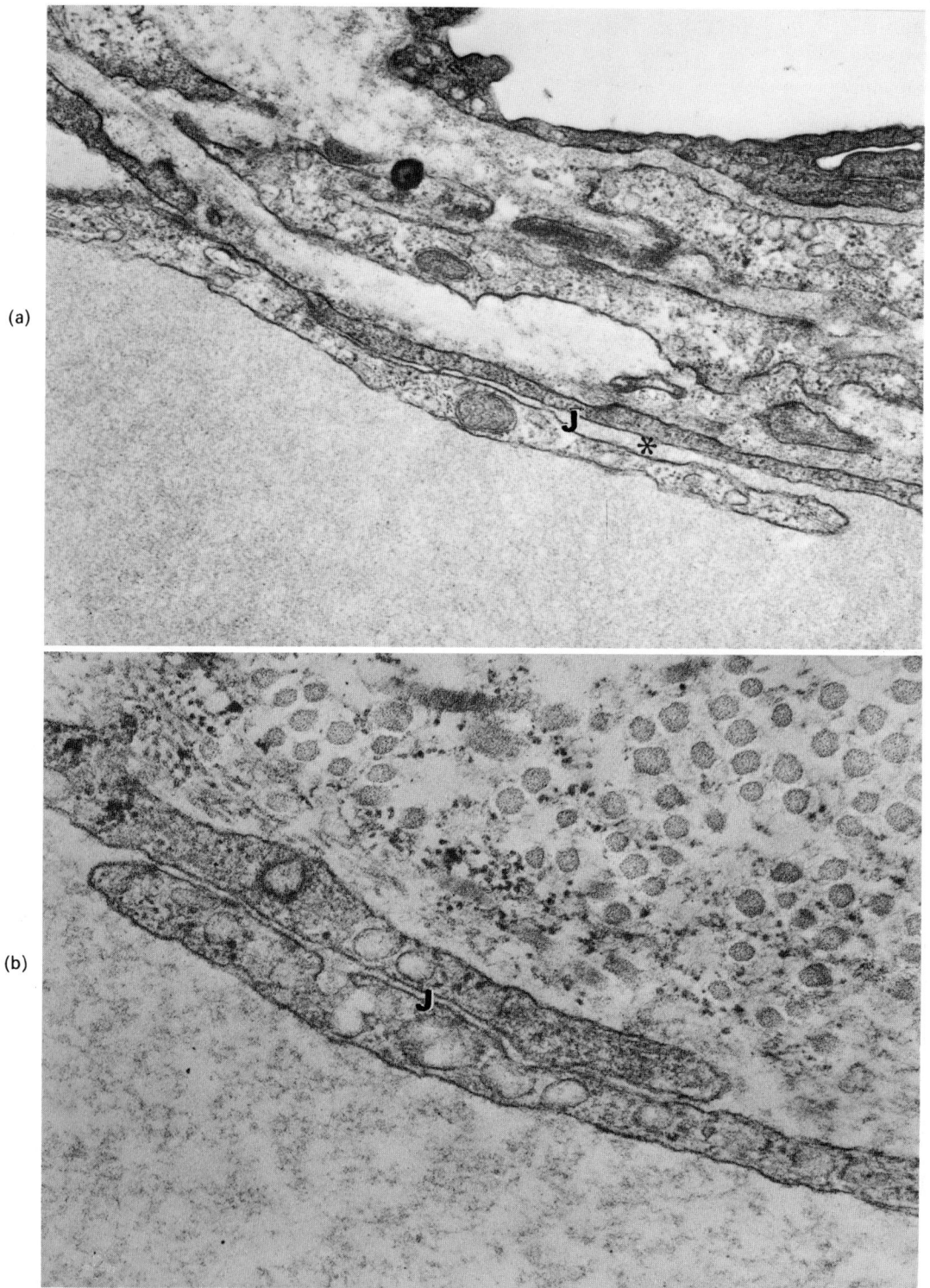

Figure 18.6. Intercellular junctions in lymphatic capillary wall (L. V. Leak).

(a), (b) The extent to which the adjacent endothelial cell margins overlap each other to form intercellular junctions (j) is clearly shown. The width of the intercellular cleft is quite variable along the intercellular junction (*). ((a) ×56,000, (b) ×73,000)

lamina are observed, it is presumed that such areas represent a transition zone between a lymphatic capillary and a larger collecting vessel since the latter possesses a continuous basal lamina. It is of interest to note that although a continuous basal lamina is observed around blood capillaries, it is very irregular and often absent from newly formed segments of regenerated blood capillaries.[17,112,113] These developing blood capillaries are also very permeable to large molecules.

18.1.4. Anchoring filaments

The earlier studies of Pullinger and Florey[102] suggested that collagen and reticular fibers provided a structural basis for connecting the lymphatic capillary wall to the surrounding extracellular elements. With the increased resolution provided by electron microscopy, collagen bundles and small fibers were described as investing the lymphatic capillaries. However, the close proximity of collagen and reticular fibers to the lymphatic endothelium described earlier by Pullinger and Florey[102] was not clearly defined in these initial electron microscopic studies.[13,38] In subsequent investigations more refined fixation and staining techniques were used to study the ultrastructure of the lymphatic capillaries. Leak and Burke[70,71,72] demonstrated that fine filaments ranging from 60 to 100 Å in diameter inserted within a densely staining substance on the external surface of the unit membrane of the endothelial cells and extended for various distances into the adjoining interstitium between collagen bundles and connective tissue cells (Figures 18.4, 18.5). The term lymphatic anchoring filaments was used to describe these structures because of their close topographical relationship to the lymphatic capillary wall and the surrounding connective tissue components. Observations of lymphatic capillaries in normal and edematous conditions suggest that these anchoring filaments provide a structural basis for maintaining a firm connection between the lymphatic capillary wall and the surrounding connective tissue areas.

In studies of the topographical relationship between lymphatic capillaries and the surrounding interstitium, Drinker and Field[27] suggested that "A further possibility for which no proof exists is that the delicate lymph capillaries are fixed to the surrounding tissue by fine strands of reticulum and that muscular movement by pulling on the strands may induce distortion and temporary openings through which fluids enter eventually to reach a valve trunk from which escape does not occur." The demonstration of anchoring filaments attached to the abluminal surface of the lymphatic capillary wall[72] provides a structural basis for "fixing" the lymphatic capillary wall to the surrounding interstitium. It is suggested that an increase in interstitial fluids and plasma proteins would also increase interstitial pressure around the circumference of the lymphatic vessel, thereby increasing the total fluid pressure within the interstitial space. There would also be an accompanying movement of collagen bundles, elastic fibers, and other connective tissue components in order to accommodate the increase in fluid volume within the connective tissue areas. This causes an expansion of the interstitial space and, therefore, produces tension on the collagen bundles and elastic fibers in which the anchoring filaments are firmly embedded. Tension would also be placed or transferred to the lymphatic capillary wall to which the anchoring filaments are inserted. Therefore, as fluids and plasma proteins accumulate within the interstitium under normal physiological conditions, there would be

(a)

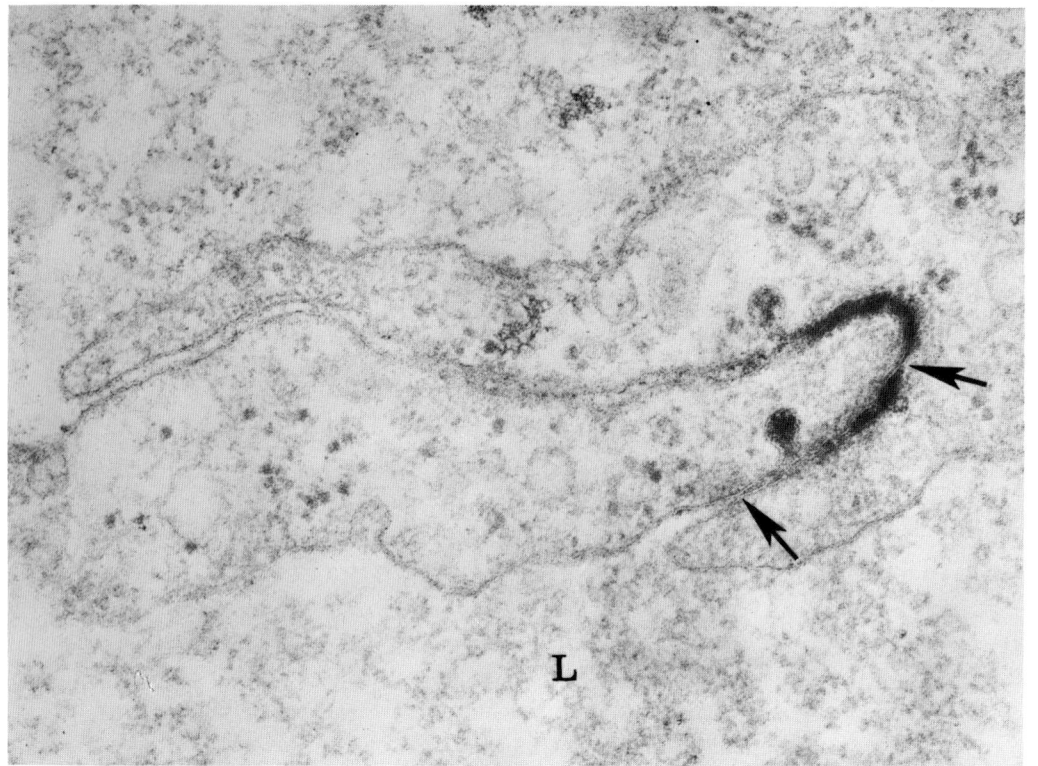

L

(b)

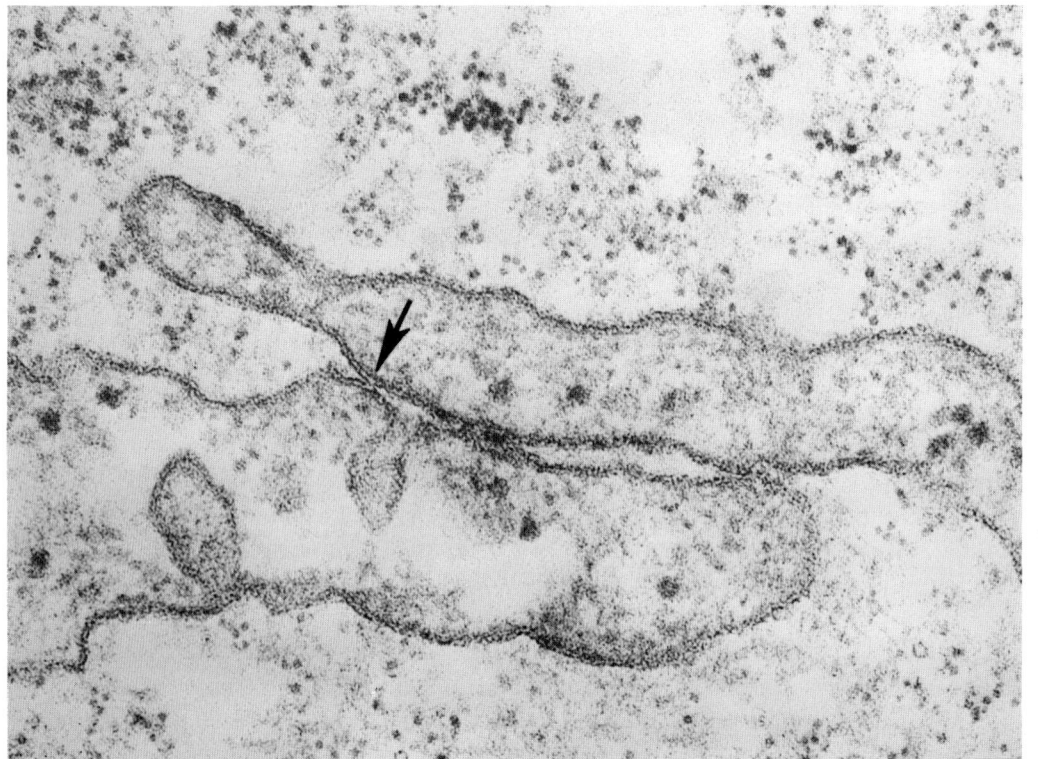

a separation of collagen and elastic fibers. The sites along the lymphatic capillary wall, to which anchoring filaments are attached, would also be pulled along with the collagen and connective tissue fibers. This would result in a widening of the lymphatic capillary lumen as the extensively overlapping and loosely adjacent endothelial cell junctions become separated to provide patent intercellular junctions (see Figure 19.2). This structural arrangement would also explain why histological evaluations of an intense inflammatory reaction demonstrate venules that are compressed while the lymphatic capillaries are greatly dilated.[102] Additional evidence which points to the stabilizing and "fixing" effect of the anchoring filaments on the lymphatic wall is obtained from studies in which hyaluronidase is injected into edematous foot pads of rats. On subsequent examination at the light and ultrastructural levels, the lymphatics are observed to be collapsed.[11] High resolution electron microscopy reveals that there is a disruption of the connective tissue ground substance (i.e., glycosaminoglycans) which is presumably due to solubilization and subsequent disruption of hyaluronate which forms the backbone of the glycosaminoglycans molecule in which anchoring filaments are embedded. Such a breakdown of ground substance components would reduce its supporting effect for the anchoring filaments.

Figure 18.7. *Maculae occludentes* (L. V. Leak).
(a), (b) The close apposition at focal points between adjacent endothelial cells (arrows) represents *maculae occludentes*. In (a) lanthanum gas used as a tracer is eliminated at several points (arrows) indicating areas of fusion between opposing cell membranes. L: lumen. ((a) ×62,000, (b) × 137,600)

19. Lymphatic Capillary Permeability and Lymph Formation

The use of electron-dense tracer substances has made it possible to monitor the movements of these substances across the blood–tissue interface at the electron microscopic level. Recent studies have demonstrated that the general flow pattern of proteins is from the blood capillary lumen into the interstitium[16, 54, 55] while a number of physiological studies[87] have demonstrated that the major direction of transport for the lymphatic capillary is from the connective tissue into its lumen as indicated by a constant removal of fluids and particulate components from the surrounding connective tissue areas. Although it was well established that these vessels are capable of rapidly removing interstitially injected vital dyes and colloidal particles,[49] the structural basis for lymphatic capillary permeability remained controversial because the resolution provided by light microscopy was not adequate to give satisfactory information on the precise relationships between adjacent endothelial cells. Subsequent studies using electron-dense tracer particles at the electron microscopic level, however, showed that the major uptake occurs by way of intercellular junctions (Figures 19.2, 19.4). There is also vesicular uptake of large molecules and particulate substances. Electron-dense particles of varying sizes have been used by a number of investigators in studying the permeability of lymphatic capillaries. These include colloidal ferritin,[13, 66] thorium dioxide,[10, 70, 71, 72] colloidal carbon,[10, 13, 37, 65, 66, 71, 89] and horseradish peroxidase.[24, 67]

Within a few seconds of injection of a suspension of tracer substances into the interstitial space, the tracer particles are observed in the interstitium and the lumen of lymphatic capillaries. In addition, particles are also observed within plasmalemmal invaginations and vesicles of various sizes (see Figures 18.4(a), 18.5). The role of micropinocytotic vesicles and the transport of substances across endothelial cells was recognized by Palade[92] who suggested that materials could pass from one side of the cell to the other. Subsequent studies of Bennett[4] led to the concept that membrane flow and vesiculation may be important transport mechanisms responsible for carrying particles, large molecules, and ions within, into, and out of the cell. Since the early investigations on capillary permeability, much evidence has accumulated from morphological and physiological studies which suggests that extracellular materials may be internalized by endothelial cells as well as by a variety of other cell types following inpocketing of the plasma membrane to form vesicles.[2, 16, 31, 55, 110, 114] It is of special interest to note that interstitially injected colloidal particles and intravenously injected tracer particles and proteins (i.e., colloidal ferritin and horseradish peroxidase) are observed within plasmalemmal vesicles within a short period of time. There is also evidence for vesicular uptake from the luminal surface of the lymphatic capillary

198

endoethelial cells. Therefore, vesicular uptake occurs at both the luminal and connective tissue fronts.

In following the movement of fluids and large molecules across the endothelium of blood capillaries, the direction of movement proceeds from the luminal to the connective tissue front.[16,55,114] However, in the lymphatic endothelial cells, particles are removed from both luminal and connective tissue fronts within vesicles that aggregate into large vacuoles. This is evidenced by the accumulation of inert particles such as carbon and thorium dioxide into aggregates within vacuoles that may reach several micromillimetres in diameter and can be observed up to twelve months following intercellular injections of the particles (Figure 19.3). These tracer experiments indicate that vesicular transport is not unidirectional in the lymphatic capillary endothelial cells, but that the transport of large molecules and proteins within vesicles proceeds from both luminal and connective tissue fronts toward the central cytoplasm (cytocentrum). Here the smaller vesicles become fused with lysosomal vacuoles that contain hydrolytic enzymes for intracellular digestion.[21,22] Exogenous protein such as peroxidase and ferritin that accumulate in large lysosomal vacuoles are broken into smaller units within 18–24 hours,[66,67] presumably for utilization by the cells.[7,36,42,104] This, however, is not the case for the inert substances such as colloidal carbon, thorium, and latex spheres which are injected interstitially. As indicated above, these inert particles accumulate into very large vacuoles which remain in the cells for an indefinite period.[66,72]

Evidence for the rapid movement of fluids and proteins across the blood–tissue–lymph interface has also come from experiments in which peroxidase is injected intravenously.[41] Peroxidase can be made visible by incubation in a medium containing 3'3'–diaminobenzidine and hydrogen peroxide in a tris buffer. The interaction of this enzyme with the substrate produces an electron-dense product whose density is considerably enhanced when the tissue is postfixed in osmium tetroxide.[41] This procedure provides a means for observing with the electron microscope the pathways for the movement of intravenously injected proteins across the blood–tissue–lymph interface at successive time intervals.

The examination of tissues within one minute after peroxidase injection shows the presence of this exogenous protein within blood capillaries and along the connective tissue fronts of blood capillaries. Within five minutes there is considerable peroxidase staining throughout the connective tissue and within vesicles of lymphatic capillaries (Figure 19.1(a)). The greatest intensity of peroxidase staining is achieved between 15 and 30 minutes as demonstrated by the dense accumulation within the lumina of lymphatic capillaries (Figure 19.1(b)). After this time, the intensity of peroxidase within the connective tissue area and within the lymphatic lumen gradually decreases (Figure 19.1(c)). These observations are significant in that they are in agreement with the findings of Clemente and Palade[16] which indicated that a concentration of peroxidase within the thoracic duct lymph was maximal at twenty minutes after intravenous injections.

In following the passage of this tracer across the connective tissue lymph interface, it is evident that intense peroxidase staining occurs within the clefts of intercellular junctions. There is also an intense peroxidase staining within plasmalemmal vesicles for periods of up to one hour. However, after one hour, the staining of plasmalemmal vesicles is minimal, but there is a large number of lysosomal vacuoles

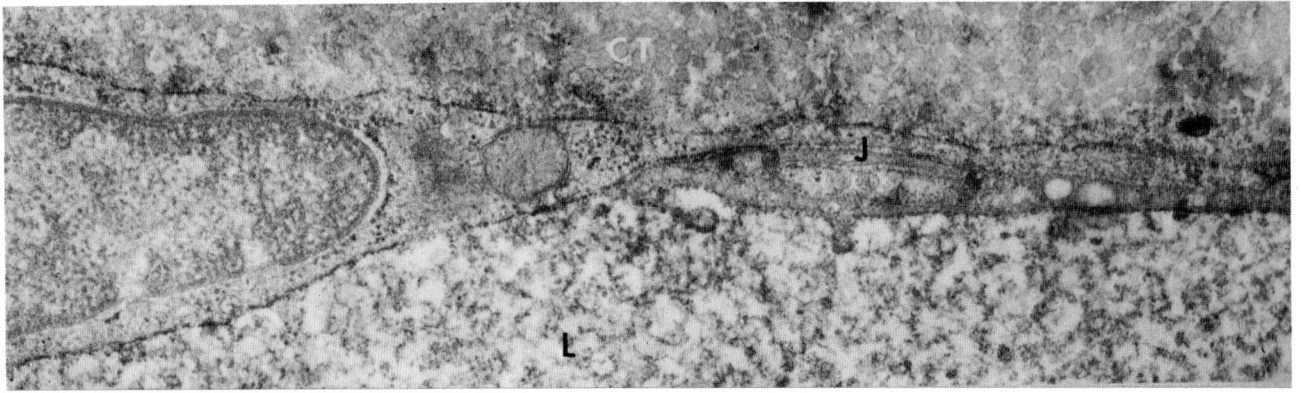

(a)

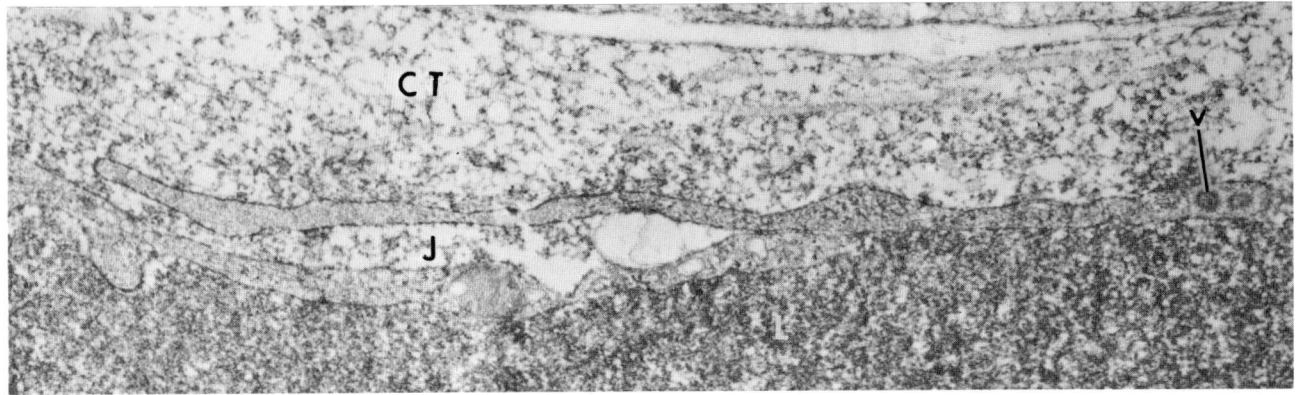

(b)

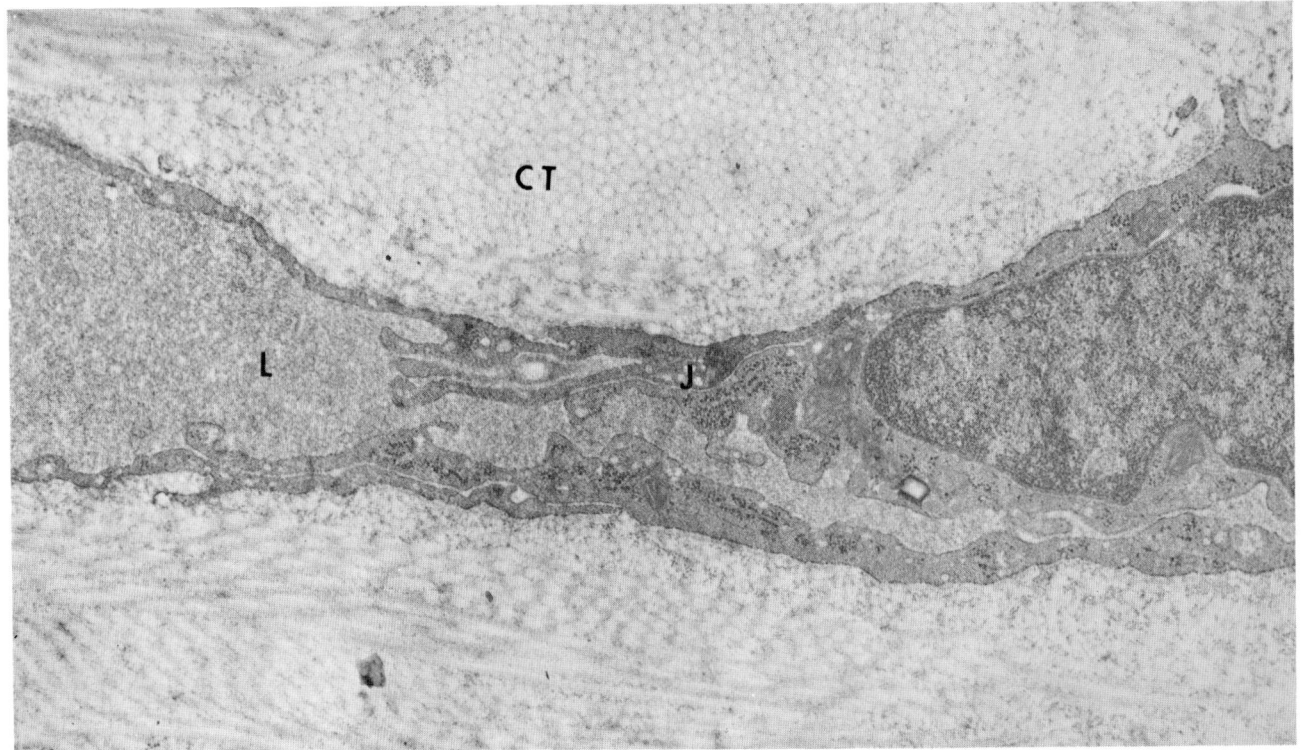

(c)

that are intensely stained for periods of up to 24 hours. The intense peroxidase staining within the interstitium and lymphatic capillaries within minutes of intravenous injections and the marked decrease of staining intensity after one hour provides morphological evidence for the rapid and constant movement of this protein and presumably other fluids and proteins across the blood–tissue–lymph interface.

To maintain a unidirectional flow process from the blood to the tissue–lymph interface the lymphatic capillary is provided with endothelial cell junctional valves. These seem to open and close the intercellular junction, depending on local pressure variations between the interstitial space and the lumen of the vessel. The response of extensively overlapping intercellular junctions to an increase in the interstitial pressure during inflammation and edematous conditions would suggest that the overlapping endothelial cell junctions open and close as a one-way flap valve system which serves to open clefts of intercellular junctions when the interstitial fluid pressure is higher than that of the lymphatic intraluminal pressure.[73] Conversely, when the intraluminal pressure is equal to or higher than the interstitial pressure, this one-way flap valve is closed. The studies of Guyton et al.[44,45] provide additional evidence for the variation in interstitial fluid pressures under normal physiological and edematous conditions. The studies of Zweifach[124] showed that the intraluminal pressure in the mesenteric lymphatic capillary was 0–2·5 cm of water and that this intraluminal pressure increased as the caliber of the vessels became larger and the thickness of the tunica media increased around the collecting vessels. This provides a condition in favor of unidirectional and centripetal flow from the lymphatic capillary to collecting lymphatics to the thoracic duct. The presence of a series of intraluminal valves serves an important role in preventing the backflow of lymph within the lumen of these vessels (see above).

The lymphatic capillary network which extends into the interstitial spaces is, therefore, a system of vessels whose walls are provided with potential one-way passage channels that directly communicate with the surrounding interstitium allowing fluids to flow from the interstitial space into the lumen without regurgitation. The structural arrangement of the extensively overlapping intercellular junctions[67,72] and a demonstration of pressure differential across the blood–tissue interface[45] suggest that these passageways are greatly influenced by an intraluminal interstitial pressure differential. Thus, higher pressures in the interstitial space would facilitate the openings of the junctional valve while higher pressures within the lymphatic capillary lumen would force the valves to close.

The lymphatic capillary is capable of responding to increased demand for fluid transport by a widening of its lumen. This is provided by the extensive overlap of adjacent endothelial cells which serves as a reserve supply of lymphatic wall that can be immediately utilized for rapid and uninterrupted expansion for dilatation of the lymphatic capillary lumen. This mechanism greatly increases the capacity for the

Figure 19.1. Movement of peroxidase across the blood–tissue–lymph interface (L. V. Leak).
Demonstration of the degree of peroxidase (exogenous protein) staining at time intervals of (a) 5 min, (b) 30 min, (c) 6h following intravenous injection. CT: connective tissue, J: intercellular junction. ((a) ×20,000, (b) ×28,000, (c) ×12,000)

lymphatic system and provides an efficient one-way drainage system for the interstitial area. The extent of lymphatic capillary dilatation and thus the volume transfer of fluid varies greatly with the physiological state. Both dilatation and volume transfer are greatly increased during the inflammatory response.

Figure 19.2. Lymphatic capillary permeability (L. V. Leak and J. F. Burke 19.2(a)).

(a) Intercellular junction in a lymphatic capillary one hour after bacterial infection. Note the electron-dense flocculent materials within the intercellular cleft (*) that is also continuous with the lymphatic lumen. The anchoring filaments (af) are found along the connective tissue (CT) fronts of the vessel.(× 36,000)

(b) Passage of colloidal carbon (c) across a patent junction and within the interstitial area at 24 h following an interstitial injection. (× 38,000)

(a)

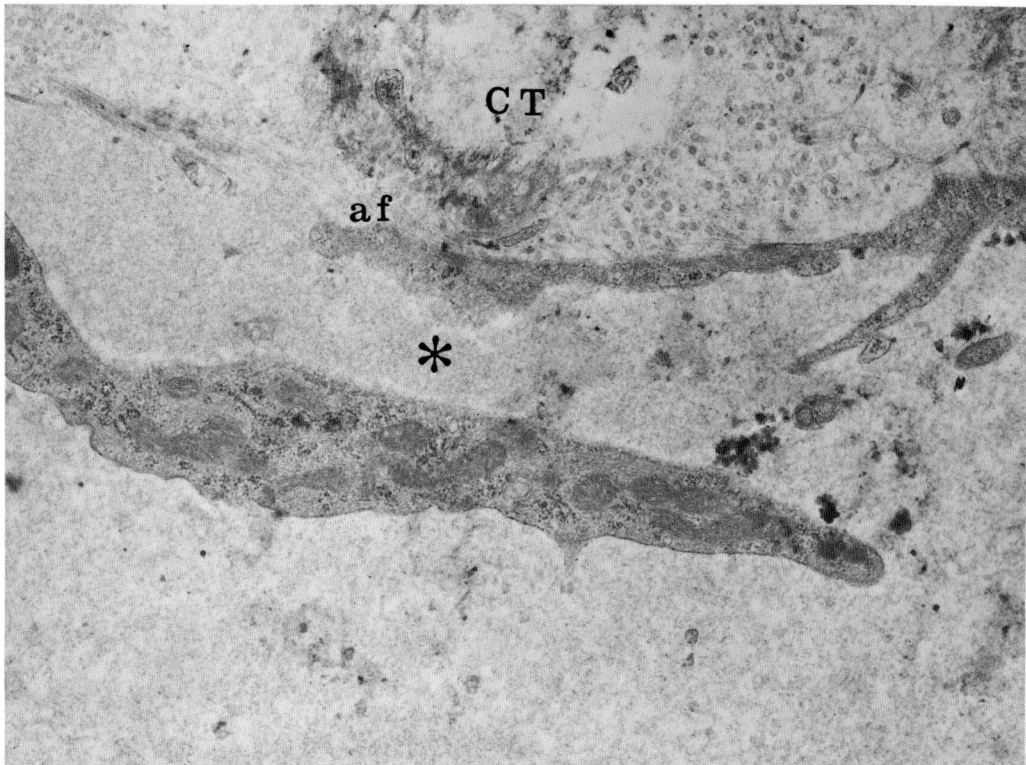

(b)

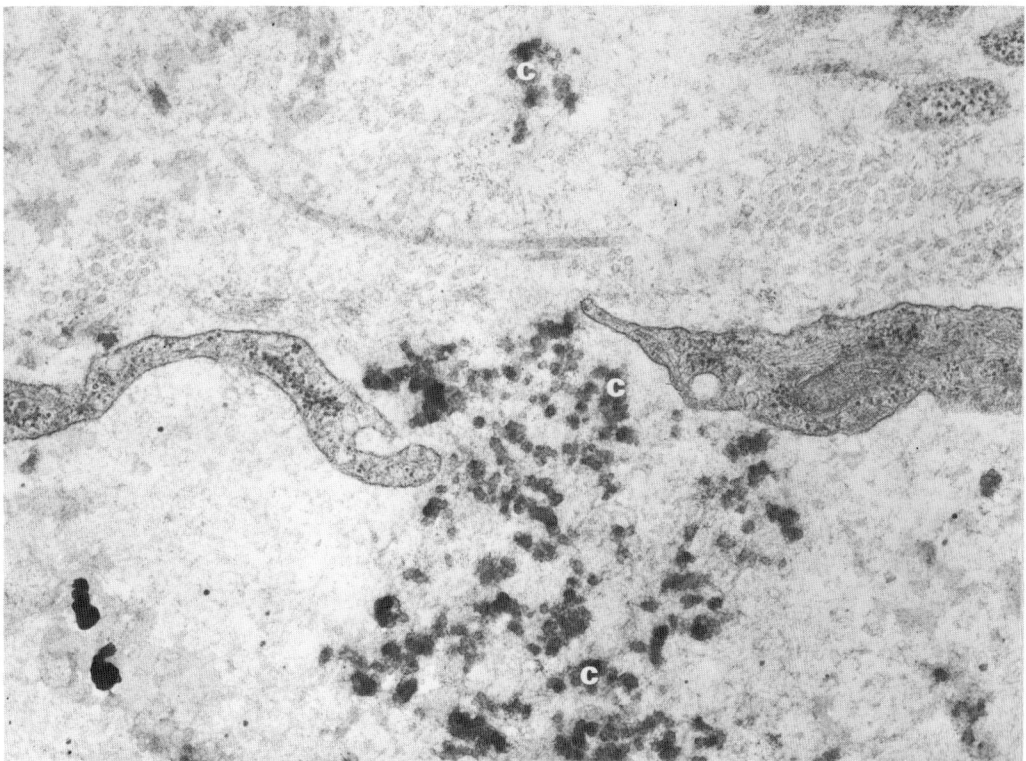

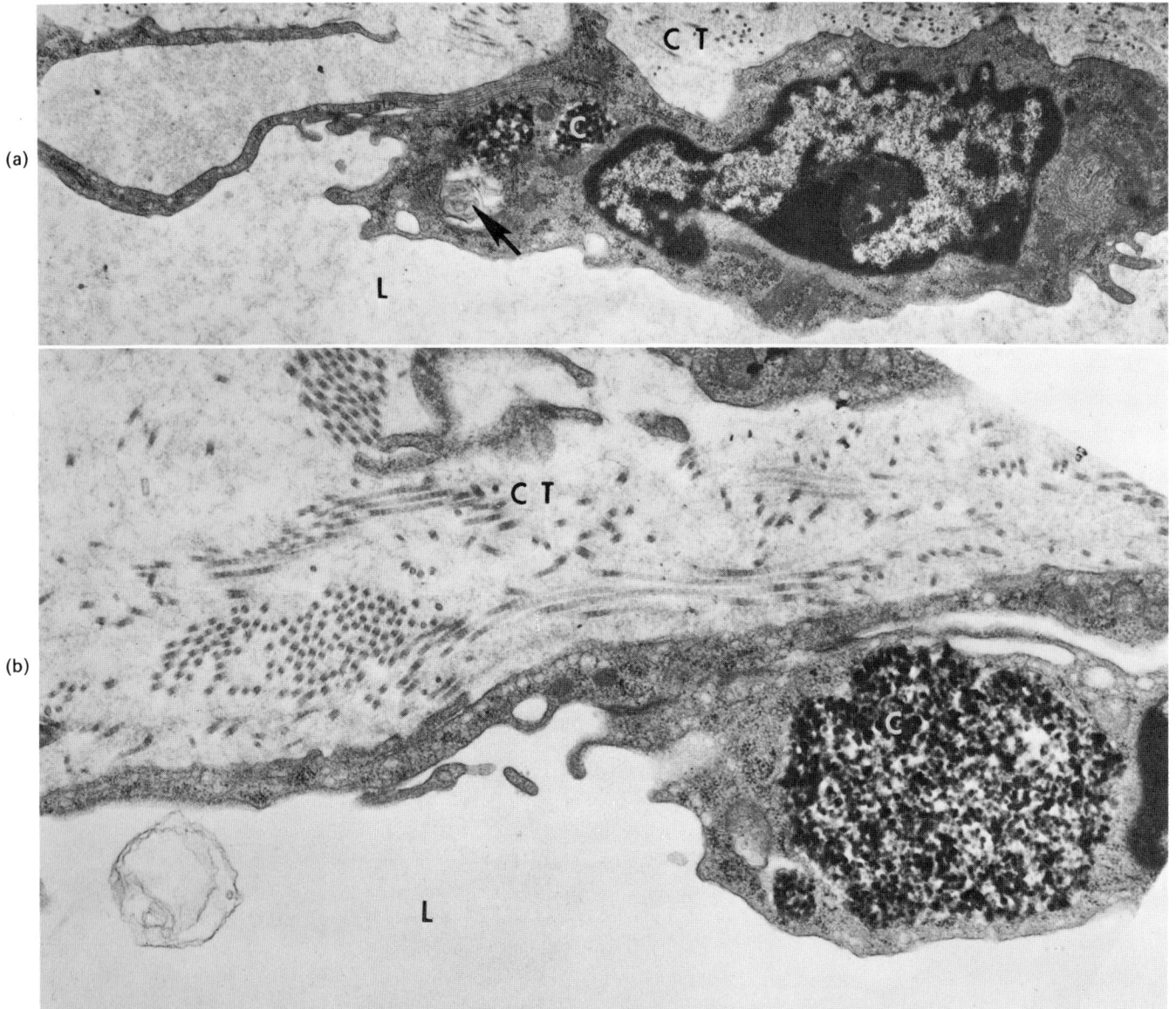

Figure 19.3. Accumulation of inert particles in lymphatic endothelial cells.
(a), (b) The accumulation of carbon (c) and membranes (arrows) within large autophagic vacuoles shown at (a) six and (b) twelve months following interstitial injections of the marker. L: lumen, CT: connective tissue. ((a) ×21,000, (b) ×22,500)

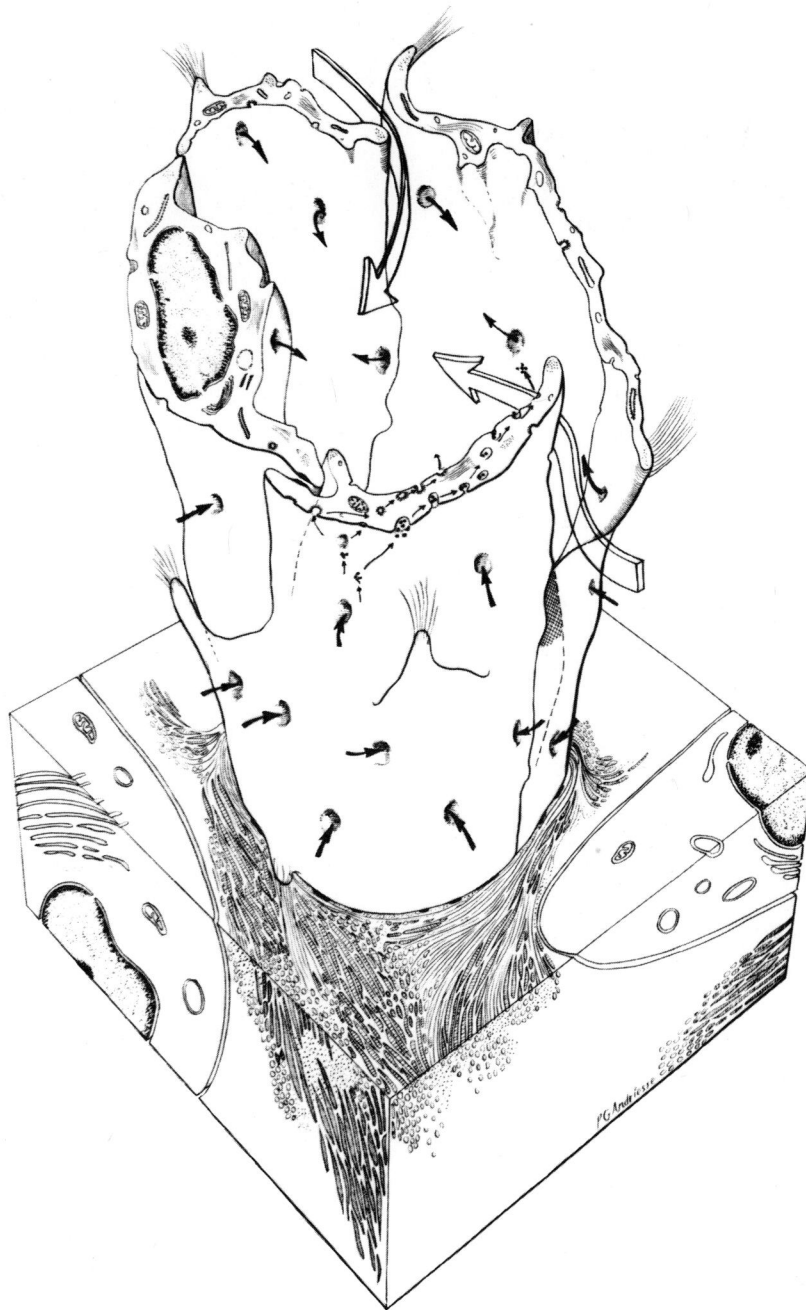

Figure 19.4. Reconstruction of lymphatic capillary to show intercellular cleft and vesicular uptake (L. V. Leak).

Three dimensional diagram of a portion of lymphatic capillary reconstructed from collated electron micrographs. The major passageway for transport of fluids and large molecules from the interstitium into the lymphatic lumen is via the intercellular cleft (long white arrows). The uptake of particulate components from both connective tissue and luminal fronts may occur within vesicles (small arrows). These move toward the central cytoplasm where they merge or aggregate and fuse with autophagic vacuoles in which intercellular digestion occurs for protein, lipids, and carbohydrates for subsequent utilization or discharge from the cell. Inert particles such as carbon remain for indefinite periods within the cell.

References to Part Three

1. Allen, L., "Lymphatics and lymphoid tissue," *A. Rev. Physiol.*, **29**, 197, 1967.
2. Anderson, E., "Oocyte differentiation and vitelogenesis in the roach *Periplaneta americana*," *J. Cell Biol.*, **20**, 131, 1964.
3. Behnke, O., Krietensen, B. J., Nillsen, L., "Electron microscopical observations on octinoid and myosenoid filaments in blood plates," *J. Ultrastruct. Res.*, **37**, 351, 1971.
4. Bennett, H. S., "The concepts of membrane flow and membrane vesiculation as mechanisms for active transport and ion pumping," *J. biophys. biochem. Cytol.*, **2**, 99, 1956.
5. Bennett, M. V. L., "Function of electrotonic junction in embryonic and adult tissues," *Fed. Proc.*, **32**, 65, 1973.
6. Benninghoff, A., "Blutgefässe und Herz," in W. von Moolendorff (ed.), *Handbuch der mikroskopischen Anatomie des Menschen*, vol. VI, part I, Springer, Berlin, 1930.
7. Bruns, R. R. and Palade, G. E., "Studies on blood capillaries. I. General organization of blood capillaries in muscle," *J. Cell Biol.*, **37**, 244, 1968.
8. Burke, J. F. and Leak, L. V. "Lymphatic capillary function in normal and inflamed states," in M. Viamonte, P. R. Kochler, M. Witte, and C. Witte (eds.), *Progress in Lymphology*, vol. II, George Thieme, Stuttgart, 1970, p. 81.
9. Caro, L. G. and Palade, G. E., "Protein synthesis, storage and discharge in the pancreatic exocrine cell. An autoradiographic study," *J. Cell Biol.*, **20**, 473, 1964.
10. Casley-Smith, J. R., "An electron microscopic study of injured and abnormally permeable lymphatics," *Ann. N.Y. Acad. Sci.*, **116**, 803, 1964.
11. ———, "Electron microscopical observation on the dilated lymphatics in oedematous regions and their collapse following hyaluronidase administration," *Br. J. exp. Path.*, **48**, 680, 1967.
12. ———, "Lymph and lymphatics," in G. Kaley and B. M. Alturo (eds.), *Microcirculation*, vol. I, University Park Press, Baltimore, 1977, p. 423.
13. ——— and Florey, H. W., "The structure of normal small lymphatics," *Q. Jl exp. Physiol.*, **46**, 101, 1961.
14. Chambers, R. and Zweifach, B. W., "Intercellular cement and capillary permeability," *Physiol. Rev.*, **27**, 431, 1947.
15. Cleary, E. G., Sandaerg, L. B., and Jackson, D. S., "The changes in chemical composition during development of the bovine nuchal ligament," *J. Cell Biol.*, **33**, 469, 1967.
16. Clementi, F. and Palade, G. E., "Intestinal capillaries. I. Permeability to peroxidase and ferritin," *J. Cell Biol.*, **41**, 33, 1969.

206

17. Cliff, W. J., "Observations on healing tissue: a combined light and electron microscope investigation," *Phil. Trans. R. Soc. B*, **246**, 305, 1963.
18. ——— and Nichol, P. A., "Structure and function of lymphatic vessel of bat's wing," *J. exp. Physiol.*, **55**, 112, 1970.
19. Collan, Y. and Kalima, T. V., "Topographical relations of lymphatic endothelial cells in the initial lymphatics of the intestine," *Lymphology*, **7**, 1975, 1974.
20. Collin, H. B., "The ultrastructure of conjunctival lymphatic anchoring filaments," *Expl Eye Res.*, **8**, 102, 1969.
21. DeDuve, C., "The lysosome concept", in A.V.S. de Reuck and M. P. Cameron (eds.), *Lysosomes,* Ciba Foundation Symposium, Little Brown, Boston, 1963, p. 1.
22. ——— and Wattiaux, R., "Function of lysosomes," *A. Rev. Physiol.*, **28**, 435, 1966.
23. Dewey, M. M. and Barr, L., "Intercellular connection between smooth muscle cells: the nexus," *Science,* **137**, 670, 1962.
24. Dobbins, W. O. and Rollins, E. L., "Intestinal mucosal lymphatic permeability: An electron microscopic study of endothelial vessels and cell junctions," *J. Ultrastruct. Res.,* **33**, 29, 1970.
25. Dreifuss, J. J., Girardier, L., and Forseman, W. G., "Etude de la propagation de l'excitation dans le ventricule de rat du moyen de solutions hypertoniques," *Pflügers Arch. ges Physiol*, **292**, 13, 1966.
26. Drinker, C. K., "The functional significance of the lymphatic system," *Harvey Lect.*, **38**, 89, 1937.
27. ——— and Field, M. E., *Lymphatics, Lymph and Tissue Fluid*, Williams and Wilkins, Baltimore, 1933.
28. ———, ———, and Ward, H. K., "The filtering capacity of lymph nodes," *J. exp. Med.*, **59**, 393, 1934.
29. ——— and Yoffey, J. M., *Lymphatic, Lymph and Lymphoid Tissue*, Harvard University Press, Cambridge, 1941.
30. Farquhar, M. G. and Palade, G. E., "Junctional complexes in various epithelia," *J. Cell Biol.*, **17**, 375, 1963.
31. Fawcett, D. W., "Intercellular bridges," *Expl. Cell Res.*, suppl., **8**, 174, 1961.
32. ———, Leak, L. V., and Heidger, P. M., "Electron microscopic observations on the structural components of the blood testis barrier," *J. Reprod. Fert.*, suppl., **10**, 105, 1970.
33. ———, Neaves, W. B., and Flores, M. N., "Comparative observation on intertubular lymphatics and the organization of the interstitial tissue of the mammalian testis," *Biol. Reprod.*, **9**, 500, 1973.
34. Faye, F. S. and Cooke P. H., "Reversible disaggregation of myofilaments in vertebrate smooth muscle," *J. Cell Biol.*, **56**, 399, 1973.
35. Florey (Lord), H. W., "Exchange of substances between blood and tissue," *Nature, Lond.*, 192, 908, 1961.
36. ———, "The uptake of particulate matter by endothelial cells," *Proc. R. Soc. B*, **166**, 375, 1967.
37. Fraley, E. E. and Weiss, L., "An electron microscopic study of the lymphatic vessels in the penile skin of the rat," *Am. J. Anat.*, **109**, 55, 1961.

38. French, J. E., Florey, H. W., and Morris, B., "The absorption of particles by the lymphatics of the diaphragm," *Q. Jl exp. Physiol.*, **45**, 88, 1960.

39. Gilula, N. B., Reeves, O. R., and Steinbach, A., "Metabolic coupling, ionic coupling and cell contacts," *Nature, Lond.*, **235**, 262, 1972.

40. Good, R. A., "Immunodeficiency in developmental perspective," *Harvey Lect.*, **67**, 1, 1971.

41. Graham, R. C. and Karnovsky, M. J., "The early stages of absorption of injected horseradish peroxidase in the proximal tubule of the mouse kidney. Ultrastructural cytochemistry by a new technique," *J. Histochem, Cytochem.*, **14**, 291, 1966.

42. Granick, S., "Ferritin, its properties and significance for ion metabolism," *Chem. Rev.*, **38**, 379, 1946.

43. Grotte, G., "Passage of dextran molecules across the blood-lymph barrier," *Act. chir. scand.*, suppl., **211**, 1, 1956.

44. Guyton, A. C., Granger, H. J., and Taylor, A. E., "Interstitial fluid pressure," *Physiol. Res.*, **51**, 527, 1971.

45. ———, Taylor, A. E., and Brace, R. A., "A synthesis of interstitial fluid regulation and lymph formation," *Fed. Proc.*, **35**, 1881, 1976.

46. Hall, J. G., "The response of a nod to stimulation with foreign tissue," *Colluq University Congress*, Liège, 1967, 45, p. 1.

47. ———, Morris, B., and Woodley, G., "Intrinsic rhythmic propulsion of lymph in the unanesthetized sheep," *J. Physiol.*, *Lond.*, **180**, 336, 1965.

48. Hortsmann, E., "Motor activity of lymphatics," *Eur. J. Physiol.*, **336**, S–43, 1972.

49. Hudack, S. S. and McMaster, P. D., "Permeability of wall of lymphatic capillary," *J. exp. Med.*, **56**, 223, 1932.

50. Huth, F., "Allgemeine Pathologie des Lymphgefäßsystems," in *Handbuch der Allgemeinen Pathologie*, Springer–Verlag, Berlin, 1972, p. 457.

51. Jamieson, J. D. and Palade, G. E., "Intracellular transport of secretory protein in the pancreatic exocrine cell," *J. Cell Biol.*, **34**, 577, 1967.

52. ——— and ———, "Condensing vacuole conversion and zymogen granule discharge in pancreatic exocrine cells: metabolic studies," *J. Cell Biol.*, **48**, 503, 1971.

53. Kalima, T. V., "The structure and function of intestinal lymphatics and the influence of impaired lymph flow on the ileum of rats," *Scand. J. Gastroenterol.*, 6, suppl. **10**, 1971.

54. Karnovsky, M. J., "A formaldehyde-glutaraldehyde fixative of high osmolarity for use in electron microscopy," *J. Cell Biol.*, **27**, 137A, 1965.

55. ———, "The ultrastructural basis of capillary permeability studied with peroxidase as a tracer," *J. Cell Biol.*, **35**, 213, 1967.

56. Kato, F., "The fine structure of the lymphatics and the passage of china ink particles through their walls," *Nagoya med. J.*, **12**, 221, 1966.

57. Kinmoth, J. B. and Taylor, G. W., "Spontaneous rhythmic contractility in human lymphatics," *J. Physiol.*, *Lond.*, **133**, 3, 1956.

58. Kolleker, A., *Handbuch der Gewebelehre des Menschen*, 1867.

59. Krogh, A., *The Anatomy and Physiology of Capillaries*, Hafner, New York, 1959.

208

60. Lauweryns, J. M., "Stereomicroscopic funnel-like architecture of pulmonary lymphatic values," *Lymphology*, **4**, 125, 1971.

61. ——— and Baert, J. H., "The role of the pulmonary lymphatics in the defenses of the diseased lung: Morphological and experimental studies of the transport mechanisms of intratracheally instilled particles," *Ann. N. Y. Acad. Sci.*, **221**, 244, 1974.

62. ———, ———, and DesLoecker, W., "Fine filaments in lymphatic endothelial cells," *J. Cell Biol.*, **68**, 163, 1976.

63. ——— and Boussauw, L. "The ultrastructure of pulmonary lymphatic capillaries of newborn rabbits and of human infants," *Lymphology*, **2**, 108, 1969.

64. Leak, L. V., "Lymphatic capillaries in tail fin of amphibian larva. An electron microscopic study," *J. Morphol.*, **125**, 419, 1968.

65. ———, "Electron microscopic observations on lymphatic capillaries and the structural components of the connective tissue-lymph interface," *Microvasc. Res.*, **2**, 361, 1970.

66. ———, "Studies on the permeability of lymphatic capillaries," *J. Cell Biol.*, **50**, 300, 1971.

67. ———, "The transport of exogenous peroxidase across the blood-tissue-lymph interface," *J. Ultrastruct. Res.*, **39**, 24, 1972.

68. ———, "The structure of lymphatic capillaries in lymph formation," *Fed. Proc.*, **35**, 1863, 1976.

69. ———, "Pulmonary lymphatic and interstitial fluid," in J. Brain, D. Proctor, and L. Reid (eds.), *Respiratory Defense Mechanisms,* vol. II, Marcel Dekker, New York, 1977, pp. 631–685.

70. ——— and Burke, J. F., "Ultrastructure of lymphatic capillaries," *J. Appl. Phys.*, **36**, 2620, 1965.

71. ——— and ———, "Fine structure of the lymphatic capillary and the adjoining connective tissue area," *Am. J. Anat.*, **118**, 785, 1966.

72. ——— and ———, "Ultrastructural studies on the lymphatic anchoring filaments," *J. Cell Biol.*, **36**, 129, 1968.

73. ——— and ———, "Early events of tissue injury and the role of the lymphatic system in early inflammation," in B. W. Zweifach, L. Grant, and R. I. McCluskey (eds.), *The Inflammatory Process*, vol. III, chap. 4, Academic Press, New York, 1974, p. 163.

74. ——— and Rahil, K., "Permeability of the diaphragmatic mesothelium: The ultrastructural basis for 'stomata'," *Am. J. Anat.*, **151**, 557, 1978.

75. ———, Shannahan, A., and Sculley, H., "Electron microscopic studies on lymphatics in the mammalian heart," *Anat. Rec.*, **169**, 365, 1971.

76. Lindner, H. R., "Partition of androgen between the lymph and venous blood of the testis in the ram," *J. Endocr.*, **25**, 483, 1963.

77. Ljungqvist, A., Mandoche, E., and Unge, G., "Ultrastructural aspects of cardiac lymphatic capillaries in experimental cardiac hypertrophy," *Microvasc. Res.*, **10**, 1, 1975.

78. Loewenstein, W. R., "Permeability of membrane junctions," *Ann. N. Y. Acad. Sci.*, **137**, 441, 1966.

79. ———, "Permeability of the junctional membrane," in B. R. Brinkley and

K. R. Porter (eds.) *International Cell Biology*, Rockefeller University Press, New York, 1977, p. 70.

80. Lowy, J. and Hanson, J., "Ultrastructure of invertebrate smooth muscles," *Physiol. Rev.*, **5**, 34, 1962.

81. McCuskey, R. S., "Sphincters in the microvascular system," *Fed. Proc.*, **30**, 713, 1971.

82. McMaster, P. D., "Lymphatic participation in cutaneous phenomena," *Harvey Lect.*, **37**, 227, 1941, 1942.

83. ———, "Conditions in skin influencing interstitial fluid movement lymph formation and lymph flow," *Ann. N. Y. Acad. Sci.*, **46**, 743, 1946.

84. ——— and Hudack, S. S., "Induced alterations in the permeability of the lymphatic capillary," *J. exp. Med.*, **56**, 239, 1932.

85. Majno, G. and Leventhal, M., "Pathogenesis of histamine type vascular leakage," *Lancet*, **2**, 99, 1967.

86. ———, Shea, S. M., and Leventhal, M., "Endothelial contraction induced by histamine type mediators. An electron microscopic study," *J. Cell Biol.*, **42**, 647, 1969.

87. Mayerson, H. S., "The physiologic importance of lymph," in W. F. Hamilton and P. Dow (eds.), *Handbook of Physiology*, section 2, vol. II, *Circulation*, American Physiological Society, Washington, 1963, p. 1035.

88. Miles, A. A. and Miles, E. M., "The state of lymphatic capillaries in acute inflammatory lesions," *J. Path. Bact.*, **76**, 21, 1958.

89. Morris, B. and Sass, M. B., "The formation of lymph in the ovary," *Proc. R. Soc. B*, **164**, 577, 1966.

90. Nachmias, V. T., Huxley, H. E., and Kessler, D., "Electron microscope observations on actomyosin and actin preparations from *Physarum polycephalum*, and their interaction with heavy meromyosin subfragment I from muscle myosin," *J. molec. Biol.*, **50**, 83, 1970.

91. Namura, Y., "Myofilaments in smooth muscle of guinea pig *Taenia coli*," *J. Cell Biol.*, **39**, 741, 1968.

92. Palade, G. E., "Fine structure of blood capillaries," *J. appl. Phys.* **24**, 1424, 1953.

93. ———, "Transport in quanta across the endothelium of blood capillaries," *Anat. Rec.*, **136**, 254, 1960.

94. ———, Siekevitz, P., and Caro, L. C., "Structure, chemistry and function of the pancreatic exocrine cell," in A. V. S. de Reuck and M. P. Cameron (eds.), *The Exocrine Pancreas: Normal and abnormal functions*, Ciba Foundation Symposium, 1962, p. 23.

95. Palay, S. L. and Karlin, K. J., "An electron microscopic study of the intestinal villus. I. The foslery animal," *J. Biophys. biochem. Cytol.*, **5**, 363, 1959.

96. Partridge, S. M. and Davis, H. F., "The chemistry of connective tissues. The composition of the soluble proteins derived from elastin," *Biochem. J.*, **61**, 21, 1955.

97. Pease, D. C., "Structural features of unfixed mammalian smooth and striated muscle prepared by glycol dehydration," *J. Ultrastruct. Res.*, **23**, 280, 1968.

98. ——— and Molenari, S., "Electron microscopy of muscular arteries, pial vessels of the cat and monkey," *J. Ultrastruct. Res.*, **3**, 447, 1960.

210

99. Piez, K. A., Miller E. J., and Martin, G. R., "The chemistry of elastin and its relationship to structure," *Adv. Biol. Skin*, **6**, 245, 1964.

100. Pollard, T. D., Shelton, E., Weihing, R., and Korn, F. D., "Ultrastructural characterization of F. actin isolated from *Acanthamoeba castellanii* and identification of cytoplasmic filaments as F. actin by reaction with heavy meromyosin," *J. molec. Biol.*, **50**, 91, 1970.

101. ——— and Weihing, R. R., "Actin and myosin and cell movement," *CRC Crit. Rev. Biochem.*, **2**, 1, 1974.

102. Pullinger, P. D. and Florey, H. W. "Some observations on the structure and function of lymphatics: Their behavior in local edema," *Br. J. exp. Path.*, **16**, 49, 1935.

103. Revel, J. P. and Karnovsky, M. J., "Hexagonal array of subunits in intercellular junction of the mouse heart and liver," *J. Cell Biol.*, **33**, C7, 1967.

104. Richter, G. W., "Electron microscopy of hemosiderin: presence of ferritin and occurrence of crystalline lattice in hemosiderin deposits," *J. biochem. biophys. Cytol.*, **4**, 55, 1958.

105. Rhodin, J. A. G., "Fine structure of vascular walls in mammals with special reference to smooth muscle components," *Phys. Rev.*, **42**, 48, 1962.

106. ———, "Ultrastructure of mammalian venous capillaries venules and small collecting veins," *J. Ultrastruct. Res.*, **25**, 452, 1968.

107. Robertson, J. D., "The ultrastructure of cell membranes and their derivatives," *Biochem. Soc. Symp.*, **16**, 3, 1959.

108. ———, "The occurrence of a subunit pattern in the unit membranes of club endings in mauther cell synapse in goldfish brains," *J. Cell Biol.*, **19**, 201, 1963.

109. Ross, R. and Bornstein, P., "The elastic fibers. I. The separation and partial characterization of its macromolecular components," *J. Cell Biol.*, **40**, 366, 1969.

110. Roth, T. F. and Porter, K. R., "Yolk protein uptake in oocyte of the mosquito *Aedes aegypti L.*", *J. Cell Biol.*, **20**, 313, 1964.

111. Sandberg, L. B., "Biochemical studies of elastic tissue," Doctorate thesis, University of Oregon, 1966.

112. Schoefl, G. I., "Studies on inflammation. III. Growing capillaries: their structure and permeability," *Virchows Arch. Path. Anat,* **337**, 97, 1963.

113. ———, "Electron microscopic observations on the regeneration of blood vessels after injury," *Ann. N. Y. Acad. Sci.*, **116**, 789, 1964.

114. Simionescu, M., Simionescu, N., and Palade, G. E., "Segmental differentiation of cell junction in the vascular endothelium: the microvasculature," *J. Cell Biol.*, **67**, 863, 1975.

115. Uehara, Y., Campbell, G. R., and Burnstock, G., "Cytoplasmic filaments in developing an adult vertebrate smooth muscle," *J. Cell Biol.*, **50**, 484, 1971.

116. Virach, Sz., Papp, M., Toro, E., and Rusznyak, I., "Cutaneous lymphatic capillaries in dextran induced oedema of the rat," *Br. J. exp. Path.*, **47**, 563, 1966.

117. Webb, R. L. and Nichol, P. A., "Behavior of lymphatic vessels in the living rat," *Anat. Rec.*, **88**, 351, 1944.

118. ——— and Starzl, T. E., "The effect of blood vessel pulsations on lymph pressure in large lymphatics," *Bull Johns Hopkins Hosp.*, **93**, 401, 1953.

119. Weber, R., "Behavior and properties of acid hydrolase in regressing tails of tadpoles during spontaneous and induced metamorphosis in vitro," in A. V. S.

de Reuck and M. P. Cameron (eds.), *Lysosomes*, Ciba Foundation Symposium, Little Brown, Boston, 1963, p. 281.

120. Wohlfarth-Bottermann, K. E., in R. D. Allen and N. Kamiya (eds.), *Primitive Motile Systems in Cell Biology*, Academic Press, New York, 1964, p. 79.

121. Yoffey, J. M. and Courtice, F. C., *Lymphatics, Lymph and Lymphomyeloid Complex*, Academic Press, New York, 1970.

122. Zimmermann, K. W., "Der feinere Bau der Blutkapillaren," *Z. Anat. EntwGesch.*, **68**, 29, 1923.

123. Zweifach, B. W., "Functional behavior of the microcirculation," Thomas, Springfield, Illinois, 1961.

124. —— and Prather, J. W., "Pressures in terminal lymphatics of mesentery," *Fed. Proc.*, **30**, 718, 1971.

Part Four

The Thymus

Gerald D. Levine
Robert M. Bearman

20. Introduction to Part Four

The essential role played by the thymus in T-lymphocyte function is now well established and has been the subject of numerous publications. However, pathologic changes in the thymus have received much less attention. This section demonstrates how a knowledge of normal thymic fine structure may be applied in the evaluation of the microarchitecture of thymic hyperplasia and provides a basis for the orderly classification of thymic neoplasms.[37] Human material (glutaraldehyde fixed and stained with uranyl acetate and lead citrate) has been the source of all illustrations in this section. Olah, Rolich, and Toro[49] provide a detailed bibliography and well-illustrated account of the normal animal thymus.

21. The Normal Thymus

21.1. Epithelial cells

The framework of the thymus is formed by epithelial cells and is established by the ninth week of fetal life.[14] These cells have extensively ramifying attenuated processes which form a meshwork enclosing lymphocytes (Figures 21.1, 21.2(a)).[4,5,13,19,21,26] Because of this appearance the term "epithelial-reticular" or "reticulum" is often used to describe these cells. While this is descriptively accurate, these epithelial cells should not be confused with the *mesenchymal*-reticular supportive cells of spleen and lymph nodes.[77]

The epithelial cells contain mitochondria, ribosomes, microvesicles, tonofilaments, and lysosomes in varying proportions (Figures 21.2(b), 21.2(c), 21.3(a), 21.3(b)). Although found in the fetal thymus, glycogen[14] and cilia[61] are inconspicuous postnatally.

Tonofilaments are a particularly distinctive feature of thymic epithelium. They are often grouped into broad, branching bundles (Figures 21.2(c), 21.3(a)) and insert into typical desmosomes (maculae adherentes) (Figure 21.2(b)). Tonofilaments may be concentrated around the nucleus but also extend into cell processes. Some cells have many desmosomes but only scant tonofilaments.

Basal lamina is found at the epithelial-connective tissue interface (Figures 21.1, 21.2(a), 21.5). Epithelial cells and their basal lamina form a continuous surface layer on the thymus. No basal lamina is present between epithelial cells and lymphocytes.

While the overall epithelial framework is similar in both cortex and medulla, the epithelial cells of Hassall's corpuscles have a different configuration (Figure 21.3(a),(b). They are arranged in concentric rings which show increasing nuclear and cytoplasmic degeneration toward the center of the corpuscle. Some are predominantly cystic and contain keratinizing epithelial cells admixed with rare lymphocytes, macrophages, and polymorphonuclear leukocytes, while others are solid and keratinized. The process of keratinization mimics that found in the squamous epithelium of the skin.[48] Epithelial cells at the periphery of Hassall's corpuscles contain numerous tonofilament bundles and cytoplasmic microcysts. The latter may be lined by microvilli (Figure 21.2(c)).

The function of Hassall's corpuscles is poorly understood. They have been proposed as a site of secretion,[19,75] and as a site of lymphocyte death.[3]

The thymus produces a number of hormones.[1] Of these, thymosin has been localized by immunocytochemical techniques to the epithelium.[12,40,69] The following organelles may be involved in the formation and secretion of thymic hormones.

1. The golgi apparatus is prominent in some epithelial cells and is closely associated with microvesicles containing electron-dense material (Figure 21.2(c)).

216

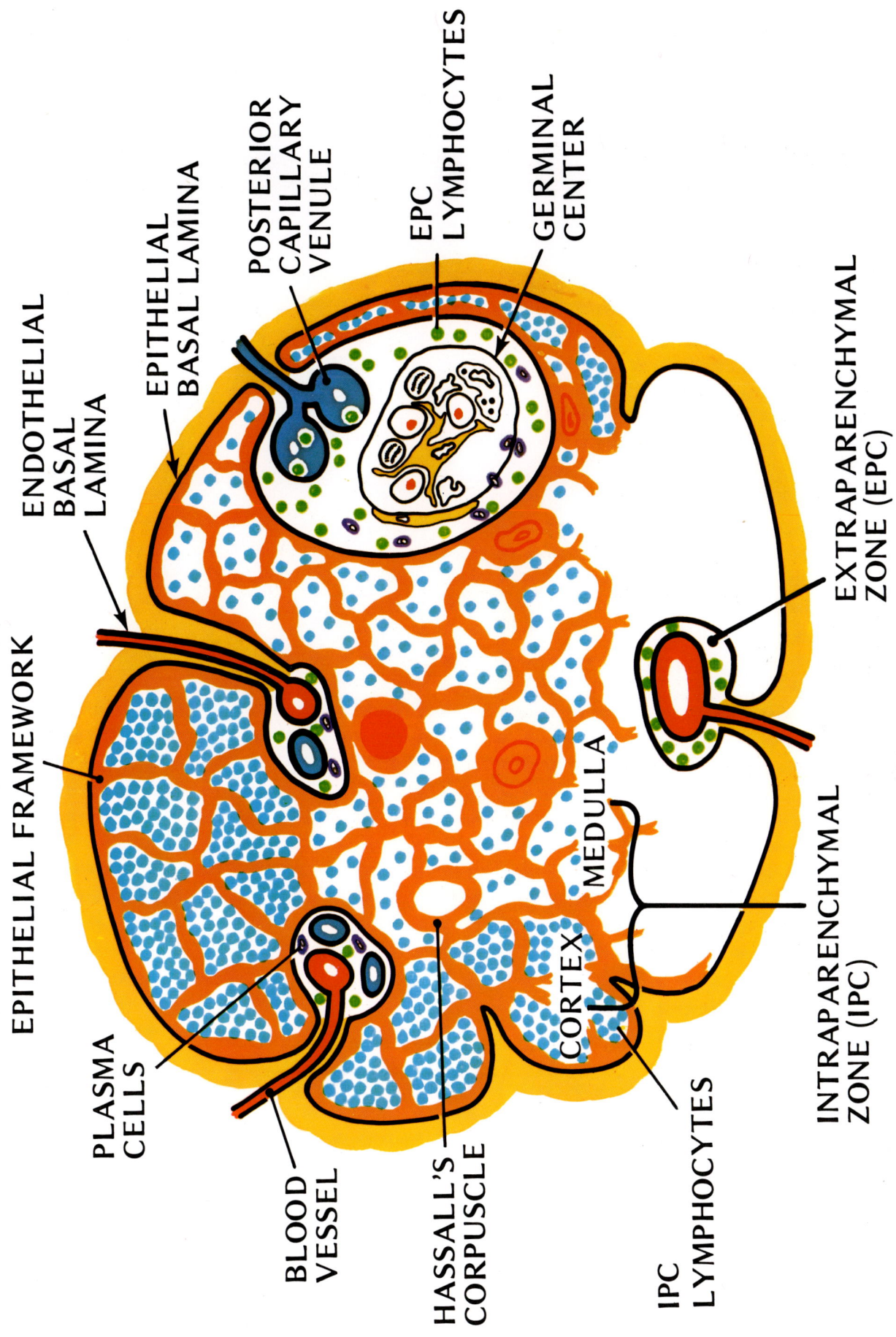

EPITHELIAL FRAMEWORK

ENDOTHELIAL BASAL LAMINA

EPITHELIAL BASAL LAMINA

POSTERIOR CAPILLARY VENULE

EPC LYMPHOCYTES

GERMINAL CENTER

EXTRAPARENCHYMAL ZONE (EPC)

PLASMA CELLS

BLOOD VESSEL

HASSALL'S CORPUSCLE

CORTEX

MEDULLA

IPC LYMPHOCYTES

INTRAPARENCHYMAL ZONE (IPC)

Figure 21.1. Thymic microarchitecture.
Note delineation of true thymic parenchyma from extraparenchymal zone by thymic epithelium and basal lamina. Germinal center lies in an expanded EPC. Dendritic cell (yellow) ramifies amongst lymphoid cells and partly separates germinal center from mantle.

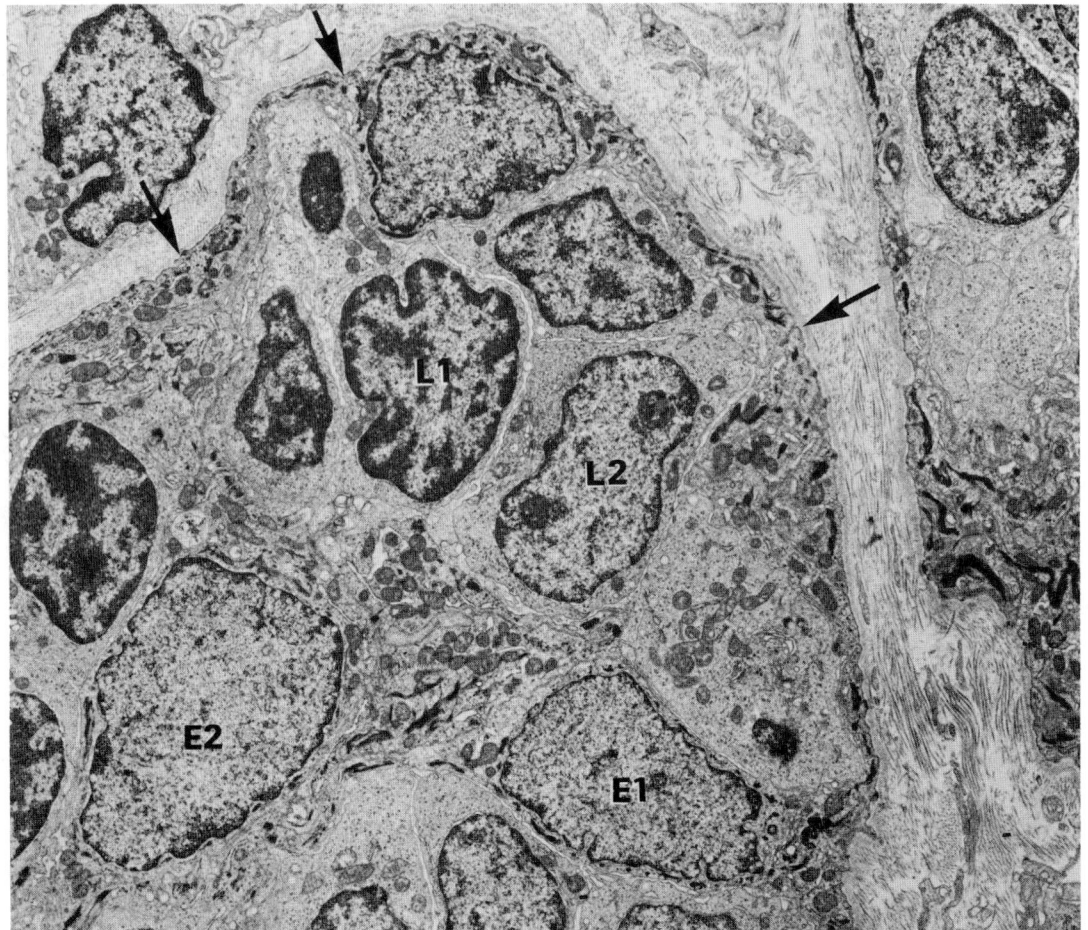

Figure 21.2. Epithelial cells of normal thymus.

(a) Thin, tonofilament-rich epithelial processes delimit thymic surface and connect to deeper epithelium (E1 and E2). Epithelial basal lamina is present at interface with collagen septa (arrows). Quiescent (L1) and activated (L2) lymphocytes are separated from surface by epithelium. (× 2,300)

2. Microvillous cysts have been proposed as a site of secretion in the mouse thymus.[8] These cysts are much more prominent in the human fetal than in the adult thymus.[21] Medullary epithelial cells, including those in Hassall's corpuscles, secrete a sulfated acid mucopolysaccharide.[16]

3. Secretory-like, dense-core granules (1,390 Å) have been described in Hassall's corpuscle epithelium[75] and we have observed granules of comparable size (1,750 Å) in this location in one of 36 normal thymuses examined ultrastructurally. The ultrastructural counterparts of the argyrophil cells described by Rosai and Higa[55] remain to be determined.

The role of these or other organelles[4] is speculative and awaits evaluation by electron microscopic, immunocytochemical, or other techniques.

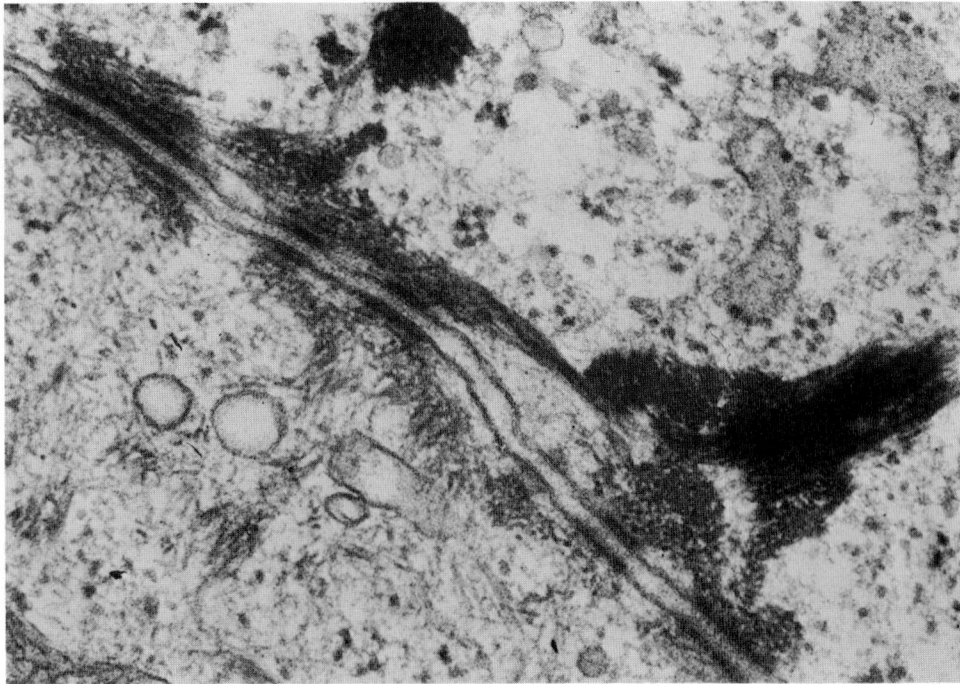

Figure 21.2. Epithelial cells of normal thymus.
(b) Well-formed desmosomes, with inserting tonofilaments seen in longitudinal and cross sections, connect two epithelial cells. (× 74,000)

21.2 Lymphocytes

These comprise the majority of thymic cells, especially in the cortex. They vary from large "transformed" lymphocytes and lymphocytes in mitosis to small, round, morphologically inactive forms (Figure 21.2(a)). The large lymphoid cells predominate near the cortical surface. Nuclear blebs (pockets) are found in a few fetal lymphocytes[60] and rarely postnatally.[24,37] Degenerating lymphocytes are numerous even in apparently normal thymuses (Figure 21.3(a)); they lie free or ingested within macrophages. We have not observed morphologic transitions between epithelial cells and lymphocytes[65] and it now appears to be established that lymphocytes initially migrate into the thymus rather than arising *in situ*.[31] There is an intimate association between the two cell types, an arrangement which may enhance the effects of thymic epithelium on lymphocyte maturation.

21.3 Macrophages and "reticulum" cells

The ultrastructure of thymic macrophages is essentially similar to that found elsewhere (see Chapter 31). Cortical macrophages phagocytose lymphocyte debris and in the mouse thymus appear to have a role in thymocyte mitogenesis.[44] Langerhans granules have been observed in cells in the human thymus.[22]

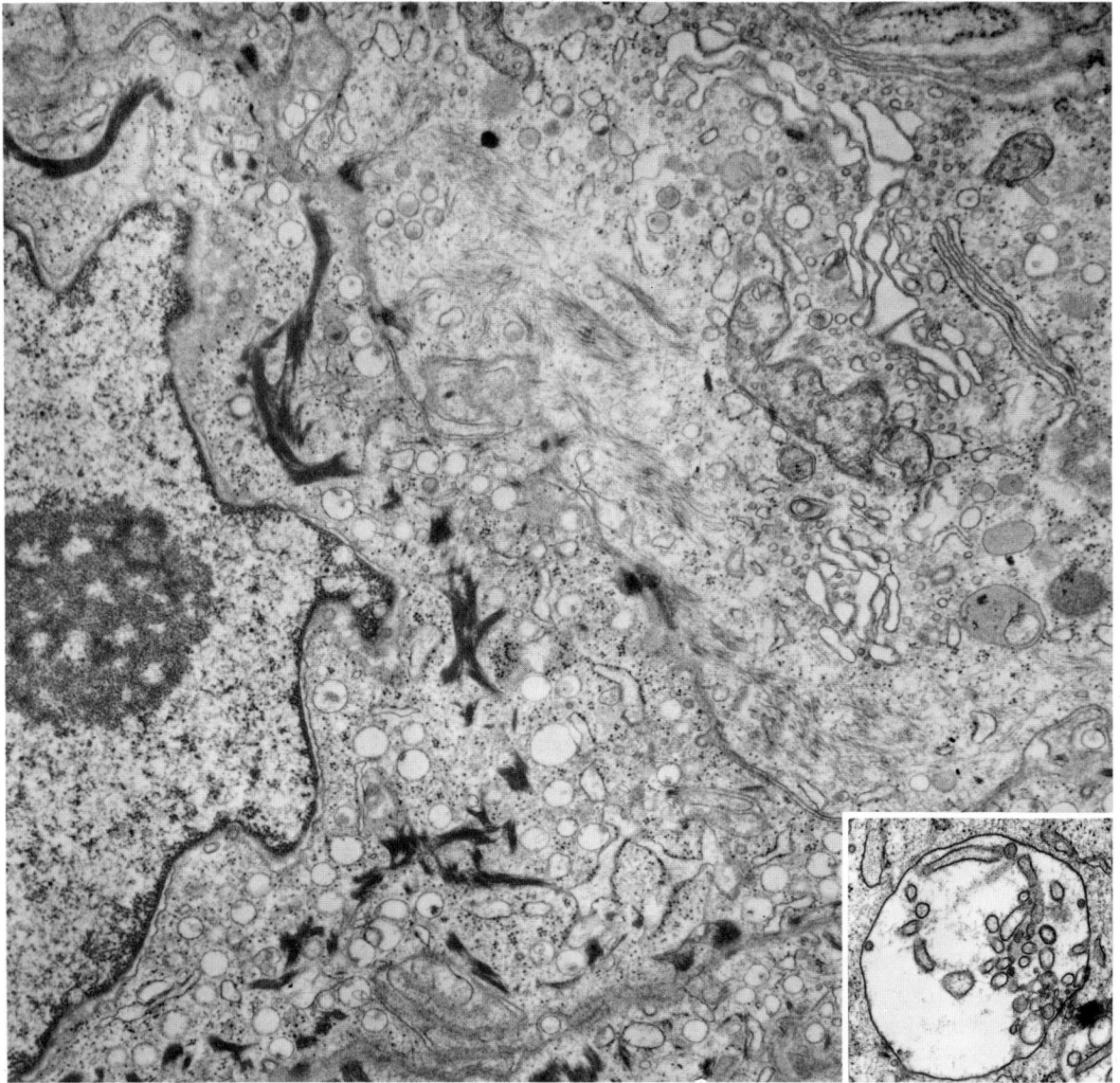

Figure 21.2. Epithelial cells of normal thymus.

(c) Prominent golgi apparatus and secretory vesicles well seen upper right. Note branching perinuclear tonofilament bundles. (× 11,000)

Inset: Microvillous lined cyst. (× 20,000)

Kaiserling *et al.*[25] have described a characteristic human thymic cell that forms complex interdigitations with lymphocytes. This is located in the medulla and inner cortex and is ultrastructurally similar to the interdigitating cell in the periartenolar lymphatic sheath of rabbit spleen,[10] and the paracortical area of rabbit lymph nodes.[73] Kaiserling has proposed that these "interdigitating reticulum cells" play a role in the differentiation of T-cells. Jones *et al.*[24] also observed an intimate relationship between thymic lymphocytes and cells they interpreted as macrophages and they attributed a functional significance to this.

21.4. Myoid cells and eosinophils

Although myoid cells are more numerous in the human fetal thymus,[15] they are also found postnatally.[9,19] Myosin and actin filaments and primitive Z-bands are present but usually do not form well-organized sarcomeres (Figure 21.4). While we have not observed desmosomes between thymic epithelium and myoid cells, Henry[18] has reported the occurrence of such attachments and that transitional forms may be observed between these two cell types. It has been suggested that thymic myoid cells may play a role in the initiation of an autoimmune response against acetylcholine receptors in myasthenia gravis.[27]

Mature eosinophils and eosinophilic myelocytes are present in the fetal[14] and neonatal thymus.[68] The dense myelocyte granules may be readily confused with those of hormone secreting cells. We have not ultrastructurally identified the erythroblasts detected by Taylor in normal thymuses.[68]

21.5. Blood vessels

Blood vessels run within the connective tissue septae. The thymic epithelium and blood vessels are consistently arranged in the following layers (Figures 21.1, 21.5).[2]

1. An epithelial layer.
2. Epithelial basal lamina.
3. Perivascular zone and contents, including lymphocytes, plasma cells, macrophages, fibroblasts, and mast cells.
4. Endothelial basal lamina.
5. Endothelium.

The epithelial layer and its basal lamina appear to be important components of the "thymic-blood barrier". The basal lamina may be disrupted by migrating lymphocytes.

Thymic capillaries are normally nonfenestrated. We agree with Soderstrom[63] who states that normal thymus contains no venules of postcapillary type (high endothelial venules) and that lymphocytes migrate across vessels having a relatively low endothelial lining (Figure 21.6). Lymphatic vessels are located within the connective tissue septae (Figure 21.7). While they are known to be a route of emigration of lymphocytes from the guinea pig thymus,[30] their role in the export of lymphocytes from the human thymus is uncertain.

21.6. Thymic microarchitecture terminology

This is illustrated in Figure 21.1. The thymic cortex and medulla form a continuum and are distinguished mainly by the more numerous lymphocytes in the cortex and

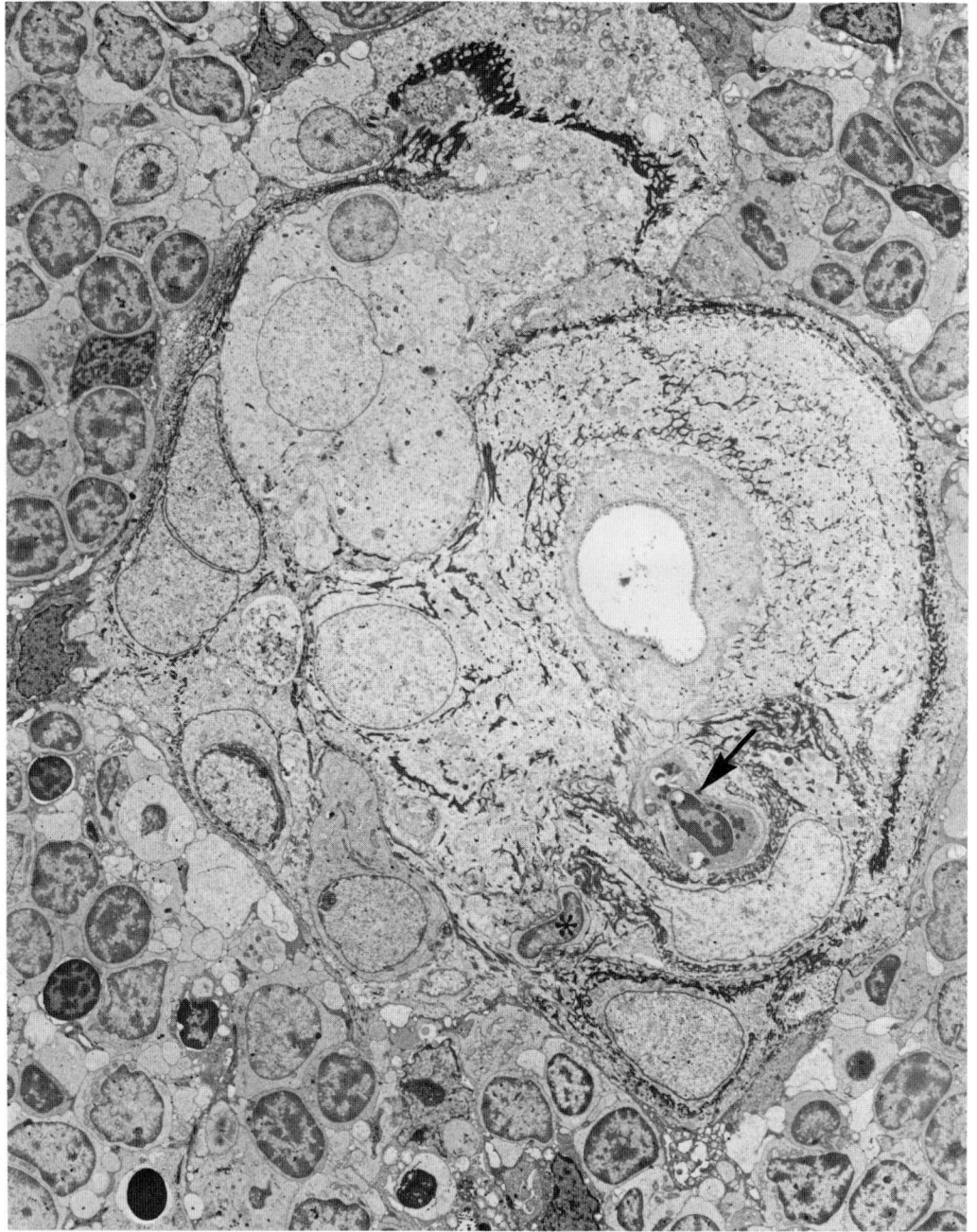

Figure 21.3. Hassall's corpuscle.

(a) Concentric epithelial cells from the corpuscle. Microvilli line central space. Note lymphocyte (asterisk) and granulocyte (arrow) within corpuscle. Two necrotic lymphocytes are visible in lower field. (× 2,100)

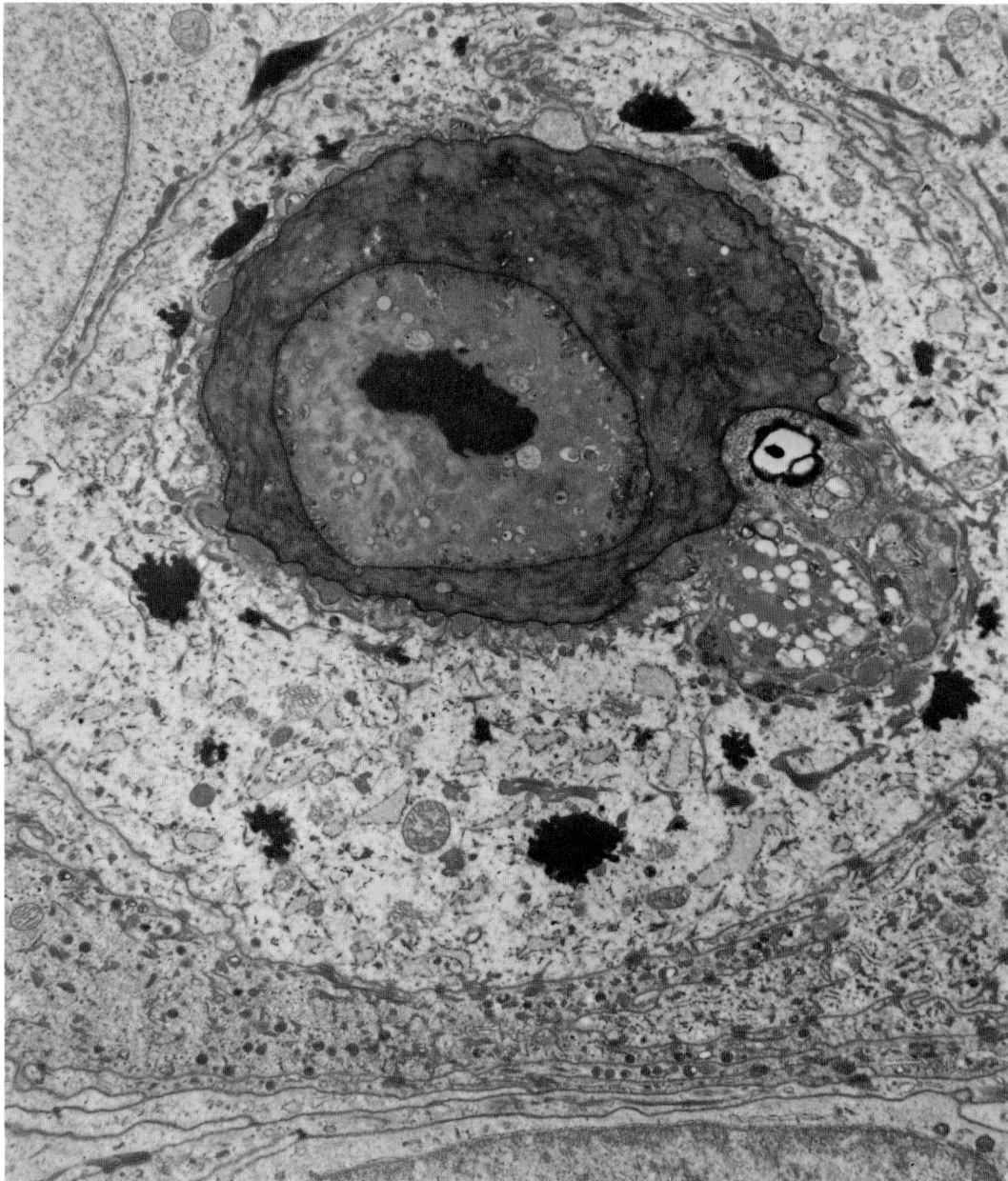

Figure 21.3. Hassall's corpuscle.

(b) Solid keratinized corpuscle. Numerous granules in lower field (possibly secretory or lyso-somal). (×3,500)

the Hassall's corpuscles in the medulla. No connective tissue is interposed between cortex and medulla and both zones are delimited by an outer layer of epithelium and basal lamina. The cortex and medulla together constitute the thymic *intraparenchymal compartment* (IPC). The *extraparenchymal compartment* (EPC) is composed of blood vessels and surrounding connective tissue and cells and is easily demonstrated by light microscopy with the aid of silver stains for reticulin fibres.

223

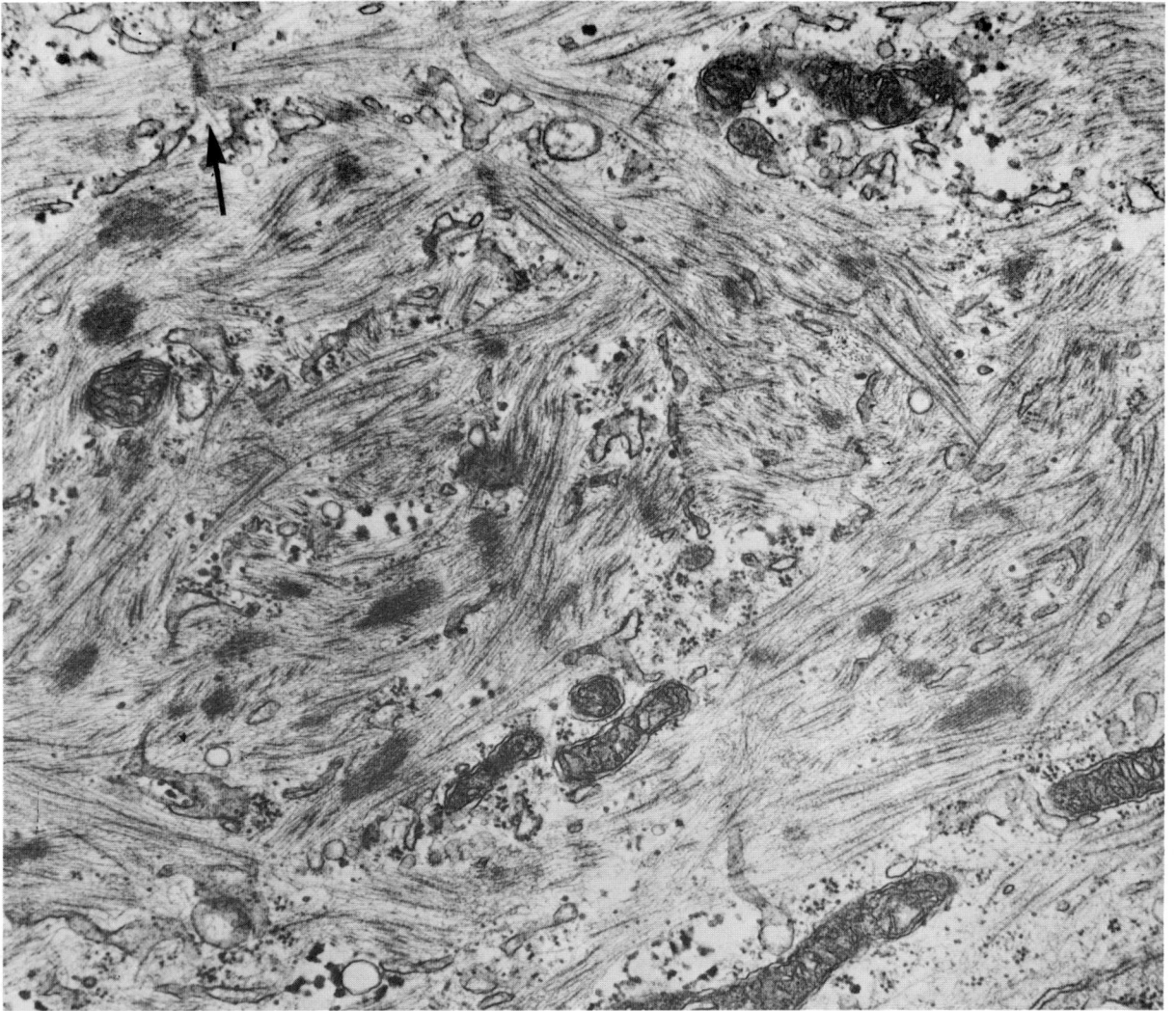

Figure 21.4. Myoid cell.
Portion of cell with scattered Z-band material and myofilaments. Primitive sarcomere formation is present (arrow). (×30,000)

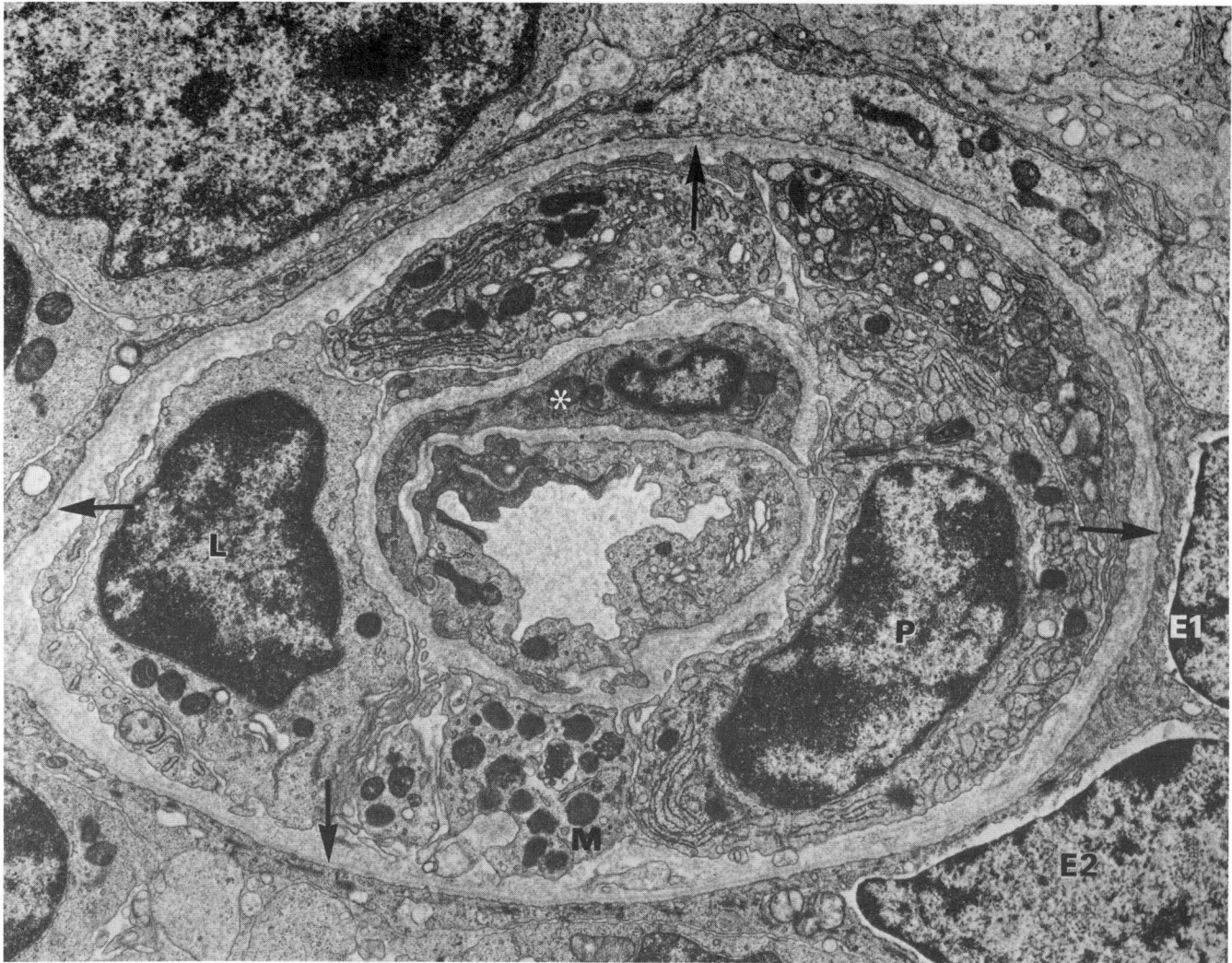

Figure 21.5. Thymic epithelium and blood vessel.
Epithelial cells (E1 and E2) and attenuated epithelial processes and basal lamina (arrows) separate thymic parenchyma from perivascular space. Cells in this space include a lymphocyte (L), a plasma cell (P), a mast cell (M), and a pericyte (asterisk) which follows the outer endothelial contour. (× 10,000)

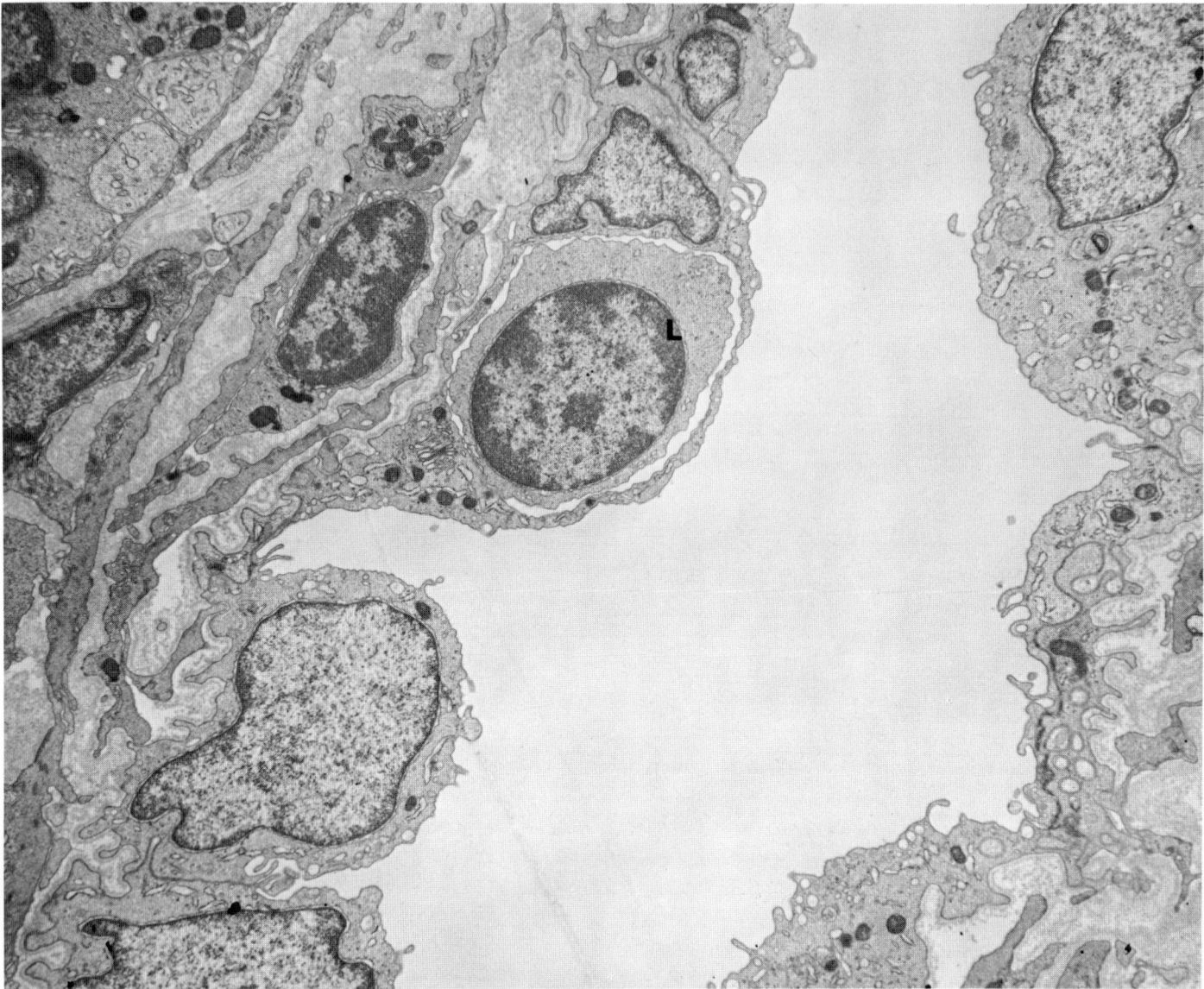

Figure 21.6. Migrating lymphocyte.
Lymphocyte (L) migrating between endothelial cells of thymic venule. (× 6,200)

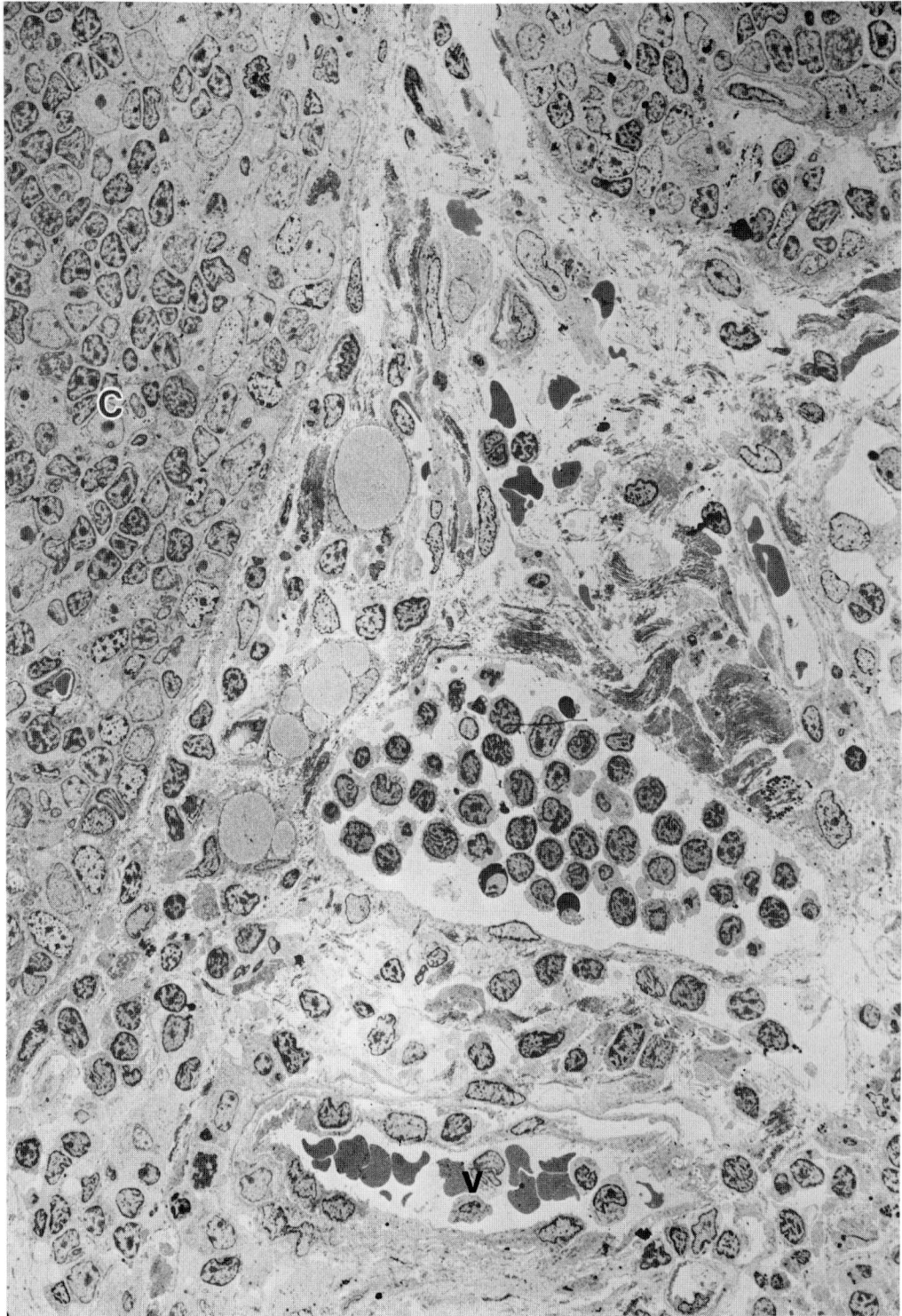

Figure 21.7. Thymic lymphatic vessel.
Surface lymphatic packed with lymphocytes (possibly emigrating?). Note venule (V). C: thymic cortex. (×1,000)

22. The Pathological Thymus

22.1. Thymic involution

In acute steroid-induced (stress) involution, the cortical lymphocytes undergo necrosis and lymphocytolysis. Consequently, lymphocytes in various stages of degeneration are found within macrophages (producing the ultrastructural equivalent of the cortical "starry-sky"). The shrinkage of the involuting thymus is reflected in the folded configuration of its outer basal lamina.[5]

In age involution associated with fatty replacement there is extreme loss of thymic parenchyma. Residual thymus may be represented only by double rows of cuboidal cells bearing little resemblance to the original organ. Electron microscopy confirms the epithelial nature of these remnants (Figure 22.1).

22.2. Thymic germinal center "hyperplasia"

In certain conditions, most notably myasthenia gravis, germinal centers are prominent in the thymus. They may also be present in the "normal" thymus.[43,74] Traditionally, germinal centers are regarded as being "medullary" in location.[19] However, our studies[36] and those of Tamaoki *et al.*[66] indicate that the germinal centers are located in the EPC adjacent to, but not truly within, the thymic medullary parenchyma. It is perhaps pertinent that plasma cells are normally found in the human EPC.[36] In mice the EPC venules at the corticomedullary boundary are permeable to macromolecules (e.g., horseradish peroxidase)[54] and this could explain antigen access to this zone.

The germinal centers (Figure 22.2) are ultrastructurally identical to those found in tonsils, lymph nodes, and spleen.[34,46,66] They are composed of a heterogeneous population including large and small lymphoid cells ("cleaved" and "noncleaved"), lymphocytes in mitosis, macrophages with ingested nuclear debris, and long-branching, desmosome-associated dendritic reticulum cells (Figure 22.3). The latter lack basal lamina and tonofilament bundles and are thus distinguishable from thymic epithelium (Figure 22.4). Furthermore, dendritic cells, unlike epithelial cells, contain alkaline phosphatase within their cytoplasmic processes.[66] These alkaline phosphatase-containing cells are said to be absent from the normal thymus and are presumed to originate from perivascular mesenchyme. No epithelial cells are present within germinal centers.

Although in our studies[36] polar orientation of the germinal centers was apparent on light microscopic examination (with the pale region aligned toward Hassall's corpuscles and the dark toward high endothelial venules) we could not distinguish these zones ultrastructurally.[45]

228

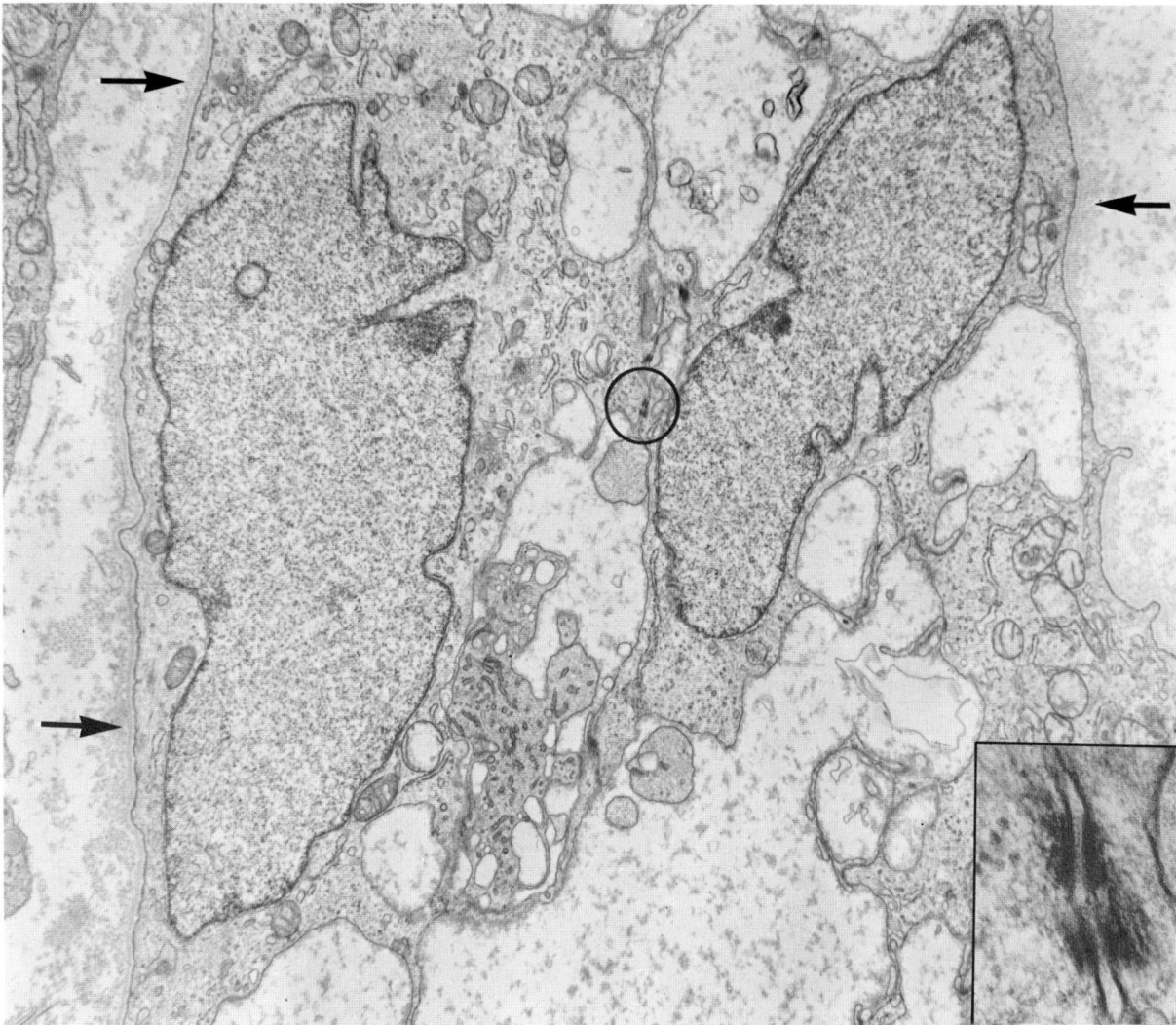

Figure 22.1. Severely atrophic thymus.
Double-layer of residual epithelium is visible. Note basal lamina (arrows) and desmosomes (circle). ($\times$ 16,000)
Inset (bottom right): Desmosomes depicted by circle in greater detail. ($\times$ 64,000)

Thymic epithelial processes and basal lamina clearly separate the germinal centers in the EPC from the thymic parenchyma (IPC) (Figures 21.1, 22.4).

Postcapillary venules (high endothelial venules) are often found adjacent to the germinal centers[6,63] and we have observed lymphocytes migrating between (not through) the lining endothelial cells.[59,70,78]

The role, if any, of thymic germinal centers in myasthenia gravis is unknown. Of obvious interest is the report of the transfer of myasthenia gravis from humans to mice by a serum IgG fraction.[71] This raises the possibility of deleterious antibody production by the thymic germinal centers. Vincent et al.[79] have demonstrated production of antibody to acetylcholine receptor in cultures of non-neoplastic thymuses from patients with myasthenia gravis.

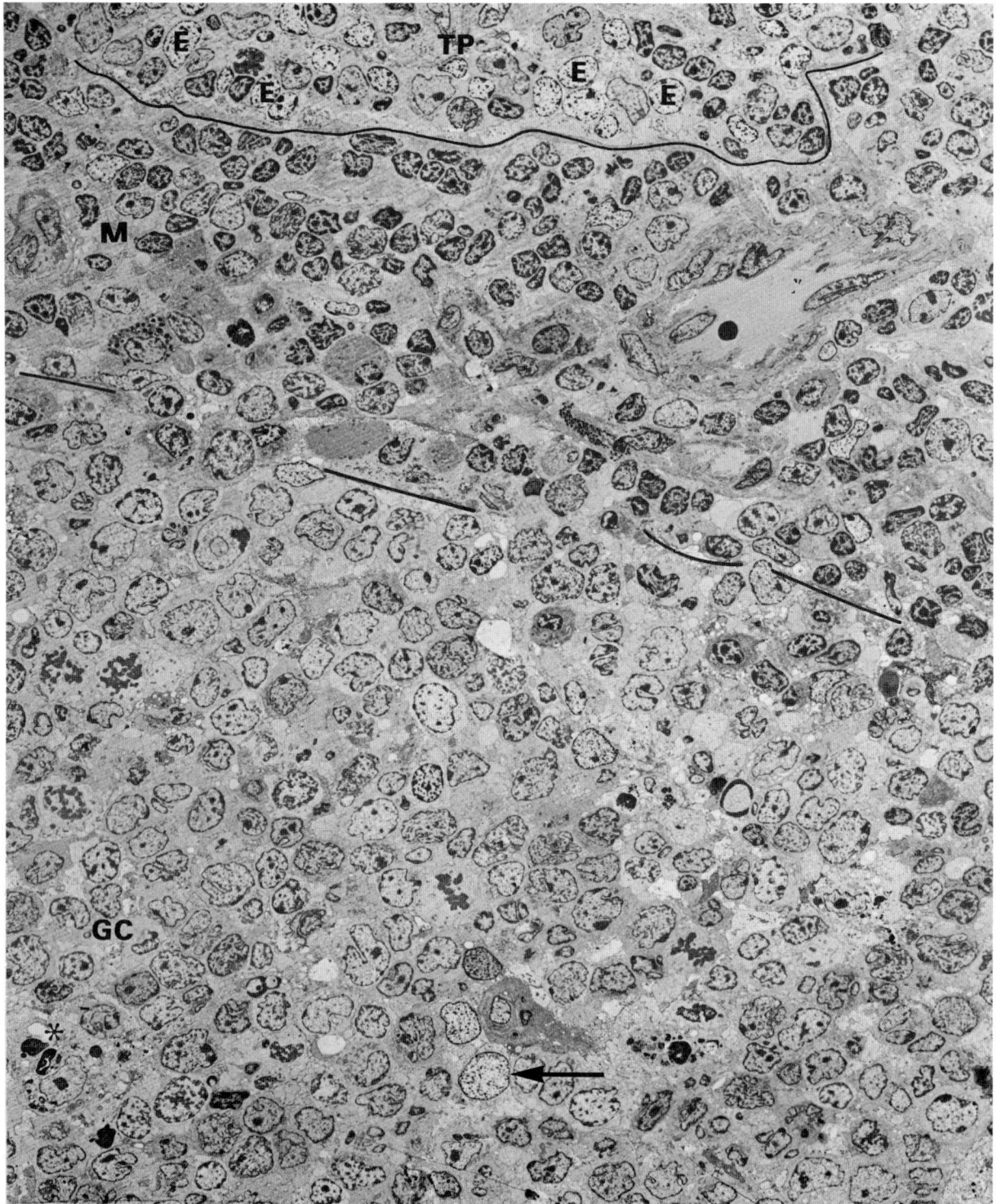

Figure 22.2. Thymic germinal center.
Artist's lines delineate thymic parenchyma (TP) from mantle (M) and mantle from germinal center (GC). Epithelial cells in thymic parenchyma have open nuclei with coarse chromatin clumps (E). Lymphocytes in mantle are mostly small and round. Within germinal center mitotic figures, nuclear phagocytosis (asterisk), many cleaved cells, and a dendritic cell (arrow) are visible. (× 1,800)

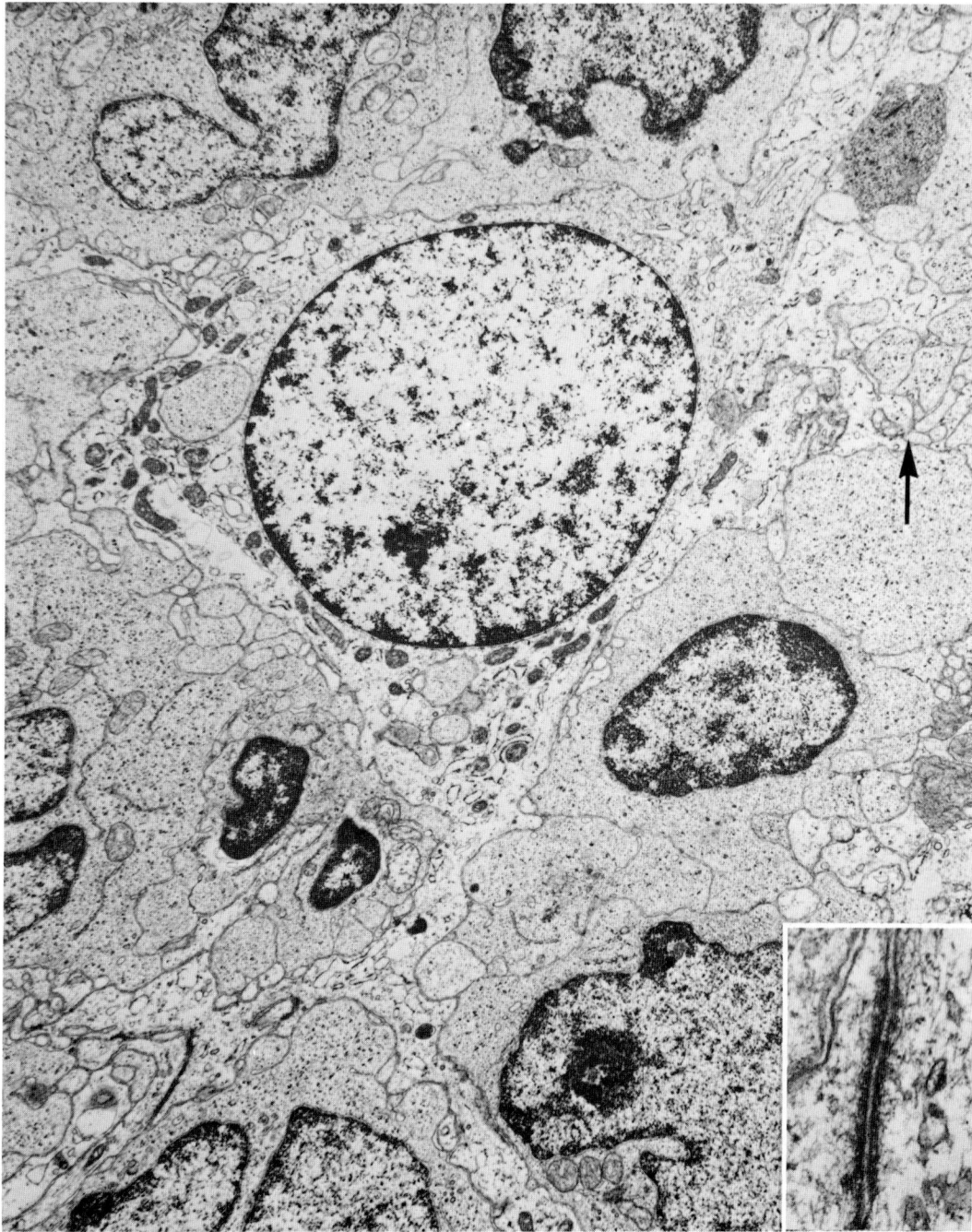

Figure 22.3. Dendritic reticulum cell in germinal center.
Ramifying cytoplasmic processes and complex interdigitations (arrow) are visible. Myasthenia gravis. (×4,000)
Inset: Desmosome (lower right field) in greater detail. (×36,000)

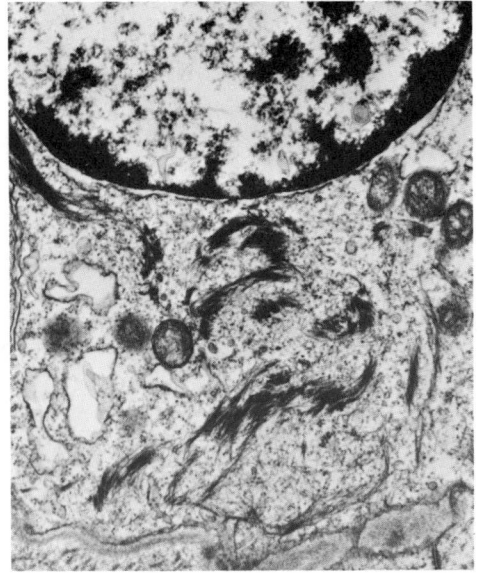

Figure 22.4. Epithelial cell at thymus-mantle interface.
Note bundles of tonofilaments and basal lamina. Myasthenia gravis. (× 15,000)

22.3. Thymic dysplasia

In thymic dysplasia the thymus is minute and is composed of spindle-shaped cells which fail to form Hassall's corpuscles.[57] There is no corticomedullary differentiation and lymphocytes are absent. These appearances are common both to a variety of combined immunodeficiency states and isolated T-cell defects. The epithelial nature of the spindle cells is appreciable only on electron microscopic examination (Figure 22.5).

22.4. Thymic neoplasia

Many different neoplasms have been erroneously grouped under the term "thymoma" merely because they share a location within the thymus. The important clinical reasons for separating these various entities have been discussed elsewhere.[57]

22.4.1. Thymoma

This neoplasm is essentially composed of epithelial cells which mimic either the overall epithelial-reticular framework or the more polyhedral and highly tonofilamentous epithelium of Hassall's corpuscles.[4, 11, 13, 17, 26, 32, 33, 35, 37, 38, 50, 62, 76] Variable

Figure 22.5. Dysplastic thymus.
Spindle-shaped epithelial cells with clearly visible desmosomes and convoluted basal lamina (arrow). (× 16,000)
Inset: Desmosomes depicted in greater detail (bottom right). (× 52,000)

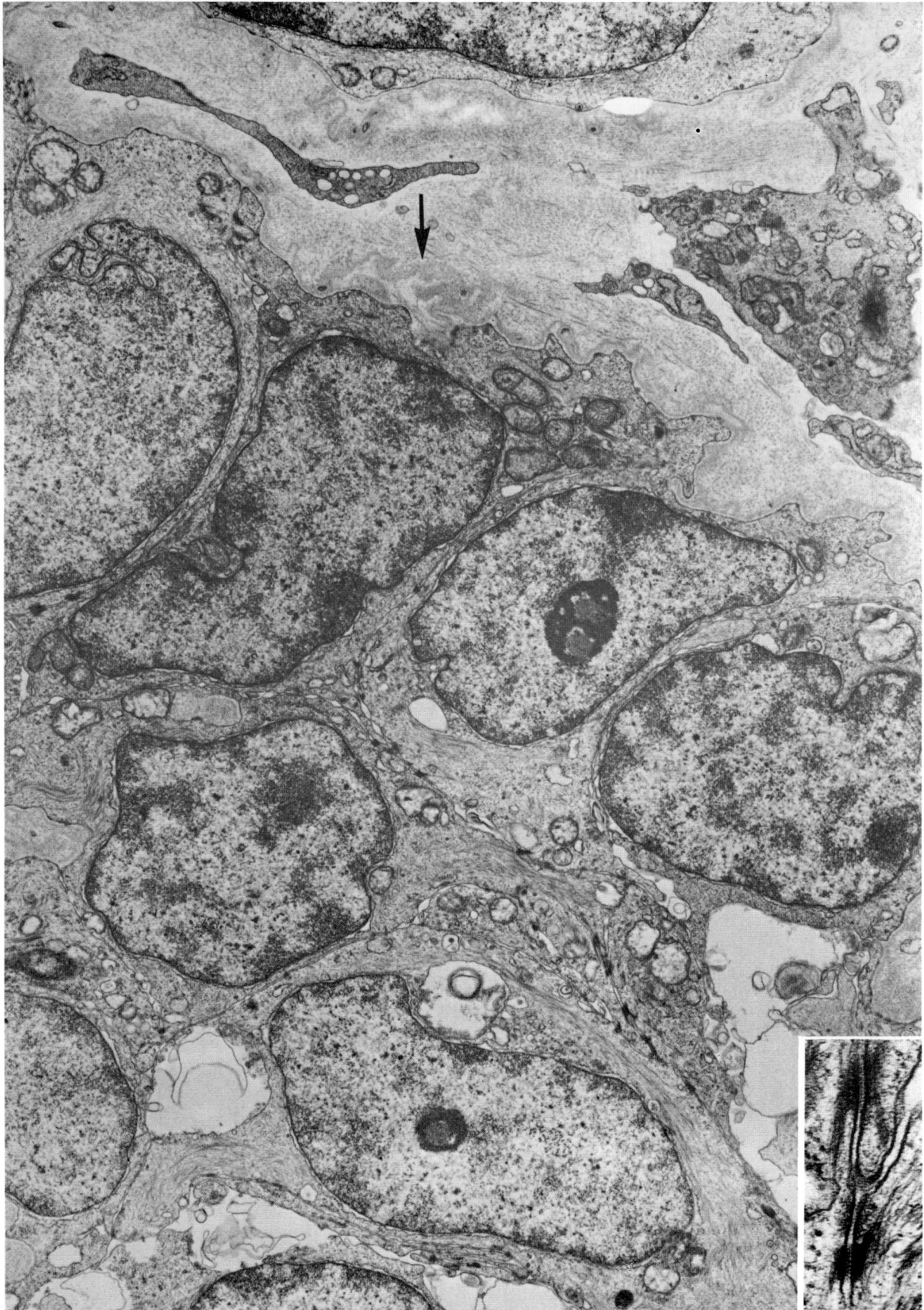

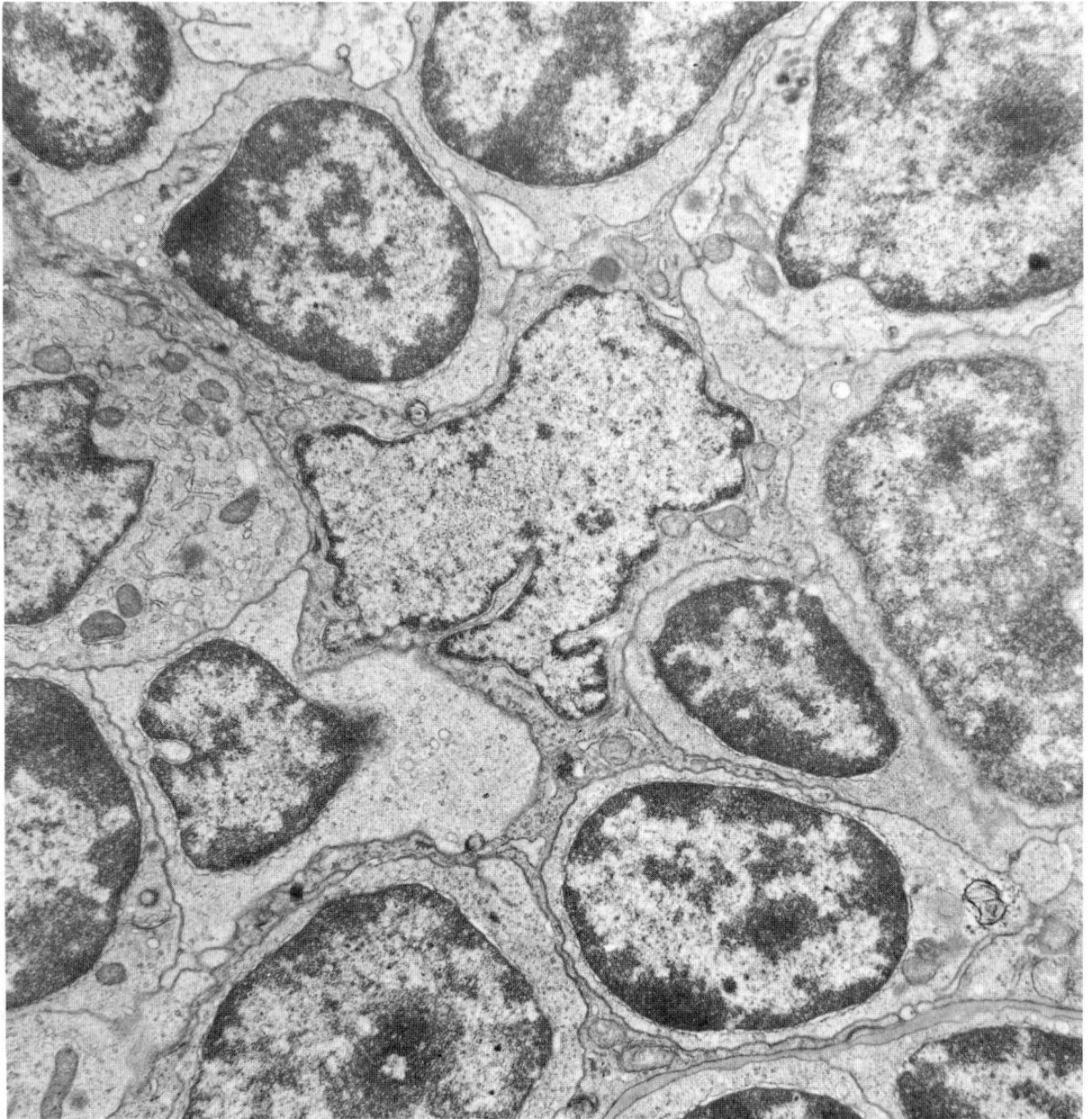

Figure 22.6. Epithelial processes in thymoma.

(a) Attenuated epithelial processes from central epithelial cell ramify amongst surrounding, closely applied, lymphocytes. (× 10,000)

numbers of lymphocytes from rare to numerous are admixed with the epithelium. These lymphocytes do not behave in a leukemic or lymphomatous manner.

Thymoma, as defined here, excludes Hodgkin's and non-Hodgkin's lymphomas, acute and chronic lymphocytic leukemia, germ cell tumors, and neoplasms whose cells contain dense-core secretory granules.[57]

The ultrastructural features of thymoma may closely mimic those of normal thy-

234

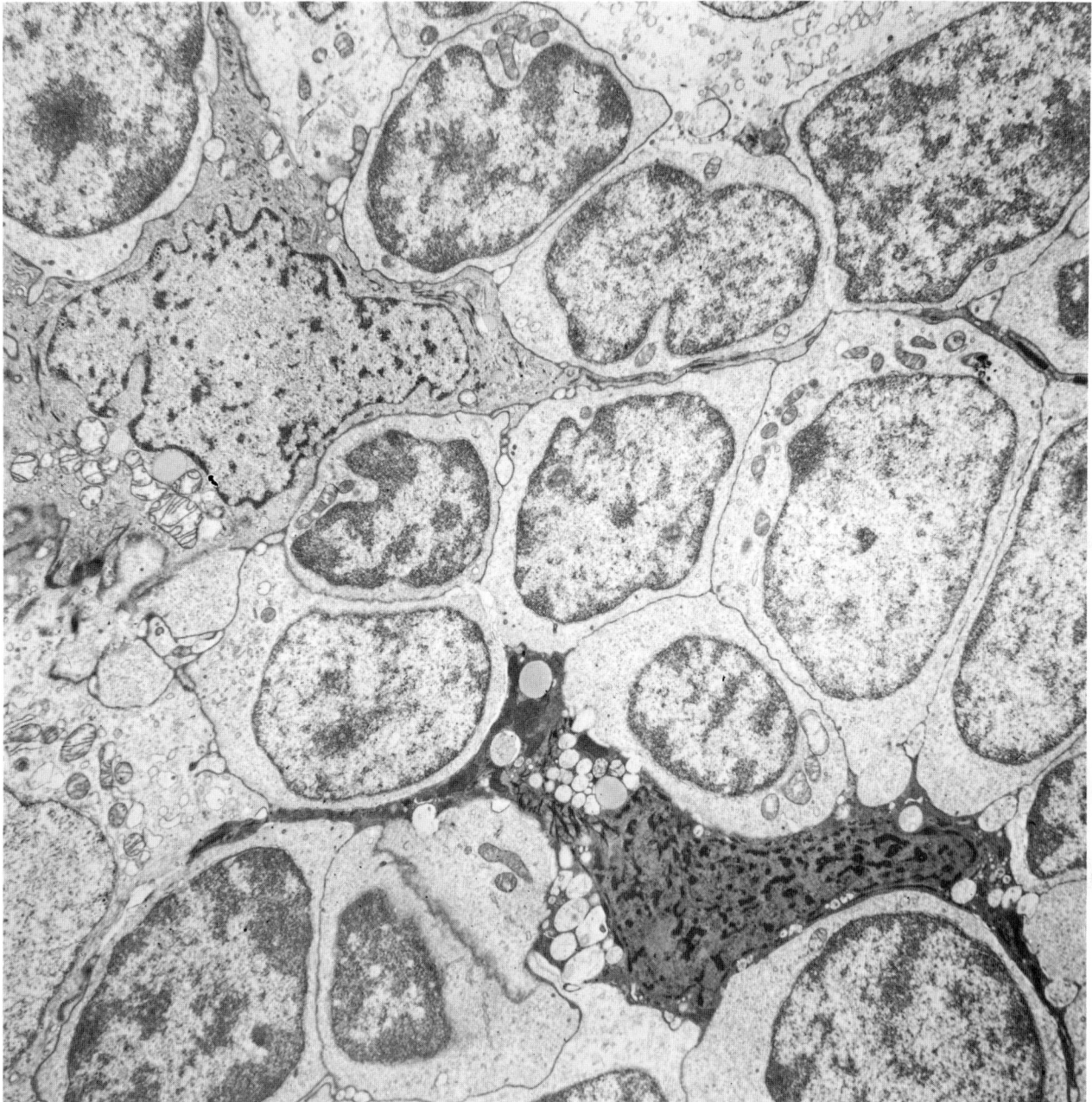

Figure 22.6. Epithelial processes in thymoma.

(b) Thin cytoplasmic processes originate from the two epithelial cells depicted here. Note electron-dense, degenerate, lower epithelial cell. (×5,500)

mus. In many thymomas, epithelial processes ramify through groups of lymphocytes (Figure 22.6(a),(b)). These processes are accentuated in degenerating electron-dense cells (Figure 22.6(b)). Attenuated epithelial cytoplasm and basal lamina surround blood vessels (Figure 22.7(a),(b)).[4,37,76] In some thymomas the epithelial cells are rounded or polyhedral and cytoplasmic processes are inconspicuous (Figure 22.8).

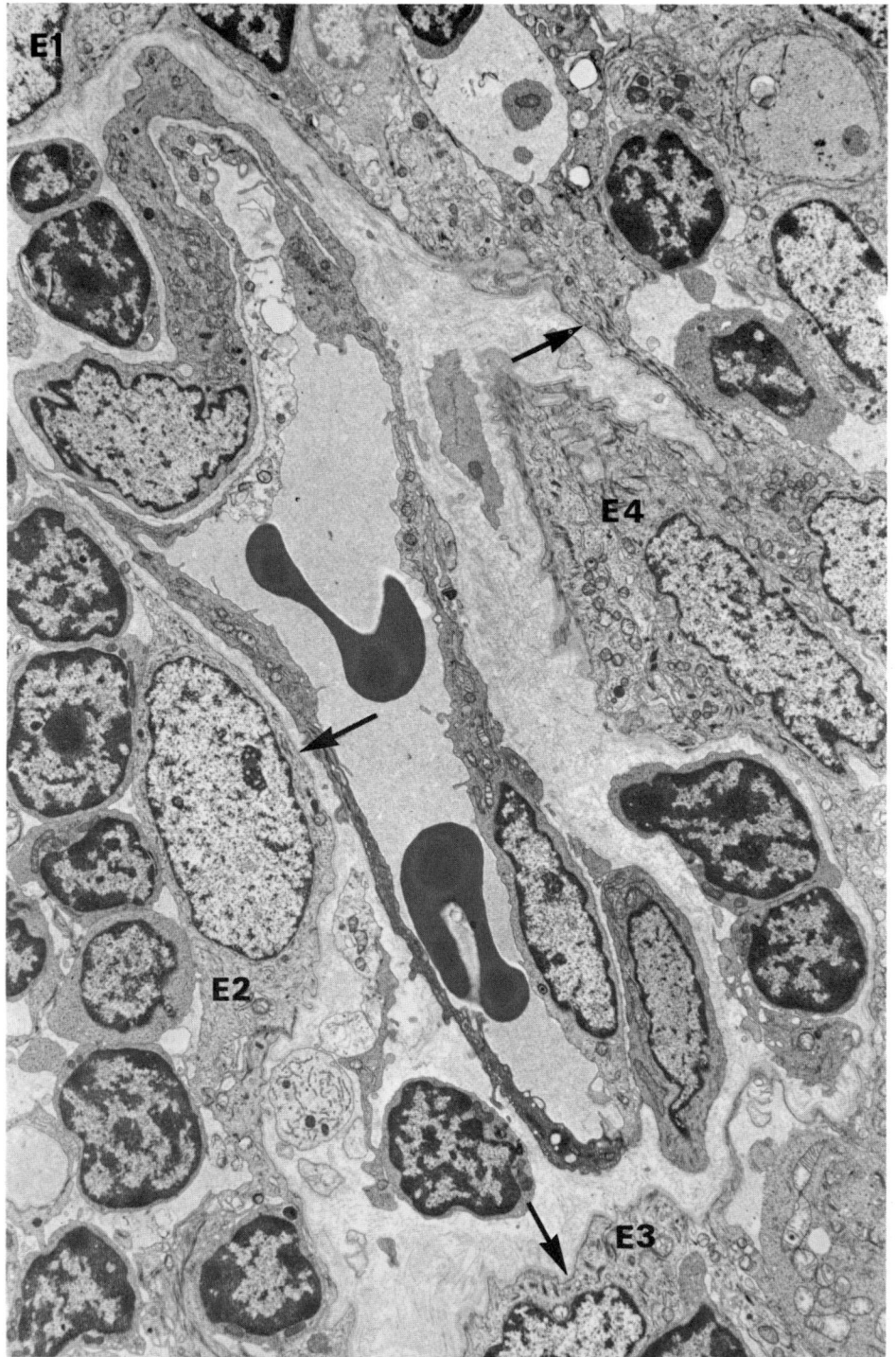

Figure 22.7. Epithelial–vessel relationship.

(a) Epithelial cells (E1, E2, E3, E4), their processes, and basal lamina (arrows), surround perivascular space containing lymphocytes. (×6,500)

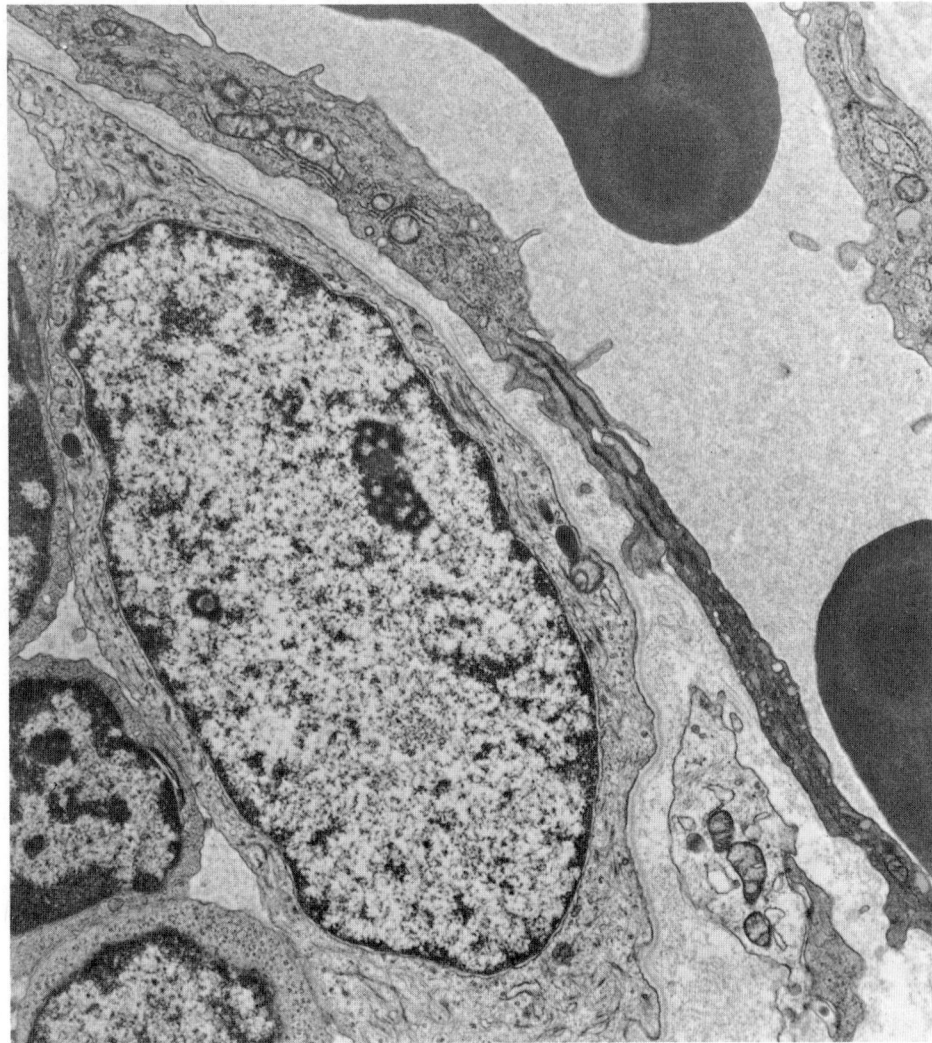

Figure 22.7. Epithelial–vessel relationship.
(b) Relationship depicted in greater detail. Basal laminae of epithelium and endothelium are easily identified. (× 15,000)

It is helpful to examine the perivascular region in such cases, since epithelial extensions and basal lamina are more readily identified in this location (Figure 22.7(a),(b)). Basal lamina is present at the epithelial–connective tissue interface (Figure 22.7(b)). It may run between closely apposed epithelial cells, halting abruptly where these cells are joined by desmosomes (Figure 22.10). Pascoe[50] described basal lamina reduplication around vessels.

The most constant and characteristic features of the epithelial cells are their tonofilaments and desmosomes (Figures 22.8, 22.9(a),(b), 22.10(a),(b), 22.12) which occur in varying proportions to each other. Some cells are electron-lucent, containing only

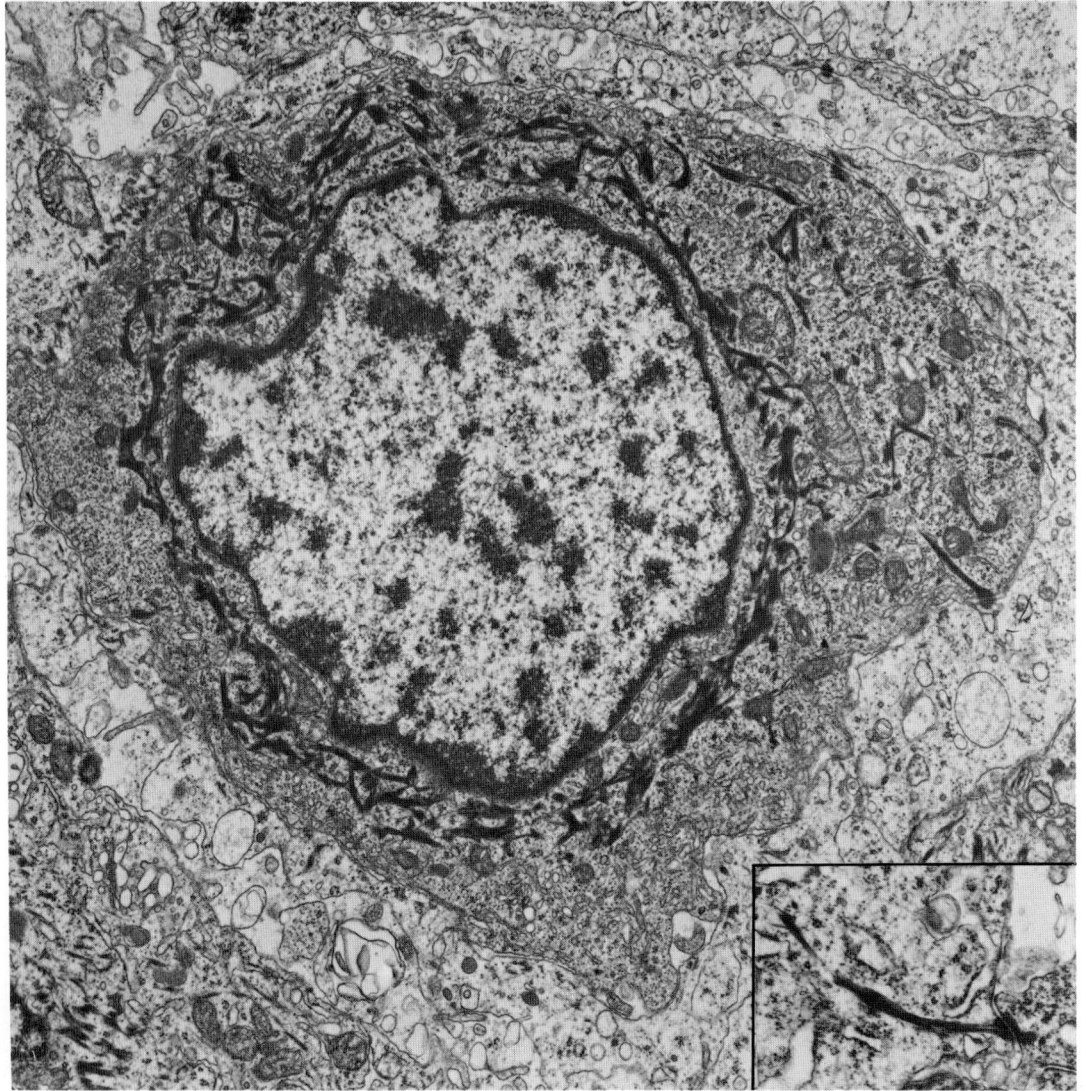

Figure 22.8. Rounded thymoma epithelial cell (G. D. Levine, J. Rosai, R. M. Bearman, and A. Polliack).
Many tonofilament bundles and a heterogeneous array of organelles are contained in the cell. (× 16,500)
Inset (bottom right): Desmosome. (× 20,000)

few tonofilaments but many desmosomes (Figure 22.9(a)), while in others tonofilaments form dense perinuclear bundles (Figure 22.8) which may extend into cytoplasmic processes. Complex interdigitations of the cytoplasmic membranes are frequently seen and desmosomes are often most prominent in such regions (Figure 22.9(b)). Spindle cell thymoma illustrates this especially well (Figure 22.10(a), (b)). Hemangiopericytoma-like areas within a thymoma prove on ultrastructure to be composed of epithelial cells.[33,62] The existence of a true hemangiopericytoma of the thymus has yet to be documented.

238

Epithelial nuclei are often markedly indented with subnuclear condensation of heterochromatin (Figure 22.6(a), (b)). While the nucleolonema may be well developed it does not approach the complexity seen in thymic seminoma.[32]

As with normal thymic epithelium, cytoplasmic organelles vary greatly in different neoplasms and from one region to another in the same neoplasm. Mitochondria, ribosomes, the golgi apparatus and vesicles, and microcysts may each be prominent in a particular cell. Lysosomes, lipid droplets, and rough endoplasmic reticulum are seldom conspicuous. Cytoplasmic glycogen and cilia formation are unusual features.[38]

Intraepithelial microcyst formation is prominent in ten percent of thymomas (Figure 22.11).[37,38] These cysts virtually replace the epithelial cell leaving only delicate cytoplasmic remnants. The cysts contain lymphocytes in various stages of degeneration. This phenomenon has been interpreted as representing emperipolesis.[38]

In 20 percent of thymomas the epithelial cells form gland-like lumina (Figure 22.12).[57] These contain microvillous projections, amorphous, electron-dense material, and degenerating cell remnants. Unlike true glands, these lumina are not surrounded by a continuous basal lamina. The lining cells show no obvious secretory characteristics.

We have been unable to correlate any of the above ultrastructural features with functional changes, e.g., myasthenia gravis.

The epithelial–vascular relationship closely reduplicates that of the normal thymus. Between the epithelial and endothelial basal laminae lies the perivascular zone (Figure 22.7). This is dilated in approximately 56 percent of thymomas.[57] Lymphocytes, red blood cells, macrophages, mast cells, or fibroblasts may be numerous in this space. It may also be filled with proteinaceous fluid or be obliterated by collagen. Lymphocytes are seen in transit across the epithelial basal lamina or between capillary endothelial cells.[37] The endothelial cells are occasionally fenestrated.[33,62]

Lymphocytes lie within the complex framework of epithelial cells. Their morphology is more variable than is generally recognized. While many are "quiescent" with abundant heterochromatin, inconspicuous nucleoli, monoribosomes, and electron-dense mitochondria, there are also large numbers of "transformed" lymphocytes (Figure 22.13).[24,37] These have euchromatin-rich nuclei, prominent nucleoli, electron-lucent mitochondria, and abundant polyribosomes. Lymphocyte nuclear blebs are rare in thymomas.[37] In all cases with at least a moderate lymphocyte component, lymphocyte mitotic figures are easily detected (four to five per high power field). Many necrotic lymphocytes, free and within macrophages, are often present. Langerhans granules have been identified in macrophages within a thymoma.[62]

Myoid cells are only rarely identified within thymomas.[72] Henry[18] has described a "thymic blastoma" with apparent transition between the epithelial and myoid component. Chopek et al.[7] have described embryonal rhabdomyosarcoma of the thymus and suggested a similar transition.

22.5. Differential diagnosis

The following neoplasms must be distinguished from thymoma.

22.5.1. Thymic carcinoid-like neoplasm

This neoplasm is usually nonfunctional but may cause Cushing's syndrome[52] or be

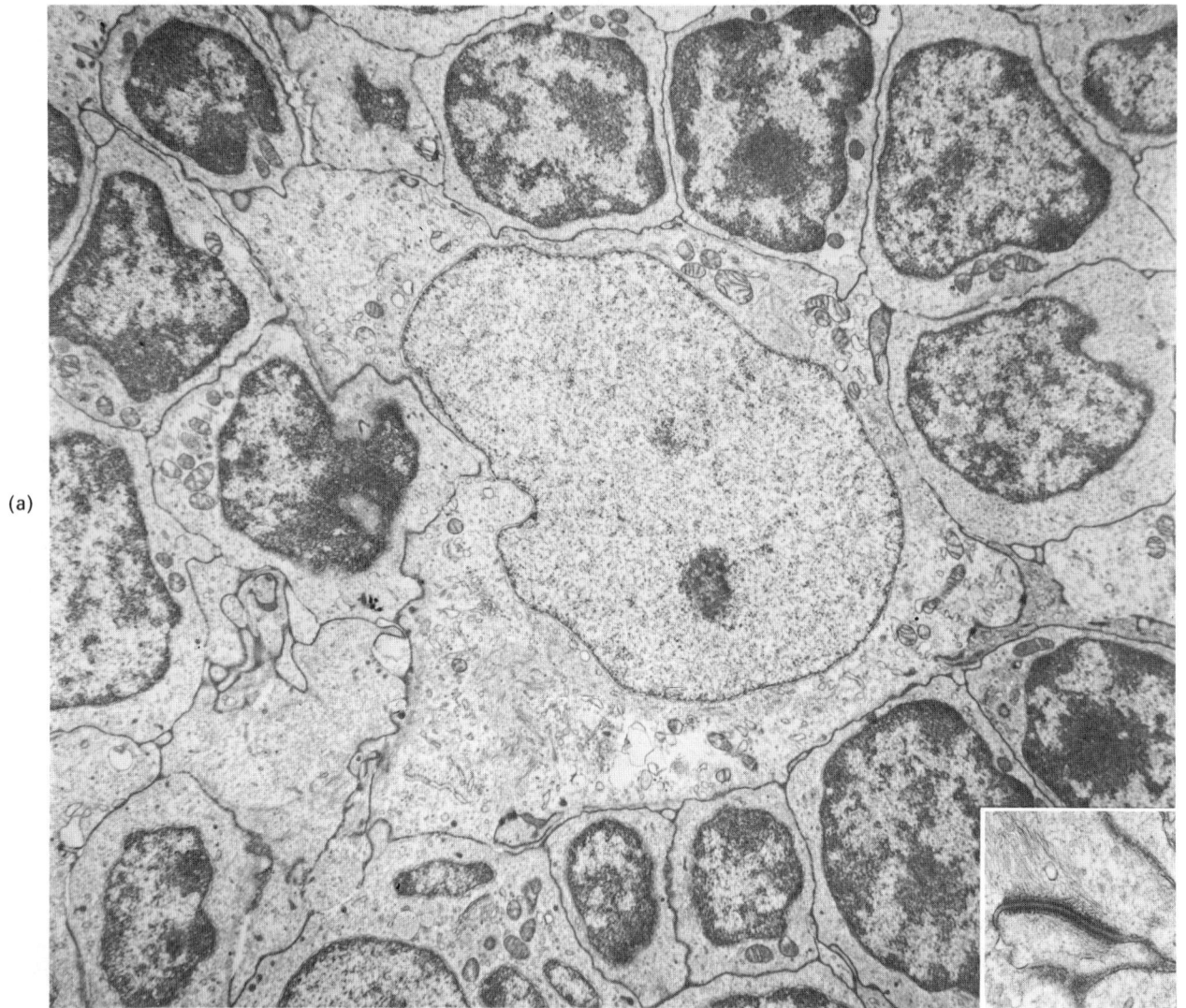

(a)

Figure 22.9. Examination of epithelial cells in differential diagnosis (G. D. Levine, J. Rosai, R. M. Bearman, and A. Polliack 22.9(b) inset).

(a) Epithelial cell with only scant tonofilaments is intimately surrounded by lymphocytes. ($\times 5,300$)
   Inset: Desmosomes, critical in establishing epithelial nature of cells. Light microscopic differential diagnosis of this case was histiocytic lymphoma versus thymoma. ($\times 25,500$)
(b) Interdigititating epithelial processes with many desmosomes. Basal lamina well seen. ($\times 16,500$)
   Inset (bottom right): Desmosome. ($\times 80,000$)

part of the multiple endocrine adenomatosis syndrome.[56] It is distinguishable from thymoma by means of both light and electron microscopic features.[57] A histologic spectrum between thymic carcinoid and thymic oat cell carcinoma has been described.[57] Numerous dense-core secretory granules are the hallmark of the thymic carcinoid (Figure 22.14); these granules have varied greatly in size according to different reports (Kay and Willson,[28] 4,000–5,000 Å; Rosai, Higa, and Davie,[56]

240

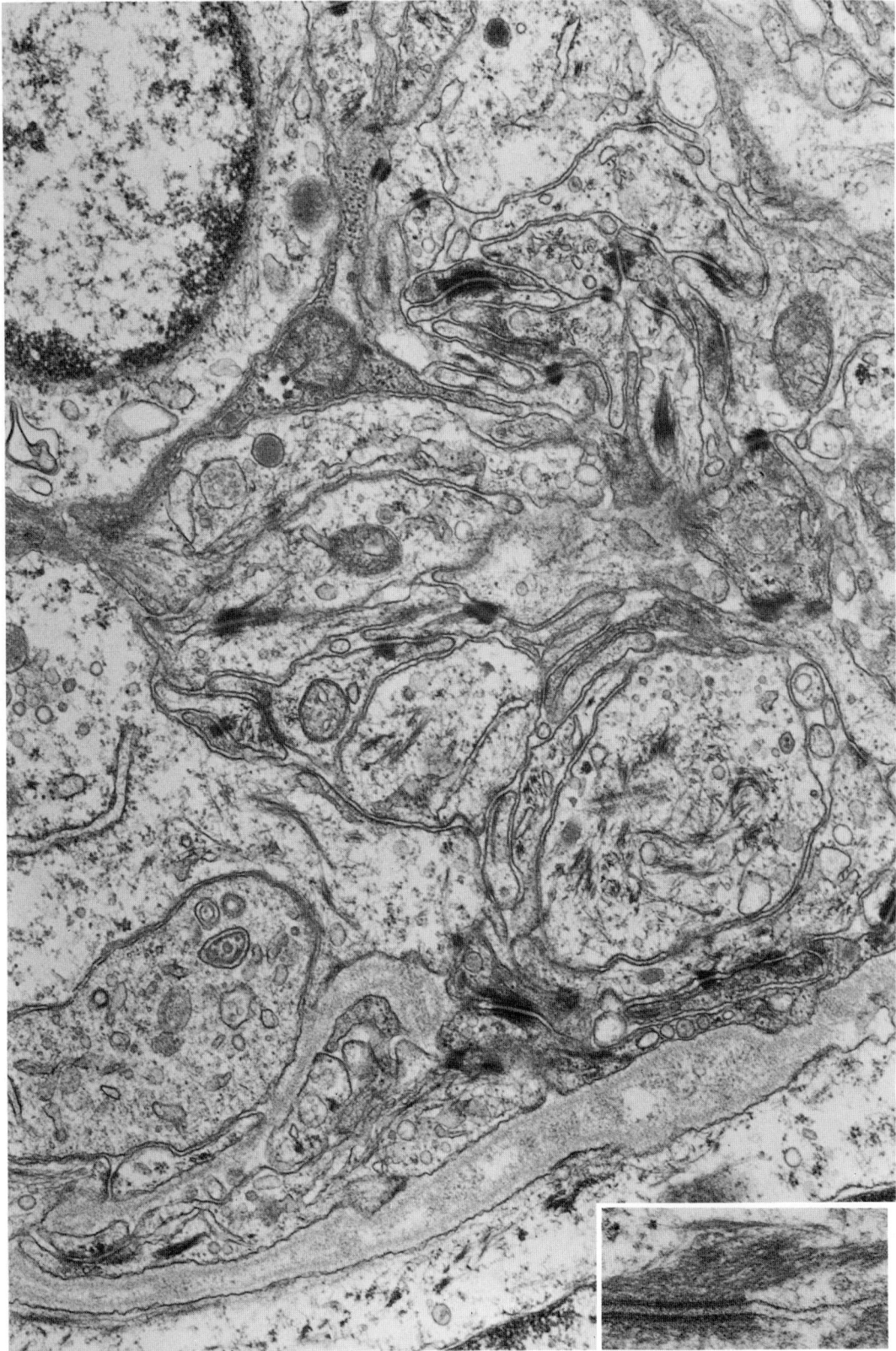

(b)

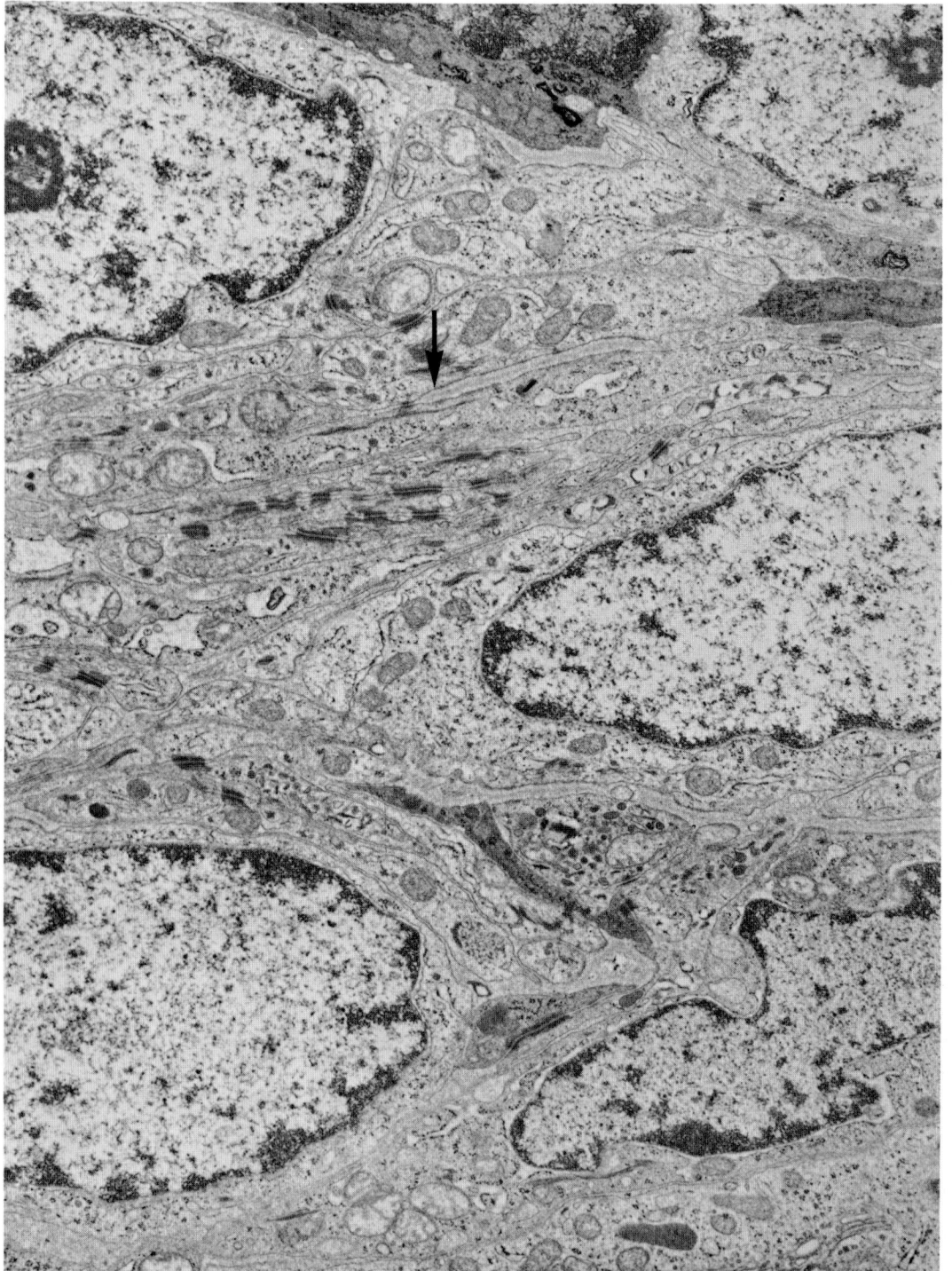

Figure 22.10. Spindle cell thymoma (G. D. Levine and K. G. Bensch).

(a) Numerous desmosomes are present. Basal lamina ends abruptly at desmosomal attachment (arrow). (× 15,500)

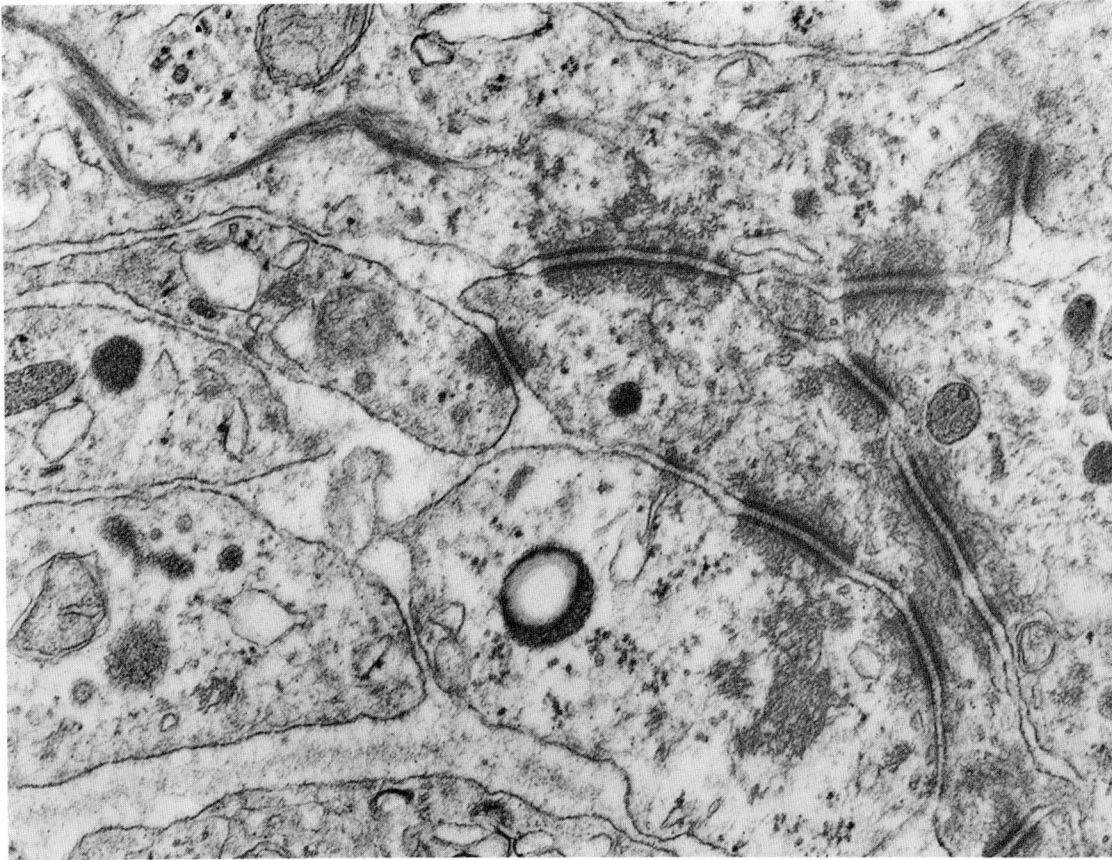

Figure 22.10. Spindle cell thymoma (G. D. Levine and K. G. Bensch).
(b) Desmosomes and tonofilament bundles (in longitudinal and cross section). Basal lamina also present. (×54,000)

600–4,000 Å; Manes and Taylor,[41] 700–3,600 Å; Tanaka *et al.*,[67] 1,500–2,000 Å; Hosoda *et al.*,[23] 2,000 Å; Rosai and Levine,[57] 1,085–4,500 Å; Macadam and Vetters,[39] 1,260 Å). Although prominent tonofilaments and well-formed desmosomes are usually absent in thymic carcinoids, we have seen two cases in which they were focally prominent. Basal lamina is found at the connective tissue interface. Lymphocytes are absent or scanty.

Ultrastructural examination is especially helpful in the diagnosis of the spindle-cell variant of thymic carcinoid.[57]

22.5.2. Thymic seminoma

Primary thymic seminoma[32] is ultrastructurally similar to testicular[51] or pineal seminoma.[42] The nucleolonema is prominent and ramifies across the nucleus (Figure 22.15). Although thymoma epithelial cells may have prominent nucleoli, the complex configuration regularly seen in seminoma cells has not occurred in the thymomas we

243

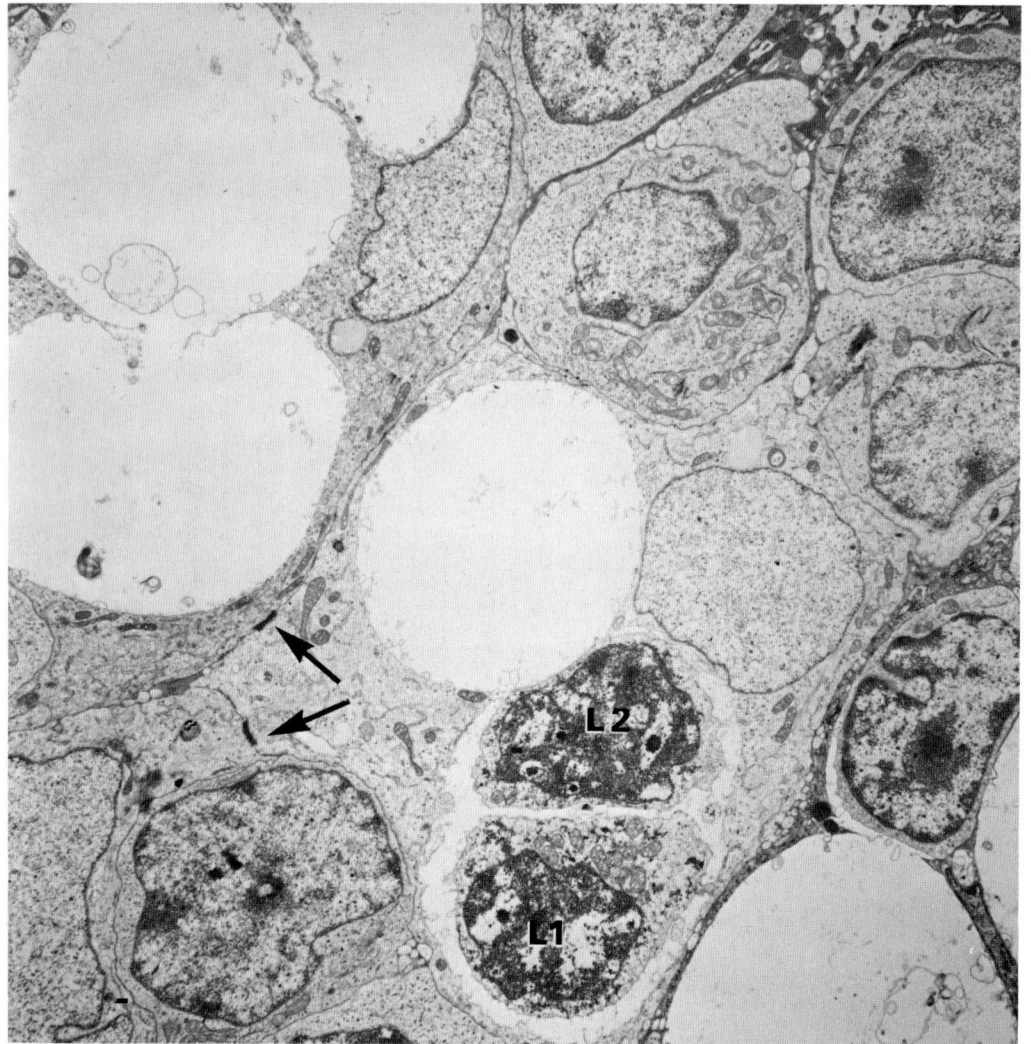

Figure 22.11. Intraepithelial cyst formation in thymoma.
Note desmosomes (arrows) and degenerating lymphocytes (L1, L2). (×3,000)

have examined ultrastructurally. Tonofilaments and maculae adherentes are inconspicuous in thymic seminoma. The seminoma cells have electron-lucent cytoplasm with few organelles and abundant glycogen. We disagree with Bloodworth[4] who states that seminoma is a variant of thymoma.

22.5.3. Thymic lymphoma

Hodgkin's disease may present localized to the thymus.[29] Unfortunately, the term granulomatous thymoma is still occasionally applied to thymic Hodgkin's disease. As with thymic carcinoid and seminoma, there are persuasive clinical and morphologic features that allow distinction from thymoma. In our experience, the Reed–Sternberg cells of thymic and extra-thymic Hodgkin's disease are ultrastructurally identical and

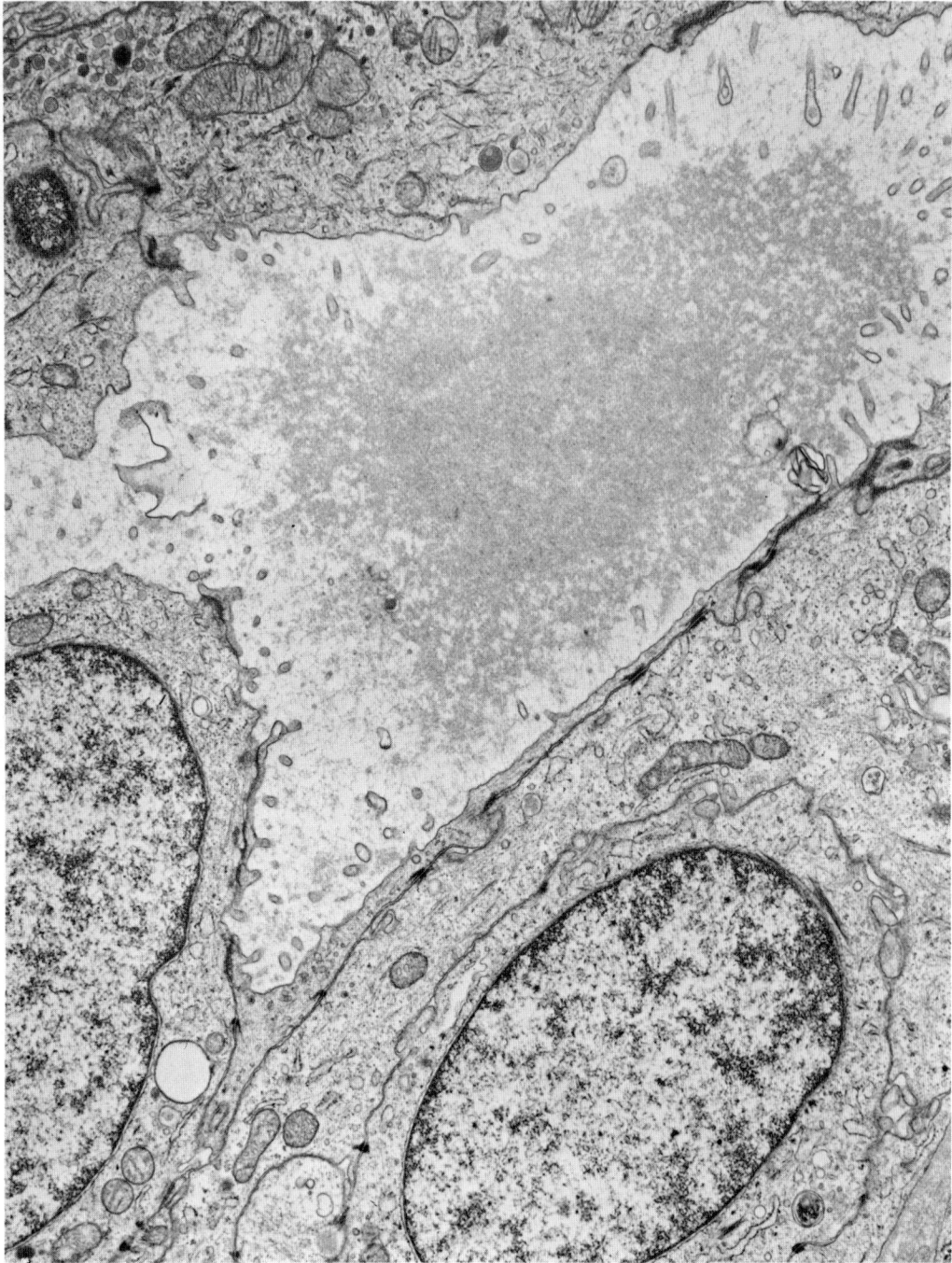

Figure 22.12. Gland-like space in thymoma.
(×20,700)

we find no evidence of epithelial derivation for these cells. Epithelial lined cysts in the thymus in Hodgkin's disease are nonspecific and accompany a variety of thymic neoplasms.

Convoluted and nonconvoluted lymphoblastic lymphoma cells[47] have irregular or

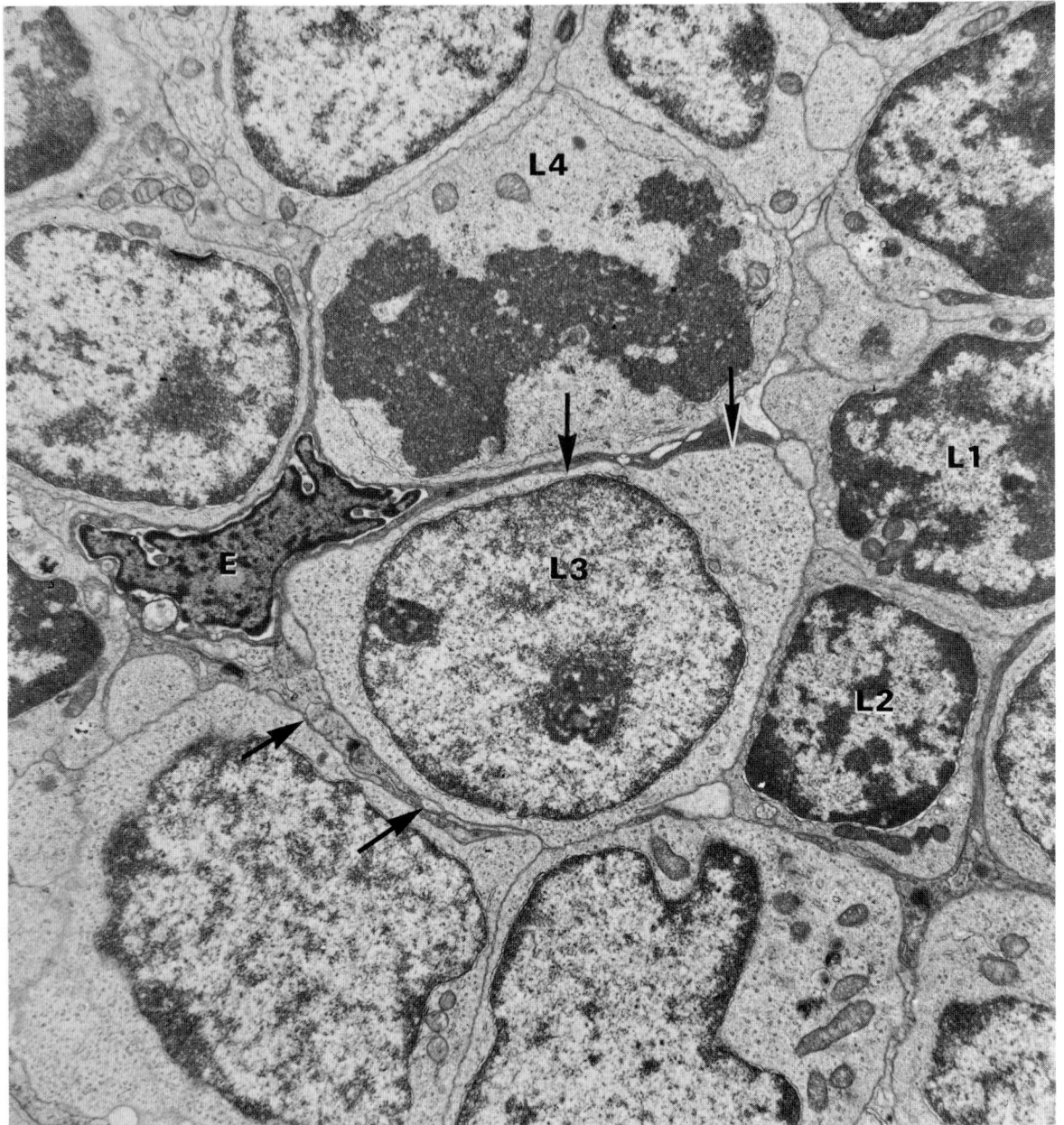

Figure 22.13. Lymphocyte–epithelial cell relationship (G. D. Levine, J. Rosai, R. M. Bearman, and A. Polliack).

Epithelial cell (E) processes lie adjacent to lymphocytes, depicted in various degree of morphologic "activation." L1 and L2 "quiescent", L3 "transformed," and L4 a lymphocyte mitotic figure. (×8,000)

rounded nuclei with evenly dispersed chromatin and numerous nuclear blebs (Figure 22.16). Thymic lymphoblastic lymphoma may represent a true malignancy of thymic lymphocytes.[64]

Thymic "histiocytic" lymphoma is composed of large lymphoid cells with abundant euchromatin and many nuclear blebs. Sclerosis characterizes these neoplasms

246

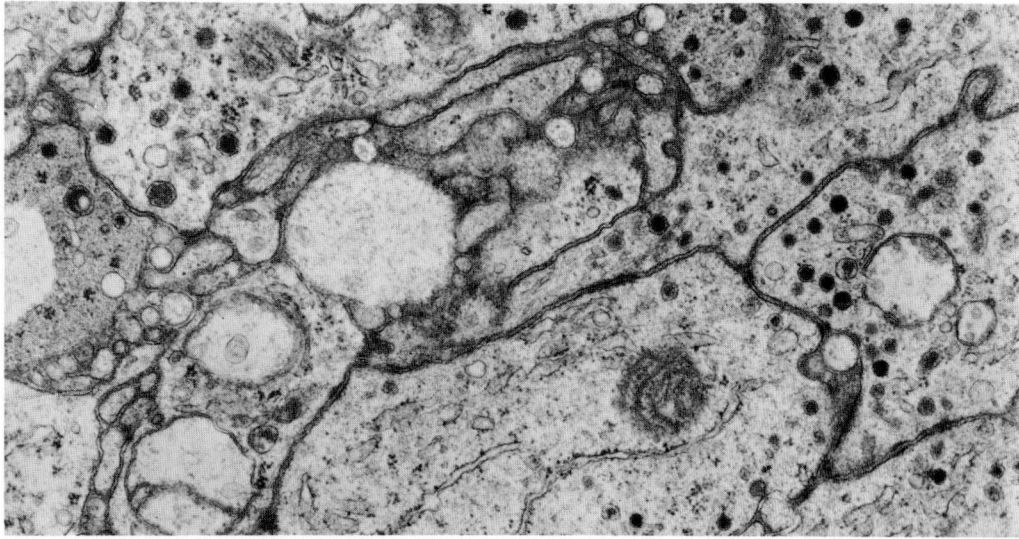

Figure 22.14. Thymic carcinoid.
Dense core granules are prominent. Complex interdigitating cell membranes reveal slight thickening but no formation of maculae adherentes. (× 22,000)

and the tumor cells lie in packets surrounded by sheets of collagen. Thymoma and thymic histiocytic lymphoma may be difficult to distinguish on light microscopy. Ultrastructural examination is especially valuable in such instances and Figure 22.9(a) illustrates such a case.

Residual thymic epithelium may be found in any of the lymphomas and should not be misinterpreted as being neoplastic.

22.5.4. Mesothelioma

Anterior mediastinal fibrous mesothelioma mimics spindle-cell thymoma. However, the spindle-cells in mesothelioma ultrastructurally resemble fibroblasts and lack desmosomes and tonofilaments.[20]

22.5.5. Conclusion

The different neoplasms that occupy the thymic region can usually be distinguished on light microscopic examination. In some instances this may be difficult and it is strongly recommended that a routine part of the morphologic evaluation of anterior mediastinal tumors includes ultrastructural examination of appropriately fixed tissue. This will do much to ensure accurate diagnosis and appropriate clinical management. Of particular value in establishing the diagnosis of thymoma is the demonstration of dense bundles of tonofilaments, desmosomes, extensively ramifying cell processes, and basal lamina at the connective tissue interface.

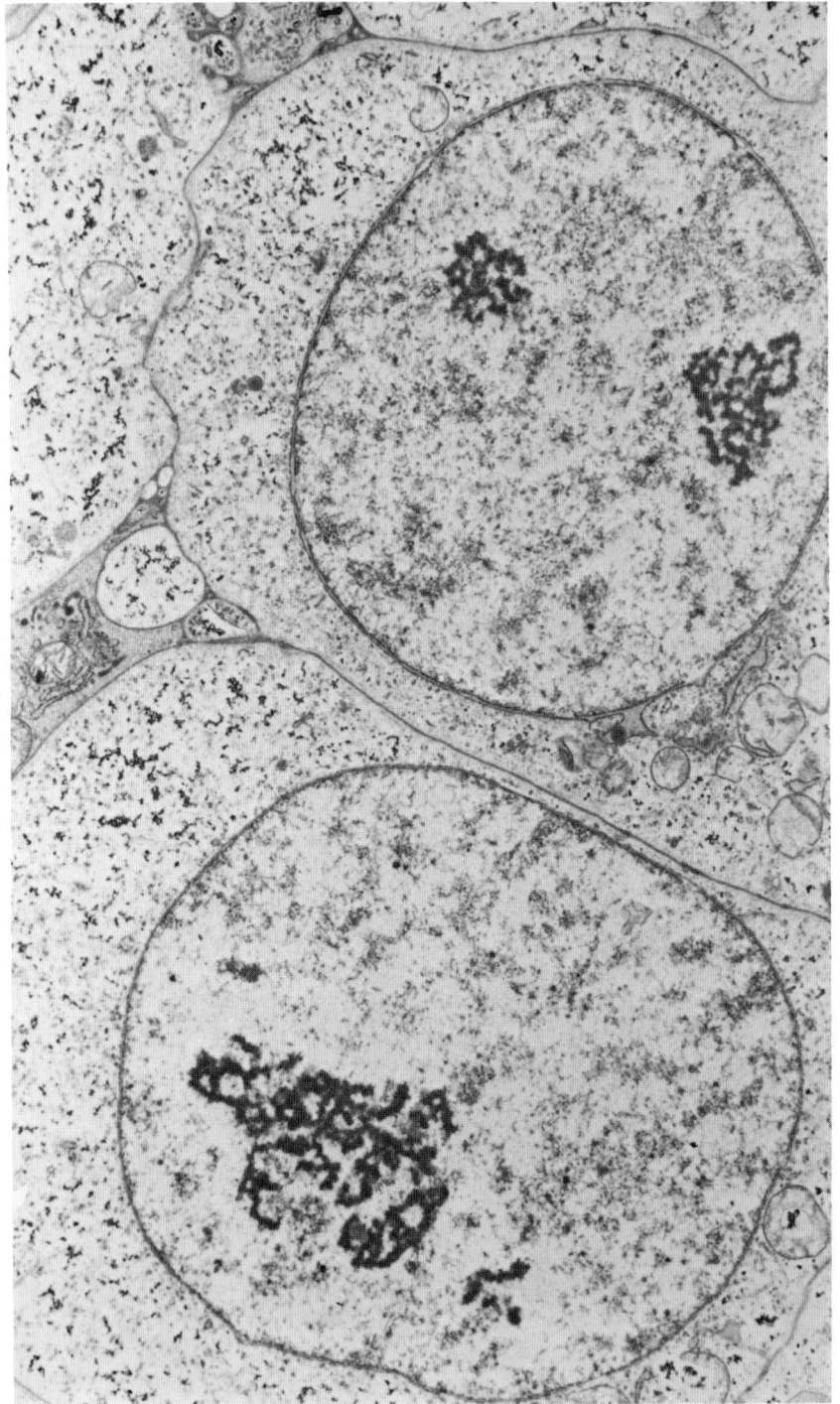

Figure 22.15. Thymic seminoma.
Neoplastic cells demonstrating complex nucleolonema and glycogen. Note absence
of tonofilaments and desmosomes. (× 13,300)

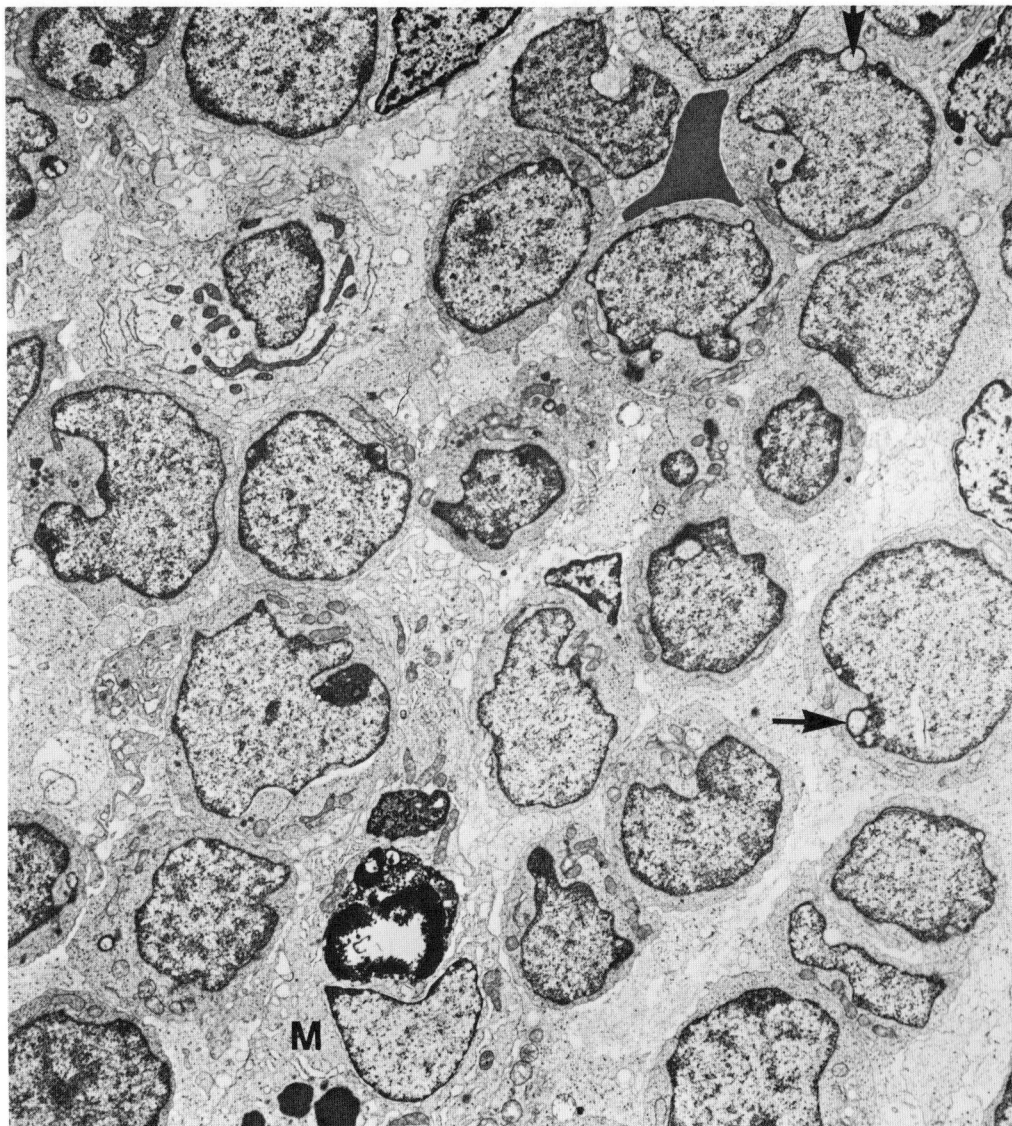

Figure 22.16. Thymic lymphoblastic lymphoma.
Note convoluted nuclei with even chromatin distribution, nuclear blebs (arrows), and a macrophage (M) containing nuclear debris. (× 5,600)

References to Part Four

1. Bach, J. P. and Carnaud, C., "Thymic factors," in P. Kallos, B. H. Waksman, and A. de Weck (eds.), *Progress in Allergy*, vol. 21, 1976, pp. 342–408.
2. Bearman, R. M., Bensch, K. G., and Levine, G. D., "The normal human thymic vasculature: An ultrastructural study," *Anat. Rec.*, **183**, 485, 1975.
3. Blau, J. N., "Hassall's corpuscles – a site of thymocyte death," *Br. J. exp. Path.*, **54**, 634, 1973.
4. Bloodworth, J. M. B., Jr., Hiratsuka, H., Hickey, R. C., and Wu, J., "Ultrastructure of the human thymus, thymic tumors, and myasthenia gravis," in S. C. Sommers (ed.), *Pathology Annual*, vol. X, Appleton-Century Crofts, New York, 1975, pp. 329–391.
5. Bockman, D. E., Lawton A. R., and Cooper, M. D., "Fine structure of thymus after bone marrow transplantation in an infant with severe combined immunodeficiency," *Lab. Invest.*, **26**, 227, 1972.
6. Bradfield, J. W. B. "Altered venules in the stimulated human thymus as evidence of recirculation," *Clin. Exp. Immunol.*, **13**, 243, 1973.
7. Chopek, M. W., Rosai, J., and Levine, G. D., "Malignant thymoma with rhabdomyosarcomatous ("myoid cell") differentiation: Report of a case and review of the literature," *Lab. Invest.*, **36**, 5, 1977 (abstract).
8. Clark, S. L., "Incorporation of sulphate by the mouse thymus: Its relation to secretion by medullary epithelial cells and to thymic lymphopoeisis," *J. exp. Med.*, **128**, 927, 1968.
9. Clarke, R. R. and Van de Velde, R. L., "Congenital myasthenis gravis," *Am. J. Dis. Child*, **122**, 356, 1971.
10. Ewijk, W. van, Verzijden, J. H. M., Kwast, T. H. and van der Luijex-Meijer, S. W. M., "Reconstitution of the thymus dependent area in the spleen of lethally irradiated mice," *Cell Tiss. Res.*, **149**, 43–60, 1974.
11. Fernandez, B. B. and Hartman, C., "Thymoma, erythroid hypoplasia and myasthenia gravis: Report of a case with ultrastructural study," *Illinois Med. J.*, **145**, 121, 1974.
12. Goldstein, G., "The isolation of thymopoietin (thymin)," *Ann. N.Y. Acad. Sci.*, **249**, 177, 1975.
13. Goldstein, G., Abbot, A., and Mackay, T. R., "An electron microscopic study of the human thymus: Normal appearances and findings in myasthenia gravis and systemic lupus erythematosus," *J. Pathol.*, **95**, 211, 1968.
14. Haar, J. L., "Light and electron microscopy of the human fetal thymus," *Anat. Rec.*, **179**, 463, 1974.

15. Hayward, A. R., "Myoid cells in the human foetal thymus," *J. Path.*, **106**, 45, 1972.

16. Henry, K., "Mucin secretion and striated muscle in human thymus," *Lancet*, **1**, 183, 1966.

17. ——, in R. Greene (ed.), *Myasthenia gravis*, Heinemann Medical Books, London, 1968, pp. 70–96.

18. ——, "An unusual thymic tumor with a striated (myoid) component (with a brief review of the literature on myoid cells)," *Br. J. Dis. Chest*, **66**, 291, 1972.

19. ——, in C. V. Harrison and K. Weinbien (eds.), *Recent Advances in Pathology*, 1975, Churchill Livingstone, Edinburgh, London, New York, 1975, pp. 30–72.

20. Hernandez, F. J. and Hernandez, B. B., "Localized fibrous tumors of pleura: A light and electron microscopic study," *Cancer*, **34**, 1667, 1974.

21. Hirokawa, K., "Electron microscopic observations of human thymus of the fetus and the newborn," *Acta Path. jap.*, **19**, 1, 1969.

22. Hoshino, T., Kukita, and Sato, S., "Cells containing Birbeck granules (Langerhans cell granules) in the human thymus," *J. Electron Microsc., Tokyo*, **19**, 271, 1970.

23. Hosoda, S., Suzuki, H., Kito, H., Hiai, H., and Akammey, Y., "Argyrophilic thymic carcinoid; clinico-pathologic study of four cases," *Acta Path. jap.*, **25**, 717, 1975.

24. Jones, D. L., Thomas K., and Jones Williams, W., "A fine structure of human thymus," *Beitr. Path. Bd.*, **156**, 387, 1975.

25. Kaiserling, E., Stein, H., and Muller-Hermelink, H. K., "Interdigitating reticulum cells in the human thymus," *Cell Tiss. Res.*, **155**, 47, 1974.

26. Kameya, T. and Watanabe, Y., "Electron microscopic observations on human thymus and thymomas," *Acta Path. jap.*, **15**, 223, 1965.

27. Kao, I. and Drachman, D. B., "Thymic muscle cells bear acetylcholine receptors: Possible relation to myasthenia gravis," *Science*, **195**, 74, 1977.

28. Kay, S. and Willson, M. A., "Ultrastructural studies of an ACTH-secreting thymic tumor," *Cancer*, **26**, 445, 1970.

29. Keller, A. R. and Castleman, B., "Hodgkin's disease of the thymus gland," *Cancer*, **33**, 1615, 1974.

30. Kotani, M., Seiki, K., Yamashita, A., and Horii, J., "Lymphatic drainage of thymocytes to the circulation in the guinea pig," *Blood*, **27**, 511, 1966.

31. Le Douarin, N. M. and Jotereau, F. V., "Tracing of cells of the avian thymus through embryonic life in interspecific chimeras," *J. exp. Med.*, **142**, 17, 1975.

32. Levine, G. D., "Primary thymic seminoma: A neoplasm ultrastructurally similar to testicular seminoma and distinct from epithelial thymoma," *Cancer*, **31**, 729, 1973.

33. —— and Bensch, K. G., "Epithelial nature of spindle-cell thymoma: An ultrastructural study," *Cancer*, **30**, 500, 1972.

34. —— and Dorfman, R. F., "Nodular lymphoma: An ultrastructural study of its relationship to germinal centers and a correlation of light and electron microscopic findings" *Cancer*, **35**, 148, 1975.

35. —— and Polliack, A., "The T-cell nature of the lymphocytes in 2 human

epithelial thymomas: A comparative immunologic, scanning and transmission electron microscopic study," *J. Immunol. Immunopathol.*, **4**, 199, 1975.

36. ―――― and Rice, D. F., "A revised concept of the location of thymic germinal centers in myasthenia gravis: An ultrastructural and immunologic study," *Lab. Invest.*, **36**, 17, 1977 (abstract).

37. ―――――, Rosai, J., Bearman, R. M., and Polliack, A., "The fine structure of thymoma, with emphasis on its differential diagnosis," *Am. J. Path.*, **81**, 49, 1975.

38. Llombart-Bosch, A., "Epithelioreticular cell thymoma with lymphocyte emperipolesis: An ultrastructural study," *Cancer*, **36**, 1794, 1975.

39. Macadam, R. F. and Vetters, J. M., "Fine structural evidence for hormone secretion by a human thymic tumour," *J. clin. Path.*, **22**, 407, 1969.

40. Mandi, B. and Glant, T., "Thymosin producing cells of the thymus," *Nature: New Biology*, **246**, 25, 1973.

41. Manes, J. L. and Taylor, H. B., "Thymic carcinoid in familial multiple endocrine adenomatosis," *Archs Pathol.*, **95**, 252, 1973.

42. Markesbery, W. R., Brooks, W. H., Milson, L., and Mortara, R. H., "Ultrastructural study of the pineal germinoma *in vivo* and *in vitro*," *Cancer*, **37**, 327, 1976.

43. Middleton, G., "The incidence of follicular structures in the human thymus at autopsy," *Aust. J. exp. Biol. med. Sci.*, **45**, 189, 1967.

44. Mills, G. Monticone, V., and Paetkau, V., "The role of macrophages in thymocyte mitogenesis," *J. Immunol.*, **117**, 1325, 1976.

45. Mori, M., Ishii, Y., and Onoe, T., "Studies on the germinal center. I. Ultrastructure of germinal centers in human lymph nodes with correspondence to the zonal differentiation," *J. Reticuloendothel. Soc.*, **6**, 140, 1969.

46. Mori, Y. and Lennert, K., *Electron Microscopic Atlas of Lymph Node Cytology and Pathology*, Springer, New York, 1969.

47. Nathwani, B. N., Kim, H., and Rappaport, H., "Malignant lymphoma, lymphoblastic," *Cancer*, **38**, 964, 1976.

48. Odland, G. F., "Histology and fine structure of the epidermis," in E. B. Helwig and F. K. Mostofi (eds.), *The Skin*, Williams and Wilkins, Baltimore, 1971, pp. 28–46.

49. Olah, I., Rohlich, P., and Toro, I., *Ultrastructure of Lymphoid Organs: An Electron-Microscopic Atlas*, Lippincott, Philadelphia, Toronto, 1975.

50. Pascoe, H. R. and Miner, S. M., "An ultrastructure of nine thymomas," *Cancer*, **37**, 317, 1976.

51. Pierce, G. D., "Ultrastructure of human testicular tumors," *Cancer*, **19**, 1963, 1966.

52. Pimstone, B. L., Uys, C. J., and Vogelpoel, L., "Studies in a case of Cushing's syndrome due to an ACTH-producing thymic tumor," *Am. J. Med.*, **53**, 521, 1972.

53. Pinkel, D., "Ultrastructure of the human fetal thymus," *Am. J. Dis. Child.*, **115**, 222, 1968.

54. Raviola, E. and Karnovsky, M. J., "Evidence for a blood-thymus barrier using electron-opaque tracers," *J. exp. Med.*, **136**, 466, 1972.

55. Rosai, J. and Higa, E., "Mediastinal endocrine neoplasm of probable thymic

origin, related to carcinoid tumor: Clinicopathologic study of eight cases," *Cancer*, **29**, 1061, 1972.

56. ———, ———, and Davie, J., "Mediastinal endocrine neoplasm in patients with multiple endocrine adenomatosis," *Cancer*, **29**, 1075, 1972.

57. ——— and Levine, G. D., "Tumors of the thymus," *Atlas of Tumor Pathology*, 2nd series, Armed Forces Institute of Pathology, Washington, D.C., 1976.

58. ———, ———, Weber, W. R., and Higa, E., "Carcinoid tumors and oat cell carcinomas of the thymus," in S. C. Sommers (ed.), *Pathology Annual*, vol. XI, Appleton-Century Crofts, New York, 1976, pp. 201–226.

59. Schoefl, G. I., "The migration of lymphocytes across the vascular endothelium in lymphoid tissue: A reexamination," (with an appendix by R. E. Miles), *J. exp. Med*, **136**, 568, 1972.

60. Sebuwufu, P. H., "Nuclear blebs in the human foetal thymus," *Nature*, **212**, 1388, 1966.

61. ———, "Ultrastructure of human fetal thymic cilia," *J. Ultrastruct. Res.*, **24**, 171, 1968.

62. Seemayer, T. A., Jerry, L. M., Shapiro, L., and Sullivan, A. K., "Spindle-cell epithelial thymoma. Fine-structural and tumor lymphocyte observations," *Am. J. clin. Path.*, **65**, 612, 1976.

63. Soderstrom, N., Axelsson, J. A., and Hagelqvist, E., "Postcapillary venules of the lymph node type in the thymus in myasthenia," *Lab. Invest.*, **23**, 451, 1970.

64. Stein, H., Petersen, N., Gaedicke, G., Lennert, K., and Landbeck, G., "Lymphoblastic lymphoma of convoluted or acid phosphatase type. A tumor of T precursor cells," *Int. J. Cancer*, **17**, 292, 1976.

65. Tachibana, F., Imai, Y., and Kojima, M., "Development and regeneration of the thymus: The epithelial origin of the lymphocytes in the thymus of the mouse and chick," *J. Reticuloendothel. Soc.*, **15**, 475, 1974.

66. Tamaoki, N., Habu, S., and Kameya, T., "Thymic lymphoid follicles in autoimmune diseases," *Keio J. Med.*, **20**, 57, 1971.

67. Tanaka, T., Tanaka, S., Kimura, H., and Ito, J., "Mediastinal tumor of thymic origin and related to carcinoid tumor," *Acta. Path. jap.*, **24**, 413, 1974.

68. Taylor, C. R. and Skinner, J. M., "Evidence for significant hematopoiesis in the human thymus," *Blood*, **47**, 305, 1976.

69. Toedorczyk, J. A., Potoworowski, E. F., and Sviculis, A., "Cellular localization and antigenic species specificity of thymic factors," *Nature*, **258**, 617, 1975.

70. Toro, I. and Olah, I., "Penetration of thymocytes into the blood circulation," *J. Ultrastruct. Res.*, **17**, 439, 1967.

71. Toyka, K. V., Drachman, D. B., Griffin, D. E., Pestronk, A., Winkelstein, J. A., Fischbeck, K. H., and Kao, I., "Myasthenia gravis. Study of humoral immune mechanisms by passive transfer to mice," *New Engl. J. Med.*, **296**, 126, 1977.

72. Van de Velde, R. L. and Friedman, N. B., "Thymic myoid cells and myasthenia gravis," *Am. J. Path.*, **59**, 347, 1970.

73. Veldman, J. E., Histophysiology and electronmicroscopy of the immune response. Ph.D. Thesis, Groningen, 1970.

74. Vetters, J. M. and Barclay, R. S., "The incidence of germinal centres in thymus glands in patients with congenital heart disease," *J. clin. Path.*, **26**, 583, 1976.

75. ——— and Macadam, R. F., "Fine structural evidence for hormone secretion by the human thymus," *J. clin. Path.*, **26**, 194, 1973.

76. Watanabe, H., "A pathological study of thymomas," *Acta Path. jap.*, **16**, 323, 1966.

77. Weiss, L., *The Cells and Tissues of the Immune System. Structure, Functions, Interactions*, Prentice-Hall, Englewood Cliffs, 1972.

78. Wenk, E. J., Orlie, D., Reith, E. J., and Rhodin, J. A. G., "The ultrastructure of mouse lymph node venules and the passage of lymphocytes across their walls," *J. Ultrastruct. Res.*, **47**, 214, 1974.

Supplementary reference

79. Vincent, A., Scadding, G. K., Thomas, H. C., and Newsom-Davis, J., "*In vitro* synthesis of anti-acetylcholine-receptor antibody by thymic lymphocytes in myasthenia gravis," *Lancet*, **1**, 678, 1978.

Part Five

Blood and Bone Marrow

Richard D. Brunning
Jorge E. Maldonado

23. Introduction to Part Five

Electron microscopy has had wide application in the study of diseases of the hematopoietic system. These studies have contributed greatly to our understanding of the biology of the hematopoietic cells and to the processes which result in functional disturbances in these cells. Conversely, studies of the functional characteristics of hematopoietic cells also contribute to our understanding of their ultrastructure, both normal and abnormal. As a result, the contribution of electron microscopy to hematology and hematopathology will be influenced to a considerable extent by the context in which ultrastructural studies are placed. Electron microscopic studies of normal and abnormal hematopoiesis will achieve greatest significance when they are considered in relationship to all the data available in an individual case, including clinical findings, light microscopic studies, both routine and cytochemical, membrane surface marker studies, chromosome analysis, cell enzyme levels, cell culture results, and immunoglobulin studies. The application of cytochemical and immunocytochemical techniques to electron microscopy has been an important advance in the ultrastructural study of hematopoietic tissue and has enhanced the role of electron microscopy in the study and diagnosis of diseases of the hematopoietic system.

The selection of hematology cases to be studied is of considerable importance. In general, more information will be derived from the study of several examples of one disease process than of one example of several disease processes. Naturally, there are exceptions to this generalization and the opportunity to study a single case with unique morphologic and clinical features should not be missed.

From a practical point of view, it is possible to fix and embed a large number of specimens for electron microscopy with a relatively minor expenditure of time and effort as compared to the sectioning and examination of specimens. As a result, the routine preparation of all potentially interesting specimens for electron microscopy obviates the necessity of performing a second biopsy after determination from other studies that electron microscopy might contribute to the diagnosis or understanding of a disease process. Those specimens which are not immediately examined can be stored for later study.

The preparation of peripheral blood and marrow specimens for electron microscopy, because of their fluid state and the necessity of separating the cellular elements from the plasma, requires a method of handling different to those used for other tissues. Several different techniques can be utilized to accomplish this. In this laboratory blood specimens are processed in the following manner. Ten ml of blood drawn in a plastic syringe and placed in a glass tube containing 0·04 ml of 30 per cent ethylenediamine-tetraacetic acid (EDTA) are centrifuged in Wintrobe tubes at 2,000g for 15 minutes. The plasma layer is withdrawn and a modified Karnovsky fixative is added over the packed leukocyte layer. The tube is scored at the lower margin of the packed leukocytes and the portion of the tube with the exposed leukocyte layer is placed in a vial of fixative. After 10 minutes the leukocyte layer is gently ejected into a vial of fresh fixative. The specimens are fixed for at least 12 hours at 4° C in a modified Karnovsky fixative[73] of 2 percent paraformaldehyde and 2 percent glutaraldehyde in 0·1 M sodium cacodylate-HCL buffer with 9·5 mg/ml calcium chloride at pH 7·3. The fixed specimens are washed for 12 hours at 4° C in 0·05 M sodium cacodylate-HCL buffer with 0·2 M sucrose at pH 7·3. Postfixation is carried out at 0° C for 1½ hours in 1 percent osmium tetroxide buffered with veronal acetate at pH 7·4.[27] The samples are then dehydrated in a graded series of ethanol, followed by two changes of propylene oxide and embedded in Maraglas (Marblette Company, Division of Allied Products Corporation, Long Island, New York) and polymerized at 52° C for 48 hours. All specimens are double stained with uranyl acetate and lead citrate.

The bone marrow specimen is placed in anticoagulant immediately after aspiration. In the laboratory the specimen is poured onto a clean watchglass. The bone marrow particles are separated from the fluid portion of the specimen and placed directly into fixative. The fluid portion of the specimen is then processed in a manner identical to that used for the peripheral blood. The nucleated cell layer is handled in the same way as the packed leukocyte layer. In addition to fixation of the particles and packed nucleated cell layer, portions of trephine biopsy specimens can also be placed in fixative for ultrastructural study. Because of the large portions of tissue with large bone trabeculae, this type of specimen does not give results as satisfactory as those for the other two specimens.

The following seven chapters cover the ultrastructural features of a wide spectrum of hematologic disorders, the five major topics being the anemias, the leukemias, plasma cell dyscrasias, reactive leukocyte processes, and hereditary anomalies. We have placed emphasis on those disorders which are most commonly encountered in diagnostic hematopathology; these include, primarily, the various types of leukemias and the plasma cell dyscrasias. Most of the diseases discussed are introduced with a brief résumé of relevant light microscopic features of the disorder. For more complete descriptions of these disease processes, the reader should refer to the standard textbooks and atlases of hematology (see, for example, p. 381).

Because of the heterogeneous nature of the hematopoietic cells, no description of the normal ultrastructural characteristics of these cells will be attempted. For detailed descriptions of normal ultrastructure, the reader is referred to *Living Cells and Their Ultrastructure* by Dr. Marcel Bessis (see p. 380).

24. Anemias

24.1. Cytoplasmic maturation defects

The cytoplasmic maturation defects are disorders of erythrocyte production which are characterized by disturbances in the synthesis of hemoglobulin. There are three primary groups of diseases in this category: iron deficiency anemia, the sideroblastic anemias, and the thalassemia syndromes. Ultrastructural studies have focused primarily on the thalassemia syndromes and the sideroblastic anemias.

24.1.1. Thalassemia syndromes

The thalassemia syndromes are genetically determined disorders of the biosynthesis of the alpha and beta polypeptide chains of the hemoglobin molecule, presumably due to a quantitative defect in messenger RNA.[6] The alpha thalassemias result from defects in the synthesis of the alpha polypeptide chains and the beta thalassemias result from defects in the synthesis of the beta polypeptide chains. The decrease in production of one or other of the polypeptide chains results in unbalanced chain production. In beta thalassemia compensatory increases in the production of gamma and delta chains give rise to elevated levels of fetal and A_2 hemoglobins. In the alpha thalassemias the gamma chains and beta chains form tetramers giving rise to hemoglobin Barts and hemoglobin H. The homozygous states are referred to as thalassemia major and the heterozygous states, thalassemia minor. This classification oversimplifies the thalassemia syndromes which show considerable variation in clinical and laboratory manifestations.[6]

Polliack et al.[127,128] have described the ultrastructural findings in the erythroid series of patients with beta thalassemia major. The red cells from the blood of these patients show striking findings (Figure 24.1), more marked in splenectomized than non-splenectomized patients. The most prominent feature in the cytoplasm is the presence of Heinz bodies in various stages of development (Figure 24.1). In contrast to the Heinz bodies in phenylhydrazine-induced anemia, there are no large marginated Heinz bodies in the thalassemic red cells. The cytoplasm also shows marked accumulations of iron in different forms, either as free particles or as aggregates of ferritin within membrane-bound particles or mitochondria. There are many bizarre membrane forms and myelin figures. Some reticulocytes show parallel arrays of tubules resembling cisternae at the periphery. Some cells are greatly distorted and deformed with indentations and infolding of the plasma membrane and marked vacuole formation. Glycogen is often found in the cytoplasm of erythroblasts.

The nuclear changes in thalassemia major are predominantly alterations in the nuclear membranes or findings related to the loss of nuclear membrane structure.

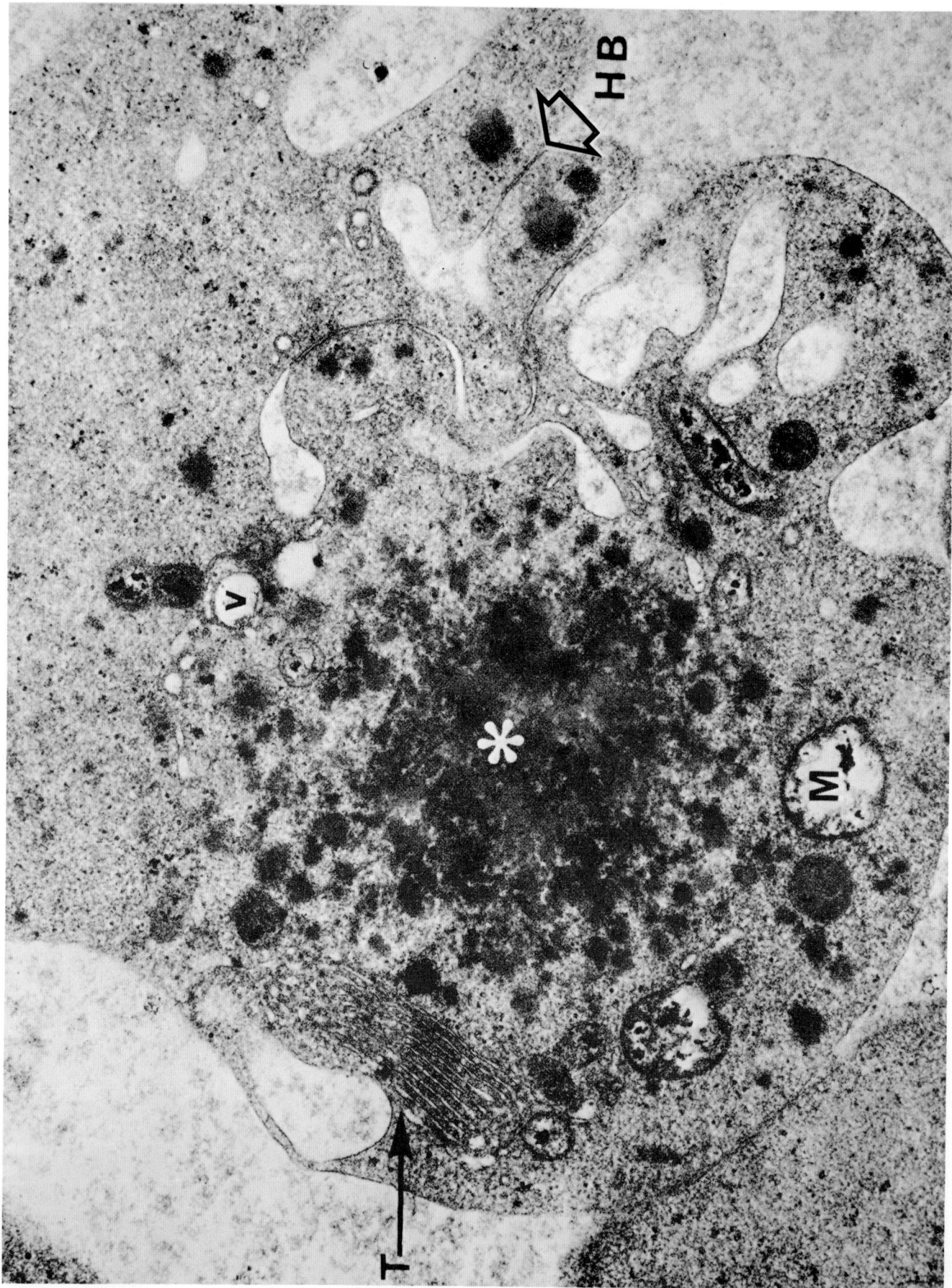

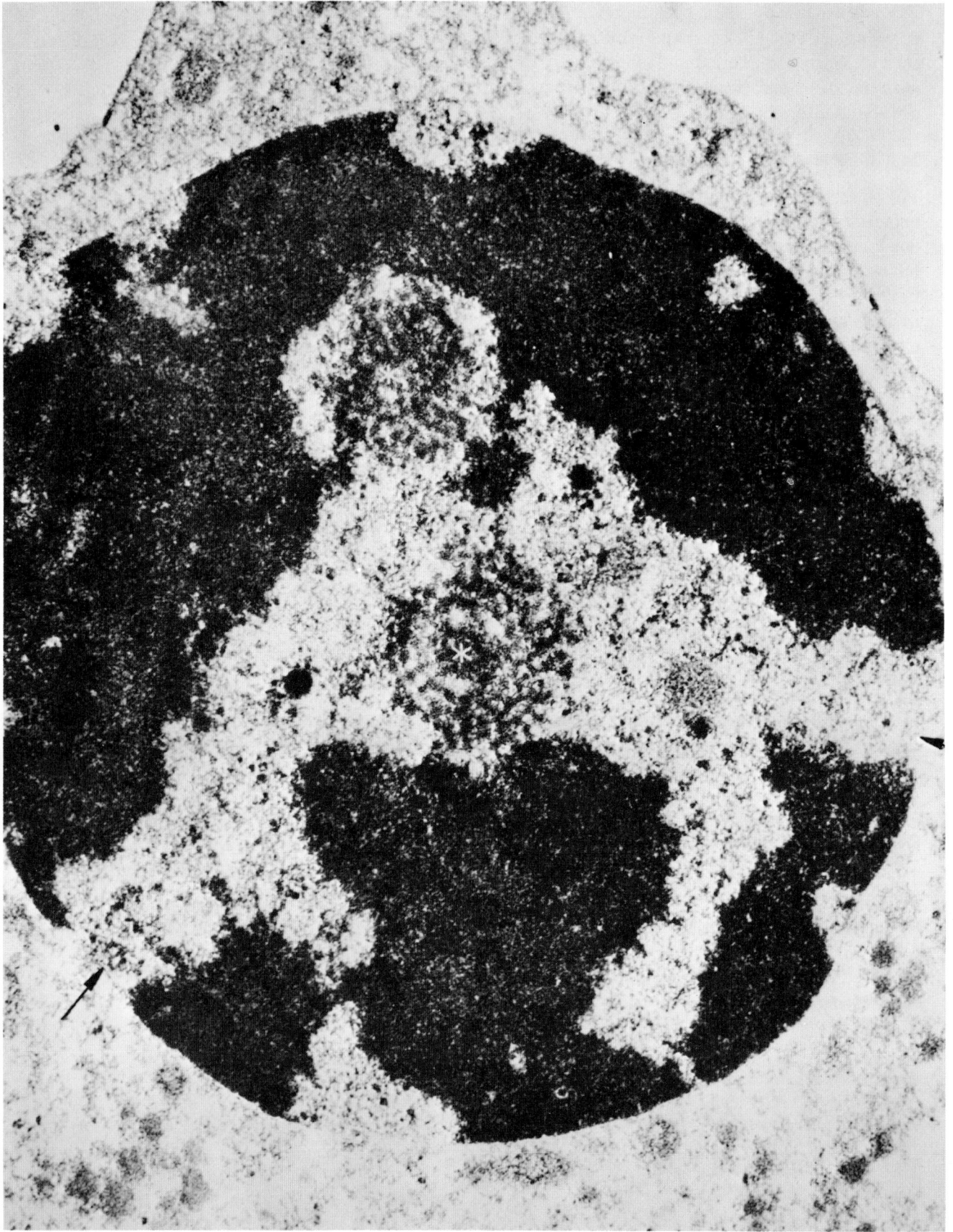

There is widening of the nuclear pores (Figure 24.2); partial absence and areas of duplication of the nuclear membrane may also be present. Intranuclear inclusions such as Heinz bodies are found; some nuclei appear to contain portions of cytoplasm with the inclusions. Nuclear alterations are most prominent when inclusion bodies are abundant in the cytoplasm.

24.1.2. Sideroblastic anemias

The sideroblastic anemias are a heterogeneous group of hematologic diseases of both hereditary and acquired types which have as a unifying feature the presence in the bone marrow of "ringed" sideroblasts, erythroblasts which in Prussian blue stains have a nucleus partially or completely encircled by iron granules.[111] The red cells in these various diseases are generally characterized by some degree of hypochromasia; in many instances the red cell population is dimorphic, both hypochromic and normochromic red cells being present. In approximately 5 percent of the cases of acquired idiopathic refractory sideroblastic anemia there is an evolution of the process to a form of acute myelogenous leukemia.[80]

Ultrastructural examination of the erythroblasts shows a striking accumulation of iron in the mitochondria (Figure 24.3(a), (b));[11,39,125] the iron is located in the matrix between the cristae (Figure 24.3(b)). The iron-laden mitochondria are frequently in a perinuclear location but there may be no clear association with the nucleus. Iron may also be found in scattered particles within single walled small vesicles and as particles within the cytoplasm. Bessis and Breton-Gorius[10] and Bessis and Jensen[11] have characterized abnormal sideroblasts as manifesting both quantitative and qualitative changes in intracellular iron. There is an increased quantity of non-heme iron present and there are two types of iron within the cell: ferritin which is similar to that found in normal erythroblasts and an abnormal morphological type of iron referred to as ferruginous micelles, either dust like or occuring as plaques with no constant conformation. Ferruginous micelles are observed only in mitochondria. Crystallized ferritin is found in the mitochondria in abnormal sideroblasts. In addition to the intraerythrocytic iron, ferritin particles can also be found on or adjacent to the plasma membranes of erythroblasts, particularly in the narrow space separating groups of developing erythroblasts.[151]

24.2. Nuclear maturation defects

The megaloblastic anemias result from disordered DNA synthesis due primarily to deficiencies of vitamin B12 or folic acid; RNA and protein synthesis remain undisturbed. This defect in nuclear maturation with unimpaired hemoglobin synthesis results in a macrocytic red cell, well filled with hemoglobin, i.e., nuclear cytoplasmic asynchrony. Asynchronous development also occurs in the neutrophil and megakaryocyte series.

Figure 24.1. Deformed reticulocyte in beta thalassemia major (A. Polliack and E. Rachmilewitz).
Irregular indentation of the membrane and cytoplasmic projections containing Heinz bodies (HB) are visible. Amorphous, partially confluent Heinz bodies (*), hemosiderin-containing mitochondria showing degenerative changes (M), small vacuoles (V), and parallel arrays of tubules (T) are also present.(× 25,000)

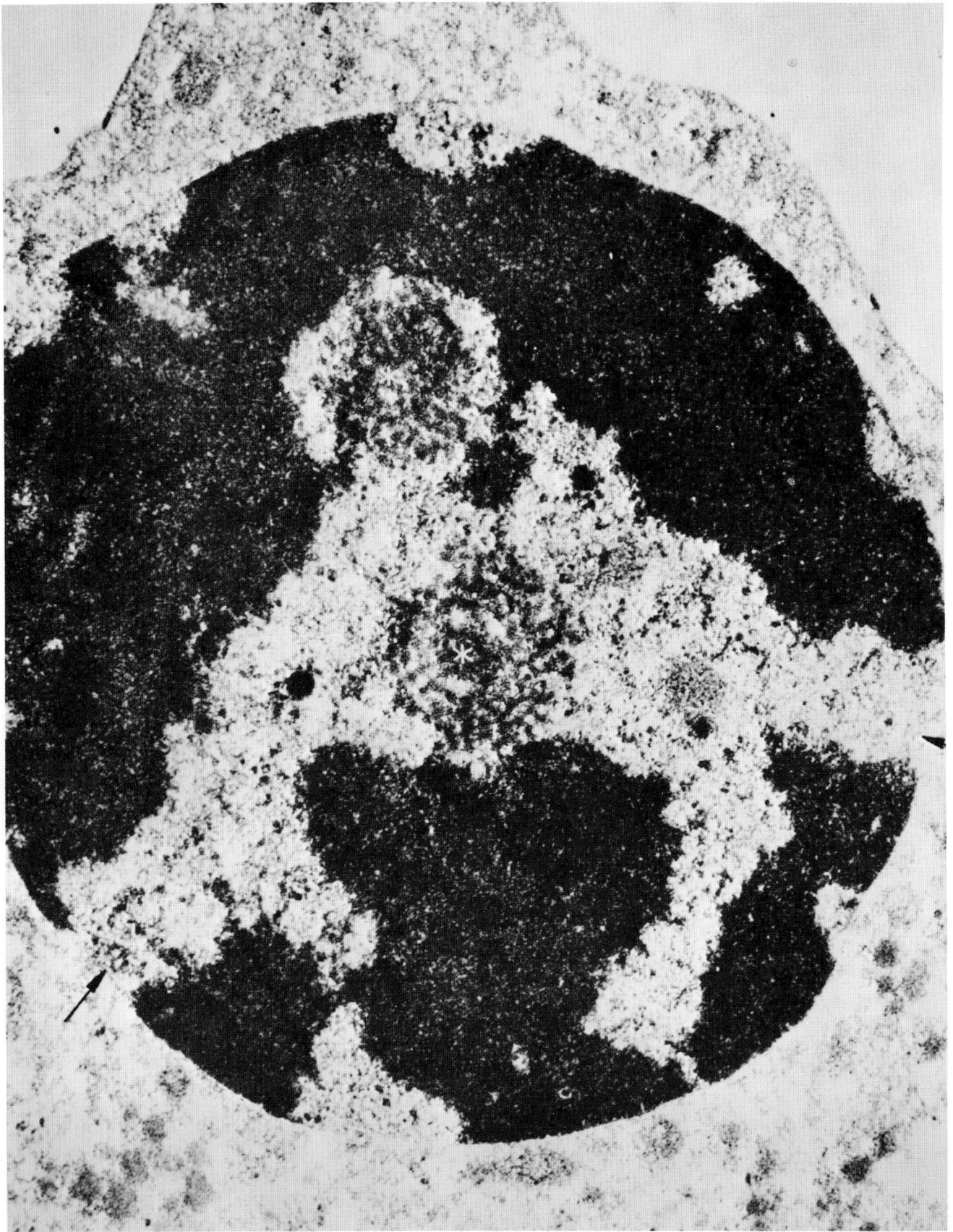

The characteristic findings in the bone marrow by light microscopy are large erythroid precursors with an open nuclear chromatin pattern, the megaloblasts. The nuclei of the neutrophil precursors also show evidence of a degree of indentation and segmentation which is discordant with the chromatin pattern; the degree of condensation of the nuclear chromatin is consistent with a promyelocyte or a myelocyte stage of development while the nuclear configuration is that of a metamyelocyte.

The principal ultrastructural alteration in the megaloblastic anemias is in the nucleus although cytoplasmic abnormalities have been noted.[152] The nuclear development is characterized by an extremely fine nuclear chromatin pattern in the early stages of development (Figure 24.4). In the proerythroblast stage there is only very slight condensation of the chromatin at the nuclear margin with occasional small scattered chromatin clumps. Development into later stages is accompanied by some increase in the chromatin condensation at the nuclear margin and large scattered clumps of chromatin. The chromatin in the central portion of the nucleus remains finely granular. Nucleoli may be prominent even in late stages of development.[74] Some megaloblasts may manifest nuclear clefts, intranuclear inclusions and abnormalities of the nuclear membrane.[170] The ultrastructural alterations in the neutrophil precursors (Figure 24.5) parallel the light microscopic findings; the nuclear chromatin pattern is asynchronous with the nuclear configuration. Nuclei with fairly fine nuclear chromatin may have deep indentations of the nuclear structure; granule development appears normal. Although the primary alterations in megaloblastic anemia are related to the nucleus, the ribosomes in megaloblasts have been described as being rather smaller than in normal erythroid precursors.[152] Additionally, the cytoplasm may contain long strands of endoplasmic reticulum, annulate lamellae, large siderosomes and inclusions of nuclear material.[170]

24.3. Congenital dyserythropoietic anemias

The term dyserythropoiesis incorporates both morphologic and kinetic aspects of erythropoiesis and embraces a number of conditions which primarily affect either the nucleus or the cytoplasm of the erythroblast, or the environment in which erythropoiesis takes place. The term implies the production of abnormal erythroblasts with the destruction of a proportion of the developing erythroid cells within the marrow. Dyserythropoiesis is an accompaniment of several of the red cell maturation defects and also occurs as a primary congenital disorder.[85]

Three main types of congenital dyserythropoietic anemia have been described. The distinction between these three primary types is based on morphologic and serologic findings;[85] there is, however, some degree of overlap between the various types.[140,159]

Congenital dyserythropoietic anemia type I is characterized by macrocytosis, megaloblastoid changes, and internuclear chromatin bridges in the developing erythroid series. On ultrastructural examination[84,85,106] the nuclear alterations are the most noteworthy and involve anomalies of nuclear division, including binucleated

Figure 24.2. Erythroblast nucleus in beta thalassemia major (A. Polliack, X. Yataganas, B. Thorell, and E. A. Rachmilewitz).
Nucleus shows widened nuclear pores (↑) and aggregates of electron-dense particles (*). There appears to be direct contact between the nucleus and cytoplasm. (×30,900)

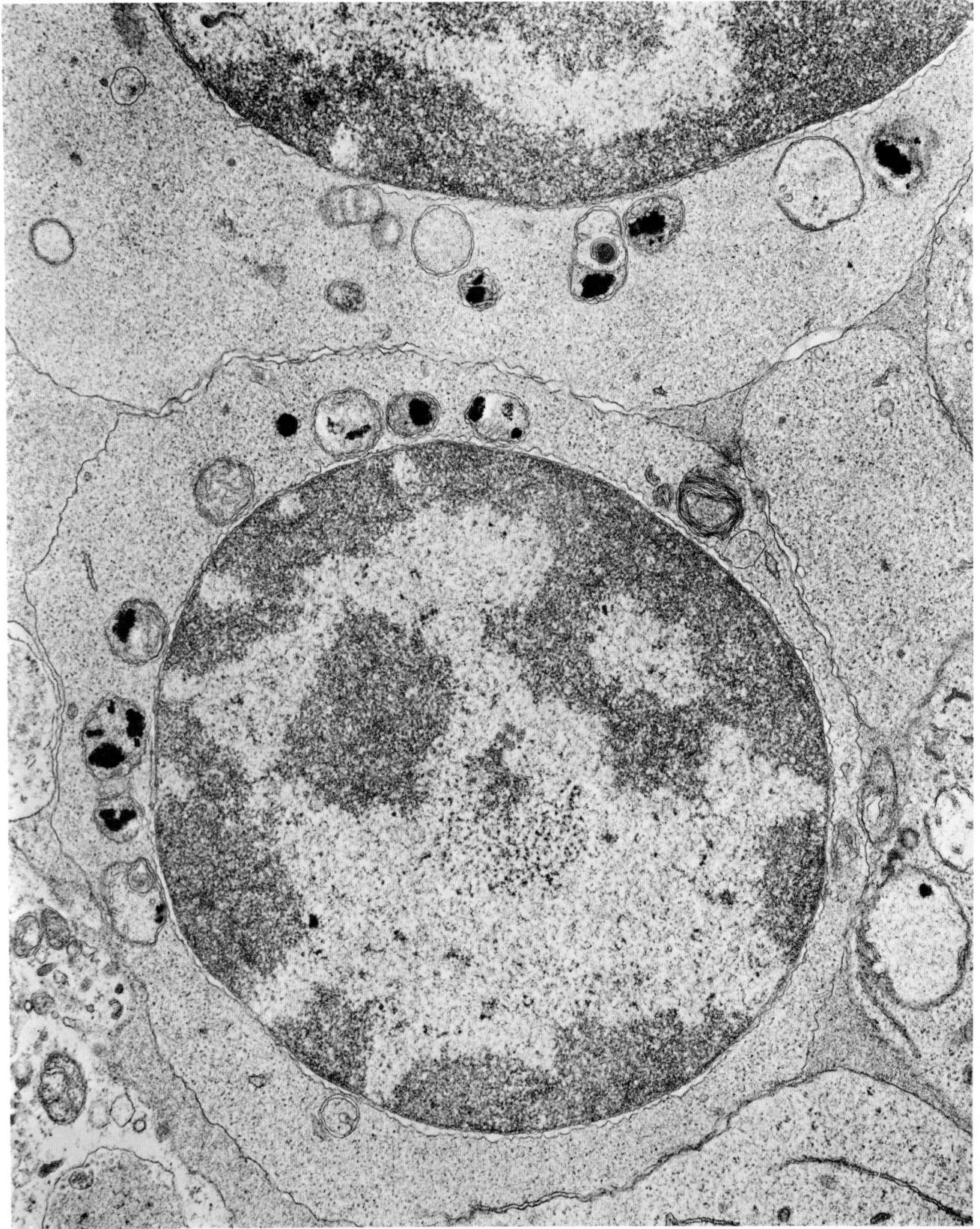

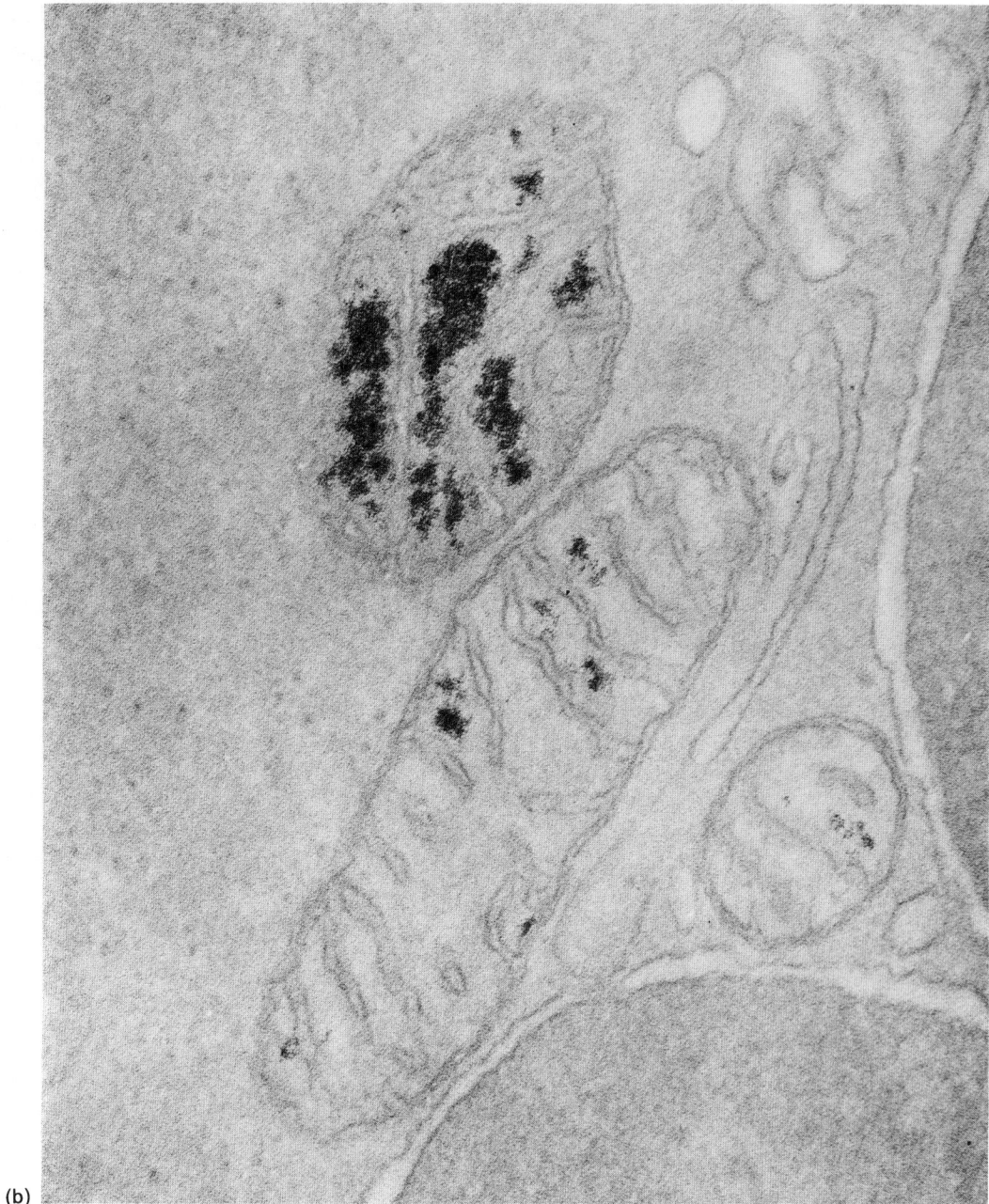

(b)

Figure 24.3. Iron-laden mitochondria in sideroblastic anemia.

(a) Sideroblast from a case of idiopathic refractory sideroblastic anemia showing iron particles present in several of the mitochondria. (×24,600)

(b) At high magnification of erythroblast the iron is seen to be located between the cristae of the mitochondria. (×125,000)

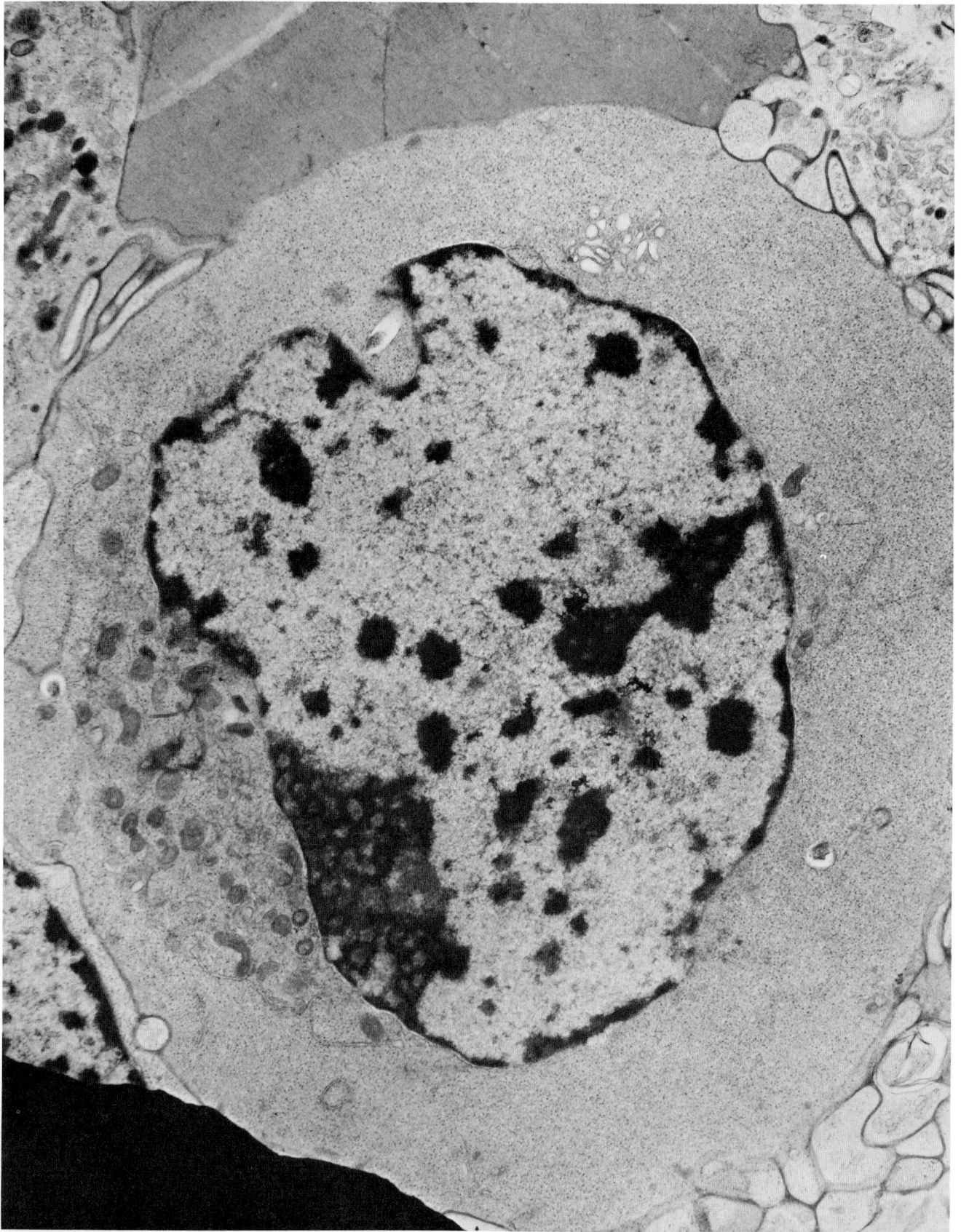

cells and cells with incomplete separation of the nuclei. Binucleated cells tend to be at an earlier stage of cell maturation than the more numerous cells containing incomplete separation of the nuclei. In some instances, there is a narrow band of cytoplasm traversed by a chromatin bridge between two incompletely divided cells. A different form of connection is a spindle bridge containing bundles of microtubules.

Nuclear abnormalities in polychromatic and orthochromatic erythroblasts include uneven condensation and spongy appearance of the chromatin and the presence of numerous holes (Figure 24.6). The nuclear envelope is frequently missing but a similar envelope can be found in many places on the interior aspects of the chromatin masses. Cytoplasmic organelles are found within the nuclear space. In some cells there are numerous cytoplasmic inclusions including vacuoles, myelin figures and membrane residue. Microtubules are frequently found in bundles and single units.

Congenital dyserythropoietic anemia type II is characterized in light microscopy by binuclearity and multinuclearity, pleuripolar mitoses, and karyorrhexis of the erythroid precursors. Ultrastructurally, the erythroid precursors in congenital dyserythropoietic anemia type II[65, 77] show excessive cytoplasmic membranes arranged as cisternae of smooth surfaced endoplasmic reticulum. All nucleated erythroid cells have abnormal cisternae, frequently separated by a narrow rim of hemoglobin from the plasma membrane and following its entire circumference. The cisternae are continuous with the perinuclear space; about 2 percent of the mature erythrocytes show remnants of these cisternae, Erythroblasts are present with incompletely separated nuclei, the perinuclear spaces being connected by one cisterna. Occasional cells have nuclei with multiple protrusions giving them a cloverleaf appearance (Figure 24.7(a)). There are breaks and extended gaps in the nuclear envelopes that seem to unwind into cisternae of endoplasmic reticulum (Figure 24.7(b)); as a consequence, there is continuity between cytoplasmic and nuclear contents.

Congenital dyserythropoiesis type III is characterized by macrocytosis in the blood smear and the presence of giant erythroblasts and multinucleated erythroblasts in the bone marrow. Breton-Gorius et al.,[14] on ultrastructural examination, found abnormalitites to be present in cells from the proerythroblast to the later stages of development. The nuclear membrane is disrupted and some split segments appear inside the nucleus.

24.4. Hemoglobinopathies

24.4.1. Sickle hemoglobin

The erythroid precursors from the bone marrows of patients with sickle cell anemia which are not subjected to deoxygenation show no evidence of formation of hemoglobin polymers or other indications of sickling on ultrastructural examination; there are no features to distinguish them from the erythroid precursors of normal individuals. Exposure of bone marrow specimens from patients with sickle cell disease to nitrogen

---

Figure 24.4. Nuclear alteration in megaloblastic anemia.
Megaloblast from the bone marrow of patient with vitamin B12 deficiency. The nuclear chromatin is extremely finely dispersed with only slight condensation at the nuclear margin. Scattered clumps of chromatin are present. The nucleolus, adjacent to the nuclear outline, is slightly irregular in configuration. (× 18,000)

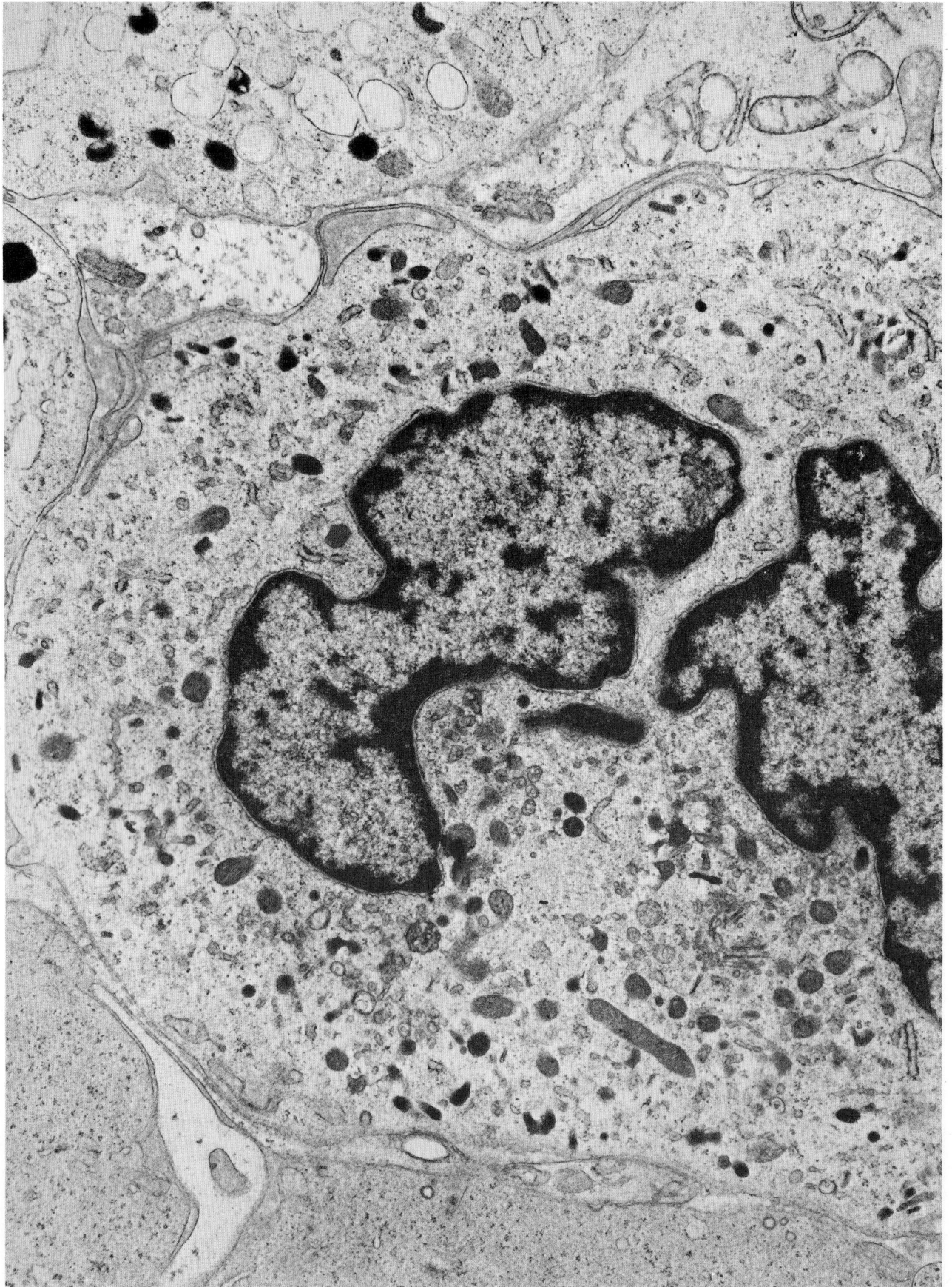

at 37° C for 30 minutes results in polymerization of the hemoglobin of most erythrocytes and reticulocytes; however, only 10–20 percent of the nucleated erythroid precursors show this phenomenon. Hemoglobin polymers are absent in basophilic normoblasts and pronormoblasts, cells which would have a very low hemoglobin content.[60]

When subjected to deoxygenation, hemoglobin S undergoes a sol–gel transformation. The polymers of hemoglobin S are unique because they differ in molecular organization from hemoglobin aggregates, microtubules, and crystals.[8,41,163,164,169] The sol–gel transformation is attended by progressive changes in the conformation of the sickle hemoglobin-containing erythrocytes as shown by scanning electron microscopy (Figure 24.8).[167] Deoxygenated hemoglobin S on transmission electron microscopy is condensed into long rods of approximately 170–190 Å in diameter.[169] The rods are usually arranged in parallel bundles oriented to the longer axis of the sickle cell (Figure 24.9(a)) and extruded spicules. Hemoglobin polymers, even in the most tightly packed bundles, are always separated from each other by a distance of 40–60 Å (Figure 24.9(a), (b)). The hemoglobin S can also be found as a layer of rods in rigid bundles forming parallel polymers oriented at an angle of 90° to the long axis. Frequently the bundles of parallel equidistant polymers show wavelike patterns. At times the polymers radiate in several different directions. In cross section, some of the polymers have small clear areas, 30–40 Å in diameter in their center, but the majority are dense. Each polymer is electron dense and always separated from its neighbor by a clear zone. Polymers are roughly hexagonal in cross section and when organized in tightly packed bundles resemble a paracrystalline array.

24.4.2. Hemoglobins Nottingham and Hammersmith

Frisch *et al.* have extensively detailed the ultrastructural characteristics of hemoglobins Hammersmith and Nottingham.[52] Bone marrows from patients with both of these hemoglobinopathies contain morphologically normal and abnormal erythroblasts but the incidence of dyserythropoietic cells is higher in hemoglobin Nottingham.

The developing erythroid cells in hemoglobin Hammersmith are characterized by islands of normal and abnormal erythroid cells occurring in adjacent areas. Some of the abnormal erythroblasts are connected by intercellular bridges containing microtubules (Figure 24.10); similar microtubules are found in bundles in the cytoplasm. Some nuclei of joined cells are irregular or elongated in shape; other nuclei are mulberry shaped or possess protuberances. Widened nuclear pores are present. Occasional nuclei have a condensed spongy appearance, similar to the findings in congenital dyserythropoietic anemia, and contain inclusions in the form of granules, ribosomes, membranes, and structures resembling Heinz bodies. Ferritin is present in many cells as an accumulation of granules lying free or contained within vesicles in the cytoplasm or in the mitochondria. The number of ribosomes varies in cells at the same stage of development.

Figure 24.5. Neutrophil precursor in megaloblastic anemia.
Neutrophil precursor from the case illustrated in Figure 24.4. The segmenting nucleus has chromatin which is finely dispersed. The cytoplasm contains scattered azurophil granules, numerous mitochondria, and strands of rough endoplasmic reticulum. (× 18,000)

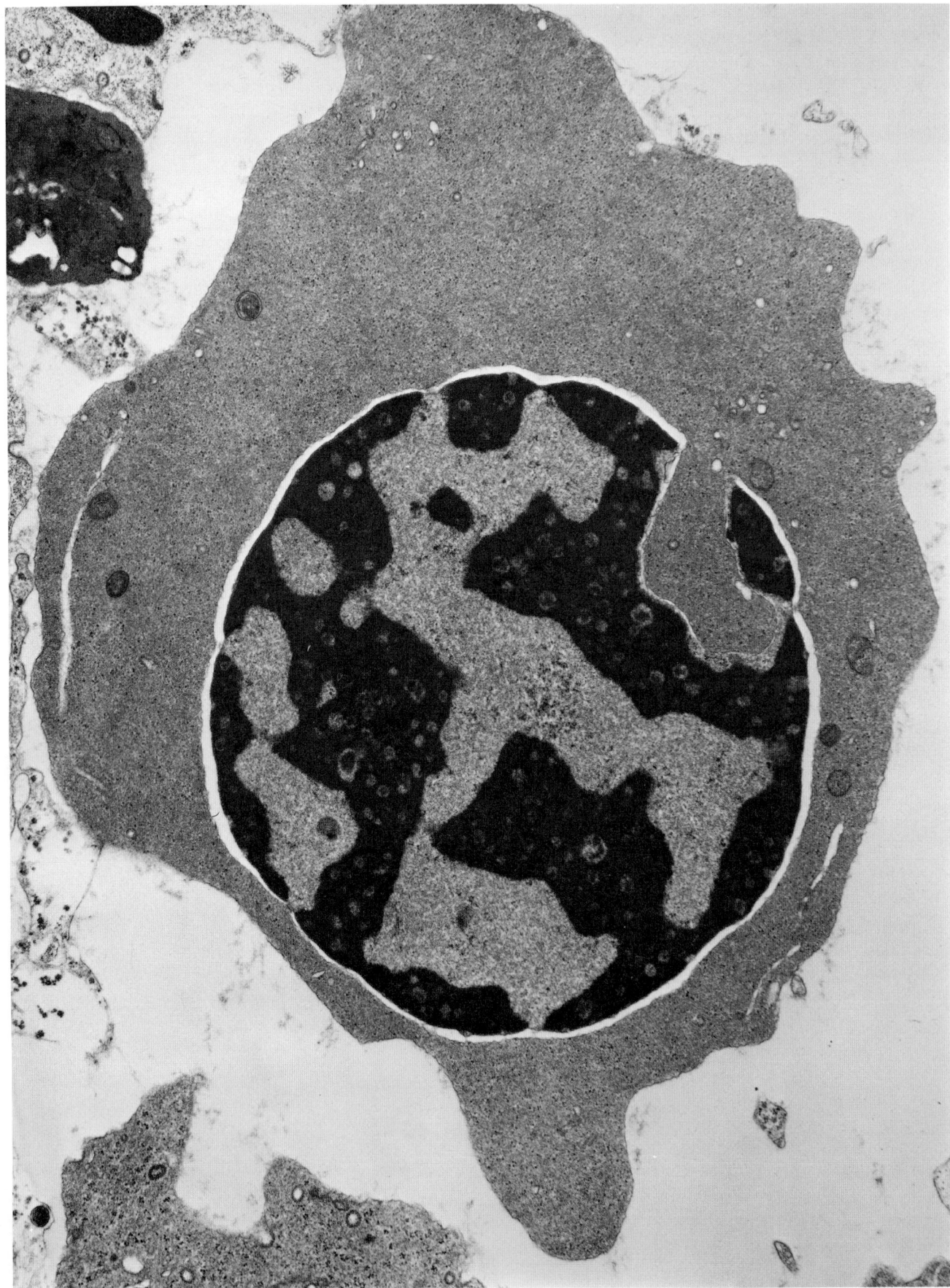

Hemoglobin Nottingham, like hemoglobin Hammersmith, manifests many features of dyserythropoiesis including bi- and multinucleated erythroblasts and intercellular bridges. The changes are present at all stages of development but primarily in the later stages. Cytoplasmic bridges are common; the bridges sometimes contain microtubules connecting nuclear regions of joined cells. In the bi- and trinucleated cells, the nuclei are unequal in size; the nuclei in some of the binucleated cells are joined by broad or narrow chromatin bridges. Many nuclei have a compact, spongy, and fenestrated appearance, similar to the findings in congenital dyserythropoietic anemia.

The nuclear envelope shows a number of aberrations; large nuclear pores are present and the nuclear envelope is incomplete. Polyribosomes and membranous structures are seen within the nuclei. The nuclear envelope occasionally encloses small or larger areas of cytoplasm containing hemoglobin and occasionally cytoplasmic organelles; whorls of endoplasmic reticulum, sometimes in concentric arrangements with an apparent connection to the nuclear envelope, are also found. In many erythroblasts the nuclear membranes have additional membranes in close apposition, sometimes as a single layer, but often in stacks of up to six layers (Figure 24.11). Many erythroblasts contain a variety of small and large vesicles, some empty, some filled with remains of membranes, myelin bodies, mitochondria, and other debris.

Figure 24.6. Erythroblast in congenital dyserythropoietic anemia type 1 (J. E. Maldonado and H. F. Taswell).
The nuclear chromatin has a "spongy" appearance. A widely dilated nuclear pore permits penetration of the nucleus by the cytoplasm. Erythroblast from bone marrow. ($\times$ 18,000)

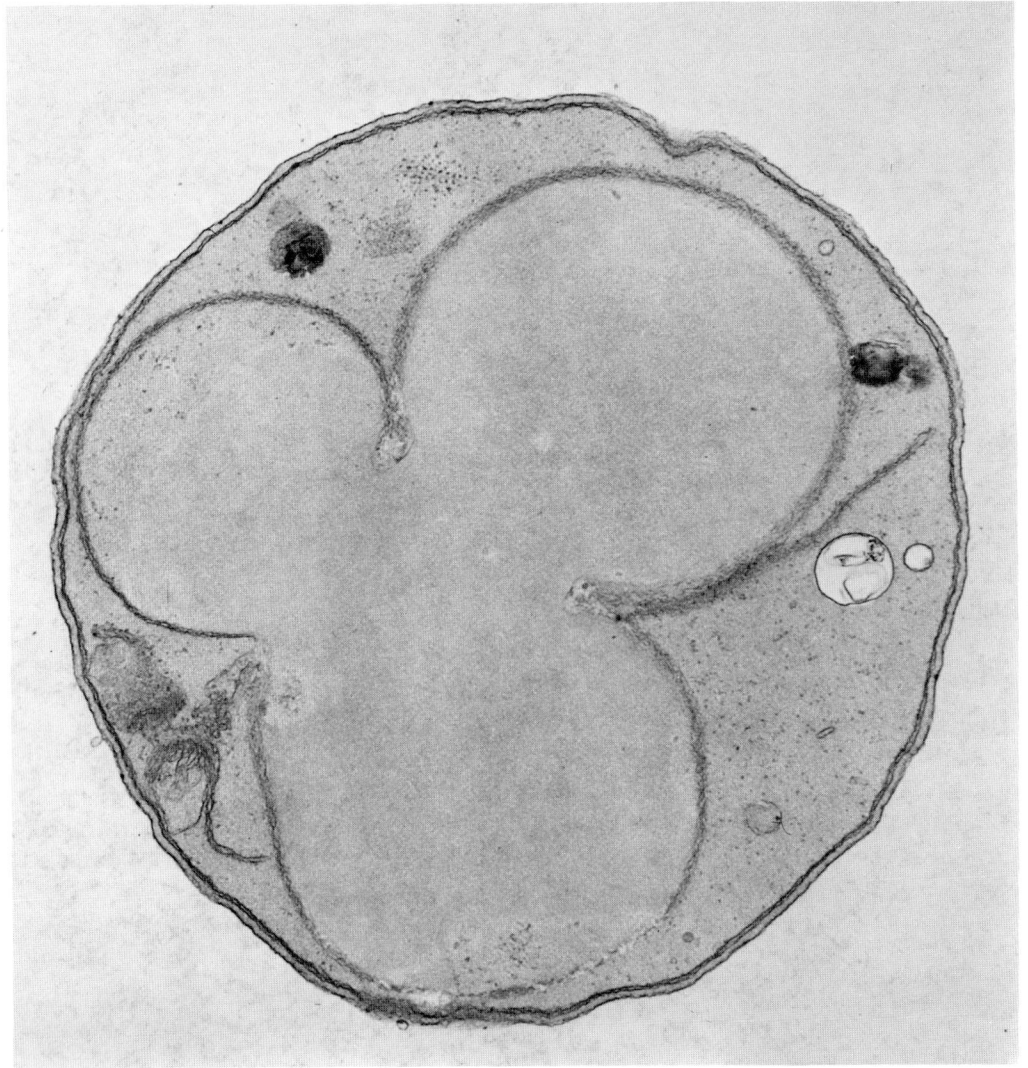

Figure 24.7. Erythroid cells in congenital dyserythropoietic anemia type II (P. Kerkhoven, H. R. Marti, and G. Hug).

(a) Late erythroblast showing a continuous peripheral cisterna and three abnormal protrusions in the form of a clover leaf. (× 10,000)

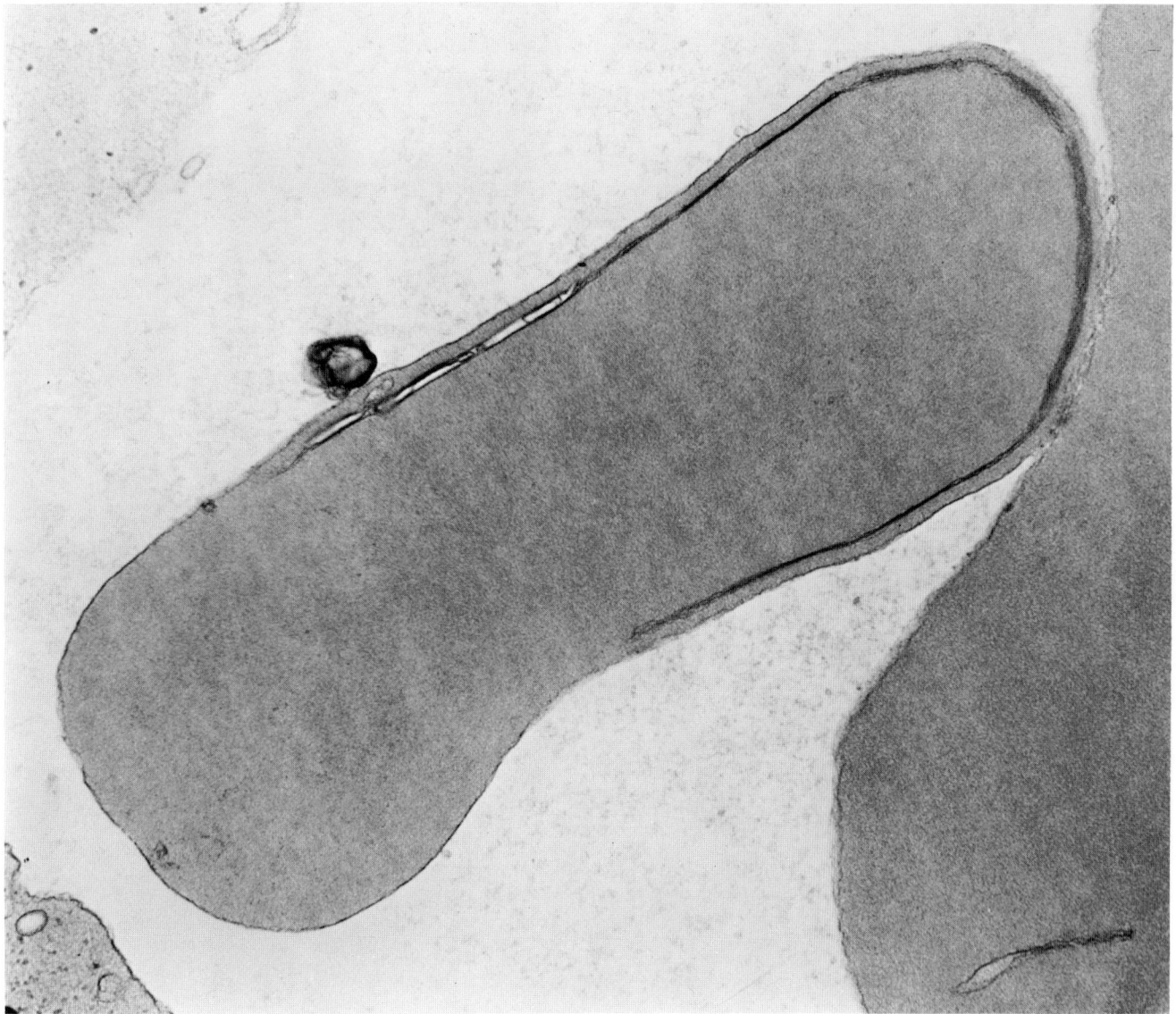

Figure 24.7. Erythroid cells in congenital dyserythropoietic anemia type II. (G. Hug, Kwan Yuen Wong, and B. Lampkin).

(b) Mature erythrocyte showing a peripheral abnormal cisterna. (× 14,000)

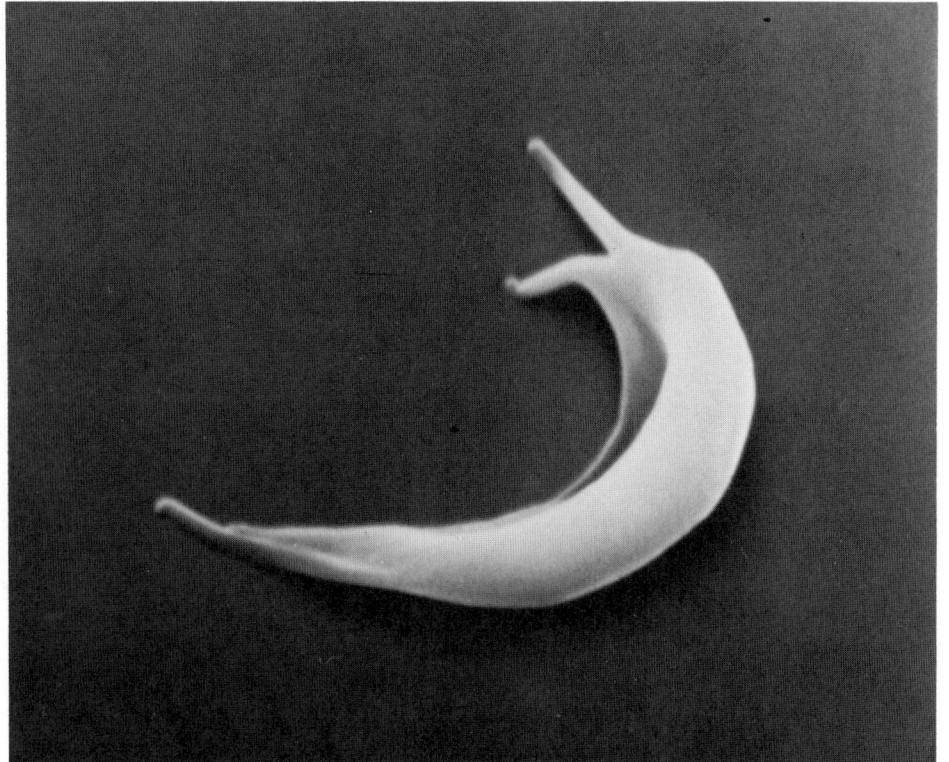

Figure 24.8. Sickled erythrocyte (J. G. White).
SEM. (×6,000)

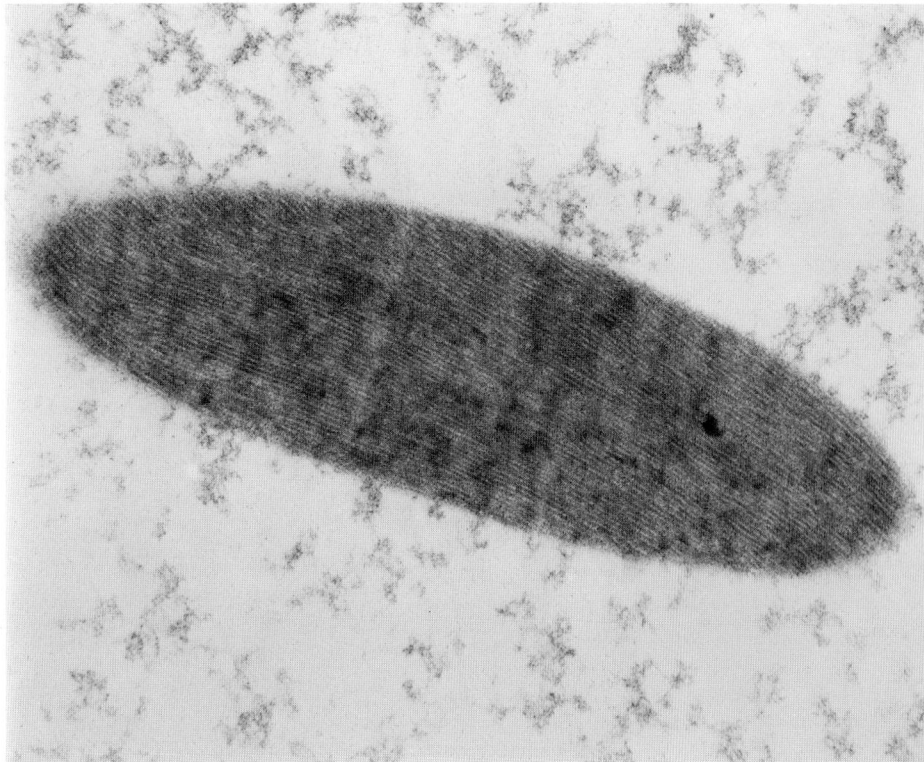

Figure 24.9. Sickled erythrocyte (J. G. White).

(a) TEM of thin section of erythrocyte. The sickled hemoglobin polymers appear as parallel bundles running in the long axis of the cell. The rods are separated by a clear space of 40–90 Å. (× 14,500)

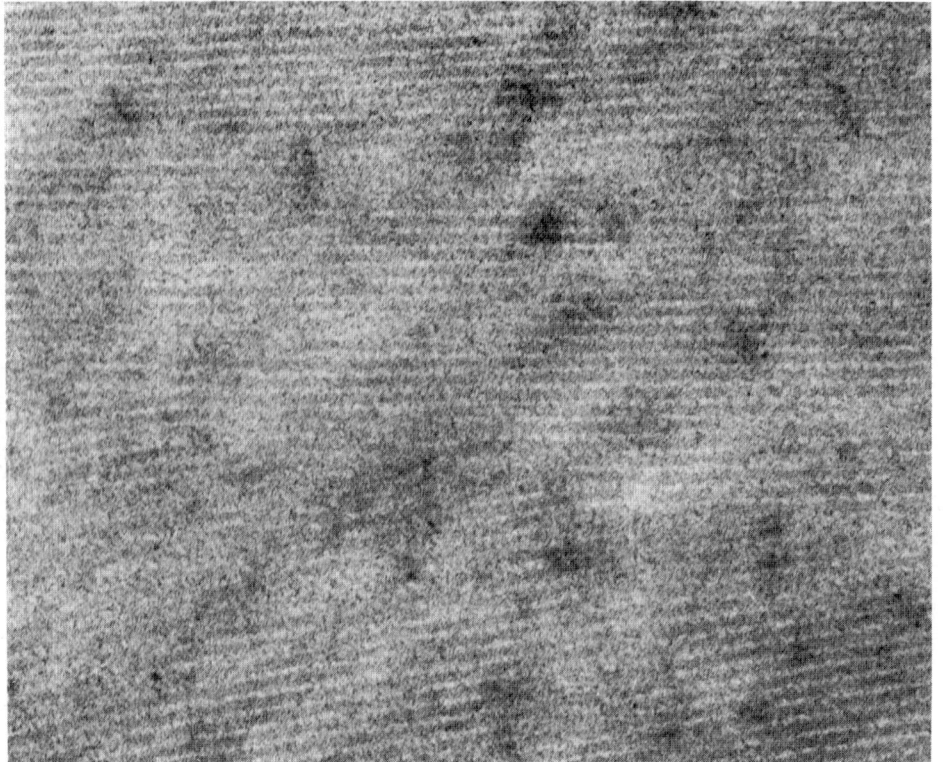

Figure 24.9. Sickled erythrocyte (J. G. White).
(b) High power TEM of sickled hemoglobin polymers. (× 130,000)

Figure 24.10. Hemoglobin Hammersmith (B. Frisch *et al.*).
Two erythroblasts joined by cytoplasmic bridges showing a midbody with microtubules (↑).
(× 13,000)

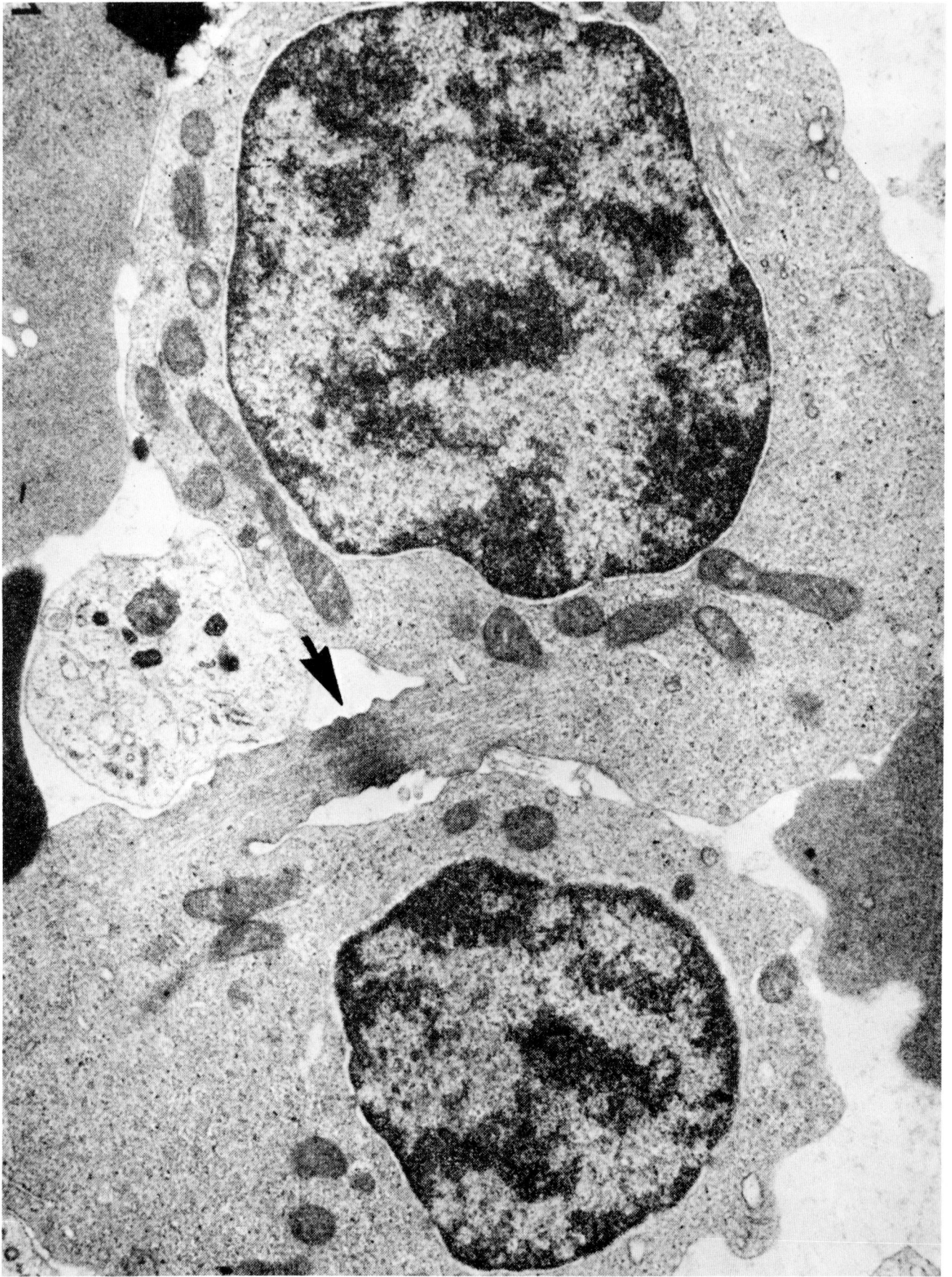

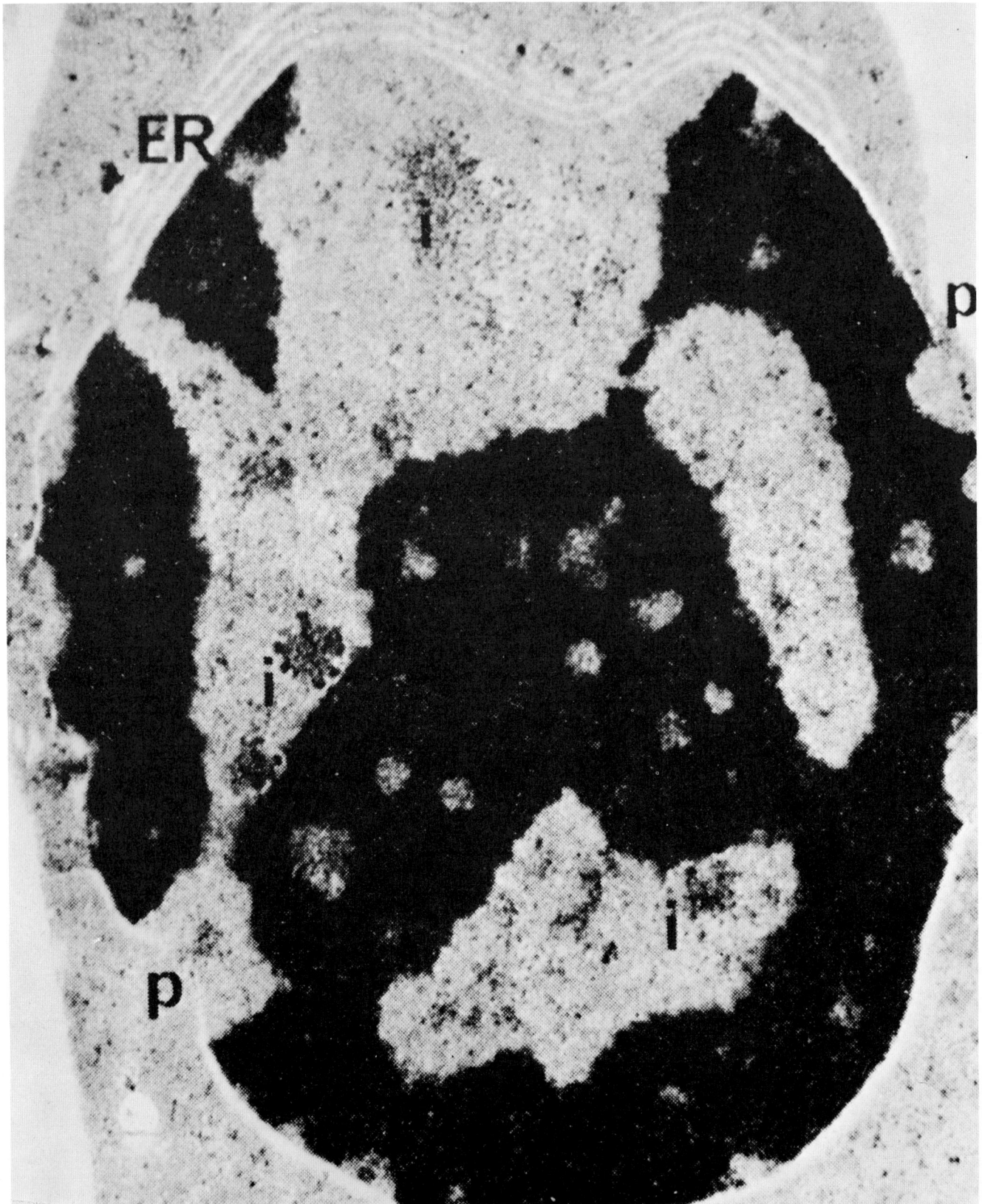

Figure 24.11. Hemoglobin Nottingham (B. Frisch *et al.*).
Erythroblast showing stacked membranes adjacent to the nucleus (ER), wide nuclear pores (p), and nuclear inclusions (i). (×21,500)

25. Leukemias

The leukemias are generally divided into two major cell types, myelocytic and lymphocytic. Within each of these two groups the leukemias are further subdivided into acute and chronic forms; this division is based on the cytologic maturity of the proliferating cell types.

25.1. Myelocytic leukemias

The myeloid stem cell gives rise to several different cell lines, the neutrophil, erythrocyte, megakaryocyte, monocyte, basophil, and eosinophil. As a result, the morphologic manifestation of acute myeloid leukemia can be quite heterogeneous. Many different cytomorphologic classifications of the acute myeloid leukemias have been proposed. Although there are differences in the various classifications, there is fairly general recognition of four subtypes of acute myelocytic leukemia.

1. Acute myeloblastic leukemia.
2. Acute monocytic and myelomonocytic leukemias.
3. Acute promyelocytic leukemia (hypergranular).
4. Erythroleukemia (erythromegakaryocytic).

The several other subtypes of acute myeloid leukemia that have been proposed can be categorized with one of the four primary subtypes listed.

25.1.1. Acute myeloblastic leukemia

The acute myeloblastic leukemias are characterized by a proliferation of myeloblasts. The proportion of myeloblasts in the blood and bone marrow varies generally from 30–100 percent. There may be evidence of maturation of the blasts into neutrophil promyelocytes and later stages. The maturing neutrophils frequently show abnormalities of nuclear and granule development. The nuclear abnormality most frequently manifested is hypolobulation, the pseudo-Pelger–Huet change. The granulation abnormality is primarily manifest as hypogranularity or the development of abnormal granule forms. The most commonly encountered abnormal granule form is the Auer rod which is thought to represent a fusion of the azurophil or nonspecific granules. Auer rods are found in varying percentages of myeloblasts in approximately 50 percent of cases of acute myeloblastic leukemia. From one to several Auer rods may be found in a myeloblast. Rarely, Auer rods are detected in mature neutrophils. Granule abnormalities similar to those found in the Chediak–Higashi–Steinbrinck anomaly have been reported in myeloblastic leukemia.[156]

The ultrastructural characteristics of the myeloblasts (Figure 25.1(a)) in acute myeloblastic leukemia are in general similar to those found in myeloblasts from normal bone marrow.[4] The nuclear chromatin is very finely dispersed with minimal condensation at the nuclear margin. One or more prominent nucleoli, surrounded by a ring of heterochromatin, may be identified. The nucleus may be round, ovoid, or segmented (Figure 25.2(a)). Myeloblasts with indented or segmented nuclei in light microscopy have been referred to as Rieder forms. It has been suggested from ultrastructural observations that the Rieder nucleus is the result of a microtubule or microfilament contractile process leading to constriction of the nucleus.[28,68,115,147] Nuclear appendages may be frequent and may result in nuclear blebs with sequestered areas of cytoplasm (Figure 25.1(b)) sometimes containing numerous cytoplasmic structures.[9,64,91] Nuclear bodies which consist of fibrillar strands may be present (Figure 25.2(b)).[12,79]

The number of cytoplasmic structures can vary considerably. In the most immature of the myeloblasts there may be few or no differentiating features. In more mature cells there may be clear evidence of granule formation. In many instances there are abnormalities of both azurophil and specific granule development;[3] granules with abnormal shapes, size, and internal structure may be found. The Auer rod (Figure 25.3), which appears to represent a fusion of azurophil granules, is a striking example of abnormal granule development.[50,51] Azurophil granules appear to coalesce into a linear form in which parallel tubular structures exhibiting a periodicity can be demonstrated on high magnification. Fukushi et al.[53] have classified Auer rods into three types based on ultrastructural characteristics. The type A Auer rod is characterized by the presence of microtubules with a diameter of 50 to 60 Å, which are parallel, with a periodicity of 80 to 100 Å, resulting in a stripe pattern. Type B has a low density with a linear structure which runs parallel to the long axis. Type C has a moderate or high density but no stripe pattern. Ultrastructural cytochemistry has demonstrated the Auer rods to be peroxidase[78] and acid phosphatase positive.[162]

The number of ribosomes, polyribosomes, strands of rough endoplasmic reticulum, and mitochondria vary. Unusually large and misshapen mitochondria may be present.[137,138]

Discordant development of the nucleus and cytoplasm may be a prominent feature in many cases of acute myeloblastic leukemia.[55] This may be characterized by cells which have very immature appearing nuclei but cytoplasm which shows granules more typical of the promyelocyte or myelocyte stage of development. Conversely, and probably more commonly, the nucleus may exhibit the configuration and chromatin clumping of a mature neutrophil (Figure 25.4) or metamyelocyte while granule development is markedly retarded.[130] Bainton[3] has described other abnormalities of granule development in the neutrophils of acute myelogenous leukemia including neutrophils containing only azurophil and lacking specific granules, neutrophils containing only specific granules and lacking azurophil granules, and neutrophils containing both types of granules but lacking the characteristic enzyme, peroxidase. In many

---

Figure 25.1. Acute myelogenous leukemia.

(a) Myeloblasts from bone marrow showing a finely dispersed chromatin pattern. Many of the cells contain numerous mitochondria, a few strands of rough endoplasmic reticulum, and scattered ribosomes. (× 7,200)

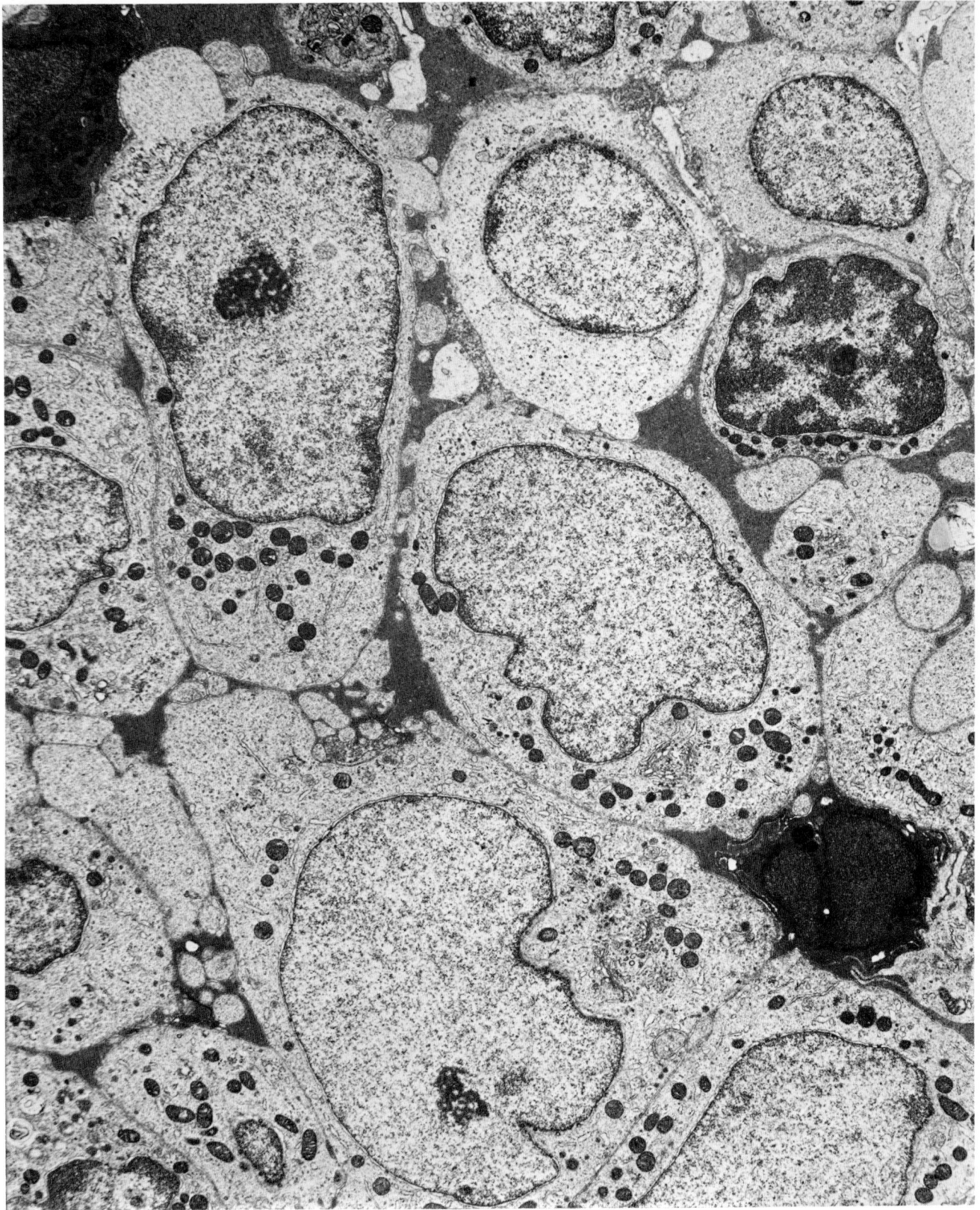

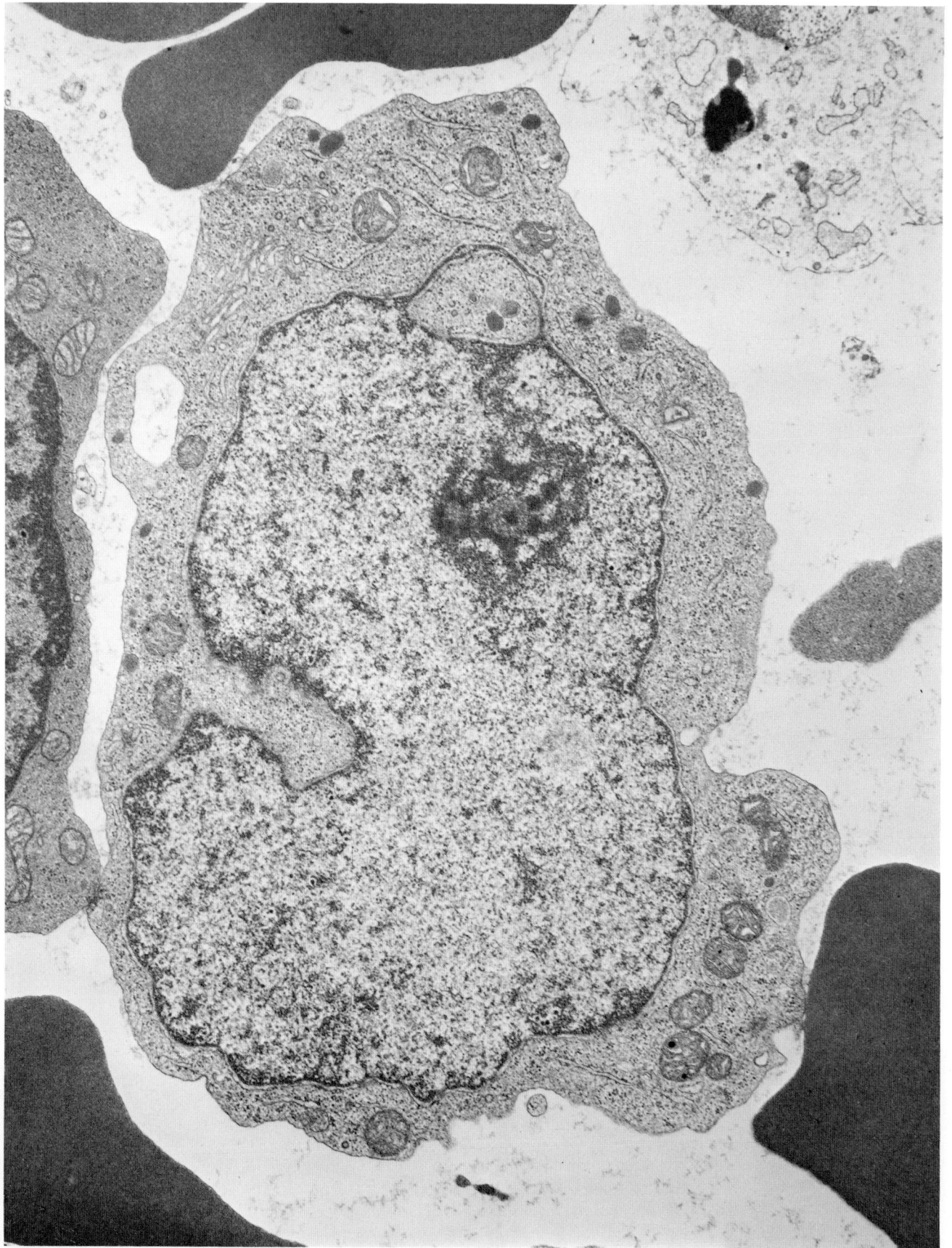

Figure 25.1. Acute myelogenous leukemia.

(b) High magnification of a myeloblast from the case illustrated in Figure 25.1(a). A nuclear bleb with sequestered cytoplasm is present; a few dense granules are visible in the cytoplasm. ($\times$ 18,450)

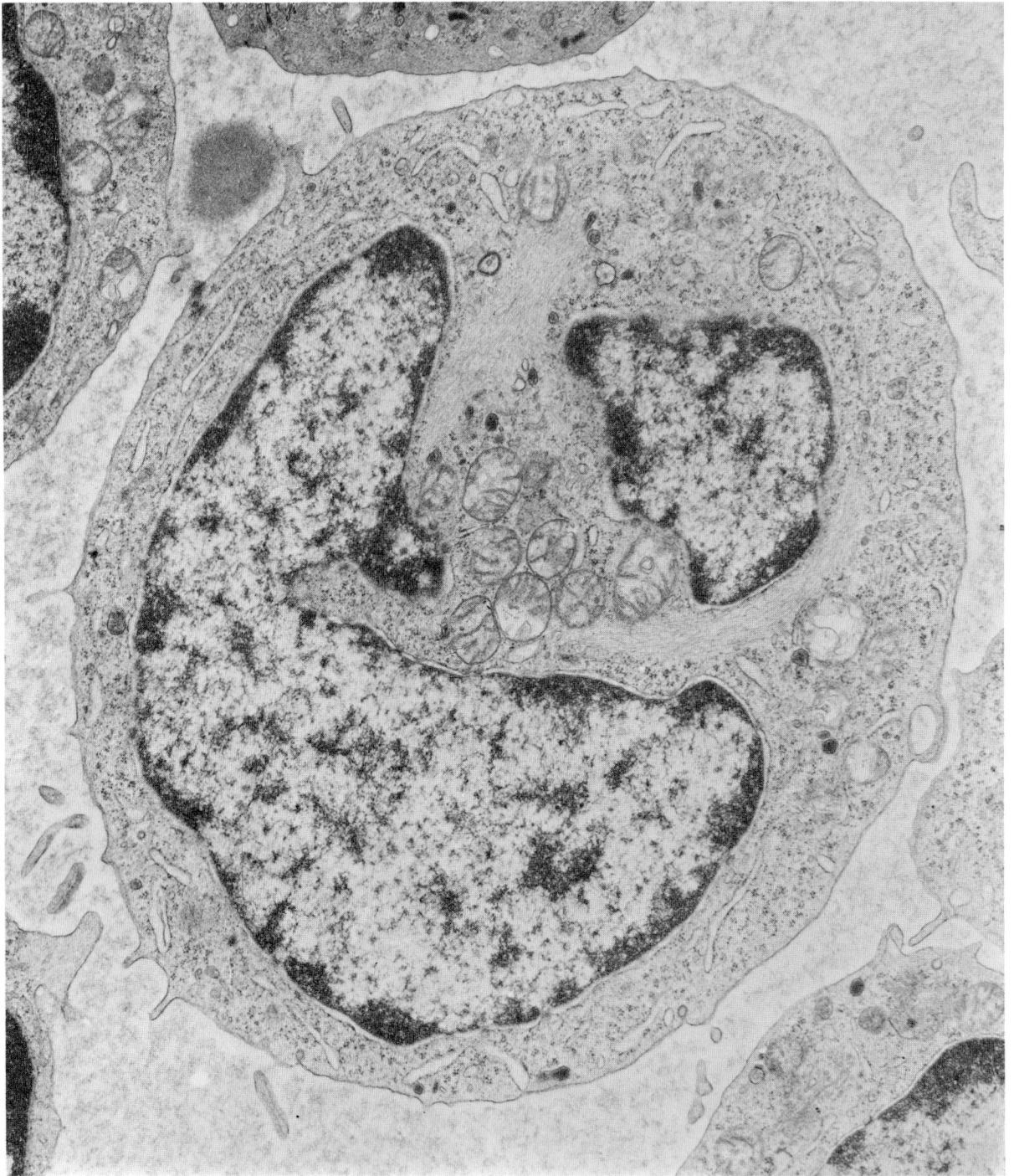

Figure 25.2. Acute myelogenous leukemia.
(a) Myeloblast from a patient with acute myelogenous leukemia. Immature in appearance, the nucleus shows segmentation and bundles of microfibrils are visible almost completely encircling portions of the nuclear segments. (× 16,000)

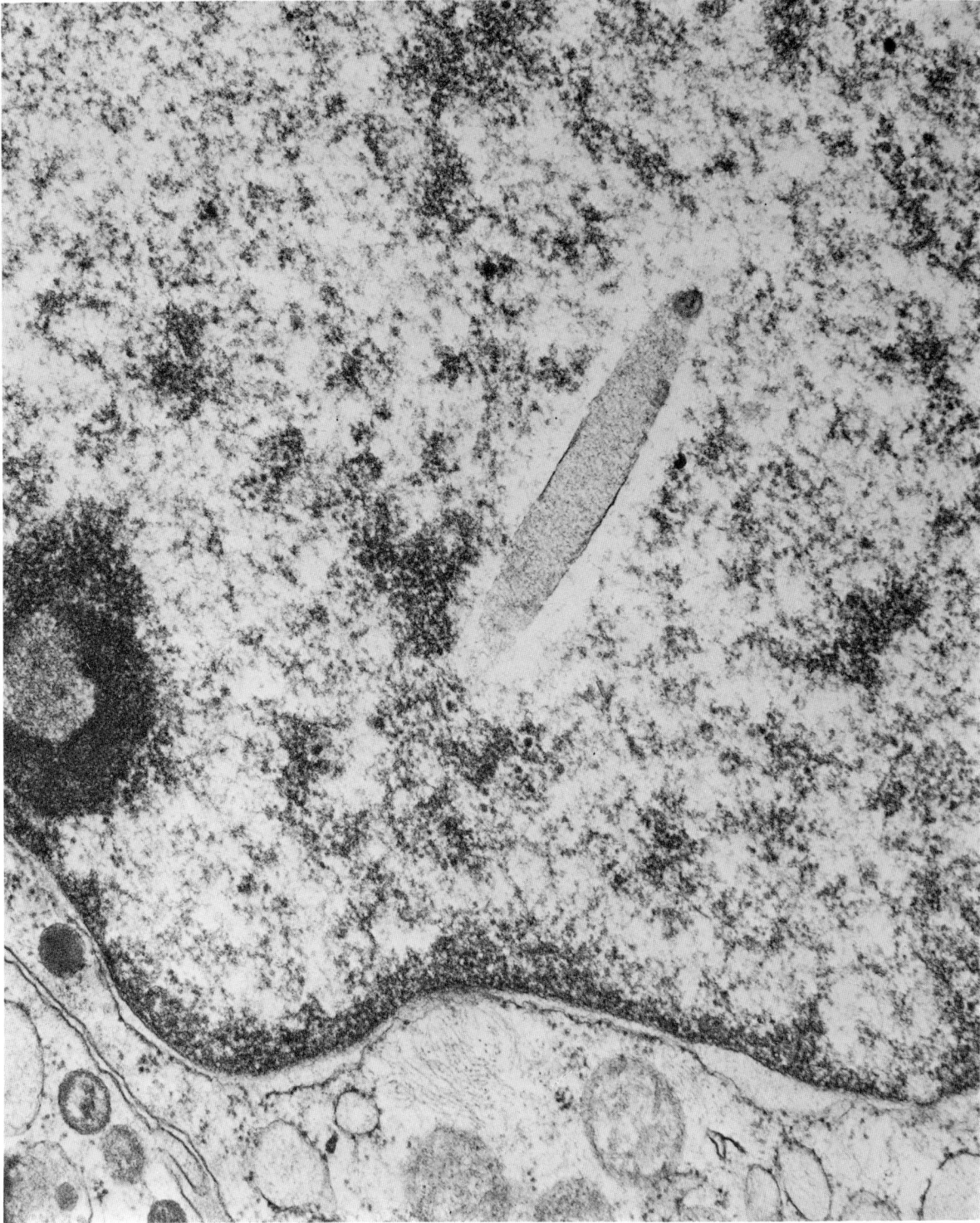

Figure 25.2. Acute myelogenous leukemia.

(b) A fibrillar intranuclear inclusion in a myeloblast from a patient with acute myelogenous leukemia. (×36,000)

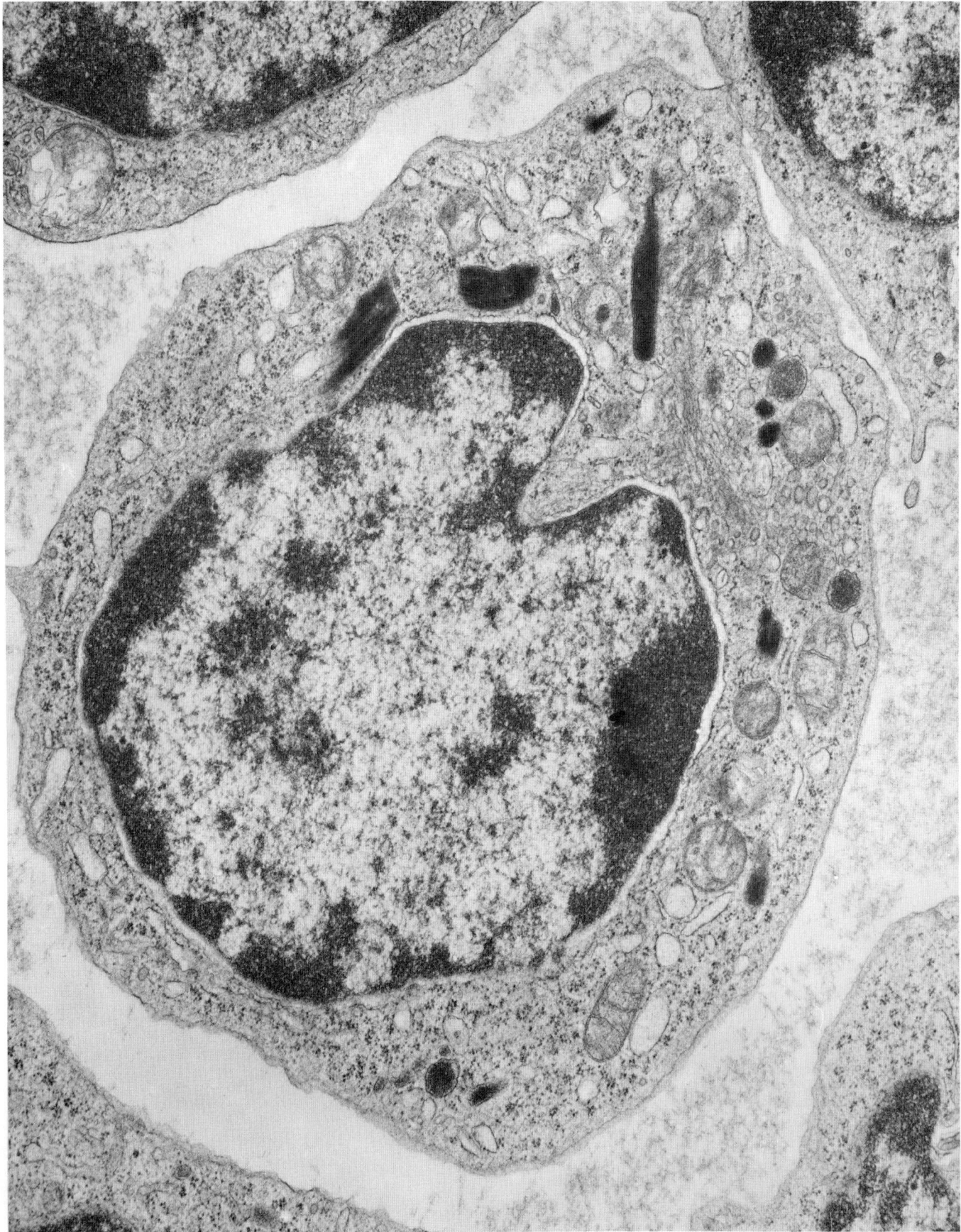

Figure 25.3. Auer rods.
A myeloblast containing Auer rods from a patient with acute myeloid leukemia. (× 29,000)

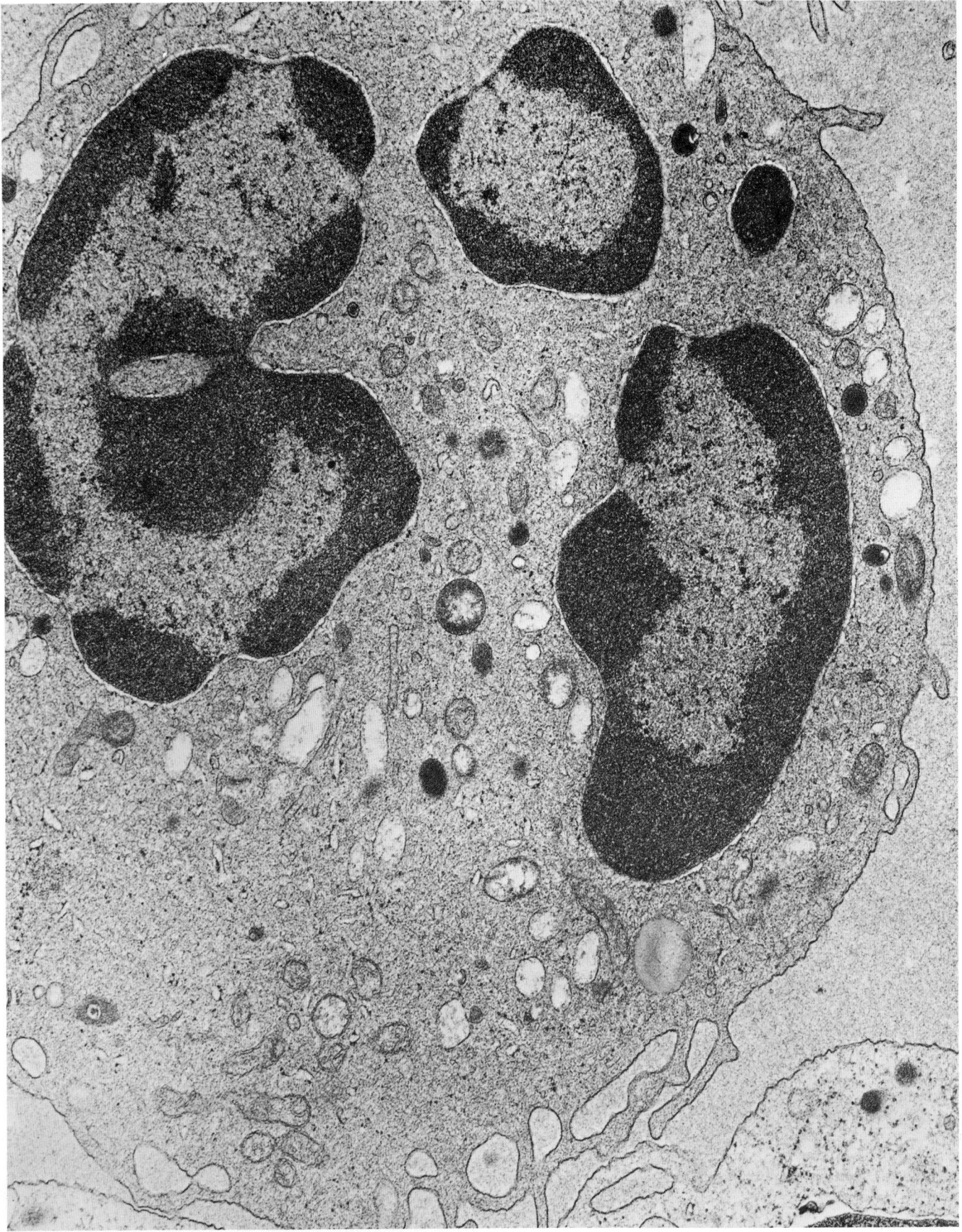

neutrophils and precursors in acute myelogenous leukemia, there may be varying sized collections of rough endoplasmic reticulum. These ultrastructural alterations have their counterparts in light microscopic findings, hypogranularity and structures resembling Dohle bodies.

25.1.2. Acute monocytic and myelomonocytic leukemias

For several decades the use of the term monocytic leukemia was qualified by the designation Schilling's monocytic leukemia or Nageli's monocytic leukemia to reflect the origin of the proliferating cell.[44] Schilling's monocytic leukemia was intended to designate a reticuloendothelial origin of the proliferating monocyte and was often referred to as pure monocytic leukemia.[142] The use of the term Nageli's monocytic leukemia implied a myeloblast origin; the Nageli's monocytic leukemias were frequently referred to as myelomonocytic leukemia. Recent ultrastructural, cytochemical, and cell culture studies have supported the myeloid origin of the monocyte.[82,113,114,155] As a result, all monocytic leukemias are generally considered at this time to be forms of myeloid leukemia in that they have their origin in the myeloid stem cell. The morphologic picture of the monocytic leukemias is extremely heterogeneous as a result of two factors: the proliferating monocyte series shows varying degrees of maturation and frequently there is concurrent proliferation of the neutrophil series. Subsequently, several terms have been used to describe monocytic leukemia, from acute monoblastic leukemia[93] to acute myelomonocytic leukemia. The first term would imply a proliferation only of very immature monocytes. The term myelomonocytic would imply a participation of both monocyte and neutrophil lines. The term myelomonocytic has also been used in a more general sense by some observers to describe the majority of the acute leukemias which originate in the myeloid tissue.[133] The nonspecific esterase stains utilizing alpha naphthyl acetate or alpha naphthyl butyrate are of considerable aid in clarifying the possible monocytic origin of leukemia cells.[86]

The light microscope heterogeneity of the monocytic and myelomonocytic leukemias is reflected in the ultrastructural findings. In cases characterized by a pure proliferation of monocyte elements, the cell population will consist solely of monocytic forms in varying stages of development, monoblasts, promonocytes, and monocytes. In the more undifferentiated forms of this type of leukemia, the cells will be primarily monoblasts. In the more differentiated types, there will be varying numbers of monoblasts, promonocytes, and monocytes. In the myelomonocytic leukemias, there will be both monocytic and neutrophilic cells present.

In acute monoblastic leukemia[93] the blasts show little evidence of differentiation to promonocytes or monocytes. The cells are large in size and possess abundant cytoplasm which may be distributed irregularly around the nucleus; pseudopod formation may be evident. There is frequently fine azurophil granulation scattered throughout the cytoplasm. The nucleus is reticular in appearance and contains one to

Figure 25.4. Mature neutrophil in acute myeloid leukemia.
The nucleus is segmented and has the chromatin pattern of a mature neutrophil. The number of azurophil and specific granules is markedly diminished compared to normal neutrophils with this degree of nuclear lobulation. (×32,000)

three usually prominent nucleoli. The peroxidase and Sudan black B stains give negative reactions. The cytoplasm is variably and frequently intensely positive with the nonspecific esterase stain utilizing alpha naphthyl acetate or alpha naphthyl butyrate.

On ultrastructural examination, the monoblasts possess abundant cytoplasm (Figure 25.5(a)) which may be irregularly distributed around the nucleus. There are numerous free ribosomes, mitochondria, strands of rough endoplasmic reticulum (Figure 25.5(b)), and varying numbers of dense granules. Fibrillar arrays frequently in a paranuclear location, are found in many of the cells. In some instances the fibrillar arrays appear to be associated with areas of nuclear indentation (Figure 25.5(c)). The cytoplasm of a high percentage of the blasts in some patients with acute monoblastic leukemia contains ribosome–lamella complexes similar to the structures noted in the cells of hairy cell leukemia.[75] The nuclei are generally round or oval; occasional nuclei exhibit folding and deep indentations. The nuclear chromatin is dispersed with some condensation at the nuclear margin; there may be decidedly more clumping of the chromatin than is found in myeloblasts or the promonocytes of some cases of acute monocytic leukemia.

In the acute monocytic leukemias there is clear evidence of differentiation of the monoblasts to promonocytes and monocytes.[49, 56] This evidence is most pronounced in the nucleus which may exhibit considerable indentation and contortion. The nuclei of many of the monocytes may show an almost cerebriform pattern on light microscopy.

Ultrastructurally, the striking feature of the acute monocytic leukemias is the extremely finely dispersed nuclear chromatin with only minimal condensation of the chromatin along the nuclear margin. The nucleoli, which may be multiple, are generally prominent. The more mature cells show considerable contortion of the nucleus; nuclear segments connected by fine chromatin strands are frequently present. Even in the nuclei which show extreme contortion, the chromatin may be very finely distributed and nucleoli may be very prominent (Figure 25.6(a)). The cytoplasm may contain numerous ribosomes and several strands of rough endoplasmic reticulum. In some of the younger forms (Figure 25.6(b)) strands of rough endoplasmic reticulum may be numerous; azurophil granules are frequently present as are pseudopod and vesicle formation. Fibrillar arrays may be prominent in many of the cells; the arrays are frequently in a paranuclear location.[49]

In the myelomonocytic leukemias, that is, those in which there is definite evidence of leukemic involvement of both neutrophils and monocytic cells, there is proliferation of both cell lines, monocyte and neutrophil. Hybrid or intermediate forms are stated not to be present.[55] The abnormalities which can be found in the neutrophils of acute myeloblastic leukemia, and the monocytes in monocytic leukemia may be present in the cell lines of acute myelomonocytic leukemia. In some of the cases of myelomonocytic leukemia, it may be possible to find abnormalities in the erythroid and megakaryocyte lines.

Figure 25.5. Acute monoblastic leukemia (R. W. McKenna *et al.*).

(a) Monoblasts in the marrow of a patient showing very abundant cytoplasm containing numerous organelles in several of the cells. The nuclei are round or ovoid and the chromatin is finely dispersed with scattered clumping. (× 7,000)

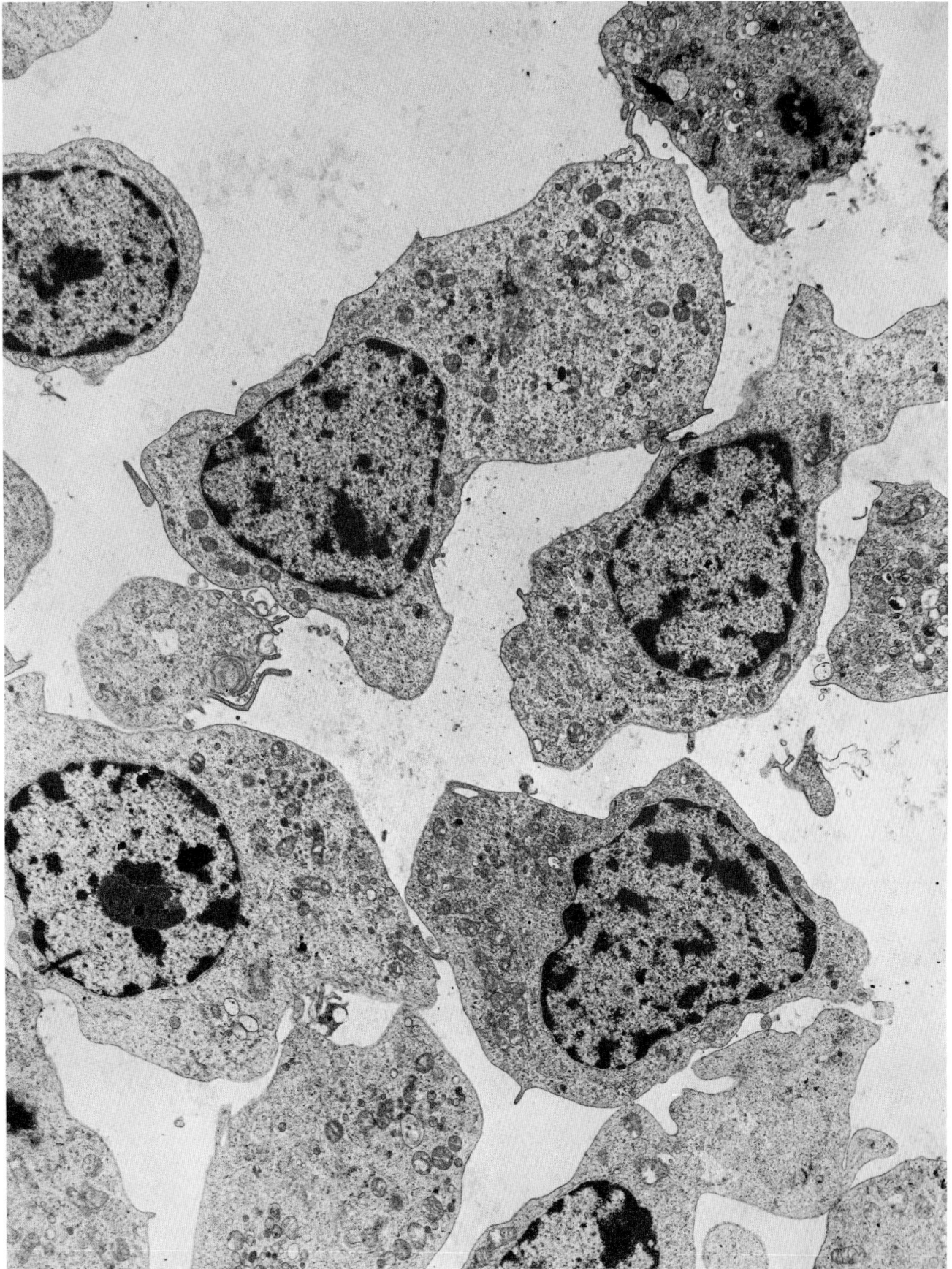

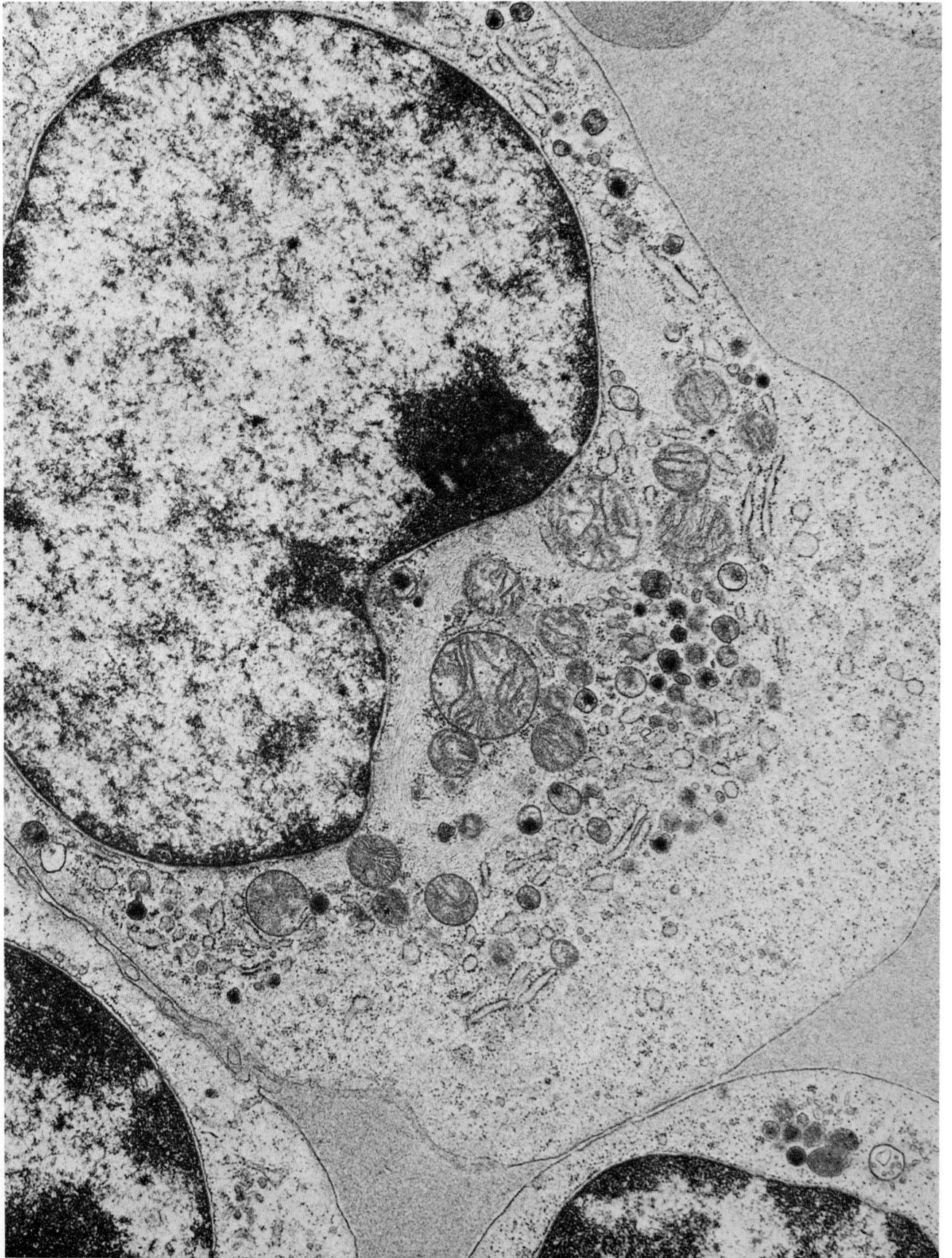

Figure 25.5. Acute monoblastic leukemia (R. W. McKenna *et al.*).

(b) Monoblast in the bone marrow of a patient showing finely dispersed nuclear chromatin
with minimal condensation at the nuclear margin. The nucleolus is compact and not unusually large. The abundant cytoplasm contains numerous granules, several mitochondria,
and strands of rough endoplasmic reticulum. Bundles of fibrils can be identified in a paranuclear location. ($\times$ 20,000)

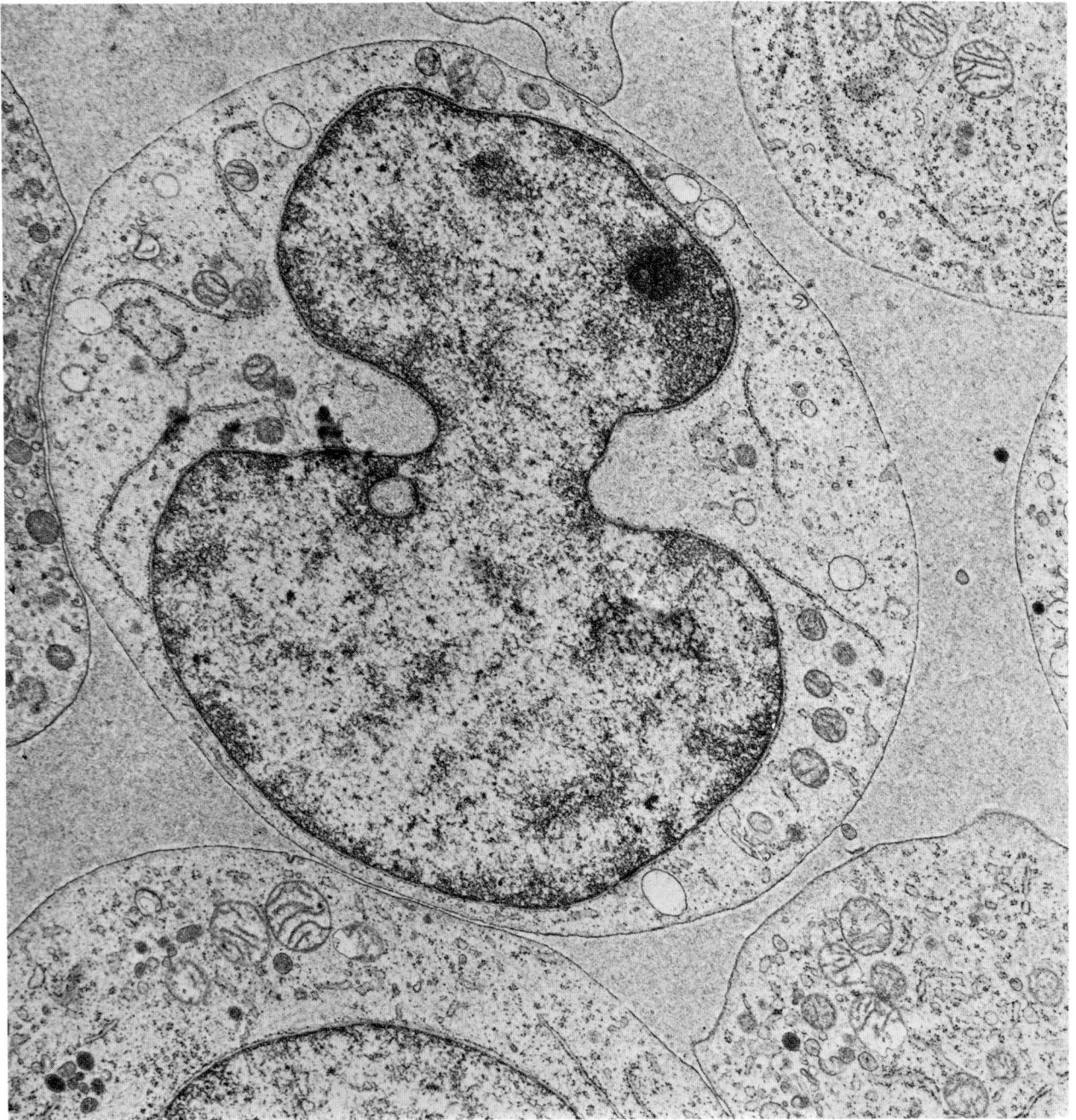

Figure 25.5. Acute monoblastic leukemia.
(c) Monoblast from a patient showing bundles of fibrils in the areas of nuclear indentation. (× 16,000)

25.1.3. Acute promyelocytic leukemia

Acute promyelocytic leukemia is a form of acute myelocytic leukemia in which there is an increased number of immature cells, both myeloblasts and neutrophil promyelocytes, which have a markedly hypergranular cytoplasm;[7] the term hypergranular leukemia has also been used as a designation for this type of leukemia. The granules in these cells are predominantly azurophilic in type. At times the increase in granules is so striking as to obscure the nuclear outline. The nuclei of these cells may be round, oval, or monocytoid in appearance. Despite the use of the term promyelocytic and the abundant azurophil granulation, the nuclei of a majority of the leukemic cells are more characteristic of a blast. One of the prominent features in most cases of acute promyelocytic leukemia is the presence of blasts which contain multiple Auer bodies. These Auer bodies may be spindle or rod shaped. Generally, the blasts with multiple Auer rods are very infrequent and may be recognized only after long and diligent search of marrow smears. Blasts with large globular inclusions of Auer material may be present. This type of leukemia is complicated by a high incidence of disseminated intravascular coagulopathy.[59,118]

Ultrastructurally, as in light microscopy, the striking feature is the greatly increased number of azurophil granules (Figure 25.7(a)) in the blasts and promyelocytes. Cells with multiple Auer rods (Figure 25.7(b)) may be found; on high magnification, the Auer rods are composed of tubular structures (Figure 25.7(c)). Breton-Gorius and Houssay[15] have suggested that the periodicity of the tubules in the Auer rods in acute promyelocytic leukemia is 260 Å, in contrast to the tubules in acute myeloblastic leukemia which have a periodicity of 60–130 Å. Fibrillar arrays and greatly dilated sacs or lamellae of endoplasmic reticulum may be present; at times, the perinuclear cisternae may also show considerable dilatation. Numerous mitochondria may be present. Similar to other forms of leukemia, the nuclei may show blebs and appendages. An unusual inclusion in the blasts of promyelocytic leukemia was described by Ogawa and Matsuoko et al.[110,117] The inclusion is a ribbon-like structure with a linear pattern. The lines are about 100 Å in width with a periodicity of 200 Å. These inclusions are stated to be present only in the leukemic cells of patients with a disseminated coagulation process.

25.1.4. Erythroleukemia

The myelocytic leukemias which are characterized by involvement of the erythroid cell line in addition to the neutrophil line, are referred to as erythroleukemia (erythromegakaryocytic leukemia) or the DiGuglielmo syndrome.[74,139] When the red cell series appears to be the exclusive cell line involved, the term erythremic myelosis or DiGuglielmo's disease is used. In erythroleukemia and erythremic myelosis, the erythroid precursors show several abnormalities of nuclear and cytoplasmic development. The nuclei are frequently megaloblastoid in appearance and giant multinucleated erythroblasts may be present. The nuclei often show evidence of lobulation and karyorrhexis. The cytoplasm, particularly of the basophilic erythroblasts, may show prominent vacuole formation; the vacuoles in these cells are usually intensely positive with the periodic acid–Schiff (PAS) stain; the orthochromatic erythroblasts frequently show a diffuse, cytoplasmic, PAS positivity. In erythroleukemia, the

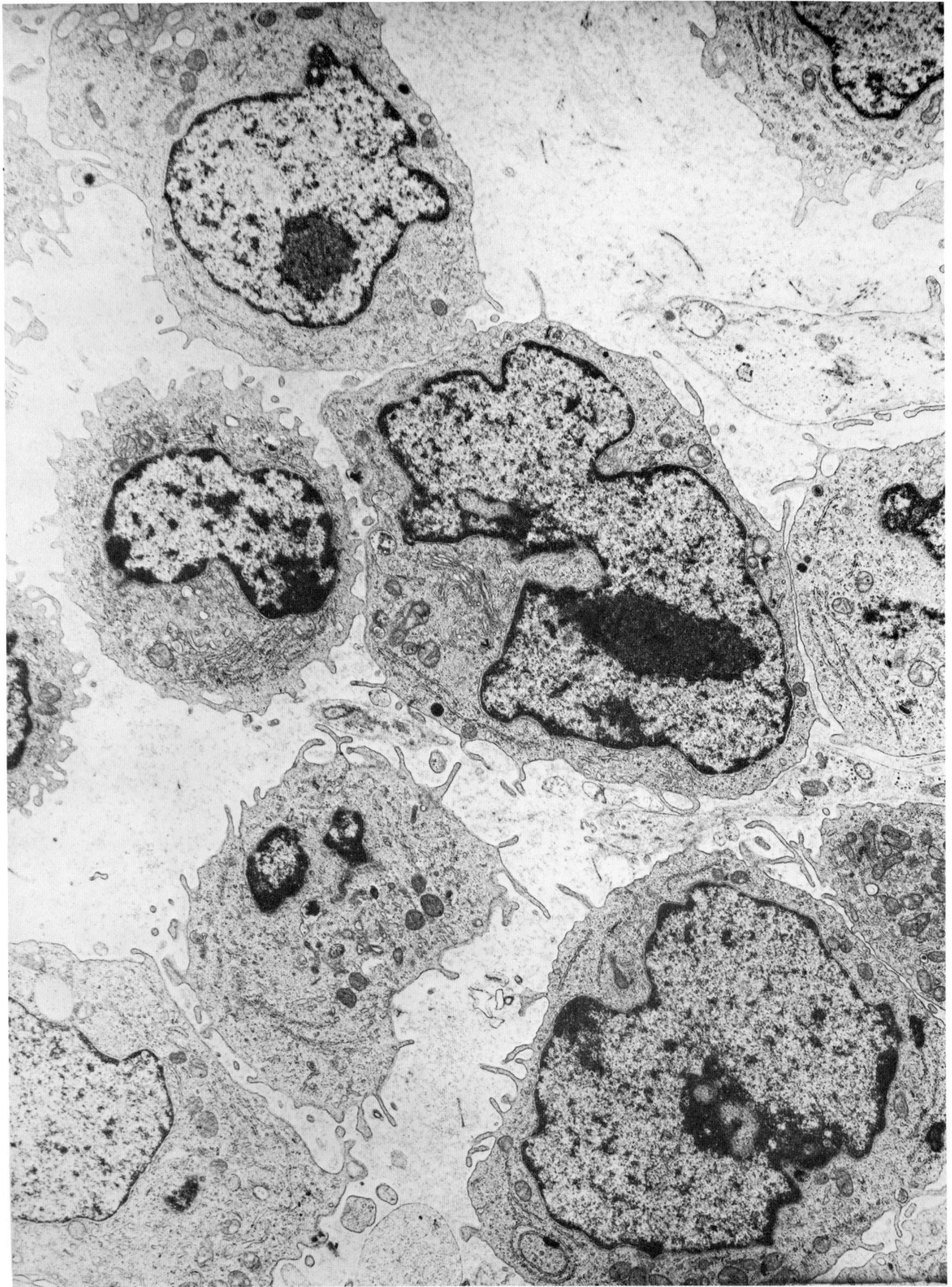

Figure 25.6. Acute monocytic leukemia.

(a) Bone marrow specimen from a patient showing the irregular nuclear outlines and the very finely dispersed nuclear chromatin. Prominent nucleoli are present in two cells. The cytoplasm contains strands of rough endoplasmic reticulum and scattered ribosomes. Some of the cells contain a few dense granules and prominent Golgi. Delicate projections are present on the surface of some of the cells. ($\times$ 10,500)

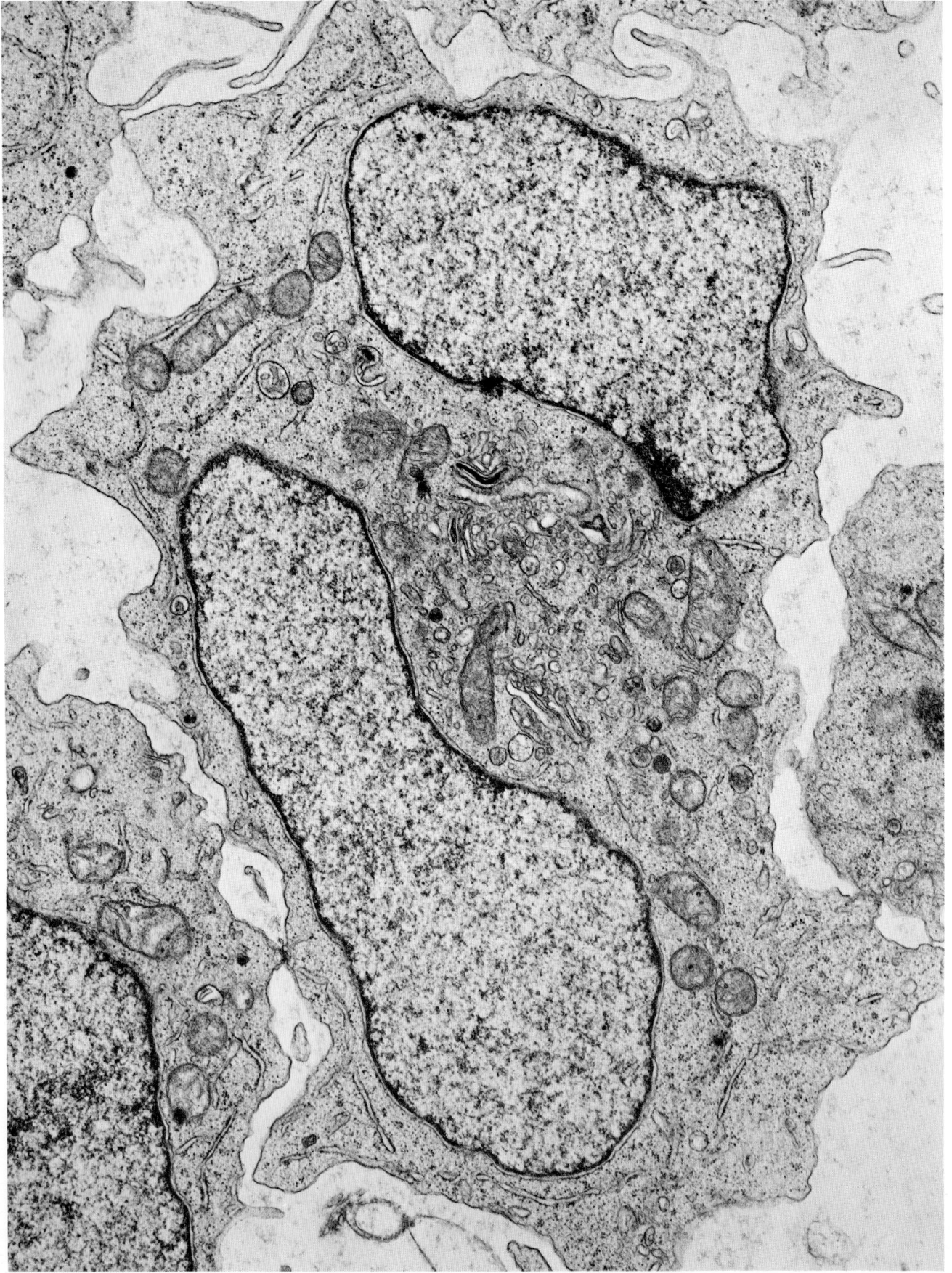

Figure 25.6. Acute monocytic leukemia.

(b) An immature cell from bone marrow. The lobulated nucleus has a very finely dispersed chromatin. ($\times$ 15,000)

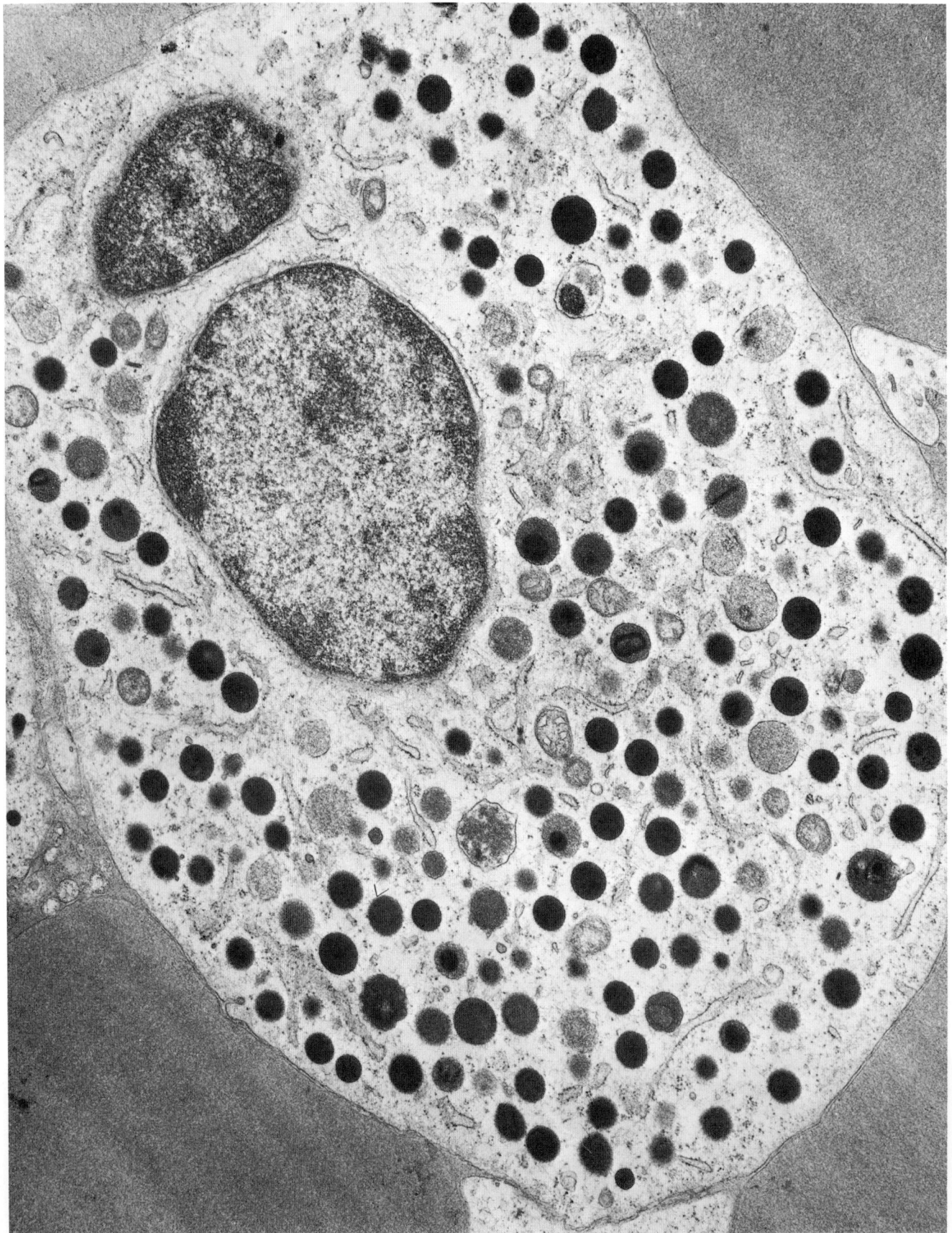

Figure 25.7. Acute promyelocytic leukemia.

(a) A neutrophil precursor from bone marrow. The cytoplasm contains a very large number of azurophil granules. (× 20,000)

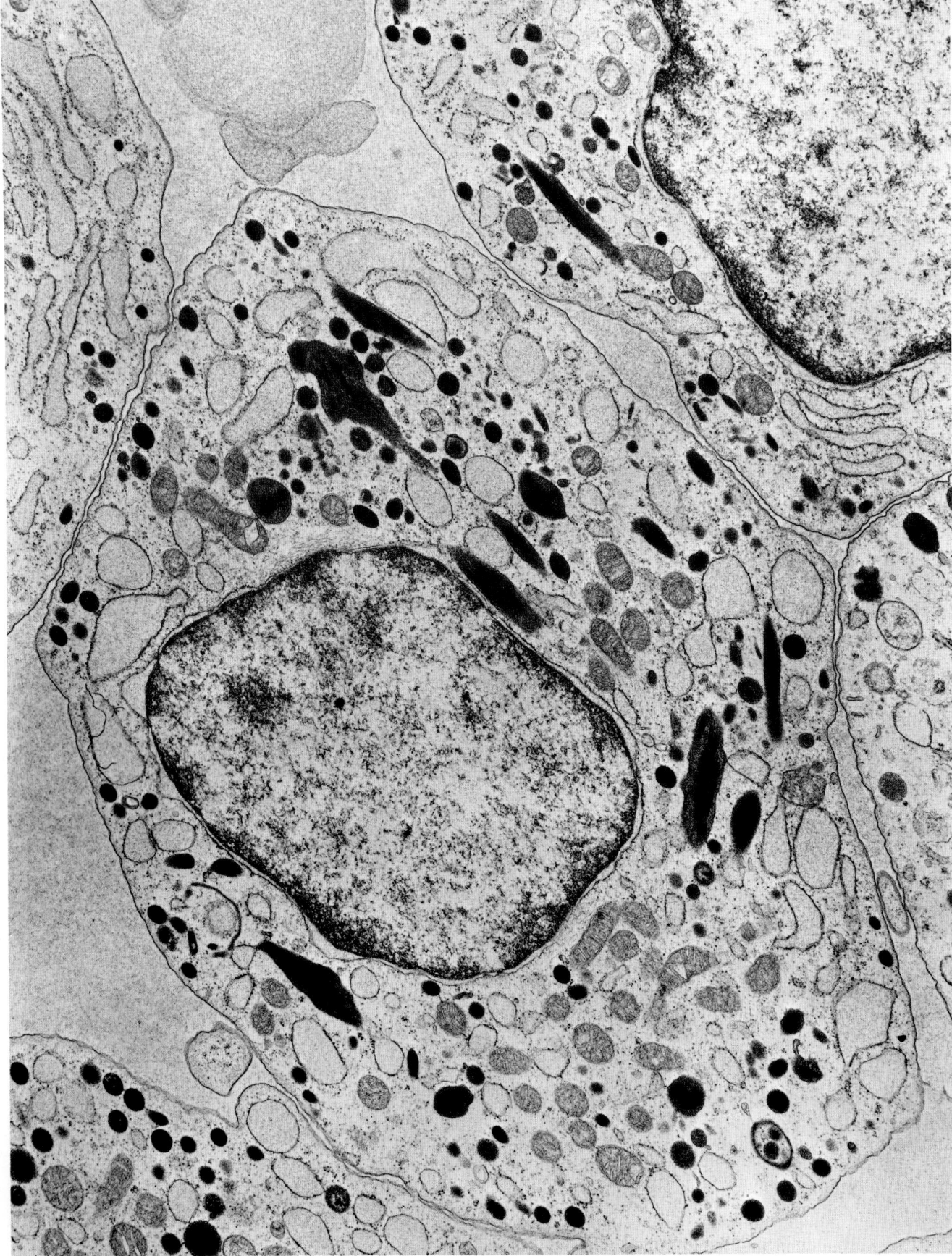

Figure 25.7. Acute promyelocytic leukemia.

(b) An early neutrophil precursor from bone marrow. The cytoplasm is marked by the presence of numerous Auer rods and dilated sacs of rough endoplasmic reticulum. The perinuclear cisternae show areas of dilatation. A bundle of fibrillary structures is present in a paranuclear location. ($\times$ 19,000)

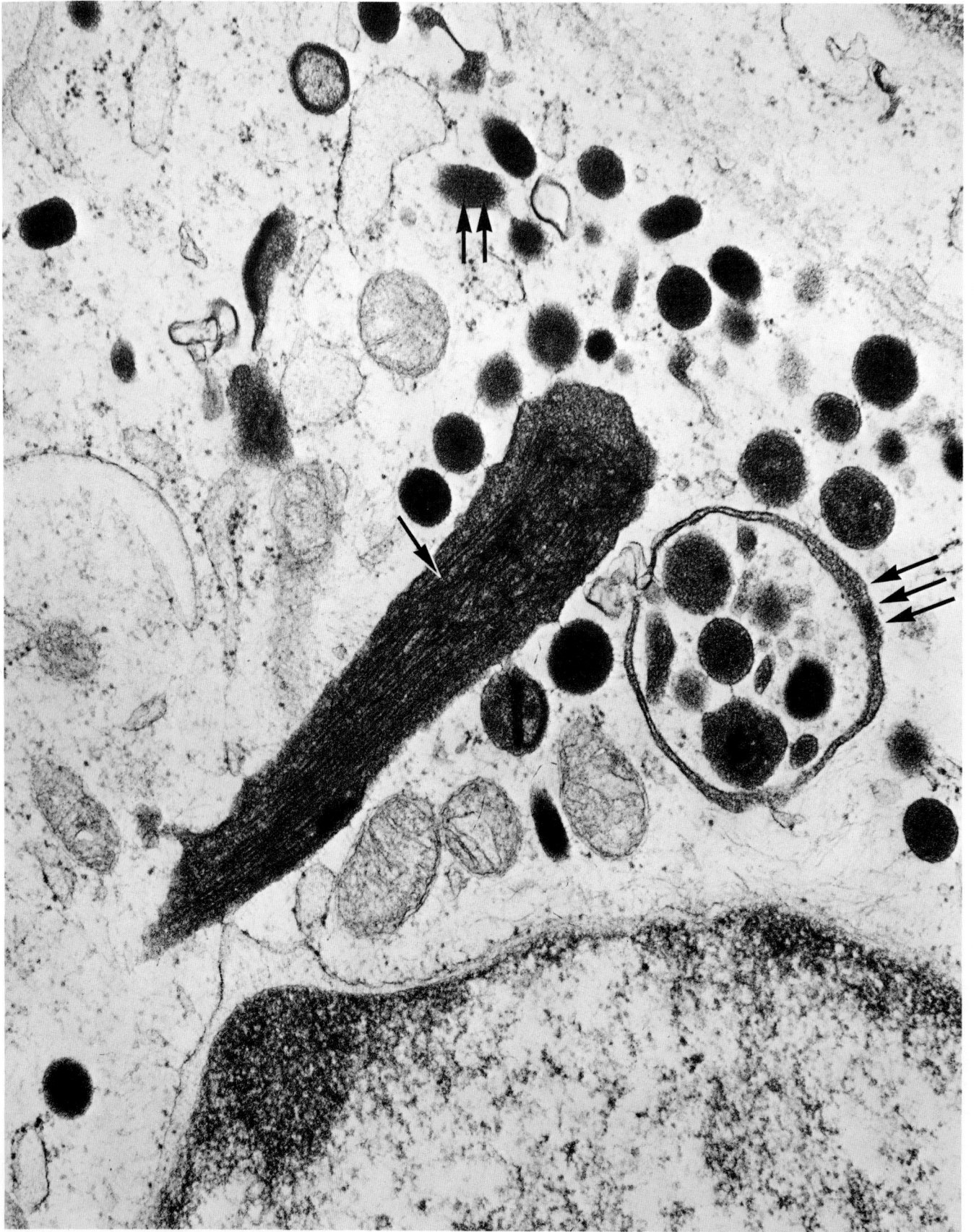

granulocyte series shows the same abnormalities which are observed in acute myeloblastic leukemia. In many of the cases of erythroleukemia, the megakaryocyte line is also involved in the leukemic process. This frequently is manifested by abnormally small forms (micromegakaryocytes) as well as nuclear and cytoplasmic abnormalities. The cases of erythroleukemia with megakaryocyte involvement are referred to as erythromegakaryocytic leukemia.

On ultrastructural examination, the erythroid precursors from patients with erythroleukemia and erythremic myelosis may exhibit nuclear cytoplasmic asynchrony which can be manifest either by chromatin clumping at relatively early stages of development or by nuclei which are less mature than the cytoplasm (Figure 25.8(a), (b)).[72, 74, 102, 103] Irregularities in nuclear outline, Figure 25.9(a), multiple nuclear profiles, and nuclear karyolysis can be seen. Alterations in the nuclear structure consisting of membrane-bound splits of the chromatin located inside the nucleus, clefts over the surface or edge, and nuclear blebs (Figure 25.9(c)) have been observed.[74, 102, 103] Erythroblasts with markedly widened nuclear pores, similar to the findings in erythroblasts in other dyserythropoietic states, may be present. Mitochondria may exhibit abnormalities of size and shape; iron deposits may be present in mitochondria (Figure 25.9(b)) but this finding is not as prominent in erythroleukemia and erythremic myelosis as it is in the sideroblastic anemias.[74] The presence of iron in the mitochondria is often accompanied by swelling, vacuolization, rupture, or separation of the cristae, and the formation of myelin figures. Cytoplasmic vacuoles and inclusions increase with cell maturation; some of the vacuoles are derived from degeneration of the mitochondria. In other instances, the vacuoles contain electron-dense masses, myelin figures, or segments of membranes of indeterminate origin. Abundant microtubules are observed in some erythroid precursors and reticulocytes; well-defined bands of peripheral microtubules may be identified.

When the megakaryocytes are involved in the leukemic process, the main ultrastructural abnormalities noted are the presence in the blood and bone marrow of small (micro) and somewhat atypical megakaryocytes (Figure 25.10),[144] nuclear cytoplasmic asynchrony, marked proliferation of the membrane demarcation system and overabundance of immature forms, as well as morphologic evidence of release of dystrophic platelets.[104]

The cytoplasm of the micromegakaryocytes in these disorders usually does not show clearly defined platelet demarcation and is frequently disorganized with haphazard distribution of the granules and the demarcation membranes. In some instances, platelet release is observed toward the periphery of the megakaryocytes but the platelets are morphologically atypical as characterized by the absence or appreciable decrease in granules, proliferation of dense tubular systems, and excess glycogen. Some megakaryocytes show large granules; these granules are noted occasionally in platelets being released from megakaryocytes.

Figure 25.7. Acute promyelocytic leukemia.

(c) A large Auer rod in a neutrophil promyelocyte. The internal architecture of the Auer rod is marked by several parallel tubular structures (↑). Similar structures can be identified in one of the azurophil granules (↑↑). Several azurophil granules are surrounded by a lamellar-like structure (↑↑↑). (× 42,000)

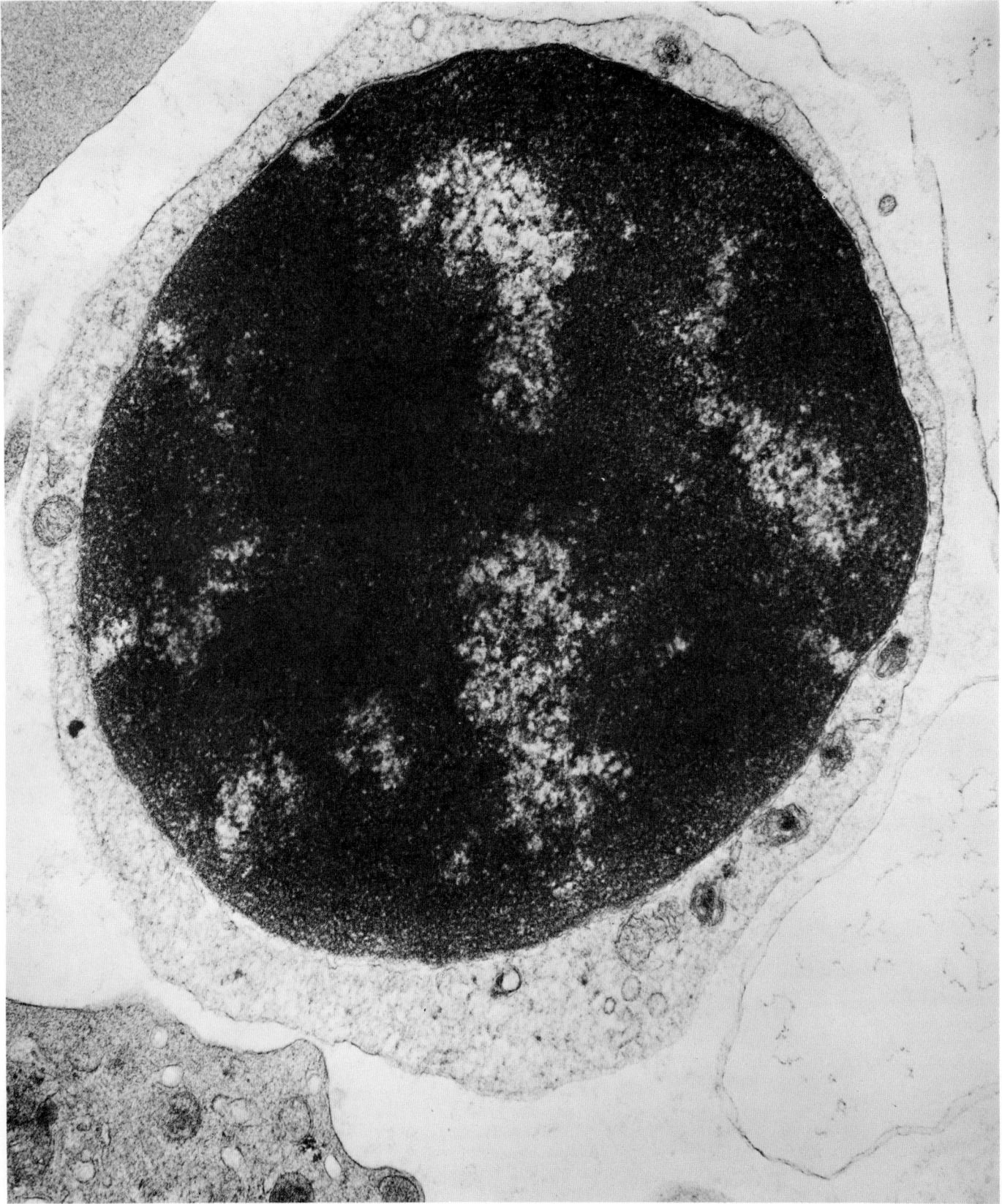

Figure 25.8.   Erythroleukemia: chromatin clumping in nucleus.

(a) Erythroblast from bone marrow manifesting markedly condensed nuclear chromatin. Particles of iron can be identified in several mitochondria. ($\times 36,000$)

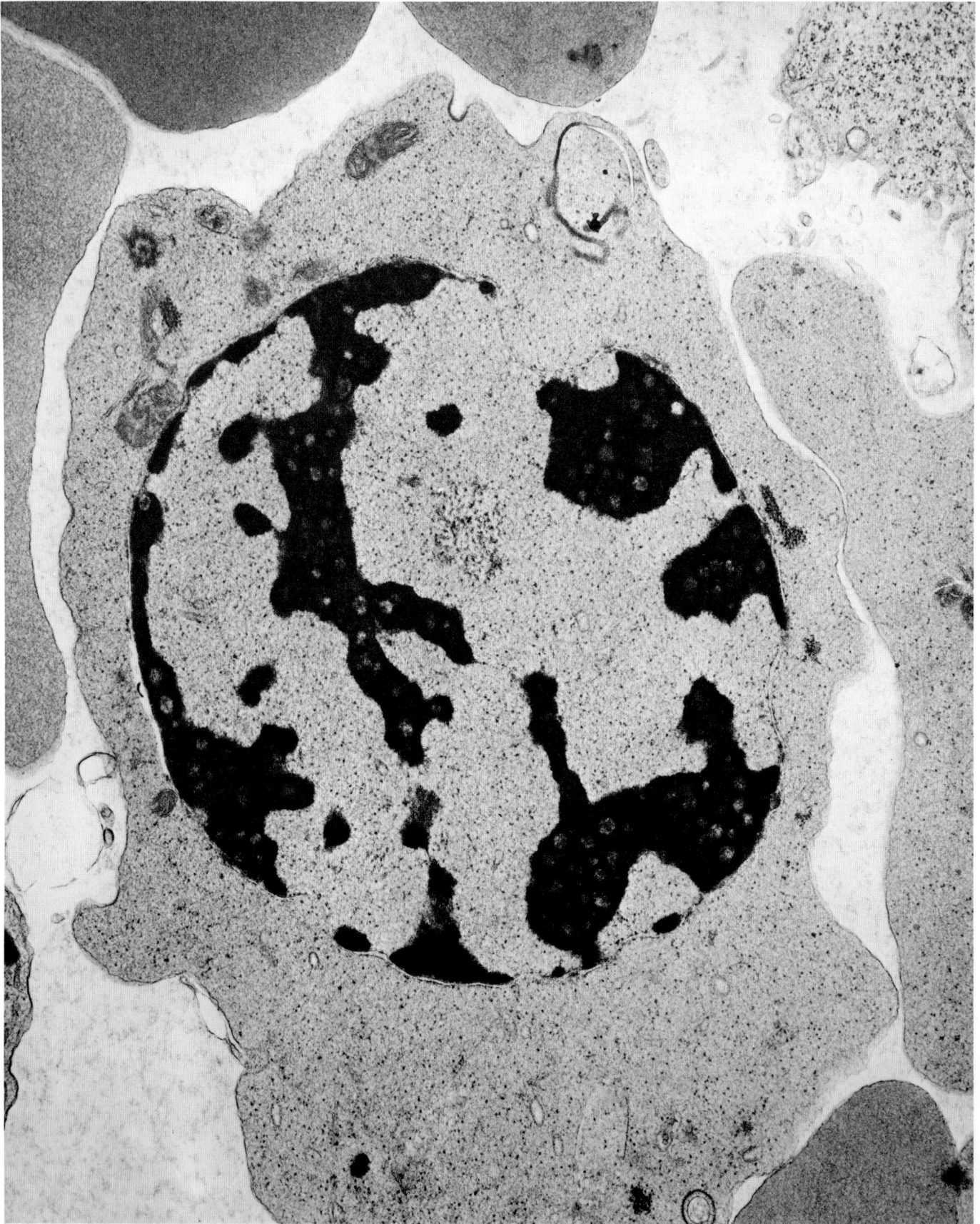

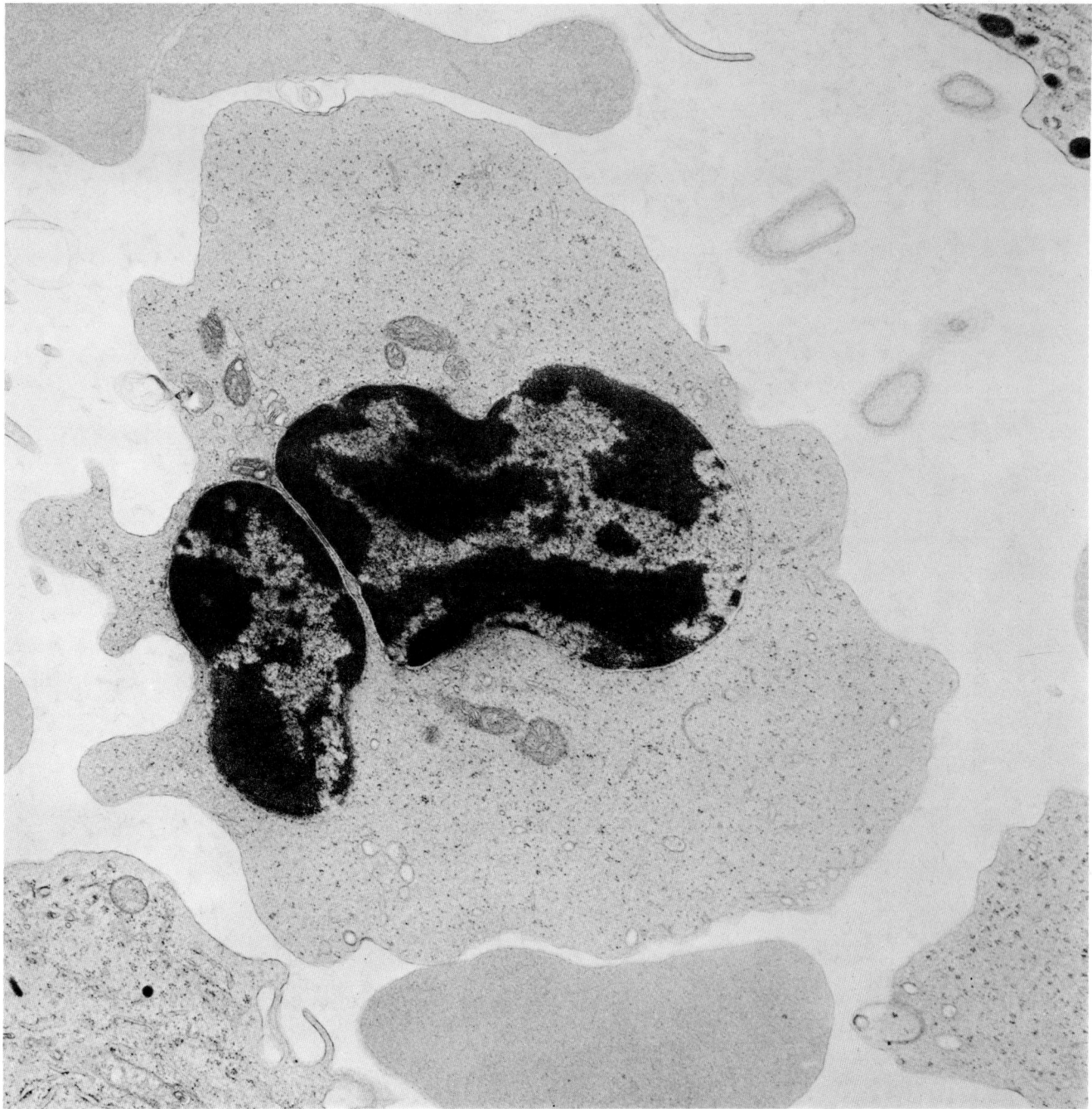

Figure 25.9. Erythroleukemia: alterations in nuclear structure and outline (J. E. Maldonado, J. Maigne, and D. Lecoq.).

(a) Large misshapen erythroblast. The double nuclear profile shows inequality in size and irregularities in outline; the chromatin manifests irregularity in the pattern of condensation. (× 18,000)

Figure 25.8. Erythroleukemia: chromatin clumping in nucleus.

(b) Late erythroblast showing very irregular chromatin condensation and markedly widened nuclear pores. The nuclear membrane shows invagination and in one area is becoming partly indistinct. (× 26,000)

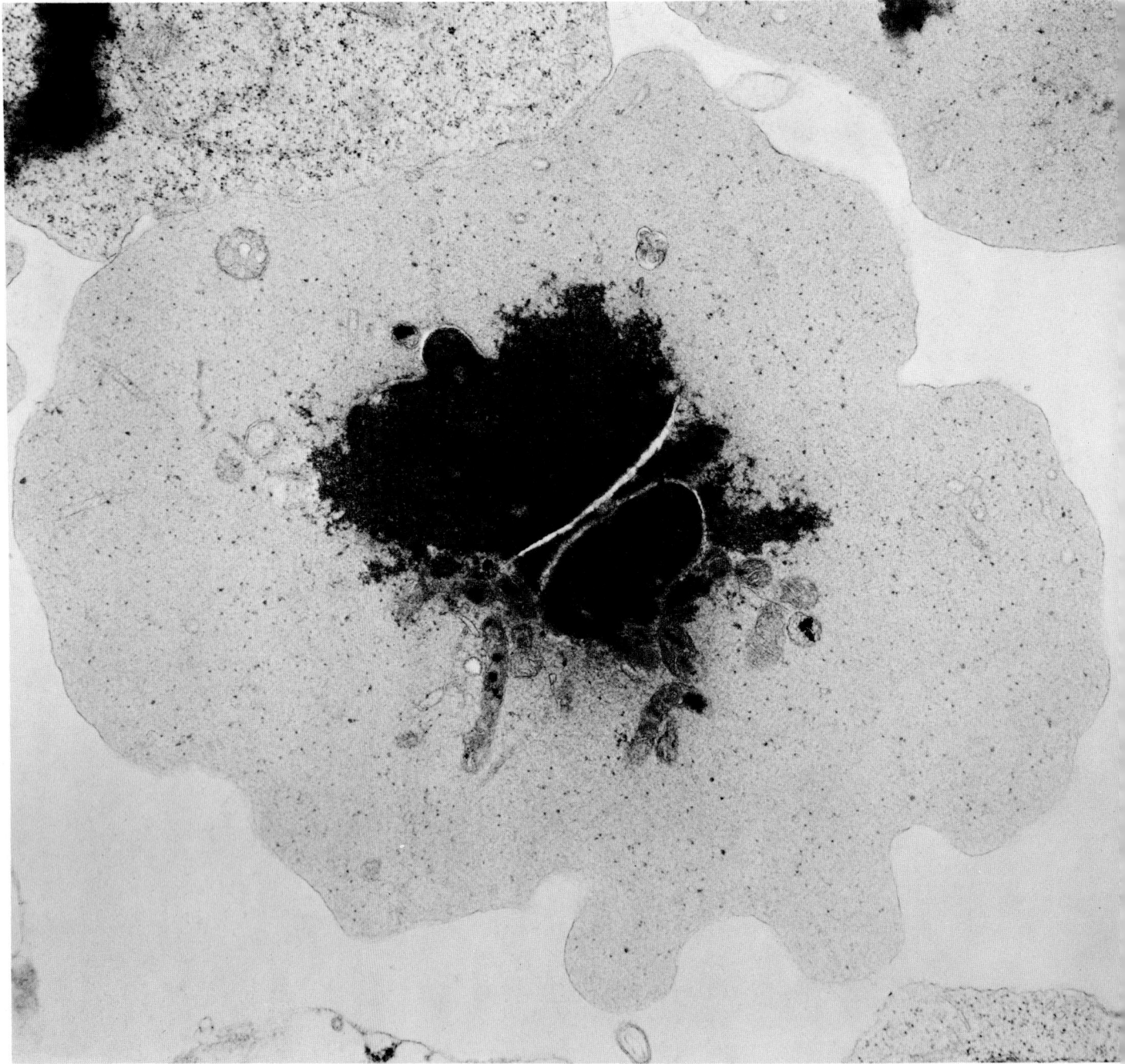

Figure 25.9. Erythroleukemia: alterations in nuclear structure and outline (J. E. Maldonado, J. Maigne, and D. Lecoq).

(b) Erythroblast with only a small portion of the nuclear membrane intact. The remainder of the nuclear outline is markedly irregular and there appears to be almost total loss of nuclear integrity. Clefts are noted in the nucleus. Several mitochondria contain particles of iron. ($\times 26,000$)

310

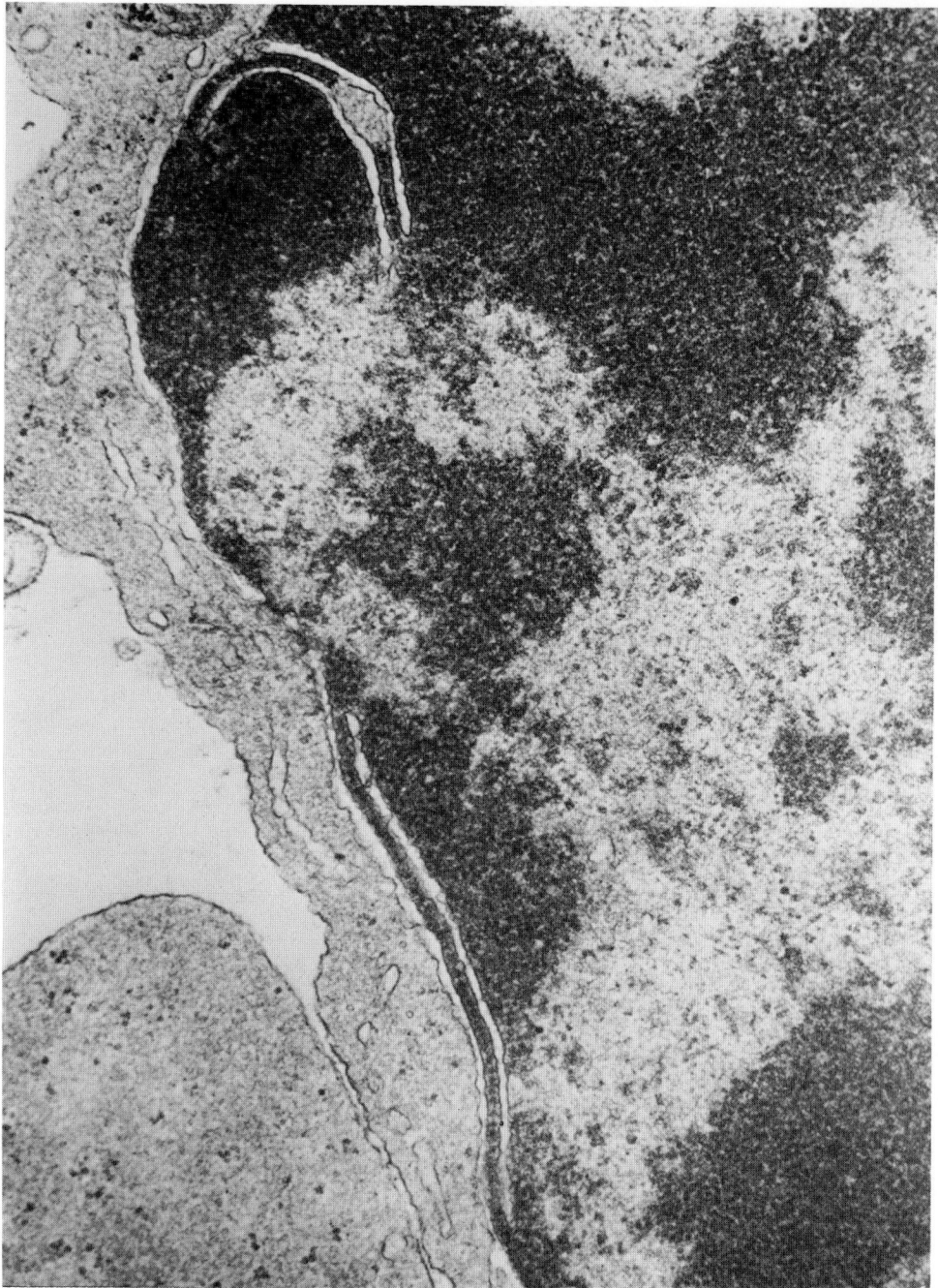

Figure 25.9. Erythroleukemia: alterations in nuclear structure and outline (J. E. Maldonado, J. Maigne, and D. Lecoq).

(c) Portions of an erythroblast showing a nuclear bleb and a nuclear cleft. (× 45,500)

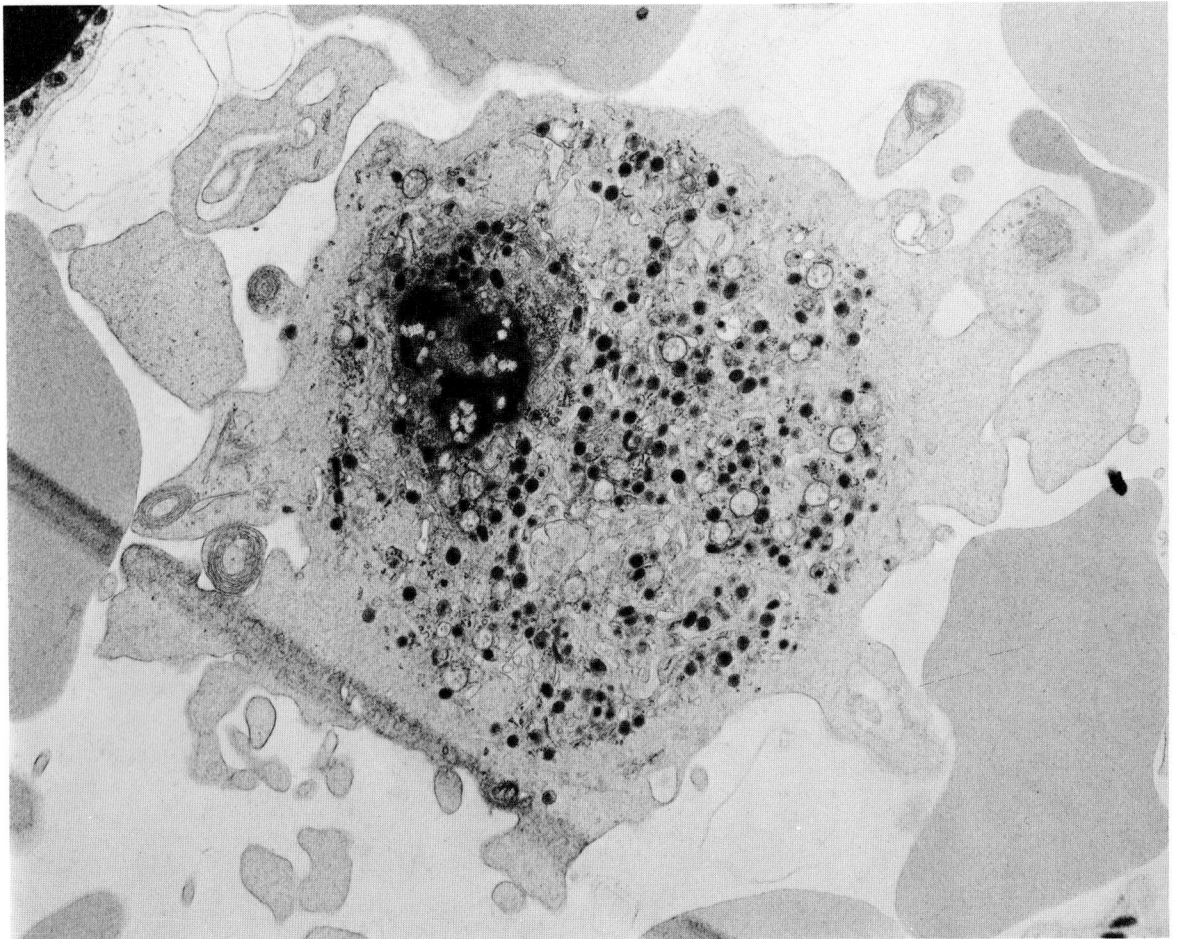

Figure 25.10. Erythromegakarocytic leukemia.
Micromegakaryocyte showing the periphery of the cytoplasm devoid of granules, tubular system, and demarcation membranes. Agranular platelets are budding from the surface. Myelin-like figures are identified in the megakaryocyte cytoplasm and in some of the platelets. (× 12,000)

The platelet changes are characterized by giant forms, paucity or absence of granulation, disorganization and scarcity of microtubules, and haphazard distribution and hypertrophy of the dense tubules and open canalicular system.[33,97] There is also evidence of platelet immaturity including abundant rough endoplasmic reticulum and ribosomes, the presence of Golgi profile, centrioles, and nuclear remnants.

The characteristics of the neutrophil series in erythroleukemia are similar to those observed in acute myeloblastic or acute myelomonocytic leukemia (Figure 25.11). Myeloblasts with Auer rods may be present.

25.1.5. Chronic myelogenous leukemia

Chronic myelogenous leukemia is a proliferative process of the granulocytes, reflected in the blood by marked leukocytosis, basophilia, and eosinophilia. The peripheral

312

blood neutrophil population in this disorder consists of all stages of development; the majority of the cells are segmented neutrophils or metamyelocytes. Lesser numbers of myelocytes and promyelocytes are present. The myeloblasts generally do not exceed 2 percent. When reacted for the enzyme alkaline phosphatase, the mature neutrophils from patients with chronic myelogenous leukemia are found to contain decreased amounts of this enzyme when compared to mature neutrophils from normal individuals. The myeloid cells of about 70–90 percent of patients with chronic myelogenous leukemia have a translocation of the long arm of chromosome 22 to the long arm of chromosome 9, the altered chromosome 22 being referred to as the Philadelphia chromosome.[132]

In contrast to the mature neutrophils, which appear normal on ultrastructural examination, the myeloblasts and neutrophil promyelocytes (Figure 25.12) from patients with chronic myelogenous leukemia are reported to manifest bundles of microfilaments, nucleosomes, deep nuclear folds, and pouches, and clustering of microfilaments and mitochondria in the cell hof.[154] The decrease in alkaline phosphatase in the mature neutrophils of chronic myelogenous leukemia does not appear to be reflected in a decrease of azurophil or specific granules.

The megakaryocytes in chronic myelogenous leukemia, on electron microscopic study, are generally hypotrophic but have a well-developed platelet demarcation system. In some patients defective development of the demarcation system is encountered in some megakaryocytes; these cells show actual demarcation of platelets in spite of very sparse development of the demarcation system.[81]

An ultrastructural histochemical alteration of the plasma membrane of the neutrophil leukocytes of chronic myelogenous leukemia has been demonstrated. Neutrophils and precursors of chronic myeloid leukemia patients show a defect in the binding of pyroantimonate.[2]

25.1.6. Chronic myelogenous leukemia – blast crisis

Chronic myelogenous leukemia generally terminates as myelofibrosis and/or a blast crisis, a situation characterized by a proliferation of blasts similar to those found in acute leukemia. The morphologic appearance of the blasts in this situation varies. In many of the cases, the blasts resemble the myeloblasts of acute myeloblastic leukemia; in other patients, monocytoid cells or megakaryocytes and erythroblasts dominate the blood and marrow picture. In a minority of the patients, the blasts resemble the lymphoblasts of acute lymphocytic leukemia.[123]

The ultrastructural characteristics parallel the light microscopic findings. The blast cells will generally show little evidence of differentiation (Figure 25.13). In those patients with blasts with well-defined myeloid or monocytic characteristics on light microscopy, there will be ultrastructural features which are similar to those observed in the blasts of acute myeloblastic or acute monocytic leukemia.[123]

Ullyot and Bainton observed abnormal mature neutrophil populations in two patients with chronic myelogenous leukemia in blast crisis.[154] In addition to the normal population of neutrophils in one case, they found neutrophils with azurophil granules which were unreactive for peroxidase. In another patient they found neutrophils with a full complement of normal appearing specific granules but no azurophil granules. Neutrophils without specific granules were also noted. Somewhat similar

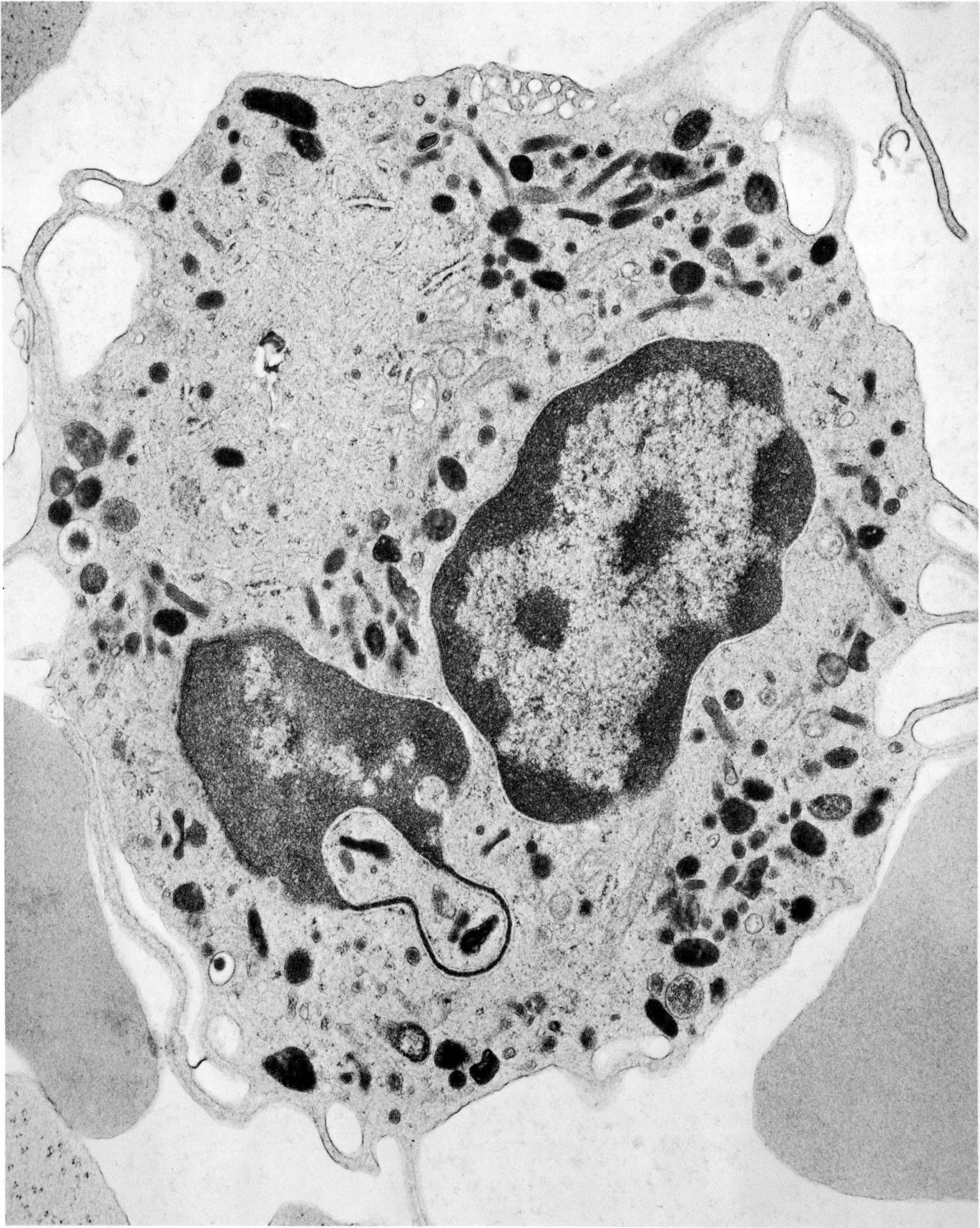

Figure 25.11. Erythroleukemia: neutrophil.

There is an area in the cytoplasm which is almost totally devoid of granules. A few strands of rough endoplasmic reticulum are present at the periphery of this area. One of the nuclear segments has a nuclear bleb which contains cytoplasmic structures. (× 28,000)

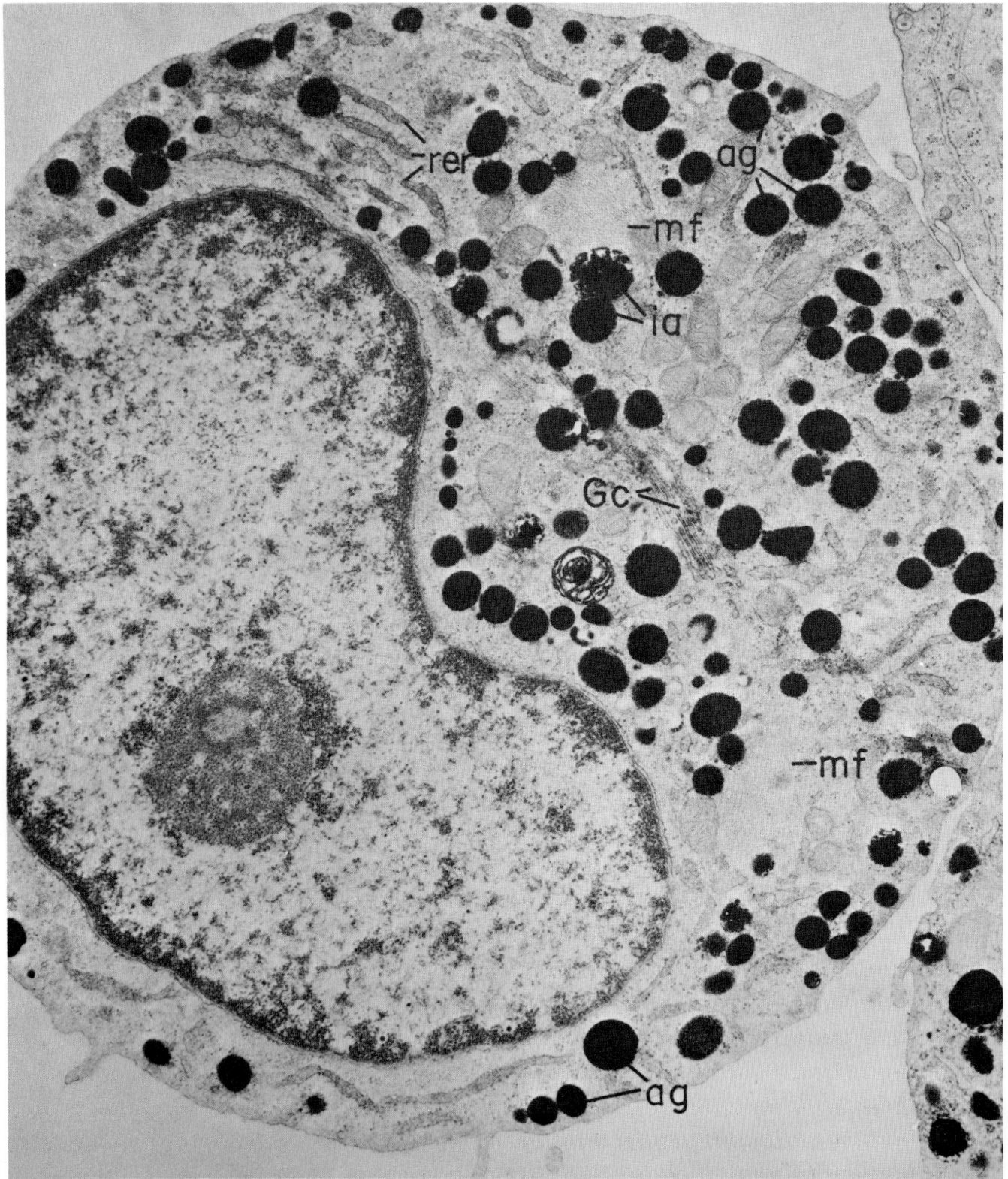

Figure 25.12. Chronic myelogenous leukemia (J. L. Ulloyt and D. Bainton).
Neutrophil promyelocyte reacted for peroxidase. Reaction product is present in the rough endoplasmic reticulum (rer), Golgi cisternae (Gc), and all immature (ia) and mature (ag) specific granules. Two bundles of microfilaments (mf) are also present. (× 13,600)

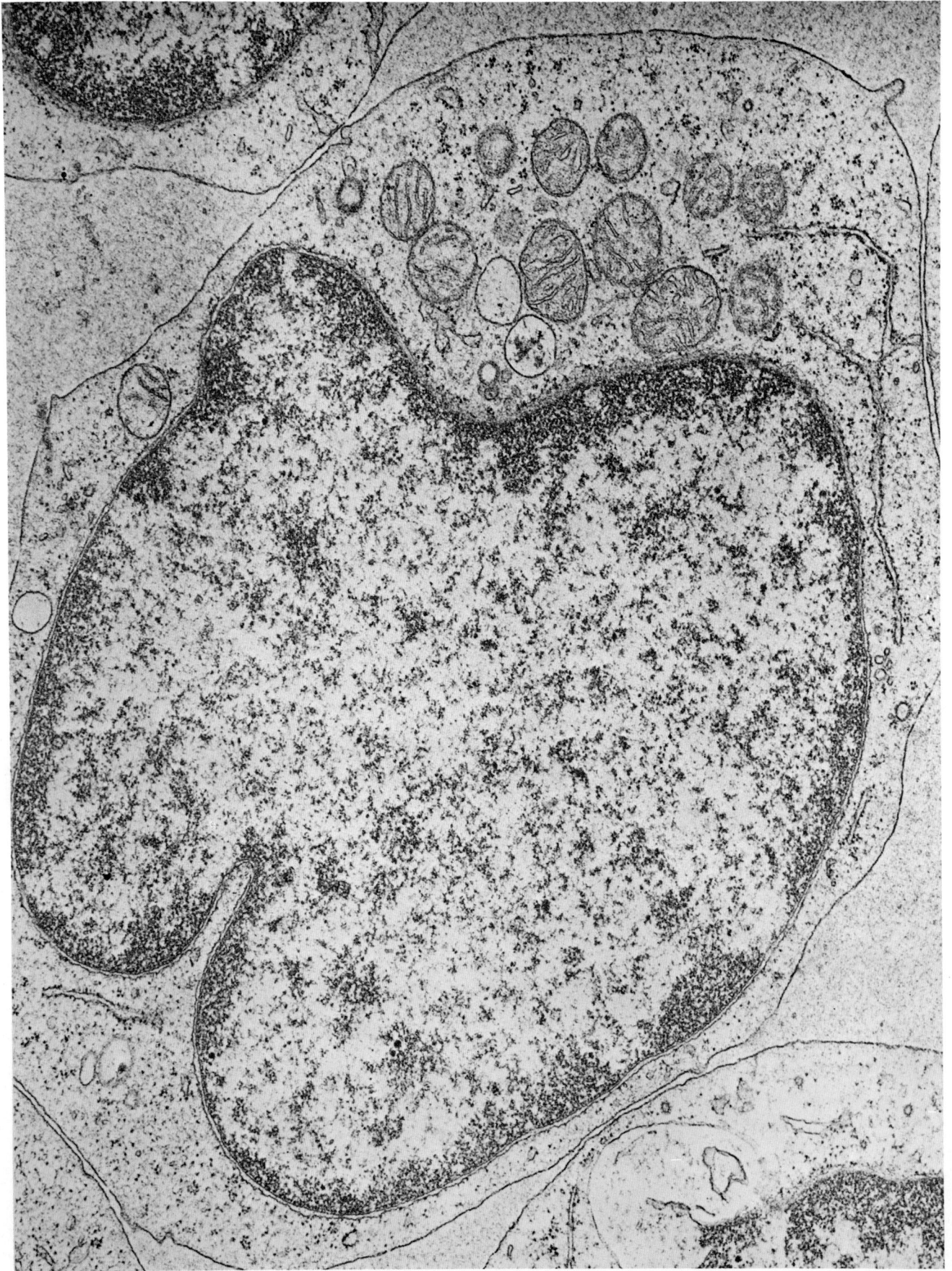

findings have been reported in the neutrophil promyelocytes from the bone marrows of patients with chronic myelogenous leukemia in blast crisis. Promyelocytes with both myeloperoxidase-positive and myeloperoxidase-negative azurophil granules were observed.[120]

25.1.7. Agnogenic myeloid metaplasia

Agnogenic myeloid metaplasia is one of the myeloproliferative syndromes closely related to chronic myelogenous leukemia and polycythemia vera; one of the characteristics of the disorder is myelofibrosis. The peripheral blood picture slightly resembles the pattern found in chronic myeloid leukemia but there are generally more pronounced changes in the red cell series as characterized by increased poikilocytosis, particularly tear drop shaped erythrocytes, and abnormalities in the size and appearance of the platelets. Megakaryocytes are frequently present in the peripheral blood and they are frequently small and abnormal in appearance. In some cases they may comprise a very high percentage of the circulating cells. Many of the megakaryocytes are small and have been referred to as micromegakaryocytes or dwarf megakaryocytes.[149] Abnormalities of the megakaryocyte cytoplasm are frequent. The abnormal megakaryocytes give rise to atypical platelet forms.[149] These are predominantly of two types: platelets with clear blue, agranular cytoplasm, often with extensive pseudopod formation at the periphery, and giant granular forms.[105] Many of the agranular platelets are also very large in size and some may be extraordinarily so.[149] Ultrastructurally, the circulating megakaryocytes in agnogenic myeloid metaplasia and related conditions have characteristic cytoplasmic features of megakaryocytes such as demarcation membranes, typical bullseye or alpha type granules, and vacuoles of the open canalicular system.[96] The cells range in size from 5–12 μm. They usually exhibit proliferation of the membranous systems; large clusters of membranes fill extensive areas of the cytoplasm and form intricate structures. Neither when clustered nor when isolated do the membranes appear to delineate or demarcate the megakaryocyte cytoplasm into individual platelets. The degree of hypertrophy of the membranous system in some patients and the accumulation of membranes without evident function as regards platelet segregation have been interpreted as evidence of asynchronous cytoplasmic maturation. Some megakaryocytes have scarcity of demarcation membranes and excess of platelet granules but no morphologic evidence of platelet production. In other instances, while the nucleus appears clearly lobulated or multisegmented and the cell is of the ovoid large size, extensive portions have few granules and are filled with hypertrophic demarcation membrane.[9]

The platelets in primary myelofibrosis manifest a wide range of alterations: large platelets (Figure 25.14(a)), platelets with abundant organelles (Figure 25.14(b)), platelets devoid of organelles, and platelets with hypertrophied endoplasmic reticulum. Three primary features of the platelets in this disorder have been characterized:

Figure 25.13. Chronic myelogenous leukemia in blast crisis (L. C. Peterson, C. D. Bloomfield, and R. D. Brunning).

An undifferentiated blast showing the nucleus with widely dispersed chromatin. The cytoplasm contains several mitochondria, scattered ribosomes, and a few strands of rough endoplasmic reticulum. ($\times$27,000)

hypoplasia of the surface connecting system with few orifices, hyperplasia of the dense tubular system, and considerable variation in the number of granules.[63]

25.2. Lymphocytic leukemias

25.2.1. Acute lymphocytic leukemia

Similar to the acute myelocytic leukemias, there is some morphologic heterogeneity to those leukemias which are classified under the term acute lymphocytic leukemia. In some patients the cell population in the blood and marrow is almost exclusively composed of lymphoblasts with few differentiating features. In other patients the leukemic population is characterized by a morphologic spectrum in which the lymphoblasts appear to progress to rather more mature appearing cells as characterized by less cytoplasm, increased condensation of the nuclear chromatin, and less prominent nucleoli. Mathe[103] has used the term macrolymphoblastic to describe those cases in which the blood and marrow reflect primarily a lymphoblast proliferation and prolymphocytic to describe those cases characterized by a predominance of more differentiated lymphocytes or prolymphocytes. The term acute lymphoblastic leukemia has been used as a designation for the predominantly lymphoblastic type of leukemia and subacute lymphocytic leukemia for those cases in which the prolymphocytes are dominant.[13,112] Others have proposed the designation L_2 for the lymphoblastic cases and L_1 for the prolymphocytic type.[5] Many observers recognize a third type of acute lymphocytic leukemia in which the proliferating blast has a more intensely basophilic cytoplasm and rather reticular nuclear structure; the cytoplasm of this type of blast frequently contains sharply defined vacuoles.[5,20] This type of acute lymphocytic leukemia has cytologic similarities to the Burkitt's lymphoma and may have a close biologic relationship to that disorder.

The introduction of membrane surface marker determinations in the study of the lymphocytic leukemias has made possible an entirely new approach to the classification of this group of disorders.[61] Whether a classification based on surface marker characteristics has more relevance for predicting the biologic course of the leukemic process than routine morphology is not completely clear from studies to date.[18,31,141]

In approximately 80 percent of the cases of acute lymphocytic leukemia, the leukemic cells do not possess detectable surface markers of normal B or T lymphocytes and are referred to as "null" cell leukemias. In about 18 percent of the cases of acute lymphocytic leukemia the cells will type as T cells, as determined by spontaneous rosette formation with sheep erythrocytes. In 1–2 percent of the cases of lymphocytic leukemia, the cells type as B cells as manifest by monoclonal surface immunoglobulin; many of these leukemias have the cytologic features of the Burkitt's lymphoma cells.[20] Focal acid phosphatase activity in lymphoblasts is stated to be more characteristic of T cells than null or B cells.[25]

Ultrastructurally, in contrast to the acute myelocytic leukemias, there are few

---

Figure 25.14. Agnogenic myeloid metaplasia (J. E. Maldonado and T. Pintado).

(a) Large, round, hypogranular platelet showing several sections of dilated or open canalicular system. ($\times 35,000$)

320

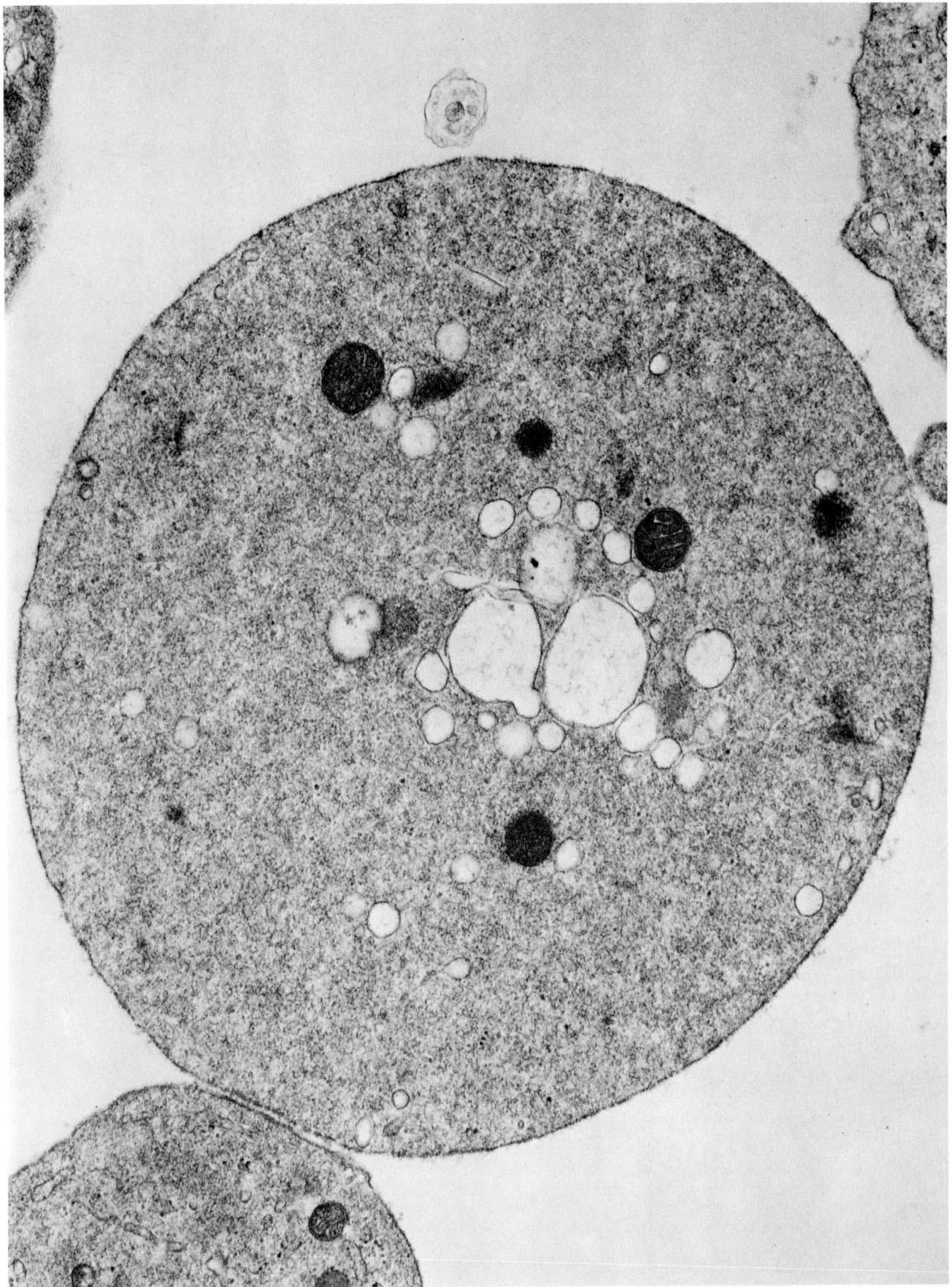

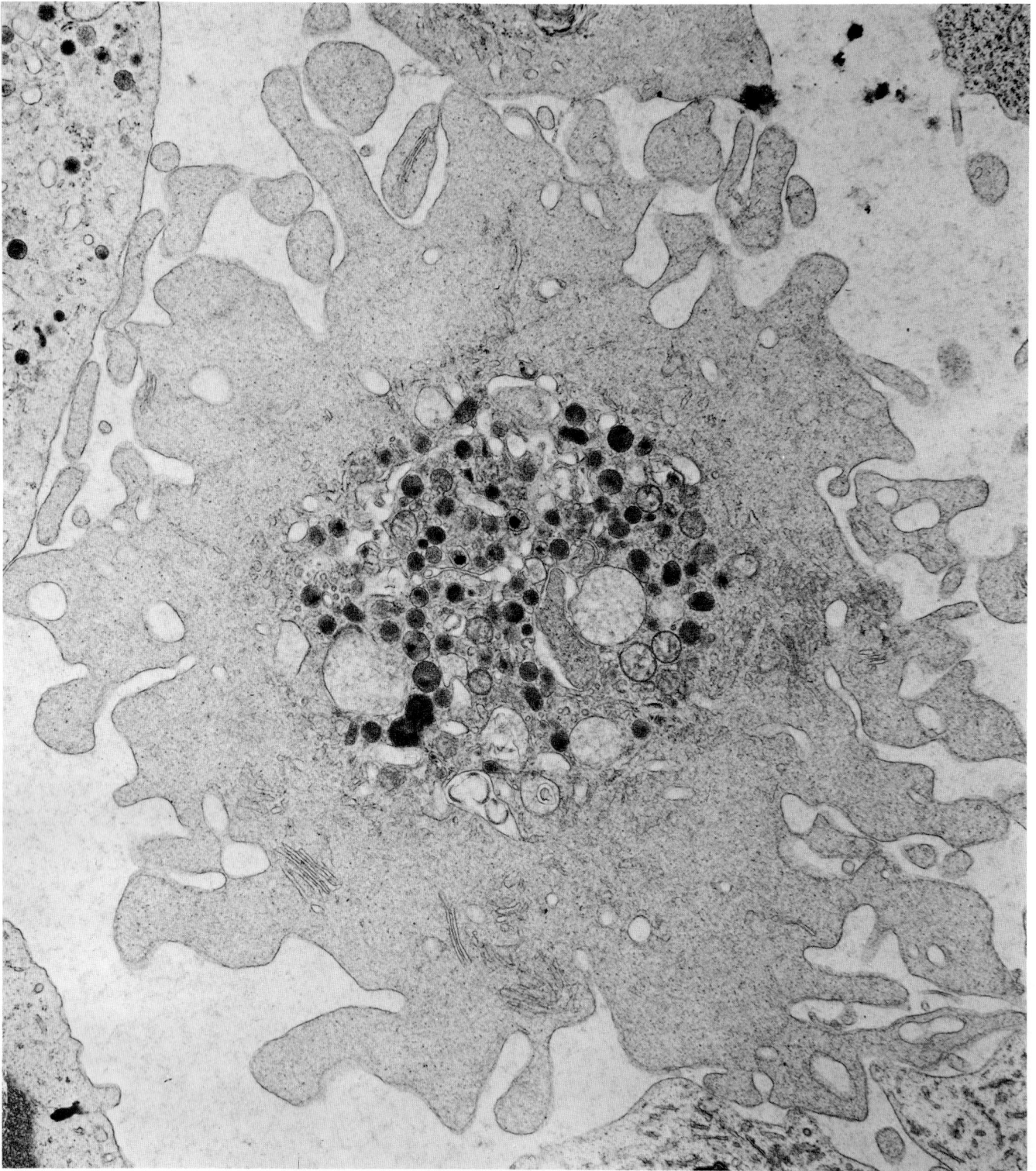

Figure 25.14. Agnogenic myeloid metaplasia.

(b) Large dystrophic platelet showing a central clustering of organelles. The peripheral portion
of the platelet is relatively free of structures.

distinctive features to the blasts in the majority of cases of acute lymphocytic leukemia. The nuclear chromatin may show considerable variation in the amount of clumping both in different cases and within a case. This is particularly true in the subacute lymphocytic leukemias (acute prolymphocytic leukemia, L_1) where populations of leukemic blasts with more clumped nuclear chromatin are seen in light microscopy.[13] Nucleoli are not always prominent. The nuclear outline may show considerable irregularity with the formation of indentations and blebs (Figure 25.15). In some cases there may be complete indentation of the nucleus resulting in two nuclear lobes (Figure 25.16(a), (b)) connected by a thin strand of nuclear chromatin. Bundles of microtubules have been observed in the areas of the nuclear indentations.[64,115]

The cytoplasm may vary considerably in its contents (Figure 25.16(a), (c)). Few or numerous mitochondria may be present in different blasts from the same case. Very large and abnormally shaped mitochondria are not infrequent. Ribosomes and polyribosomes also vary in number. Granules have been reported in lymphoblasts; however, these granules do not react for peroxidase. Particles of glycogen may be present either scattered throughout the cytoplasm or less commonly in dense accumulations. Unusual, large, membrane-bound inclusions containing membrane whorls and amorphous material have been described in the blasts in a small number of patients with acute lymphocytic leukemia.[148] Inclusions of this type have been observed in the lymphoblasts of children with Down's syndrome and acute lymphocytic leukemia (Figure 25.17).[24] In the Burkitt's type of leukemia the cytoplasm contains numerous ribosomes and polyribosomes with only a few strands of rough endoplasmic reticulum.[1] Vacuoles with amorphous, slightly osmiophilic material (Figure 25.18), presumably lipid, may be numerous.

25.2.2. Chronic lymphocytic leukemia

Chronic lymphocytic leukemia is usually described as a proliferation of normal appearing mature lymphocytes. The lymphocytes may be small with only scant cytoplasm or medium to large sized with a moderate to generous rim of very lightly basophilic cytoplasm.[124] The nucleus is characterized by a clumped nuclear chromatin pattern. Nucleoli, when present, are not usually prominent. To establish the diagnosis, the absolute peripheral blood lymphocyte count should be in excess of 5,000; usually it is substantially higher. The bone marrow manifests a varying degree of infiltration by the lymphocytes.

Cell surface marker studies have shown the proliferating lymphocytes in the vast majority of patients with chronic lymphocytic leukemia to type as B cells.[61] However, cases of T-cell chronic lymphocytic leukemia have been reported.[17] The proliferating lymphocytes in the cases typing as T cells are medium to large lymphocytes. An additional feature is the presence of coarse azurophilic granules in the cytoplasm in a high percentage of the lymphocytes.

Galton et al.[54] have described a type of chronic lymphocytic leukemia which they have referred to as prolymphocytic leukemia. This should not be confused with the prolymphocytic leukemia as described by Mathe[109] which is a form of acute lymphocytic leukemia. The prolymphocytic leukemia as described by Galton et al. is characterized by the proliferation of large lymphocytes which have relatively well-condensed

323

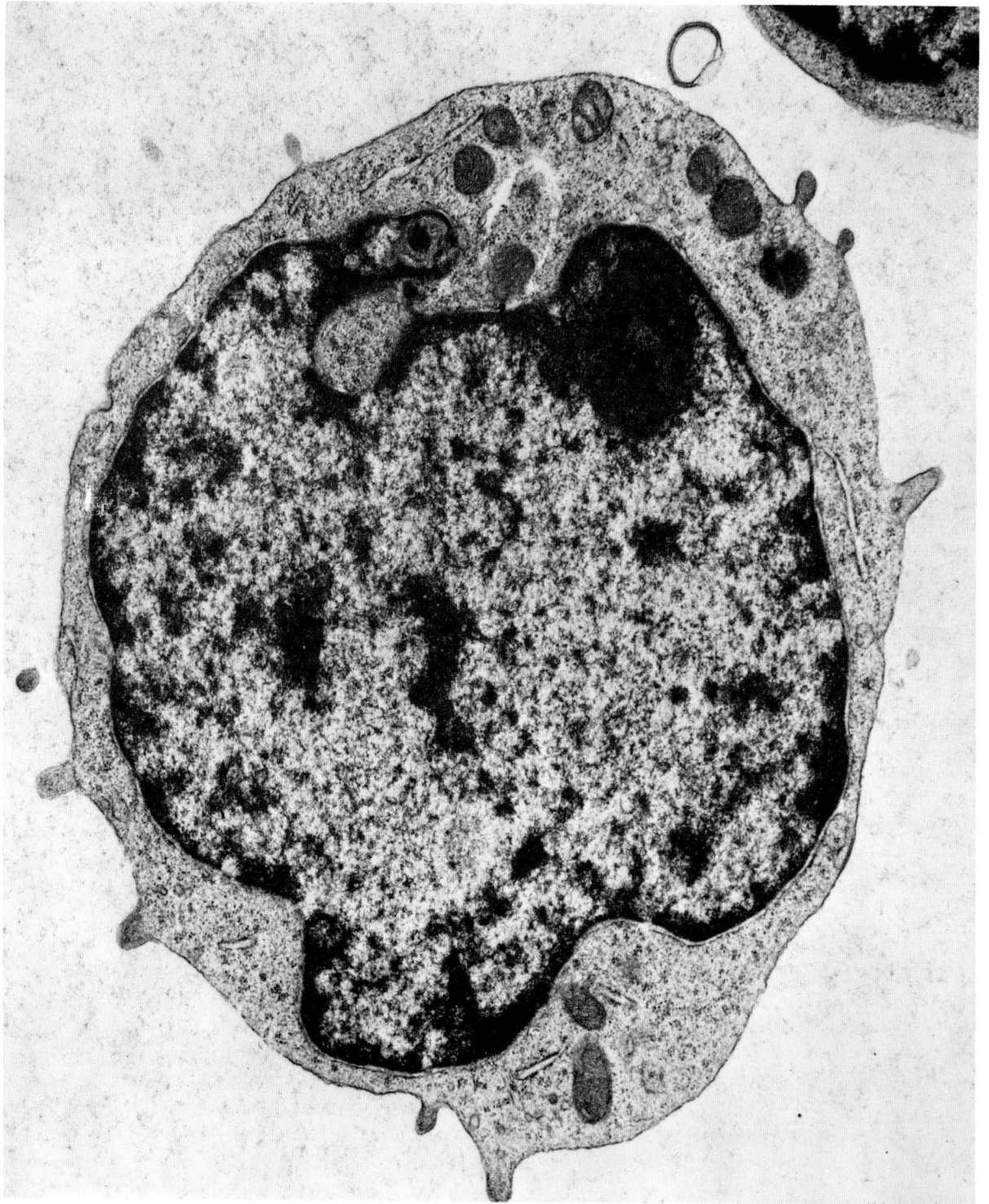

Figure 25.15. Acute lymphocytic leukemia: "null" cell type.
Lymphoblast from the peripheral blood of a patient. The nucleus has finely dispersed chromatin
with condensation at the periphery. A prominent compact nucleolus is present at the periphery
of the nucleus. A nuclear bleb is present. (×23,000)

nuclear chromatin, a large vesicular nucleolus, and a moderate amount of cytoplasm. The presenting total lymphocyte count in these patients is generally extremely high. Most of the patients also have marked splenomegaly without prominent peripheral lymphadenopathy.

Ultrastructurally, the lymphocytes in the typical small cell chronic lymphocytic leukemia exhibit a high nuclear cytoplasmic ratio; however, there is more cytoplasm than can be appreciated by light microscopy. The nuclear chromatin exhibits considerable clumping (Figure 25.19(a)). Nucleoli, which are not readily identified by light microscopy, may be found in a small number of cells and generally have a density similar to the clumped chromatin. The cytoplasmic margin is relatively smooth in outline. The cytoplasm contains scattered ribosomes and varying numbers of mitochondria. Strands of rough endoplasmic reticulum are very sparse. Occasional lymphocytes contain small granules.

In the chronic lymphocytic leukemias characterized by a proliferation of medium to large size lymphocytes, the ultrastructural findings are rather different to those found in the small cell type of chronic lymphocytic leukemia. The nuclear cytoplasmic ratio is lower and the nuclear configurations are considerably less uniform (Figure 25.19(b)) than in the small cell type. The chromatin pattern and the size of the nucleoli are very similar to the small cell type. The abundant cytoplasm may contain numerous mitochondria which show variation in size and shape. The cytoplasm contains scattered ribosomes and very few strands of rough endosplasmic reticulum. The cytoplasmic margin may have a few short projections.

The prolymphocytic leukemia of Galton is characterized by large cells which possess abundant cytoplasm (Figure 25.20(a)). The nuclear chromatin is considerably more dispersed than in the lymphocytes of the mature types of chronic lymphocytic leukemia; there is some clumping at the nuclear margin. Some of the nuclei may show indentations. Cells in midplane section may show extremely prominent nucleoli (Figure 25.20(b)).

Those cases of chronic lymphocytic leukemia which type as T cells constitute 1 percent or less of the cases of chronic lymphocytic leukemia. Ultrastructurally, the lymphocytes from some of these patients manifest an unusual finding which is not found in the lymphocytes from patients with typical B-cell chronic lymphocytic leukemia. On low power electron microscopy, the lymphocytes contain cytoplasmic inclusions (Figure 25.21(a)) which show varying degrees of density. These inclusions may be located primarily in the pericentriolar area or scattered widely throughout the cytoplasm. On high power electron microscopy, these structures consist of bundles of parallel tubular arrays (Figure 25.21(b)).[21,66] These inclusions of parallel tubular arrays exist as membrane-bound and nonmembrane-bound forms. The inclusions have been identified in 70–90 percent of lymphocytes from cases of a T-cell chronic lymphoproliferative disorder which closely resembles T-cell chronic lymphocytic leukemia.[95]

Various types of inclusions have been observed by light microscopy in the lymphocytes of patients with chronic lymphocytic leukemia. One of the most noteworthy is a clear, rod-like structure which occurs in the cytoplasm and overlying the nucleus in varying numbers of lymphocytes from a small percentage of patients with chronic lymphocytic leukemia.[30] These structures (Figure 25.22) have been shown to consist of immunoglobulin by immunofluorescent techniques. Ultrastructurally, the rods are

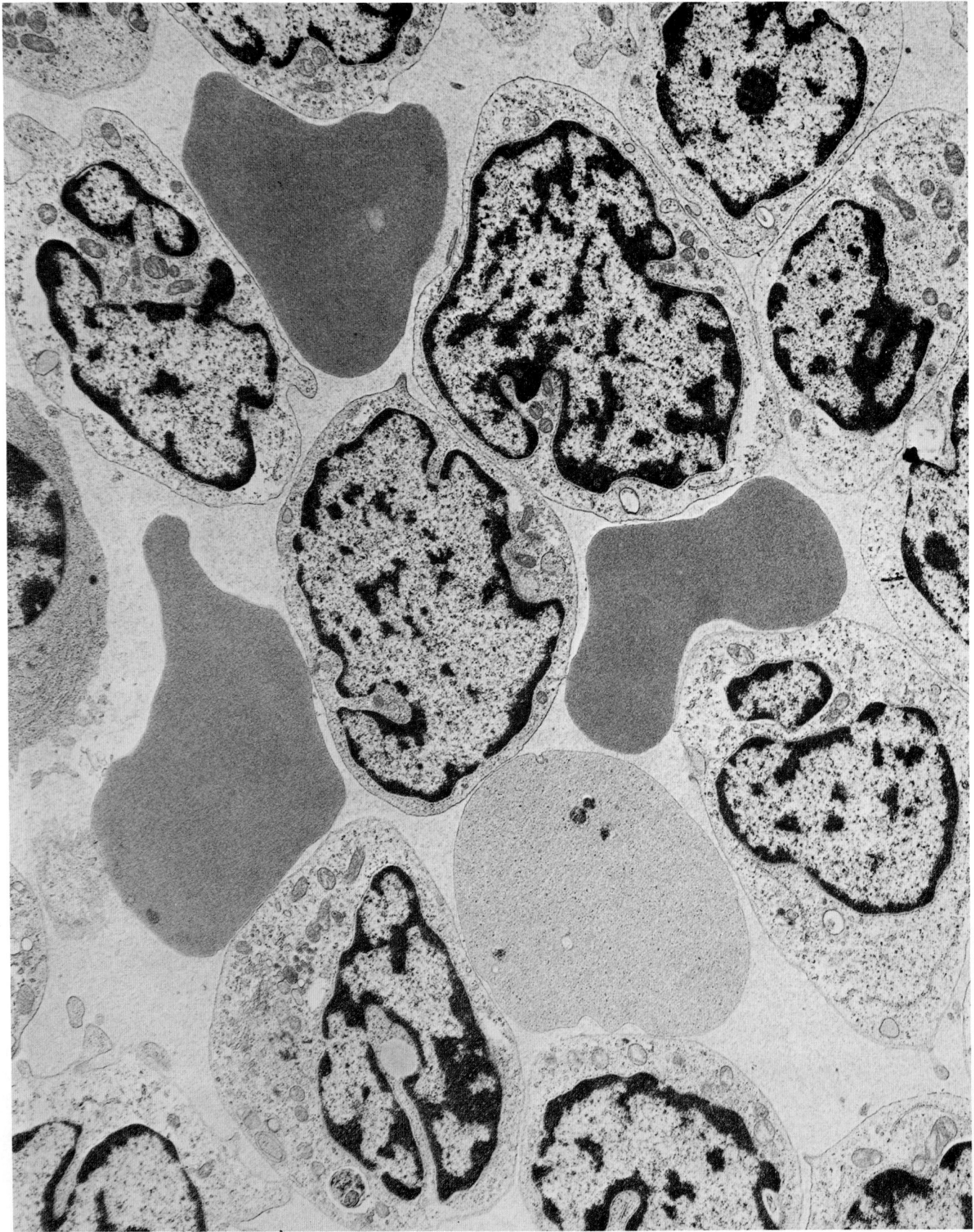

Figure 25.16. Acute lymphocytic leukemia: T-cell type.

(a) Low power view of bone marrow specimen from a patient with acute lymphocytic leukemia, T-cell type, without a mediastinal mass. Several cells have an irregular nuclear outline
with apparent lobulation. The chromatin is finely dispersed with some condensation at the
nuclear margin; a few scattered chromatin clumps are present. (× 10,000)

327

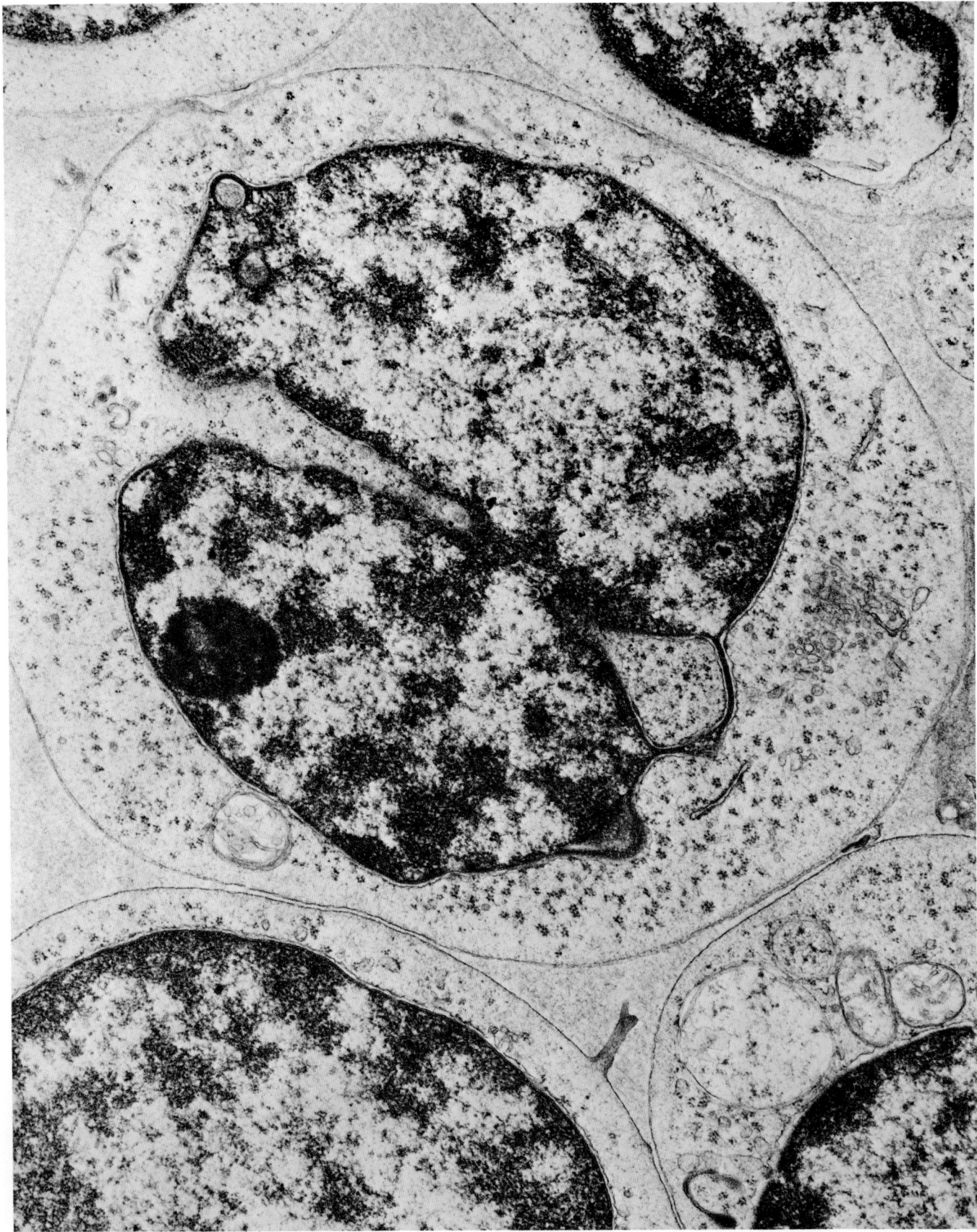

Figure 25.16. Acute lymphocytic leukemia: T-cell type.

(b) High magnification of a lymphoblast from the specimen illustrated in Figure 25.16(a). The nucleus consists of two lobes connected by a thin strand of chromatin. A compact nucleolus is present in one of the lobes. (× 24,000)

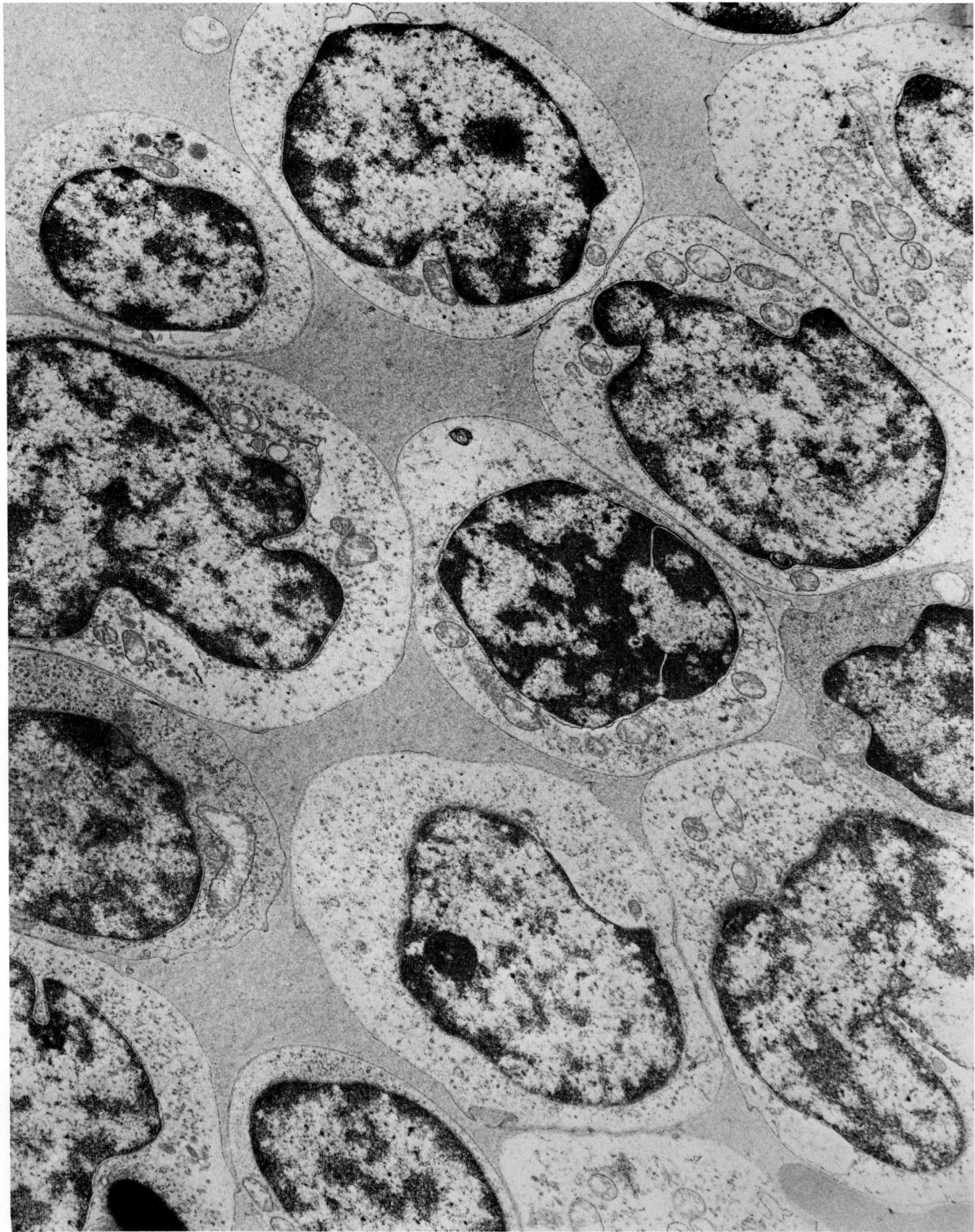

Figure 25.16. Acute lymphocytic leukemia: T-cell type.

(c) Lymphoblasts in the bone marrow specimen from a patient with acute lymphocytic leukemia, T-cell type, associated with a mediastinal mass. (× 11,000)

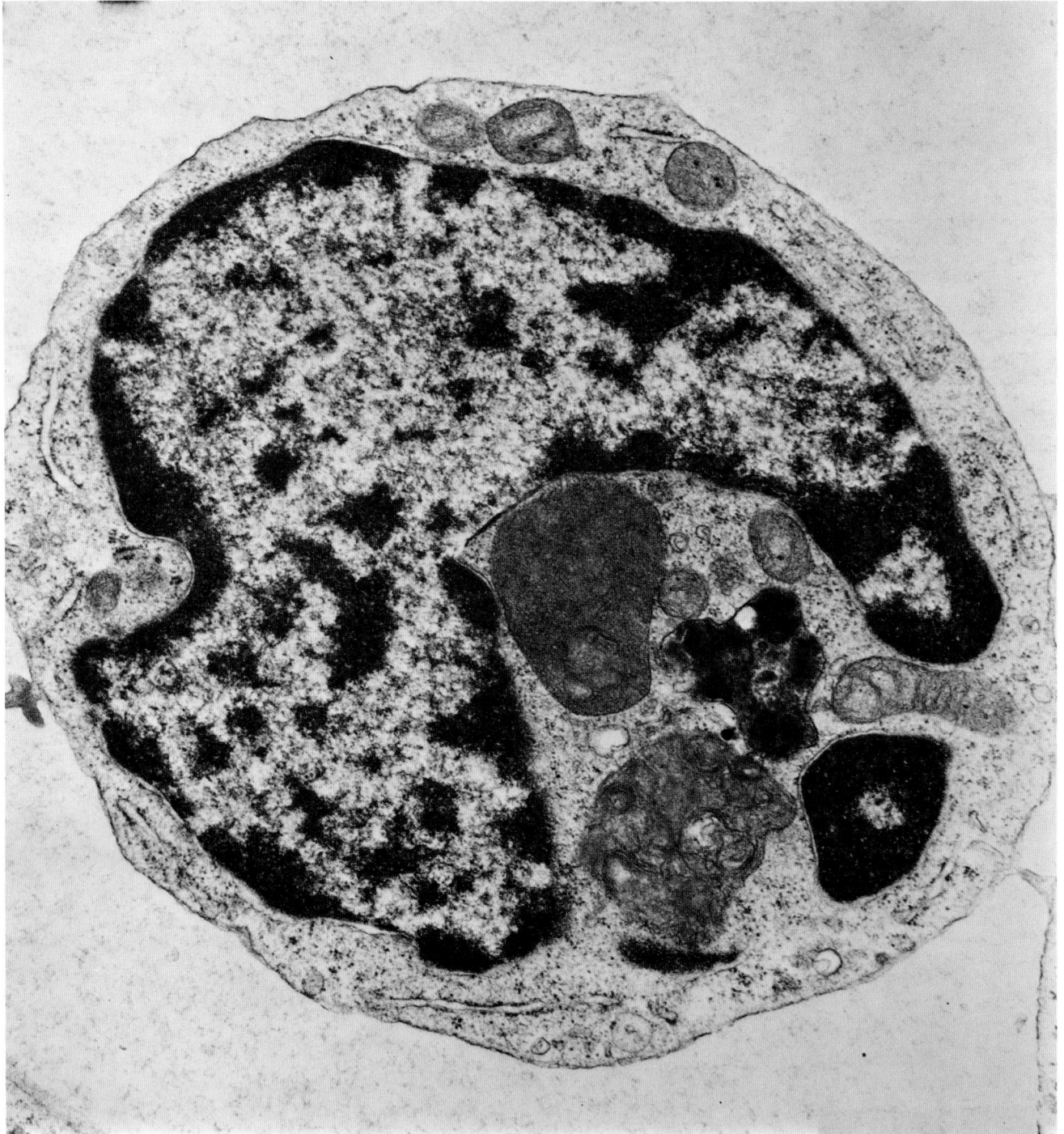

Figure 25.17. Down's syndrome and acute lymphocytic leukemia.
Lymphoblast from the blood of a child. The cytoplasm contains membrane-bound inclusions consisting of whorled membranous material and amorphous substance. (× 25,000)

bound by a membrane and consist of parallel fibers which have a periodicity of 80 Å. Depending on the plane of section, these structures may run the length of the cell. If multiple and cut in cross section, several may be identified. They appear to be crystallized immunoglobulin and serve as unique morphologic markers for B cells.

25.3. Malignant lymphomas (lymphosarcoma cell leukemia)

A relatively high percentage of the non-Hodgkin's malignant lymphomas will manifest some degree of marrow and blood involvement as part of their biologic course.[38] The term lymphosarcoma cell leukemia, at times qualified as acute or chronic, has been used as a designation for lymphoma cells in the blood.[135,172]

The appearance of lymphoma cells in the blood and marrow may be quite variable. In many cases the lymphoma cells resemble the blasts found in the lymphocytic leukemias. In other instances, such as some cases of nodular, poorly differentiated lymphocytic lymphoma, the cells appear to possess quite noteworthy characteristics, e.g., prominent nuclear folding and clefting.

Ultrastructurally, the circulating lymphoma cells from cases of nodular, poorly differentiated lymphocytic lymphoma may show striking cleavage of the nuclei; at times the nucleus consists of two segments connected by a strand of chromatin (Figure 25.23(a)). Nuclear appendages resulting in sequestered areas of cytoplasm may be present (Figure 25.23(b)). The nuclear chromatin may show peripheral condensation similar to mature lymphocytes; nucleoli are generally not prominent.[92]

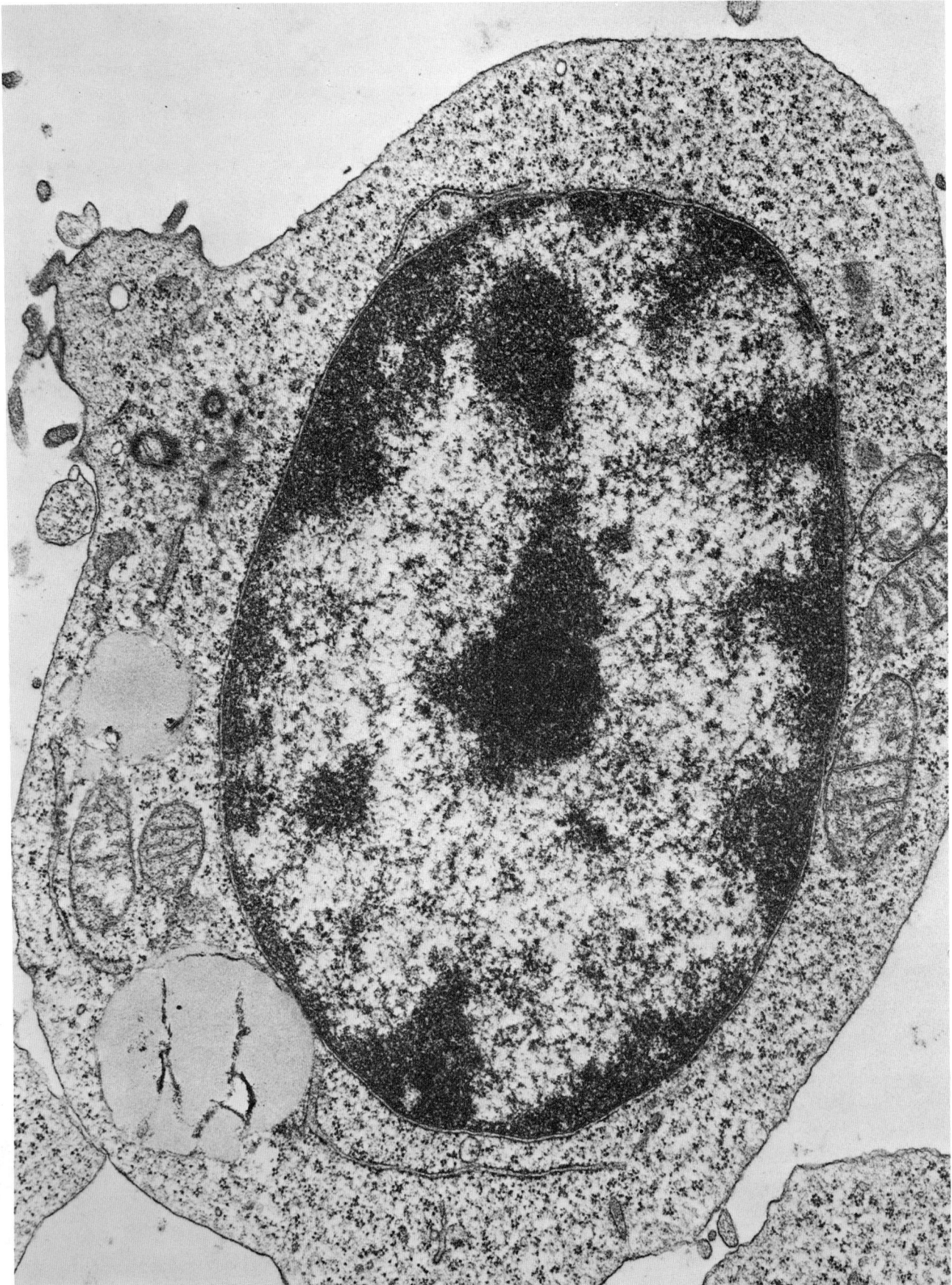

Figure 25.18. Burkitt's cell leukemia.
Blast cell showing numerous scattered ribosomes and slightly osmiophilic filled vacuoles present in the cytoplasm. A few strands of rough endoplasmic reticulum are noted. (× 28,000)

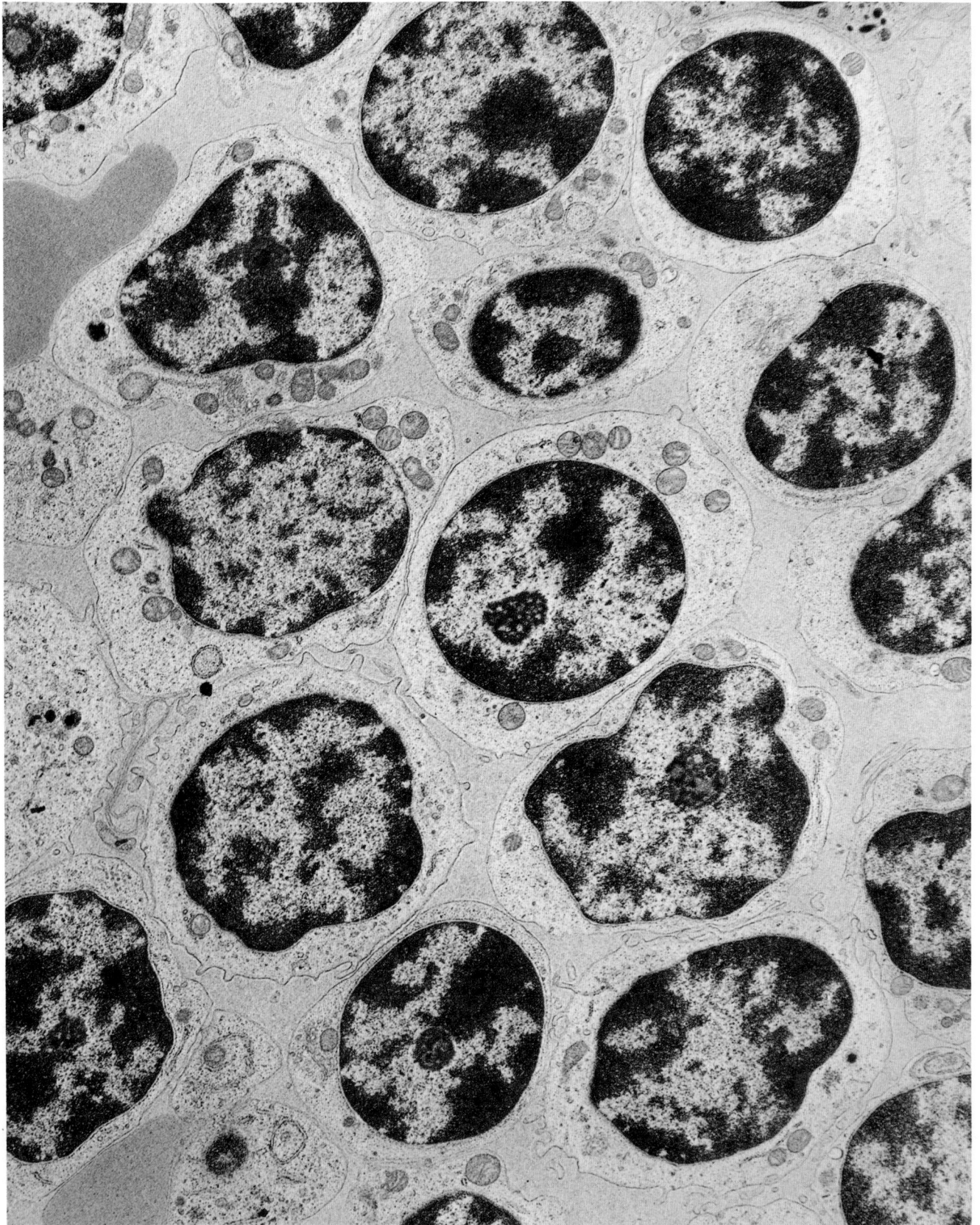

Figure 25.19. Chronic lymphocytic leukemia (L. C. Peterson *et al*.).

(a) Lymphocytes from the peripheral blood of a patient with small cell chronic lymphocytic
leukemia. The nuclear chromatin shows considerable clumping; nucleoli are identified in
several cells. (× 10,000)

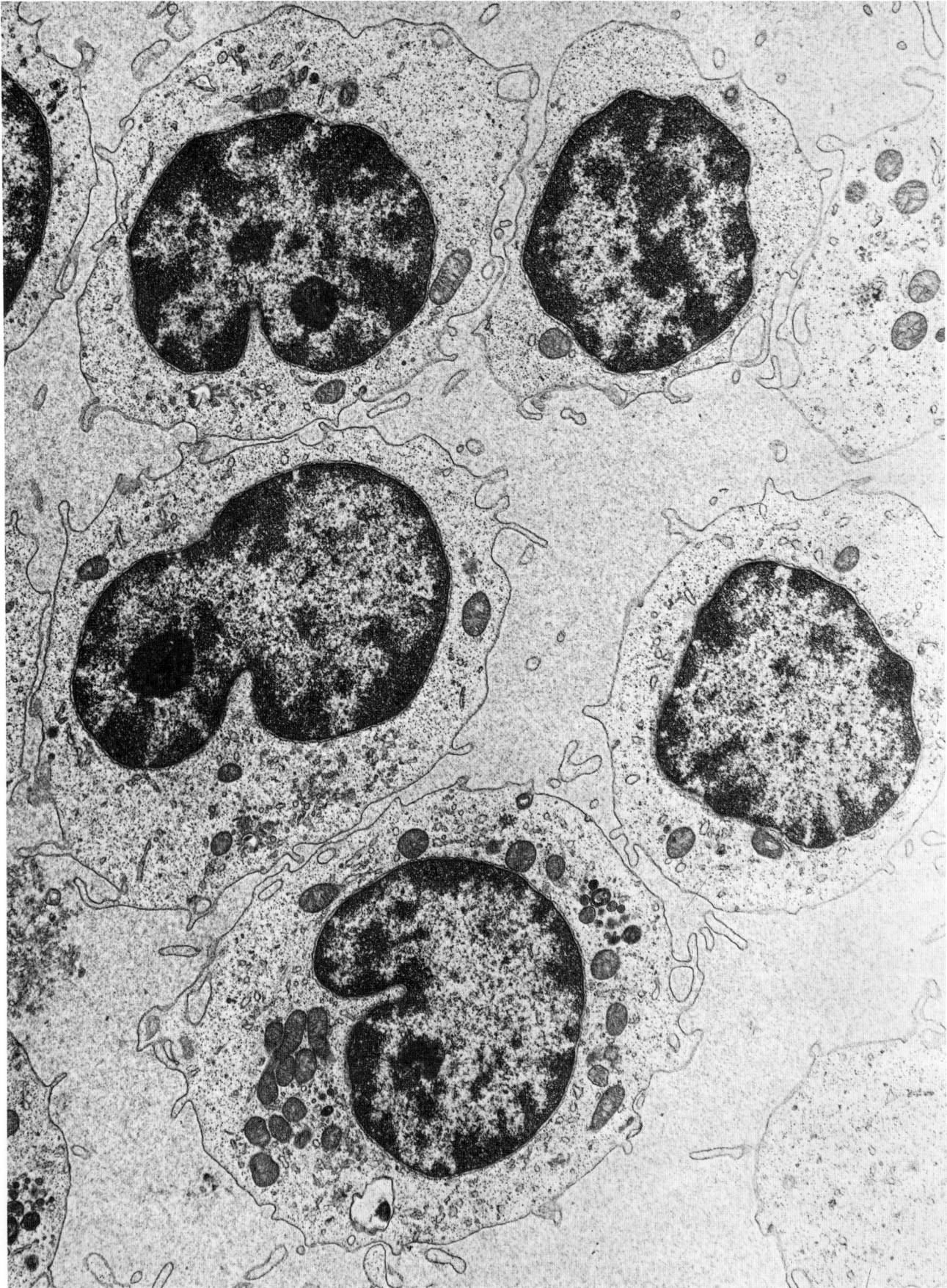

Figure 25.19. Chronic lymphocytic leukemia (L. C. Peterson *et al.*).

(b) Peripheral blood lymphocytes from a patient with a large cell variant of chronic lymphocytic leukemia. Many of the lymphocytes have an irregular nuclear outline. The nuclear chromatin is heterochromatic; nucleoli are identified in several cells. (× 11,000)

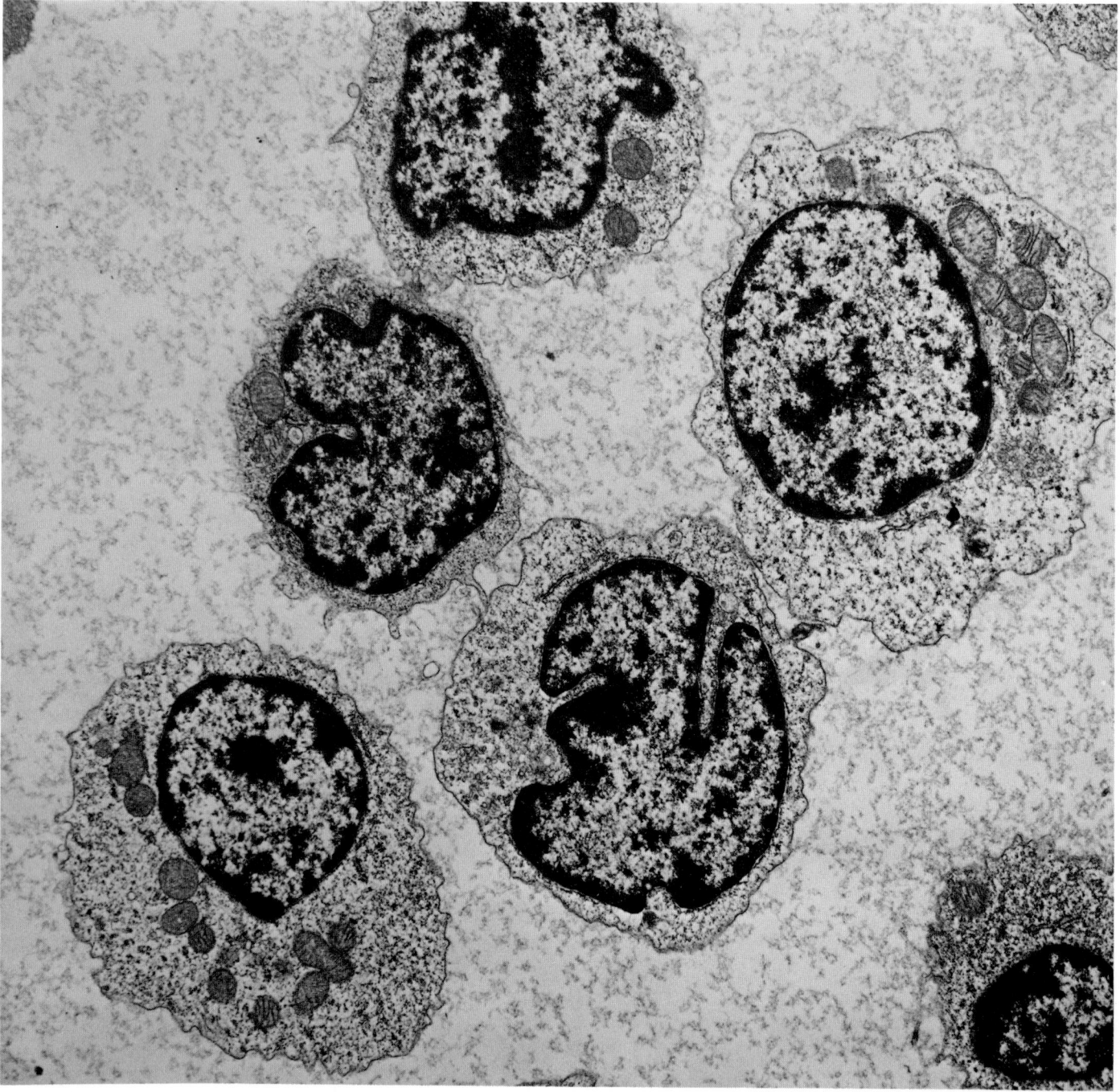

Figure 25.20. Prolymphocytic leukemia.

(a) Peripheral blood lymphocytes from an elderly male with the prolymphocytic variant of chronic lymphocytic leukemia. The nuclear chromatin is relatively finely dispersed. The abundant cytoplasm contains scattered ribosomes, several mitochondria, and a few strands of rough endoplasmic reticulum. (× 14,000)

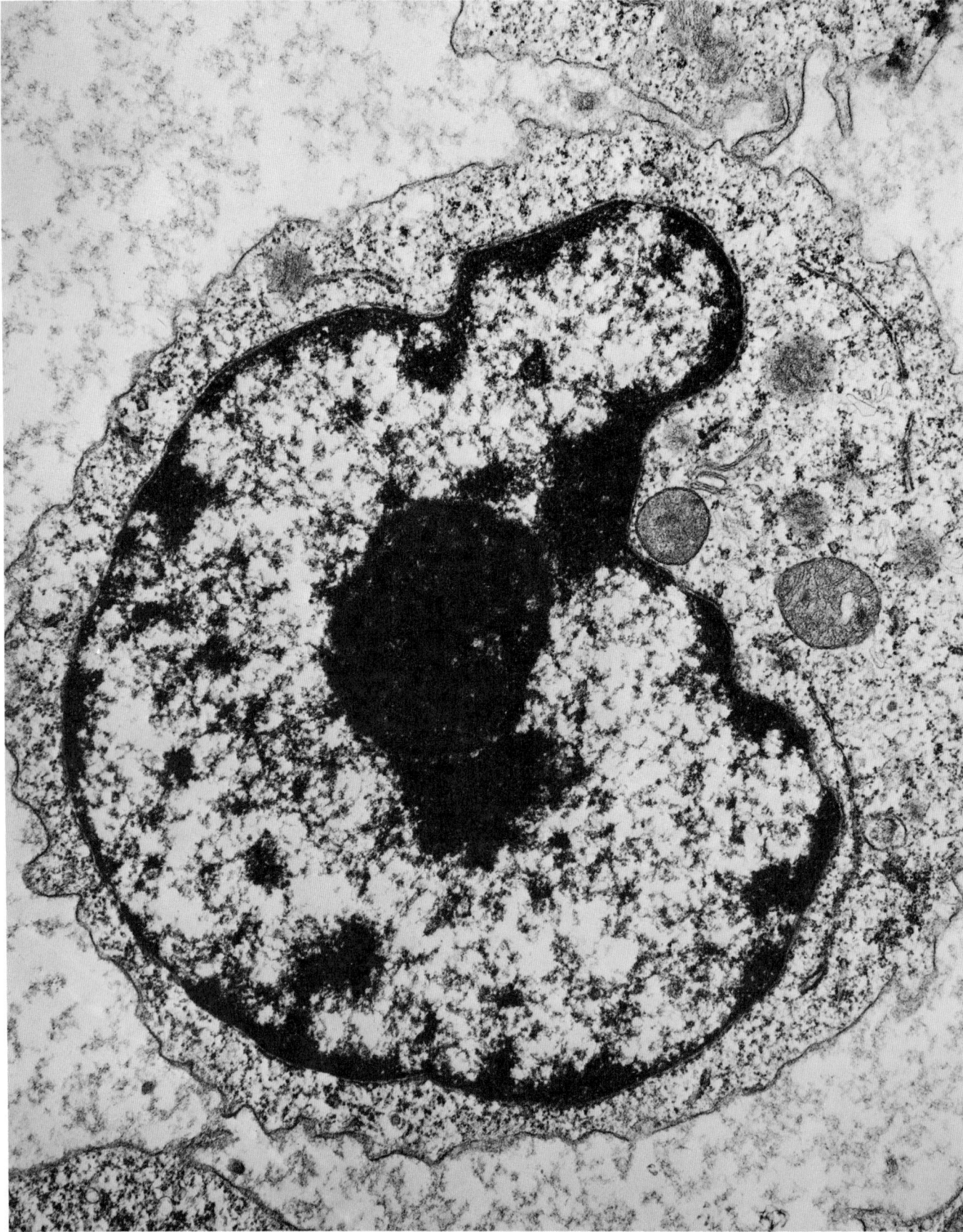

Figure 25.20. Prolymphocytic leukemia.

(b) High magnification of a prolymphocyte from a case of the prolymphocytic variant of chronic lymphocytic leukemia. The plane of section is through a prominent compact nucleolus. Some clumping of the chromatin is visible at the nuclear margin. (× 26,000)

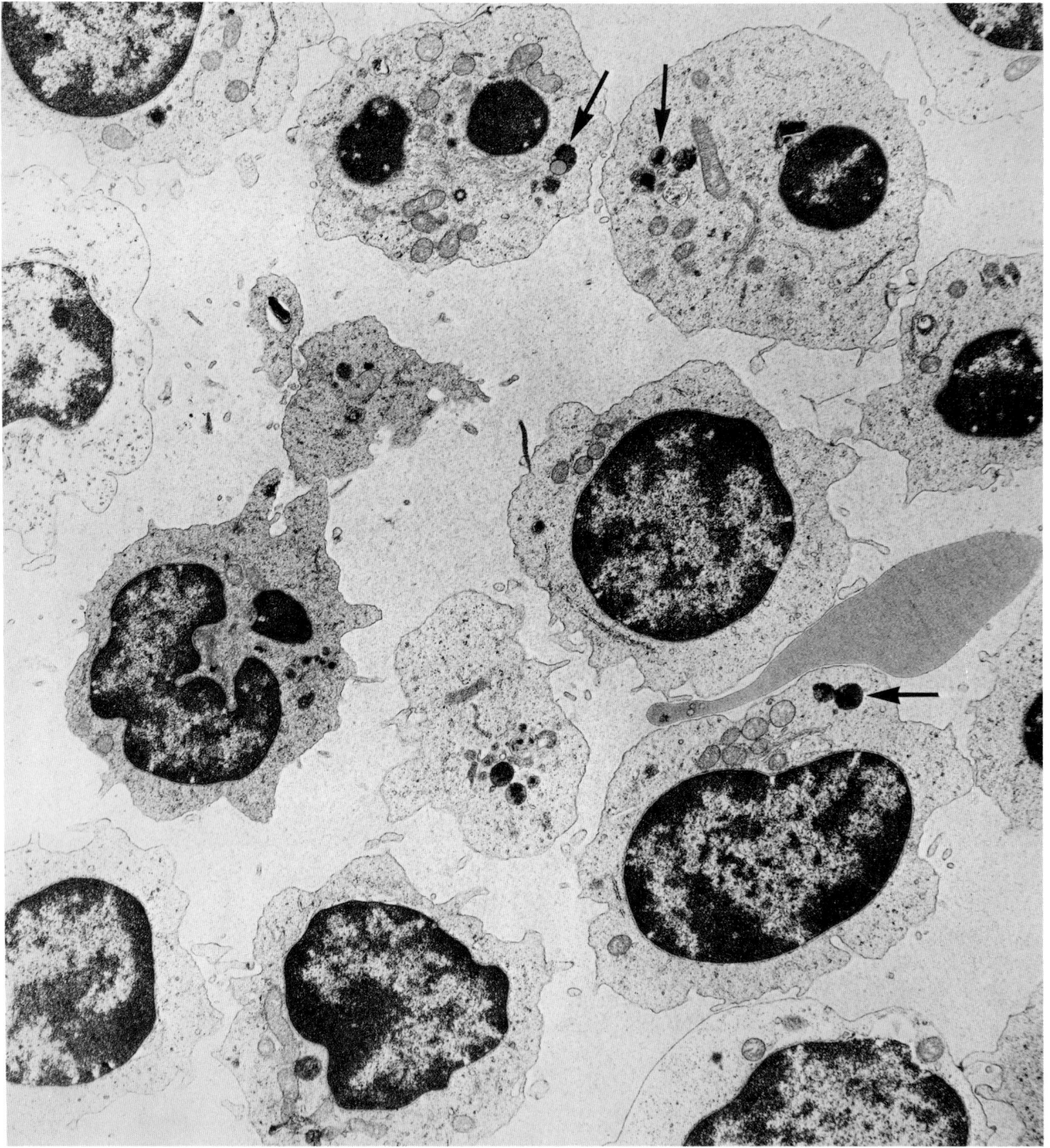

Figure 25.21. T-cell chronic lymphocytic leukemia.

(a) Peripheral blood lymphocytes from a patient with a proliferation of mature lymphocytes
    which typed as T-cells. Several of the cells contain cytoplasmic granules (↑). (× 7,000)

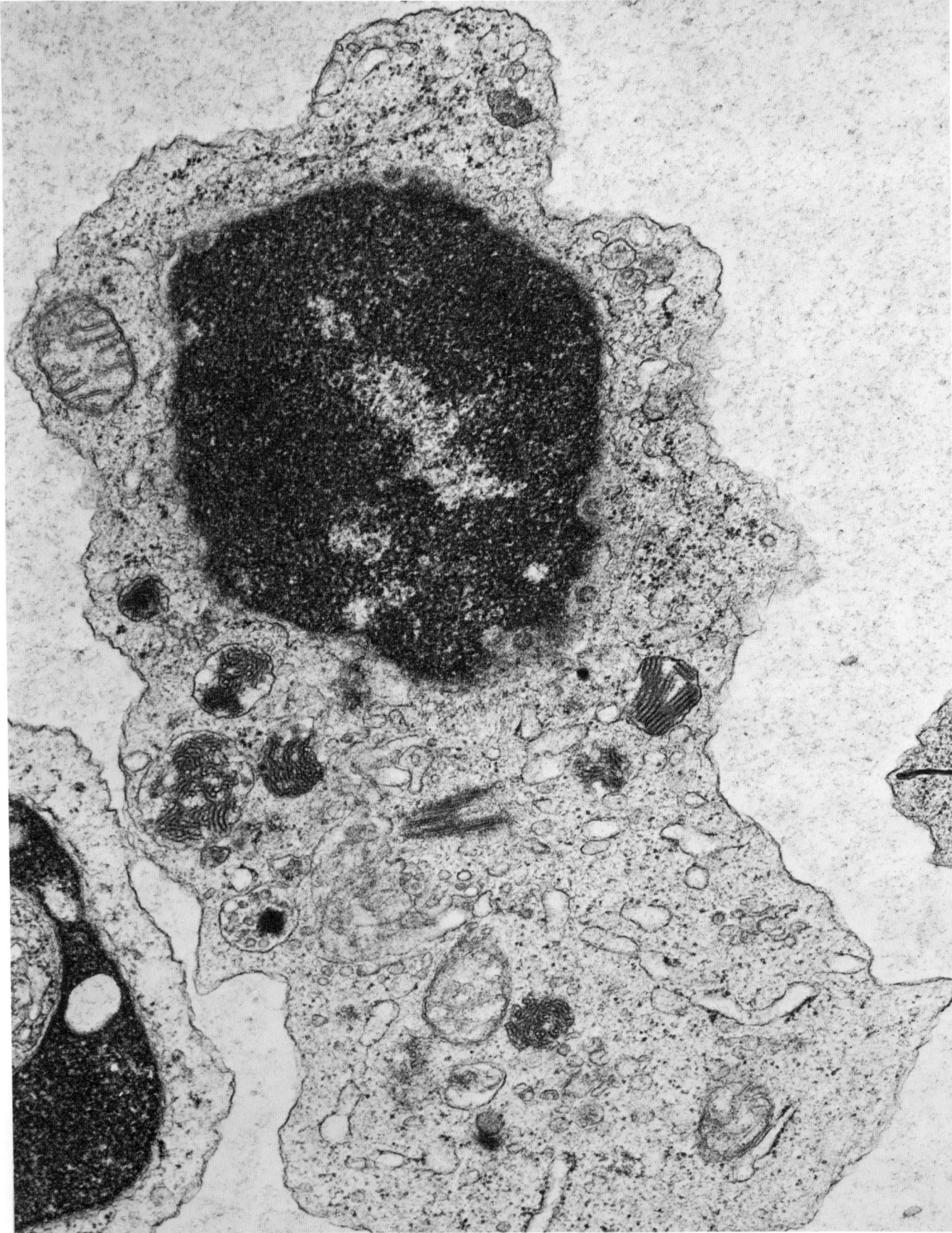

Figure 25.21. T-cell chronic lymphocytic leukemia.

(b) High magnification of a cell from the case illustrated in Figure 25.21(a). The cytoplasm contains several inclusions of undulating arrays of closely packed tubular structures, parallel tubular arrays, both membrane bound and nonmembrane bound. ($\times$36,000)

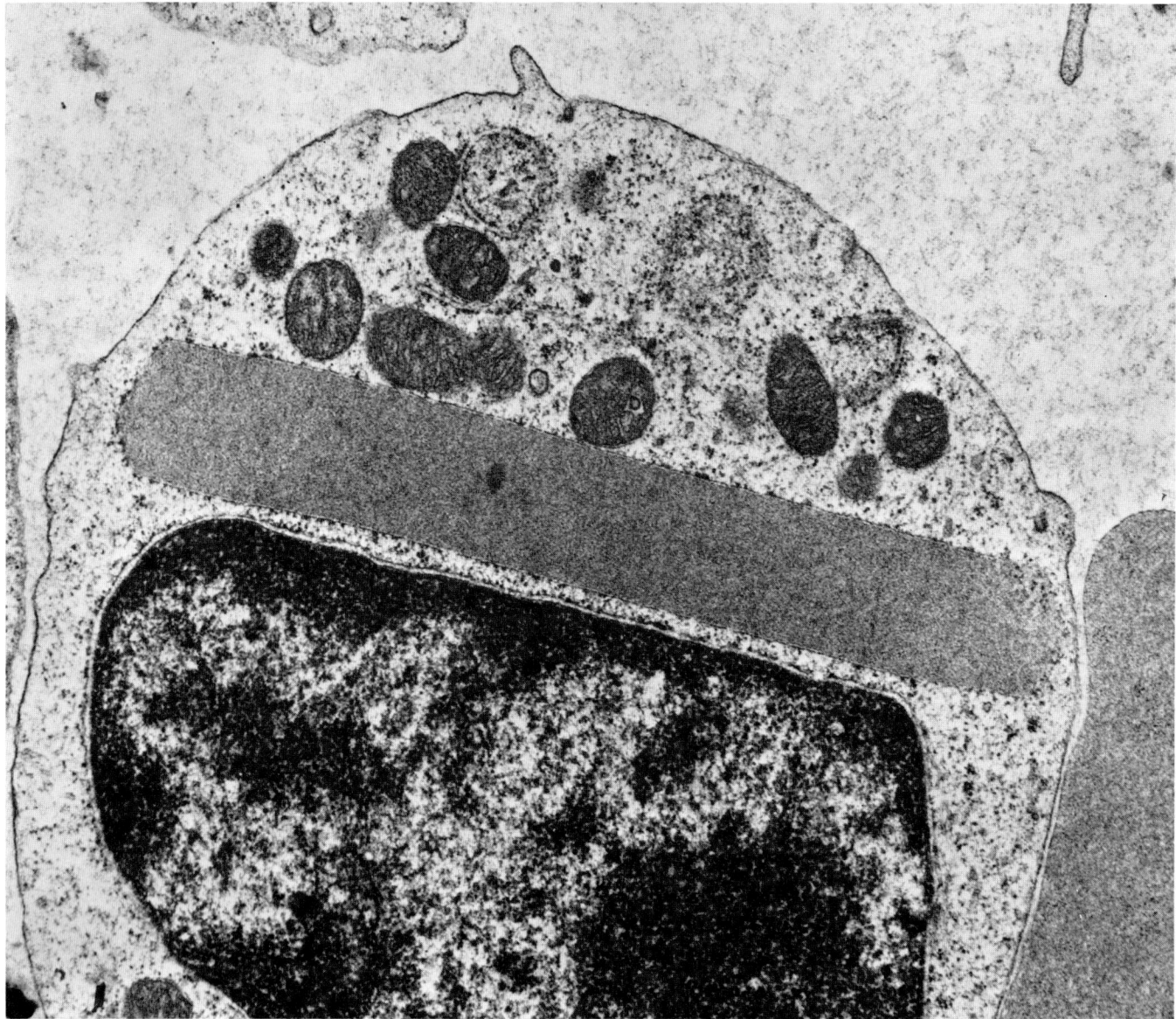

Figure 25.22. Chronic lymphocytic leukemia: cytoplasmic crystalline inclusion.
Lymphocyte with a cytoplasmic crystalline structure. These structures reacted with anti IgA
kappa antibody on immunofluorescent study. (× 28,000)

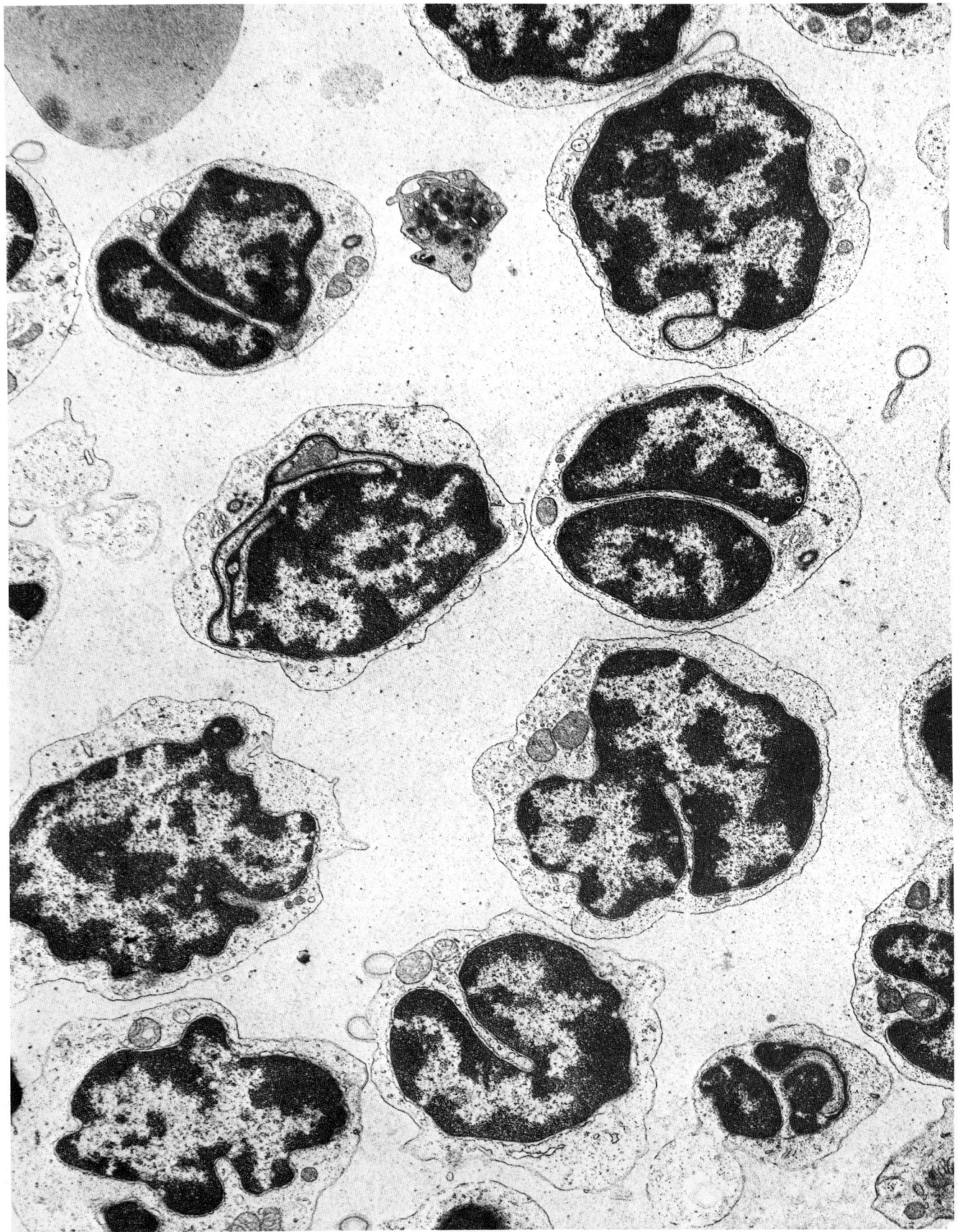

Figure 25.23. Lymphocytic lymphoma, nodular poorly differentiated (R. W. McKenna, C. D. Bloomfield, and R. D. Brunning).

(a) Low power EM of a peripheral blood specimen from a patient with nodular, poorly differentiated lymphocytic lymphoma and a leukocyte count of 30,000 with 90 percent lymphoma cells. The degree of clumping of the nuclear chromatin is characteristic of mature lymphocytes. A considerable amount of nuclear contortion, clefting, and bleb formation is visible. The nuclei of some cells are completely bisected. ($\times$ 13,000)

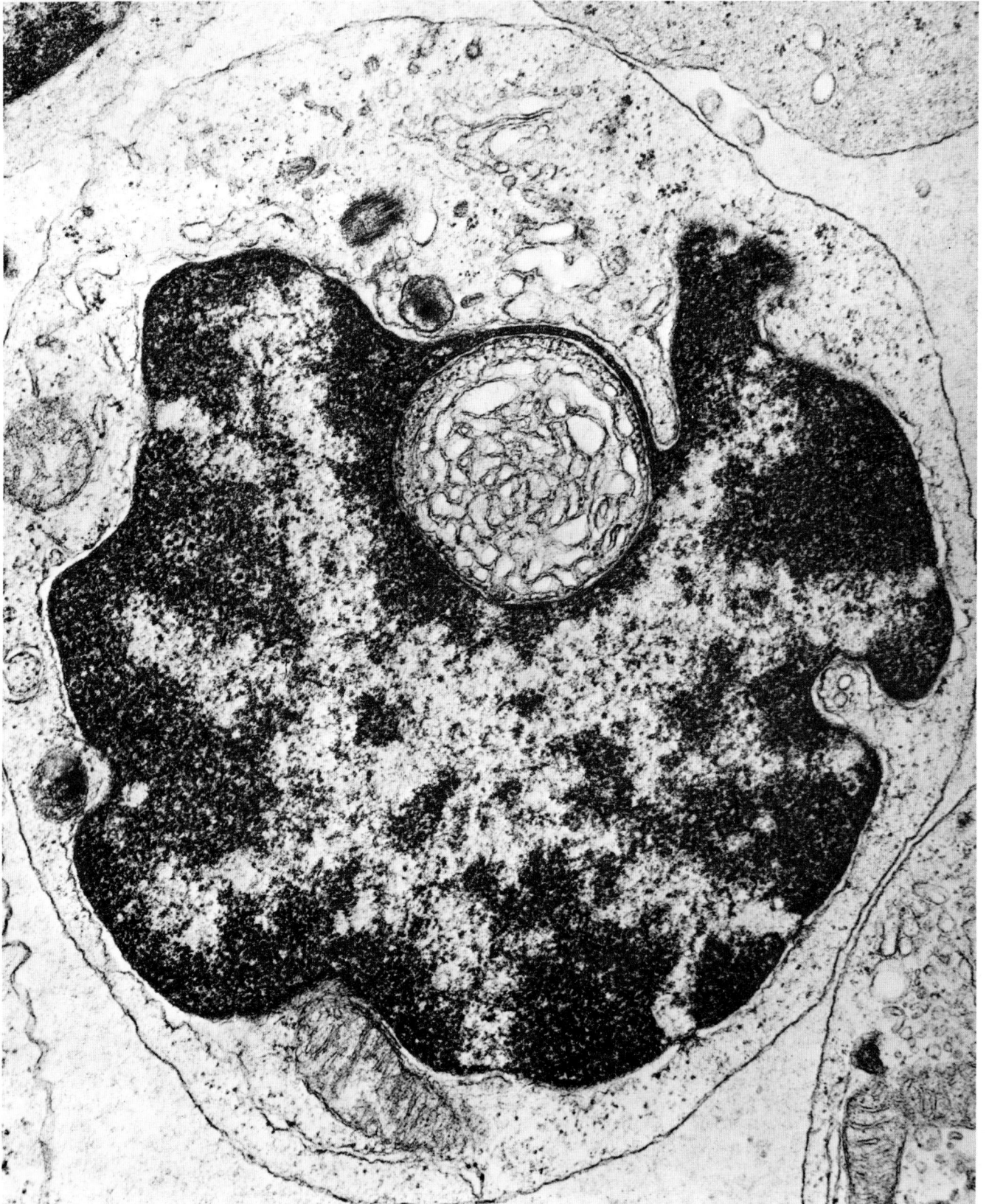

Figure 25.23. Lymphocytic lymphoma, nodular poorly differentiated (R. W. McKenna, C. D. Bloomfield, and R. D. Brunning).

(b) High power EM of nodular lymphoma cell from the blood specimen illustrated in Figure 25.23 (a) showing sequestered cytoplasm with fenestrated membranes. (× 37,000)

26. Plasma Cell Dyscrasias

The plasma cell dyscrasias are disorders of the B-cell component of the immune system which are characterized by a proliferation of immunocytes in the absence of known antigen stimulus, elaboration of a monoclonal immunoglobulin, and generally a decrease in the levels of the normal immunoglobulins.[119] Multiple myeloma, Walderstrom's macroglobulinemia, and heavy chain disease are generally recognized types of plasma cell dyscrasias.

26.1. Multiple myeloma

Multiple myeloma was the first recognized and is the most frequently occurring of the plasma cell dyscrasias. The proliferating immunocytes in multiple myeloma are generally recognized as plasma cells or as morphologic variants of the plasma cell. The morphologic spectrum of the plasma cells ranges from those myelomas in which the predominant proliferating cell has many of the cytologic features of mature plasma cells to cases where many of the malignant cells show extreme pleomorphism and immaturity and bear little resemblance to plasma cells.[101] Numerous types of cytoplasmic inclusions, both globular and crystalline, have been reported in myeloma cells and these appear to be the result of disordered immunoglobulin synthesis.[98,99,100] Attempts to correlate the type of immunoglobulin being produced with specific morphologic characteristics have not been entirely successful although the presence of large numbers of thesaurocytes (flaming plasma cells) is probably suggestive of an IgA immunoglobulin pattern.[121]

The most commonly encountered nuclear abnormalities are inclusions of varying types. They are of two main types: relatively large, pale staining inclusions and sharply defined hyalin spherule-like structures.[16,23,32] The pale staining inclusions usually are much larger than the hyalin spherules and appear to overlie a large area of the nucleus; they stain variably positive with the PAS reaction. Both types of intranuclear inclusions appear to result from cytoplasmic invagination.[23]

Ultrastructurally, the myeloma cells manifest many of the features of normal plasma cells.[100,145] The cytoplasm includes abundant rough endoplasmic reticulum which contains an amorphous, lightly electron-dense material. There is considerable variation in the degree of dilatation of the rough endoplasmic reticulum (Figure 26.1(a)). In some instances it is relatively flat while in other cells there may be marked dilatation with the accumulation of extremely large amounts of amorphous material. The latter type of finding is considered to correspond to the saurocytes of light microscopy (Figure 26.1(b)). The rough endoplasmic reticulum may contain inclusions of varying types (Figure 26.2(a), (b)); these range from dense osmiophilic spherules to crystalline structures in which periodicity can be demonstrated.[23,67,99,107,146,150]

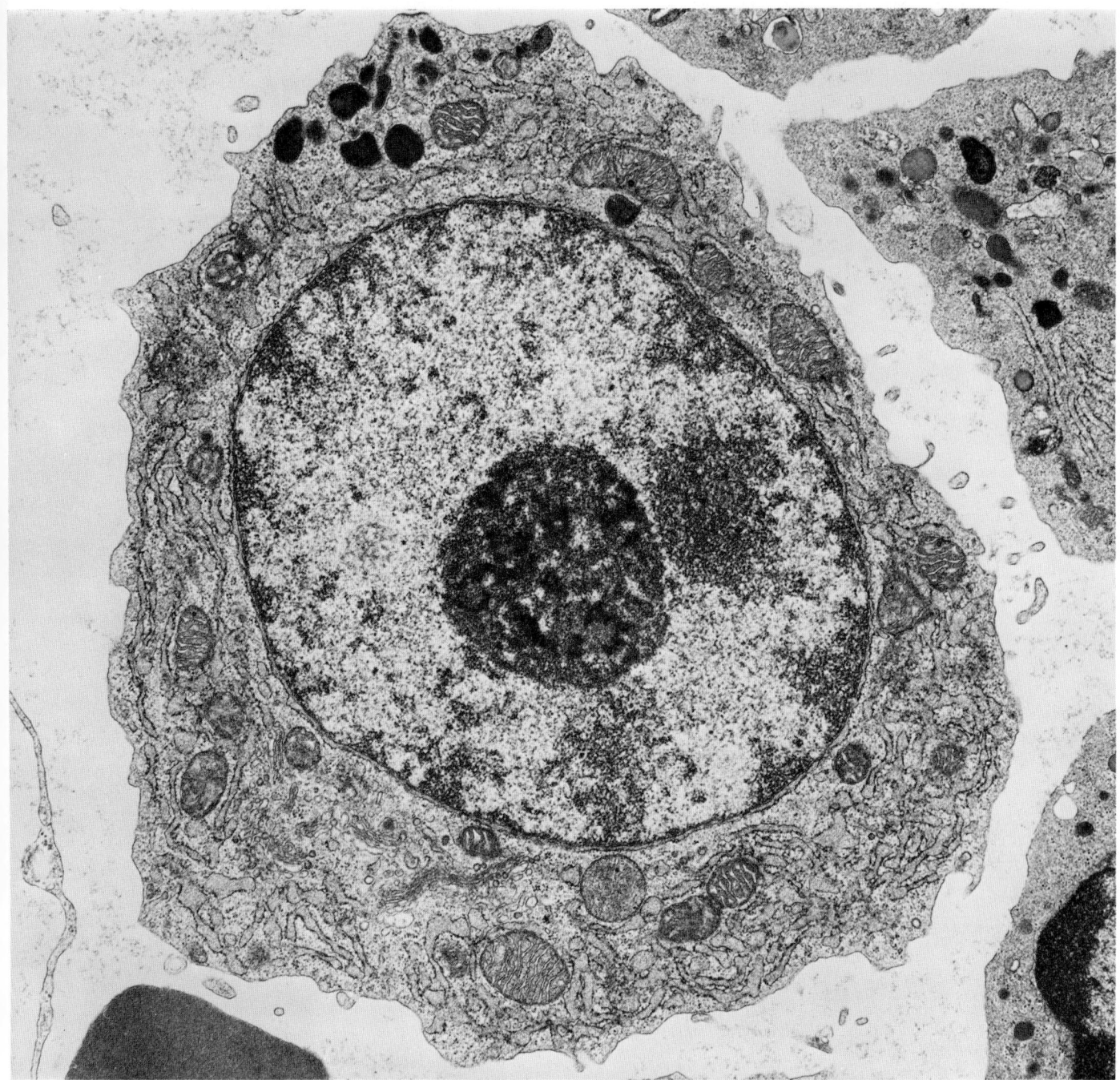

Figure 26.1. Multiple myeloma.

(a) Plasma cell with the plane of section through a prominent, compact nucleolus. The chromatin is dispersed with scattered clumping. The cytoplasm contains numerous dilated strands of rough endoplasmic reticulum, several mitochondria, and a prominent Golgi. Several dense inclusions are present in the cytoplasm. ($\times$ 18,200)

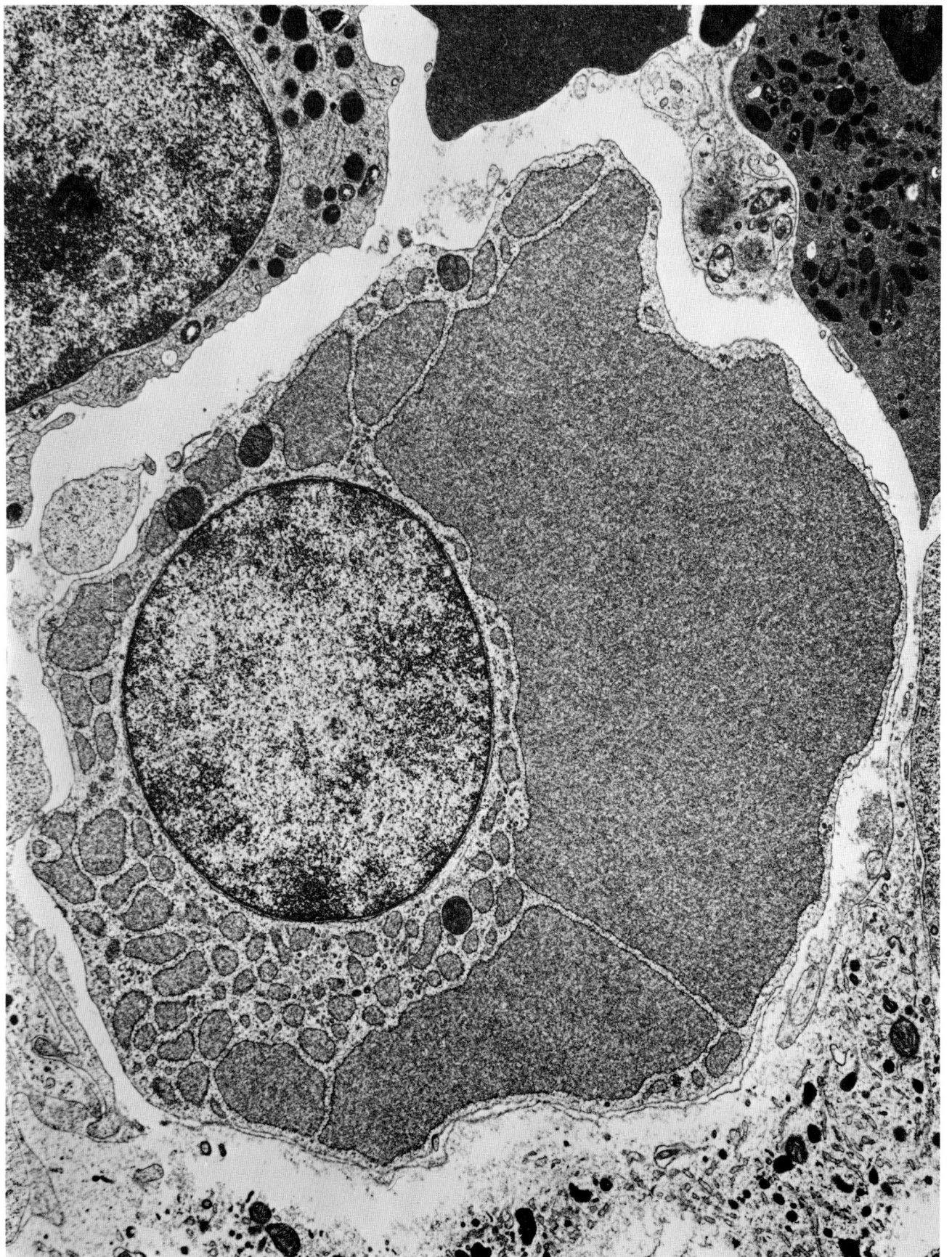

Figure 26.1. Multiple myeloma.

(b) Plasma cell with greatly dilated endoplasmic reticulum which is filled with a moderately electron-dense amorphous material. This cell corresponds to the flaming plasma cell or saurocyte seen in light microscopy. ($\times$ 12,150)

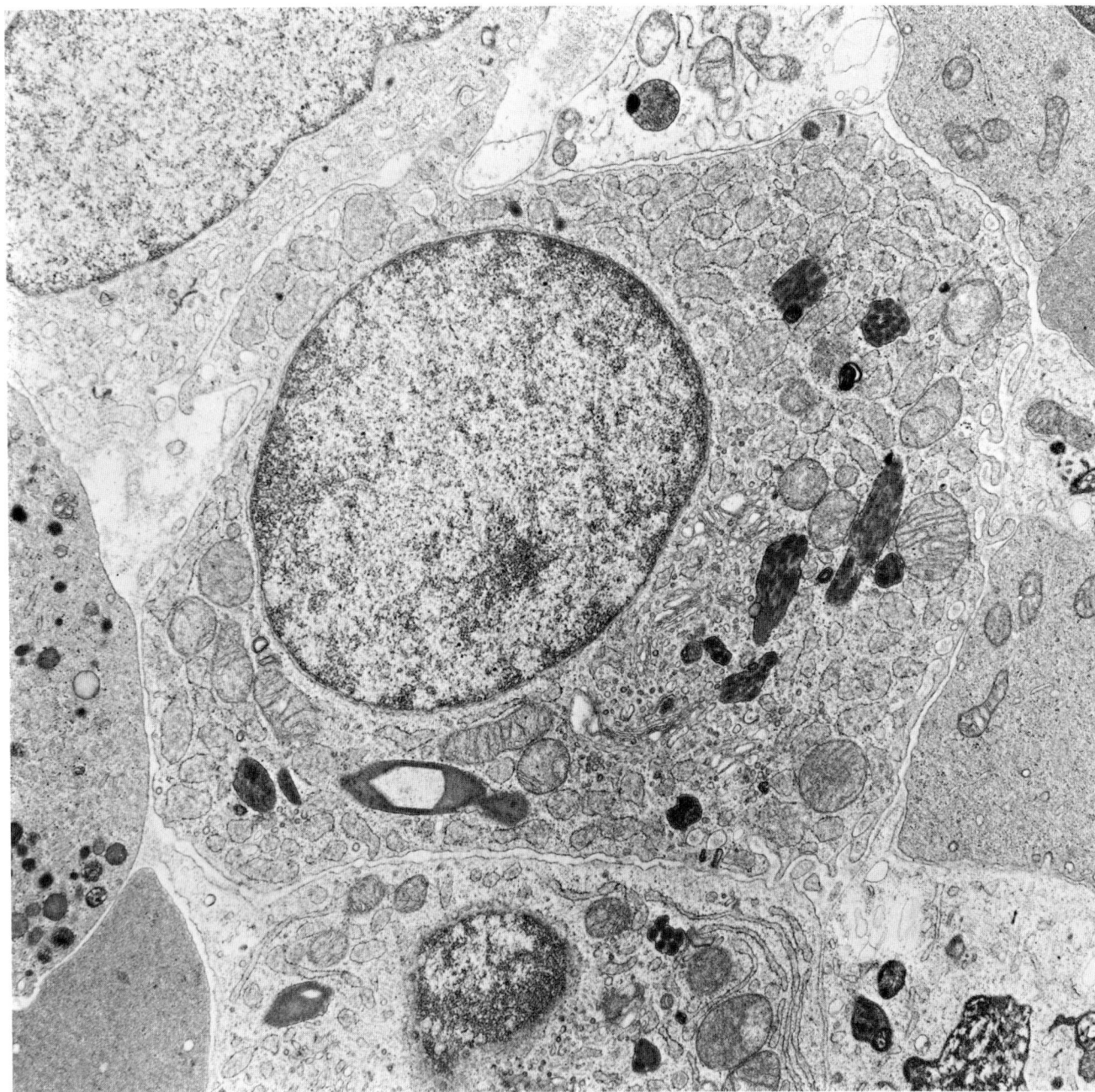

Figure 26.2. Cytoplasmic inclusions in plasma cell dyscrasia.

(a) Plasma cell showing several electron-dense inclusions in the cytoplasm. The inclusions are of variable shape and density and have a hollow central core. Numerous mitochondria and dilated sacs of endoplasmic reticulum are present. (× 14,000)

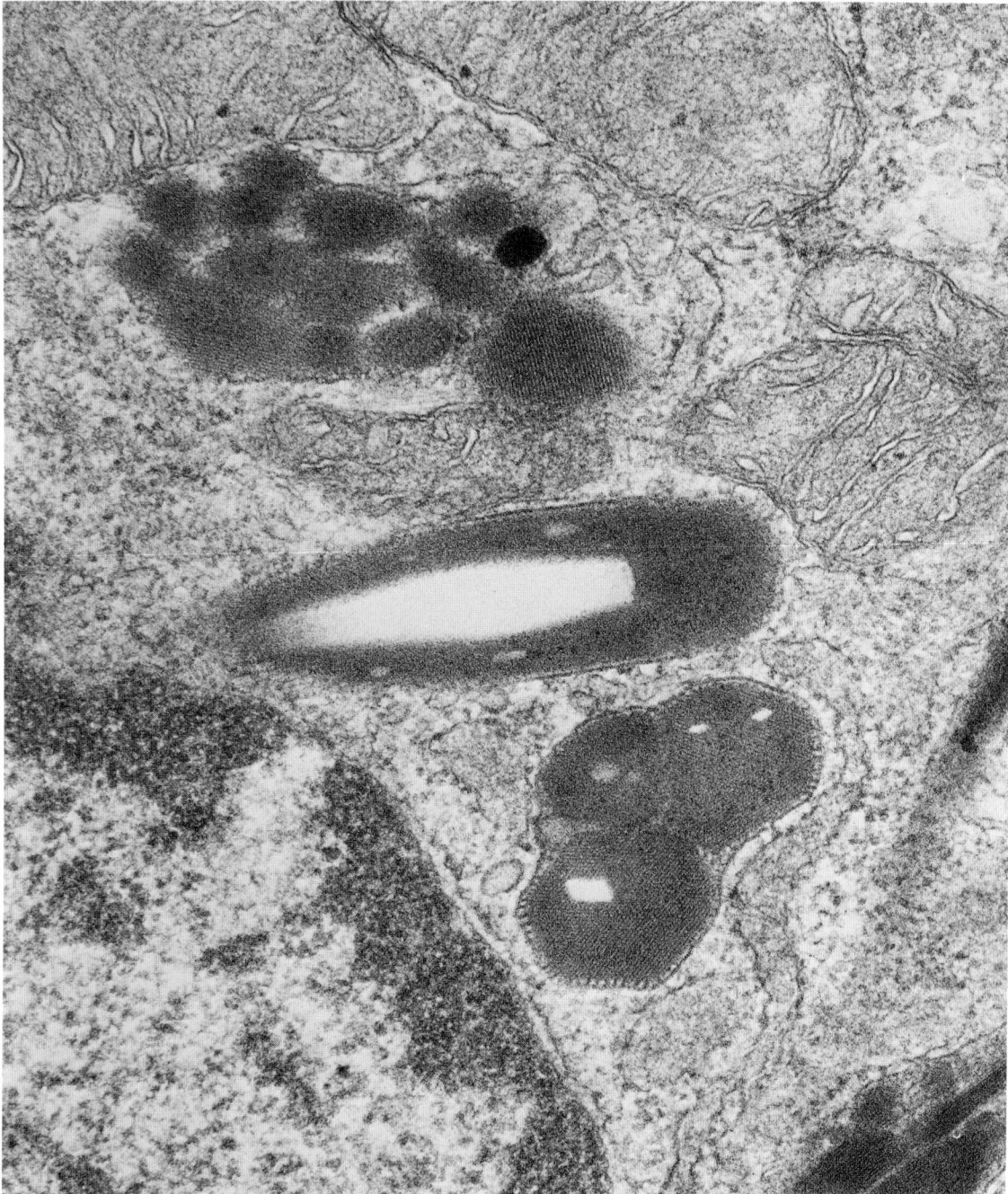

Figure 26.2. Cytoplasmic inclusions in plasma cell dyscrasia.

(b) High magnification of a portion of the plasma cell illustrated in Figure 26.2(a). The inclusion bodies are completely or partially encircled by a smooth membrane. A linear periodicity can be seen in some of the inclusions. (×67,200)

The dense osmiophilic inclusions are thought to correspond to the Russell bodies described in light microscopy.[99] These inclusions are probably the result of normal or disordered immunoglobulin synthesis. The Golgi may be very prominent (Figure 26.1(a)) with numerous vesicular structures. Mitochondria may be numerous and unusually large. Some variation in shape is frequent.

The nuclear outline is usually round or oval; in some instances there may be marked indentation and folding of the nucleus. Considerable variation in the degree of chromatin condensation occurs in different cases and to some extent in the same case. This variation corresponds to the variation found in the degree of nuclear maturity in light microscopy. In the most immature nuclei there is minimal chromatin clumping at the nuclear margin. In the more differentiated myelomas the nuclear chromatin exhibits more clumping and may resemble normal plasma cells. Despite the more mature chromatin pattern, nucleoli, usually single, may be quite prominent. Nuclear cytoplasm asynchrony, as defined by ultrastructural studies of myeloma cells and manifested by disparity between nuclear maturity and cytoplasmic development, has been proposed as an index of the clinical extent of multiple myeloma.[58]

Ultrastructurally, the pale staining, large, intranuclear inclusions of light microscopy are membrane-bound structures filled with an amorphous, lightly electron-dense material (Figure 26.3(a)) similar, and probably identical, to the amorphous substance in the dilated endoplasmic reticulum. Small, dense, osmiophilic bodies may be found scattered throughout the amorphous material (Figure 26.3(b), (c)). The second type of intranuclear inclusion, the hyalin-like spherule, ultrastructurally appears as a densely osmiophilic structure (Figure 26.3(d)) similar to the dense osmiophilic structures found in the dilated endoplasmic reticulum. Like the dense bodies in the rough endoplasmic reticulum, the intranuclear dense bodies may be surrounded by a rim of pale amorphous substance similar to that found in the other type of intranuclear inclusion. The densely osmiophilic inclusions have been observed in plasma cells from patients with reactive plasmacytoses as well as malignant immunoproliferative disorders.[23,32]

In some cases of myeloma the proliferating cell type has more the appearance of a lymphoid cell than a plasma cell (Figure 26.4(a)). The number of these cases is very small in any series and these processes bear some morphologic similarity to Waldenstrom's macroglobulinemia. In two of nine such cases observed in this laboratory, the monoclonal immunoglobulin was of IgD lambda type (Figure 26.4(a), (b)).

26.2. Waldenstrom's macroglobulinemia

Waldenstrom's macroglobulinemia is a type of plasma cell dyscrasia accompanied by a hyper-viscosity syndrome and the production of a 19s immunoglobulin.[158] The morphologic characteristics of the proliferating cells in macroglobulinemia have been a focus of considerable discussion and have been characterized as plasma cells, lymphocytoid plasma cells, plasmacytoid lymphocytes, and lymphocytes. This variation in observed morphologic patterns is probably a reflection of the true variability which can occur in macroglobulinemia. In most instances, however, the proliferating cell appears to have more the characteristics of a lymphocyte than a plasma cell.

The bone marrow shows a moderate to marked increase in lymphocytes or plasmacytoid lymphocytes. The nuclei of these cells may contain pale staining

360

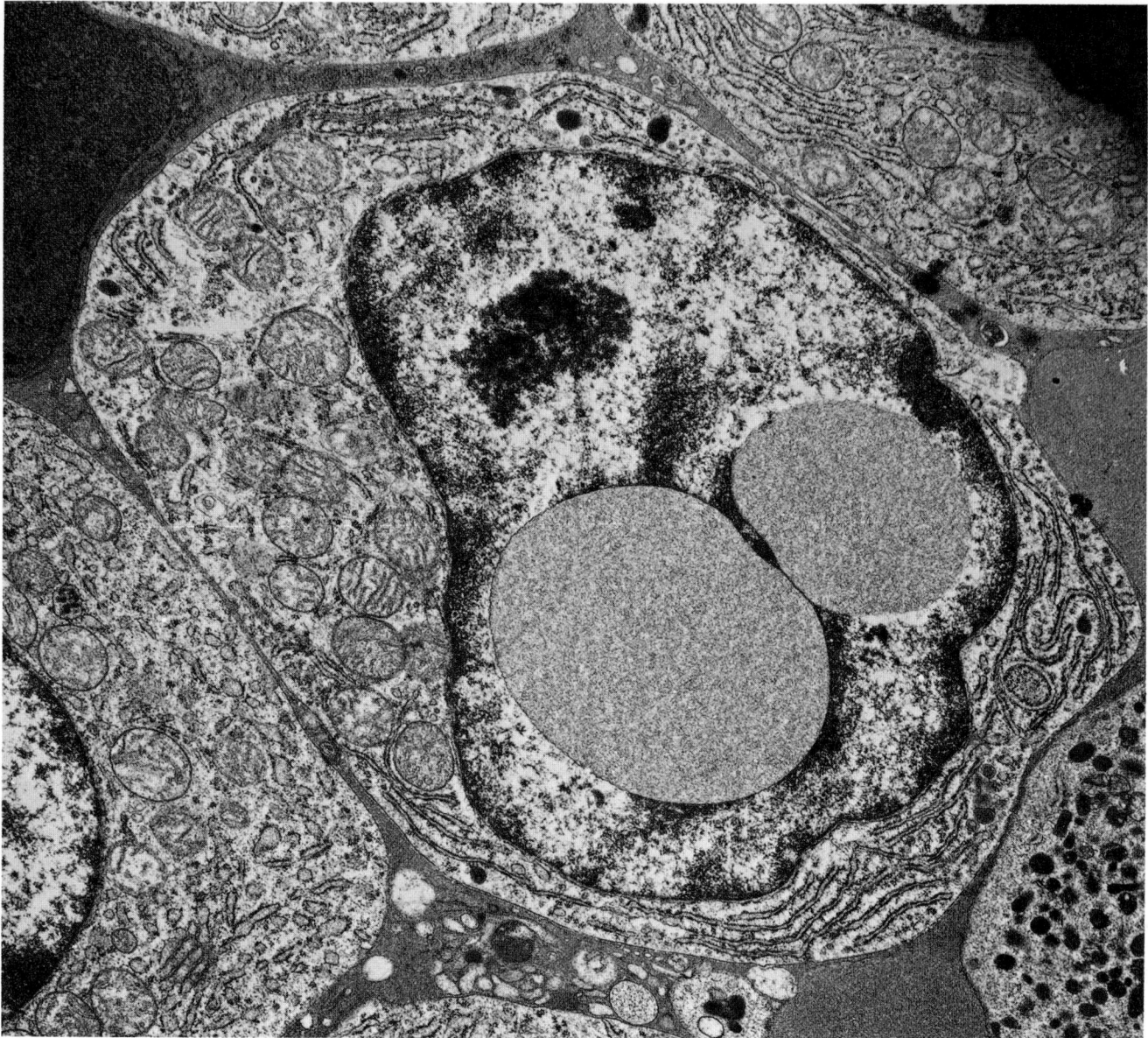

Figure 26.3. Intranuclear inclusions in plasma cell dyscrasia (R. D. Brunning and J. Parkin).

(a) Plasma cell from the marrow of a patient with multiple myeloma with an IgA lambda monoclonal protein. The nucleus exhibits two single membrane-bound inclusions which contain slightly electron-dense amorphous material. There is some condensation of chromatin at the margin of one of the inclusions. ($\times$ 14,000)

intranuclear inclusions similar to the pale staining intranuclear inclusions described in multiple myeloma. There may be an increase in plasma cells, many of which have a rather immature appearance. An increase in tissue mast cells and histiocytes may also be present.[46]

Ultrastructurally, the cells in this disorder resemble the lymphocytes of the small

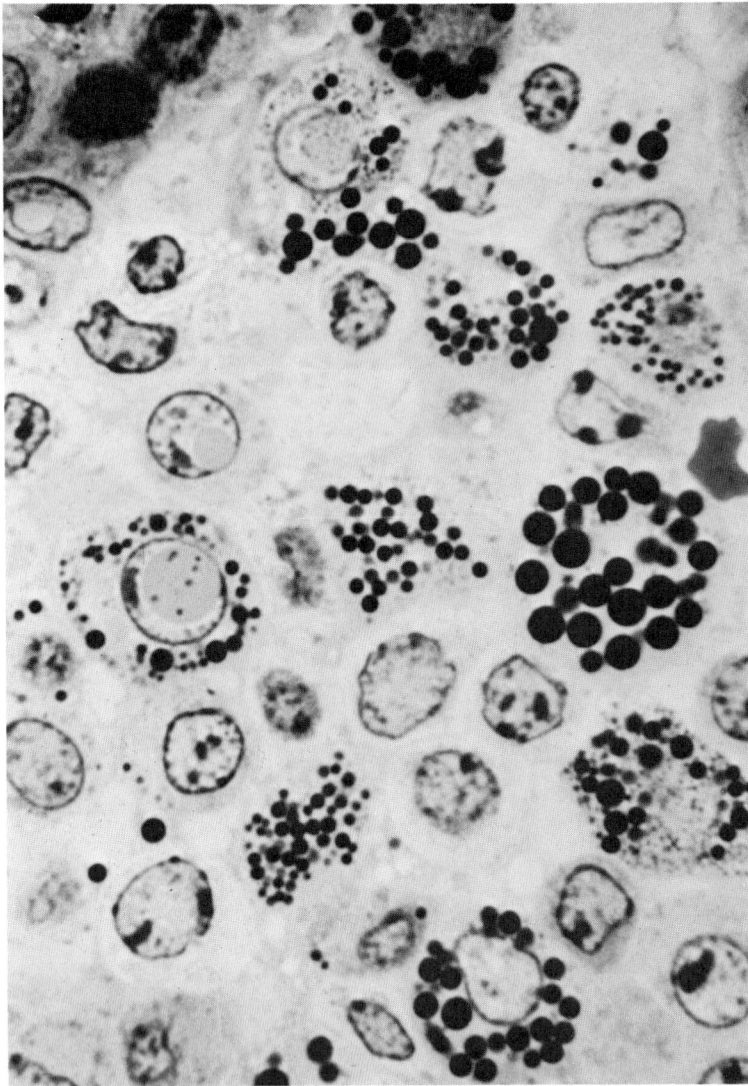

Figure 26.3. Intranuclear inclusions in plasma cell dyscrasia.

(b) Thick sections of a lymph node specimen from a case of immunoblastic
sarcoma associated with an IgM kappa monoclonal gammopathy. Several of the plasma cells contain osmiophilic inclusions in the cytoplasm.
Intranuclear inclusions of lightly osmiophilic substance are present.
Small, densely osmiophilic inclusions can be noted in the light amorphous material. (× 15,000)

Figure 26.3. Intranuclear inclusions in plasma cell dyscrasia.

(c) Plasma cell from the marrow of the case illustrated in Figure 26.3 (b). The single membrane-bound inclusion in the nucleus contains slightly electron-dense amorphous material
in which are scattered smaller densely osmiophilic deposits. The cytoplasm contains several densely osmiophilic deposits surrounded by single membranes. (× 5,000)

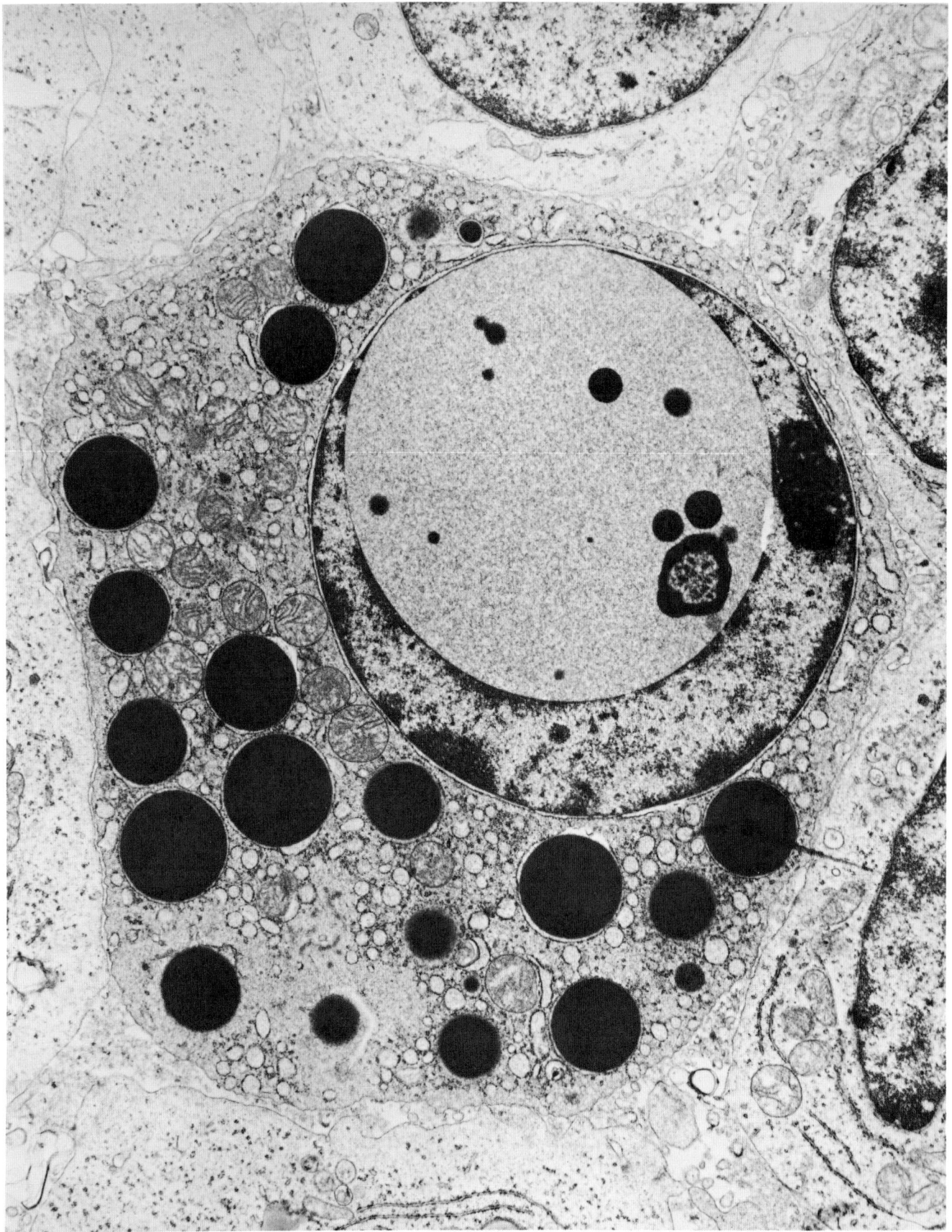

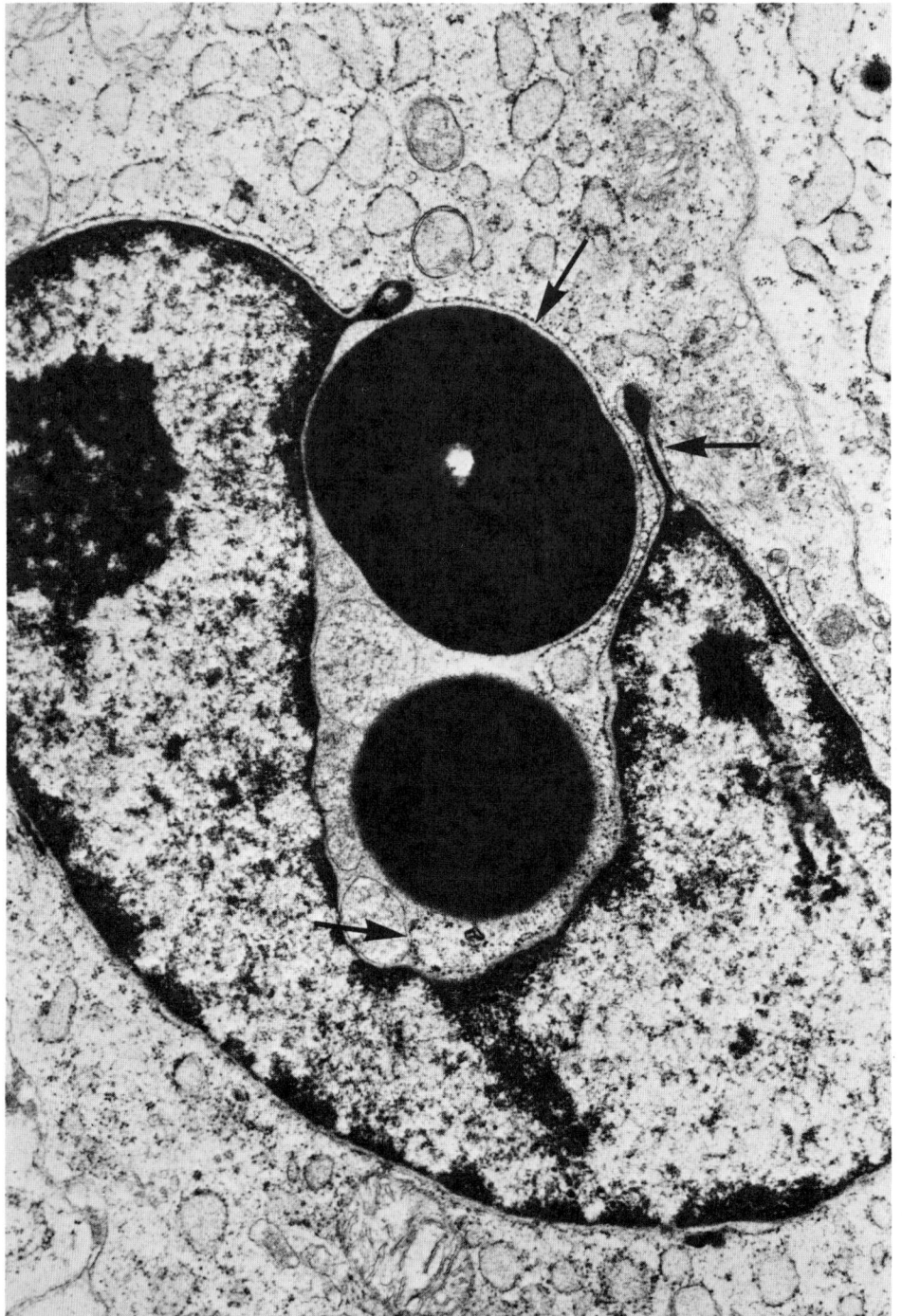

Figure 26.3. Intranuclear inclusions in plasma cell dyscrasia (R. D. Brunning and J. Parkin).

(d) Plasma cell from the specimen illustrated in Figure 26.3 (b) and (c). A very large nuclear inclusion with two densely osmiophilic structures is clearly located inside the perinuclear envelope (arrows). (× 25,000)

cell type of chronic lymphocytic leukemia. The nucleus shows considerable chromatin condensation. Nucleoli, when identified, are not prominent. Membrane-bound intranuclear inclusions of lightly electron-dense amorphous material similar to those noted in myeloma cells may be present (Figure 26.5(a)). The nuclear chromatin shows some clumping at the margin of the inclusion. Occasionally, the inclusions are surrounded by two membranes which are separated by what appears to be a cytoplasmic substance. The genesis of these nuclear inclusions appears to be invagination of the perinuclear cisternae or cytoplasm into the nucleus.[23]

The cytoplasm of the lymphocytic cells in macroglobulinemia differs from that of the lymphocytes in chronic lymphocytic leukemia by greater numbers of cytoplasmic structures. Mitochondria may be numerous and are frequently somewhat enlarged. Numerous free ribosomes are present. Strands of rough endoplasmic reticulum may be prominent although considerably less abundant than in plasma cells. Ribosome–lamella complexes (Figure 26.5(b)), similar to those found in hairy cell leukemia, have been identified in the cytoplasm of a small number of cells. The occurrence of these structures in the proliferating cells of macroglobulinemia, however, appears to be quite uncommon.

26.3. Heavy chain disease

The heavy chain diseases are plasma cell dyscrasias of extremely uncommon occurrence.[47] They are characterized by a proliferation of lymphocytes and plasma cells. The monoclonal protein produced in these disorders consists of the heavy chain portion of the various immunoglobulin molecules or a portion of the heavy chain. In μ-chain disease, there is also an elaboration of free light chains.

Zucker-Franklin has reported the morphology and ultrastructure of the plasma cells in the marrow from a patient with μ-chain disease.[173] In light microscopy, the plasma cells contained numerous vacuoles. Ultrastructurally, about 90 percent of the plasma cells appeared vacuolated (Figure 26.6). The vacuoles appeared to form in the Golgi zone and frequently extended to the periphery of the cell. Some of the vacuoles were completely empty and did not appear to be delimited by a membrane. Some contained debris, membrane fragments (Figure 26.6), and homogeneous material of variable electron density. The cisternae of rough endoplasmic reticulum was not particularly distended and the remainder of the cells had a normal appearance. Concurrent immunofluorescent studies demonstrated the plasma cells to be the source of both heavy and light chains.

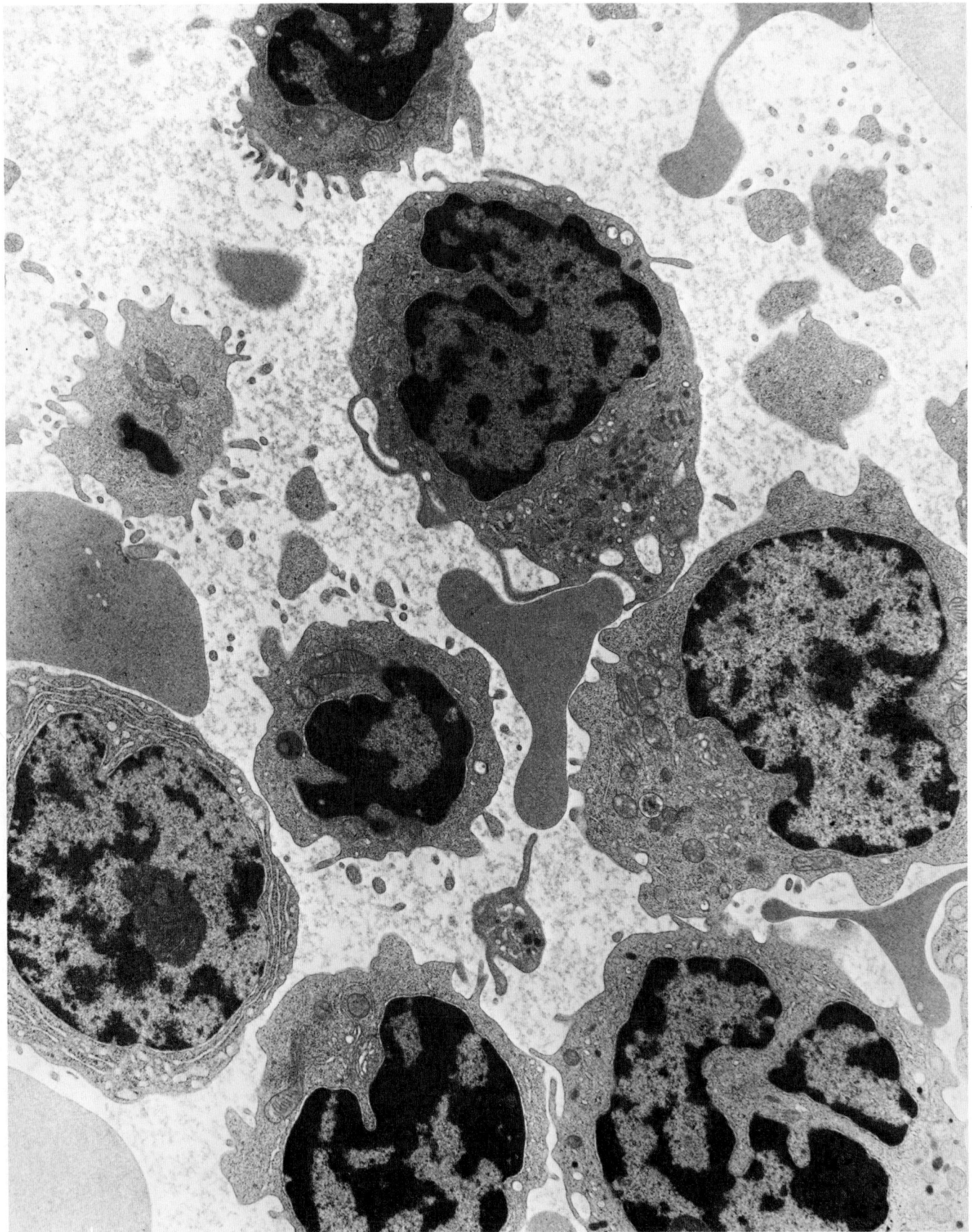

Figure 26.4. **Proliferating immunocytes in multiple myeloma.**

(a) Low power view of bone marrow specimen from a patient with an immunocytic proliferation and IgD monoclonal gammopathy. On light microscopy, the immunocytes had a lymphocytic plasma cell appearance. The nuclear chromatin shows considerable clumping and resembles the chromatin pattern of mature lymphocytes. (× 12,000)

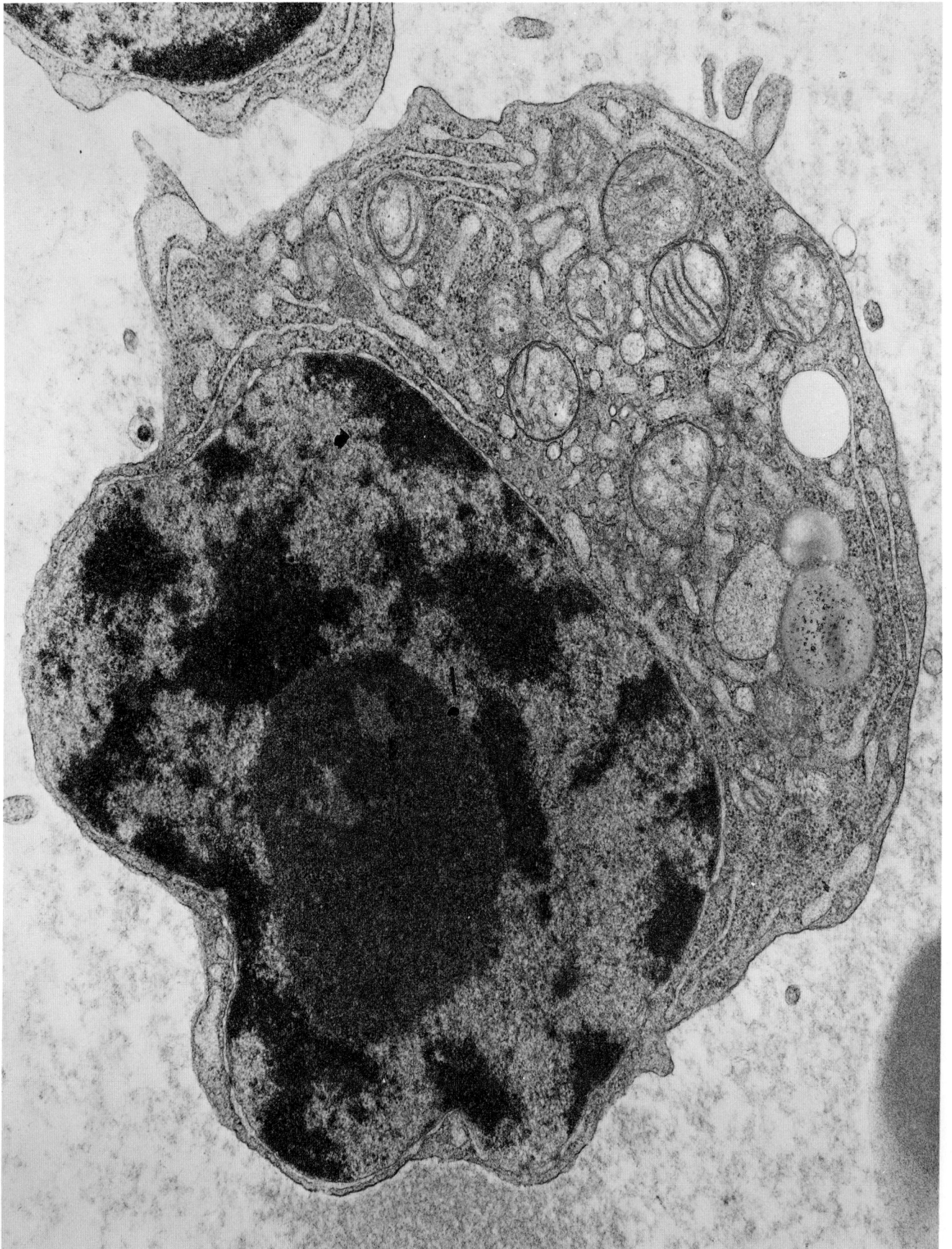

Figure 26.4. Proliferating immunocytes in mutiple myeloma.

(b) Immunocyte from the case illustrated in Figure 26.4(a). The nucleus contains a very prominent compact nucleolus. The cytoplasm contains several strands of rough endoplasmic reticulum which are dilated and contain a pale amorphous substance. Lightly osmiophilic inclusions are present. (× 27,000)

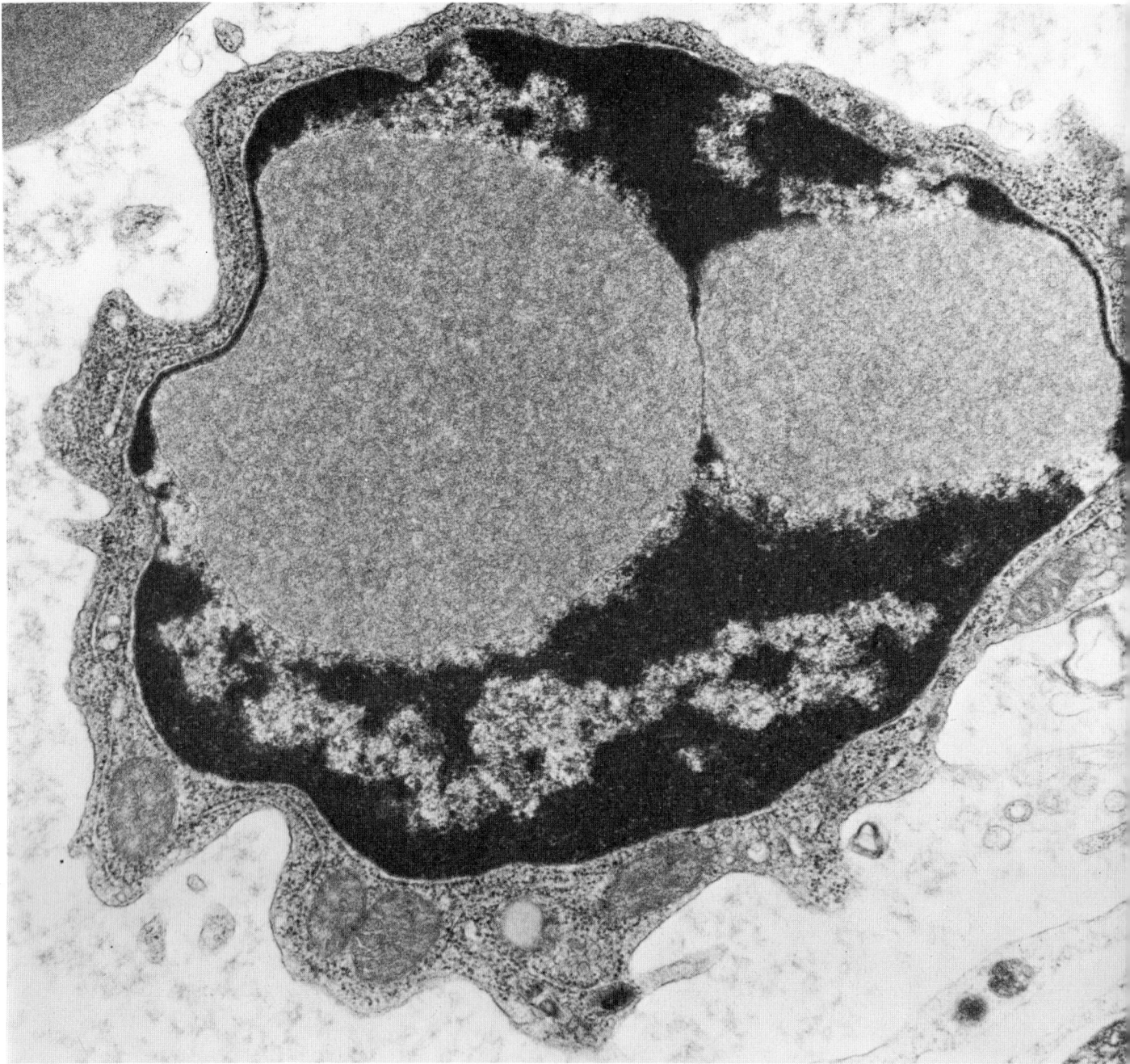

Figure 26.5. Waldenstrom's macroglobulinemia.
(a) Lymphocyte from bone marrow. This cell contains two intranuclear inclusions which contain electron-dense amorphous substance. Several strands of rough endoplasmic reticulum are visible in the cytoplasm. (×25,000)

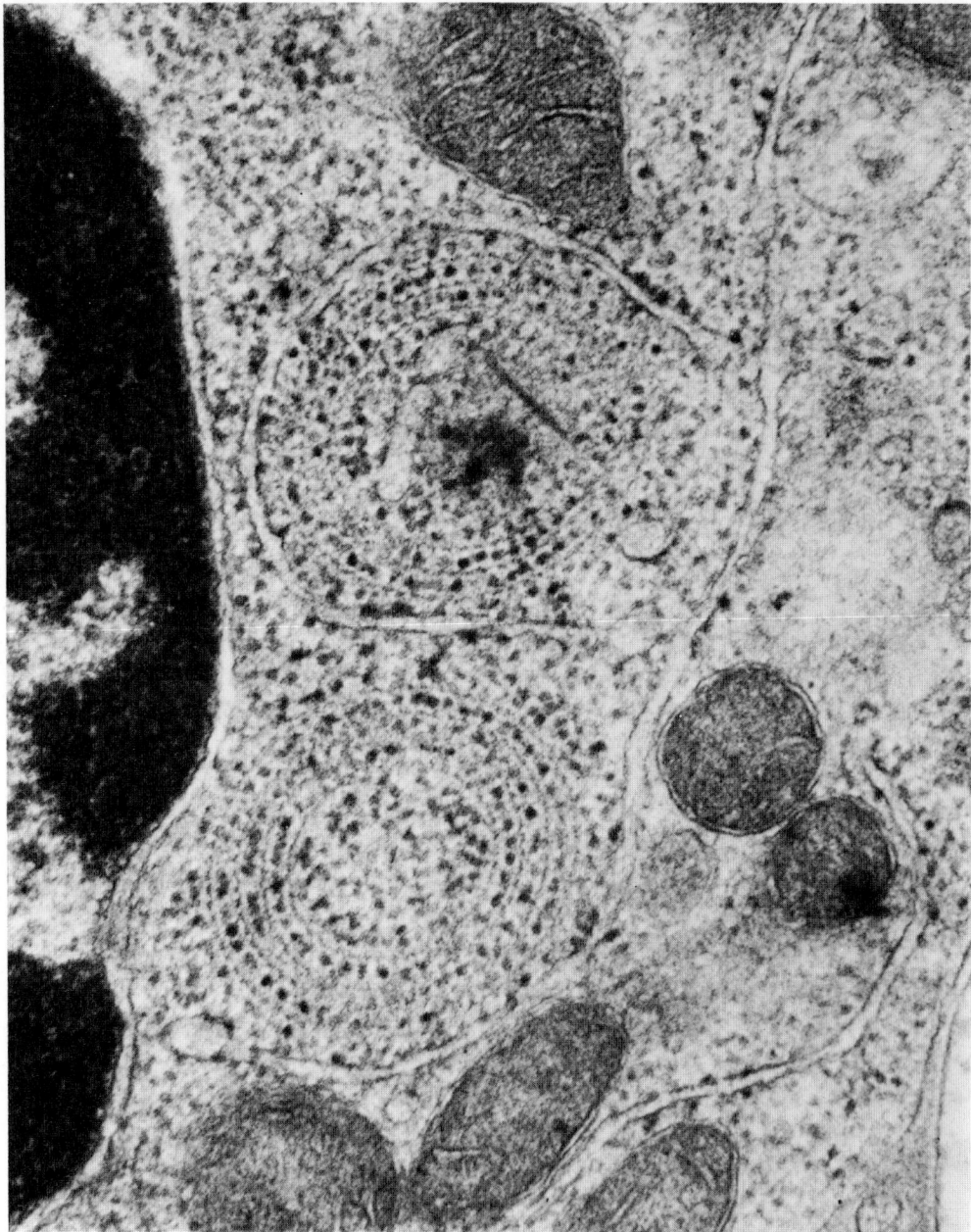

Figure 26.5. Waldenstrom's macroglobulinemia (R. D. Brunning and J. Parkin).
(b) Two ribosome–lamella complexes in the cytoplasm of a lymphocyte. (× 79,000)

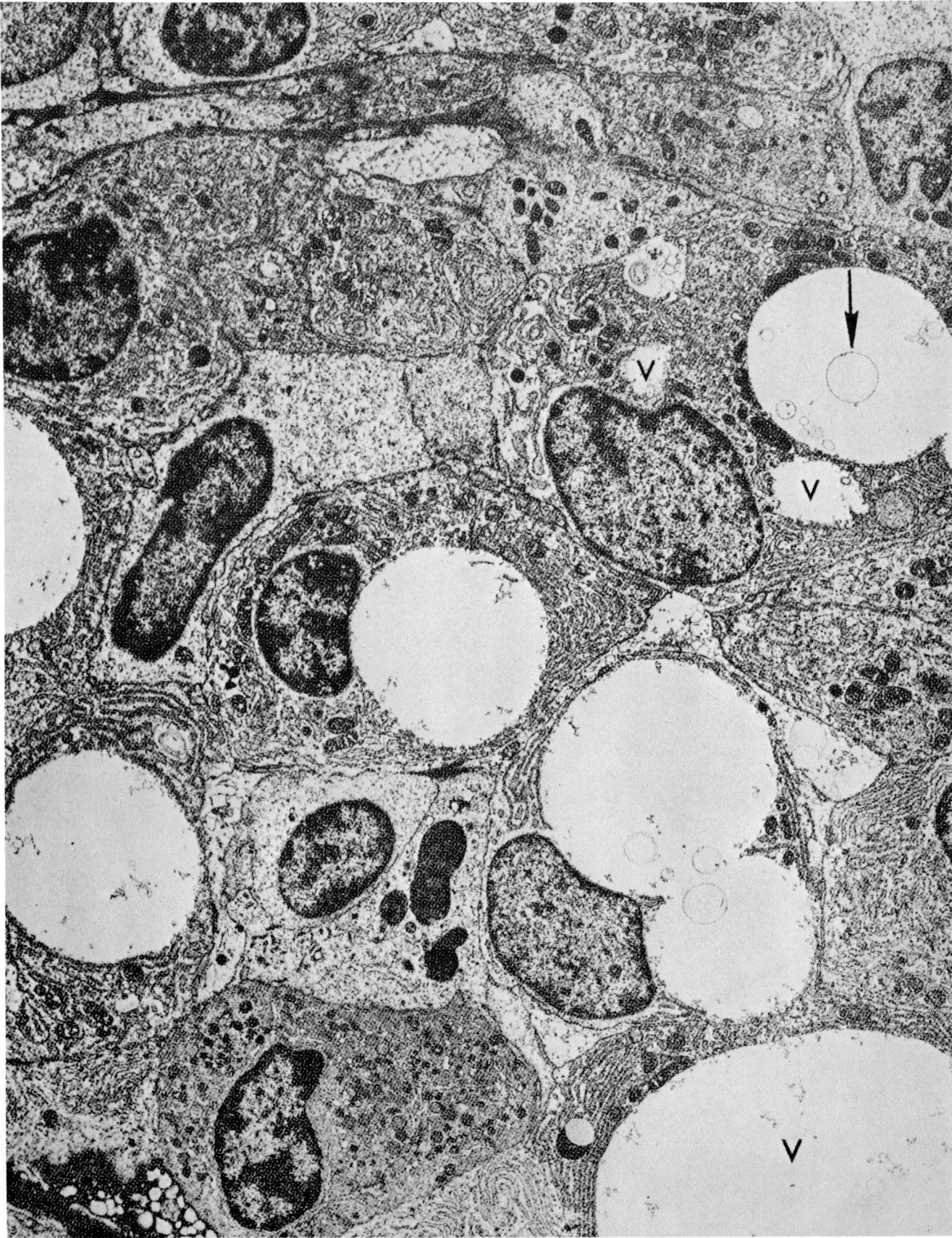

Figure 26.6. μ-Chain disease.
Low power view of bone marrow from a patient showing the majority of plasma cells with one or more varying sized vacuoles (V), some of which contain membrane fragments (↑). Some vacuoles appear confluent. (× 4,500)

27. Hairy Cell Leukemia

Leukemic reticuloendotheliosis or hairy cell leukemia is a disorder of the lymphoreticular system. Because of the morphologic characteristics of the leukemic cells in phase microscopy, the term hairy cell leukemia has been applied to this disease.[136] The cell of origin of hairy cell leukemia is in some dispute with evidence for both a B lymphocyte and a monocyte origin being advanced by different investigators.[26,36,57,69]

In Romanovsky stained smears, the hairy cell is larger than the normal lymphocyte. The nucleus has a reticular appearing chromatin pattern in which nucleoli are usually very faintly visible. The nuclear outline may be round, oval, or folded. The cytoplasm, which may appear quite vacuolated, has an indistinct and irregular border; frequently, delicate cytoplasmic projections are present. In phase microscopy, the cells manifest numerous, thin, cytoplasmic projections at right angles to the surface of the cell; the projections are usually short. An important diagnostic feature of the disorder is the presence of tartrate-resistant acid phosphatase activity in the leukemic cells.[171]

There have been several ultrastructural studies of the hairy cells of leukemic reticuloendotheliosis both by transmission and scanning electron microscopy.[35,75,76] In transmission electron microscopy the cells range from 8–10 nm in diameter. The nuclei may be round, oval, or deeply indented. Occasionally the nucleus manifests several indentations giving it a very irregular outline (Figure 27.1). The nuclear chromatin shows clumping at the margin. Nucleoli, usually single, are small in size. The cytoplasm is marked by the presence of numerous delicate projections (Figure 27.1) which range up to 4 nm in length and 0·5 nm in width. The number of these projections varies from cell to cell. Katayama has described broadly based pseudopods in addition to the more delicate projections.[76] The cytoplasm contains pinocytotic vesicles, multivesicular bodies, strands of rough endoplasmic reticulum, and occasional granules. Collections of fine fibrils may be found, frequently in a paranuclear location.

An unusual inclusion, the ribosome–lamella complex, was first described in the hairy cells of leukemic reticuloendotheliosis by Katayama et al.[75] In cross section, the ribosome–lamella complex appears as concentric round profiles of fibers with ribosomes spaced at even intervals between the fibers. In longitudinal section, they appear as parallel arrays of single fibers with ribosomes arranged in a linear pattern at regular intervals between the fibers. The ribosomes do not appear attached to the fibers.

Figure 27.1. Leukemic reticuloendotheliosis (hairy cell disease).
Several "hairy cells" showing the numerous, delicate, cytoplasmic projections in several cells. The nuclei, which are irregular in outline, are encircled by bands of microfibrils. (× 7,800)

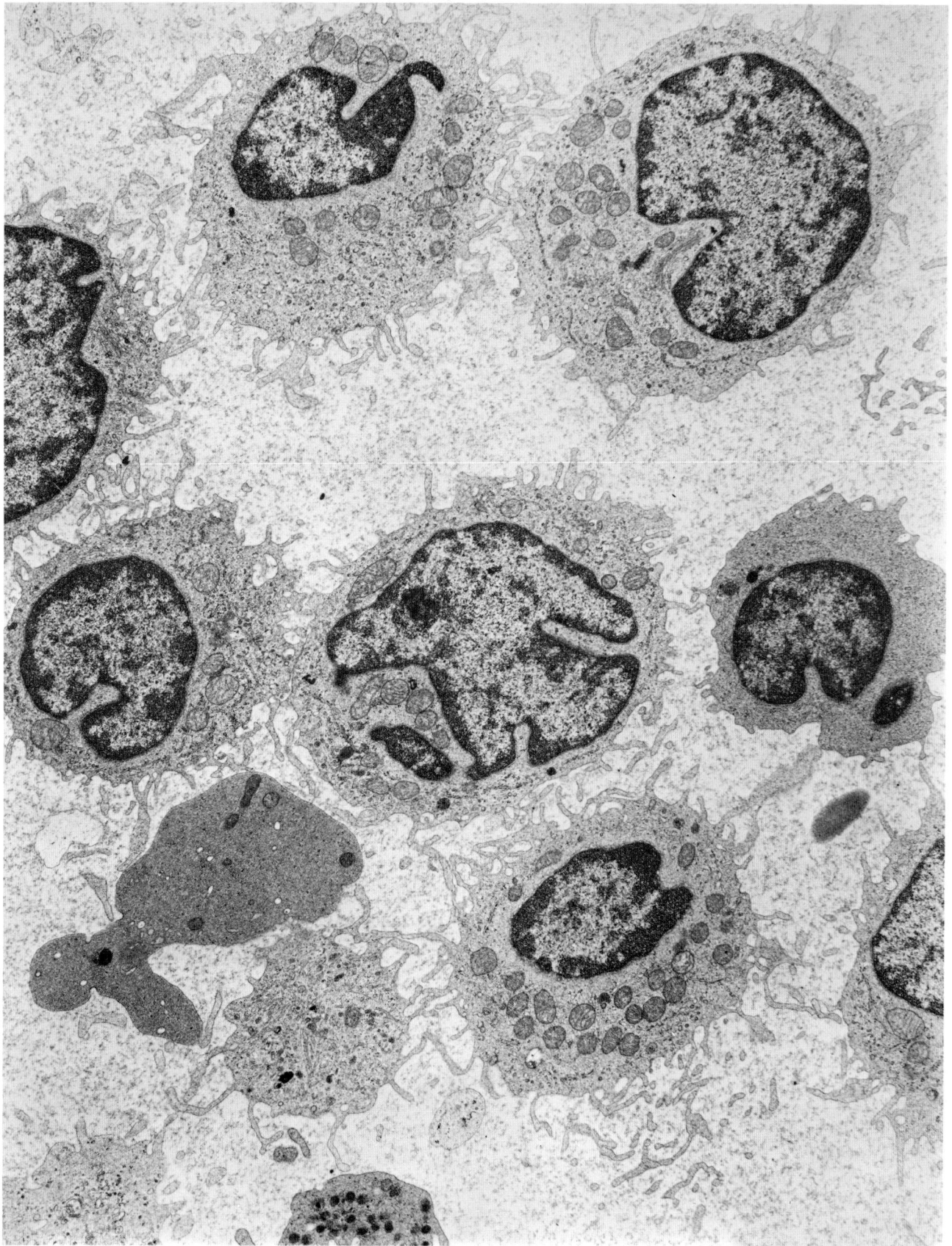

Katayama observed these structures in 0·2–90 percent of the hairy cells in 10 of 23 patients with leukemic reticuloendotheliosis.[76] The ribosome–lamella complex, however, is not pathognomonic for leukemic reticuloendotheliosis and has been detected in other conditions.[22]

In scanning electron microscopy, the hairy cell measures 5·0–6·8 nm and displays short stublike microvilli, long microvilli, and ruffled membranes.[76]

Ultrastructural abnormalities have been observed in some of the platelets from patients with leukemic reticuloendotheliosis.[83] Granules of giant size and unusual shape were found; platelets from one patient contained profiles of rough endoplasmic reticulum. Functional abnormalities were also noted; the platelets from some patients showed lack of aggregation following epinephrine stimulation and decreased platelet factor 3 availability following ADP stimulation.

28. Sezary's Syndrome

Sezary's syndrome is a disorder characterized by a generalized exfoliative erythroderma with intensive pruritus and a cutaneous infiltrate of mononuclear cells[34] which are also found in the peripheral blood and lymph nodes.[153] The atypical mononuclear cells, referred to as Sezary cells, have been characterized by membrane surface marker studies as T lymphocytes.[61,174] The relationship of Sezary's syndrome to mycosis fungoides is not completely clear, although several observers are of the opinion that the Sezary cells are a peripheral blood manifestation of mycosis fungoides.[157]

In Romanovsky stained blood films, the typical Sezary cell is large, 12–14 μm, and has a nucleus which occupies approximately four-fifths of the cell diameter. The nucleus has a folded and grooved appearance which has been characterized as cerebriform. The usually sparse cytoplasm may contain vacuoles which stain with the periodic acid–Schiff technique. Although Sezary cells are typically large in size, there is a small cell variant.[88]

Ultrastructurally, the nucleus of the Sezary cell shows a degree of indentation and lobulation which may be striking.[88,89,174] The nuclear chromatin is heterochromatic (Figure 28.1) with clumping at the nuclear margin. In addition to the nuclear lobulation, the cells may show a striking number of cytoplasmic fibrils. Clusters of glycogen granules may be present. Ultrastructural similarities between the Sezary cells and the cells in the skin in mycosis fungoides have been shown.[131]

On scanning electron microscopy[126] most of the Sezary cells have appeared spherical in shape, with a moderately to markedly villous appearance, and resembled the majority of the lymphocytes from patients with chronic lymphocytic leukemia. A proportion of the cells were larger and more irregular in shape while others had small extensions of cytoplasm.

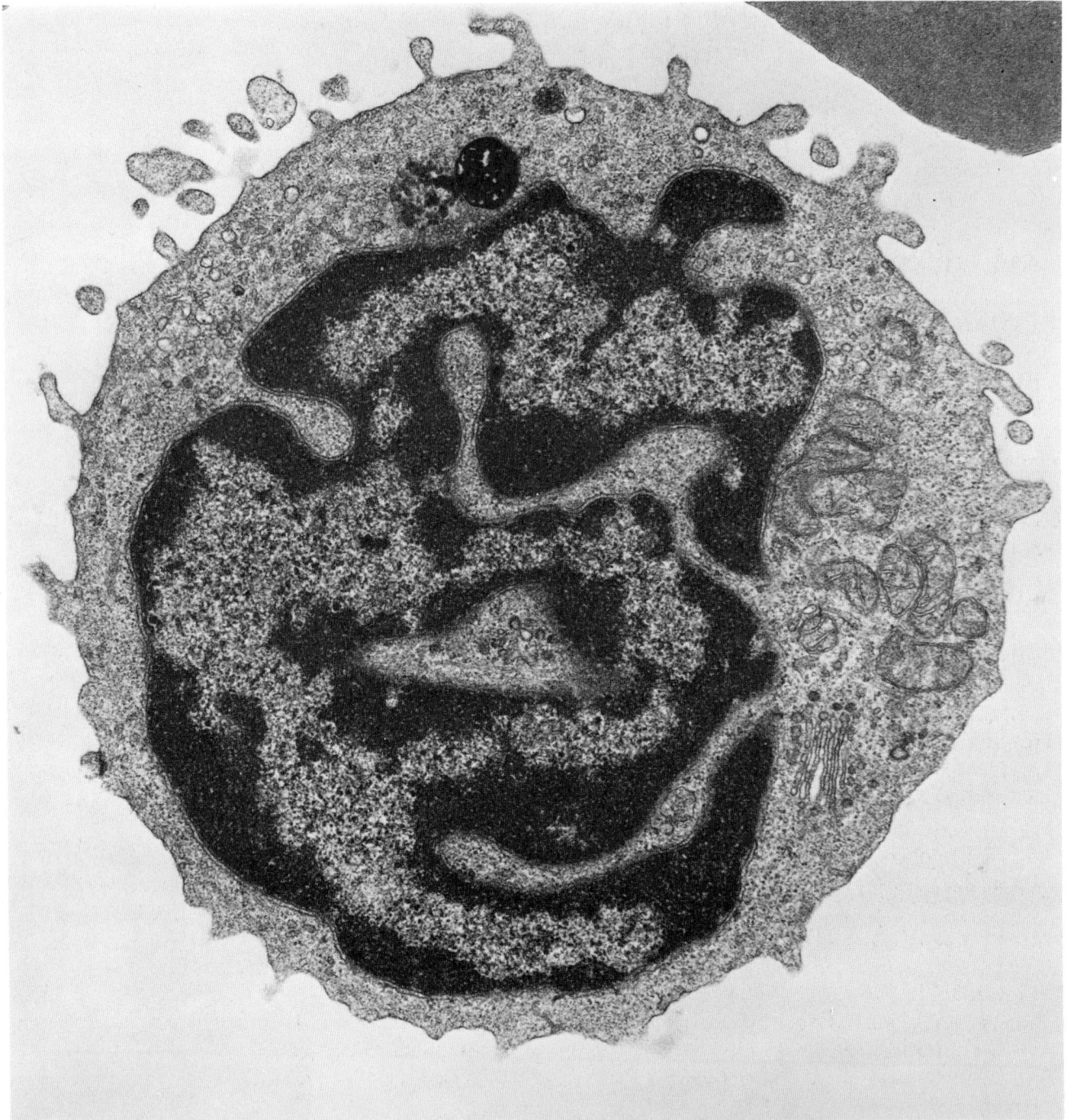

Figure 28.1. Sezary's syndrome.
A cell from the peripheral blood of a patient showing a markedly contorted, heterochromatic nucleus. (×33,600)

378

29. Reactive Leukocyte Processes

29.1. Neutrophils

The response of the neutrophil system to inflammatory processes can be manifested either as qualitative or quantitative alterations. The qualitative changes are usually referred to as toxic changes and are primarily reflected by changes in the cytoplasm contents. The most frequently encountered toxic alteration is the presence of varying numbers of prominent azurophilic granules in the cytoplasm (Figure 29.1); these are referred to as toxic granules. The other toxic alteration, which usually reflects a more severe insult, is the Döhle body, a focal area of basophilia in the neutrophil cytoplasm. Inflammatory processes accompanied by bacteremia may also result in vacuolated neutrophils.

Ultrastructurally, the toxic granulation appears identical to the azurophil granules which are part of the neutrophils' normal granule composition. For reasons which are not completely clear, these granules cannot be visualized in normal mature neutrophils in routinely stained smears, although they are readily visualized in electron micrographs. McCall *et al.*[90] could not detect any consistent ultrastructural difference in the fine structure of the several types of primary granules in normal or toxic neutrophils. The Döhle body consists of an aggregate of lamellae of rough endoplasmic reticulum (Figure 29.1). The vacuoles are membrane-bound structures which may be clear or contain amorphous debris.

29.2. Infectious mononucleosis

Infectious mononucleosis is a self-limited lymphoproliferative disorder caused by the Epstein–Barr virus. The changes in the lymphocytic cells in the peripheral blood are one of the hallmarks of the disorder;[45] the altered lymphocytes are referred to as reactive or atypical lymphocytes. Reactive lymphocytes may be found in low numbers in normal individuals and in increased numbers in patients with any type of viral infection. There is an absolute increase in the number of T lymphocytes in infectious mononucleosis.[143]

The most frequently encountered type of reactive lymphocyte in infectious mononucleosis is the Downey type II cell, a medium size lymphocyte with abundant cytoplasm which displays radiating basophilia. Such cells frequently contain coarse azurophil granules. The minority of the reactive lymphocytes will be the Downey type III lymphocyte which has a reticular nuclear pattern, relatively prominent nucleoli, and a moderate rim of hyperbasophilic cytoplasm. The latter cell has characteristics of the transformed lymphocyte.

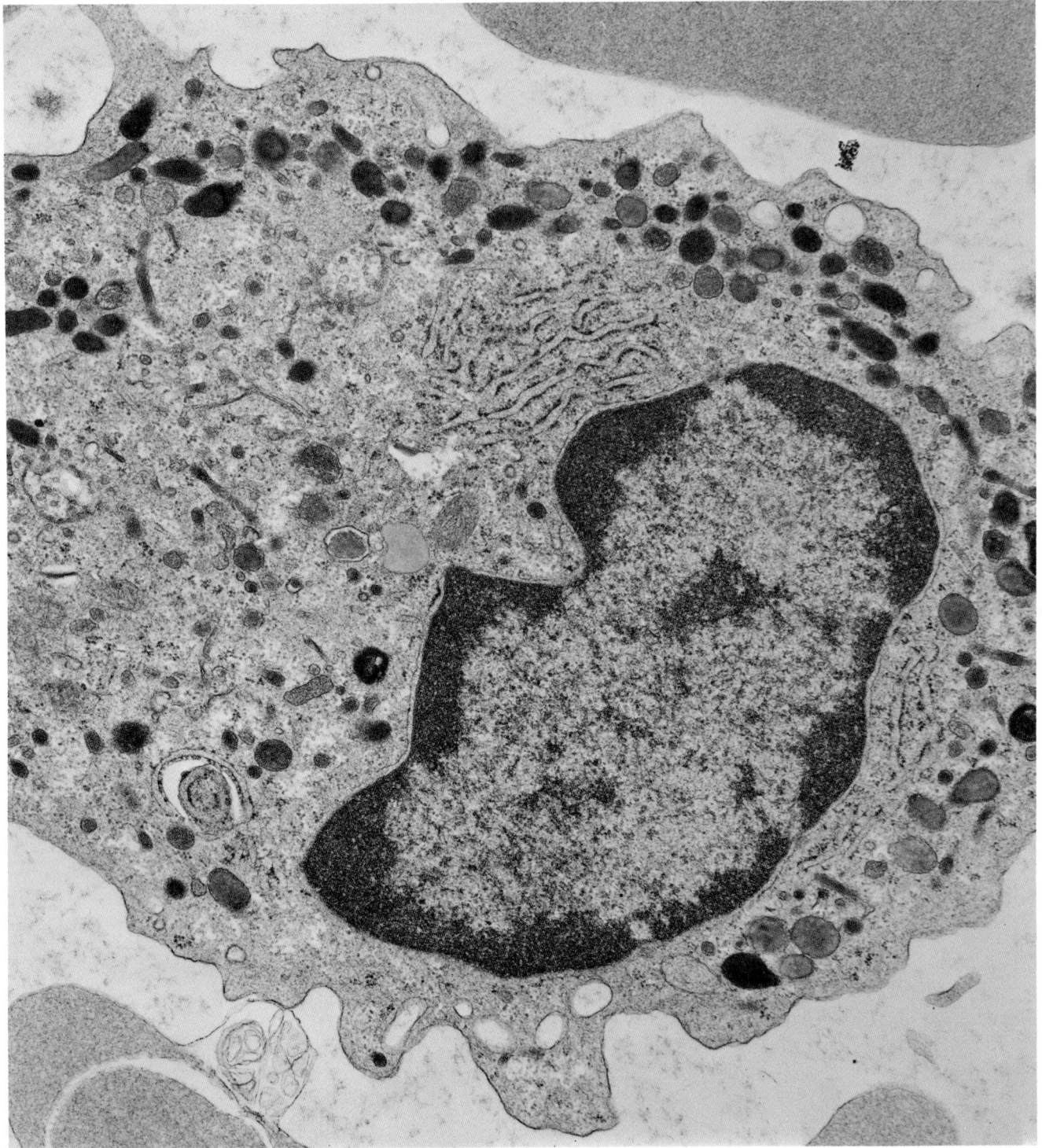

Figure 29.1. Toxic neutrophil.
Neutrophil with prominent azurophil granules and two foci of lamellae of endoplasmic reticulum from a patient with increased neutrophils showing marked toxic granulation and Döhle bodies. The lamellae of endoplasmic reticulum correspond to the Döhle bodies observed in Romanowsky stained blood films. (×27,000)

No one ultrastructural description can be applied to all the lymphocytes from patients with infectious mononucleosis. The cell which appears to correspond to the most frequently encountered cell, the Downey type II lymphocyte, is 5–8 nm in diameter, contains abundant cytoplasm, moderately clumped nuclear chromatin (Figure 29.2(a)), free ribosomes, occasional strands of rough endoplasmic reticulum, numerous large mitochondria, and a prominent Golgi. A high percentage of the lymphocytes in infectious mononucleosis, probably corresponding to the Downey II cell, possess electron-dense cytoplasmic inclusions (Figure 29.2(b)) which contain parallel arrays of microtubule-like structures (Figure 29.2(c));[94] these usually occur in the centrosome region of the cell,[21] their significance being unknown. The nuclei of these cells show a moderate degree of clumping.

Douglas *et al.*[43] in their ultrastructural studies of the peripheral blood cells from patients with infectious mononucleosis described an increase in lymphoid plasma cells. These cells are probably the ultrastructural counterpart of the hyperbasophilic Downey III lymphocytes.

29.3. Tubular reticular structure

The term tubular reticular structure, an inclusion described by Schaff *et al.*,[62,134] describes a net-like arrangement of tubules which has been observed in lymphocytes, cultured lymphoid cells, and endothelial cells. They have been observed in a variety of disorders, most notably lupus erythematosus.[108] On electron microscopy these structures are composed of arrays of undulating tubules, 200 to 300 Å in diameter, bound by a single smooth membrane which is in continuity with the rough endoplasmic reticulum. Ultracytochemical studies have shown that the tubular reticular structure (Figure 29.3) probably consists of an acidic glycoprotein. It has been suggested that they are a general cellular response to a number of stimuli, including viruses.[129] Their exact biological significance is unknown.

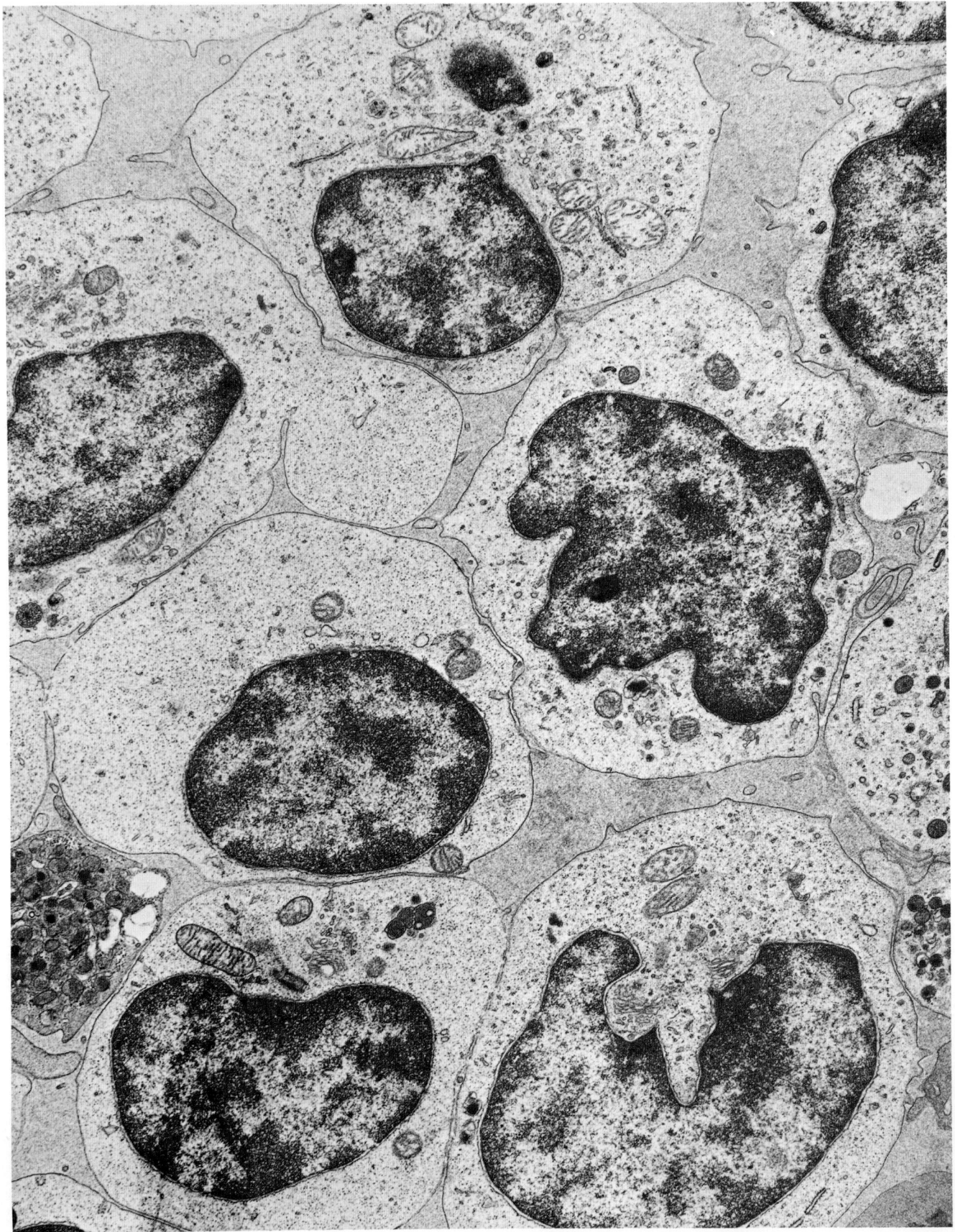

Figure 29.2. Infectious mononucleosis.

(a) Several lymphocytes from the peripheral blood of a patient showing abundant cytoplasm and moderately clumped nuclei. In light microscopy the majority of the peripheral blood lymphocytes were of the Downey II type. (× 13,000)

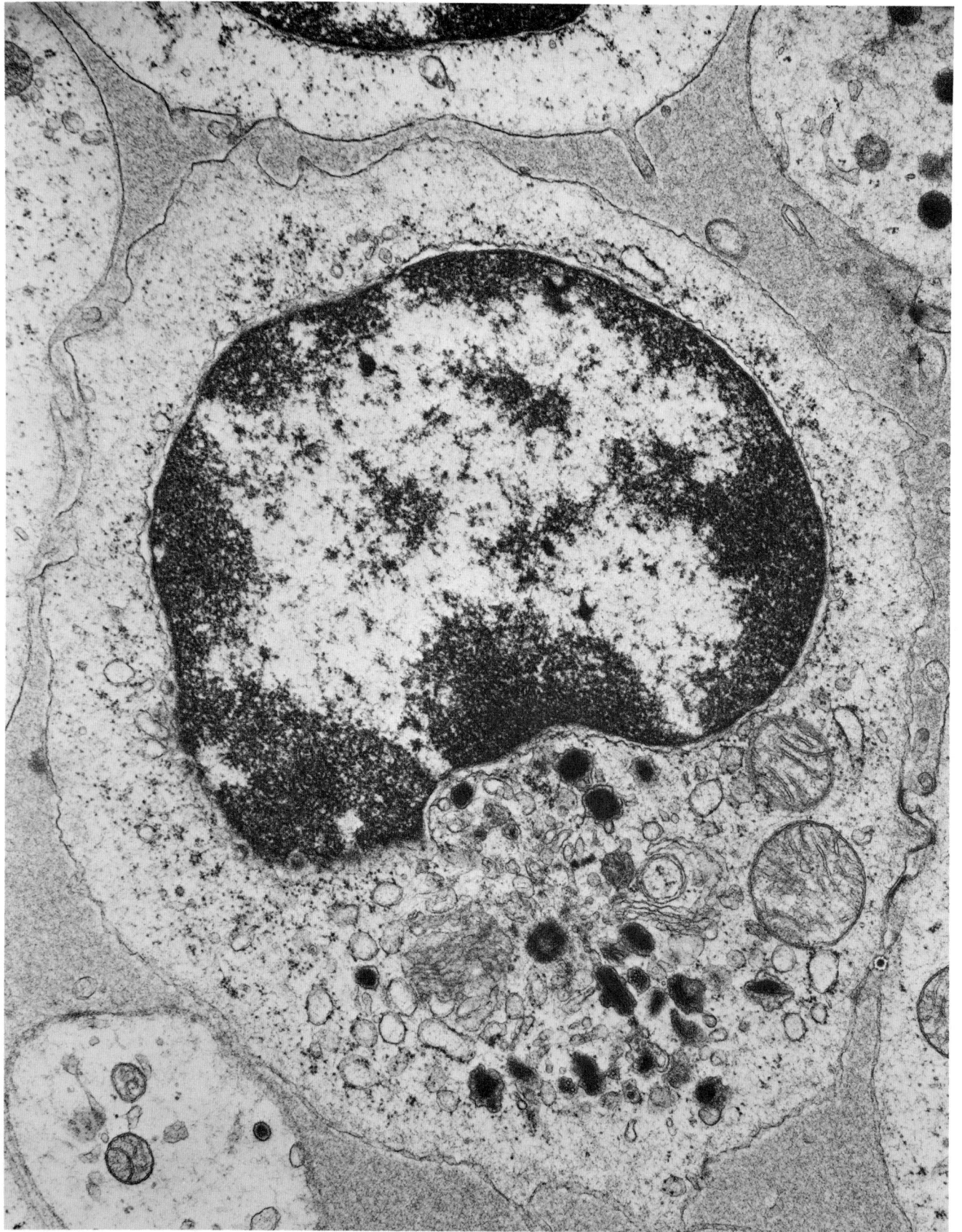

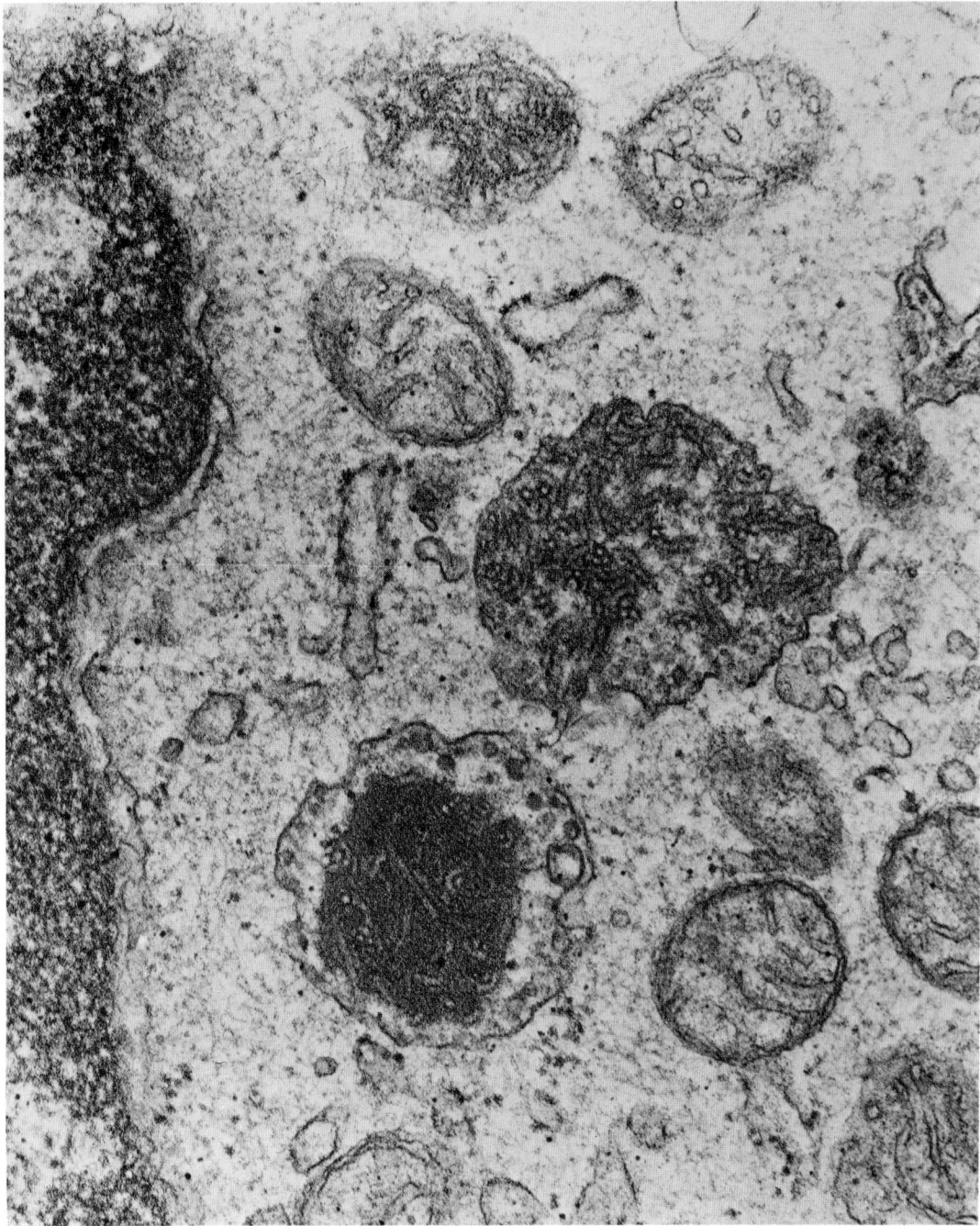

Figure 29.2. Infectious mononucleosis.

(c) High magnification of an inclusion in a lymphocyte showing bundles of parallel tubular arrays, several of which are membrane bound. ($\times 63,000$)

Figure 29.2. Infectious mononucleosis.

(b) Lymphocyte from the peripheral blood showing several cytoplasmic inclusions in the region of the centriole. ($\times 29,000$)

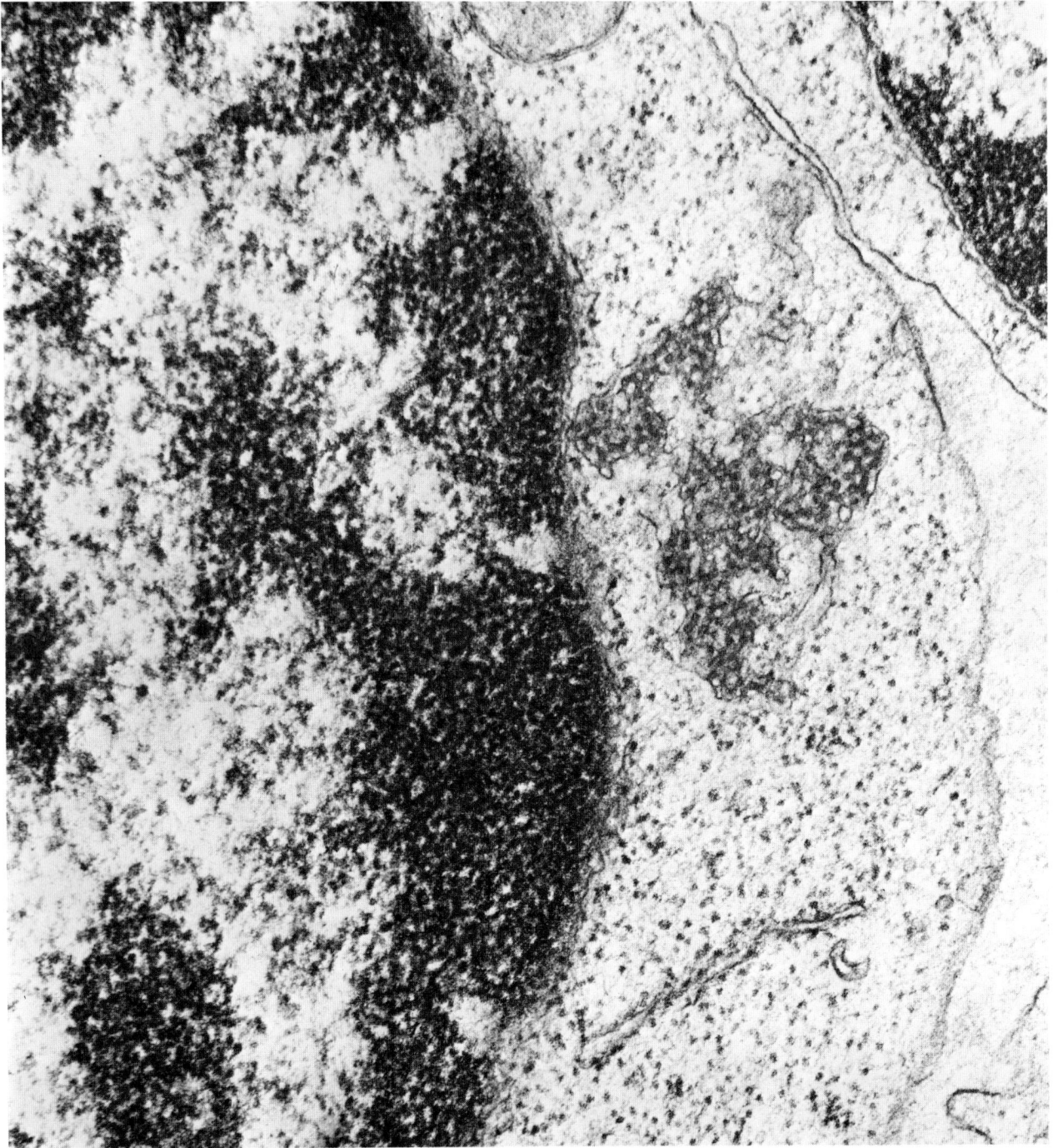

Figure 29.3. Tubular reticular structure.
Peripheral blood lymphocyte with a tubular reticular structure. (×79,000)

30. Hereditary Disorders with Manifestations in Hematopoietic Cells

30.1. Chediak–Higashi–Steinbrinck syndrome

This syndrome is a rare autosomal recessive disorder which is characterized by partial oculocutaneous albinism, photophobia, recurrent infections, neuropathies, hepatosplenomegaly, and lymphadenopathy. The peripheral blood shows thrombocytopenia, leukopenia, and a granular anomaly of the leukocytes. The size and tinctorial characteristics of the granules vary among the different cell types.[19]

On ultrastructural examination, the neutrophils from patients with the Chediak–Higashi–Steinbrinck syndrome contain azurophil and specific granules. Although the large granules (Figure 30.1(a)) in these neutrophils originate from one source,[42, 160] White has distinguished at least two different types.[166] One type is a large cytoplasmic organelle (Figure 30.1(b)), oval or round, with an uncomplicated internal structure. Except for its size it resembles the azurophil granule in normal neutrophils. This type probably arises by simple enlargement or unrestricted growth of a primary lysosome in an early promyelocyte. The second type of giant granule evolves during the late promyelocyte and early myelocyte stage by a continued fusion of azurophil granules into massive bodies. The process is not completed even in mature neutrophils. The enlarged particles are similar to the normal azurophil granules and have a unit membrane and relatively homogeneous substructure. In addition to the homogeneous material, these structures also contain lamellated sheets, rows of membranous structures, typical myelin figures, and fine granular osmiophilic material. Sequestration of cytoplasm has also been observed.[161] In the lymphocytes the giant organelles contain fenestrated structures, crystalloid material, small electron-dense spherules, lamellar stalks, and myelin figures. White was able to demonstrate localization of acid phosphatase activity in the Chediak–Higashi granules (Figure 30.2) in the neutrophils.[160] This was in contrast to the granules in normal granulocytes and normal granules in Chediak–Higashi neutrophils in which the acid phosphatase activity was irregular or absent. White also demonstrated giant inclusions of parallel tubular arrays (Figure 30.3) in the lymphocytes of patients with the Chediak–Higashi syndrome.[165] These are similar to the parallel arrays which have been observed as smaller inclusions in lymphocytes from normal individuals and in patients with several different types of disorders.[21]

30.2. Gaucher's disease

Gaucher's disease is a hereditary disorder of the metabolism of glucocerebroside.[48] Excess glucocerebroside accumulates in the reticuloendothelial cells which take on a

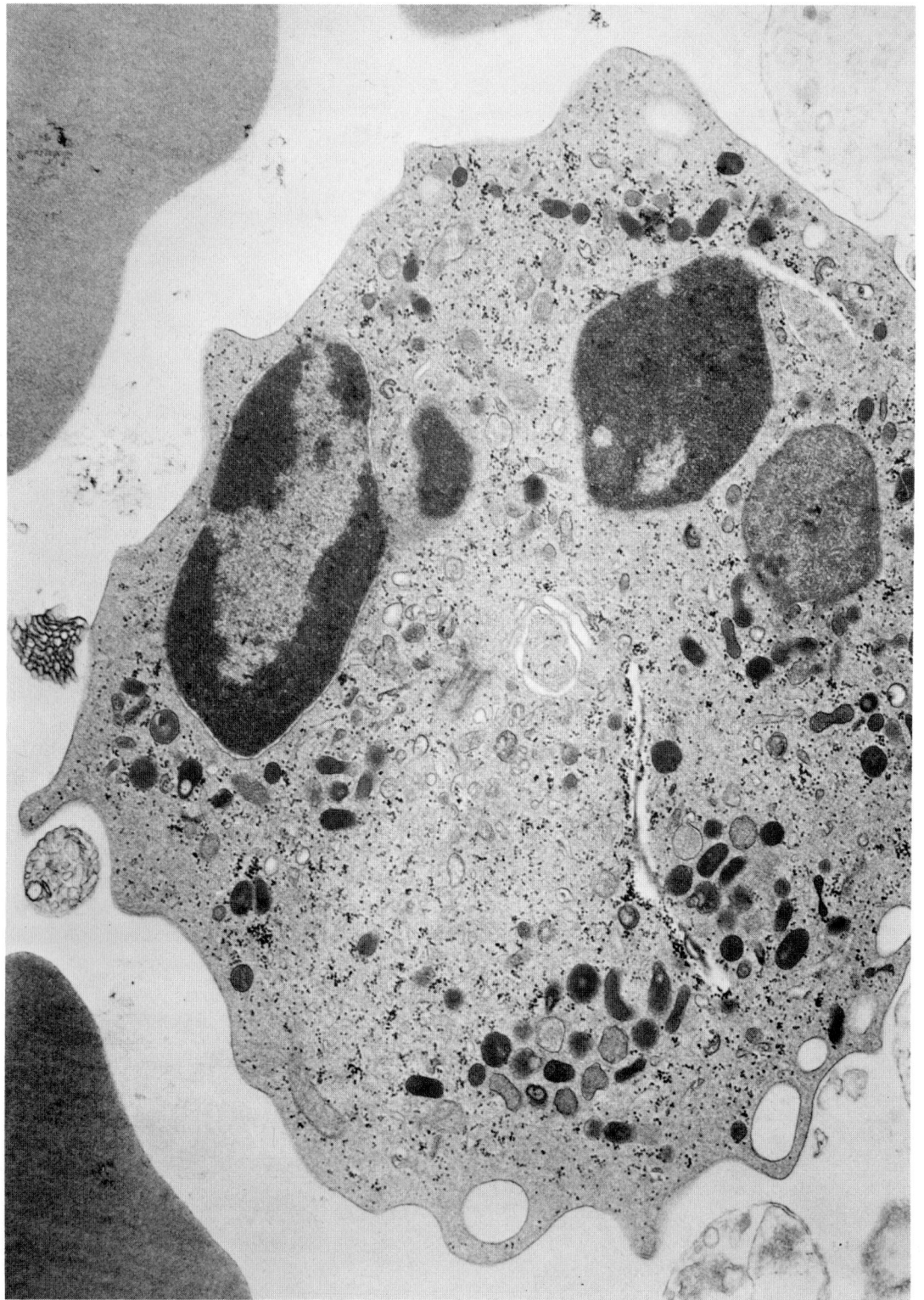

Figure 30.1. Chediak–Higashi syndrome.
(a) Peripheral blood neutrophil with an abnormally large granule in the cytoplasm. (× 30,000)

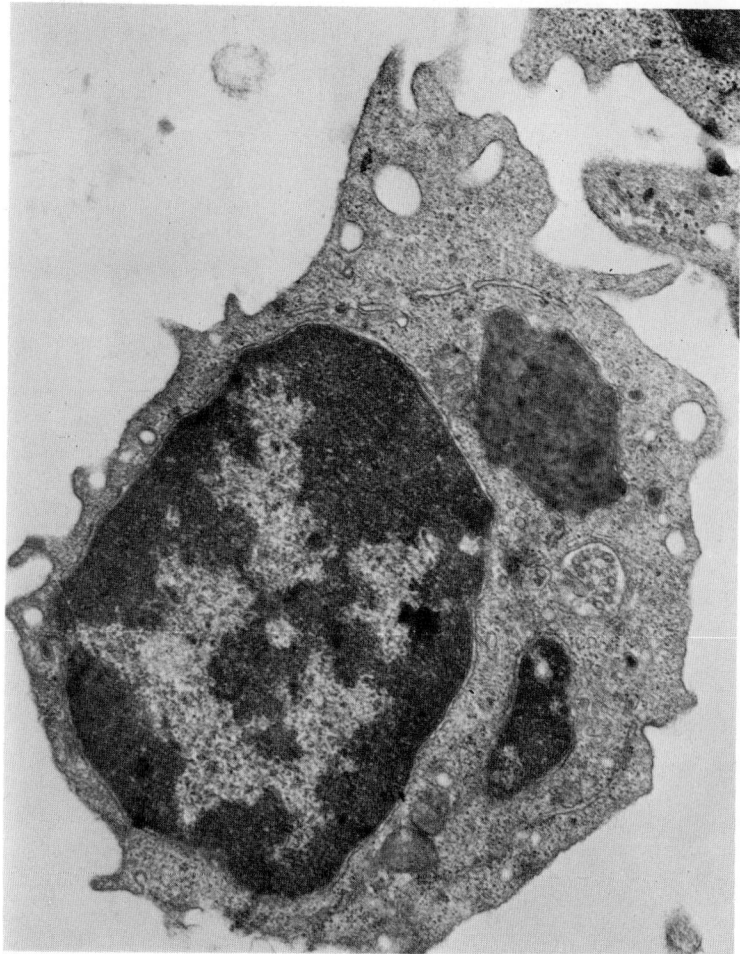

Figure 30.1. Chediak–Higashi syndrome (J. G. White).
(b) Peripheral blood lymphocyte with large irregularly shaped cytoplasmic inclusions. (× 13,900)

characteristic appearance. The Gaucher's cells accumulate in abundance in the spleen, liver, lymph node, and bone marrow. In smears and imprints, the Gaucher's cell measures 20–100 μm and has one or more eccentrically or centrally placed nuclei and a cytoplasm with a characteristic striated or fibrillary pattern.

Ultrastructurally, the Gaucher's cell has abundant cytoplasm which contains numerous oval or crescent shaped bodies of variable size (Figure 30.4(a)), generally surrounded by a single smooth membrane and with an internal tubular structure (Figure 30.4(b)).[122] On cross section, the tubules appear as rings which are moderately osmiophilic and measure approximately 400–600 Å. The tubules contain a pale staining amorphous material. They are set in a pale matrix in the largest bodies and in a rather dense substance in medium and small bodies. There are a variable number of dense erythrophagosomes (Figure 30.4(b)) in which tubular structures are some-

389

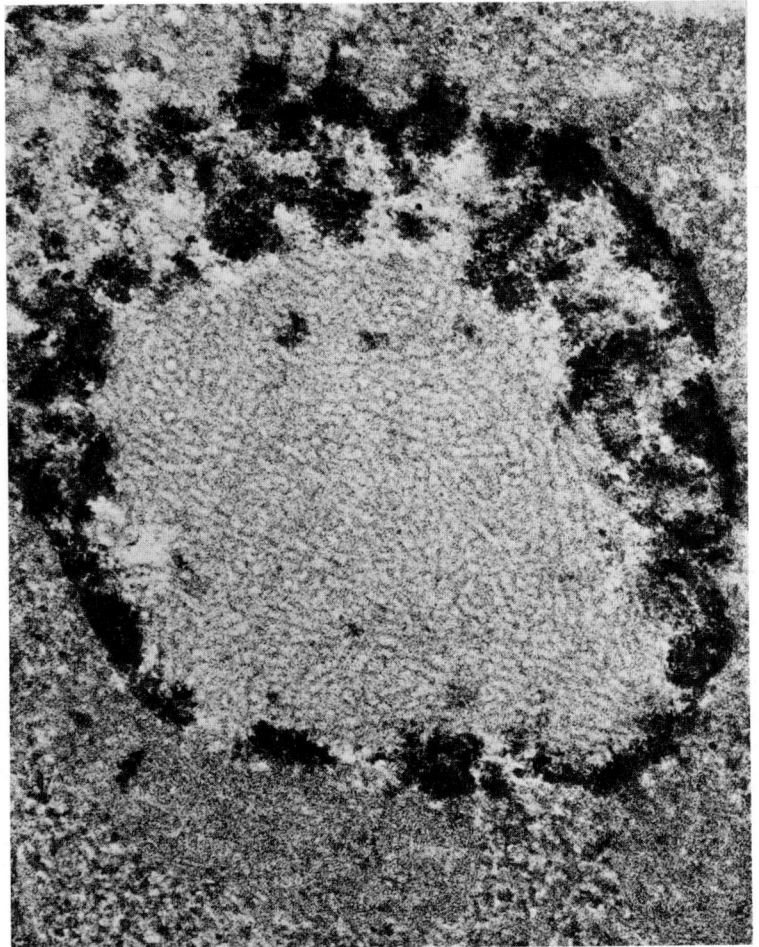

Figure 30.2. Chediak–Higashi granule (J. G. White).
Granule stained for acid phosphatase. The central portion of the inclusion, which lacks acid phosphatase activity, has a slightly cobbled framework. (× 102,500)

times detected. The cell border has small pseudopods or ridge-like projections. Frequently, erythrocyte fragments are present.

30.3. Pelger–Huet anomaly

This is an autosomal, dominant, hereditary disorder characterized by incomplete segmentation of the nuclei of the neutrophils and eosinophils.[19] The heterozygous state, which, with very rare exceptions, is the only form observed in humans, is characterized by neutrophils that have unsegmented or bilobed nuclei. The nuclear chromatin is coarse and clumped but the granules in the cytoplasm are normal in number and appearance. Ultrastructurally, the neutrophil possesses one or two lobes

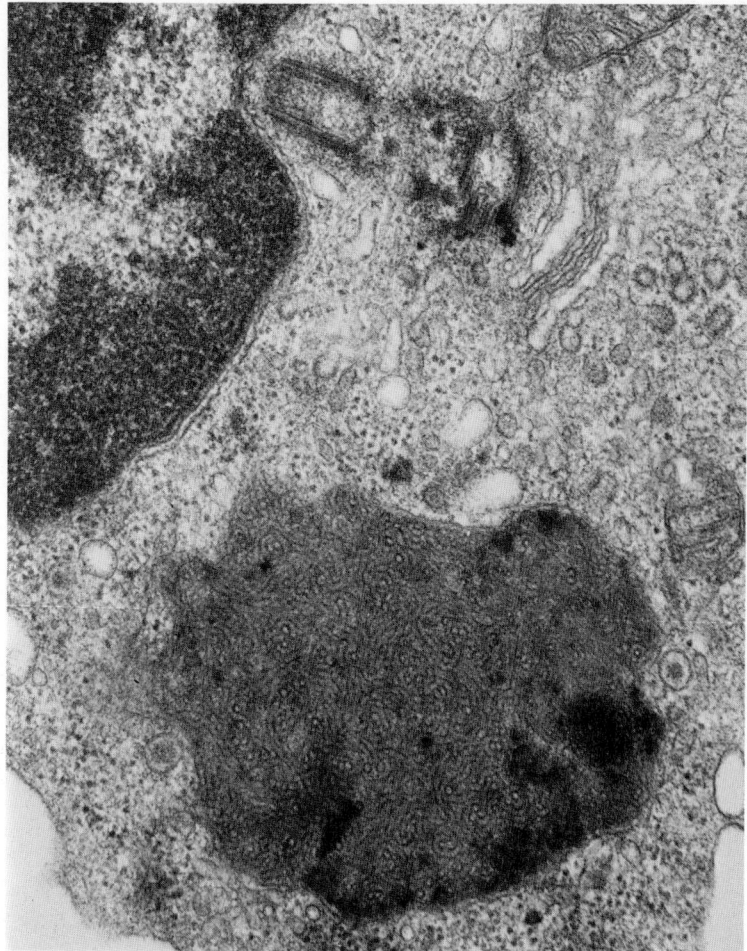

Figure 30.3. Chediak–Higashi syndrome: giant inclusion (J. G. White).

Giant inclusion, primarily composed of undulating tubules, in the cytoplasm of a lymphocyte. A few focal areas of dense amorphous substance are also present. ($\times 41,500$)

with well-preserved heterochromatin.[40] Nuclear appendages and bridges are occasionally seen. Djaldetti reported a pronounced decrease in primary and secondary granules with a marked increase in size of some of the secondary granules (Figure 30.5).[40]

30.4. May–Hegglin anomaly

The May–Hegglin anomaly is an autosomal dominant disorder, characterized by platelet abnormalities and the presence of abnormally large Döhle bodies in neutrophils, eosinophils, basophils, and monocytes.[19] In electron microscopy the neutrophils from these patients contain areas of cytoplasm which are devoid of granules.[70, 71]

391

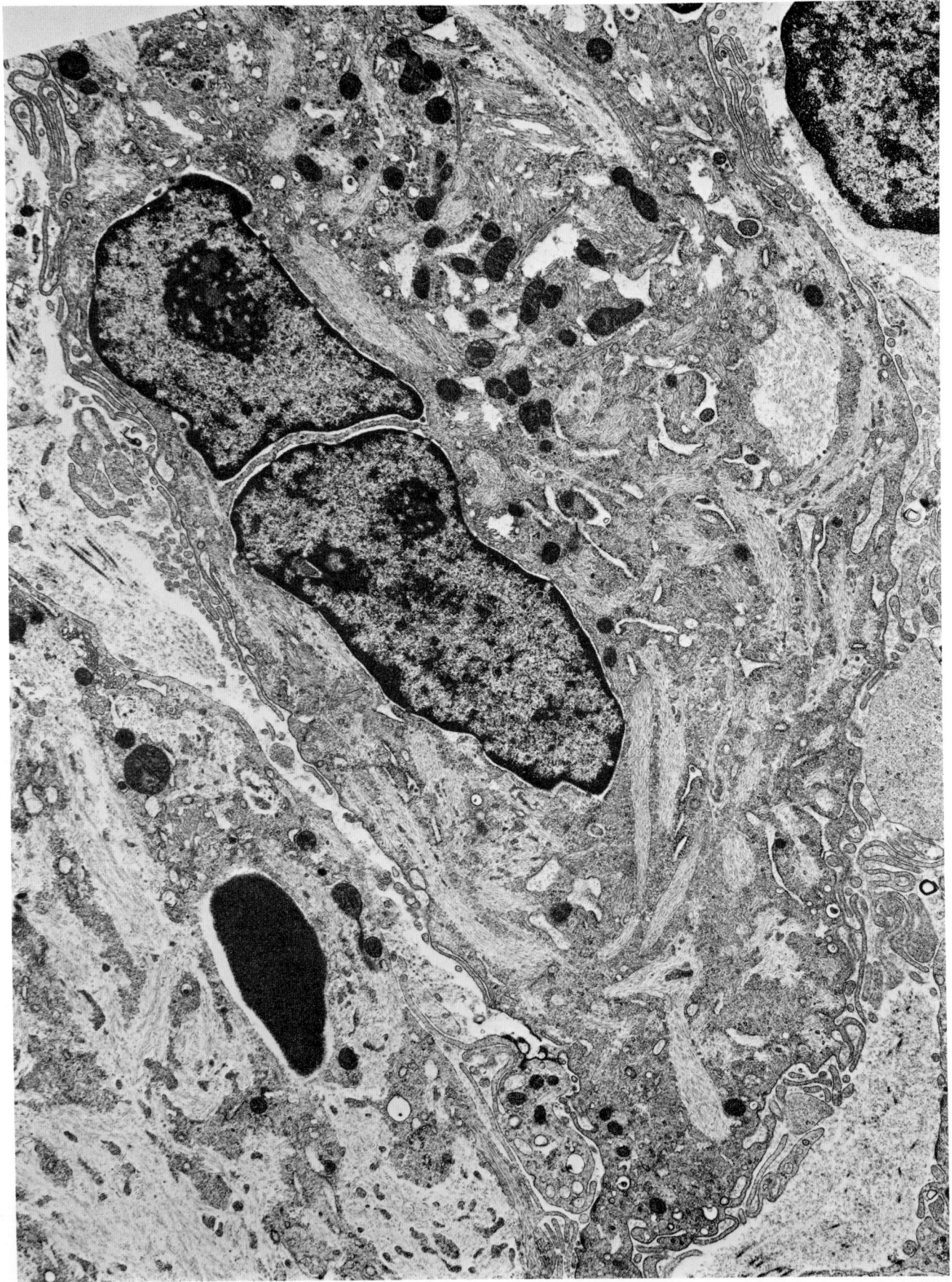

Figure 30.4. Gaucher's disease.

(a) Gaucher's cell in a bone marrow specimen. Numerous linear and crescent shaped areas containing cerebroside are noted. ($\times$ 10,500)

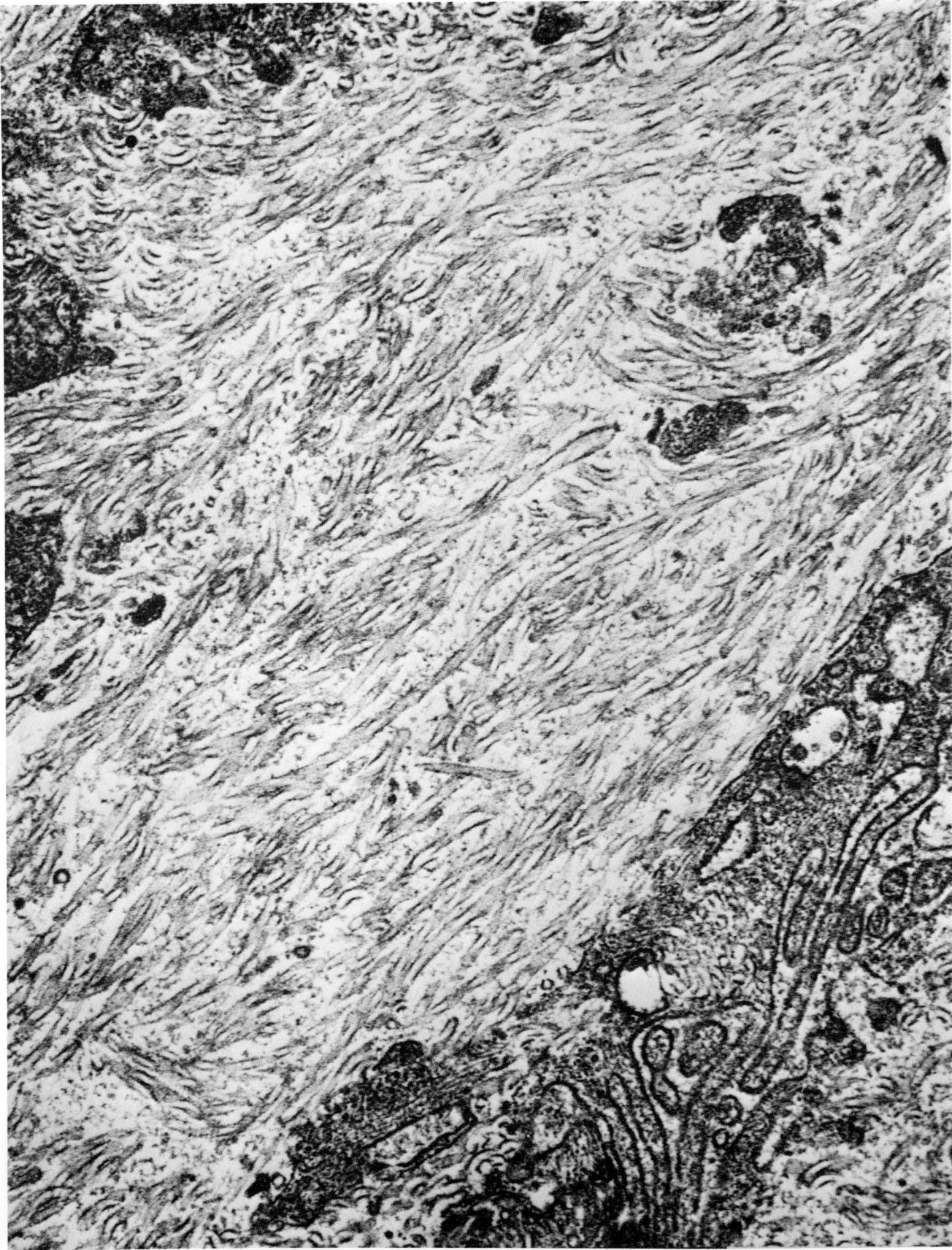

Figure 30.4. Gaucher's disease.

(b) High magnification of a Gaucher's cell showing the intertwining tubules of cerebroside. Erythrophagosomes are present. ($\times 52,000$)

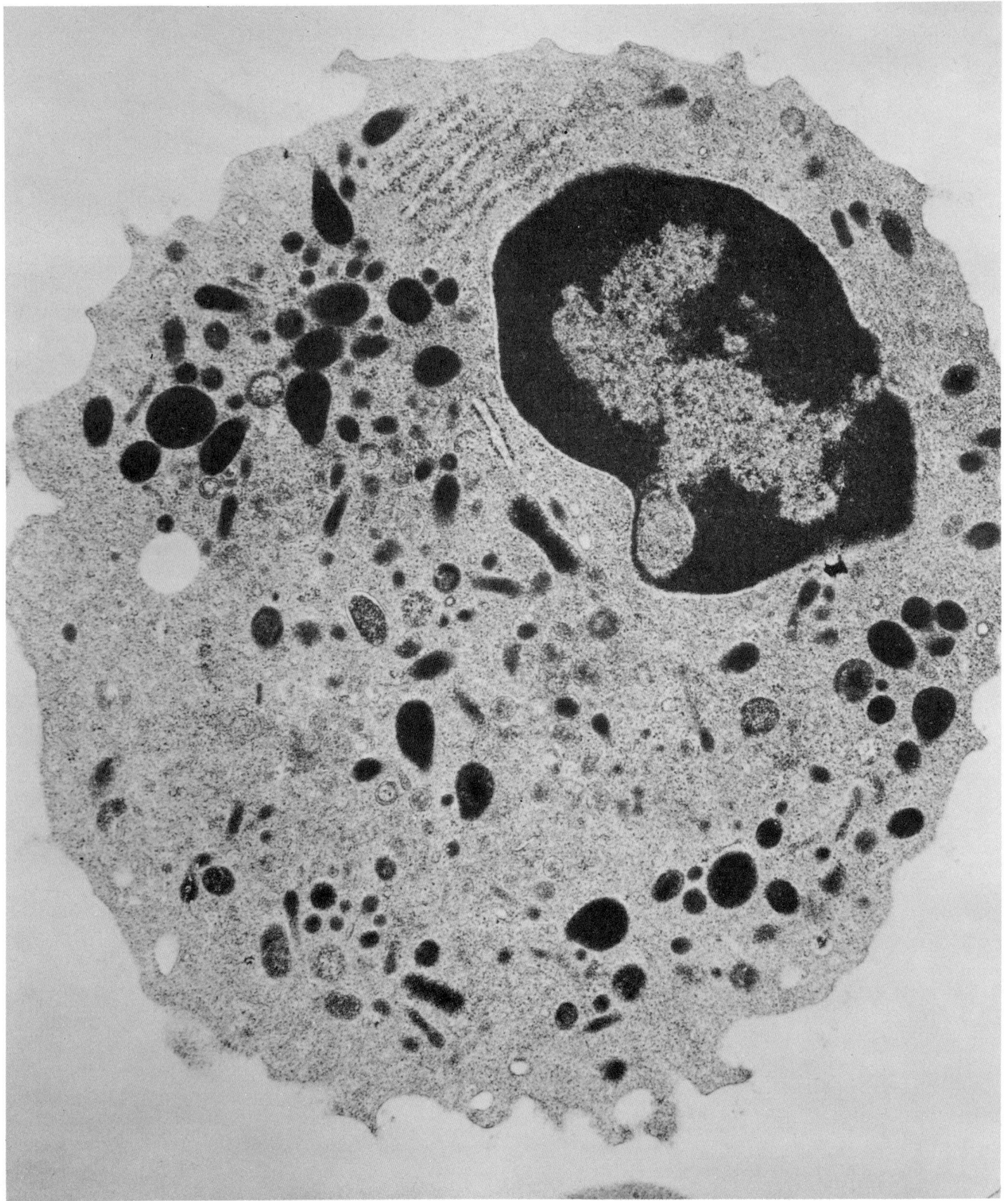

Figure 30.5. Pelger–Huet anomaly (M. Djaldetti, S. Weiss, and U. Gafter).

Peripheral blood neutrophil from a patient with the Pelger–Huet anomaly. The nucleus is uni-lobed. Some of the secondary granules are increased in size. (× 16,600)

These areas have outlines similar in shape to the Döhle bodies seen in light microscopy preparations. These structures may be detected as early as the myelocyte stage of development and may be surrounded by one to five concentric cisternae of either granular or agranular endoplasmic reticulum. In the more mature cells, the inclusions are associated with fewer cisternae of endoplasmic reticulum and in the mature neutrophil there may be only rare associated cisternae of endoplasmic reticulum. The inclusions are composed of arrays of osmiophilic beaded fibers of varying length embedded in a lightly osmiophilic amorphous matrix (Figure 30.6(a)). Scattered throughout this matrix are several polyribosomes. The structures differ from the Döhle bodies in toxic neutrophils; ultrastructurally, the latter inclusions are composed of stacked lamellae of endoplasmic reticulum.[29] Except for their large size (Figure 30.6(b)), the platelets show no significant abnormalities.[168]

30.5. GM₁ gangliosidosis

This is a rapidly progressive disorder characterized by mental and motor retardation and severe bony deformities.[116] There is cerebral and visceral storage of ganglioside GM_1, and mucopolysaccarides. The involvement of the hematopoietic tissue is manifested as vacuolated lymphocytes in the blood and marrow and by foamy macrophages in the bone marrow. On ultrastructural examination, the bone marrow macrophages from these patients contain numerous vacuoles (Figure 30.7) which may be empty or contain several osmiophilic ringlike structures. The vacuoles in the lymphocytes may have a similar appearance.

30.6. Mannosidosis

This systemic lysosomal storage disease is characterized by psychomotor retardation, facial dysmorphia, dysostosis multiplex, hepatosplenomegaly, hearing loss, recurrent infections, and autosomal recessive inheritance.[37] The lymphocytes in the peripheral blood from these patients may contain sharply defined cytoplasmic vacuoles. The bone marrow may contain numerous foamy macrophages which measure approximately 40–50 nm in diameter. On ultrastructural examination, the macrophages in the bone marrow show numerous cytoplasmic vacuoles some of which contain amorphous material. The material when present in the vacuoles is variably osmiophilic.

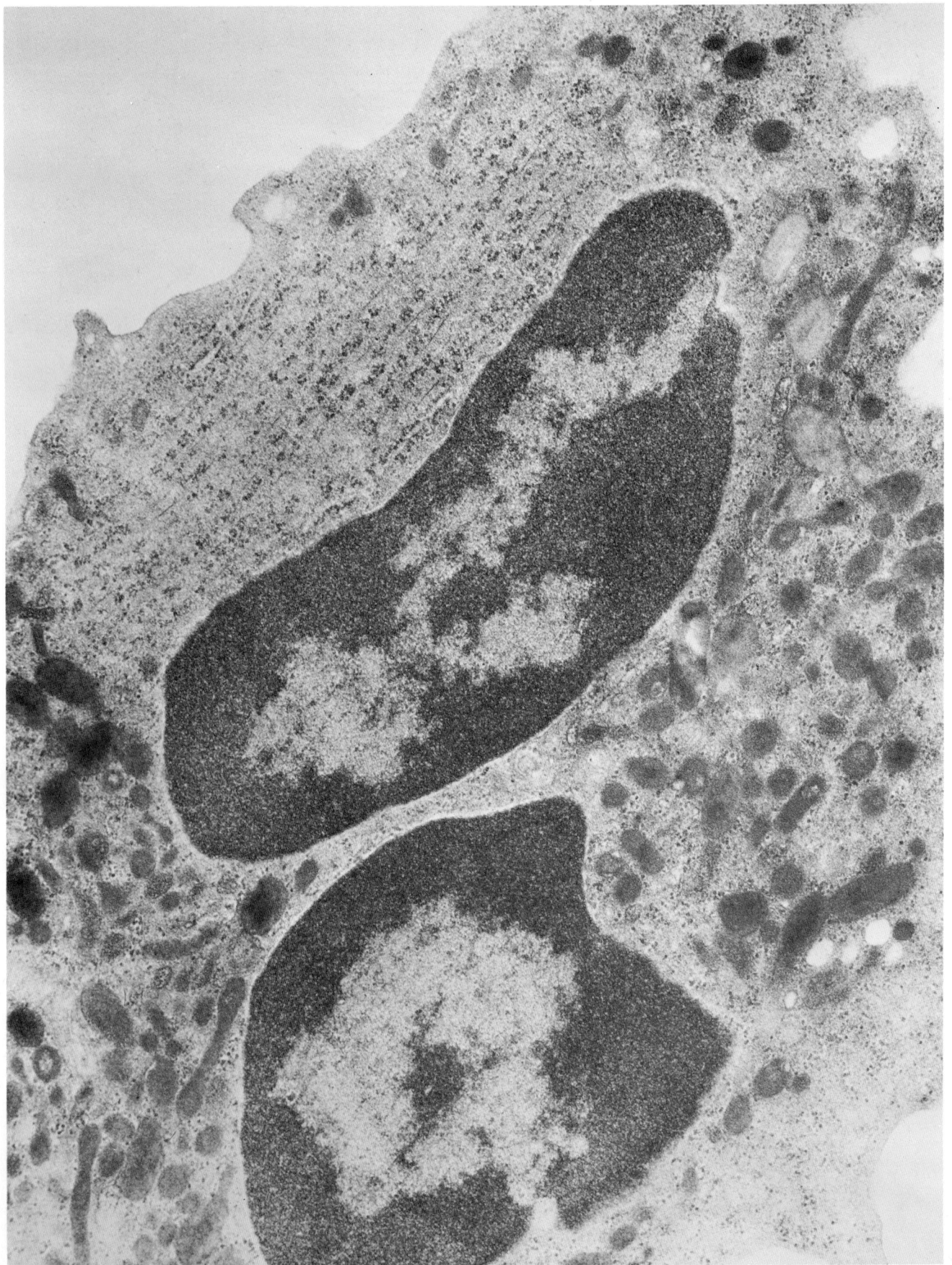

Figure 30.6. May–Hegglin anomaly.

(a) Neutrophil from a patient showing focal areas of the cytoplasm which are devoid of granules. These areas consist of lightly osmiophilic fibers embedded in amorphous material.
Numerous polyribosomes are scattered throughout these areas. ($\times 55,000$)

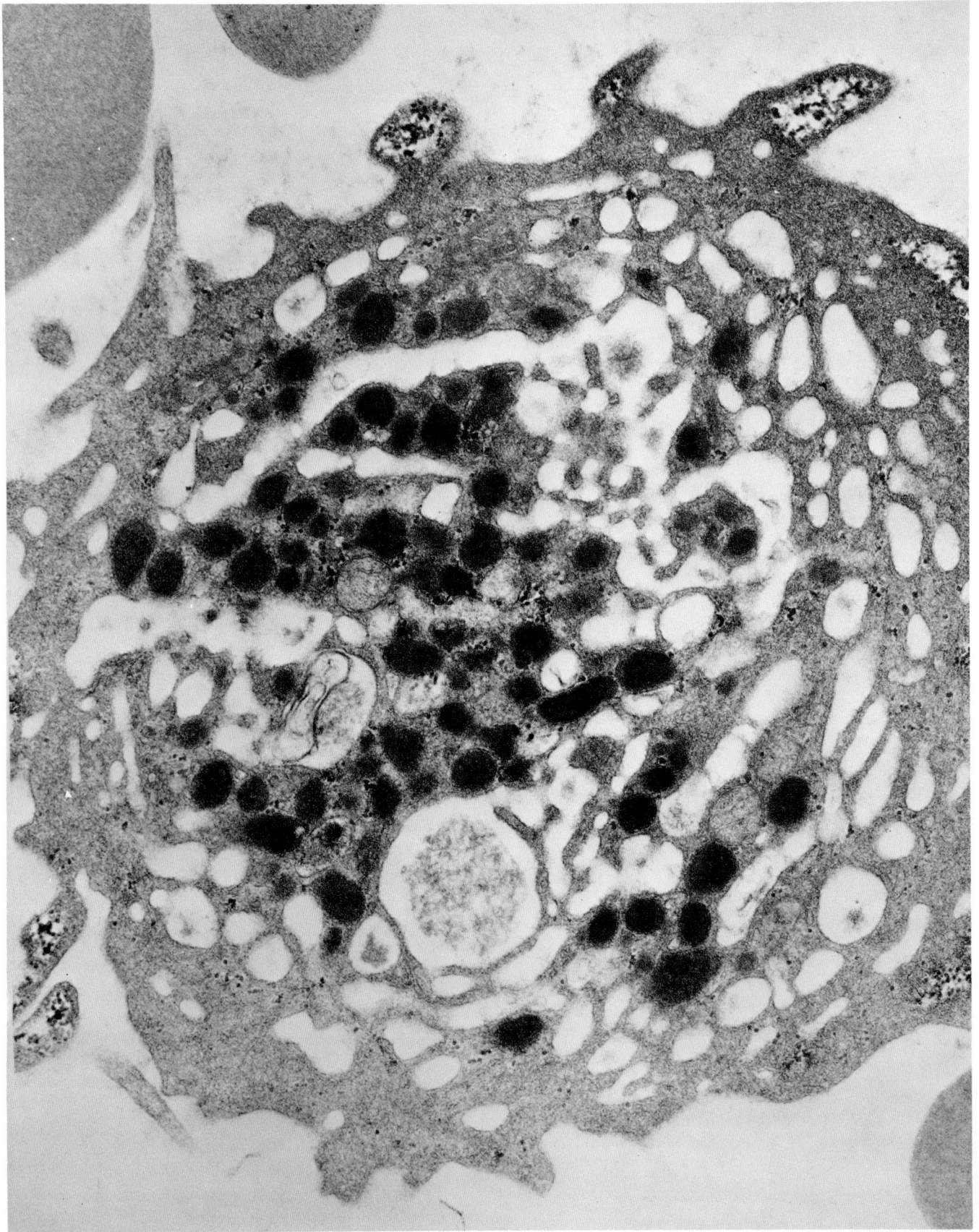

Figure 30.6. May–Hegglin anomaly.

(b) Large platelet. A dilatation of the surface-connected canicular system is visible. (× 30,000)

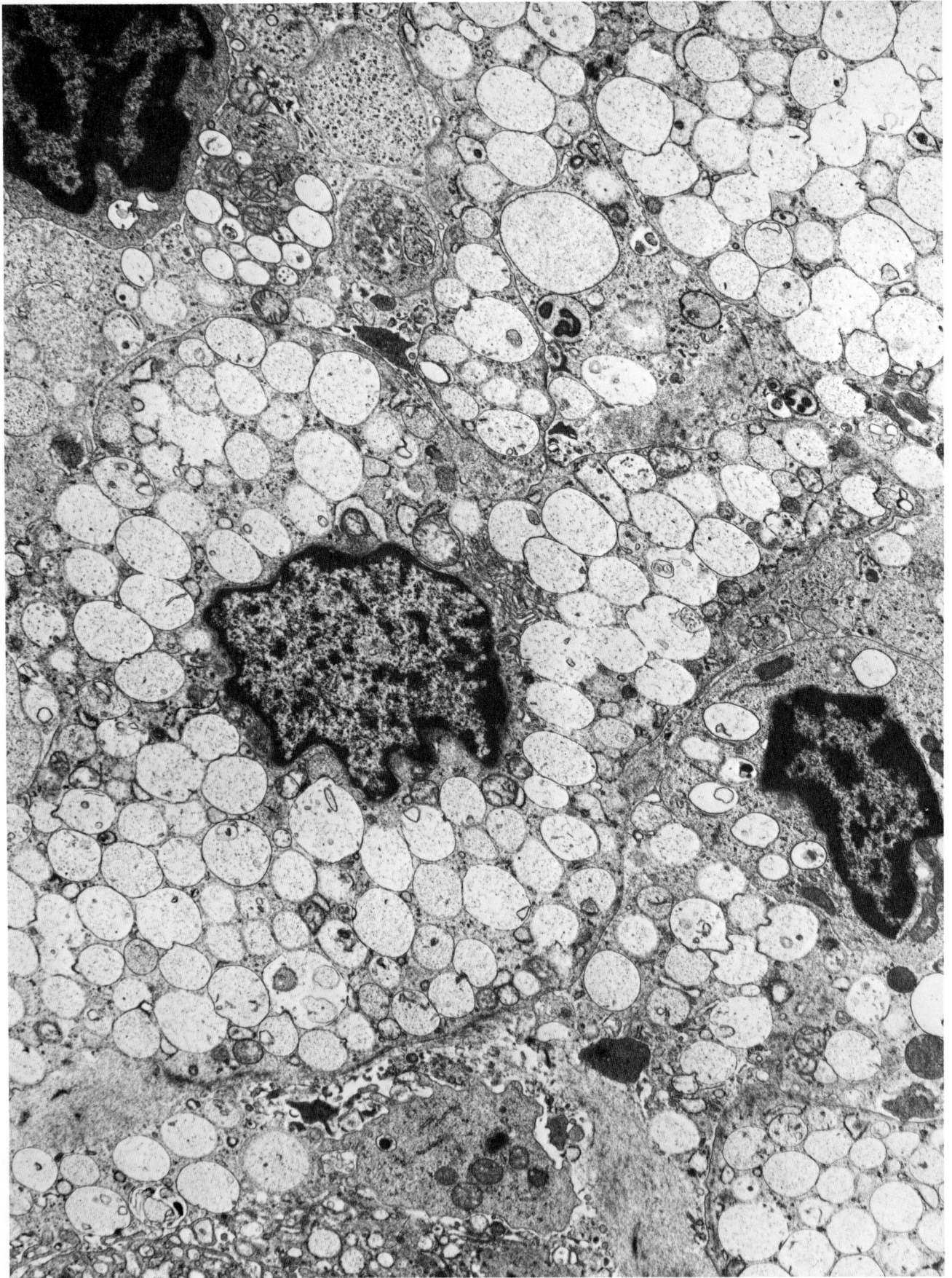

Figure 30.7. GM$_1$ gangliosidosis.
Macrophage from the bone marrow of a patient. The cytoplasm contains numerous vacuoles, some of which possess a slight amount of amorphous material. ($\times$ 11,000)

References to Part Five

1. Achong, B. C. and Epstein, M. A., "Fine structure of the Burkitt tumor," *J. natn. Cancer Inst.*, **36**, 877, 1966.
2. Ackerman, G. A., "Ultrastructural histochemical alteration of the plasma membrane in chronic myelocytic leukemia," *Blood,* **46**, 869, 1975.
3. Bainton, D. F., "Abnormal neutrophils in acute myelogenous leukemia: identification of subpopulations based on analysis of azurophil and specific granules," *Blood Cells*, **1**, 191, 1975.
4. ———, Ullyot, J. L., and Farquhar, M. G., "The development of neutrophilic polymorphonuclear leukocytes in human marrow. Origin and content of azurophil and specific granules," *J. exp. Med.*, **134**, 907, 1971.
5. Bennett, J. M., Catovsky, D., Daniel, M. T., Flandrin, G., Galton, D. A. G., Gralnick, H. R., and Sultan, C., "Proposals for the classification of the acute leukaemias," *Br. J. Haemat.*, **33**, 451, 1976.
6. Benz, E. J., Jr. and Forget, B. G., "The molecular genetics of the thalassemia syndromes" in E. B. Brown (ed.), *Progress in Hematology*, vol. IX, Grune and Stratton, New York, 1975, pp. 107–156.
7. Bernard, J., Lasneret, J., Chome, J., Levy, J. P., and Boiron, M., "A cytological and histological study of acute promyelocytic leukemia," *J. clin. Path.*, **16**, 319, 1963.
8. Bertles, J. F. and Dobler, J., "Reversible and irreversible sickling: a demonstration by electron microscopy," *Blood*, **33**, 884, 1969.
9. Bessis, M. C., "Ultrastructure of normal and leukemia granulocytes," in C. J. D. Zarafonetis (ed.), *Proceedings of the International Conference on Leukemia-Lymphoma*, Lea and Febiger, Philadelphia, 1968, pp. 281–302.
10. ——— and Breton-Gorius, J., "Ferritin and ferruginous micelles in normal erythroblasts and hypochromic hypersidermic anemias," *Blood*, **14**, 423, 1958.
11. ——— and Jensen, W. N., "Sideroblastic anemia, mitochondria and erythroblastic iron," *Br. J. Haemat.*, **11**, 49, 1965.
12. ——— and Thiery, J. P., "Etudes au microscope electonique sur les leucemies humaines. II. Les leucemies lymphocytaires. Comparison avec la leukemie de la Louris de Souche AK," *Nouv. Revue fr. Hémat.*, **2**, 387, 1962.
13. Bloomfield, C. D. and Brunning, R. D., "Prognostic implications of cytology in acute leukemia in the adult," *Human Pathol.*, **5**, 641, 1974.
14. Breton-Gorius, J., Daniel, M. T., Clauvel, J. P., and Dreyfus, B., "Anomalies ultrastructurales des erythroblastes et des erythrocytes dans six cas de dyserythropoiese congenitale," *Nouv. Revue fr. Hémat.*, **13**, 23, 1973.

404

15. ———— and Houssay, D., "Auer bodies in acute promyelocytic leukemia: demonstration of their fine structure and peroxidase localization," *Lab. Invest.* **28**, 135, 1973.
16. Brittin, G. M., Tanaka, Y., and Brecher, G., "Intranuclear inclusions in multiple myeloma and macroglobulinemia," *Blood*, **21**, 335, 1963.
17. Brouet, J., Flandrin, G., Sasportes, M., Preud-Homme, J., and Seligman, M., "Chronic lymphocytic leukemia of T cell origin," *Lancet*, **2**, 890, 1975.
18. ————, Valensi, F., Daniel, M., Flandrin, G., Preud-Homme, J., and Seligman, M., "Immunological classifications of acute lymphoblastic leukemia: evaluation of its clinical significance in a hundred patients," *Br. J. Haemat.*, **33**, 319, 1976.
19. Brunning, R. D., "Morphologic alterations in nucleated blood and marrow cells in genetic disorders," *Human Pathol.*, **1**, 99, 1970.
20. ————, McKenna, R. W., Bloomfield, C. D., Gajl-Peczalska, K. J., and Coccia, P., "Burkitt's lymphoma in the bone marrow," *Cancer*, **40**, 1771, 1977.
21. ————and Parkin, J., "Ultrastructural studies of parallel tubular arrays in human lymphocytes," *Am. J. Path.*, **78**, 59, 1975.
22. ———— and ————, "Ribosome-lamella complexes in neoplastic hematopoietic cells," *Am. J. Path.*, **79**, 565, 1975.
23. ———— and ————, "Intranuclear inclusions in plasma cells and lymphocytes from patients with monoclonal gammopathies," *Am. J. clin. Path.*, **66**, 10, 1976.
24. ————, ————, Dick, F., and Nesbit, M., "Unusual inclusions occurring in the blasts of four patients with acute leukemia and Down's syndrome," *Blood*, **44**, 735, 1974.
25. Catovsky, D., Galetto, J., Okos, A., Milliani, E., and Galton, D. A. G., "Cytochemical profile of B and T leukaemic lymphocytes with special reference to acute lymphoblastic leukaemia," *J. clin. Path.*, **27**, 767, 1974.
26. ————, Pettit, J. E., Galetto, J., Okos, A., and Galton, D. A. G., "The B-lymphocyte nature of the hairy cell of leukemic reticuloendotheliosis," *Br. J. Haemat.*, **26**, 29, 1974.
27. Caulfield, J. B., "Effects of varying the vehicle for OsO4 in tissue fixation," *J. biophys. biochem. Cytol.*, **3**, 827, 1957.
28. Cawley, J. C., "The microtubules of leukemic Rieder cells: an ultrastructural study," *Scand. J. Haematol.*, **9**, 417, 1972.
29. ———— and Hayhoe, F. G. J., "The inclusions of the May-Hegglin anomaly and Dohle bodies of infection: an ultrastructural comparison," *Br. J. Haemat.*, **22**, 491, 1972.
30. Clark, C., Rydell, R., and Kaplan, M., "Frequent associations of IgM λ with crystalline inclusions in CLL lymphocytes," *New Engl. J. Med.*, **289**, 113, 1973.
31. Coccia, P. F., Kersey, J. H., Gajl-Peczalska, K. J., Krivit, W., and Nesbit, M., "Prognostic significance of surface marker analysis in childhood non-Hodgkin's lymphoproliferative malignancies," *Am. J. Hematol*, **1**, 405, 1976.
32. Cohen, H. J. and Lefer, L. G., "Intranuclear inclusions in Bence-Jones lambda plasma cell myeloma," *Blood*, **45**, 131, 1975.
33. Cowan, D. H. and Graham, R. C., Jr., "Structural-functional relationships in platelets in acute leukemia and related disorders," *Ser. Haematol.*, **8**, 68, 1971.
34. Crossen, P. E., Mellor, J. E. L., Finley, A. G., Ravich, R. B. M., Vincent, P. C., and Gunz, F. W., "The Sezary syndrome. Cytogenetic studies and

identification of the Sezary cell as an abnormal lymphocyte," *Am. J. Med.*, **50**, 24, 1971.

35. Daniel, M. Th. and Flandrin, G., "Fine structure of abnormal cells in hairy cell (tricholeukocytic) leukemia with special reference to their in *vitro* phagocytic capacity," *Lab. Invest.*, **30**, 1, 1974.

36. Debusscher, L., Bernheim, J. L., Collard-Ronge, E., Gavaerts, A., Hooghe, R., Lejeune, F. J., Zeicher, M., and Stryckmans, P. A., "Hairy cell leukemia: functional, immunologic, kinetic, and ultrastructural characterization," *Blood*, **46**, 495, 1975.

37. Desnick, R. J., Sharp, H. L., Grabowski, G. A., Brunning, R. D., Quie, P. G., Gorlin, R. J., and Ikonne, J. U., "Mannosidosis; clinical, morphologic, immunologic, and biochemical studies," *Pediat. Res.*, **10**, 985, 1976.

38. Dick, F., Bloomfield, C. D., and Brunning, R. D., "Incidence, cytology, and histopathology of the non-Hodgkin's lymphomas in the bone marrow," *Cancer*, **33**, 1381, 1974.

39. Djaldetti, M., Bessler, H., Mandel, E. M., Weiss, S., Har-Zahav, G., and Fishman, P., "Clinical and ultrastructural observations in primary acquired sideroblastic anemia," *Nouv. Revue fr. Hémat.*, **15**, 637, 1975.

40. ———, Weiss, S., and Gafter, U., "Ultrastructural features of the blood cells in a patient with Pelger–Huet anomaly," *Am. J. clin. Path.*, **65**, 942, 1976.

41. Dobler, J. and Bertles, J. F., "The physical state of hemoglobin in sickle-cell anemia erythrocytes *in vivo*," *J. exp. Med.*, **127**, 711, 1968.

42. Douglas, S. D., Blume, R. S., and Wolff, S. M., "Fine structural studies of leukocytes from patients and heterozygotes with the Chediak-Higashi syndrome," *Blood*, **33**, 527, 1969.

43. ———, Fudenberg, H. H., Glade, P. R., Chessin, L. N., and Moses, H. L., "Fine structure of leukocytes in infectious mononucleosis: in *vivo* and in *vitro* studies," *Blood*, **34**, 42, 1969.

44. Downey, H., "Diseases of the blood," in E. T. Bell (ed.), *Textbook of Pathology*, Lea and Febiger, Philadelphia, 1938, p. 840.

45. ——— and McKinlay, C. A., "Acute lymphadenosis compared with acute lymphatic leukemia," *Arch. intern. Med.*, **32**, 82, 1923.

46. Dutcher, T. F. and Fahey, J. L., "The histopathology of the macroglobulinemia of Waldenstrom," *J. natn. Cancer Inst.*, **22**, 88, 1959.

47. Frangione, B. and Franklin, E. C., "Heavy chain disease: Clinical features and molecular significance of the disordered immunoglobulin structure," *Ser. Haematol.*, **10**, 53, 1973.

48. Frederickson, D. S. and Sloan, H., "Glucosyl ceramide lipidoses: Gaucher's disease" in J. B. Stanbury, J. B. Wyngaarden, and D. S. Frederickson, (eds.), *The Metabolic Basis of Inherited Disease*, McGraw-Hill, New York, 1972, pp. 730–759.

49. Freeman, A. I. and Journey, L. J., "Ultrastructural studies on monocytic leukemia," *Br. J. Haemat.*, **20**, 225, 1971.

50. Freeman, J. A., "The ultrastructure and genesis of Auer bodies," *Blood*, **15**, 449, 1959.

51. ———, "Origins of Auer bodies in human leukemias," *J. Cell. Biol.*, **27**, 29A, 1965.

52. Frisch, B., Lewis, S.M., Sherman, D., White, J. M., and Gordon-Smith, E. C., "The ultrastructure of erythropoiesis in two hemoglobinopathies," *Br. J. Haemat.*, **28**, 109, 1974.

53. Fukuski, K., Nakasato, N., Narita, N., and Yoshida, K., "Electron microscopic study of the Auer body," *Acta. Path. jap.*, **22**, 509, 1972.

54. Galton, D. A. G., Goldman, J. M., Wiltshaw, E., Catovsky, D., Henry, K., and Goldenberg, G. J., "Prolymphocytic leukemia," *Br. J. Haemat.*, **27**, 7, 1974.

55. Glick, A. D., "Acute leukemia: electron microscopic diagnosis," *Semin. Oncol.*, **3**, 229, 1976.

56. —— and Horn, R. G., "Identification of promonocytes and monocytoid precursors in acute leukemia of adults: ultrastructural and cytochemical observations," *Br. J. Haemat.*, **26**, 395, 1974.

57. Golde, D.W., Stevens, R. H., Quan, S. G., and Saxon, G., "Immunoglobulin synthesis in hairy cell leukemia," *Br. J. Haemat.*, **35**, 359, 1977.

58. Graham, R. C., Jr. and Bernier, G. B., "The bone marrow in multiple myeloma: correlation of plasma cell ultrastructure and clinical state," *Medicine*, **54**, 225, 1975.

59. Gralnick, H. and Tan, H. K., "Acute promyelocytic leukemia. A model for understanding the role of the malignant cell in hemostasis," *Human Pathol.*, **5**, 661, 1974.

60. Grasso, J. A., Sullivan, A. L., and Sullivan, L. W., "Ultrastructural studies of the bone marrow in sickle cell anemia. II. The morphology of erythropoietic cells and their response to deoxygenesis in vitro," *Br. J. Haemat.*, **31**, 381, 1975.

61. Greaves, M. F., "Clinical applications of cell surface markers," in E. Brown (ed.), *Progress in Hematology*, Vol. IX, Grune and Stratton, New York, 1975, p. 255.

62. Grimley, P. M. and Schaff, Z., "Significance of tubuloreticular inclusions in the pathobiology of human disease," in H. I. Ioachim (ed.), *1976 Pathobiology Annual*, vol. 6, Appleton-Century-Crofts, New York, 1976, p. 221.

63. Hattori, A., Koike, K., Ito, S., and Matsuoka, M., "Static and functional morphology of the pathological platelets in primary myelofibrosis and myeloproliferative syndrome," *Ser. Haematol.*, **8**, 126, 1971.

64. Hayhoe, F. G. J. and Cawley, J. C., "Acute leukemia: cellular morphology, cytochemistry, and fine structure," *Clin. Haematol.*, **1**, 49, 1972.

65. Hug, G. W., Wong, K. Y., and Lampkin, B. C., "Congenital dyserythropoietic anemia type II: ultrastructure of erythroid cells and hepatocytes," *Lab. Invest.*, **26**, 11, 1972.

66. Huhn, D., "Neue Organelle in peripheren Lymphozyten?," *Dt. med. Wschr.*, **93**, 2099, 1968.

67. Ito, S., Goshima, K., Niinomi, M., Horikoshi, N., Nomura, S., Sugiura, K., and Yamazaki, K., "Electron microscopic studies of the crystalline inclusions in the myeloma cells and kidney of K-Bence Jones protein type myeloma," *Acta. Haemat. jap.*, **33**, 598, 1970.

68. —— and Hattori, A., "Study on the fibrillar formation surrounding the nuclear bridge in some types of leukemia cells,' *Scand. J. Haematol.*, **12**, 321, 1974.

69. Jaffe, E. S., Shevach, E. M., Frank, M. M., and Green, I., "Leukemic reticuloendotheliosis: presence of a receptor for cytophilic antibody," *Am. J. Med.*, **57**, 108, 1974.

70. Jenis, E. H., Takeuchi, A., Dillon, D. E., Ruymann, F. B., and Rivkin, J., "The May-Hegglin anomaly: ultrastructure of the granulocyte inclusion," *Am. J. clin. Path.*, **55**, 187, 1970.

71. Jordan S. W. and Larsen, W. B., "Ultrastructural studies of the May-Hegglin anomaly," *Blood*, **25**, 921, 1965.

72. Kamiyama, R., "An electron microscopic study of erythroleukemia, with special reference to the structure of erythroblasts," *Acta Path. jap.*, **21**, 231, 1971.

73. Karnovsky, M. J., "A formaldehyde glutaraldehyde fixative of high osmolality for use in electron microscopy," *J. Cell Biol.*, **27**, 137A, 1965.

74. Kass, L. and Schnitzer, B., *Refractory Anemia*, Thomas, Springfield, Illinois, 1972.

75. Katayama, I., Li, C. Y., and Yam, L. T., "Ultrastructural characteristics of the 'hairy cells' of leukemic reticuloendotheliosis," *Am. J. Path.*, **67**, 361, 1972.

76. —— and Schneider, G. B., "Further ultrastructural characterization of hairy cells of leukemic reticuloendotheliosis," *Am. J. Path.*, **86**, 163, 1977.

77. Kerkhoven, P., Marti, H. R., and Hug, G., "Electron-microscopic and biochemical observations on erythroid cells in congenital dyserythropoietic anemia type II," *Virchows Arch Path. Anat.*, **363**, 1, 1974.

78. Kondo, K., Yoshitake, J., and Takemura, K., "The fine structure of Auer bodies," *J. Electron Microsc.*, **15**, 237, 1966.

79. Krishan, A., Uzman, B. G., and Hedley-Whyte, E. T., "Nuclear bodies: A component of cell nuclei in hamster tissues and human tumors," *J. Ultrastruct. Res.*, **19**, 563, 1967.

80. Kushner, J. P., Lee, G. R., Wintrobe, M. M., and Cartwright, G., "Idiopathic refractory sideroblastic anemia. Clinical and laboratory investigation of 17 patients and review of the literature," *Medicine*, **50**, 139, 1971.

81. Lagerlof, B. and Franzen, S., "The ultrastructure of megakaryocytes in polycythemia vera and chronic granulocytic leukaemia," *Acta. path. microbiol. scand. A*, **80**, 71, 1972.

82. Leder, L. D., "The origin of blood monocytes and macrophages," *Haematol. Blutransfus.*, **16**, 86, 1967.

83. Levine, P. H. and Katayama, I., "The platelet in leukemic reticulo-endotheliosis. Functional and morphological evidence of a qualitative disorder," *Cancer*, **36**, 1353, 1975.

84. Lewis, S. M. and Frisch, B., "Congenital dyserythropoietic anaemias," *Electron microscopy in congenital disorders of erythropoiesis*, Ciba Foundation Symposium, 37 (new series): **171**, 1976.

85. —— and Verwilghen, R. L., "Dyserythropoiesis and dyserythropoietic anemias," in E. B. Brown (ed.), *Progress in Hematology*, vol. VIII, Grune and Stratton, New York, 1973, pp. 99–129.

86. Li, C. Y., Lam, K. W., and Yam, L. T., "Esterases in human leukocytes," *J. Histochem. Cytochem.*, **21**, 1, 1973.

87. LoBuglio, A., "Leukemic reticuloendotheliosis. A defined syndrome of an ill-defined cell," *New Engl. J. Med.*, **295**, 219, 1976.

88. Lutzer, M. A., Emerit, I., Durepaire, R., Flandrin, G., Grupper, Ch., and Prunieras, M., "Cytogenetic, cytophotometric, and ultrastructural study of large cerebriform cells of the Sezary syndrome and description of a small-cell variant," *J. natn. Cancer Inst.*, **50**, 1145, 1973.

89. ———— and Jordan, H. W., "The ultrastructure of an abnormal cell in Sezary's syndrome," *Blood*, **31**, 719, 1968.

90. McCall, C. E., Katayama, I., Cotran, R. S., and Finland, M., "Lysosomal and ultrastructural changes in human toxic neutrophils during bacterial infection," *J. exp. Med.*, **129**, 267, 1969.

91. McDuffie, N. G., "Nuclear blebs in human leukemic cells," *Nature, Lond.*, **214**, 341, 1967.

92. McKenna, R. W., Bloomfield, C. D., and Brunning, R. D., "Nodular lymphoma: bone marrow and blood manifestations," *Cancer*, **36**, 428, 1975.

93. ————, ————, Dick, F., Nesbit, M. E., and Brunning, R. D., "Acute monoblastic leukemia: diagnosis and treatment of ten cases," *Blood*, **46**, 481, 1975.

94. ————, Parkin, J., Gajl-Peczalska, K. J., Kersey, J. H., and Brunning, R. D., "Ultrastructure, cytochemical and membrane surface marker characteristics of the atypical lymphocytes in infectious mononucleosis," *Blood*, **50**, 505, 1977.

95. ————, ————, Kersey, J. H., Gajl-Peczalska, K. J., Peterson, L., and Brunning, R. D., "Chronic lymphoproliferative disorder with unusual clinical, morphologic, ultrastructural and membrane surface marker characteristics," *Am. J. Med.*, **62**, 588, 1977.

96. Maldonado, J. E., "Dysplastic platelets and circulating megakaryocytes in chronic myeloproliferative diseases. II. Ultrastructure of circulating megakaryocytes," *Blood*, **43**, 811, 1974.

97. ————, "The ultrastructure of the platelets in refractory anemia ('preleukemia') and myelomonocytic leukemia," *Ser. Haematol.*, **8**, 101, 1975.

98. ————, Bayrd, E. D., and Brown, A. L., "The flaming cell in multiple myeloma," *Am. J. clin. Path.*, **44**, 605, 1965.

99. ————, Brown, A. L., Bayrd, E. D., and Pease, G. L., "Cytoplasmic and intranuclear electron-dense bodies in the myeloma cell," *Archs Path.*, **81**, 484, 1966.

100. ————, ————, ————, and ————, "Ultrastructure of the myeloma cell," *Cancer*, **19**, 1613, 1966.

101. ————, Kyle, R. A., Brown, A. L., and Bayrd, E. D., "'Intermediate' cell types and mixed cell proliferation in multiple myeloma: electron microscopic observations," *Blood*, **27**, 212, 1966.

102. ————, Maigne, J., and Lecoq, D., "Comparative electronmicroscopic study of the erythrocytic line in refractory anemia (preleukemia) and myelomonocytic leukemia," *Blood Cells*, **2**, 167, 1976.

103. ———— and Mandon, P., "The erythrocytic line in refractory anemia and myelomonocytic leukemia. II. Some unusual morphologic variants of the polychromatic normoblasts and reticulocytes," *Nouv. Revue fr. Hémat.*, **16**, 329, 1976.

104. —— and Pintado, T., "Ultrastructure of the megakaryocytes in refractive anemia and myelomonocytic leukemia," in M. G. Baldini and S. Ebbe (eds.), *Platelet Production, Function, Transfusion, and Storage*, Grune and Stratton, New York, 1974, pp. 105–114.

105. ——, ——, and Pierre, R. V., "Dysplastic platelets and circulating megakaryocytes in chronic myeloproliferative diseases. I. The platelet: ultrastructure and peroxidase reaction," *Blood*, **43**, 797, 1974.

106. —— and Taswell, H., "Type I dyserythropoietic anemia in an elderly patient," *Blood*, **44**, 495, 1974.

107. ——, Velosa, J. A., Kyle, R. A., Wagoner, R. D., Holley, K. E., and Salassa, R. M., "Fanconi syndrome in adults. A manifestation of a latent form of myeloma," *Am. J. Med.*, **58**, 354, 1975.

108. Masakatsu, I., Block, S. R., and Mellors, R. C., "Electron microscopic study of distinctive structures in peripheral blood lymphocytes obtained from twins with systemic lupus erythematous," *Am. J. Path.*, **81**, 561, 1975.

109. Mathe, G., Pouillart, P., Weiner, R., Hayat, M., Steresco, M., and Lafleur, M., "Classification and subsclassification of acute leukemia correlated with clinical expression, therapeutic sensitivity and prognosis," in G. Mathe, P. Pouillart, and O. Schwarzenberg (eds.), *Nomenclature, Methodology and Results of Clinical Trials in Acute Leukemias: Recent Results in Cancer Research*, vol. 43, New York, Springer-Verlag, 1973, pp. 6–20.

110. Matsuoka, M., Hattori, A., Mizushina, T., and Jimbo, C., "The ultrastructure of the cryofibrinogen in acute promyelocytic leukemia displaying the defibrination syndrome and fibriller inclusions in promyelocyte," *Acta Med. Biol.*, **17**, 49, 1969.

111. Mollin, D. L., "Sideroblasts and sideroblastic anaemia," *Br. J. Haemat.*, **11**, 41, 1965.

112. Nelson, D. A., "Cytomorphological diagnosis of the acute leukemias," *Semin. Oncol.*, **3**, 201, 1976.

113. Nicholls, B. A. and Bainton, D. F., "Differentiation of human monocytes in bone marrow and blood: sequential formation of two granule populations," *Lab. Invest.*, **29**, 27, 1973.

114. ——, ——, and Farquhar, M. G., "Differentiation of monocytes. Origin, nature, and fate of their azurophil granules," *J. Cell Biol.*, **50**, 498, 1971.

115. Norberg, B., "Cytoplasmic microtubules and radial-segmented nuclei (Rieder cells): ultrastructural studies," *Scand. J. Haematol.*, **7**, 445, 1970.

116. O'Brien, J., "GM_1 gangliosidosis," in J. B. Stanbury, J. B. Wyngaarden, and D. S. Fredrickson (eds.), *The Metabolic Basis of Inherited Disease*, McGraw-Hill, New York, 1972, pp. 639–667.

117. Ogawa, T., "Electron microscopic observation of leukemic cells in six cases of so-called acute promyelocytic leukemia," *J. Electron Microsc.* **17**, 260, 1968.

118. ——, "An electron microscopic study of acute promelocytic cells," *Keio J. Med.*, **18**, 163, 1969.

119. Osserman, E. F. and Fahey, J. L., "Plasma cell dyscrasias," *Am. J. Med.*, **44**, 256, 1968.

120. Palakavong, P., Teichberg, S., Vinciguerra, V., Degnan, T. J., and

Sinlaratana, P., "Ultrastructural cytochemical analysis of blastic transformation of chronic myelocytic leukemia," *Blood*, **49**, 535, 1977.

121. Paraskevas, F., Heremans, J., and Waldenstrom, J. G., "Cytology and electrophoretic pattern in γAI(B₂A) myeloma," *Acta med. scand.*, **170**, 575, 1961.

122. Pennelli, N., Scaravilli, F., and Zacchello, F., "The morphology of Gaucher cells investigated by electron microscopy," *Blood*, **34**, 331, 1969.

123. Peterson, L. C., Bloomfield, C. D., and Brunning, R. D., "Blast crisis as an initial or terminal manifestation of chronic myeloid leukemia," *Am. J. Med.*, **60**, 209, 1976.

124. ———, ———, Sundberg, R. D., Gajl-Peczalska, K. J., and Brunning, R. D., "Morphology of chronic lymphocytic leukemia and its relationship to survival," *Am. J. Med.*, **59**, 315, 1975.

125. Petz, L. D., Goodman, J. R., Hall, S. G., and Fink, D. J., "Refractory normoblastic (sideroblastic) anemia. Clinical and electron microscopic observations," *Am. J. clin. Path.*, **45**, 581, 1966.

126. Polliack, A., Djaldetti, M., Reyes, F., Biberfeld, P., Daniel, M. T., and Flandrin, G., "Surface features of Sezary cells: a scanning electron microscopy study of 5 cases," *Scand. J. Haematol.*, **18**, 207, 1971.

127. ——— and Rachmilewitz, E. A., "Ultrastructural studies on B-thalassemia major," *Br. J. Haemat.*, **24**, 319, 1973.

128. ———, Yataganas, X., Thorell, B., and Rachmilewitz, E. A., "An electron microscopic study of the nuclear abnormalities in erythroblasts in beta-thalassemia major," *Br. J. Haemat.*, **26**, 201, 1974.

129. Popoff, N. A. and Malinin, T. I., "Cytoplasmic tubular arrays in cells of American Burkitt's type lymphoma," *Cancer*, **37**, 275, 1976.

130. Repine, J. E., Clawson, C. C., and Brunning, R. D., "Abnormal pattern of bactericidal activity of neutrophils deficient in granules, myeloperoxidase and alkaline phosphatase," *J. Lab. clin. Med.*, **88**, 788, 1976.

131. Rosas-Uribe, A., Variakojis, D., Molnar, Z., and Rappaport, H., "Mycosis fungoides: An ultrastructural study," *Cancer*, **34**, 634, 1974.

132. Rowley, J. D., "Evidence for a new consistent chromosomal abnormality in chronic myelogenous leukemia identified by quinacrine fluorescence and Giemsa staining," *Nature, Lond.*, **24**, 240, 1973.

133. Saarni, M. T. and Linman, J. W., "Myelomonocytic leukemia: disorderly proliferation of all marrow cells," *Cancer*, **27**, 1221, 1971.

134. Schaff, L., Heine, J., and Dalton, D. J., "Ultramorphological and ultracytochemical studies on tuboreticular structures in lymphoid cells," *Cancer Res.*, **32**, 2696, 1972.

135. Schnitzer, B., Loesel, L. S., and Reed, R. E., "Lymphosarcoma cell leukemia," *Cancer*, **26**, 1082, 1970.

136. Schrek, R. and Donnelly, W. J., "'Hairy' cells in blood in lymphoreticular neoplastic disease and 'flagellated' cells in normal lymph nodes," *Blood*, **27**, 199, 1966.

137. Schumacher, H. R., Szekely, I. E., and Park, S. A., "Monoblasts of acute monoblastic leukemia," *Cancer*, **31**, 209, 1973.

138. ———, ———, ———, Rao, O. N. M., Fisher, D. R., and Patel, S. B., "Acute

leukemic cells. Qualitative and quantitative electron microscopy," *Am. J. Path.*, **73**, 27, 1973.

139. Scott, R. B., Ellison, R. R., and Ley, A. B., "A clinical study of twenty cases of erythroleukemia (di Guglielmo's syndrome)," *Am. J. Med.*, **37**, 162, 1964.

140. Seip, M., Skrede, S., Bjerve, K. S., Hovig, T., and Gaarder, P. I., "Congenital dyserythropoietic anemia with features of both type I and type II," *Scand. J. Haematol.*, **15**, 272, 1975.

141. Sen, L. and Borella, L., "Clinical importance of lymphoblasts with T markers in childhood acute leukemia," *New Engl. J. Med.*, **292**, 828, 1975.

142. Shaw, M. T. and Nordquist, R. D., "'Pure' monocytic or histiomonocytic leukemia: a revised concept," *Cancer*, **35**, 208, 1975.

143. Sheldon, P. J., Hemsted, E. H., Papanichail, M., and Holborow, E. J., "Thymic origin of atypical lymphoid cells in infectious mononucleosis," *Lancet*, **1**, 1153, 1973.

144. Smith, B. W., Ablin, A., Goodman, J. R., and Brecher, G., "Atypical megakaryocytes in preleukemic phase of acute myeloid leukemia," *Blood*, **42**, 535, 1973.

145. Sorenson, G. D., "Electron microscopic observations of bone marrow from patients with multiple myeloma," *Lab. Invest.*, **13**, 3, 1964.

146. Stavem, P., Vandvik, B., Skrede, S., and Hovig, T., "Needle like crystals in plasma cells in a patient with a plasma cell proliferative disorder," *Scand. J. Haematol.*, **14**, 24, 1975.

147. Stenstam, M., von Mecklenburg, C., and Norberg, B., "The ultrastructure of spontaneous radial segmentation of the nuclei in bone marrow cells from 3 patients with acute myeloid leukemia," *Scand. J. Haematol.*, **15**, 63, 1971.

148. Sun, C. N., Bryne, G., and Pinkerton, H., "Acute lymphoblastic leukemia: virus like particles in lymphatic cell inclusions from bone marrow and peripheral blood," *Exp. Path.*, **6**, 72, 1972.

149. Sundberg, R. D., "Myeloid metaplasia," in H. Klein (ed.), *Polycythemia*, Thomas, Springfield, Illinois, 1973, pp. 112–180.

150. Suzuki, I., Takahaski, M., and Itoh, S., "Ultrastructural study of human myeloma cells in relation to its function," *J. clin. Path.*, **23**, 339, 1970.

151. Tanaka, Y., Brecher, G., and Bull, B., "Ferritin localization on the erythroblast cell membrane and ropheocytosis in hypersiderotic human bone marrows," *Blood*, **28**, 758, 1966.

152. —— and Goodman, J. R., *Electron Microscopy of Blood Cells*, Harper and Row, New York, 1972, p. 59.

153. Taswell, H. F. and Winkelman, R. K., "Sezary syndrome. A malignant reticulemic erythroderma," *J. am. Med. Ass.*, **177**: 465, 1961.

154. Ullyot, J. L. and Bainton, D. F., "Azurophil and specific granules of blood neutrophils in chronic myelogeous leukemia: an ultrastructural and cytochemical analysis," *Blood*, **44**, 469, 1974.

155. Van Furth, F., "Origin and kinetics of monocytes and macrophages," *Ser. Haematol.*, **7**, 125, 1970.

156. Van Slyck, E. J. and Rebuck, J. W., "Pseudo-Chediak-Higashi anomaly in acute leukemia. A significant morphologic corollary?," *Am. J. clin. Path.*, **62**, 673, 1974.

157. Variakojis, D., Rosas-Uribe, A., and Rappaport, H., "Mycosis fungoides: pathologic findings in staging laparotomies," *Cancer*, **33**, 1589, 1974.
158. Waldenstrom, J. G., "Macroglobulinemia," *Adv. Metab. Disord.*, **2**, 115, 1965.
159. Weiss, S., Gafter, U., Van Der Lyn, E., and Djaldetti, M., "Congenital dyserythropoietic anaemia with peculiar nuclear abnormality," *Scand. J. Haematol.*, **15**, 261, 1975.
160. White, J. G., "The Chediak–Higashi syndrome. A possible lysosomal disease," *Blood*, **28**, 143, 1967.
161. ———, "The Chediak–Higashi syndrome: cytoplasmic sequestration in circulating leukocytes," *Blood*, **29**, 435, 1967.
162. ——— "Fine structural demonstration of acid phosphatase activity in Auer bodies," *Blood*, **29**, 667, 1967.
163. ———, "The fine structure of sickled hemoglobin *in situ*," *Blood*, **31**, 561, 1968.
164. ———, "Observations on the mechanism of erythrocyte sickling," *Pediat. Res.*, **3**, 220, 1969.
165. ———, "Giant organelles containing tubules in Chediak–Higashi lymphocytes," *Am. J. Path.*, **69**, 225, 1972.
166. ———, "The Chediak–Higashi syndrome. Fine structure of giant inclusions in freeze-fractured neutrophils," *Am. J. Path.*, **72**, 503, 1973.
167. ———, "Ultrastructural features of erythrocyte and hemoglobin sickling," *Arch. intern. Med.*, **133**, 545, 1974.
168. ——— and Gerrard, J. M., "Ultrastructural features of abnormal blood platelets," *Am. J. Path.*, **83**, 590, 1976.
169. ——— and Heagan, B., "The fine structure of cell-free sickled hemoglobin," *Am. J. Path.*, **58**, 1, 1970.
170. Wickramasinghie, S. N. and Bush, V. "Electron microscope and high resolution autoradiographic studies of megaloblastic erythropoiesis," *Acta Haemat.*, **57**, 1, 1977.
171. Yam, L. T., Li, C. Y., and Lam, K. W., "Tartrate-resistant acid phosphatase isoenzyme in the reticulum cells of leukemic reticulendotheliosis," *New Engl. J. Med.*, **284**, 357, 1971.
172. Zacharaski, L. R. and Linman, J. W., "Chronic lymphocytic leukemia versus chronic lymphosarcoma cell leukemia: Analysis of 496 cases," *Am. J. Med.*, **47**, 75, 1969.
173. Zucker-Franklin, D. and Franklin, E. C., "Ultrastructural and immuno-fluorescence studies of the cells associated with μ-chain disease," *Blood*, **37**, 257, 1971.
174. ———, Melton, J. W., and Quagliata, F., "Ultrastructural, immunologic, and functional studies on Sezary's cells: A neoplastic variant of thymus-derived (T) lymphocytes," *Proc. natn. Acad. Sci., U.S.A.*, **71**, 1877, 1974.

General references

Electron microscopy of blood cells

Bessis, M., *Living Blood Cells and Their Ultrastructure*, Springer-Verlag, New York, 1973.

413

Cawley, J. C. and Hayhoe, F. G. J., *Ultrastructure of Haemic Cells*, Saunders, Philadelphia, 1973.

Tanaka, Y. and Goodman, J. R., *Electron Microscopy of Human Blood Cells*, Harper and Row, New York, 1972.

Laboratory and clinical hematology

Miale, J. B., *Laboratory Medicine: Hematology*, Mosby, St. Louis, 1972.

Williams, W. J., Beutler, E., Erslev, A. J., and Rundles, R. W., *Hematology*, McGraw-Hill, New York, 1972.

Wintrobe, M. M., Lee, G. R., Boggs, D. R., Bithell, T. C., Athens, J. W., and Foerster, J., *Clinical Hematology*, Lea and Febiger, Philadelphia, 1974.

414

Part Six

The Lymph Node

Harry L. Ioachim

31. The Normal Lymph Node

In the course of the lymphatic pathways are the lymph nodes, peripheral lymphoid organs performing major functions of lymphopoiesis, filtration of lymph, and processing of antigens. This chapter provides a brief light microscopical view of the lymph node followed by ultrastructural description of lymphocyte, lymphoblast, histiocyte, and reticular cell. For description of plasma and endothelial cells, see Chapter 33, p. 441.

Light microscopy reveals a dense capsule of connective tissue surrounding the lymphatic tissues which include cortex, medulla, and sinuses (Figure 31.1). Collecting lymphatic vessels, termed afferent lymphatics, discharge lymph into the subcapsular sinus, from where a system of interconnecting sinuses (Figure 31.2) drains the lymph node into the efferent lymphatics situated in the hilar region. The supporting framework of the lymph nodes is formed by the connective tissue capsule, by trabeculae projecting from it (Figure 31.2), and by a finer meshwork of reticulin fibers between the trabeculae (Figure 31.1). The sinuses, lined by flat, elongated, endothelial cells, form passageways through the network of reticulin, between the capsule and the hilus.[41,51] The cortex is composed of lymphoid follicles and interfollicular lymphoid tissue. The follicles include the germinal centers which consist of stem cells, lymphoblasts, macrophages, and reticular cells. The lymphoid cells of the cortical follicles display surface immunoglobulins and are of B-cell type. In contrast, the lymphoid cells of the parafollicular areas and particularly of the deep cortex have surface markers for sheep erythrocytes and are of T-cell type.

The medulla is composed of lymphocytes, plasma cells, macrophages, and reticular cells located between the sinuses.

31.1. Lymphocyte

It is also designated as small, circulating, or mature lymphocyte. In sections, the cell diameter averages 6 μm (larger in smears) with a round nucleus about 5 μm in diameter, resulting in a high nuclear–cytoplasmic ratio.[55] The surface shows shallow indentations and occasional short microvilli. The cytoplasm contains a high number of mono- and few polyribosomes. It also includes a small Golgi body, few mitochondria, and a few strands of endoplasmic reticulum. The nucleus is almost entirely composed of highly condensed heterochromatin.[48,60]

31.2. Lymphoblast

Also referred to as large lymphocyte, germinal center lymphocyte, or activated lymphocyte, the lymphoblast is round or slightly oval with an average diameter of 13 μm

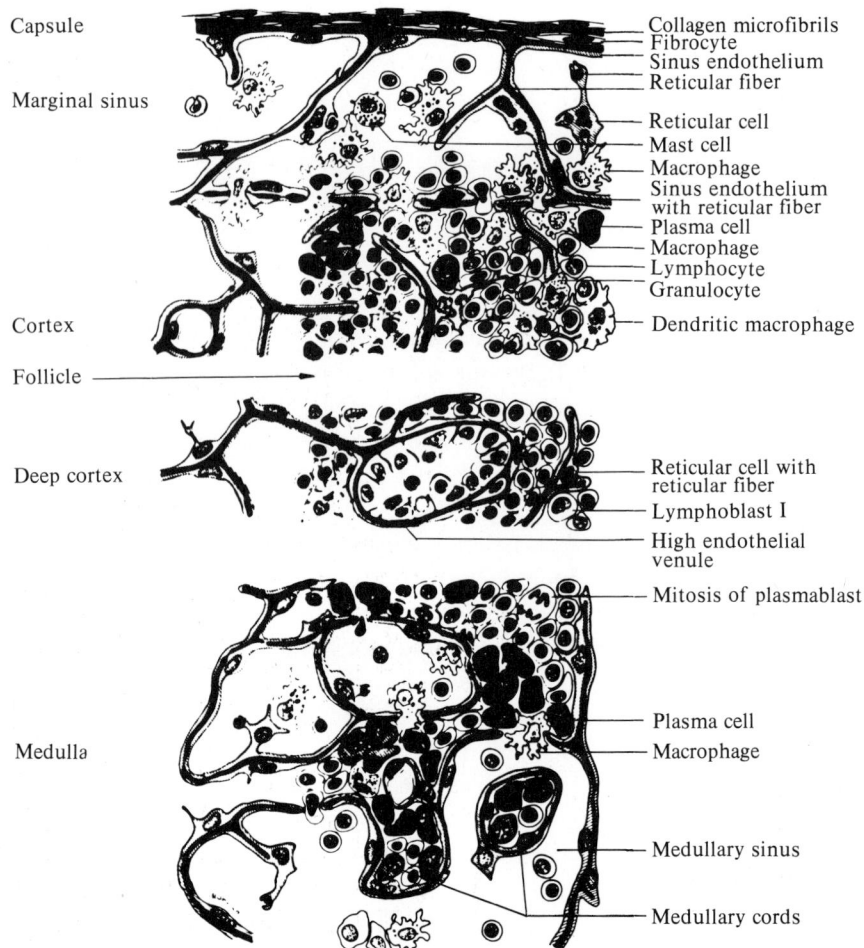

Figure 31.1. Structure of normal lymph node (I. Olah, P. Röhlich, and I. Törö).

(Figure 31.3).[55] The cell surface is irregular, often indented and covered by occasional short microvilli. The cytoplasm contains numerous polyribosomes, mitochondria, and a few strands of endoplasmic reticulum but a Golgi body is not observed.[55] The nucleus is large, cleaved or noncleaved,[42] sometimes with surface indentations. The heterochromatin is marginated, forming a thin rim along the nuclear membrane. The nucleoli are prominent and usually connected to the peripheral heterochromatin.[48,60]

31.3. Histiocyte

This major cellular component of the mononuclear phagocyte system (MPS)[2,19,58] is ubiquitous in the reticuloendothelial tissues where it is also referred to as a macrophage and in the general circulation where it is referred to as a monocyte. Under pathologic conditions the histiocyte may change into an epithelioid cell which, in contrast with its macrophage precursor, has primarily secretory functions.[2,19,58] The phagocytic histiocyte is the largest cell in the lymph node, sometimes up to 20 μm in diameter. The shape is markedly irregular with many pseudopodal processes branching between the cells which enables the histiocytes to easily contact foreign

418

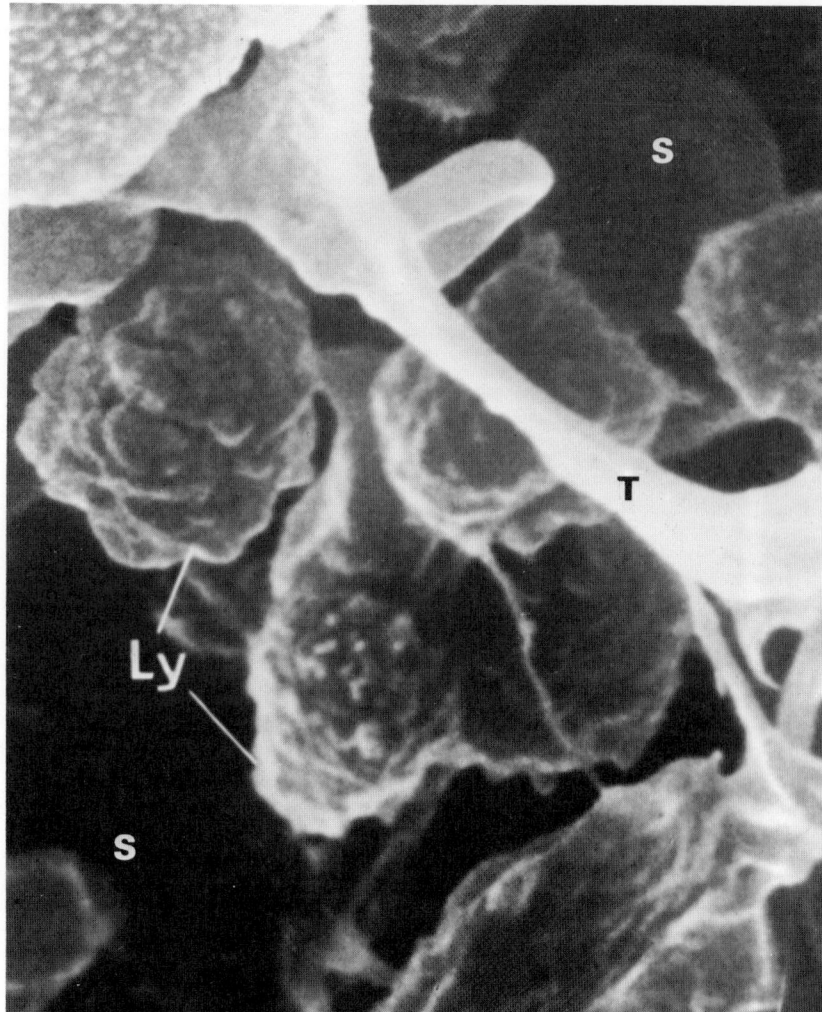

Figure 31.2. Lymphocytes in lymph node sinus.
Lymphocytes (Ly) clinging to the surface of trabeculae (T) in the sinuses (S).
(×5,000)

material.[48] The cytoplasm contains a large Golgi body, unevenly distributed mitochondria, and a large number of vesicular profiles of smooth endoplasmic reticulum.
Characteristic is the large number of lysosomes and phagosomes.[60] The latter contain
engulfed cells, cellular debris, or amorphous dark granules. The lysosomes derived
from the Golgi sacs[55] are membrane-bound vesicles or dense bodies containing various proteolytic enzymes, mainly hydrolases.

31.4. Reticular cell

In association with reticulin and fine collagen fibers, the reticular cells form the
stroma of lymphoid tissues. The cell is also referred to as a fixed or dendritic macrophage.[55] The shape is extremely variable with lengthy dendritic processes extending
for long distances between the lymphoid cells. The abundant cytoplasm contains a
large number of vesicles, large Golgi body, free ribosomes, mitochondria, and a few
profiles of endoplasmic reticulum.

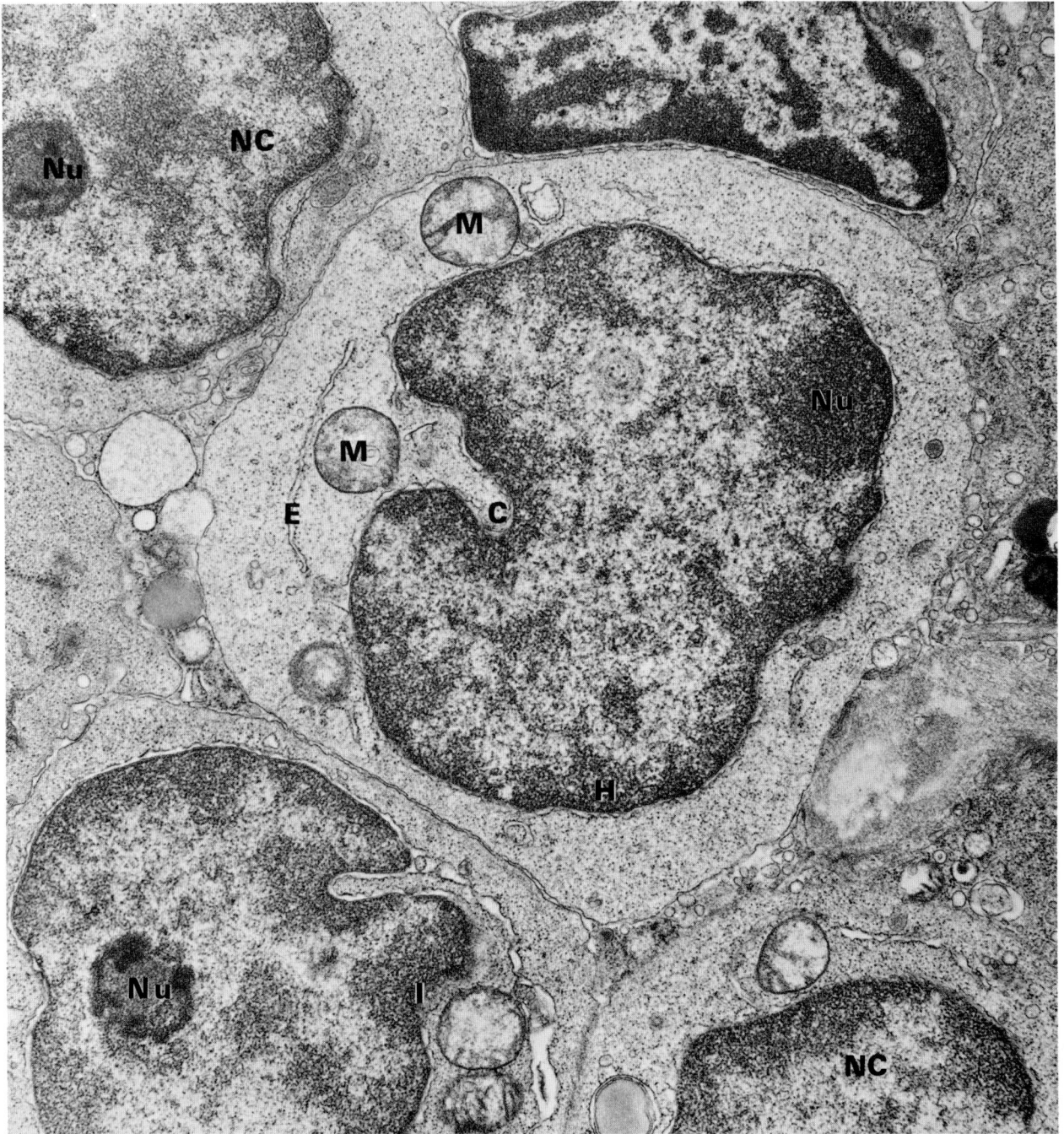

Figure 31.3. Lymphoblasts in germinal center.
The fairly abundant cytoplasm is filled with mono- and polyribosomes. Note few mitochondria (M) at one pole of cell, few strands of endoplasmic reticulum (E), absence of Golgi body. Nuclei are indented (I), cleaved (C), or noncleaved (NC) with marginated heterochromatin (H) and large nucleoli (Nu) frequently connected to marginal chromatin. (× 14,000)

420

32. The Pathological Lymph Node

32.1. Non-neoplastic disorders

32.1.1. Sarcoidosis

This is a systemic granulomatous disease of unknown etiology, predominantly involving the reticuloendothelial system. The lymph nodes are affected in almost all cases with concomitant lesions in lungs, skin, eyes, spleen, and bones. Hypergammaglobulinemia and impairment of cell-mediated immunity are usually associated.[32]

Light microscopically, the lymph node and/or spleen architecture are obliterated by numerous, round, occasionally confluent nodules, sharply demarcated by collagen fibers. Epithelioid cells are concentrically oriented, forming a typical granuloma (Figure 32.1). The center includes one or several multinucleated giant cells while the periphery is occupied by a mantle of mature lymphocytes and occasional plasma cells. Necrosis is rare and limited to a central focus that undergoes early fibrosis.

EM studies show that the epithelioid cells are large, mononuclear cells about 20 μm in diameter, with abundant cytoplasm extending into multiple processes that interdigitate with those of other epithelioid cells in zipper-like arrays (Figure 32.2).[2] The nuclei are eccentrically located, elongated, and indented. Young epithelioid cells contain heterochromatin while more mature cells have mostly euchromatin. Nucleoli are multiple, small, and fine. The cytoplasm contains numerous ovoid or rod-shaped mitochondria, multicentric Golgi bodies,[21,48] a large amount of smooth endoplasmic reticulum, multiple lysosomal bodies containing various enzymes, and no phagocytic vacuoles. The structure is that of an immunologically activated secretory cell and there is no evidence of phagocytosis.[21,32]

Multinucleated giant cells with a diameter of about 300 μm and as many as 30 nuclei (Figure 32.3)[48] arise by fusion of epithelioid cells.[2,48] The general structure resembles that of the epithelioid cells. The nuclei are usually peripheral and the cytoplasm is filled with numerous, randomly dispersed organelles.[2]

32.1.2. Infectious mononucleosis

This is a benign, self-limiting, lymphoproliferative disease caused by the Epstein–Barr virus (EBV). The clinical manifestations are systemic and in addition to lymph nodes, the spleen, tonsils, bone marrow, liver, and central nervous system may be involved. Heterophile antibodies, anti-EBV antibodies, auto- and isoantibodies are commonly detected in significant titers.[22]

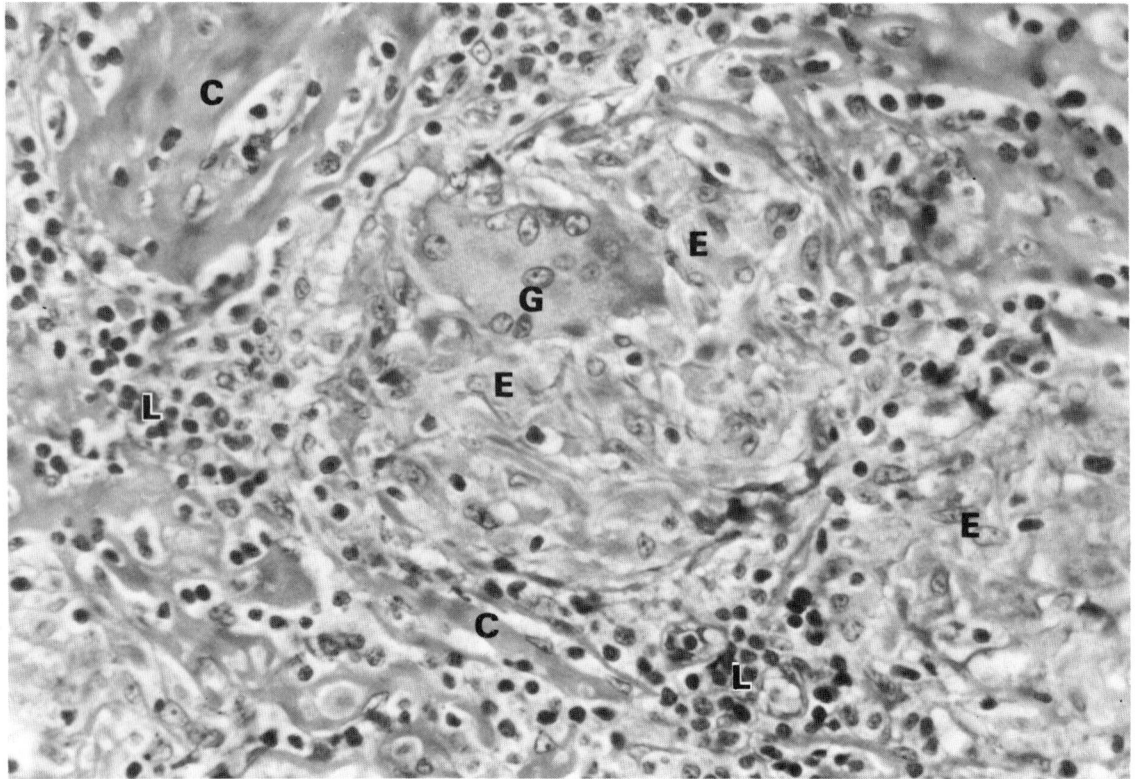

Figure 32.1. Mediastinal lymph node in sarcoidosis.
The structure is obliterated by characteristic multiple granulomata. Epithelioid cells (E), multinucleated giant cell (G), lymphocytes (L), bands of collagen (C) are visible. (× 250)

Light microscopy shows that the lymph node architecture is distorted but not entirely effaced (Figure 32.4). The characteristic feature is the presence in large numbers of activated lymphocytes (immunoblasts) that infiltrate extensively and diffusely the cortex and medulla, with greatest concentration in the parafollicular areas. The cells are large, intensely basophilic, with big nuclei and prominent nucleoli. Occasional binucleated, Reed–Sternberg-like cells can be observed. Pyronin staining of the cytoplasm is positive. Similar cells infiltrate the spleen, liver, and bone marrow and may be identified in the peripheral blood (Downey cells).

Electron microscopy reveals that the large lymphocytes of infectious mononucleosis (immunoblasts) are morphologically similar to the lymphocytes activated by phytohemagglutinin or other mitogens (Figure 32.5).[4] The cell is one and a half to three times the size of a small lymphocyte,[12] with a lower nuclear–cytoplasmic ratio. The nucleus is indented or cleaved, and the chromatin is less dense and more uniformly distributed.[65] One or two nucleoli are present. The cytoplasm contains numerous

422

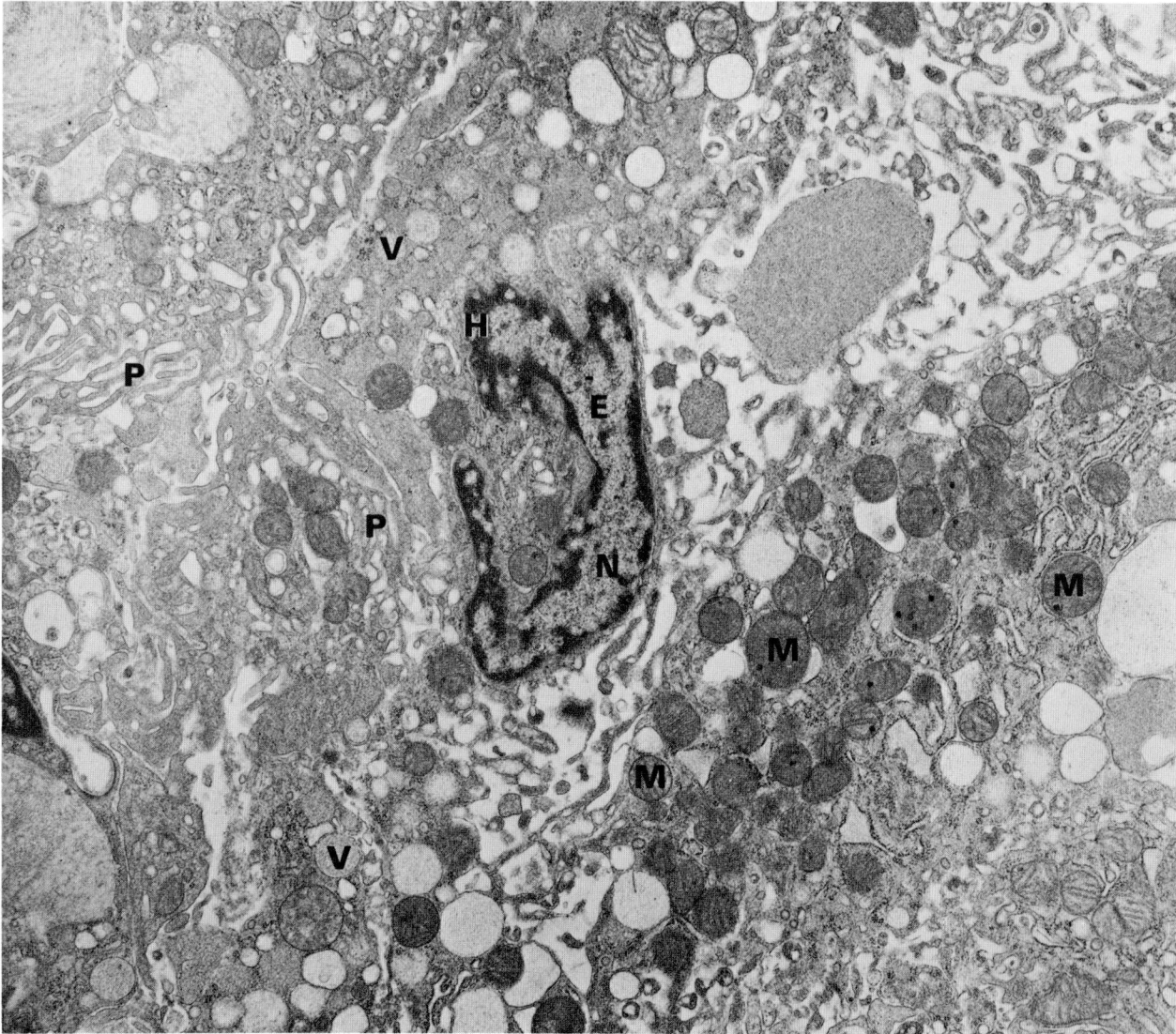

Figure 32.2. Epithelioid cells in sarcoidosis (S. C. Luk, C. Nopajaroonsri and G. T. Simon).
Epithelioid cells in lymph node depicted in Figure 32.1. Note interlocked processes (P), mitochondria (M), secretory vacuoles (V), elongated, indented nucleus (N) with euchromatin (E) and marginated heterochromatin (H). (× 12,000)

ribosomes,[65] few mitochondria, and a well-developed, granular, endoplasmic reticulum with dilated cisternae. Mitoses are occasionally seen.

32.1.3. Toxoplasma lymphadenitis

Acute acquired toxoplasmosis often affects lymph nodes, creating difficult problems of differential diagnosis with Hodgkin's disease and other lymphomas. The posterior

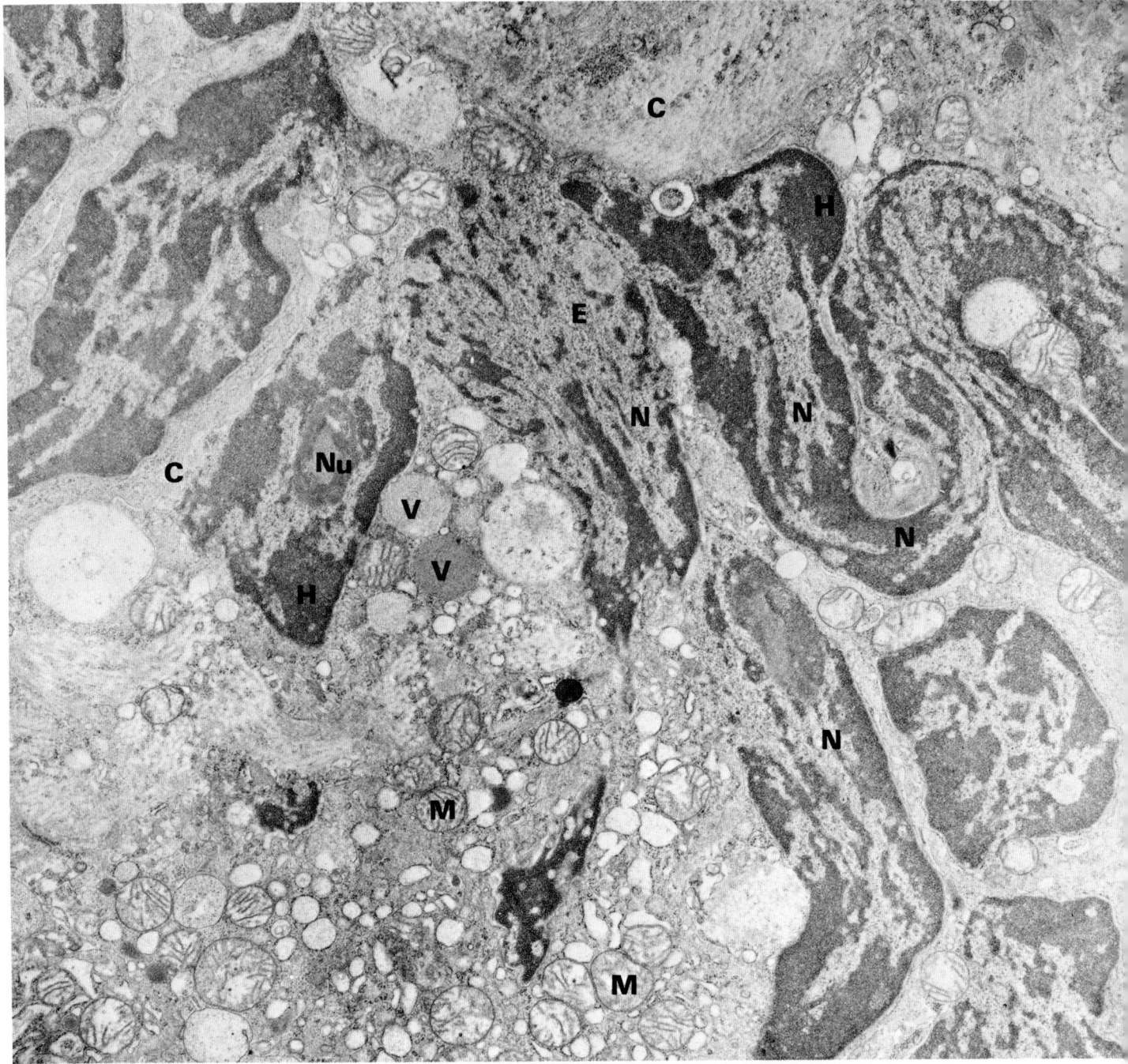

Figure 32.3. Multinucleated giant cell in sarcoidosis.

From lymph node illustrated in Figure 32.1. Note multiple, irregularly shaped nuclei (N) with heterochromatin (H), euchromatin (E), and occasional nucleoli (Nu). Numerous mitochondria (M), secretory vacuoles (V), and bands of collagen (C) are also visible. (× 12,000)

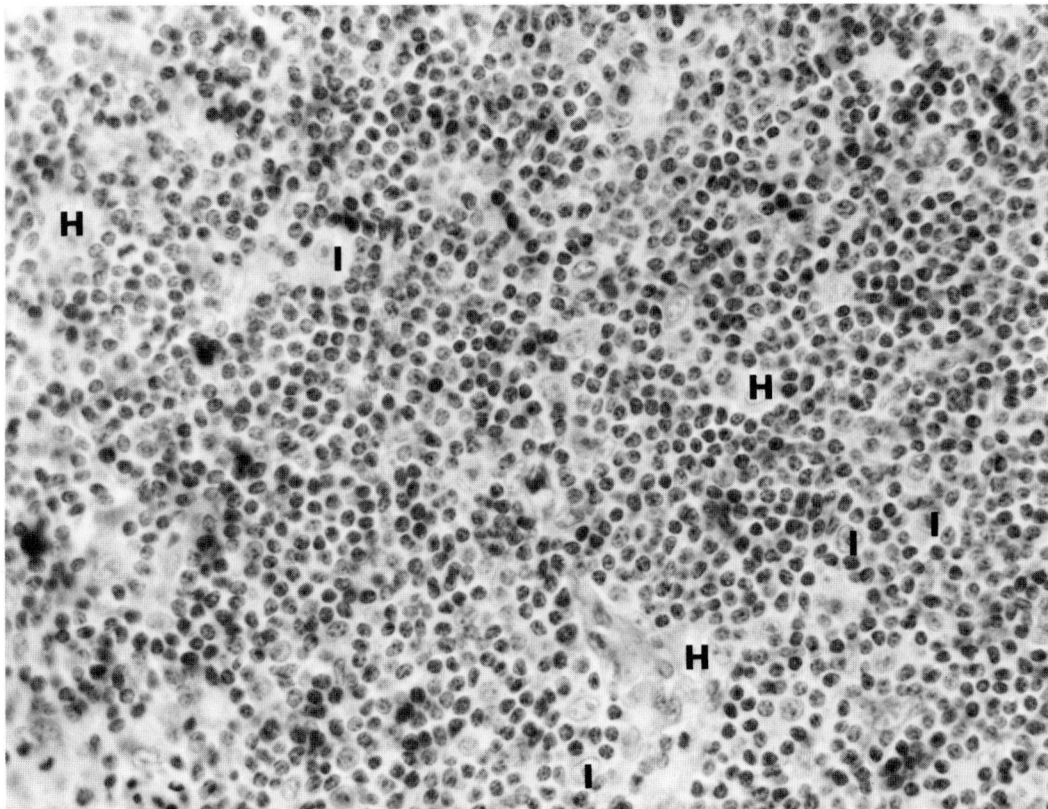

Figure 32.4. Cervical lymph node in infectious mononucleosis.
Note the effaced cortical structure, numerous, scattered, immunoblasts (I) with large nuclei and prominent nucleoli, phagocytic histiocytes (H). (× 250).

cervical lymph nodes are frequently involved.[23] A presumptive histologic diagnosis can be confirmed by a positive Sabin–Feldman dye test with a titer over 1:256 and/or a positive immunofluorescence test for IgM antibodies.[15, 59]

With the light microscope the enlarged lymph nodes show reactive hyperplasia of lymphoid follicles associated with the presence of large, clear histiocytes, singly or in clusters, scattered through the cortical and paracortical zones (Figure 32.6).[15, 17, 59] The histiocytes encroach and infiltrate the lymphoid follicles and frequently contain phagocytosed nuclear debris. The sinuses are distended and contain numerous hyperplastic histiocytes.[15, 59]

EM studies of the small aggregates of epithelioid cells show that they contain abundant cytoplasm, rod-shaped mitochondria, and vesicular smooth endoplasmic reticulum. Large histiocytes with marked phagocytic activity are present in the germinal centers and contain numerous phagosomes and residual bodies of variable size and composition (Figure 32.7). They include myelin figures, granular material of varying electron density, or coarse, amorphous, electron-opaque debris.[48]

Toxoplasma gondii in the lymph node is difficult to identify unless a longitudinal section is obtained. The organism can also be recognized by its bizarre, large mitochondria, small, round nuclei, and double-layered cytoplasmic membrane.[48]

425

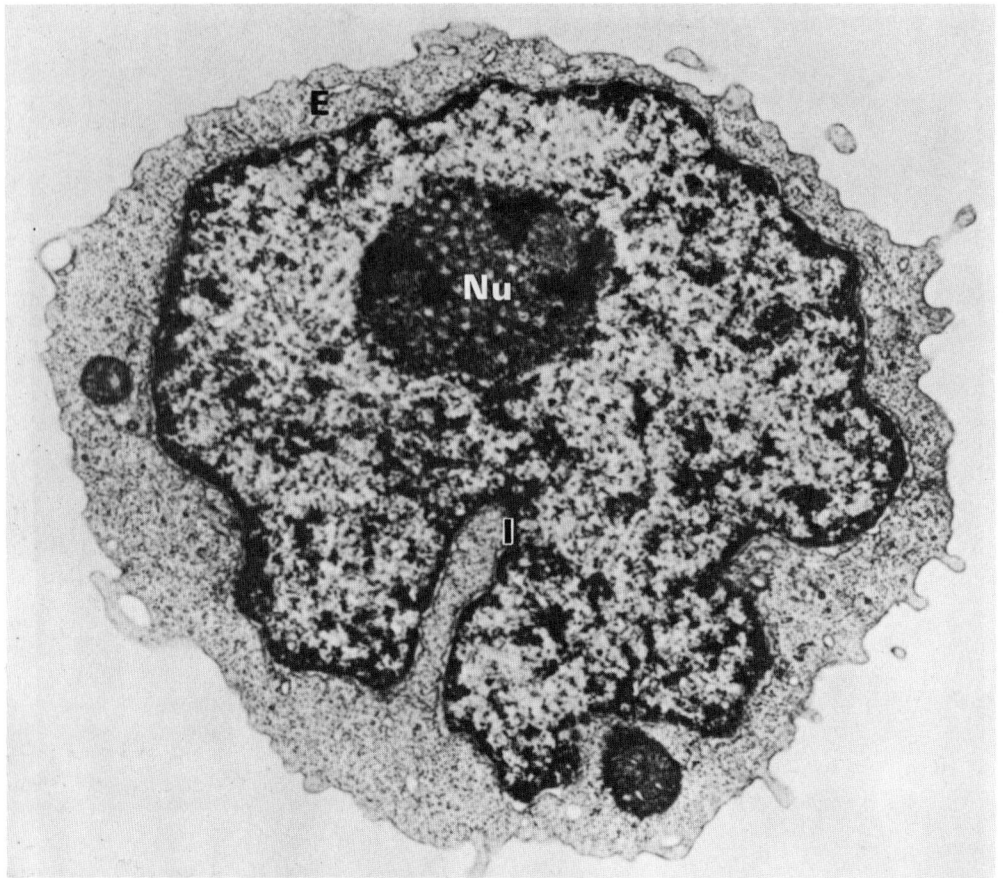

Figure 32.5. Immunoblast (activated lymphocyte) in infectious mononucleosis (M. Bessis.)

The fairly abundant cytoplasm contains strands of endoplasmic reticulum (E), large, indented nucleus (I), dispersed chromatin, and prominent reticulated nucleolus (Nu). (×8,000)

32.1.4. Rheumatoid lymphadenitis

During the long course of rheumatoid arthritis, 50 to 75 percent of patients may exhibit significant lymphadenopathies.[50] Clinically and histologically, the differential diagnosis with lymphoma, particularly of nodular type, is often difficult.

In the light microscope the lymphoid follicles are markedly hyperplastic, including large germinal centers and thick, peripheral lymphocytic mantles. Aggregates of lymphocytes as well as lymphoid follicles with germinal centers are often present in the perinodal adipose tissue.[50] The dilated sinuses are lined by hyperplastic endothelial cells and contain polymorphonuclears (Figure 32.8). The interfollicular areas and medullary cords include numerous plasma cells, isolated and in large clusters.

Ultrastructurally, the cellular changes are not specific and may be seen in part, in infectious mononucleosis, postvaccinial[26] or luetic lymphadenopathies.[10,17,27] Capillaries and sinuses show hyperplastic endothelial cells protruding into the lumina

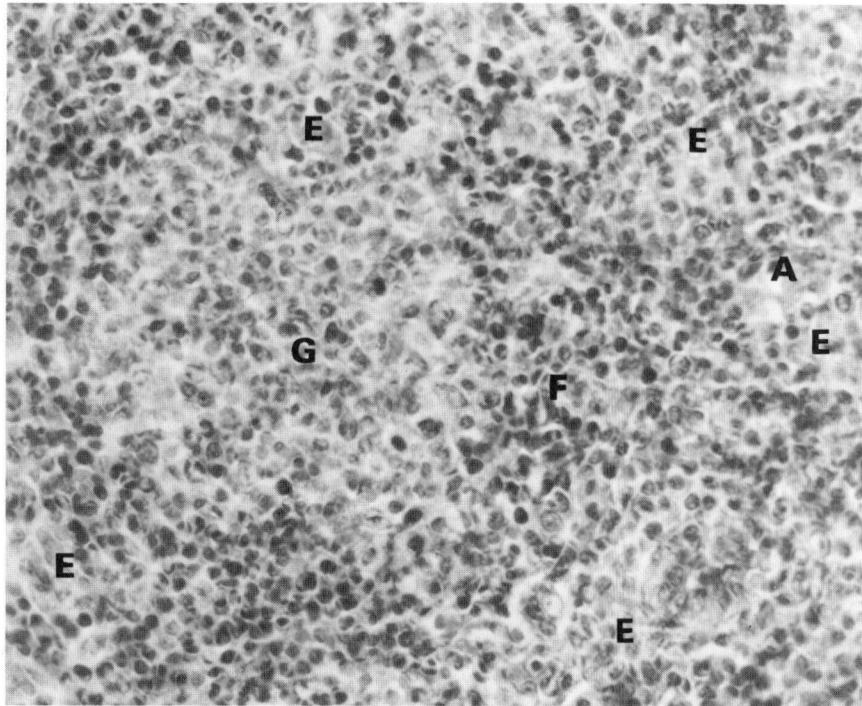

Figure 32.6. Posterior cervical lymph node of toxoplasmosis.
Large epithelioid cells (E) infiltrating a lymphoid follicle (F) and its germinal centre (G) as well as the perifollicular area (A). (×250)

which often contain polymorphonuclears. The cortical follicles comprise markedly enlarged germinal centers composed of activated lymphocytes (immunoblasts) with morphologic features previously described. Plasma cells of usual appearance in the lymph node medulla are frequent (Figure 32.9).

32.1.5. Luetic lymphadenitis

It may accompany primary or secondary stages of syphilis and is probably due to the persistence of spirochaetes in the tissues and particularly in the lymph nodes, providing continuous antigenic stimulation.[61]

Light microscopically, the lymph node cortex shows marked follicular hyperplasia and diffuse infiltration of histiocytes in the paracortical area. Clusters of epithelioid cells and multinucleated giant cells forming small granulomata are scattered throughout the parenchyma. The capsule is inflamed and fibrosed. There is proliferation of capillaries, lined by hyperplastic endothelial cells and surrounded by cuffs of plasma cells and lymphocytes (Figure 32.10). Spirochaetes are usually present, particularly in the walls of blood vessels.[28]

Electron microscopy reveals the frequent occurrence of capillaries with hyperplastic endothelial cells that protrude into the lumina (Figure 32.11). Surrounding them are plasma cells and lymphocytes of usual morphology. The enlarged lymphoid

427

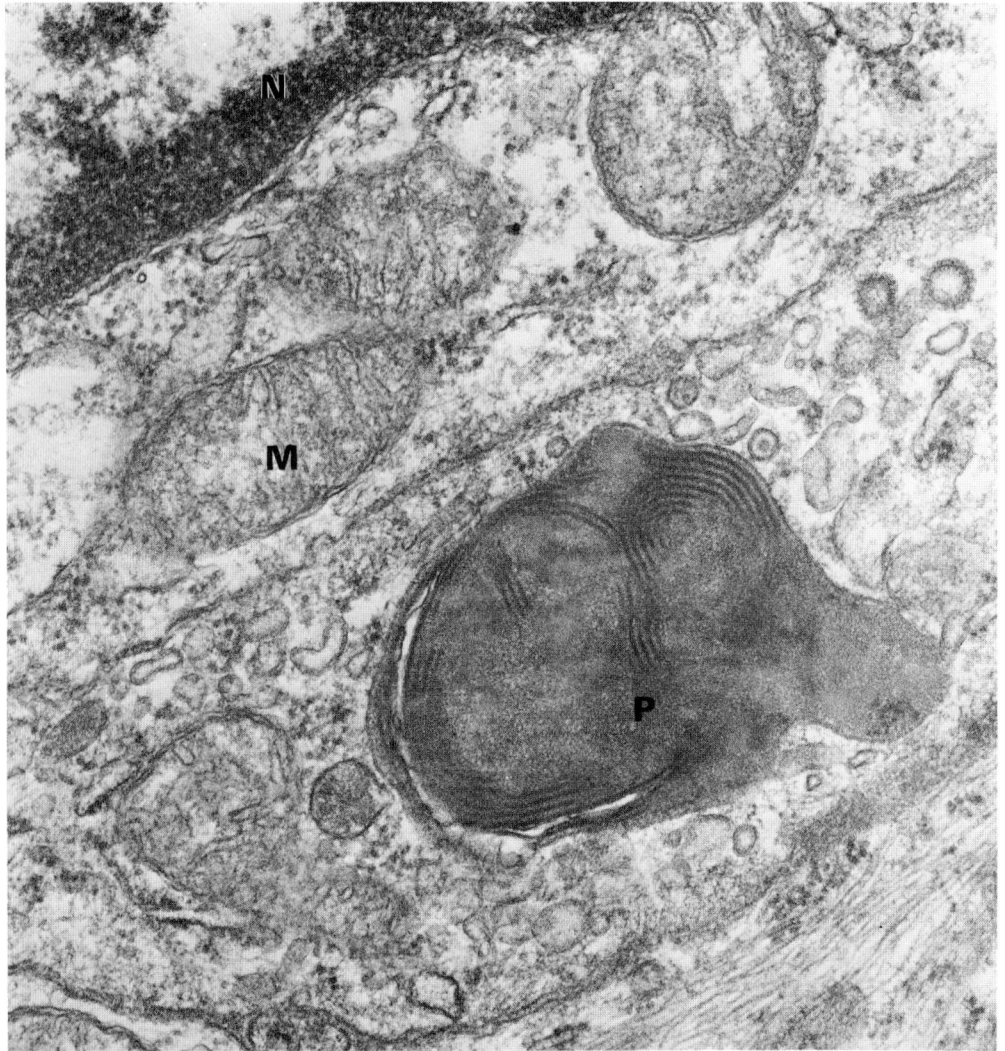

Figure 32.7. Large histiocyte with macrophage activity in toxoplasmosis.
It includes nucleus (N), mitochondria (M), large phagosome with myelin figure (P).
(× 40,000)

follicles include activated lymphocytes and histiocytes not dissimilar to those observed in other lymphadenopathies.

32.1.6. Immunoblastic lymphadenopathy

A non-neoplastic, generalized lymphadenopathy is associated with hepatosplenomegaly, abnormal immune reactivity, and polyclonal hypergammaglobulinemia.[20,45]

With light microscopy enlarged lymph nodes show diffuse alteration of normal architecture due to cellular and vascular proliferation (Figure 32.12). Arborizing small

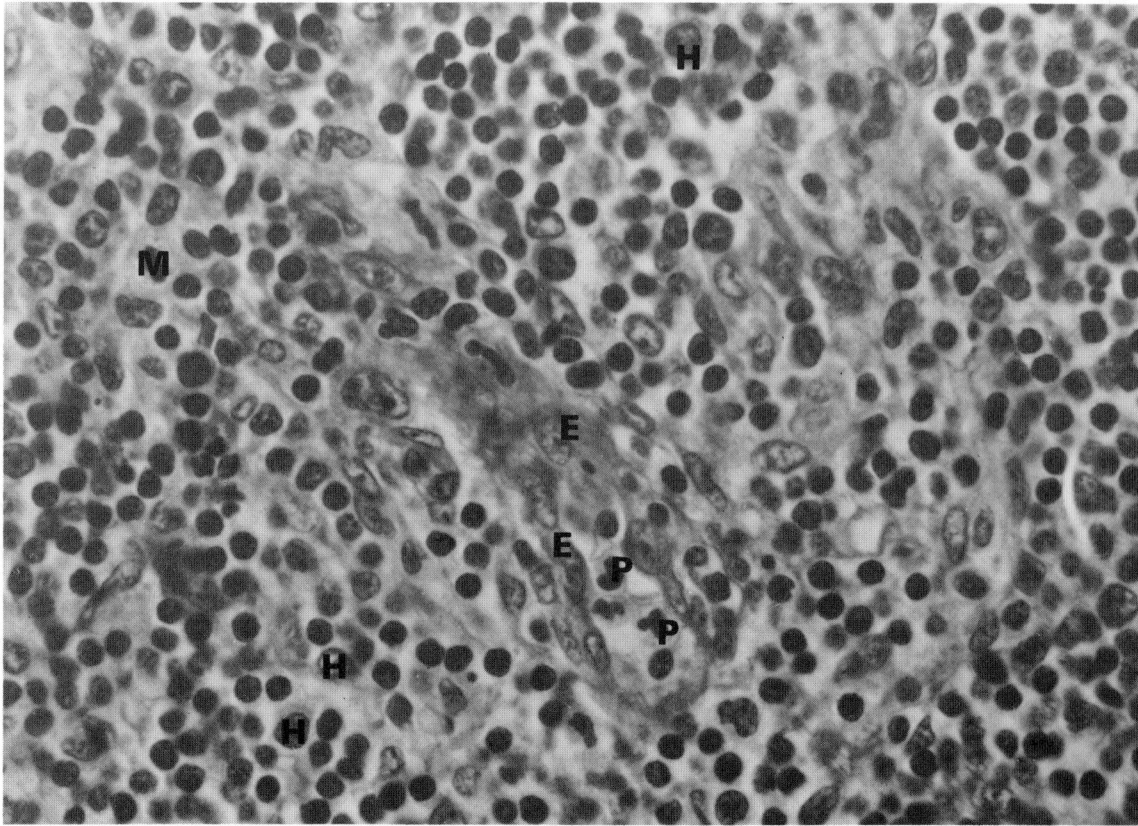

Figure 32.8. Hyperplastic endothelial cells in rheumatoid lymphadenitis.
Axillary lymph node showing hyperplastic endothelial cells (E) lining a sinus that contains polymorphonuclears (P). Large histiocytes (H) and immunoblasts, some in mitosis (M), are scattered throughout. (×400)

vessels lined by hyperplastic endothelial cells are numerous. The cellular infiltrates consist of lymphocytes and, particularly, immunoblasts, the latter being numerous and characteristic for this entity. They consist of large lymphoid cells (activated lymphocytes) with abundant cytoplasm, indented nuclei, and prominent nucleoli. Intercellular, PAS-positive, amorphous material is also present.

Ultrastructurally, with the exception of immunoblasts, all cells appear normal and exhibit their usual morphologic features.

The immunoblasts range from 15 to 25 μm in size and have been erroneously interpreted in the past as reticulum cells (Figure 32.13).[45] They resemble the lymphocytes activated by mitogens *in vitro*. The cytoplasm is abundant and, in contrast to the small, nonactivated lymphocytes, includes fairly numerous mitochondria, profiles of endoplasmic reticulum, and a dilated Golgi body.[65] The nucleus has multiple indentations and a prominent nucleolus.

Reacted with labeled anti-immunoglobulin sera the cellular membrane shows positive staining, revealing the presence of surface immunoglobulins (Figure 32.13). This demonstrates the B-lymphocyte origin of the immunoblasts in this lymphadenopathy.

429

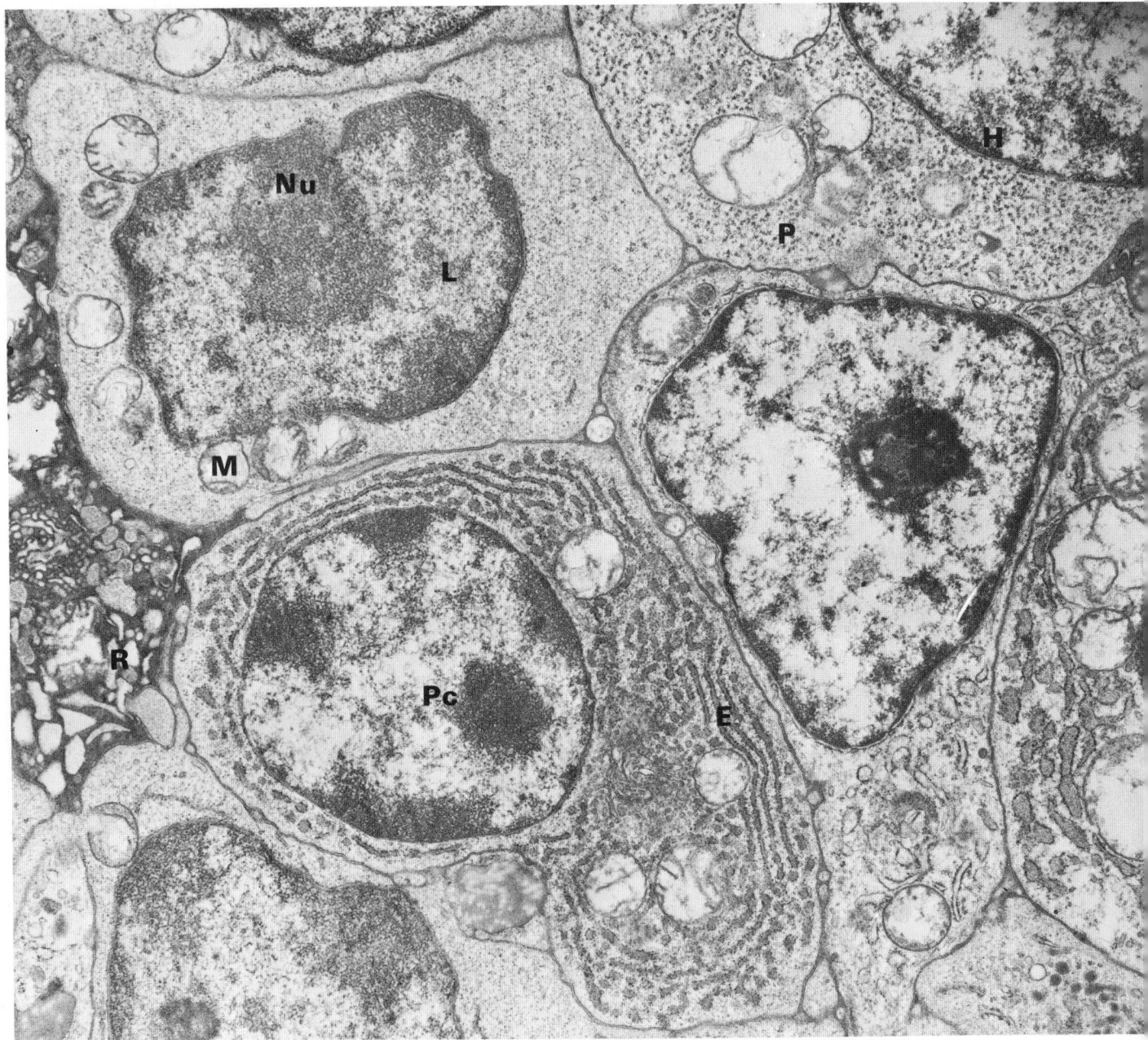

Figure 32.9. Lymph node medulla in rheumatoid lymphadenitis.
EM shows plasma cell(Pc) with well-differentiated granular endoplasmic reticulum (E), activated lymphoctye (L) with mitochondria (M) clustered at one pole of the cell and nucleus with
marginated nucleolus (Nu), large histiocyte (H) with abundant polyribosomes (P), reticular
cell (R) with dendrite including multiple vesicles. (× 12,600)

430

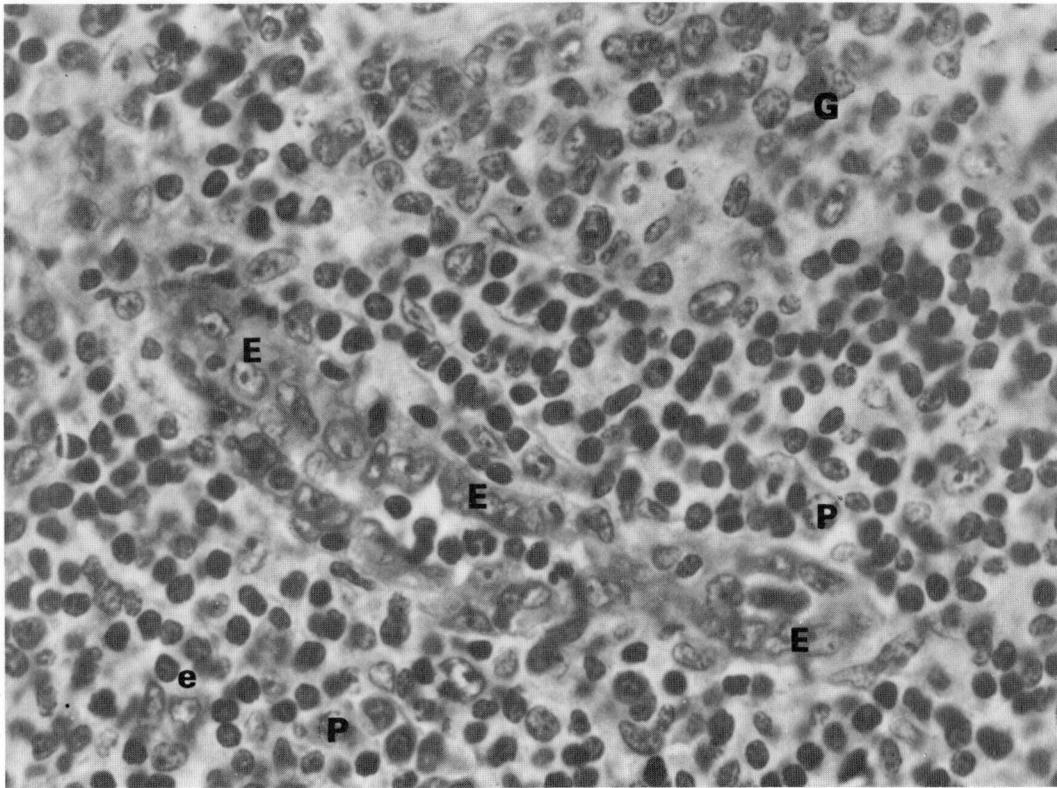

Figure 32.10. Luetic lymphadenitis of inguinal lymph node.
Dilated capillary with markedly hyperplastic endothelial cells is visible (E). Note hyperplastic germinal center (G), frequent plasma cells (P), and epithelioid cells (e) in addition to polymorphonuclears. (×400)

32.1.7. Sinus histiocytosis with massive lymphadenopathy

This reactive, non-neoplastic lymphadenopathy is characterized by massive, painless, cervical lymph node enlargement. Described by Rosai and Dorfman,[17, 56] it occurs mostly in Negro children and is accompanied by fever, leukocytosis, and hypergammaglobulinemia. Spontaneous regression occurs after a protracted course.

Important changes revealed by light microscopy are marked dilatation of lymph node sinuses and hyperplasia of histiocytes and endothelial cells. The histiocytes form large cellular aggregates and are mixed with plasma cells, lymphocytes, and granulocytes (Figure 32.14). The histiocytes have abundant cytoplasm, vesicular nuclei, and fine nucleoli. Nuclear pleomorphism and mitoses are not noted. Active cellular phagocytosis is commonly noted and a characteristic feature is the presence of large histiocytes containing engulfed lymphocytes and granulocytes (Figure 32.14).[56] The lymphoid follicles are effaced and there is no formation of granulomas.

Electron microscopy shows that well-differentiated histiocytes are the predominant cells (Figure 32.15). They exhibit abundant cytoplasm containing numerous osmiophilic inclusions of varying size and outline, probably representing residual

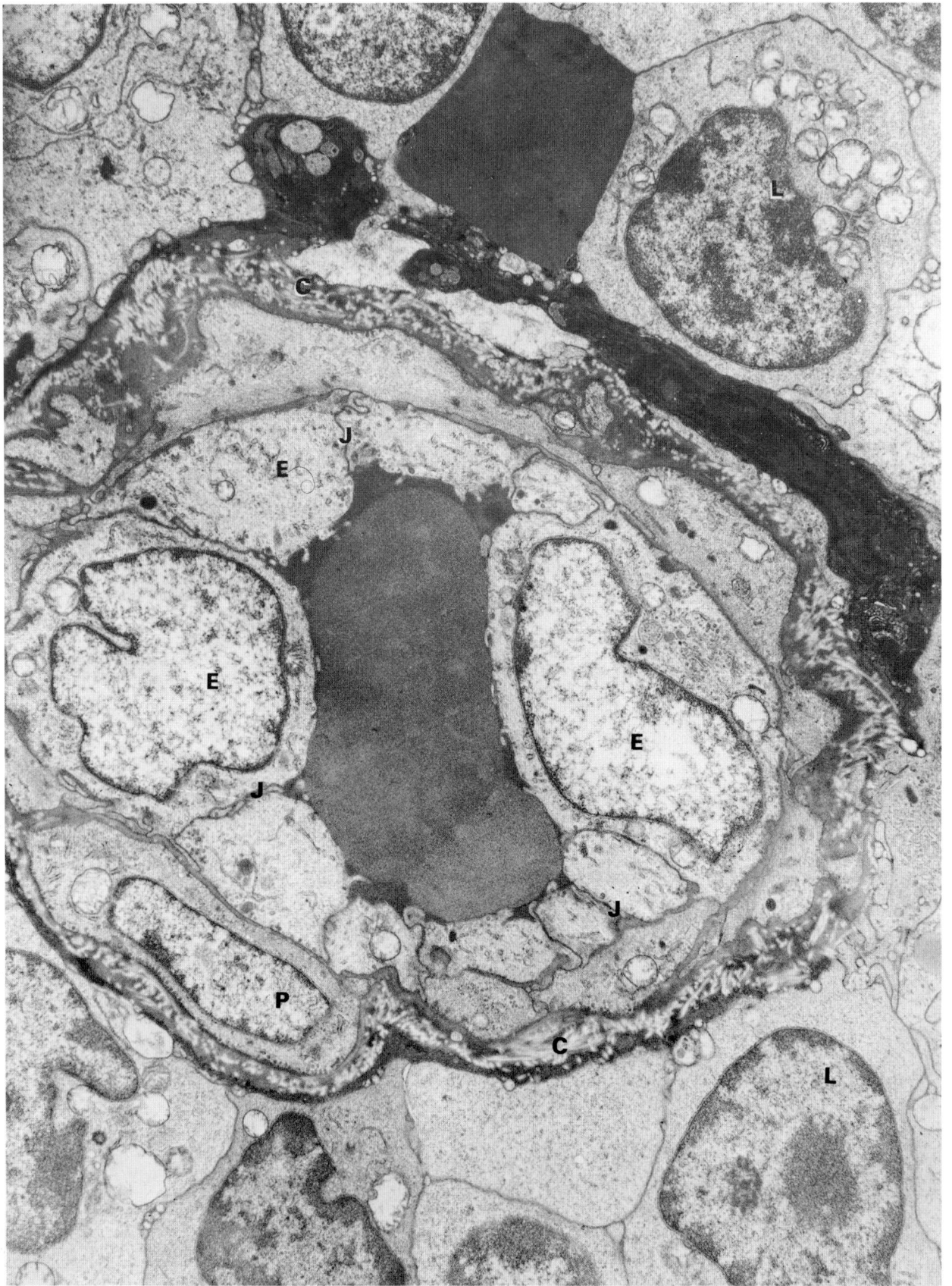

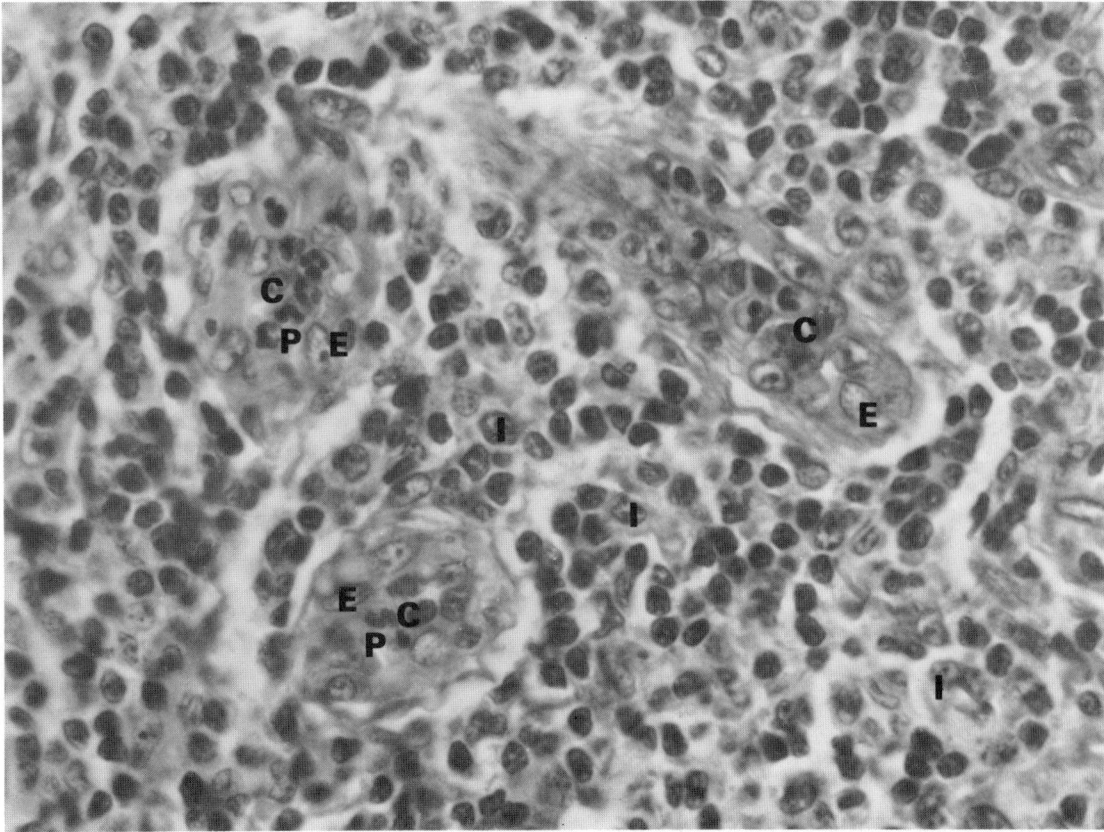

Figure 32.12. Axillary lymph node in immunoblastic lymphadenopathy.
Enlarged node shows arborization of capillaries (C) lined by hyperplastic endothelial cells (E) containing polymorphonuclears (P) and lymphocytes. Surrounding lymphoid tissue includes frequent immunoblasts (I). (×400)

Figure 32.11. Capillary in luetic lymphadenitis.
Large, protruding endothelial cells with cytoplasm contain few organelles and large nuclei with abundant euchromatin (E). Note intercellular junctions (J), pericyte (P), perivascular bundles of collagen (C), activated lymphocytes (L). (×9,000)

433

bodies.[37] Many histiocytes also contain engulfed lymphocytes, erythrocytes, neutrophiles or plasma cells in variable stages of degradation, sequestered within membrane-bound phagosomes, $0 \cdot 3$ to $1 \cdot 0$ μm in diameter.[39] Rod-shaped mitochondria as well as short strands of endoplasmic reticulum are numerous. The nuclei have multiple indentations and contain moderate, marginated heterochromatin and a large, prominent nucleolus.

The sinuses are dilated and lined by endothelial cells that are enlarged and contain a few dense bodies. The cells of the pulp include numerous plasma cells, lymphocytes, and neutrophils. External to the endothelial cells there is an increase in basal lamina substance and collagen.[39]

32.2. Neoplastic disorders

32.2.1. Non-Hodgkin lymphomas

The classification of lymphomas is presently controversial. Under the stimulus of new immunologic concepts,[42] earlier classifications[53] have been challenged[42,43] and new definitions of pathologic entities have been proposed.[5,14,43,54] The T- or B-cell origin of most lymphomas and leukemias has been determined by studies of cell surface markers resulting in tentative functional classifications.[42,43] However, at the present time, the consensus of pathologists and clinicians[34,35] is that the classification of Rappaport is most widely used and offers high reproducibility and clinical significance. In the following six sections, 32.2.2 to 32.2.7, the classification and nomenclature of Rappaport[53] with recent modifications[5,14,54] and additions of new entities is used (Table 32.1).

Table 32.1. Non-Hodgkin's lymphoma (modified classification of Rappaport)

Nodular (Follicular) Lymphomas
Lymphocytic, poorly differentiated
Mixed lymphocytic – histiocytic
Histiocytic

Diffuse Lymphomas
Lymphocytic, well differentiated
Lymphocytic, plasmacytoid type
Lymphocytic, poorly differentiated
Mixed lymphocytic – histiocytic
Undifferentiated, Burkitt's type
Undifferentiated, pleomorphic (non-Burkitt's)
Histiocytic
Lymphoblastic
Unclassified

Lymphocytic lymphoma, well differentiated

Lymphoid neoplasia involving lymph nodes, spleen, other lymphatic tissues, and/or bone marrow; additionally, it may involve the peripheral blood (chronic lymphocytic

434

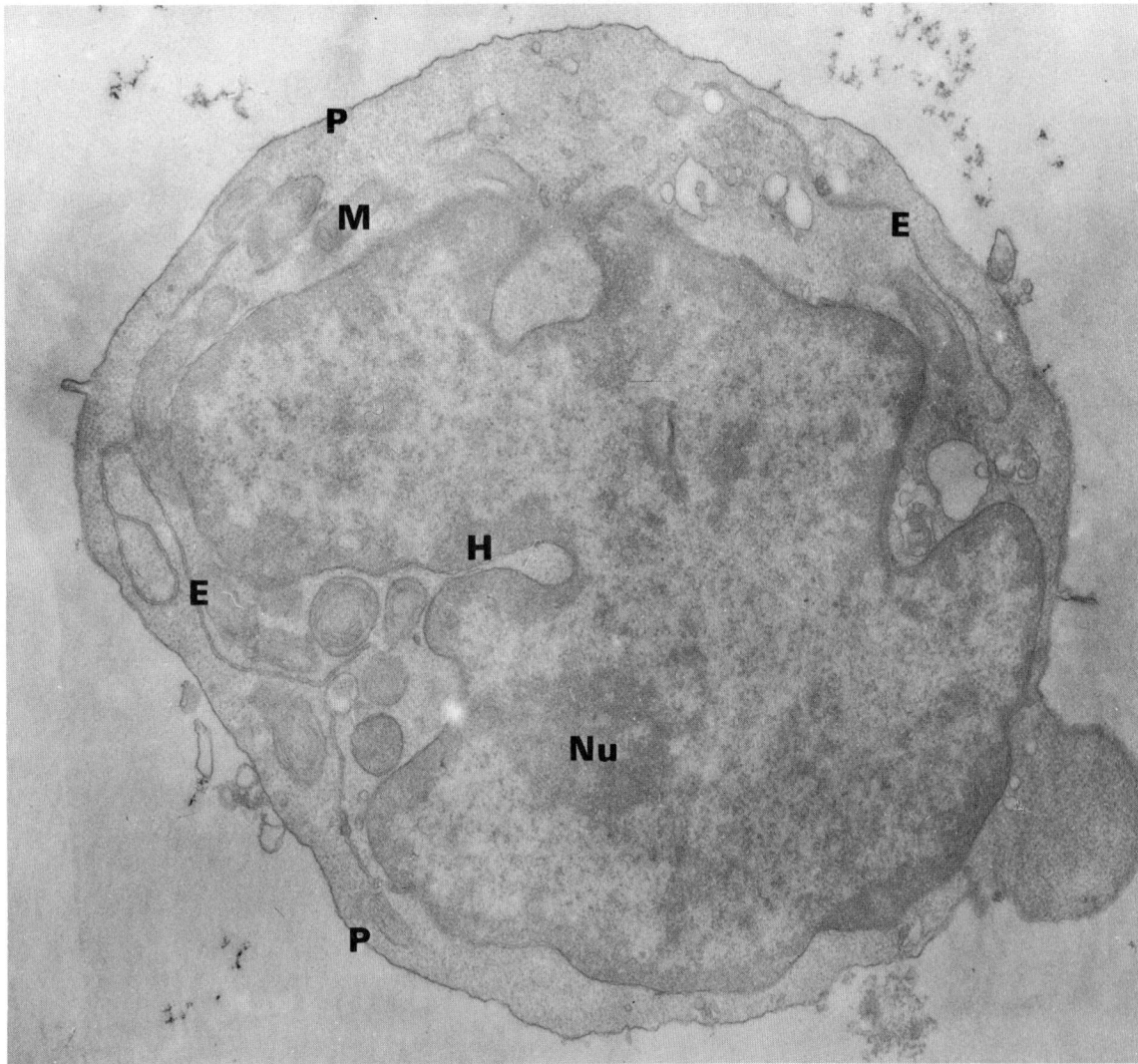

Figure 32.13. Activated lymphocyte in immunoblastic lymphadenopathy.
Immunoblast from axillary lymph node. Cells were unstained and reacted with peroxidase-labeled antihuman IgM antiserum. Precipitate of peroxidase (P) on cell membrane indicates presence of IgM. Very large, indented nucleus contains marginated heterochromatin (H) and large reticulated nucleolus (Nu). Cytoplasm includes rod-shaped mitochondria (M) and profiles of endoplasmic reticulum (E). (× 18,000)

leukemia) in 43 percent of cases.[52] or be associated with a monoclonal gammopathy in 18 percent of cases.[52] It affects primarily individuals after the fifth decade of life and is slowly progressive[52, 53] with usually good therapeutic response and long survivals.

The histologic pattern is almost always diffuse. The lymph node follicular structure is replaced by sheets of monomorphous, closely packed, mature lymphocytes (Figure 32.16). The cytoplasm is scarce, the nuclei are round and hyperchromatic, the nucleoli are inconspicuous, and mitoses are infrequent.

435

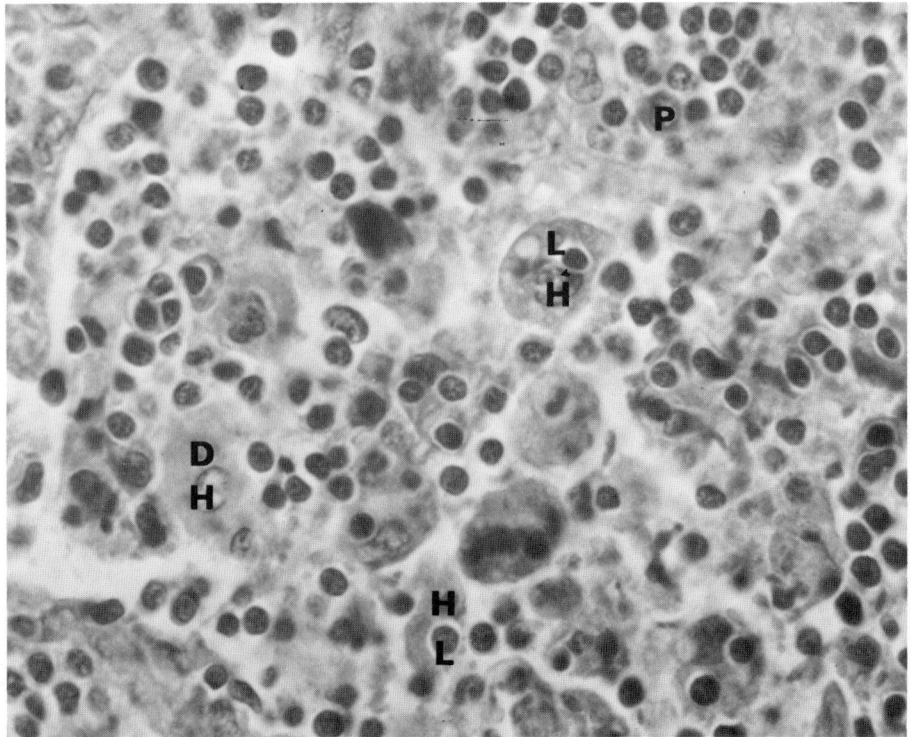

Figure 32.14. Sinus histiocytosis.
Cervical lymph node in black, 11-year-old boy. Note large histiocytes (H) with multiple engulfed lymphocytes (L) and cellular debris (D). Cellular infiltrate also includes plasma cells (P) and polymorphonuclears. (×400)

The cells are more often of B-cell type[6, 7, 42] and surface marker studies show monoclonality with the predominant presence of IgM-kappa chains.[7, 33]

Electron microscopy shows monotonous sheets of cells, similar to each other, closely packed, and without intercellular junctions (Figure 32.17). Occasional dendritic processes of intervening reticular cells separate the neoplastic lymphocytes. The latter show small amounts of cytoplasm including few mitochondria, rare cisternae of endoplasmic reticulum, and polysomes. Nuclei exhibit compact chromatin and the nucleoli are small.

Lymphocytic lymphoma, poorly differentiated

Lymphoid neoplasia involving any or all lymphatic tissues; frequently the bone marrow and/or the peripheral blood are included.

Figure 32.15. Histiocytes in sinus histiocytosis.
The histiocytes are large with abundant cytoplasm containing large amounts of ribosomes and polyribosomes, numerous mitochondria (M), and few stands of endoplasmic reticulum (E). Nuclei are irregularly shaped with prominent nucleoli (Nu) and marginated, moderately dense heterochromatin. (×12,600)

436

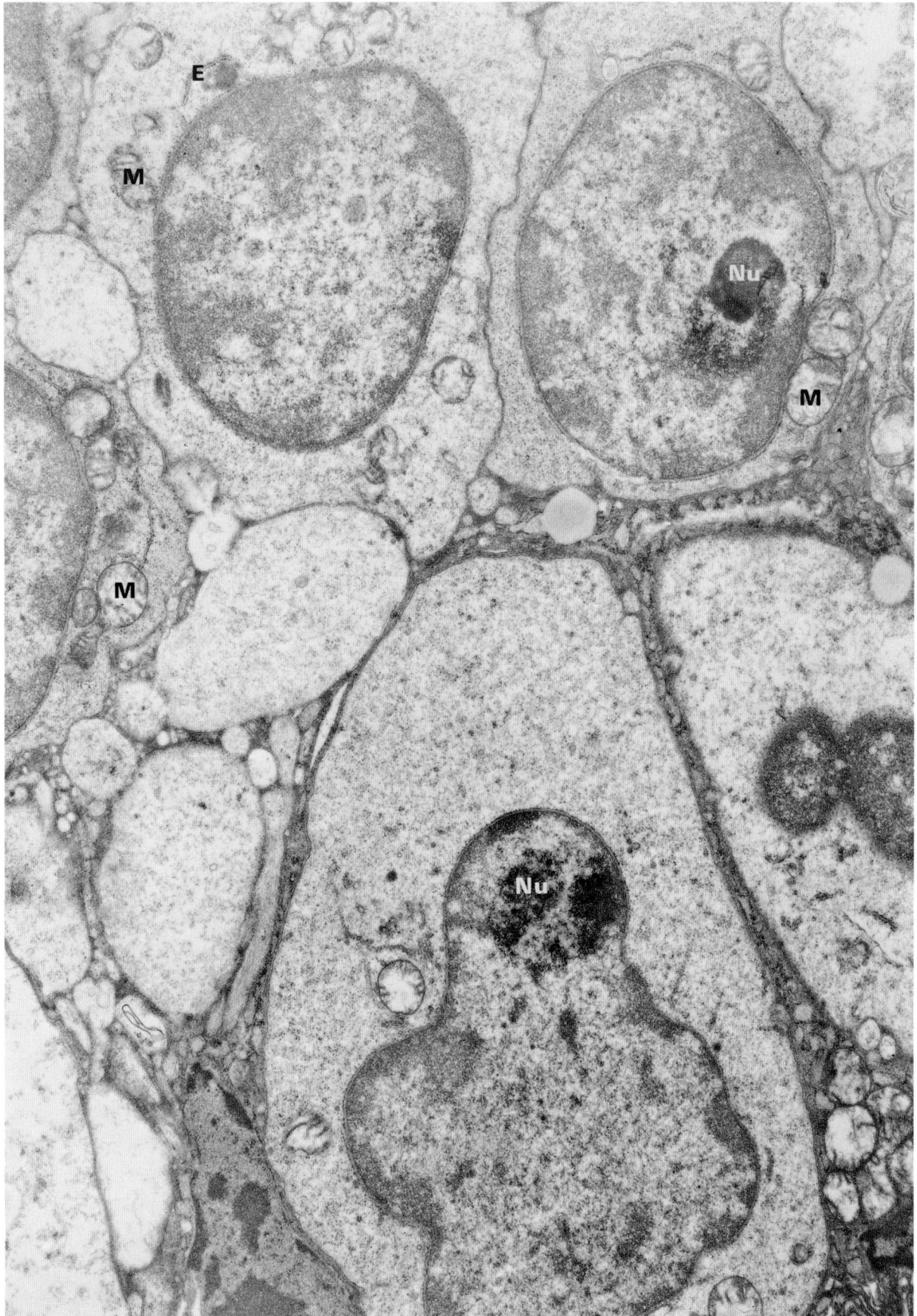

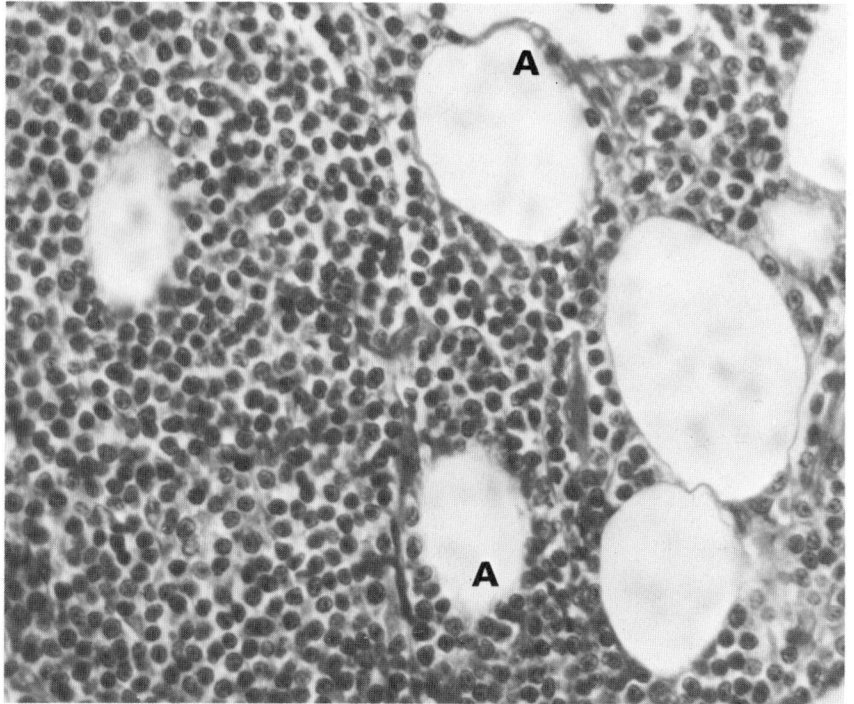

Figure 32.16. Lymphocytic lymphoma, well differentiated, of axillary lymph node.
Monotonous structure composed of well-differentiated, mature lymphocytes invading perinodal adipose tissue (A). (×250)

The histologic pattern can be nodular or diffuse,[49, 53] resulting in two distinct clinicopathologic entities.

1. Nodular lymphomas, arising usually in older individuals, originate in the immature center cells of the germinal centers.[31, 40] Progression is slower and survival is relatively long.
2. Diffuse lymphomas (Figure 32.18(a)), affecting younger individuals, originate in immature cells of germinal centers or parafollicular areas. Progression is faster and survival is shorter.

Both types may be associated with peripheral blood involvement, giving the clinical appearance of lymphosarcoma cell leukemia. Immunologic studies indicate that lymphomas of both patterns are monoclonal, of B-cell type, and expressing more often IgM-kappa surface immunoglobulins (Figure 32.19).[6, 7, 33]

Ultrastructurally, the neoplastic lymphoid cells of germinal center origin are aggregated in nodules or arranged diffusely. Cells are large, with distinct plasma membranes and abundant cytoplasm containing numerous mitochondria (Figure 32.18(b)), numerous cisternae of endoplasmic reticulum, well-developed Golgi body. Nuclei may be large, noncleaved (Figure 32.20) with occasional indentations or cleaved (Figure 32.18(b)). Dilated perinuclear cisterna, dense marginated heterochromatin, huge nonhomogeneous nucleoli are also seen (Figure 32.20).[3]

438

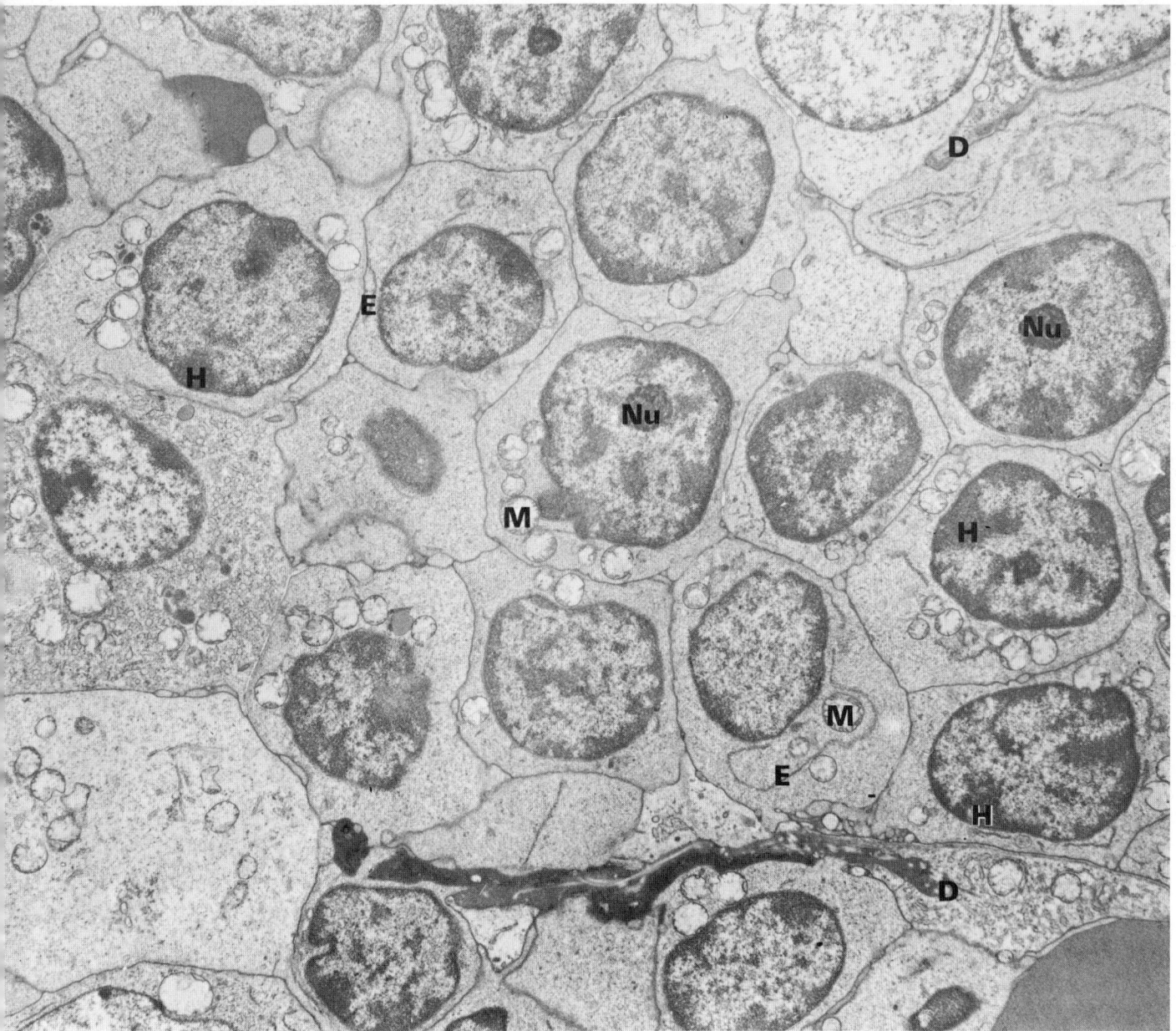

Figure 32.17. Lymphocytic lymphoma, well differentiated, of supraclavicular lymph node.

Sheet of monomorphous lymphocytes with round, noncleaved nuclei containing marginated, dense heterochromatin (H) and occasional nucleoli (Nu). Cytoplasm shows distinct plasma membrane, mitochondria (M), and rare profiles of endoplasmic reticulum (E). D: dendritic process of reticular cell. ($\times$ 6,000)

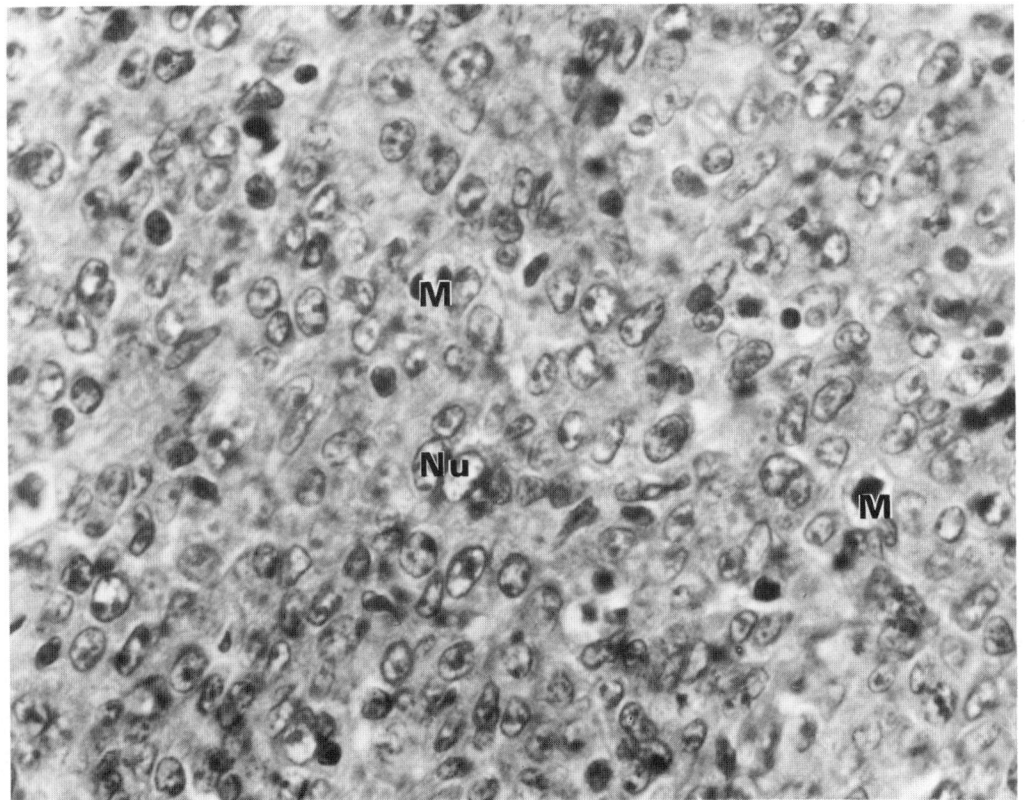

Figure 32.18. Lymphocytic lymphoma, diffuse, poorly differentiated, of axillary lymph node.

(a) Nuclei with thick nuclear membrane and prominent nucleoli (Nu) are shown. Mitoses (M) are frequent. (×400)

Lymphoma, undifferentiated, Burkitt's type

Malignant lymphoid neoplasia mainly of children (median age 7 years)[64] occurs endemically in tropical Africa and occasionally in other areas. The Epstein–Barr virus is the suspected etiologic agent. Major localizations are in the jaws, ovaries, and brain.

Light microscopy shows sheets of tightly packed, primitive lymphoid cells with interspersed large, palely-stained histiocytes giving the "starry-sky" pattern (Figure 32.21). The lymphoid cells are relatively uniform in size and shape with scarce, intensely basophilic cytoplasm and round or clefted nuclei. Nucleoli are two to five, and inconspicuous.[63] Intracytoplasmic vacuoles containing neutral lipids, probably as a result of high cell death rate, are frequent. The histiocytes display intense phagocytosis expressed by engulfed pyknotic nuclei and other cell debris.

On ultrastructural examination large, rounded cells (approximately 12 μm in diameter) with high nuclear–cytoplasmic ratio are visible (Figure 32.22). There are few mitochondria and poorly developed Golgi body and endoplasmic reticulum. The most prominent cytoplasmic feature is the presence of large numbers of polysomes.[1,63] The chromatin is clumped and marginated, with a frequent accumulation of granular

440

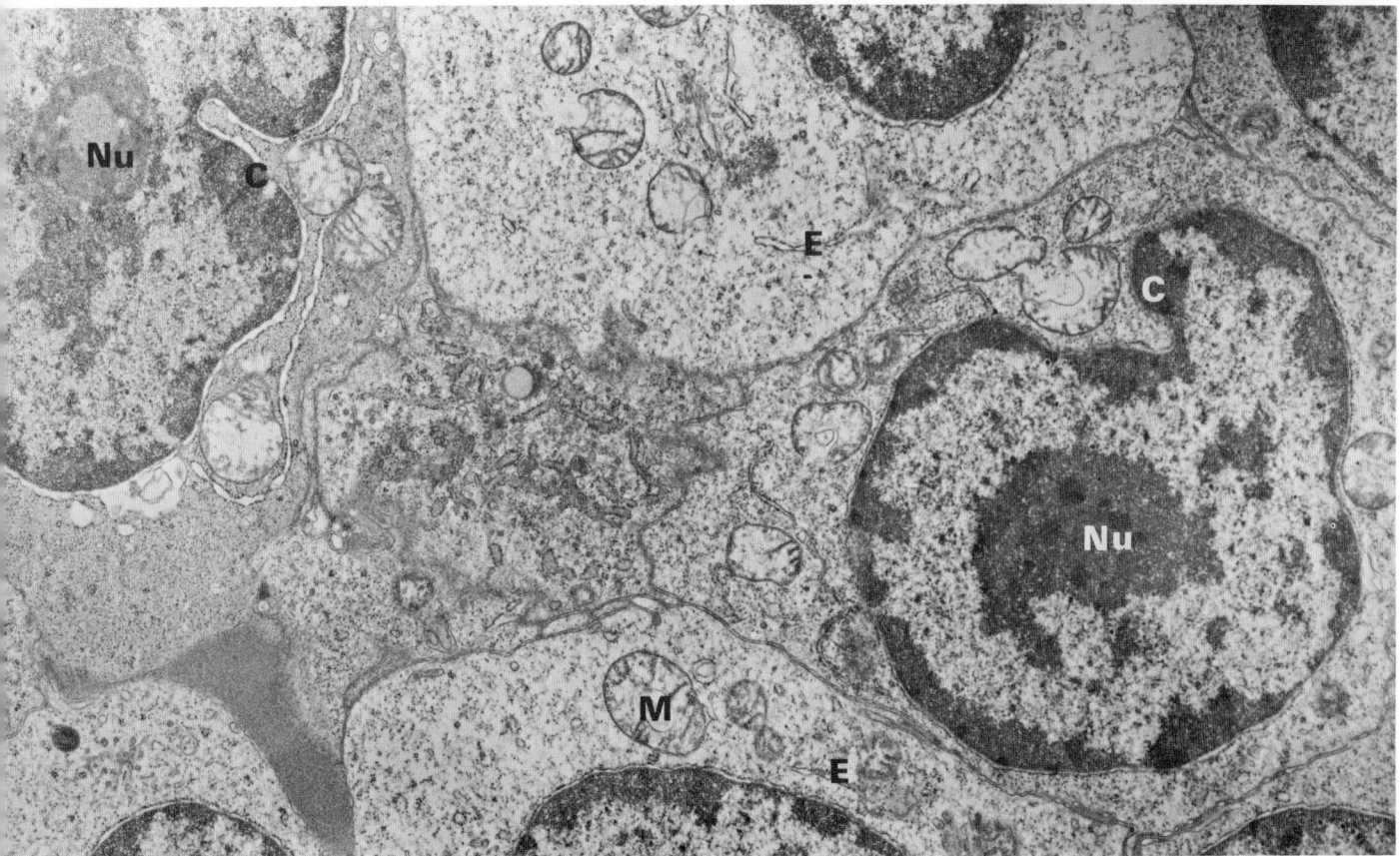

Figure 32.18. Lymphocytic lymphoma, diffuse, poorly differentiated, of axillary lymph node.

(b) Cleaved nuclei (C) with nonhomogeneous nucleoli (Nu) are shown. Cytoplasm contains numerous mitochondria (M) and dilated endoplasmic reticulum (E). (× 13,200)

material in the nuclear center.[1,63] The appearance is that of a stem cell. The histiocytes contain multiple phagosomes and exhibit the usual, non-neoplastic morphology with monomorphous nuclei and fine nucleoli.

Lymphoblastic lymphoma

The T-cell lymphoma (lymphoblastic lymphoma with convoluted nuclei) is an entity recently described[24,43,46,49] occurring in teenagers and young adults, with the main location in the anterior mediastinum. It has a relentless, aggressive, malignant course and a tendency to early generalization with involvement of various lymph nodes, bone marrow, peripheral blood, and central nervous system.

Light microscopy reveals that the lymph node structure is effaced and the histologic pattern is diffuse. The component cells are closely packed and monomorphous, with indistinct cytoplasm and round or ovoid, fairly large nuclei (Figure 32.23). On thin sections, nuclear convolutions and indentations are noted.[42] Mitoses are fre-

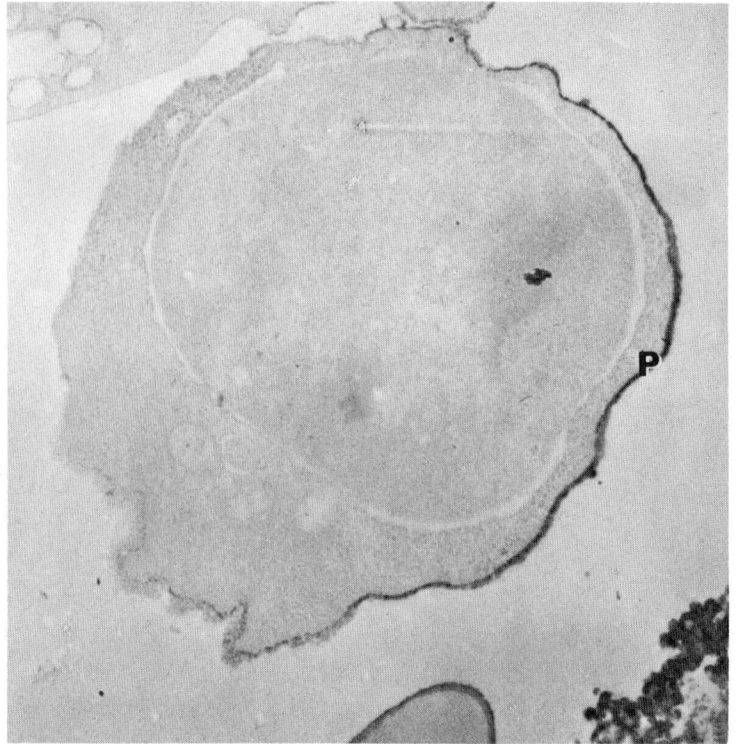

Figure 32.19. Lymphocytic lymphoma; poorly differentiated, diffuse.

Positive staining (P) of membrane immunoglobulins with peroxidase-labelled antihuman IgM serum is shown.

quent. Giant or bizarre cellular elements are rare and the degree of cellular differentiation is poor.

Using immunological techniques the neoplastic lymphoid cells form rosettes with sheep erythrocytes, thus being identified as T cell. They do not show surface immunoglobulins when stained with fluorescein- or peroxidase-labeled anti-Ig sera (Figure 32.24) and do not form EAC rosettes.

Electron microscopy shows that the cells are moderately sized with scarce cytoplasm and a paucity of organelles including a few mitochondria, Golgi body, rare profiles of endoplasmic reticulum, and free ribosomes. The nuclei are very large and markedly cleaved (Figure 32.25(a), (b)) with dense, peripheral condensations of chromatin. Perinuclear cisterna is prominent. The nucleolus is conspicuous and often peripheral.

Figure 32.20. Lymphocytic lymphoma, diffuse, poorly differentiated, of cervical lymph node.

Very large, noncleaved nuclei with marginated, dense heterochromatin (H), nonhomogeneous nucleoli (Nu), and distended perinuclear cisterna (C) are shown. (× 18,000)

442

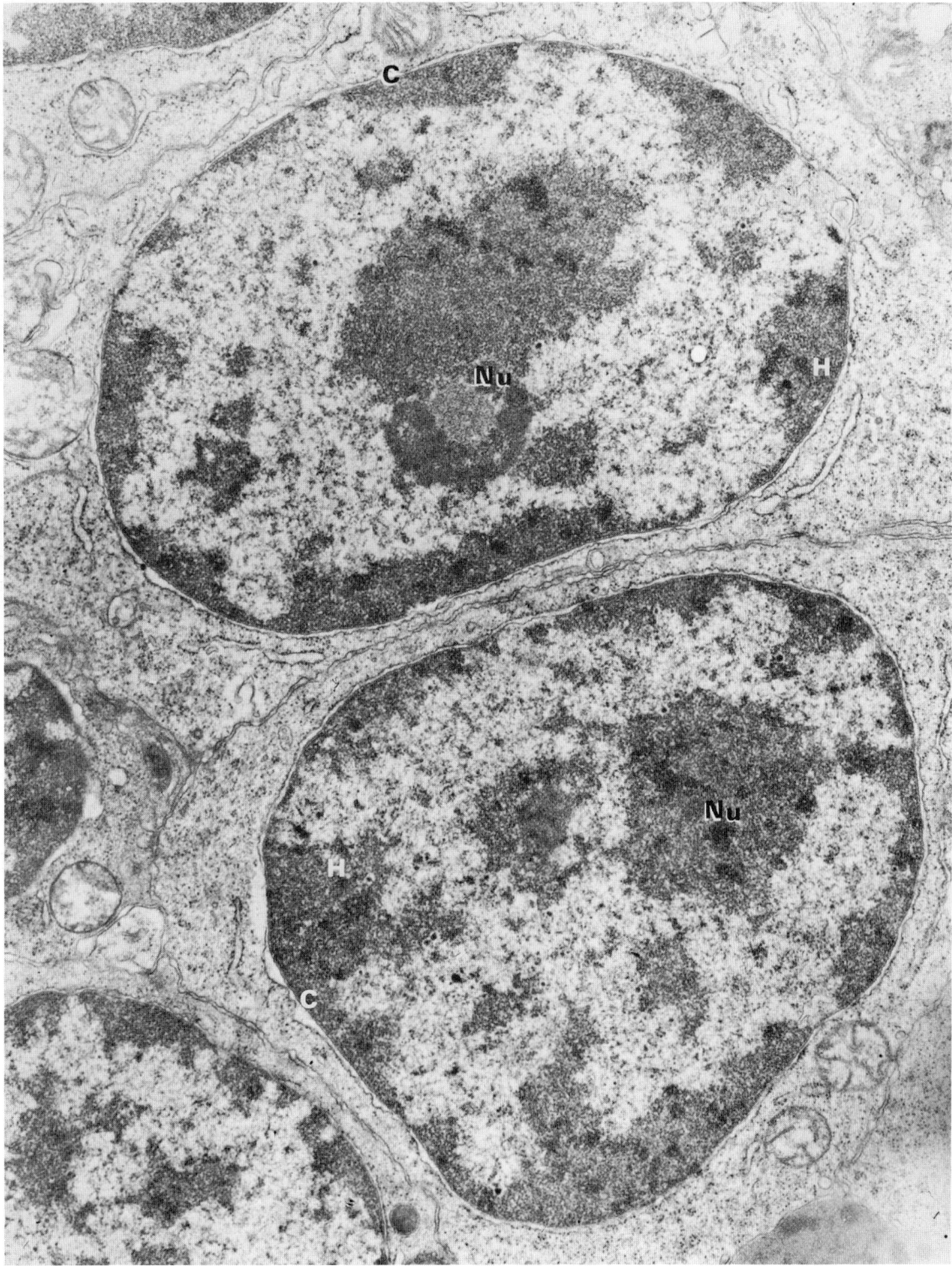

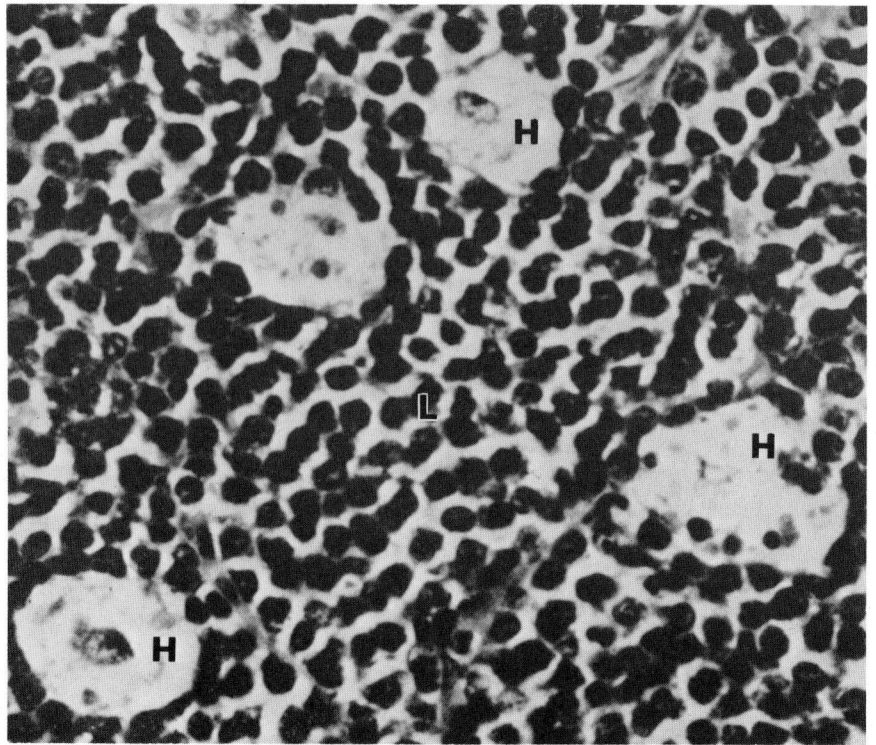

Figure 32.21. Burkitt's lymphoma (J. L. Ziegler and I. T. Magrath).
Sheet of undifferentiated lymphoid cells (L) with interspersed, large, clear histiocytes (H) giving the "starry-sky" pattern. Case from Uganda. (×535)

Lymphocytic lymphoma, plasmacytoid type

The neoplastic proliferation of immunoglobulin-producing cells (B-lymphocytes and plasma cells) is usually accompanied by overproduction of anomalous proteins that can be identified in the serum or urine. Because the neoplastic process involves a single clone of cells, the immunoglobulins that they secrete belong to one of five classes of immunoglobulins or to their heavy or light polypeptide chains and appear on electrophoresis as a characteristic, homogeneous spike.[18,62] The most common neoplasias associated with a monoclonal gammopathy are: multiple myeloma, lymphocytic lymphoma, and chronic lymphocytic leukemia. Of these, lymphocytic lymphomas, involving the cell populations normally responsible for the synthesis of IgM globulins, are primarily localized in lymph nodes and constitute the macroglobulinemia of Waldenström.[62] Subsequently, bone marrow, spleen, liver (portal spaces), and other organs may be involved.

Involved lymph nodes are enlarged, and light microscopy shows effacement of their architecture with lymphocytic infiltration of the capsule and perinodal fibroadipose tissues. The cortical follicles are indistinct, however, the sinuses may remain patent.[18,25] The lymphocytic infiltrate has a diffuse pattern and includes well-differentiated lymphocytes, plasmacytoid lymphocytes, plasma cells, hemosiderin-laden

444

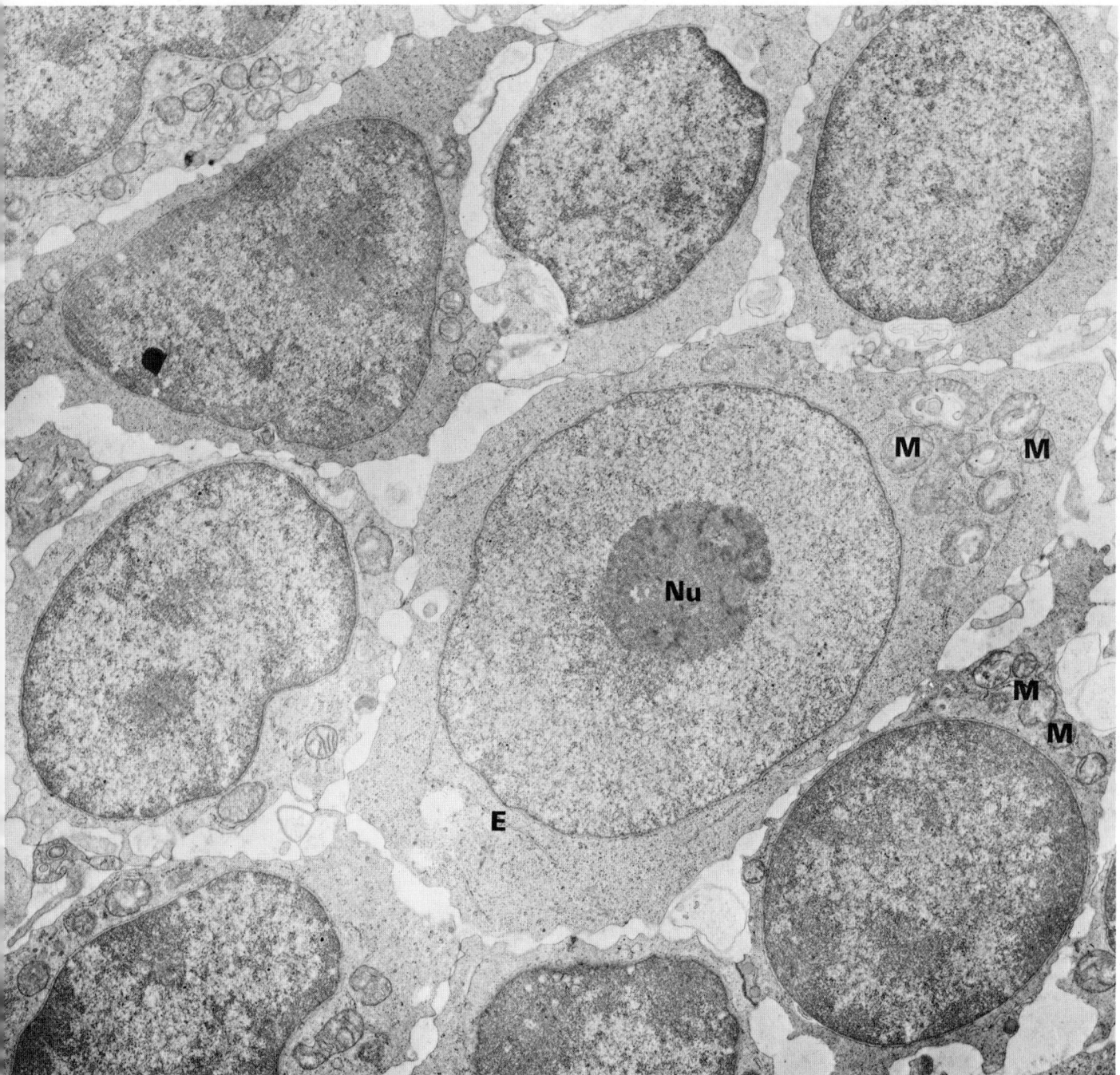

Figure 32.22. Burkitt's lymphoma in cervical lymph node (B. Mackay).

Cells are large and rounded, with few processes. Cytoplasm contains abundant ribosomes and polysomes and a few long threads of endoplasmic reticulum (E). Large mitochondria are concentrated at one pole of the cell (M). Note nuclei with fine euchromatin, occasional clumps of heterochromatin, and large nucleolus (Nu). (× 12,600)

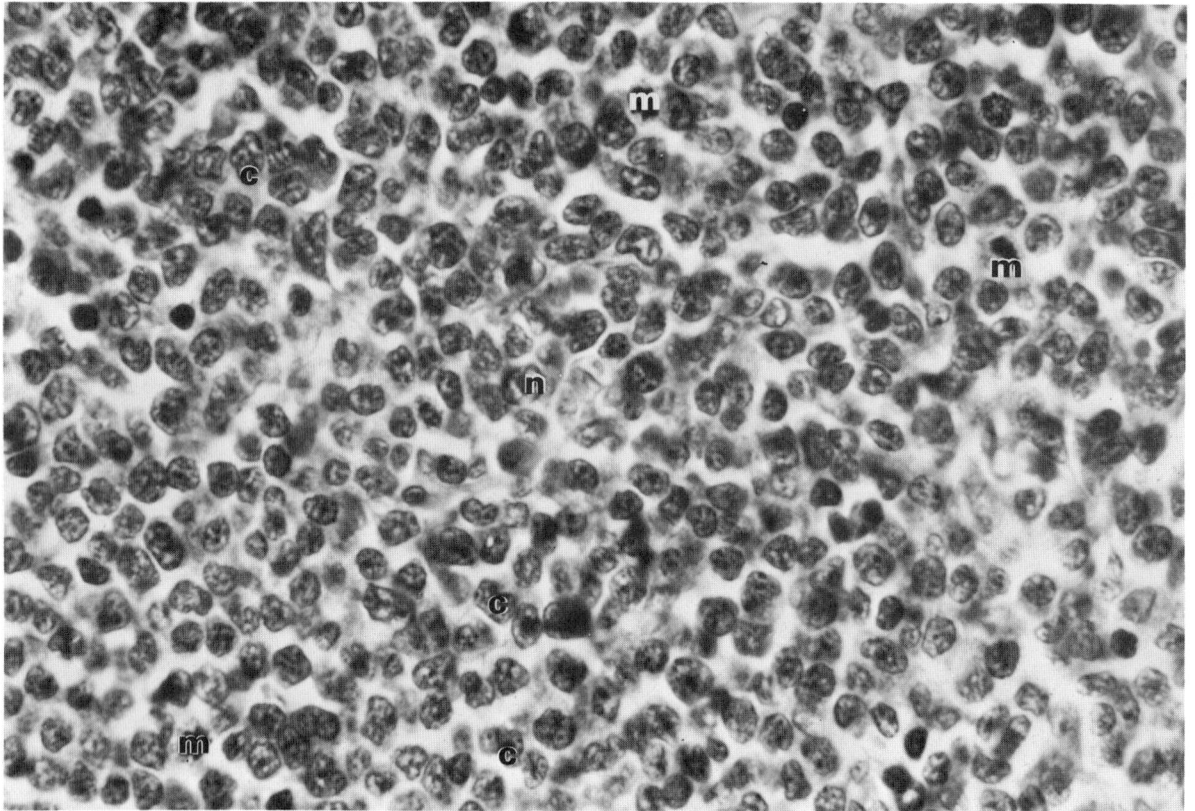

Figure 32.23. Lymphoblastic lymphoma, mediastinal.
Uniform infiltrate of closely packed neoplastic lymphoid cells. Cytoplasm is indistinct, nuclei are large, cleaved (c) with occasional large nucleoli (n) and frequent mitoses (m). (×400)

histiocytes, and occasional mast cells (Figure 32.26). The plasma in blood vessels appears darkly stained due to its high viscosity.

The plasmacytoid lymphocytes, characteristic cellular components of Waldenström's macroglobulinemia,[18] are transitional forms between B lymphocytes and plasma cells. The cytoplasm is ample, the nucleus eccentric, the chromatin structure is clumped.[18] Nuclear pleomorphism is low and mitoses infrequent. PAS-positive inclusion bodies are present both in the nucleus and in the cytoplasm of a variable number of cells (Figure 32.26).

Cytochemistry studies demonstrate that the intracellular inclusion bodies are diastase PAS-positive,[18] similar to the intravascular plasma. They are glycoproteins with a hexose content greater than 4 percent and with the aid of fluorescein-labeled monospecific sera, using the immunofluorescence technique, can be identified as IgM globulins.

Ultrastructural studies show that the plasmacytoid lymphocytes are slightly larger than the mature lymphocytes and contain abundant, stacked cisternae of rough endoplasmic reticulum (Figure 32.27(a), (b)). Even the cells identifiable as lymphocytes

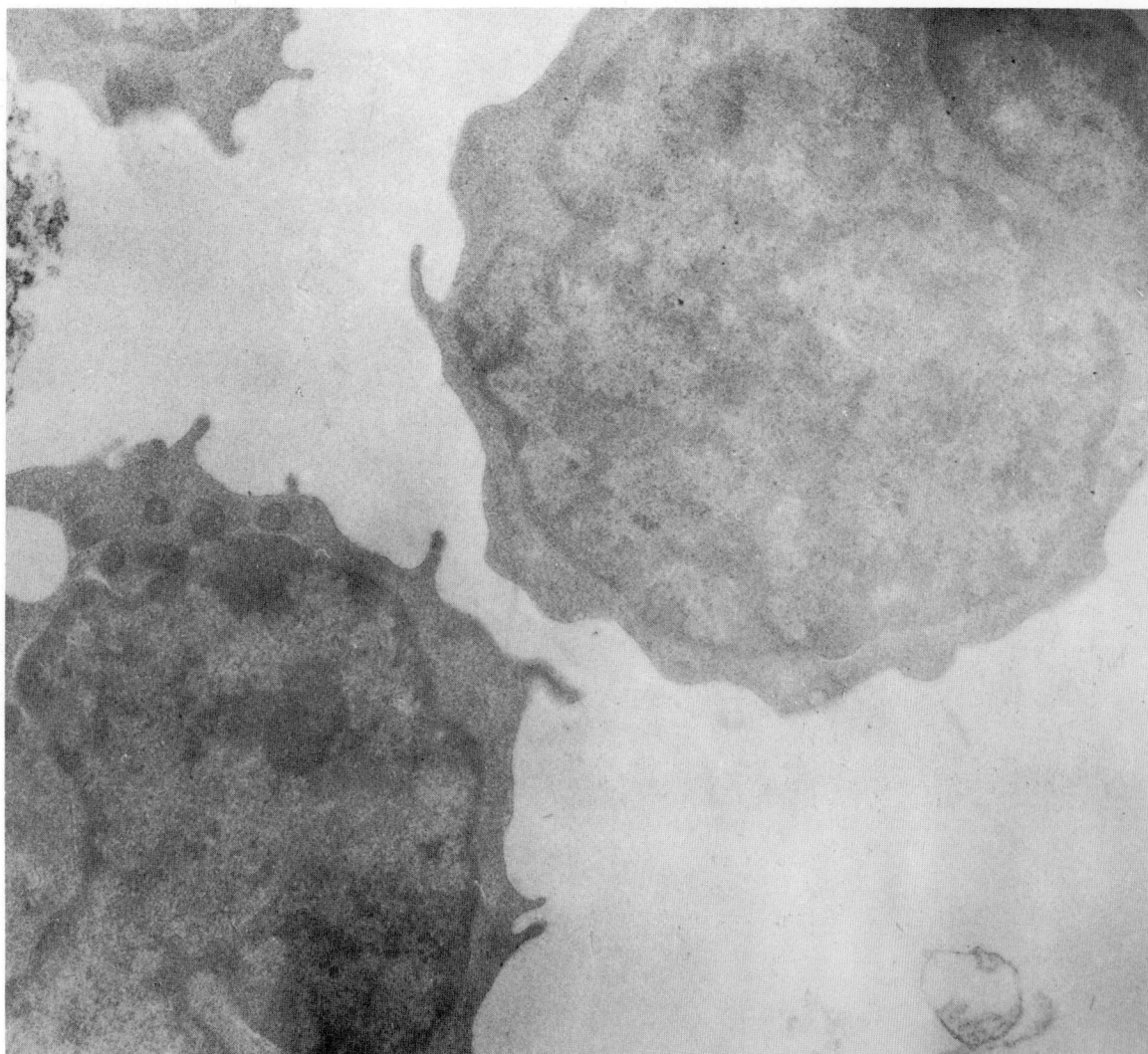

Figure 32.24. Lymphoblastic lymphoma.
Neoplastic lymphoblasts from cervical lymph node stained with peroxidase-labeled antihuman polyvalent 1g serum. Large cleaved nuclei. Negative peroxidase reaction, indicating lack of surface Ig. (× 15,000)

have more rough endoplasmic reticulum than normal lymphocytes, suggesting that they are engaged in active antibody synthesis. The nuclei have the clumped hetero-chromatin structure of lymphocytes. The intracytoplasmic inclusion bodies are mem-brane-bound and contain a flocculent material (Figure 32.27(a)). In the nucleus, the inclusions are eccentrically placed, and usually apposed to the nuclear membrane (Figure 32.27(b)). Multiple inclusions can be present in one nucleus and attain large proportions, deforming the nucleus and protruding into the cytoplasm.[4] Their relation with the perinuclear cisterna is variable, sometimes entirely separated, at other times in continuity due to fusion of the two membranes.[38] The content of intranuclear

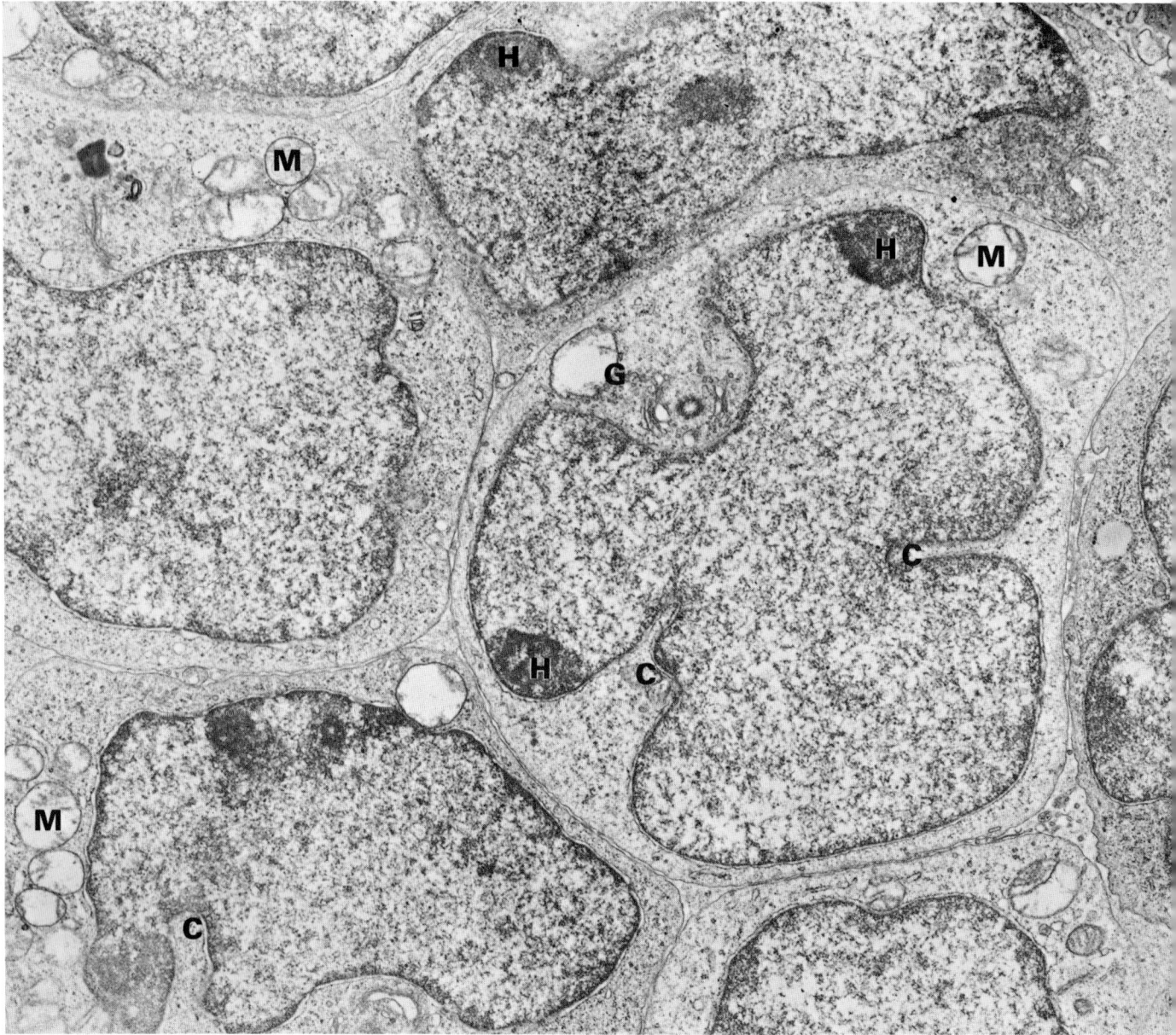

(a)

Figure 32.25. Lymphoblastic lymphoma.

(a) Lymph node section showing closely apposed neoplastic lymphoid cells. Cytoplasm contains mitochondria (M), Golgi body (G). Note markedly cleaved nuclei (C) and dense,
peripheral heterochromatin (H). (× 12,600)

(b) Neoplastic lymphoblast in cervical lymph node. Note cytoplasm with mitochondria (M)
and free ribosomes (R), and the cleaved nucleus (N) with dense, peripheral heterochromatin (H) and nucleolus (Nu). (× 24,600)

448

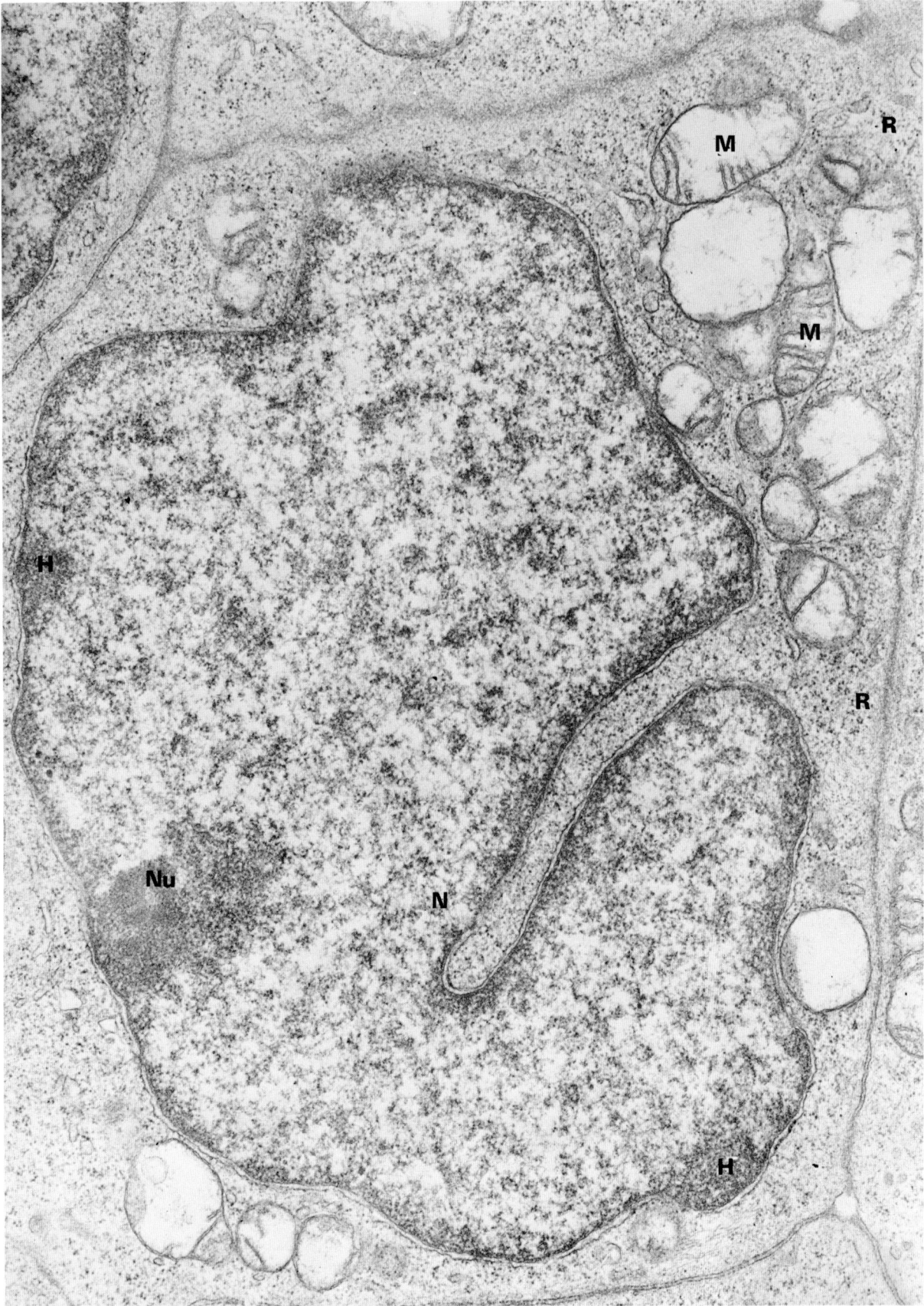

(b)

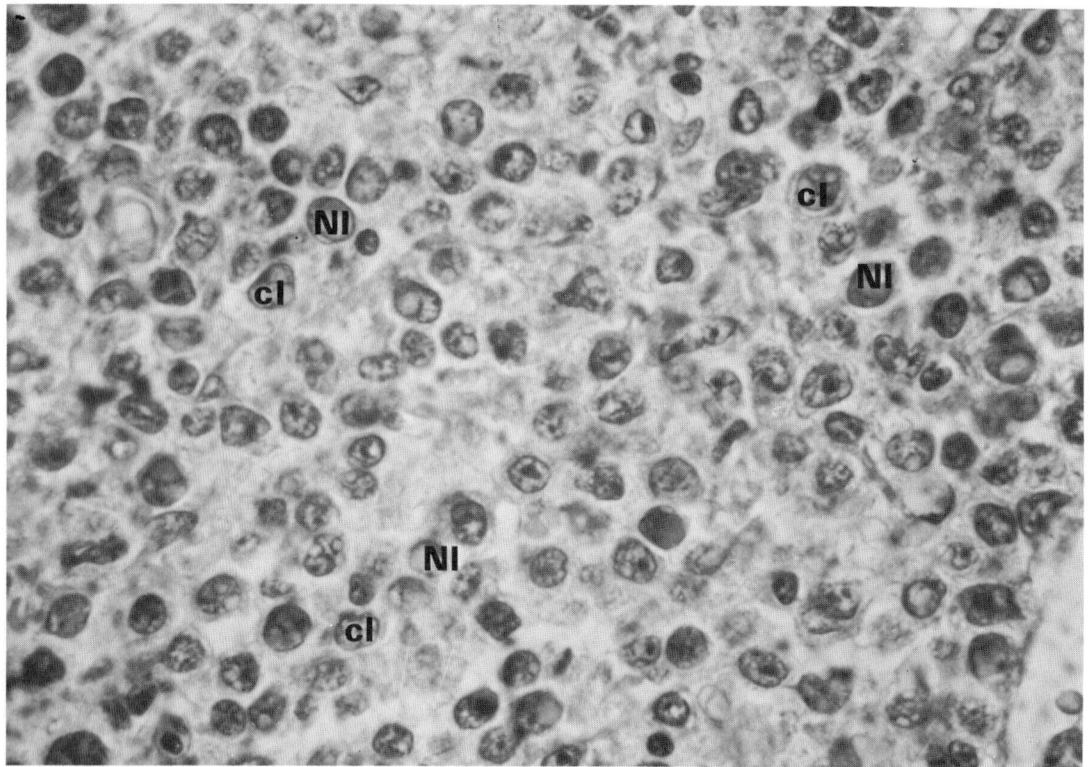

Figure 32.26. Lymphocytic lymphoma, plasmacytoid type, (Waldenstrom's macroglobulinemia).
Node infiltrated by plasmacytoid lymphocytes containing multiple intracytoplasmic and intranuclear inclusion (NI) bodies. (× 400)

inclusions is finely granular or flocculent like that of the intracytoplasmic inclusions.[9] However, on occasion, the inclusions are nonhomogeneous and include finely granular as well as strongly osmiophilic areas.[38] Smaller inclusions may be surrounded by concentric layers of a fibrillar material.[38] While the content of the intranuclear inclusions has been identified as IgM, their mode of origin is not entirely clear. It is believed that they arise by intranuclear invaginations of the perinuclear cisterna. Other observations, however, support the idea of intranuclear bodies as sites of globulin synthesis.[38]

Histiocytic lymphoma

According to the original description,[53] this entity is characterized by large, irregularly shaped neoplastic cells with abundant, palely stained cytoplasm, pleomorphic

---

Figure 32.27. Lymphocytic lymphoma plasmacytoid type, (Waldenstrom's macroglobulinemia).

(a) Lymph node infiltrated by plasmacytoid lymphocytes with interlocked cytoplasmic processes (P). Note multiple stacks of rough endoplasmic reticulum (ER), intracytoplasmic (CI) and intranuclear (NI) membrane-bound inclusion bodies, containing finely granular or nonhomogeneous material, large reticulated nucleolus (Nu). (× 7,100)

450

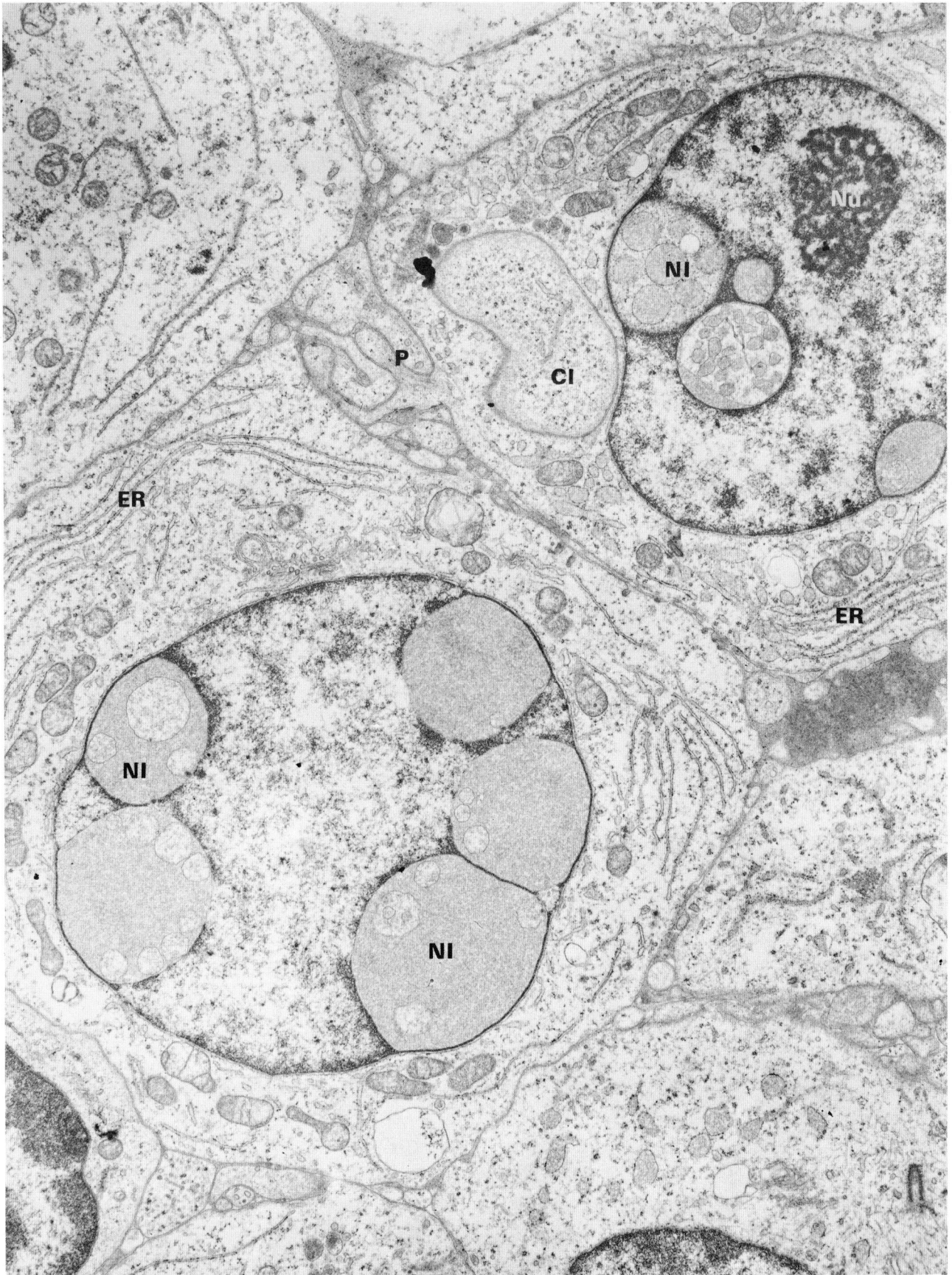

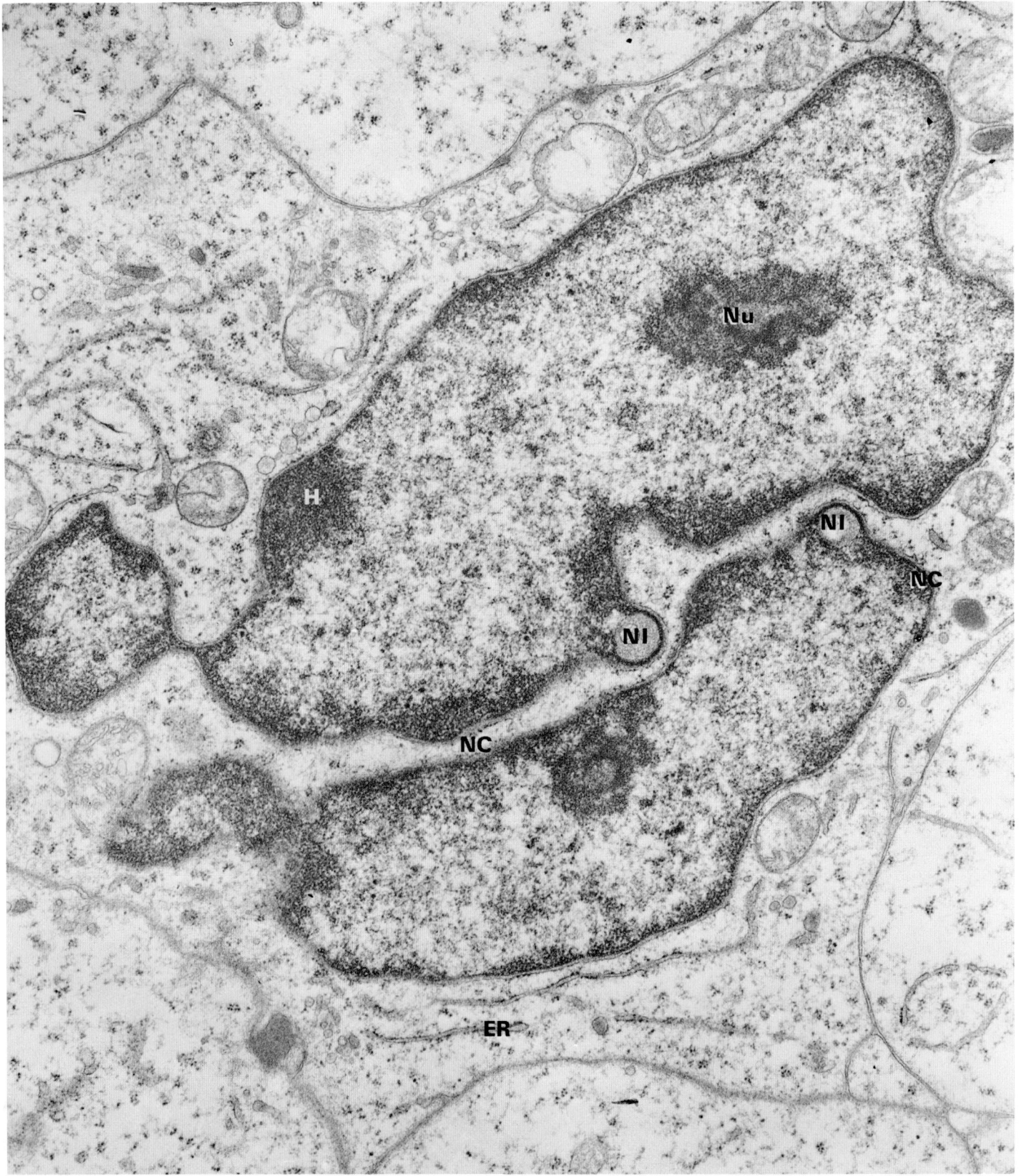

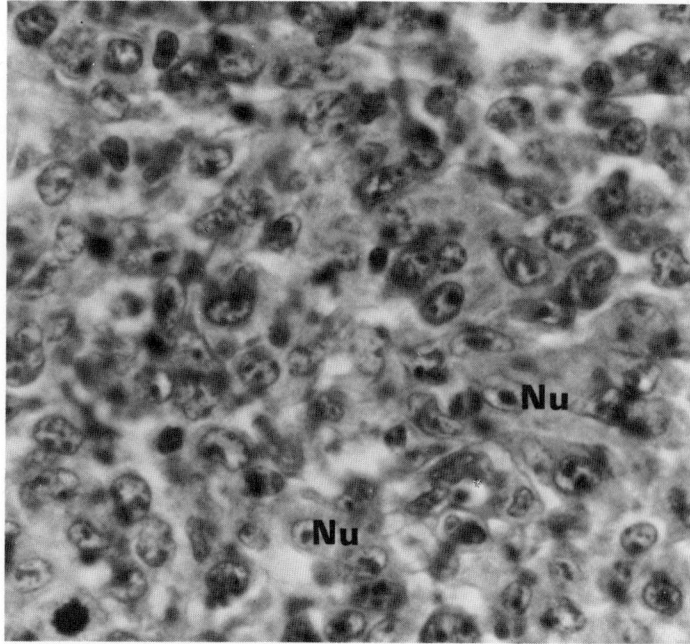

Figure 32.28. "Histiocytic" lymphoma of axillary lymph node. Sheets of large neoplastic cells containing round or ovoid nuclei with thick nuclear membranes and prominent nucleoli (Nu) indicative of germinal center cell origin. (×400)

nuclei, and prominent nucleoli. Presently, it is recognized that this category is heterogeneous[8,14,43,54] including, in addition to the lymphomas originating in histiocytes, other lymphoid neoplasms derived from activated lymphocytes of the germinal centers. A distinction between these two entities is often impossible to make by conventional light microscopy.[47] Therefore, immunologic investigation of cell surface markers is used to determine the lymphocytic or histiocytic origin of large cell lymphomas. In addition, in most cases, the electron microscopic study of such lymphomas permits a correct diagnosis based on ultrastructural features.

Lymphomas that originate in immunoblasts of center cell origin comprise large neoplastic cells with abundant cytoplasm, pleomorphic nuclei, and prominent nucleoli (Figure 32.28). However, the nuclear structure is characteristically lymphoid, with clumped, peripheralized heterochromatin.

Figure 32.27. Lymphocytic lymphoma, plasmacytoid type, (Waldenstrom's macroglobulinemia).

(b) Plasmacytoid lymphocytes with multiple endoplasmic reticulum cisternae (ER) and polyribosomes. Bizarre, neoplastic nucleus contains clumped heterochromatin (H) and a large nucleolus (Nu). Note protruding intranuclear inclusion bodies (NI) apposed to the dilated perinuclear cisterna (NC). (×18,000)

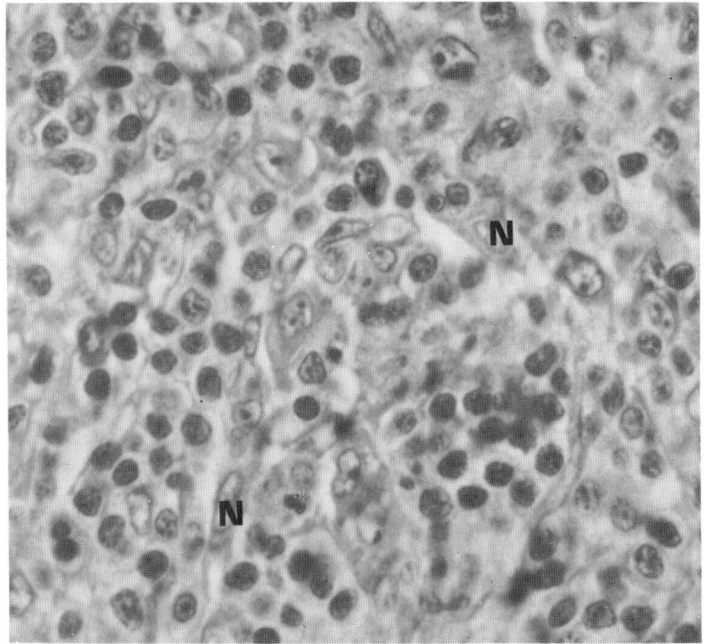

Figure 32.29. Histiocytic lymphoma of inguinal lymph node.

(a) Neoplastic cells contain abundant cytoplasm and elongated nuclei (N) with fine nucleoli indicative of histiocytic origin. (× 400)

Lymphomas that originate in histiocytes (Figure 32.29(a)) are composed of cells that may also be unusually large and contain bizarre pleomorphic nuclei with voluminous nucleoli (Figure 32.29(b)). However, the nuclear structure includes mostly euchromatin,[57] the nucleolus is more reticulated, and the cytoplasm contains lysosomes and phagosomes (Figure 32.29(c)). Cellular processes are frequently present. Thus electron microscopic examination is useful in the differentiation of large cell lymphomas.

32.2.2 Hodgkin's lymphoma

It is the commonest form of cancer in young adults and the commonest type of lymphoma of any age group in the United States.[13] Epidemiologic and immunologic studies have suggested a viral etiology.[29] It involves various groups of lymph nodes by contiguous progression[36] and spreads subsequently to spleen, liver, and bone marrow.

Figure 32.29. Histiocytic lymphoma of axillary lymph node.

(b) EM of lymph node represented in Figure 32.28(a). Neoplastic large cells contain abundant cytoplasm, numerous mitochondria (M), distended Golgi complex (G). Nuclei are pleomorphic and nucleoli (Nu) are prominent, but the nuclear structure is of lymphoid type with clumped, peripheralized heterochromatin (H).(× 12,600)

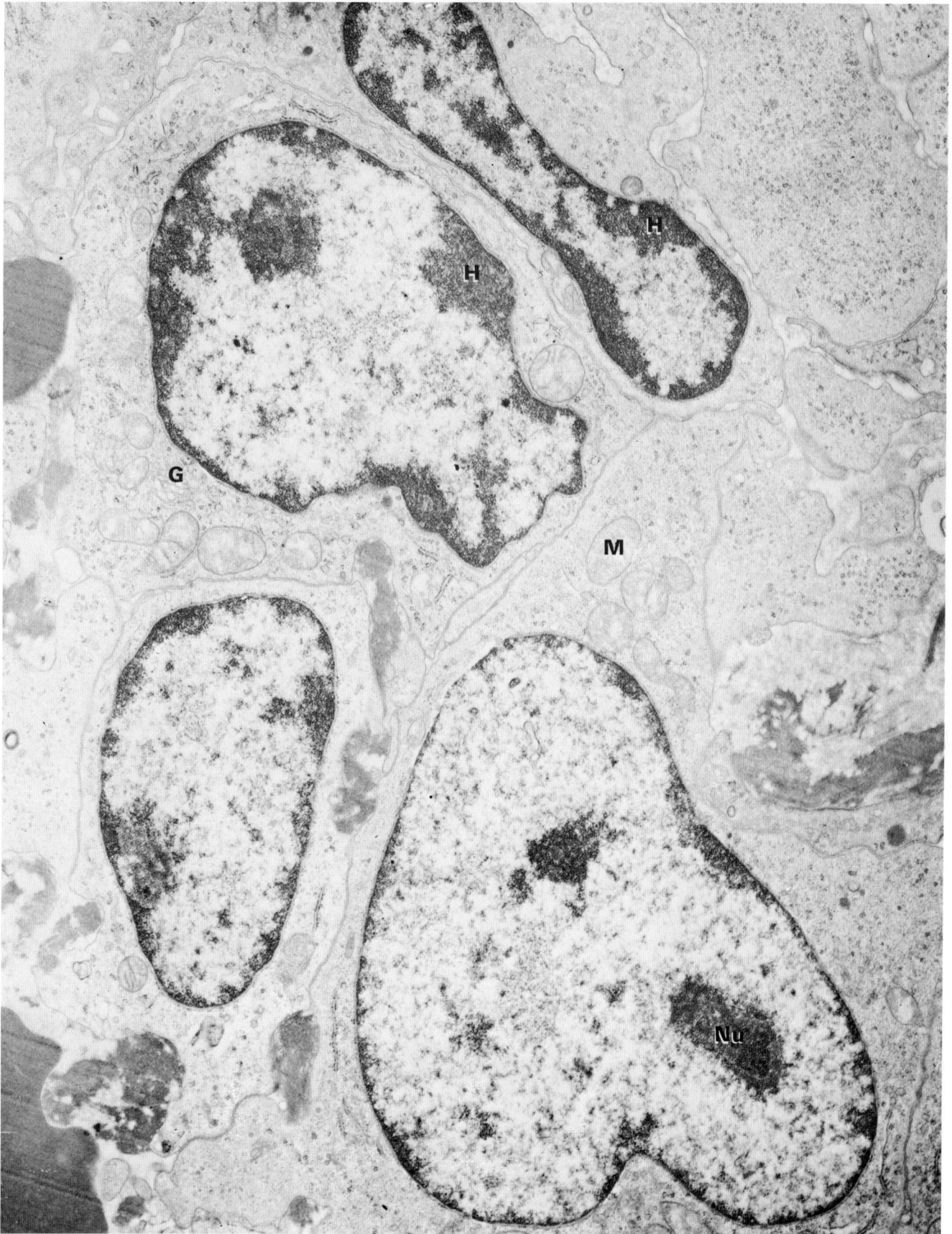

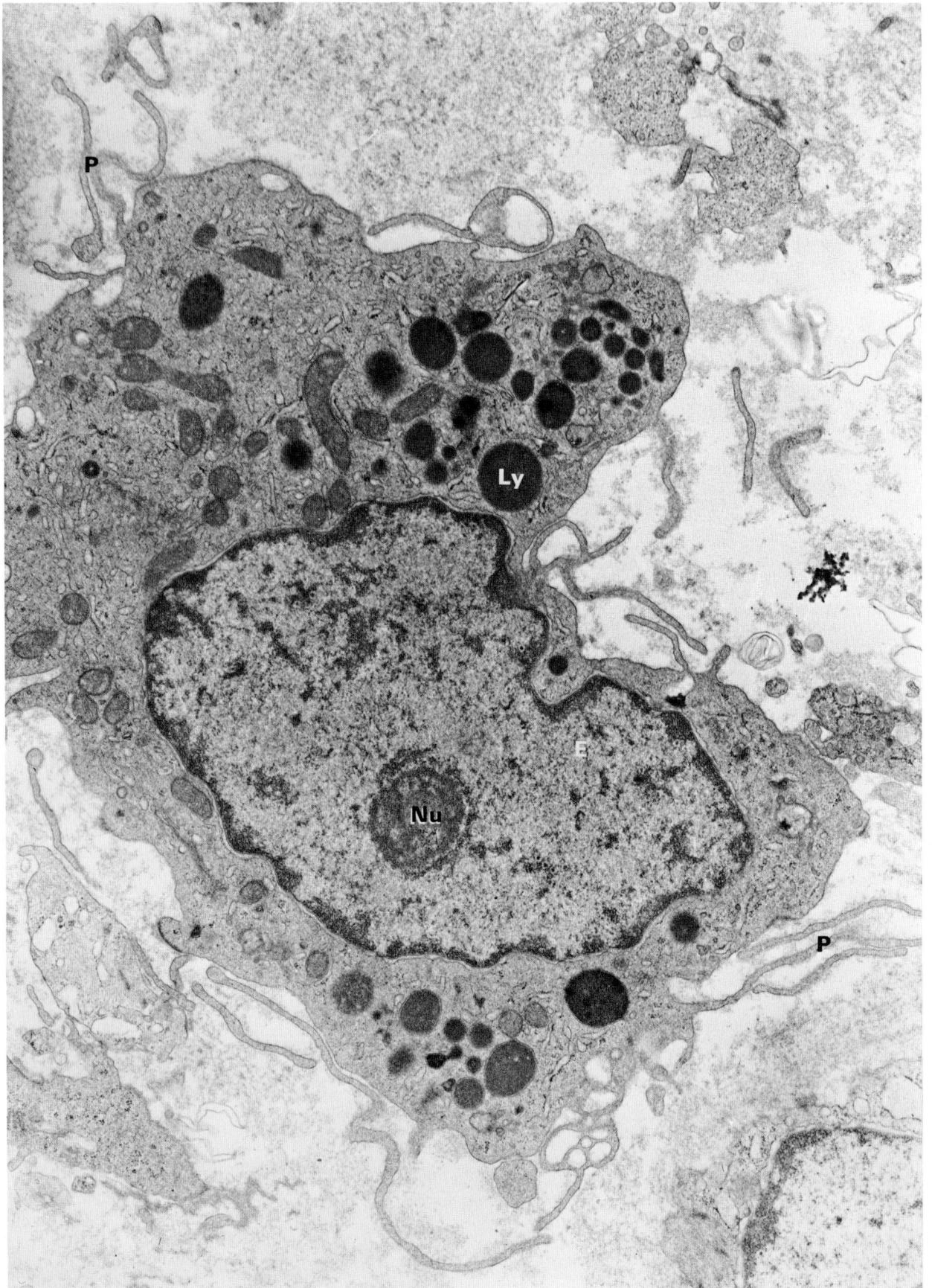

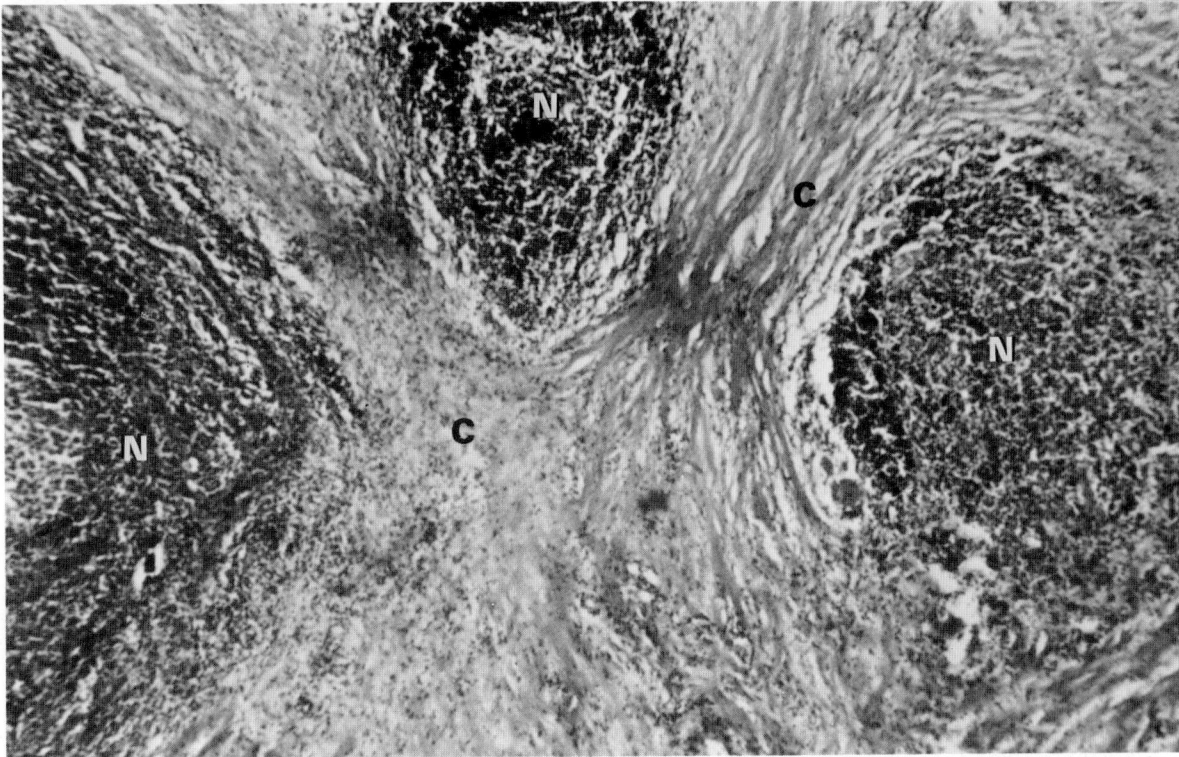

Figure 32.30. Hodgkin's disease, nodular sclerosis type.
Mediastinal lymph node. Nodules of cellular aggregates (N) including mainly lymphocytes and Reed–Sternberg cells separated by broad, dense, poorly cellular bands of fibrocollagen (C). (×210)

The histologic classification generally accepted is that proposed by a Nomenclature Committee at Rye, New York, in 1965[44] (Table 32.2):

Table 32.2. Hodgkin's lymphoma (Rye classification)

Lymphocyte predominance
Nodular sclerosis
Mixed cellularity
Lymphocyte depletion

1. Lymphocyte predominance: lymph node with partial architectural effacement due to diffuse proliferation of lymphocytes and histiocytes. Reed–Sternberg cells are infrequent.

Figure 32.29. Histiocytic lymphoma of inguinal lymph node.
(c) EM of lymph node represented in Figure 32.29(a). Neoplastic large cells show abundant cytoplasm, numerous organelles, pleiomorphic nucleus, and prominent nucleolus (Nu) but cytoplasm includes multiple lysosomes (Ly) and displays elongated processes (P). The nucleus has a fine structure of euchromatin (E). (×14,400)

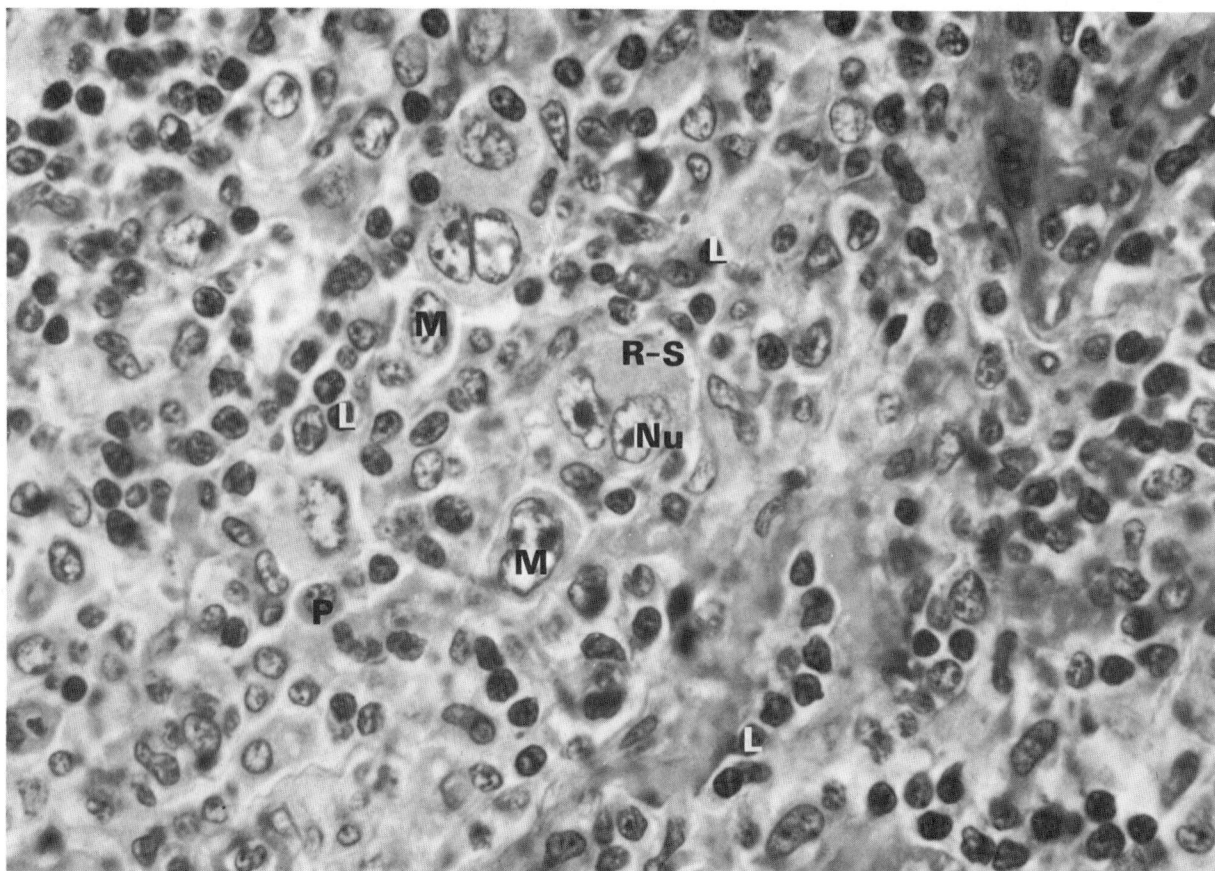

Figure 32.31. Hodgkin's disease, mixed cellularity type.
Cervical lymph node. Cellular infiltrate includes plasma cells (P), lymphocytes (L), neoplastic mononuclear cells (M), and Reed–Sternberg cell (R–S) with mirror-image nucleus containing prominent nucleoli (Nu). (×420)

2. Nodular sclerosis: characterized by broad bands of dense collagen fibers that circumscribe cellular nodules composed of lymphocytes, histiocytes, and Reed–Sternberg cells (Figure 32.30). In formalin-fixed specimens, the latter display a characteristic pericellular halo-like area (lacunar cells).[11]

3. Mixed cellularity: the most typical and easiest recognizable histologic type of Hodgkin's disease. The normal structure of tissues is obliterated and replaced by infiltrates of lymphocytes, eosinophils, neutrophils, plasma cells, neoplastic mononuclear cells (possibly neoplastic immunoblasts), and Reed–Sternberg cells (Figure 32.31). The neoplastic mononuclear cells show distinct cellular borders, thick nuclear membranes and huge, hyperchromatic pyroninophilic nucleoli.[11,29] The Reed–Sternberg cell, probably deriving from the mononuclear cells, is larger in size and similar in staining characteristics. The nucleus is bizarrely shaped with multiple indentations and lobulations, and contains prominent inclusion-like nucleoli (Figure 32.31).

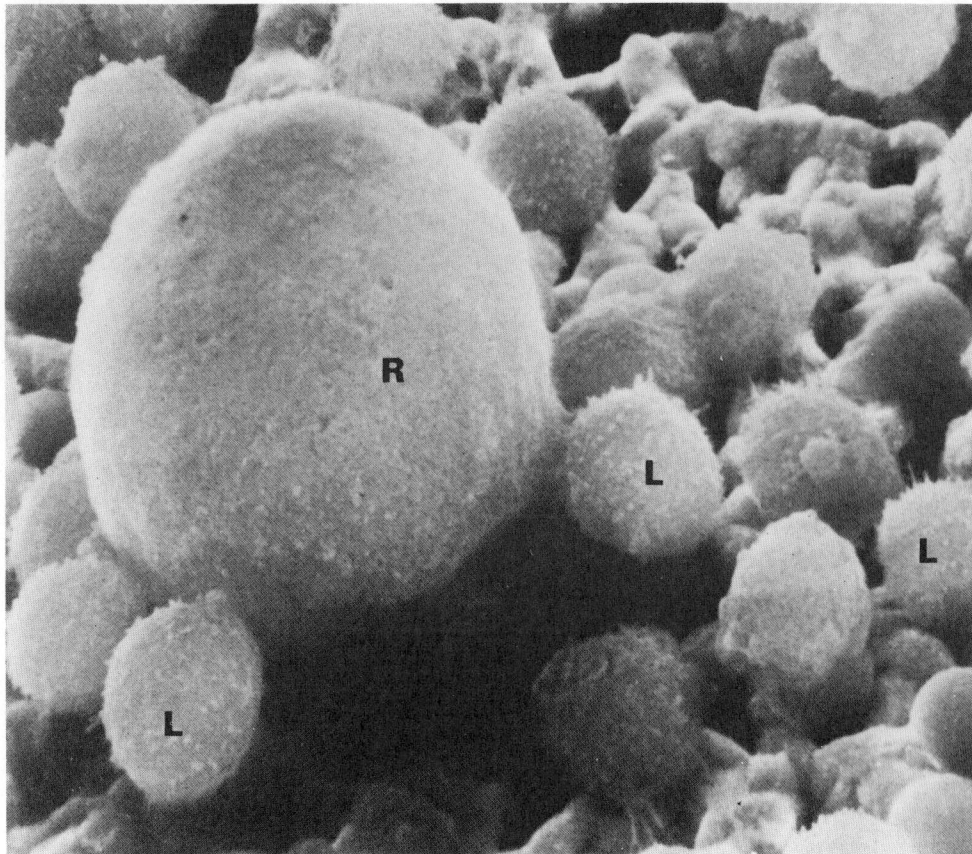

Figure 32.32. Lymph node cell suspension in Hodgkin's disease (R. C. Braylan, E. S. Jaffe, and C. W. Berard).

Large cell presumed to be a Reed–Sternberg cell (R) and small cells lymphocytes (L). SEM. (×2,950)

4. Lymphocyte depletion: advanced stage of disease with few lymphocytes and no plasma cells or eosinophils. The infiltrate is composed of neoplastic mononuclear cells and Reed–Sternberg cells (Figure 32.32).

Ultrastructurally, the neoplastic mononuclear cells are large and mostly rounded although occasional indentations can be noted. The cell membrane is sharply delineated and the cytoplasm contains numerous mitochondria and polysomes but poorly developed Golgi area and endoplasmic reticulum. The nuclei are very large and rounded. The heterochromatin is abundant and condensed around the nuclear membrane as well as in irregularly distributed clumps (Figure 32.35). The nucleolus is huge and nonhomogeneous. The general appearance is that of neoplastic immunoblasts of follicular center origin (Figures 32.34 and 32.35).

The Reed–Sternberg cell is significantly larger (Figures 32.33, 32.34 and 34.10) and irregularly shaped with abundant cytoplasm containing numerous mitochondria, some rod-shaped (Figures 32.33 and 32.34), polysomes, and dense bodies. Profiles of endoplasmic reticulum are rare. The nucleus is multilobated and irregularly shaped

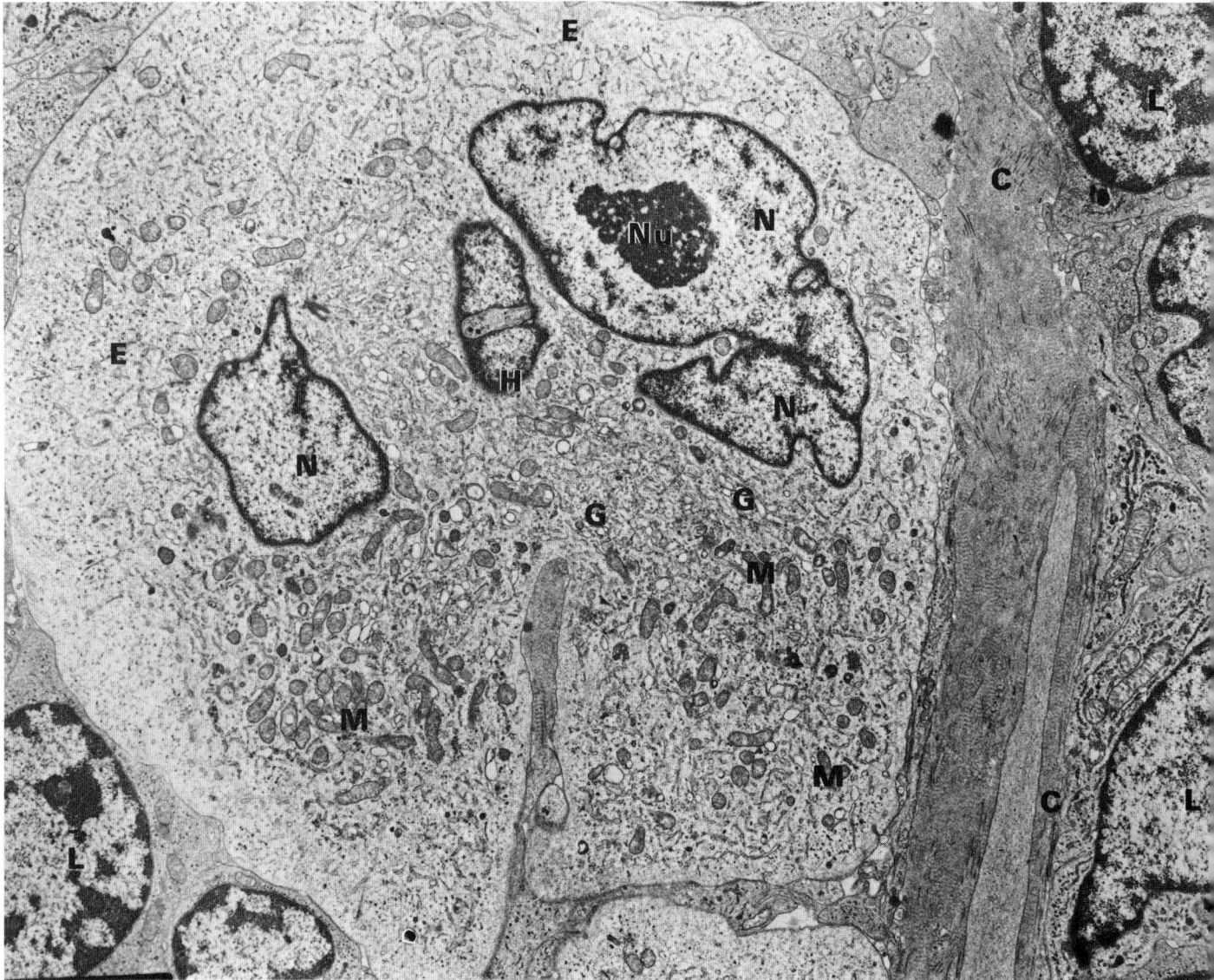

Figure 32.33. Hodgkin's disease, nodular sclerosis type, in mediastinal lymph node.
Reed–Sternberg cell with multilobated (apparently multinucleated) nucleus (N) including
prominent reticulated nucleolus (Nu) and peripheral heterochromatin (H). Cytoplasm contains
numerous rod-shaped mitochondria (M), scarce endoplasmic reticulum (E), and Golgi body
(G). Lymphoid cells (L) and bands of fibrocollagen (C) are also visible. (× 12,000)

Figure 32.34. Hodgkin's disease, mixed cellularity type in mesenteric lymph node.
Reed–Sternberg cell with lobated nucleus showing marginated heterochromatin (H) and
prominent nucleolus (Nu). The cytoplasm includes mitochondria (M) and few other organelles.
Note also plasma cell with well-developed endoplasmic reticulum (ER), activated lymphocytes
with interlocked processes (P), abundant cytoplasm, rod-shaped mitochondria (M), distended
Golgi body (G), large nucleus with marginated heterochromatin (H). Collagen fibers (C) are
also visible. (× 12,000)

460

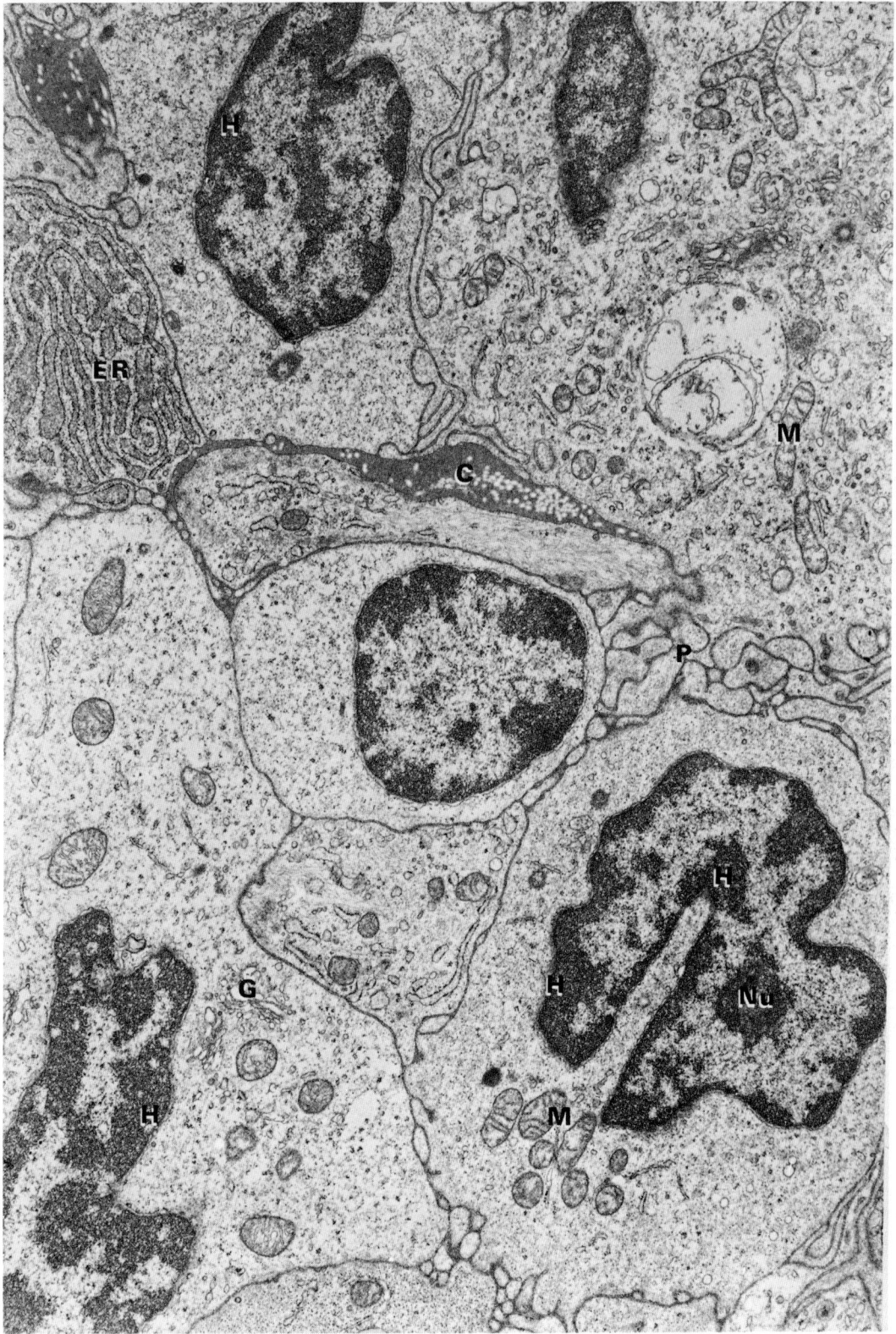

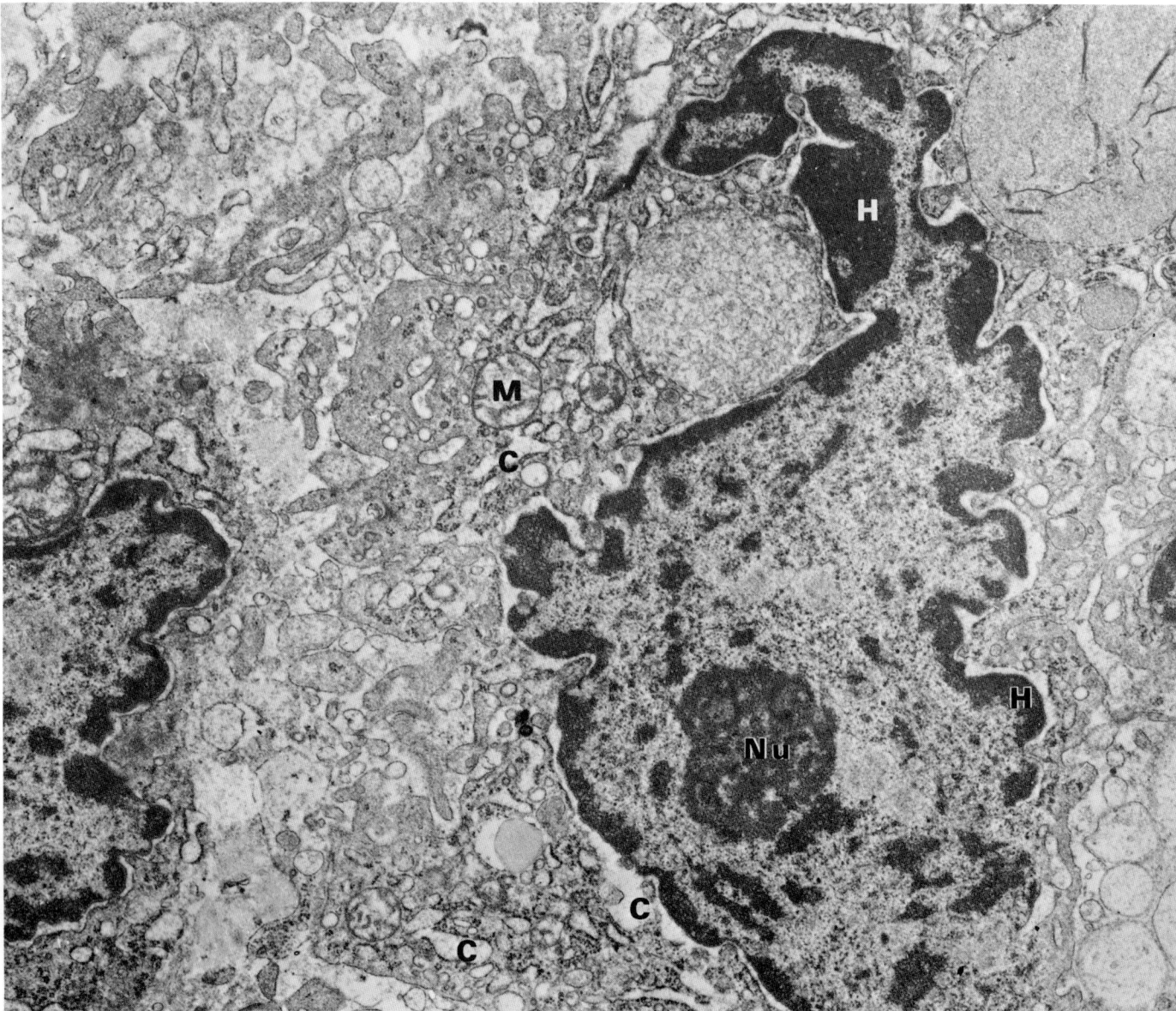

Figure 32.35. Hodgkin's disease, mixed cellularity type in cervical lymph node.
Large neoplastic mononuclear cell with abundant cytoplasm containing dilated cisternae (C). Irregularly shaped nucleus with marginated, clumped heterochromatin (H) and huge, reticulated nucleolus (Nu). M: mitochondria. (×24,000)

with sometimes thin bridges (inapparent in the plane of section) linking the nuclear lobes (see Figure 34.10). There is more euchromatin in the nuclear mass with marginated heterochromatin[3] and huge, dense, reticulated nucleoli (Figures 32.33, 32.34 and 34.10).

The lymphocytes show various degrees of cellular maturation expressed by the nuclear–cytoplasmic ratio, cytoplasmic organelles, chromatin structure, and presence

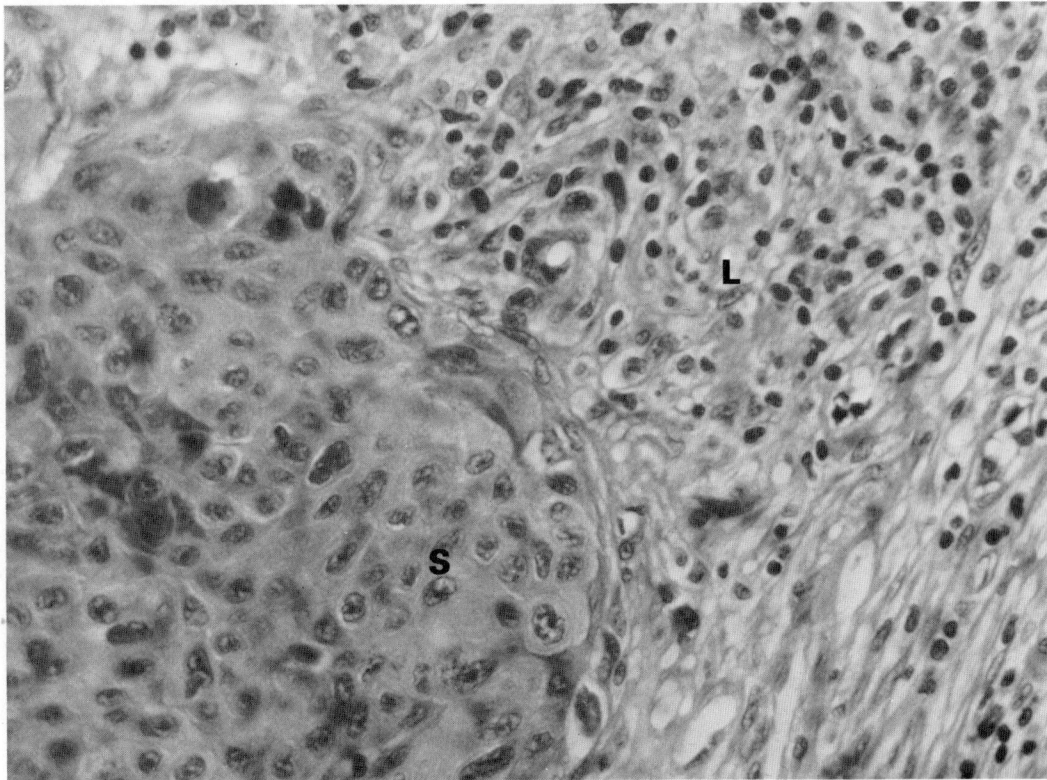

Figure 32.36. Metastatic squamous cell carcinoma of lung in mediastinal lymph node.

(a) Large island of neoplastic squamous epithelial cells (S) replacing lymphoid tissue (L). (×250)

of nucleoli. The plasma cells, eosinophils and neutrophils are of normal appearance. Interrelations between Reed–Sternberg cells and lymphocytes, expressed by clustering, juxtaposition, and interdigitation of processes, are frequently observed[16] (Figures 32.33, 32.34 and 34.10).

In nodular sclerosis, lymphocytes, neoplastic mononuclear cells, and Reed–Sternberg cells similar to those described are closely circumscribed by bands of collagen fibers showing the characteristic periodic structure (Figure 32.33).

32.2.3. Lymph node metastases

The lymph nodes are the most common metastatic site of malignant tumors. Spreading predominantly through the lymphatic vessels, carcinomas and melanomas invade the lymph nodes through the marginal sinuses where the first clusters of metastatic tumor cells can be detected.

Light microscopy shows cords, islands, or single tumor cells present in the lymph node sinuses from where extension into the lymphoid parenchyma occurs.[47] Variable areas of lymphoid tissues are thus replaced by neoplastic cells that exhibit various

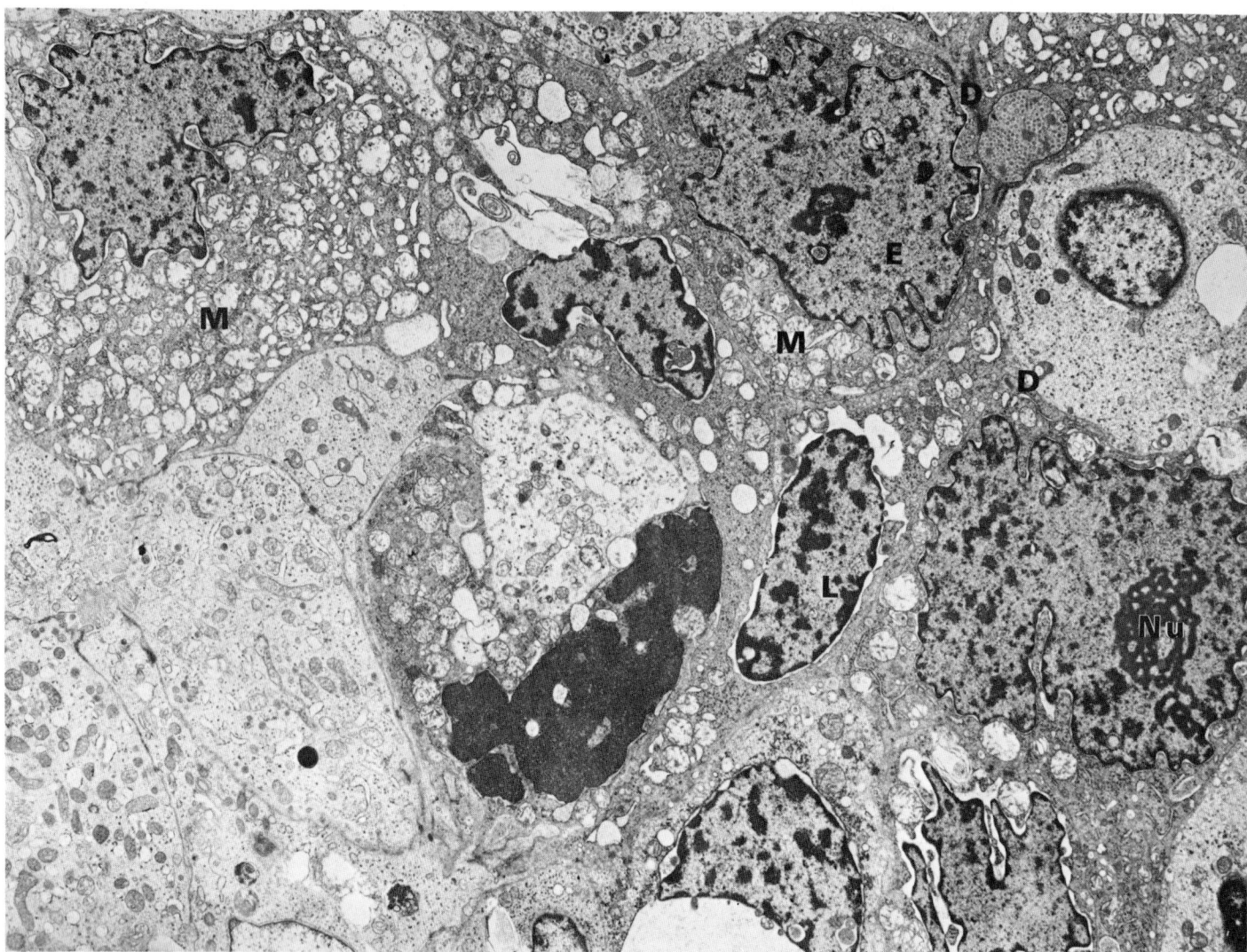

Figure 32.36. Metastatic squamous cell carcinoma of lung in mediastinal lymph node.

(b) Neoplastic cells joined by desmosomes (D) containing large numbers of mitochondria (M) and irregularly shaped nuclei with abundant euchromatin (E) and reticulated nucleoli (Nu). L: residual cortical lymphoid cells. (× 7,200)

histologic patterns according to their relative degree of cellular differentiation (Figures 32.36(a) and 32.37(a)).

The ultrastructural features of metastatic squamous cell carcinoma are in accordance with the grade of tumor differentiation. Metastases of well-differentiated squamous cell carcinoma are composed of large tumor cells with numerous, interlocked cellular processes and multiple desmosomes. The cytoplasm is abundant and contains numerous, fine tonofilaments. The nuclei are large and irregularly shaped, sometimes huge and bizarre with marginated clumps of heterochromatin (Figure 32.36(b)).

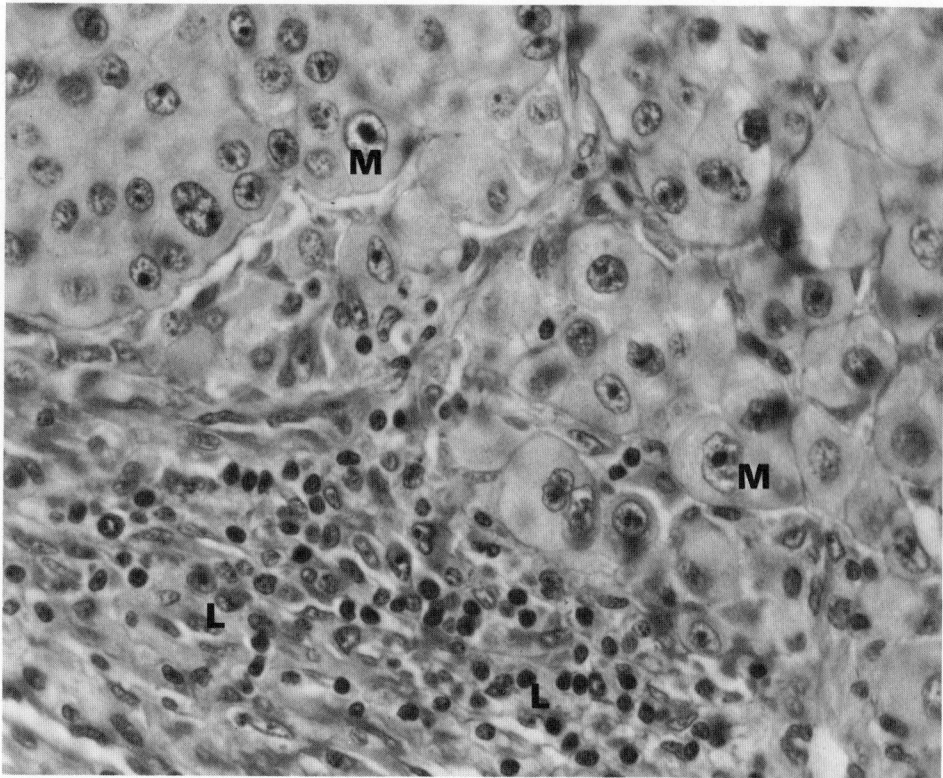

Figure 32.37. Metastatic melanoma in axillary lymph node.

(a) Islands of large melanoma cells (M) with abundant cytoplasm, and round or ovoid nuclei with prominent nucleoli. Residual cortical lymphoid cells (L) are also visible. (×250)

Ultrastructurally, the cells of metastatic melanoma are ovoid or polyhedral with smooth plasma membrane. The cytoplasm includes rod-shaped mitochondria, branching cisternae of endoplasmic reticulum and fine, electron-dense granules identified as melanosomes. The latter, not present in poorly differentiated cells, represent the characteristic feature of melanomas (Figure 32.37(b)). Melanosomes are of variable size, shape, and electron density. Some are round and strongly osmiophilic with no apparent internal structure. Others are ovoid, less darkly stained and show fine, parallel, cross-banded filaments.

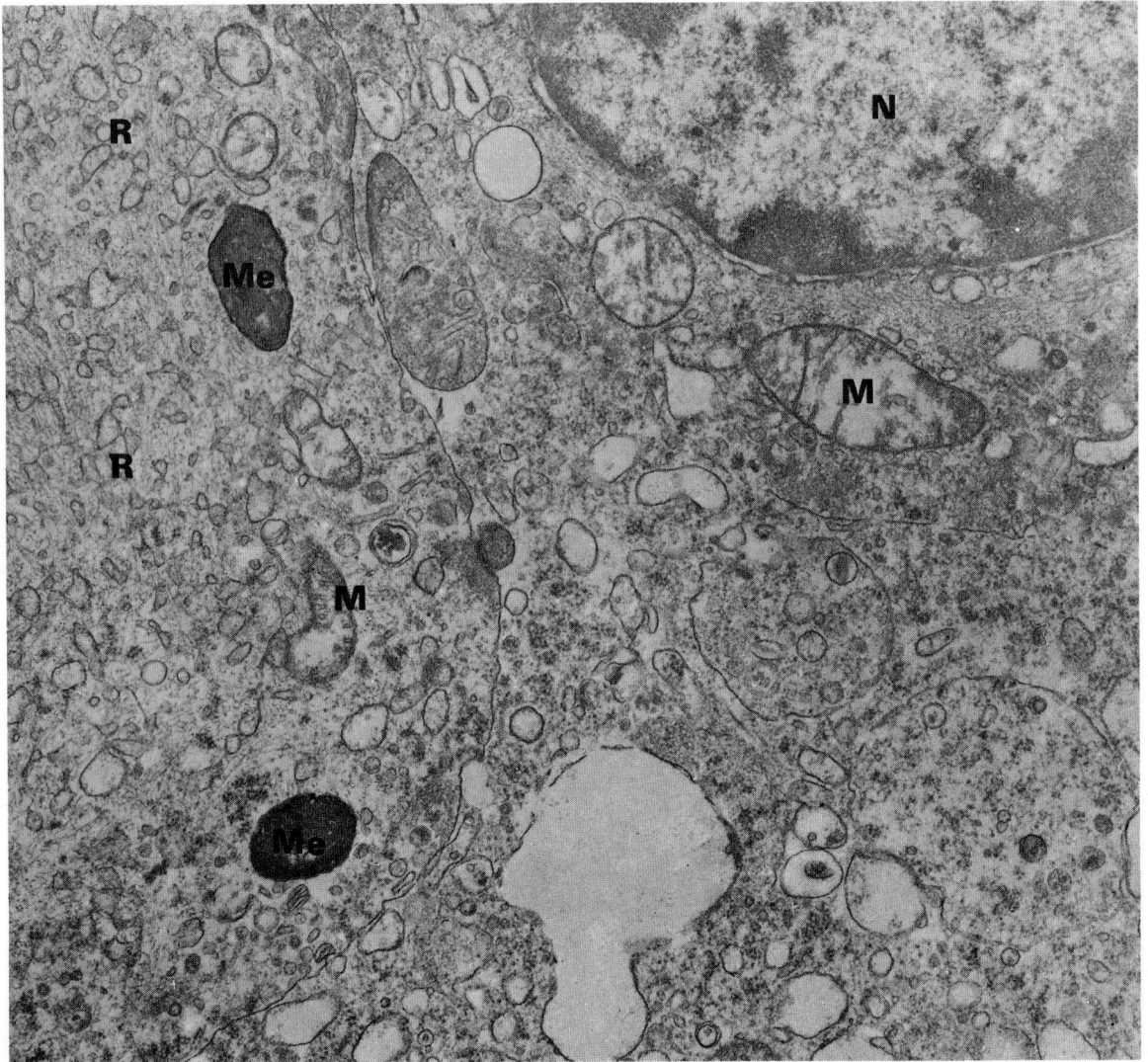

Figure 32.37. Metastatic melanoma in axillary lymph node.

(b) Melanoma cells with large nucleus (N), irregularly shaped mitochondria (M), abundant agranular endoplasmic reticulum (R), and melanosomes (Me). (× 17,500)

References to Part Six

1. Achong, B. G. and Epstein, M. A., "Fine structure of the Burkitt tumour," *J. natn. Cancer Inst.,* **36**, 877, 1966.
2. Adams, D. O., "The granulomatous inflammatory response," *Am. J. Path.,* **84**, 164, 1976.
3. Bernhard, W., "Some problems of fine structure in tumor cells," *Prog. Exp. Tumor Res.,* **3**, 1, 1963.
4. Bessis, M., *Living Blood Cells and Their Ultrastructure,* Springer-Verlag, New York, 1973.
5. Braylan, R. C., Jaffe, E. S., and Berard, C. W., "Malignant lymphomas: current classification and new observations," in S. C. Sommers (ed.), *Pathology Annual,* Appleton-Century-Crofts, New York, **10**, 213, 1975.
6. ——, ——, Burbach, J. W., *et al.,* "Similarities of surface characteristic of neoplastic well-differentiated lymphocytes from solid tissues and from peripheral blood," *Cancer Res.,* **36**, 1619, 1976.
7. Brouet, J. C., Labaume, S., and Seligmann, M., "Evaluation of T and B lymphocyte membrane markers in human non-Hodgkin malignant lymphomata," *Br. J. Cancer,* **31**, suppl. II, 121, 1975.
8. ——, Preud'Homme, J. L., Flandrin, G., *et al.,* "Membrane markers in histiocytic lymphoma," *J. natn. Cancer Inst.,* **56**, 631, 1976.
9. Brunning, R. D. and Parkin, J., "Intranuclear inclusions in plasma cells and lymphocytes from patients with monoclonal gammopathies," *Am. J. clin. Path.,* **66**, 10, 1976.
10. Butler, J. J., "Non-neoplastic lesions of lymph nodes of man to be differentiated from lymphomas," *J. natn. Cancer Inst., Monogr.,* **32**, 233, 1969.
11. ——, "The natural history of Hodgkin's disease and its classification," in J. W. Rebuck, C. W. Berard, and M. R. Abell (eds.), *The Reticulo Endothelial System,* Williams and Wilkins, Baltimore, 1975, pp. 184–213.
12. Cline, M. J., *The White Cell,* Harvard University Press, Cambridge, Massachusetts, 1975.
13. Doll, R., Muir, C., and Waterhouse, J. (eds.), *Cancer Incidence in Five Continents,* vol. 2, Springer-Verlag, Berlin, New York, 1970.
14. Dorfman, R. F., "The non-Hodgkin's lymphomas," in J. W. Rebuck, C. W. Berard, and M. R. Abell (eds.), *The Reticulo Endothelial System,* Williams and Wilkins, Baltimore, 1975, pp. 262–282.
15. —— and Remington, J. S., "Value of lymph node biopsy in the diagnosis of acute acquired toxoplasmosis," *New Engl. J. Med.,* **289**, 878, 1973.
16. ——, Rice, D. F., Mitchell, A. D., *et al.,* "Ultrastructural studies of Hodgkin's disease," *J. natn. Cancer Inst. Monogr.,* **36**, 221, 1973.

467

17. ———— and Warnke, R., "Lymphadenopathy simulating the malignant lymphomas," *Human Pathol., 5*, 519, 1974.

18. Dutcher, T. F. and Fahey, J. L., "The histopathology of the macroglobulinemia of Waldenstrom," *J. natn. Cancer Inst., 22*, 887, 1959.

19. Epstein, W. L., "Granuloma formation in Man," in H. L. Ioachim (ed.), *Pathobiology Annual,* Appleton-Century-Crofts, New York, 7, 1, 1977.

20. Frizzera, G., Moran, E. M., and Rappaport, H., "Angio immunoblastic lymphadenopathy with dysproteinemia," *Lancet, 1*, 1070, 1974.

21. Fukushiro, R., Hirone, T., and Eryn, Y., "Ultrastructural and cytochemical observations on sarcoid granulomas," in K. Iwai and Y. Hosoda (eds.), *Proceedings of International Conference on Sarcoidosis,* 1974, pp. 276–279.

22. Gowing, N. F. C., "Infectious mononucleosis: histopathologic aspects," in S. C. Sommers (ed.), *Pathology Annual,* Appleton-Century-Crofts, New York, 10, 1, 1975.

23. Gray, G. F., Jr., Kimball, A. C., and Kean, B. H., "The posterior cervical lymph node in toxoplasmosis," *Am. J. Path., 69*, 349, 1972.

24. Greenberg, B. R., Peter, C. R., Glassy, F., and McKenzie, M. R., "A case of T-cell lymphoma with convoluted lymphocytes," *Cancer, 37*, 1602, 1976.

25. Harrison, C. V., "The morphology of the lymph node in the macroglobulinemia of Waldenstrom," *J. clin. Path., 25*, 12, 1972.

26. Hartsock, R. J., "Postvaccinial lymphadenitis," *Cancer, 21*, 632, 1968.

27. ————, "Reactive lesions in lymph nodes," in J. W. Rebuck, C. W. Berard, and M. R. Abell (eds.), *The Reticulo Endothelial System,* Williams and Wilkins, Baltimore, 1975, pp. 153–184.

28. ————, Halling, L. W., and King, F. M., "Luetic lymphadenitis," *Am. J. clin. Path., 53*, 304, 1970.

29. Ioachim, H. L., "New vistas in Hodgkin's disease," in S. C. Sommers (ed.), *Pathology Annual,* Appleton-Century-Crofts, New York, 10, 419, 1975.

30. ————, Schmidt, E. C., and Keller, S. E., "Morphologic studies of cell receptors of lymphocytes and lymphomas," *Biblphy. Haematol., 43*, 29, 1976.

31. Jaffe, E. S., Shevach, E. M., Frank, M. M., Berard, C. W., and Green, I., "Nodular lymphoma. Evidence for origin from follicular B lymphocytes," *New Engl. J. Med., 290*, 813, 1974.

32. James, D. G. and Neville, E., "Pathobiology of sarcoidosis," in H. L. Ioachim (ed.), *Pathobiology Annual,* Appleton-Century-Crofts, New York, 7, 31, 1977.

33. Johansson, B., Klein, E., and Haglund, S., "Correlation between the presence of surface localized immunoglobulin (Ig) and the histological type of human malignant lymphomas," *Clin. Immunol. Immunopathol., 5*, 119, 1976.

34. Jones, S. E., Butler, J. J., Byrne, G. E., Jr., *et al.,* "Histopathologic review of lymphoma cases from the Southwest Oncology Group," *Cancer, 39*, 1071, 1977.

35. ————, Fuks, Z., Bull, M., *et al.,* "Non Hodgkin's lymphomas. Clinico-pathologic correlation in 405 cases," *Cancer, 31*, 806, 1973.

36. Kaplan, H. S., *Hodgkin's Disease,* Harvard University Press, Cambridge, Massachussetts, 1972.

37. Karpas, A., Arno, J., and Cawley, J., "Sinus histiocytosis with massive lymphadenopathy. Properties of cultured histiocytes," *Eur. J. Cancer, 9*, 729, 1973.

468

38. Kuhn, C., "Nuclear bodies and intranuclear globulin inclusions in Waldenstrom's macroglobulinemia," *Lab. Invest.,* **17**, 404, 1967.

39. Lennert, K., Niedorf, H. R., and Blümcke, S., "Lymphadenitis with massive hemophagocytic sinus histiocytosis," *Virchows Arch Path. Anat.,* **10**, 14, 1972.

40. Levine, G. D. and Dorfman, R. F., "Nodular lymphoma: An ultrastructural study of its relationship to germinal centers and a correlation of light and electron microscopic findings," *Cancer,* **35**, 148, 1975.

41. Luk, S. C., Nopajaroonsri, C., and Simon, G. T., "The architecture of the normal lymph node and hemolymph node," *Lab. Invest.,* **29**, 258, 1973.

42. Lukes, R. J. and Collins, R. D., "Immunologic characterization of human malignant lymphomas," *Cancer,* **34**, 1488, 1974.

43. ——— and ———, "A functional classification of malignant lymphomas," in J. W. Rebuck, C. W. Berard, and M. R. Abell, *The Reticulo Endothelial System,* Williams and Wilkins, Baltimore, 1975, pp. 213–243.

44. ———, Craver, L. F., Hall, T. C., Rappaport, H., and Ruben, P., "Report of the Nomenclature Committee," *Cancer Res.,* **26**, 1311, 1966.

45. ——— and Tindle, B. H., "Immunoblastic lymphadenopathy," *New Engl. J. Med.,* **292**, 1, 1975.

46. Mann, R. B., Jaffe, E. S., Braylan, R. C., *et al.,* "Immunologic and morphologic studies of T-cell lymphoma," *Am. J. Med.,* **58**, 307, 1975.

47. Miale, J. B., "Hemopoietic system," in W. A. D. Anderson (ed.), *Pathology,* vol. 2, Mosby, St. Louis, 1971, pp. 1297–1387.

48. Mori, Y. and Lennert, K., *Electron Microscopic Atlas of Lymph Node Cytology and Pathology,* Springer-Verlag, New York, 1969.

49. Nathwani, B. N., Kim, H., and Rappaport, H., "Malignant lymphoma, lymphoblastic," *Cancer,* **38**, 964, 1976.

50. Nosanchuk, J. S. and Schnitzer, B., "Follicular hyperplasia in lymph nodes from patients with rheumatoid arthritis," *Cancer,* **24**, 343, 1969.

51. Olah, I., Röhlich, P. and Törö, I., *Ultrastructure of Lymphoid Organs,* Lippincott, Philadelphia, 1975.

52. Pangalis, G. A., Natwani, B. N., and Rappaport, H., "Malignant lymphoma, well differentiated, lymphocytic," *Cancer,* **39**, 999, 1977.

53. Rappaport, H., *Tumors of the Hematopoietic System, Atlas of Tumor Pathology,* Armed Forces Institute of Pathology, Washington, 1966.

54. ———, Braylan, R. C., "Changing concepts in the classification of malignant neoplasms of the hematopoietic system," in J. W. Rebuck, C. W. Berard, and M. R. Abell (eds.), *The Reticulo Endothelial System,* Williams and Wilkins, Baltimore, 1975, pp. 1–19.

55. Rhodin, J. A. G., *Histology,* Oxford University Press, London, 1974.

56. Rosai, J. and Dorfman, R. F., "Sinus histiocytosis with massive lympha-denopathy: A pseudolymphomatous benign disorder," *Cancer,* **30**, 1174, 1972.

57. Schnitzer, B. and Kass, L., "Leukemic phase of reticulum cell sarcoma (histiocytic lymphoma)," *Cancer,* **31**, 547, 1973.

58. Spector, W. G., "The macrophage: Its origins and role in pathology," in H. L. Ioachim (ed.), *Pathobiology Annual,* Appleton-Century-Crofts, New York, **4**, 33, 1974.

59. Stansfeld, A. G., "The histological diagnosis of toxoplasmic lymphadenitis," *J. clin. Path.,* **14**, 565, 1961.

60. Tanaka, Y. and Goodman, J. R., *Electron Microscopy of Human Blood Cells,* Harper and Row, New York, 1972.

61. Turner, D. R. and Wright, D. J., "Lymphadenopathy in early syphilis," *J. Path.,* **110**, 305, 1973.

62. Waldenstrom, J., "Studies on conditions associated with disturbed gamma globulin formation (gammopathies)," *Harvey Lect.,* **56**, 211, 1961.

63. Wright, D. H., "Burkitt's lymphoma: A review of the pathology, immunology and possible etiologic factors, in S. C. Sommers (ed.), *Pathology Annual,* Appleton-Century-Crofts, New York, **6**, 337, 1971.

64. Ziegler, J. L. and Magrath, I. T., "Burkitt's lymphoma," in H. L. Ioachim (ed.), *Pathobiology Annual,* Appleton-Century-Croft, New York, **4**, 128, 1974.

65. Zuckerman, S. H. and Douglas, S. D., "The lymphocyte plasma membrane: markers, receptors and determinants," in H. L. Ioachim (ed.), *Pathobiology Annual,* Appleton-Century-Crofts, New York, **6**, 119, 1976.

Part Seven

The Spleen

Harry L. Ioachim

33. The Normal Spleen

The spleen is the largest lymphoid organ, connected directly with the general circultation. It performs the major functions of lymphopoiesis, antibody formation, and erythrophagocytosis. Following a summary of the light microscopic appearance of normal spleen, this chapter presents an ultrastructural description of the endothelial and plasma cells. For description of lymphocytes, lymphoblasts, histiocytes, and reticular cells, see Chapter 31.

Light microscopy shows a fibroelastic capsule, trabecular network composed of connective tissue and smooth muscle cells, and splenic parenchyma divided into white pulp and red pulp (Figure 33.1).

The white pulp is organized into lymphoid follicles (Malpighian corpuscles) and lymphoid sheaths surrounding the arteries. The lymphoid follicles, comprising germinal centers of a size related to their state of responsiveness, surround an eccentrically placed central artery.[21] The follicles include lymphoblasts, lymphocytes, and reticular cells.

The red pulp consists of a vast system of interconnecting venous sinuses separated by the pulp cords composed of reticular cells, macrophages, lymphocytes, and plasma cells. The sinus walls comprise a loose network of reticulin fibers and basal lamina on which rest the lining endothelial cells.[18]

33.1. Endothelial cell

Also called littoral cell, the endothelial cell, according to some,[21] is a modified, less phagocytic reticular cell (Figure 33.2). Elongated elements with long processes attached to each other by desmosomes[16] form the lining of sinuses. In the splenic red pulp sinuses, frequent gaps (Figure 33.2) between the endothelial cell processes give rise to stomata through which blood elements pass freely. The cytoplasm of endothelial cells is thin and of a simple organization. The filamentous elements are arranged along the longitudinal axis and numerous pinocytotic vesicles may be present at the periphery. The nucleus is elongated and contains marginated chromatin and fine, small nucleoli.

33.2. Plasma cell

These cells, reponsible for the synthesis and temporary storage of immunoglobulins, are pear-shaped with a maximum diameter of 10 μm. The cell surface is smooth. The eccentrically placed nucleus contains abundant heterochromatin distributed in a

473

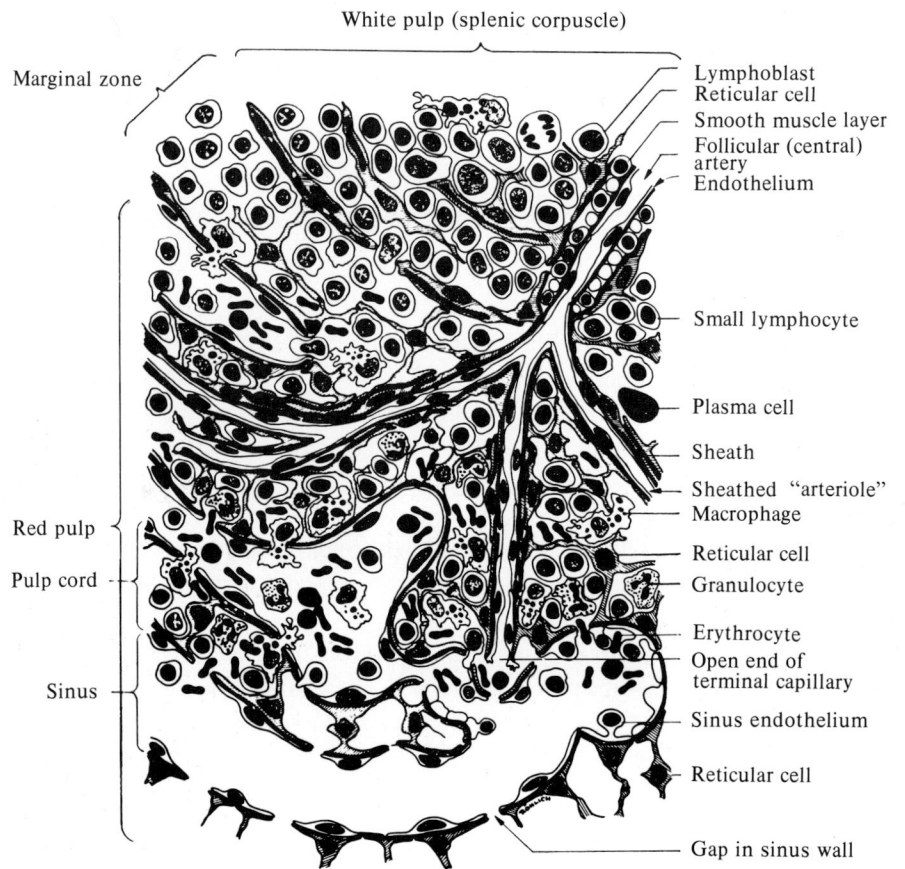

Figure 33.1. Normal spleen (I. Olah, P. Röhlich, and I. Törö).

characteristic, spoked-wheel pattern. The cell includes an extensive, elaborately developed granular endoplasmic reticulum (Figure 33.3) which fills the entire cytoplasm, with the exception of the paranuclear region. This region is occupied by a large Golgi apparatus which includes both membranous sacs and vesicles. The cisternae of the endoplasmic reticulum may appear flat or largely distended, filled with a finely granular material and lined by numerous ribosomes. A pair of centrioles is always present.[21] The mitochondria are large and surrounded by ergastoplasmic lamellae.[16]

474

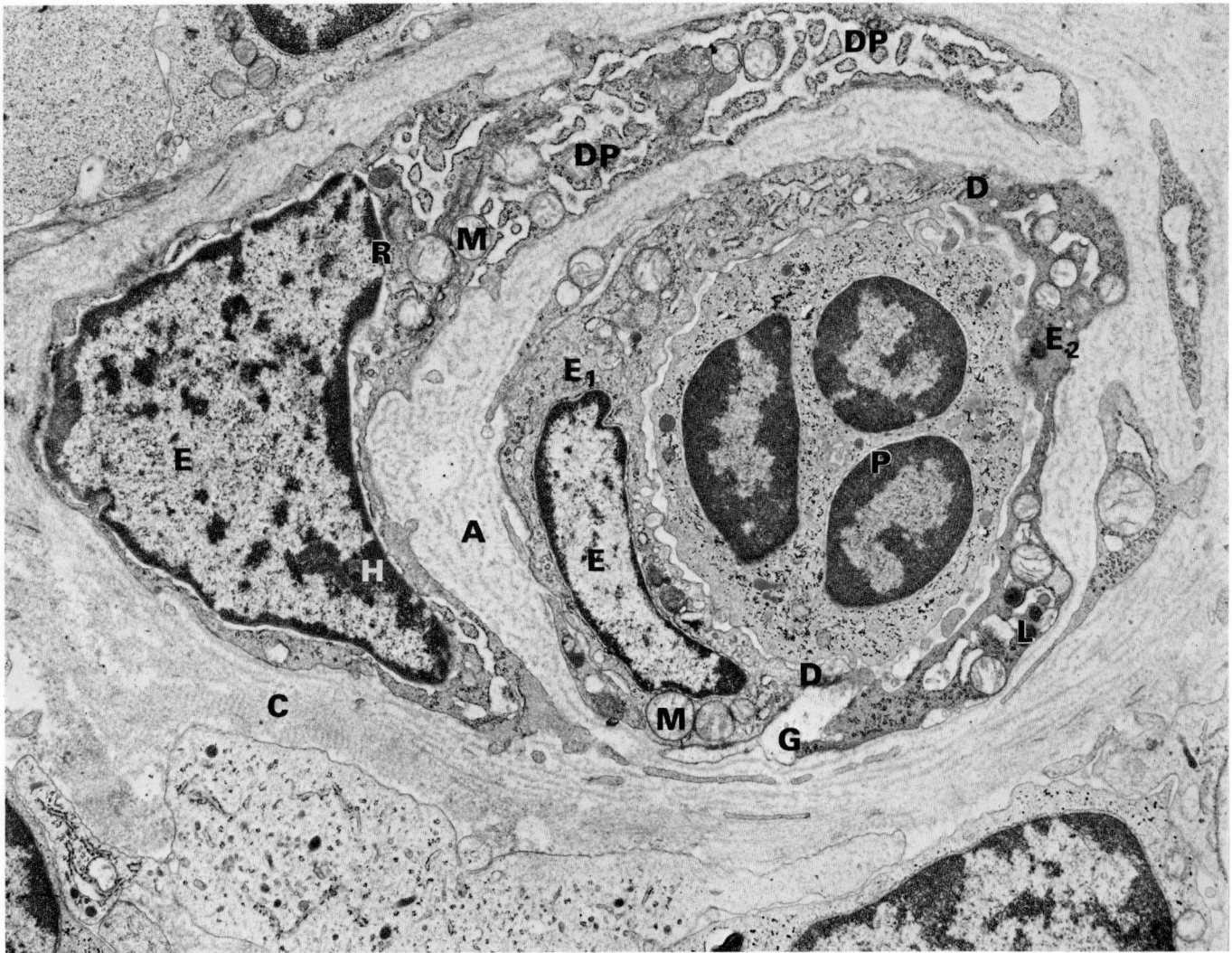

Figure 33.2. Splenic sinusoid lined by endothelial cells.

Two endothelial cells (E_1, E_2) are visible, connected by desmosomes (D), and with an intercellular gap (G). Nuclei contain euchromatin (E) and marginated heterochromatin (H). Cytoplasm contains mitochondria (M) and lysosomes (L). Note also polymorphonuclear in the lumen (P), reticular cell (R) with numerous dendritic processes (DP), collagen fibers (C), and amorphous intercellular material (A). ($\times 4,000$)

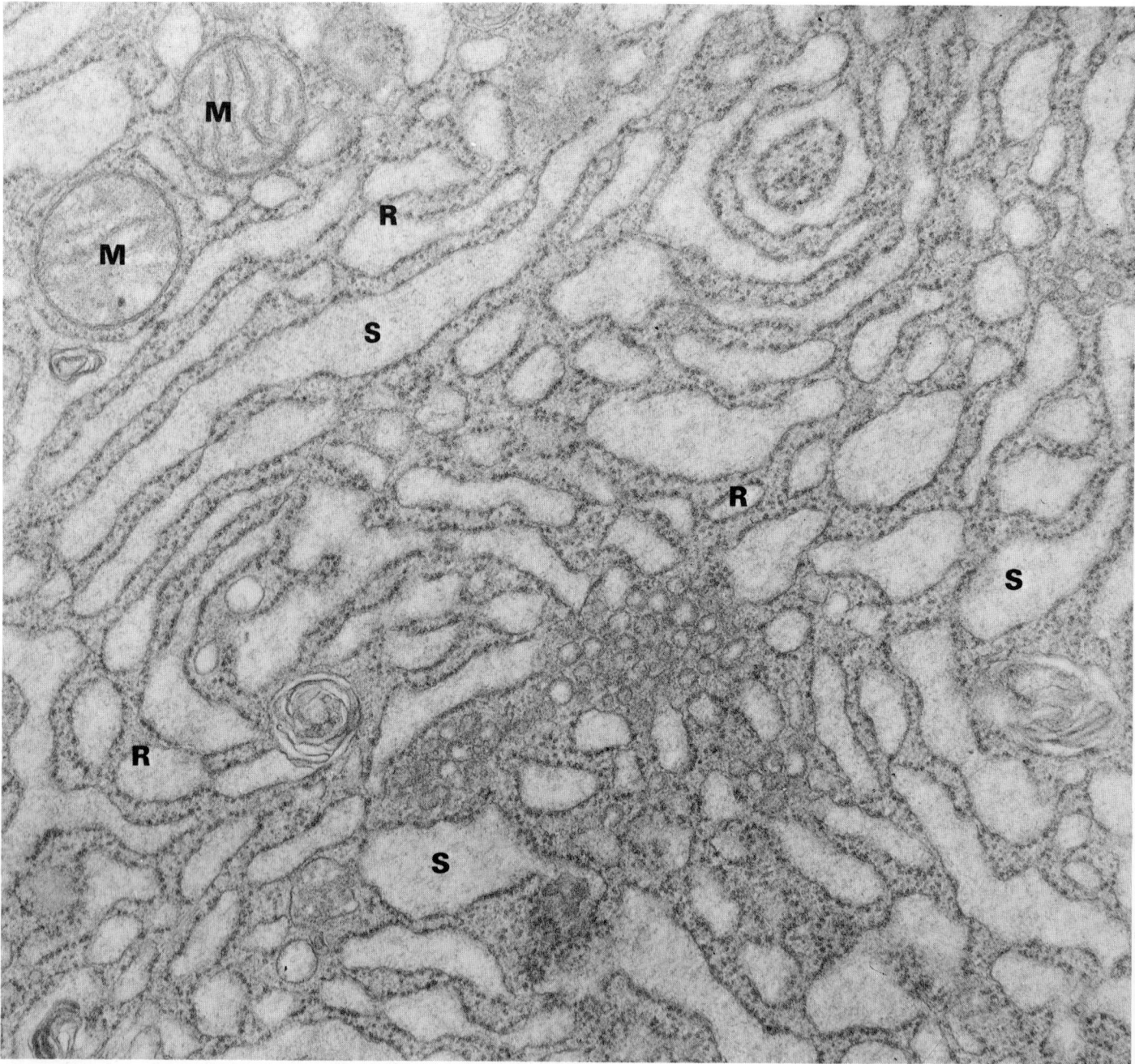

Figure 33.3. Plasma cell of red pulp.
Cytoplasm of plasma cell in normal spleen showing well-developed intercommunicating, largely distended cisternae of granular endoplasmic reticulum, studded with ribosomes (R) and containing a fine, granular product of secretion (S) apparently immunoglobulins. M: mitochondria. (×36,000)

34. The Pathological Spleen

34.1. Hypersplenism

This syndrome is characterized by splenomegaly associated with the reduction in the number of one or more cellular elements of the peripheral blood. Although the etiology of hypersplenism is multiple, the mechanism for cytopenia (anemia, leukopenia, thrombocytopenia, or combinations thereof) appears to be the hypersequestration of the circulating cells in the spleen.[9]

The large size of the spleen which can increase over tenfold its normal weight is due to red pulp hyperplasia and congestion. The white pulp is markedly reduced. Light microscopy shows that in the early stages the lymphoid follicles show three concentric lymphocytic areas including an additional peripheral mantle of large, activated lymphocytes (Figure 34.1). In later states, the lymphoid follicles are reduced to only one, small, residual, periarteriolar area of small lymphocytes.

The red pulp shows largely distended and congested sinuses lined by markedly hyperplastic endothelial cells. The splenic cords comprise variable amounts of plasma cells, macrophages, and fibrosis.

Ultrastructurally, the sinuses are seen to be dilated and to contain numerous erythrocytes (Figure 34.2). Endothelial cells are hyperplastic and protrude in the lumina of sinuses. Macrophages are numerous and include phagocytosed erythrocytes as well as products of hemoglobin breakdown.[15] Erythrocytes of varying electron density due to hemolysis are frequently seen.[15] Platelets are occasionally present within endothelial cells. Clusters of ferritin granules are commonly observed in macrophages, endothelial cells, and platelets.

34.2. Acute leukemias

A heterogeneous group of neoplasias is subclassified into lymphoblastic, myeloblastic, myelomonocytic, and erythremic,[7,17] according to the cytologic features of the component cells. Due to cellular immaturity, the characteristic features of the major cytologic types are sometimes difficult to establish.[14] However, an important contribution to their differential diagnosis has been made by the application of modern immunologic techniques to the characterization of cell membrane markers.[13]

34.2.1. Acute lymphoblastic leukemia

The spleen may be affected by any type of acute leukemia but is most commonly involved in acute lymphoblastic leukemia, the predominant form of leukemia in early childhood.

477

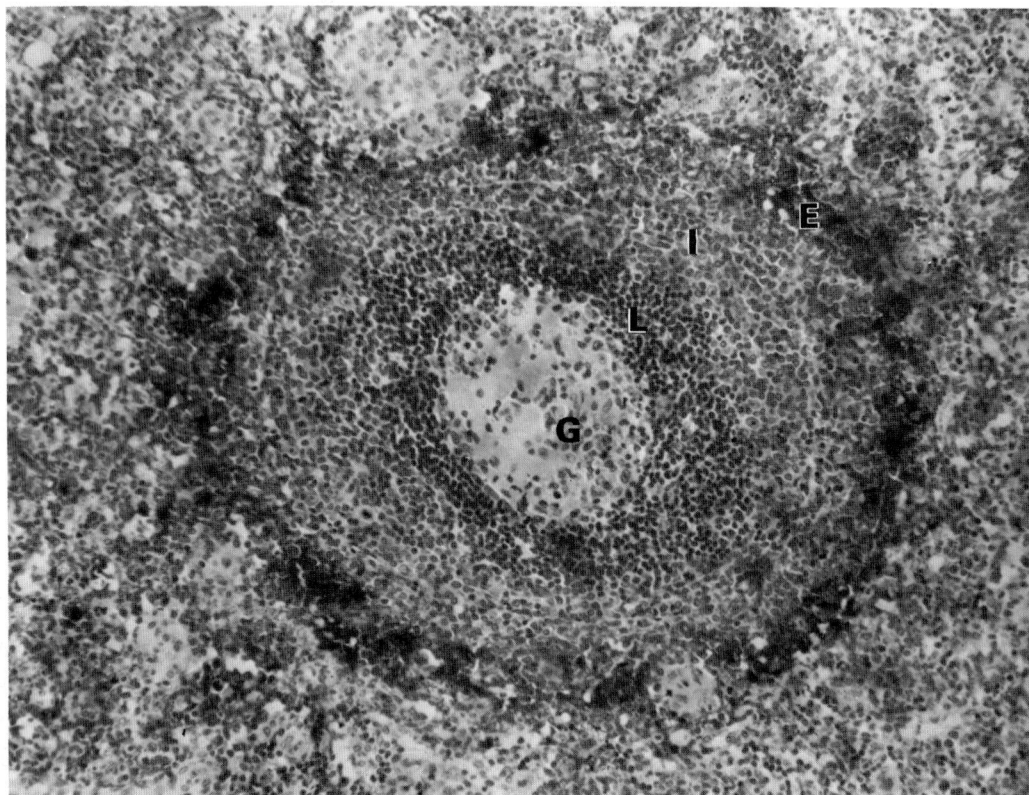

Figure 34.1. White pulp in hypersplenism.
Lymphoid follicle in splenic white pulp including germinal center (G), mantle of mature lymphocytes (L), and area of activated lymphocytes (I). A peripheral concentric layer of erythrocytes (E) is present in this case of hypersplenism due to congenital hemolytic anemia. (× 100)

Light microscopy shows that in the early stages, there is involvement of malpighian corpuscles by immature neoplastic lymphoblasts with relative preservation of red pulp. The corpuscles are large, irregularly shaped and often confluent, without distinction between germinal centers and periphery.[20] In later stages, extensive replacement of all splenic structures takes place (Figure 34.3).

Ultrastructurally, the cells are round to ovoid 10–12 μm in diameter, with an almost smooth cellular outline. The nuclei (Figure 34.4) are markedly pleomorphic with numerous deep indentations, folds, bridges, and pockets. The chromatin is coarse and clumped along the nuclear borders. The nucleoli are large and dense (Figure 34.4). The cytoplasm contains mitochondria that are of variable shapes with unevenly arranged cristae, usually located at one pole of the cell.[16] There is an abundance of uniformly dispersed ribosomes, polysomes, and clusters of glycogen granules. Long threads of endoplasmic reticulum and occasional bundles of cytoplasmic microfilaments in a perinuclear location[7] are also noted. The peroxidase reaction is negative in electron microscopy.[1]

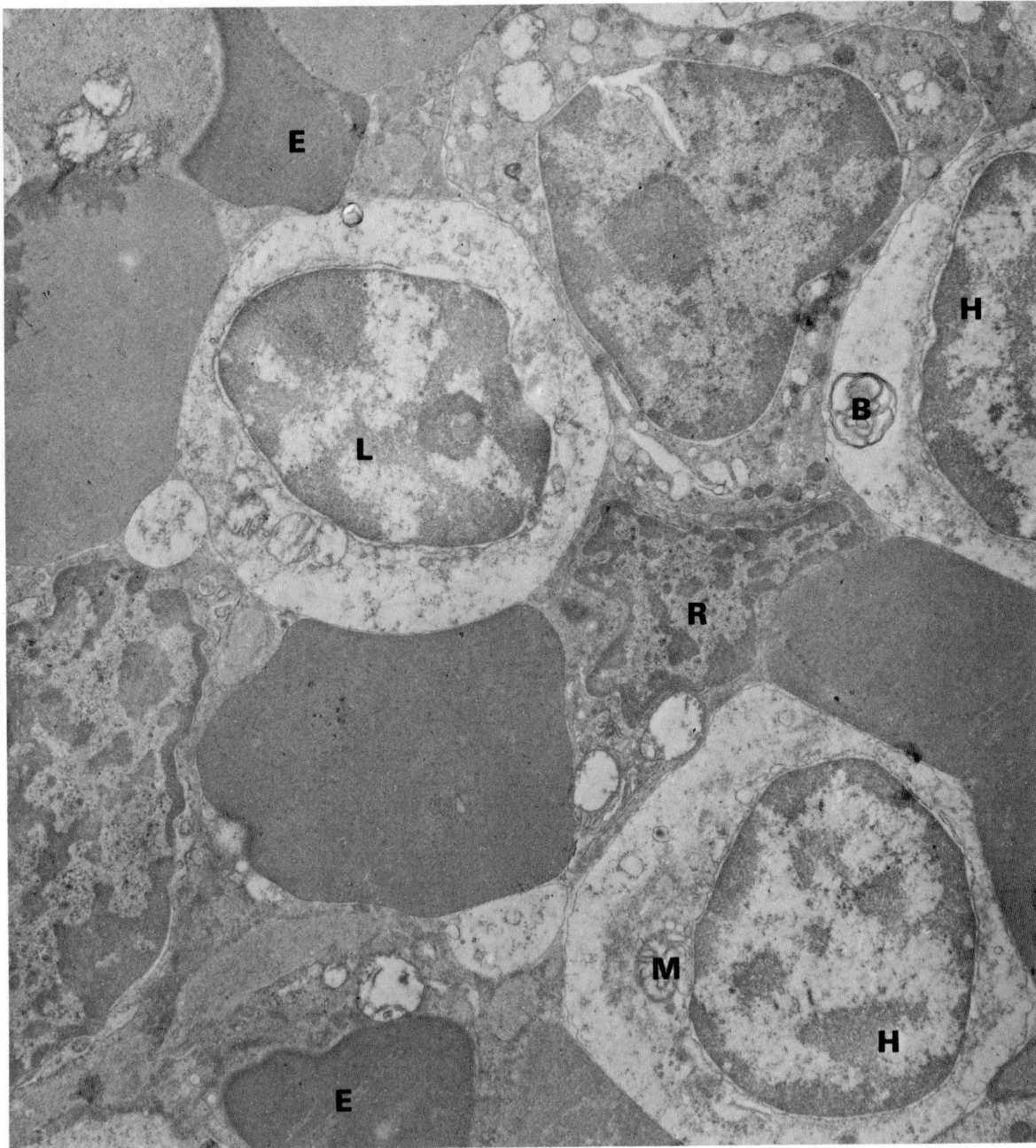

Figure 34.2. Red pulp in hypersplenism.
Erythrocytes (E), reticular cells (R), macrophagic histiocytes (H) with intracytoplasmic myelin
bodies (B), and lymphoblast (L) are visible. (×8,000)

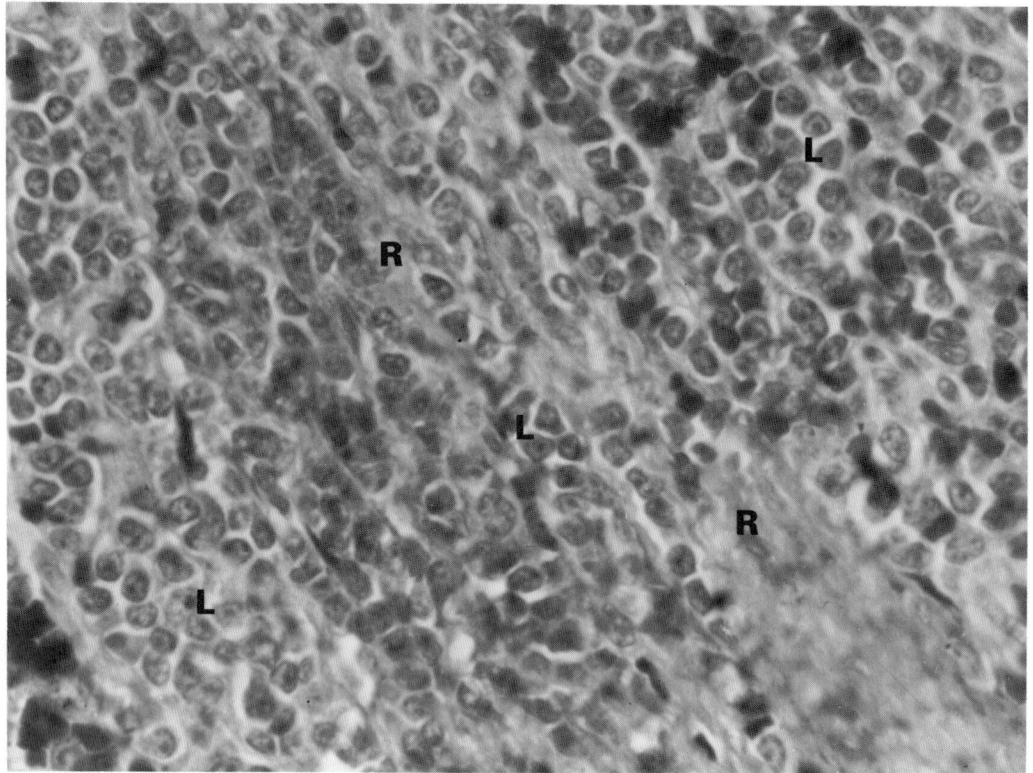

Figure 34.3. Acute lymphoblastic leukemia.
Diffuse infiltration of splenic red pulp (R) by neoplastic lymphoblasts (L). (× 400)

34.3. Leukemic reticuloendotheliosis (hairy cell leukemia)

Malignant, lymphoreticular, proliferative disease, predominantly involving the bone marrow and spleen, characterized by the presence of typical "hairy cells" in the peripheral blood.

Cytological investigations reveal moderately large (20 μm) monocytoid cells with abundant, palely stained cytoplasm and multiple villous projections producing the hairy aspect.[2, 3, 23] The nucleus is ovoid, occasionally indented, with a sharp nuclear membrane, dispersed chromatin, and fine nucleolus.

Cytochemistry studies provide the following information on the cells: Alkaline phosphatase negative;[22] acid phosphatase strongly positive; tartrate-resistant acid phosphatase isozyme 5 positive;[25] α-naphthyl acetate esterase positive;[22] PAS slightly positive[23] peroxidase negative.[3, 22]

Immunogloblin surface markers are present (most frequently heavy chain-gamma; light chain-lambda).[6] Also present are receptors for activated C_3 (EAC complexes) and F_c fragment of IgG (cytophilic antibody).[4]

The spleen, which grossly appears meaty and weighs an average of 2,000 g, displays microscopically (Figure 34.5) the effacement of its histologic structure. The Malpighian follicles and the cords of the red pulp are replaced by neoplastic

480

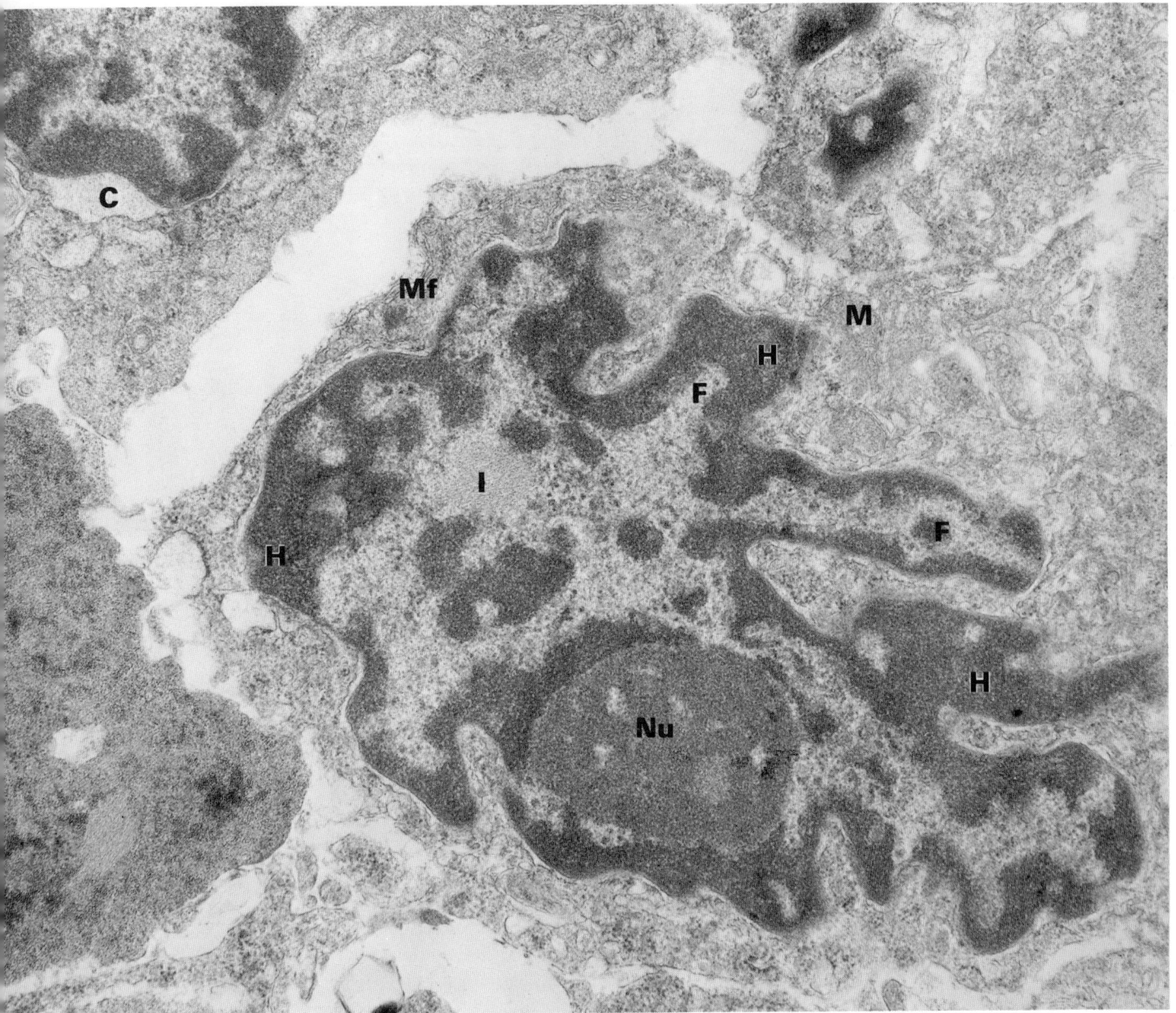

Figure 34.4. Undifferentiated leukemic cells in splenic sinuses.
Large, folded (F) nucleus with deep indentations and huge, dense nucleolus (Nu). Note marginated, clumped heterochromatin (H), intranuclear inclusion (I), and perinuclear dilated cisterna (C). The cytoplasm contains mitochondria with uneven cristae (M) and perinuclear microfilaments (Mf). (×24,000)

mononuclear cells. The penicillate arteries lack the surrounding lymphoid sheaths and the contrast between white and red pulp is inapparent. The infiltrating cells are diffusely arranged and obliterate follicles, cords, and sinuses. The cells are monomorphous and do not show giant elements or bizarre nuclei. Phagocytosis is not observed and mitoses are infrequent.

481

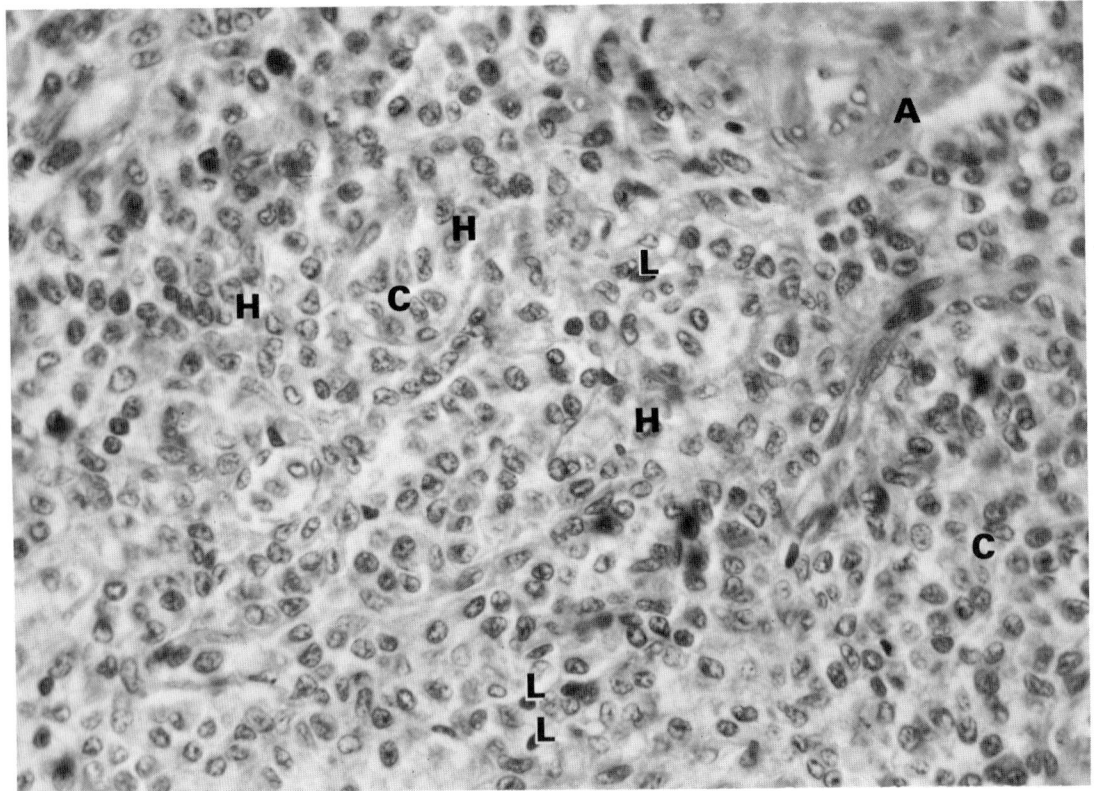

Figure 34.5. Hairy cell leukemia.
Spleen with cords (C) and sinuses infiltrated by hairy cells (H). Penicillate arteriole (A) lacking Malpighian corpuscle is visible and there are few residual lymphocytes (L). (×250)

Scanning electron microscopy of hairy cells from peripheral blood shows cells covered by long, thin, villous processes.[4] Transmission electron microscopy of splenic tissue (Figure 34.6) shows closely apposed cells with interlocked, long, slender cytoplasmic processes. Some cells are free, floating in the still patent splenic sinuses.[2] *In vitro,* hairy cells are able to phagocytose particulate matter[3] and develop zipper-like junctions composed of juxtaposed parallel membranes separated by a 400 Å electron-lucent space.[3] The nuclei (Figure 34.6) are indented and contain a small but conspicuous nucleolus. The heterochromatin is scarce and peripheral. The cytoplasm (Figure 34.7(a), (b)) includes a moderate number of ovoid mitochondria, few ribosomes, small Golgi body, short profiles of rough endoplasmic reticulum, occasional centrioles, and some vesicular structures. Characteristic for hairy cells is the presence of ribosome–lamellar complexes[11] in about 50 percent of cases in 20 to 100 percent of the cells examined.[3] They appear as multiple parallel lamellae separated by regular 450 Å interlamellar spaces.[3] The spaces are lined by a single row of regularly arranged, ribosome-like round granules. In a tridimensional reconstruction,[3] the complexes appear to be hollow cylinders of about 3 μm length composed of concentric circles of a fibrillar nature. The large ribosome-like granules inserted on the circular lamellae are of RNA nature.[3]

482

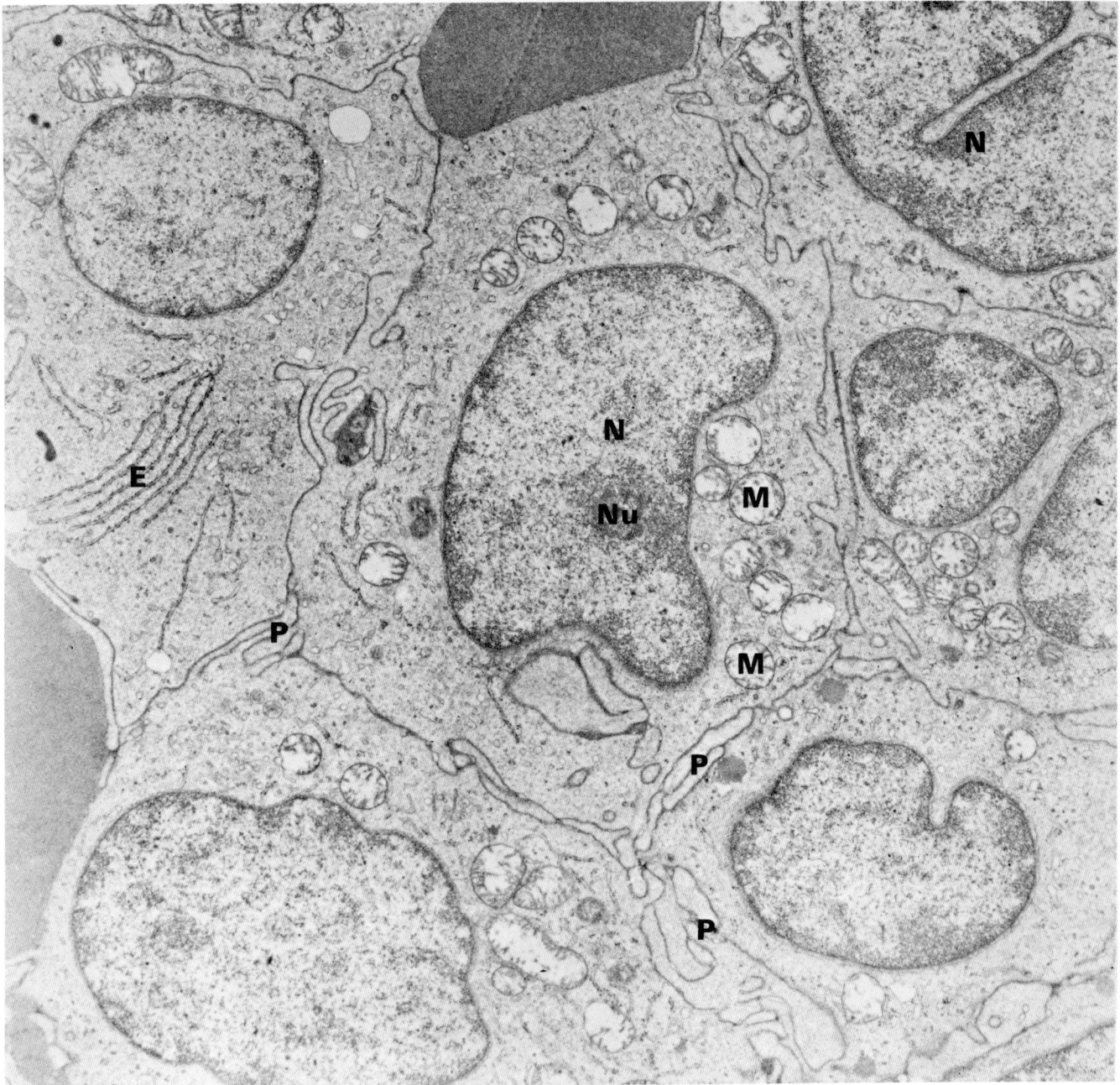

Figure 34.6. Splenic paraenchyma replaced by hairy cells.
The cells are closely packed. Note interlocked processes (P), few round mitochondria (M), large, deeply indented nucleus (N) with conspicuous nucleolus (Nu), and few profiles of endoplasmic reticulum (E). (× 12,600)

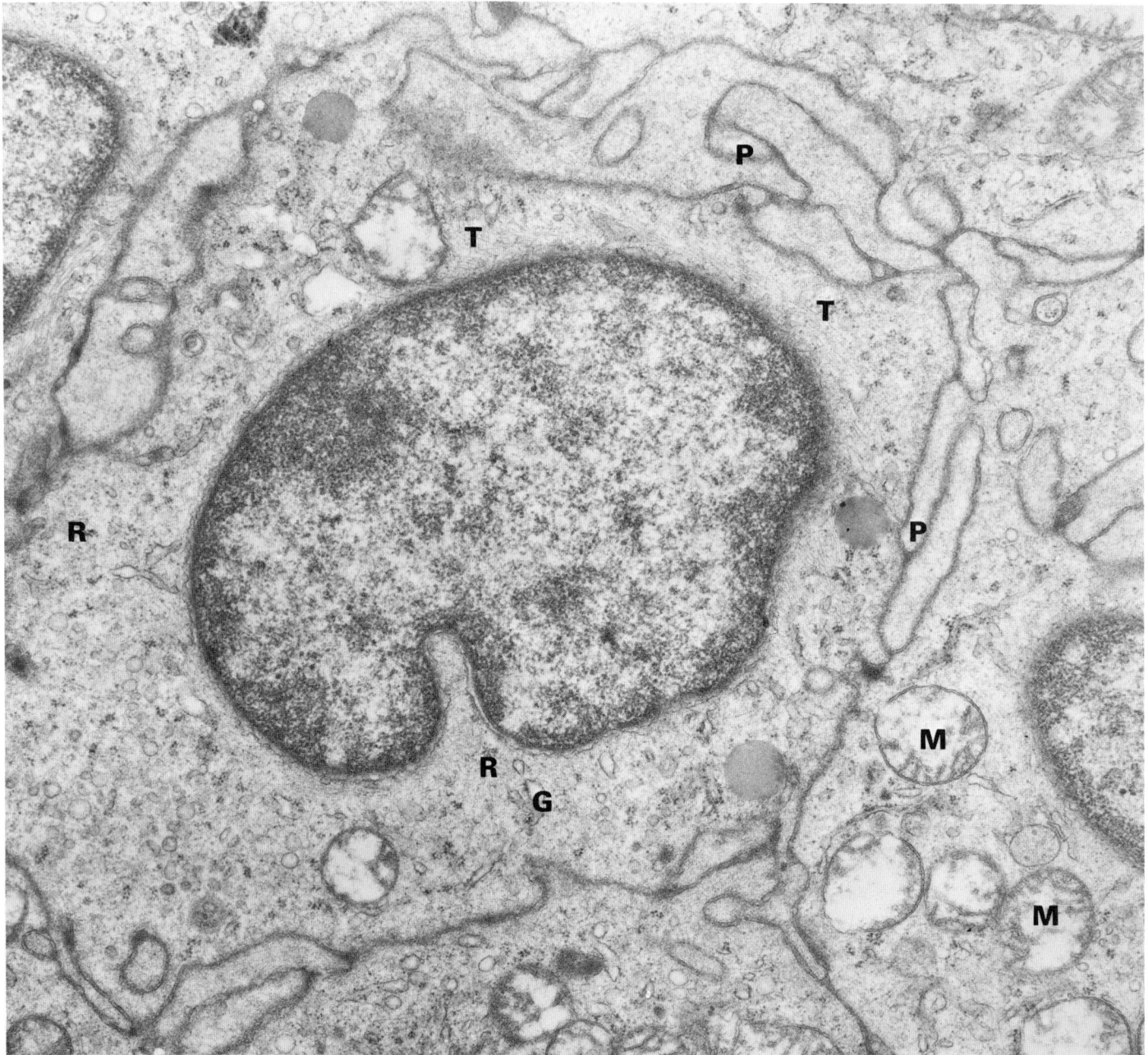

Figure 34.7. Hairy cell in spleen.

(a) The cell has long, tortuous, interlocked processes (P). Cytoplasm contains few, round mitochondria (M), polyribosomes (R), Golgi complex (G), and tubular inclusions (T). (×23,400)

484

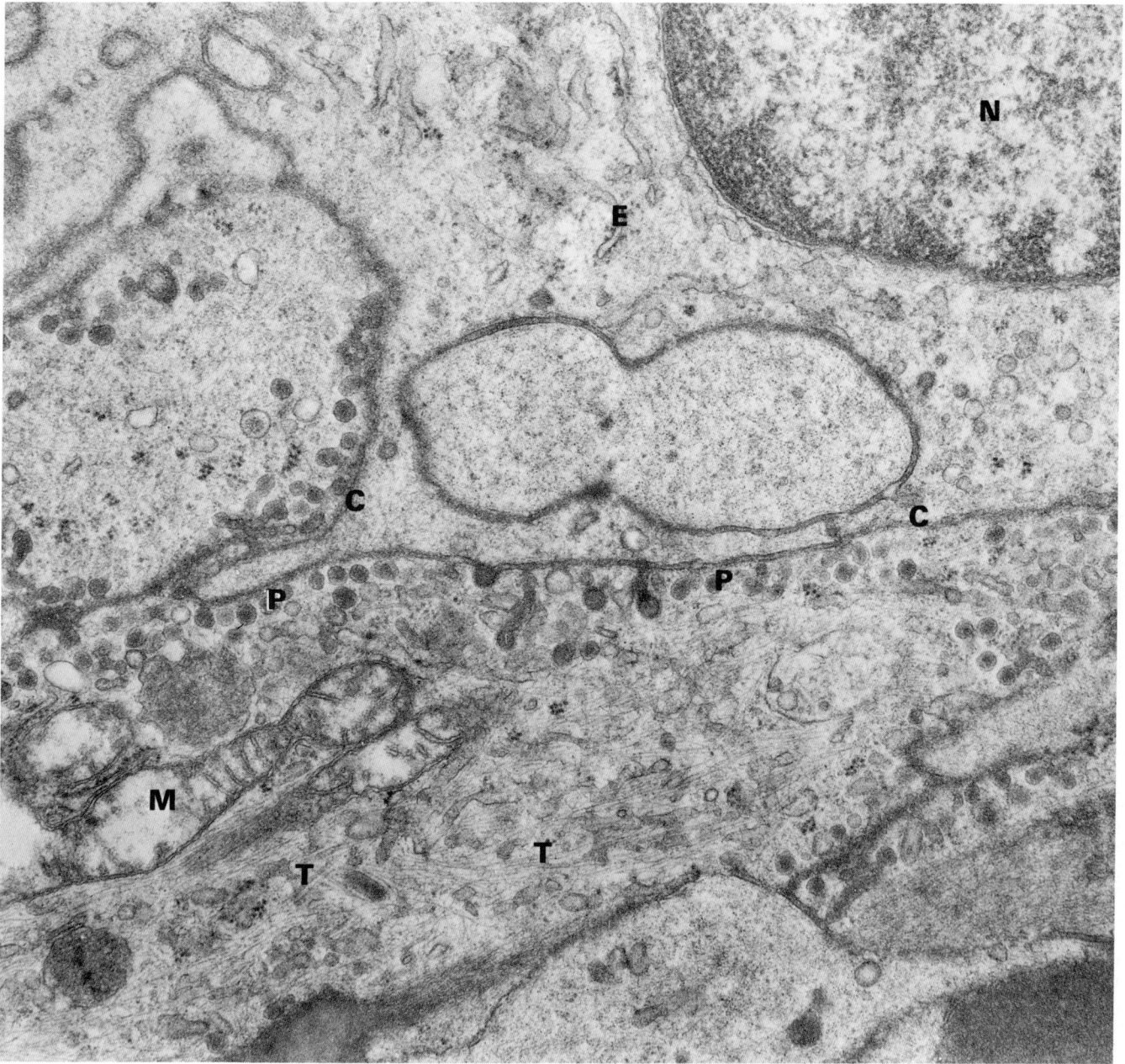

Figure 34.7. Hairy cell in spleen.

(b) Nucleus (N), mitochondria (M), rough endoplasmic reticulum (E), and tubular inclusions (T) are clearly visible. Round particles (P) contain dense nucleoids, some of which are inserted on cylindric structures (C), possible expansions of the plasma membrane. (×27,000)

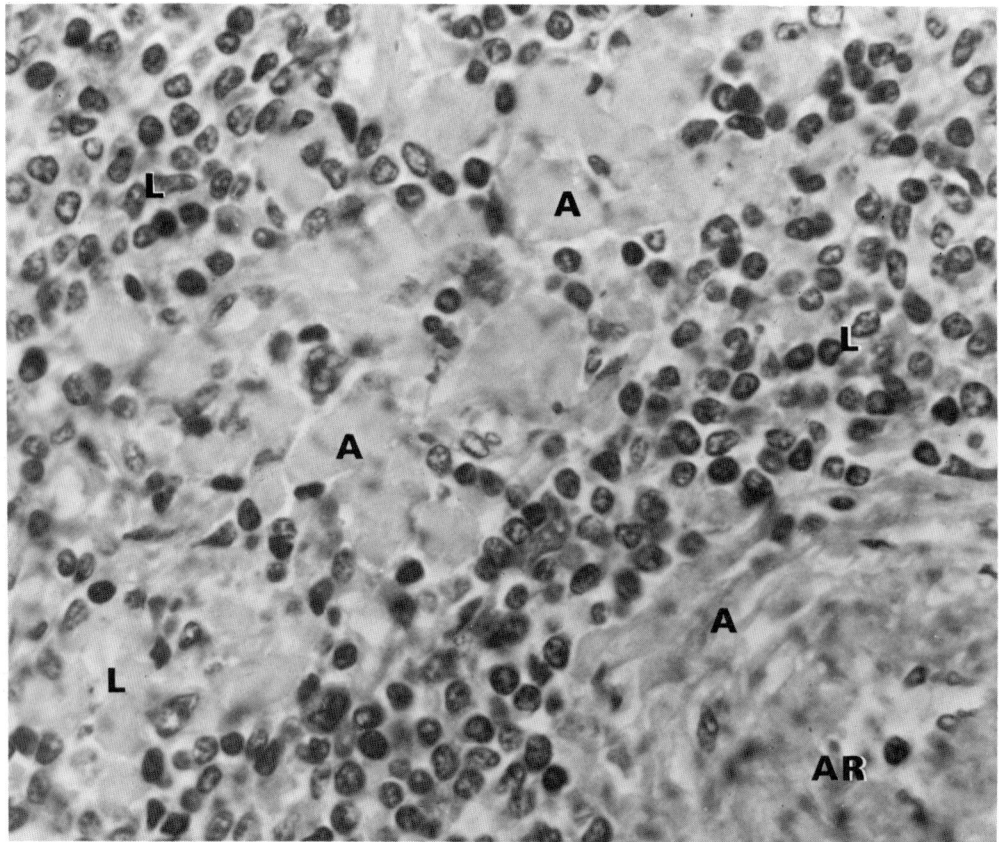

Figure 34.8. Amyloidosis.

(a) Amorphous deposits of amyloid (A) in wall of arteriole (AR) and in red pulp of spleen replacing the lymphoid cells (L). (×400)

The origin of the hairy cell is still controversial. A histiocytic origin[1-3] is suggested by its localization in spleen cords, size, cytoplasmic enzymes, tubular inclusions, cytoplasmic processes, and reticulin network; a B lymphocytic origin[4,23] is suggested by nuclear pattern, surface immunoglobulins, and lack of phagocytosis *in vivo*.

34.4. Amyloidosis

Amorphous, eosinophilic, extracellular substance identified by metachromatic staining with crystal violet and birefringence in the polarized light after staining with Congo red. Consists of a fraction of immunoglobulin light chains[6] that is deposited in various organs. The current classification of amyloidosis[19] recognizes several categories according to organ distribution. However, the various types of amyloidosis exhibit similar ultrastructure and chemical composition.[5]

Splenic amyloidosis may be focal or diffuse and the organ variably enlarged. Light microscopically, the amyloid appears as masses of an amorphous substance deposited

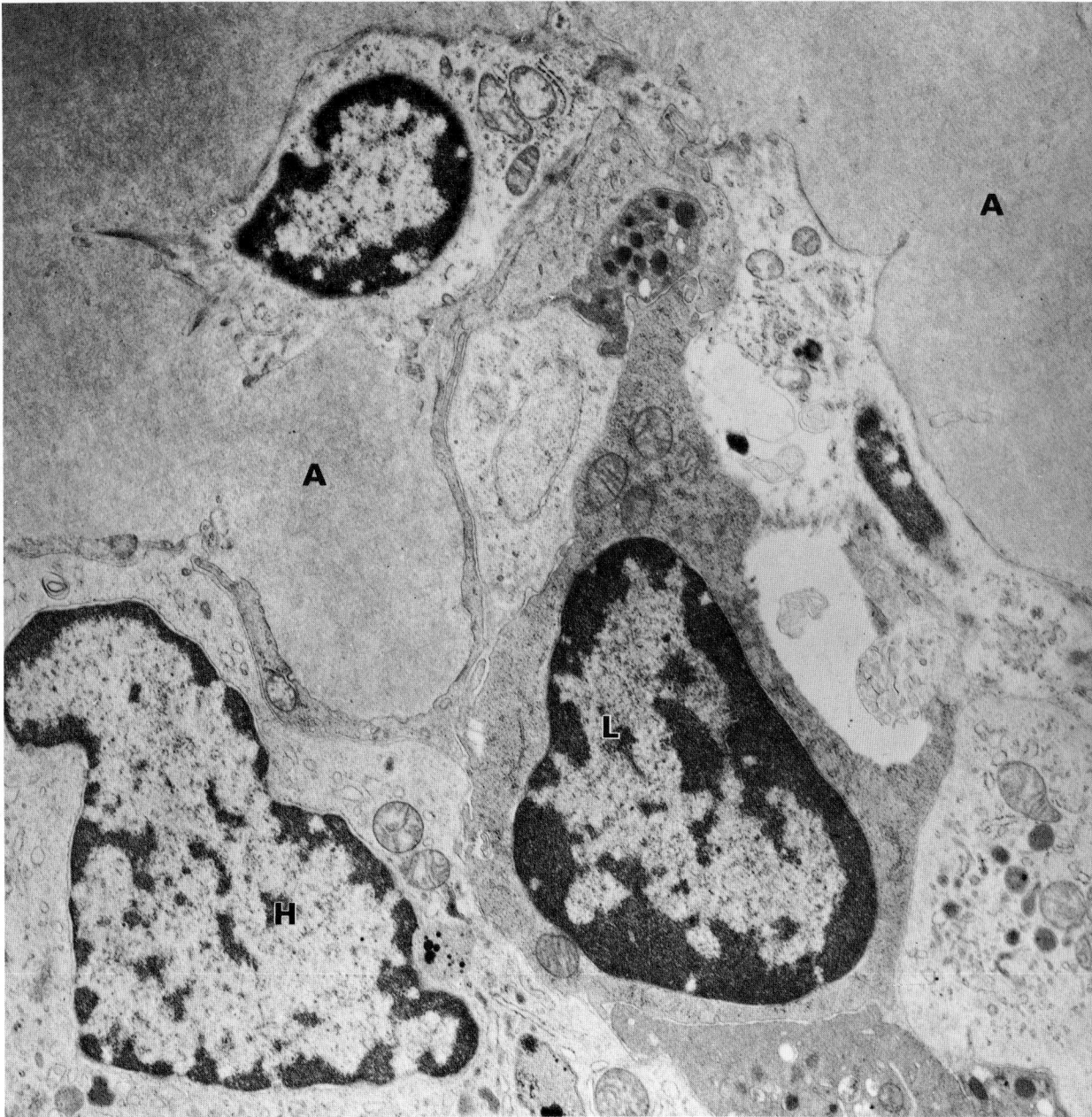

Figure 34.8. Amyloidosis.
(b) Lymphoid cell (L) and histiocyte (H) in spleen red pulp. Masses of amorphous deposits identified as amyloid (A) displacing the splenic parenchyma. (× 20,600)

in the vessel walls, in the connective tissue of trabeculae and capsule and eventually in the splenic pulp, replacing cells and sinuses (Figure 34.8(a), (b)).

Ulstrastructurally, the masses of amyloid are composed of a multitude of randomly oriented individual fibrils measuring about 120 Å in diameter (Figure 34.9).[5] The fibrils do not bend or branch but crisscross in all directions. On occasion, amyloid

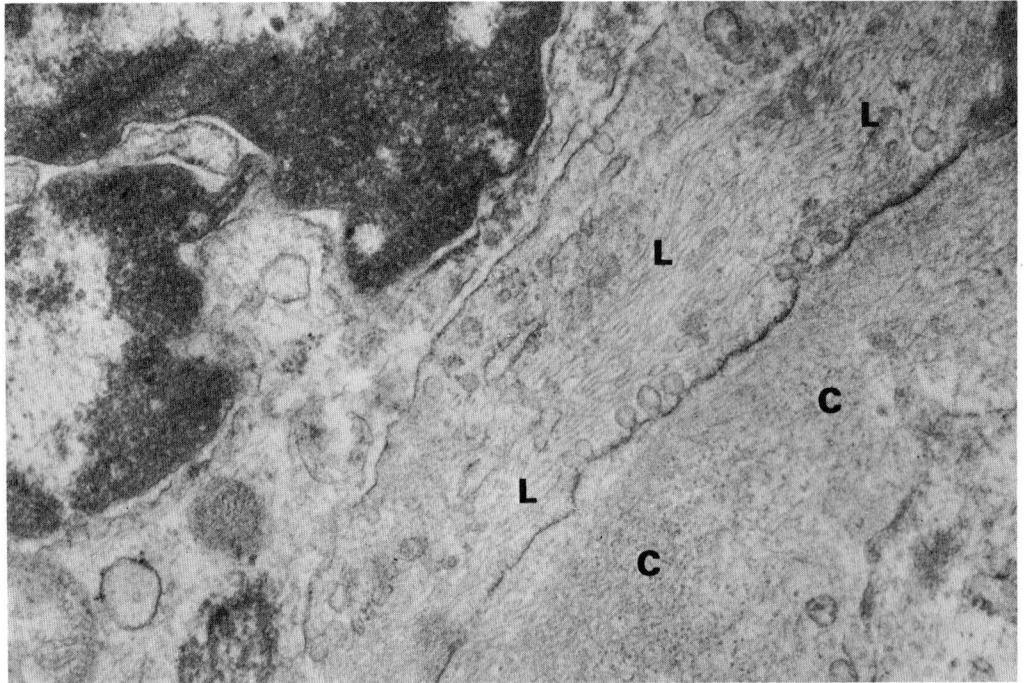

Figure 34.9. Amyloid fibrils (B. Mackay).
The fibrils are seen in longitudinal (L) and cross sections (C). (× 30,000).

fibrils are situated at right angles or in parallel with adjacent cell membranes or bundles of collagen fibers. Intracellular amyloid fibrils have also been observed in reticular cells and plasma cells.[5]

34.5. Hodgkin's disease

The general features, histology, and ultrastructure are described in Chapter 32, in relation to the pathology of lymph nodes. The spleen, more frequently involved than previously suspected, as revealed by the current staging procedures, shows similar light and electron microscopic changes (Figure 34.10).

Figure 34.10. Hodgkin's disease, mixed cellularity type, in spleen.
Reed–Sternberg cell with multilobated, mirror-image nucleus (N) containing marginated heterochromatin (H) and huge, reticulated nucleoli (Nu). The two nuclear lobes are linked by an interlobular bridge (B). Cytoplasm contains a large number of mitochondria and few lysosomal bodies. Activated lymphocytes (L) with large nuclei and nucleoli are also visible. (× 14,000)

488

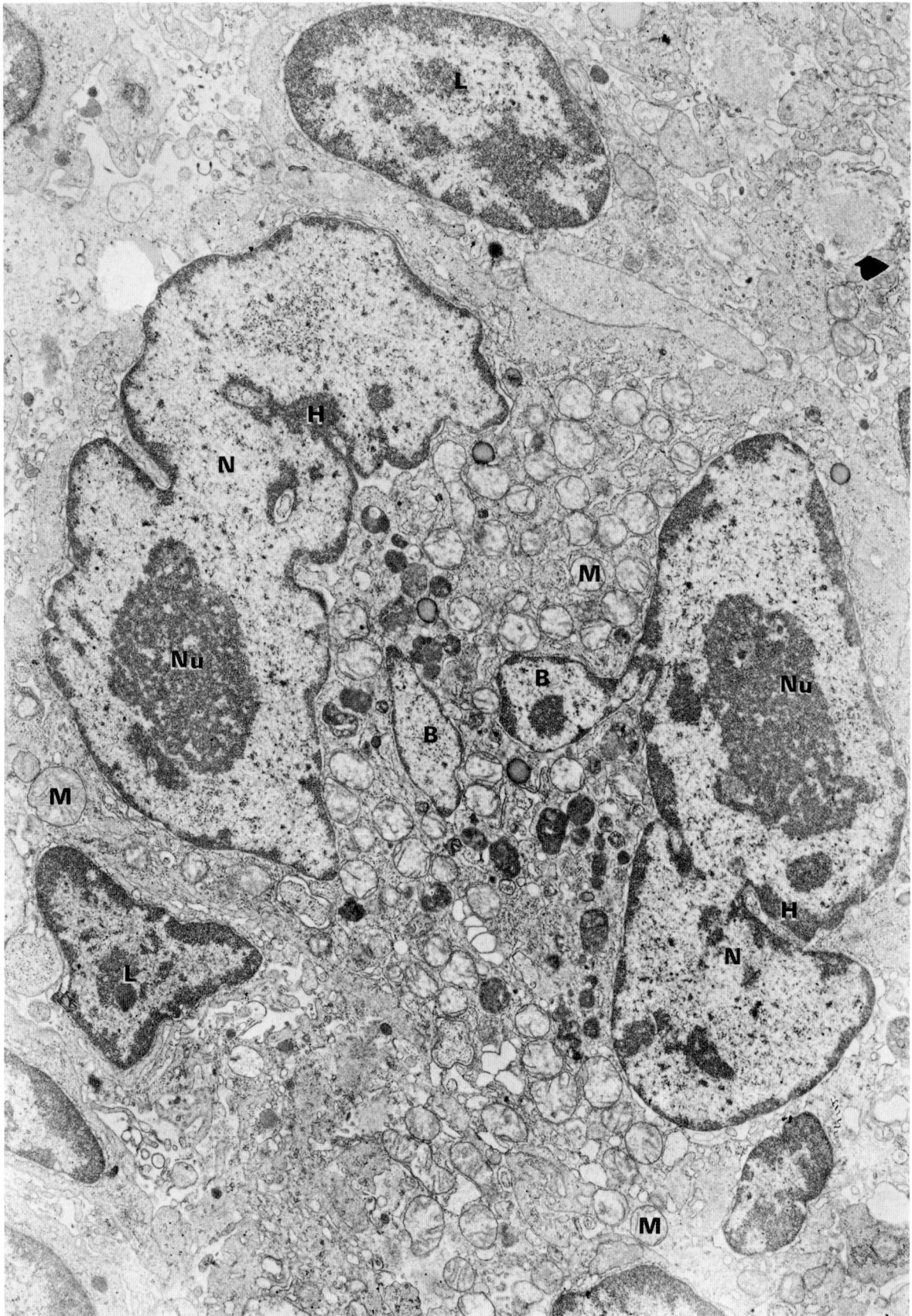

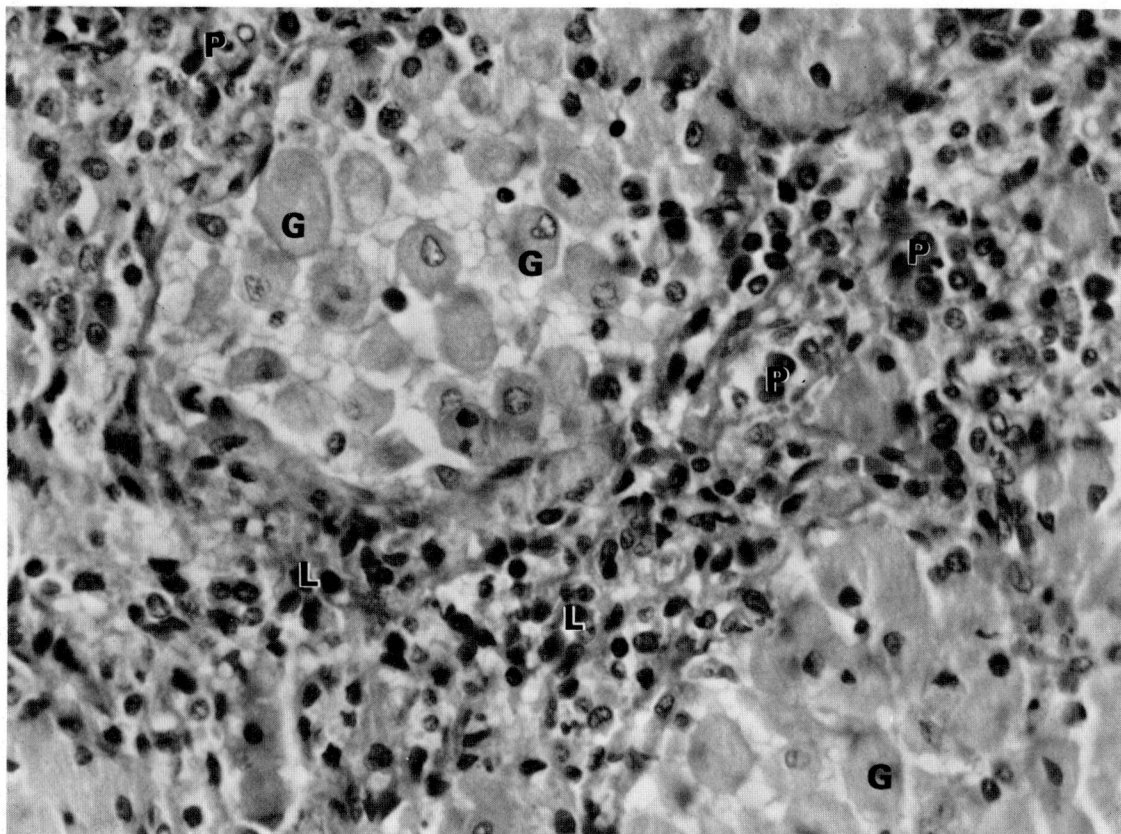

Figure 34.11. Spleen with Gaucher's cells.

(a) Nests of Gaucher's cells (G) showing abundant cytoplasm and small, fine nuclei. Residual lymphocytes (L) and plasma cells (P) separate the aggregated Gaucher's cells. (× 250)

34.6. Gaucher's disease

This is an inborn lysosomal disease due to the genetic deficiency of glucocerebrosidase in the lysosomes of reticuloendothelial macrophages.[8] As a result, glucocerebrosides derived from the degradation of erythrocytes are stored in the cytoplasm of histiocytes in the spleen, liver, bone marrow, and lymph nodes.

Cytological studies reveal large (50–100 μm), irregularly-shaped reticulum cells or histiocytes with abundant palely-stained cytoplasm and eccentric one to four nuclei. The cytoplasm has a typical fibrillar appearance due to parallel unstained striations.

Cytochemistry studies indicate that Gaucher's cells are characterized by the storage of glucocerebrosides. They are PAS positive,[8] iron positive, esterases and acid phosphatase intensely positive,[8] and lactic dehydrogenase strongly positive.[8]

The spleen is massively enlarged with its histologic structure partially or totally obliterated by large aggregates of Gaucher's cells (Figures 34.11(a), (b)).

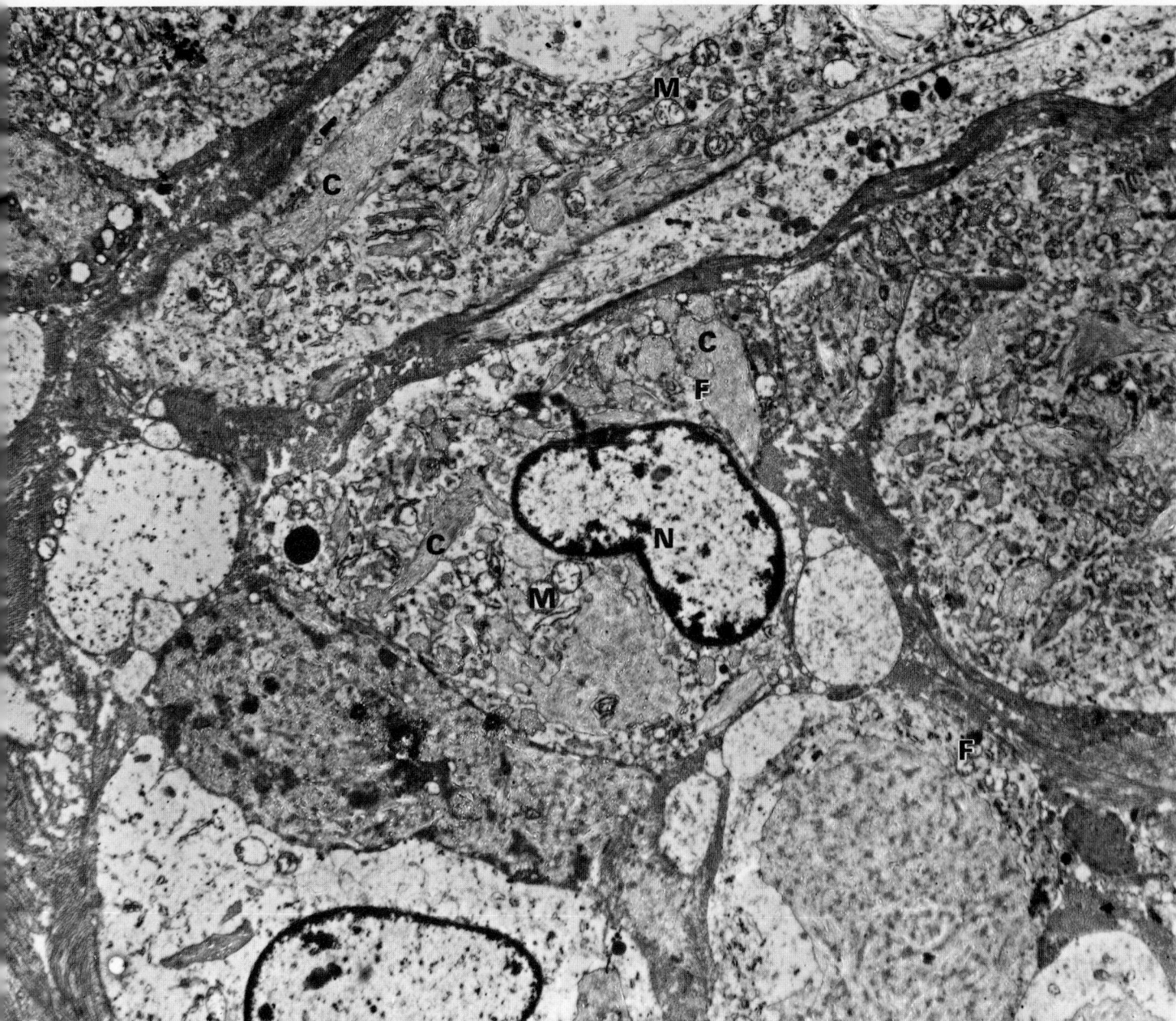

Figure 34.11. Spleen with Gaucher's cells.

(b) Multiple Gaucher's cells. Abundant cytoplasm containing numerous cytoplasmic bodies (C). Note indented nucleus (N), mitochondria (M), and clusters of ferritin (F). ($\times$ 6,750)

EM studies confirm that the cells are large with abundant cytoplasm containing numerous organelles.[24] The nucleus is single or multiple, deeply indented (Figure 34.12(a), (b)), with dense heterochromatin, and a prominent nucleolus (Figure 34.12(b). The cytoplasm includes mitochondria of variable sizes and density of matrix, vesicles containing dense bodies (ferritin), free ferritin particles, Golgi

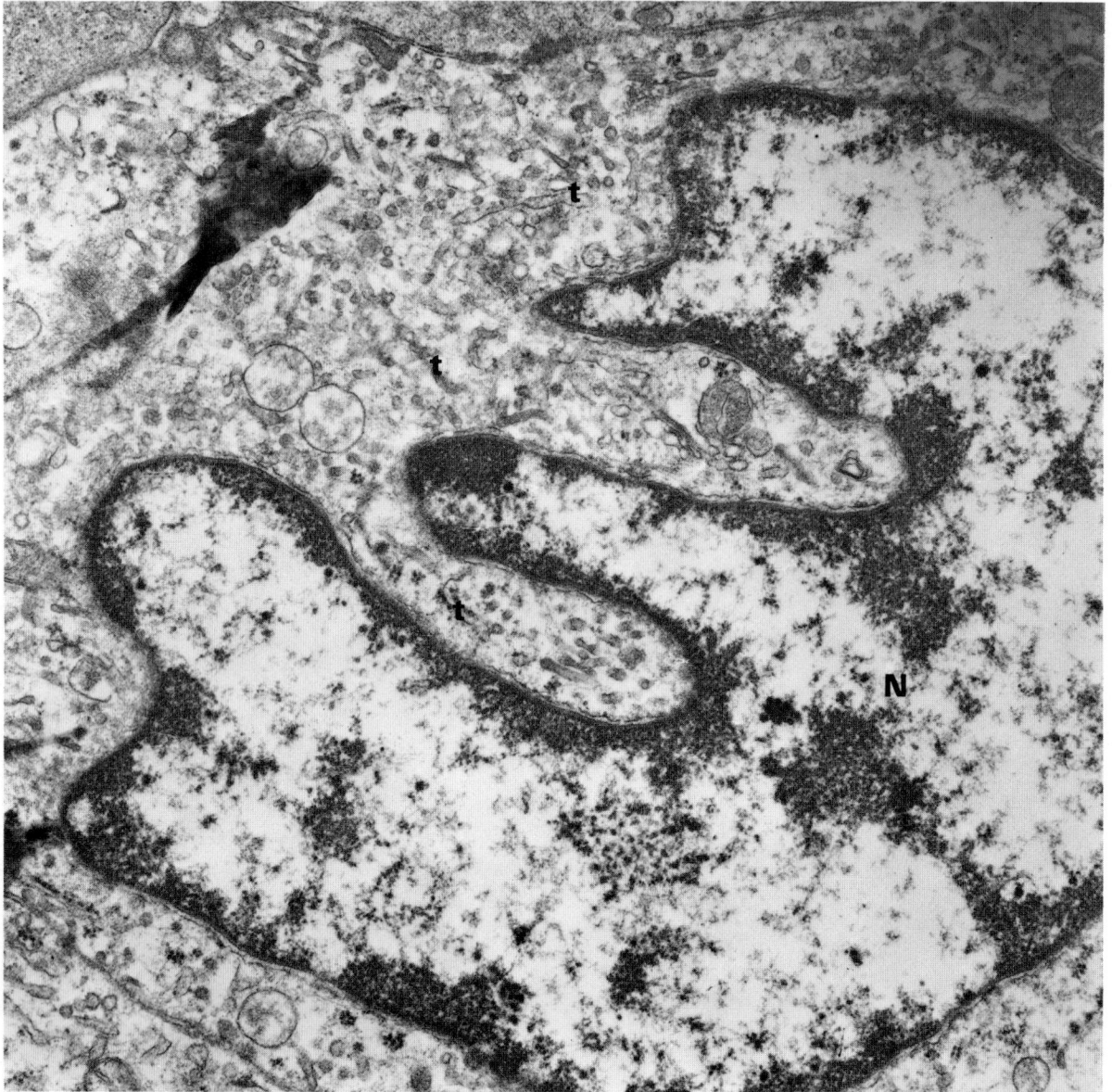

Figure 34.12. Gaucher cell.
(a) The nucleus (N) is deeply indented by protruding cytoplasmic bodies. Longitudinal and cross sections of tubules (t) in cytoplasmic bodies are visible. (× 7,000)

complex in the perinuclear area. The rich, rough endoplasmic reticulum with dilated cisternae is studded by ribosomes. Phagosomes containing erythrocytes or their fragments (Figure 34.12(a), (b)) all also present.[10]

The cytoplasmic bodies, characteristic of Gaucher's cells [1, 8, 9, 12] (Figure 34.12(a), (b), (c)), are numerous, filling the cytoplasm and distorting the nucleus. They are spindle-shaped, with a diameter of 200–400 Å (Figure 34.12(b), (c)),[12] limited by a

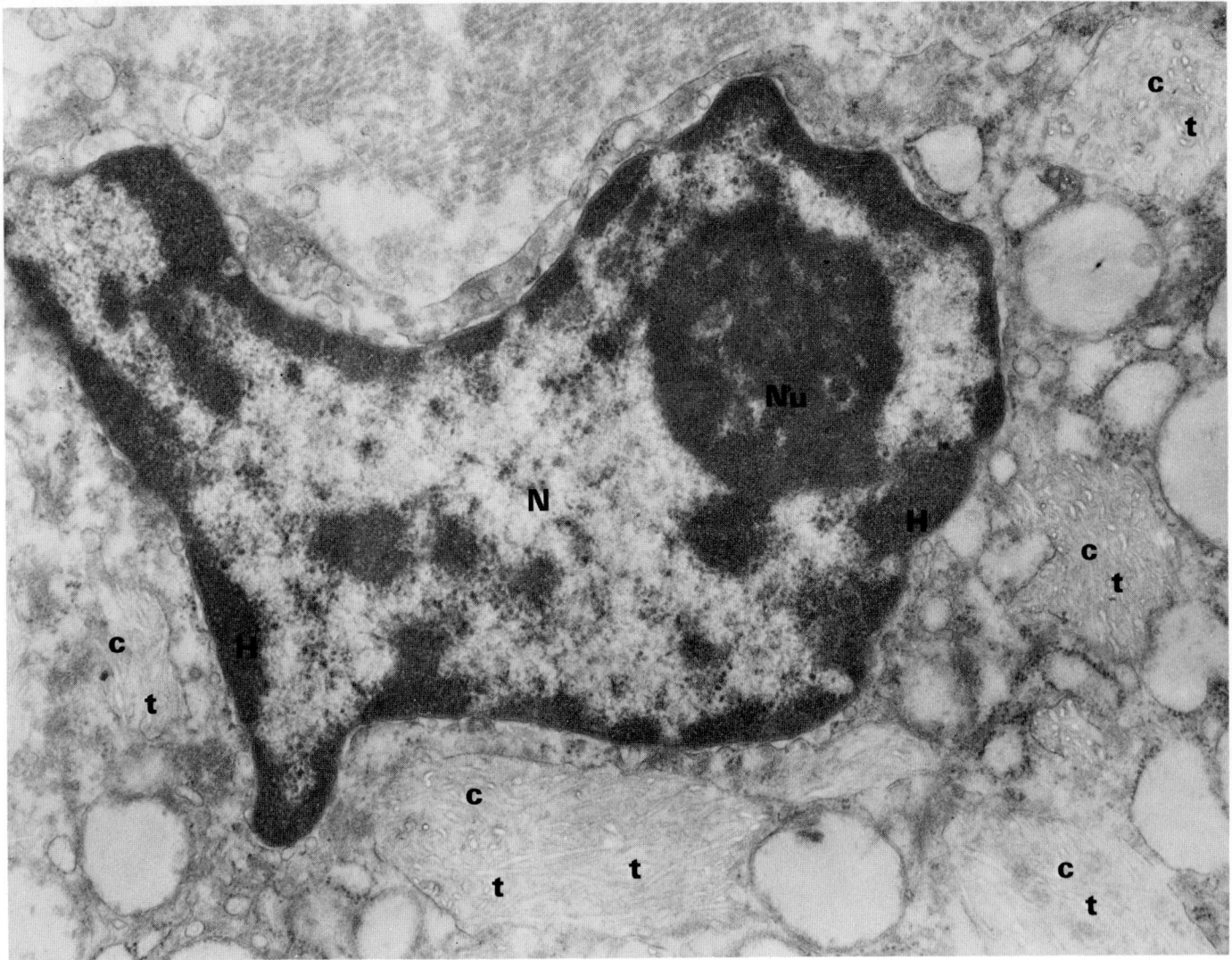

Figure 34.12. Gaucher cell.
(b) The large, irregularly shaped nucleus (N) contains dense heterochromatin (H) and a huge nucleolus (Nu). Cytoplasmic bodies (c) are filled with branching tubules (t). (× 18,000)

thick membrane and composed of numerous, fine branching tubules. These are randomly oriented and separated by an osmiophilic matrix. The tubules represent aggregates of cerebroside molecules[12] while the matrix contains the acid phosphatase.[8] The enzyme is more abundant in the smaller, more compact cytoplasmic bodies.[8]

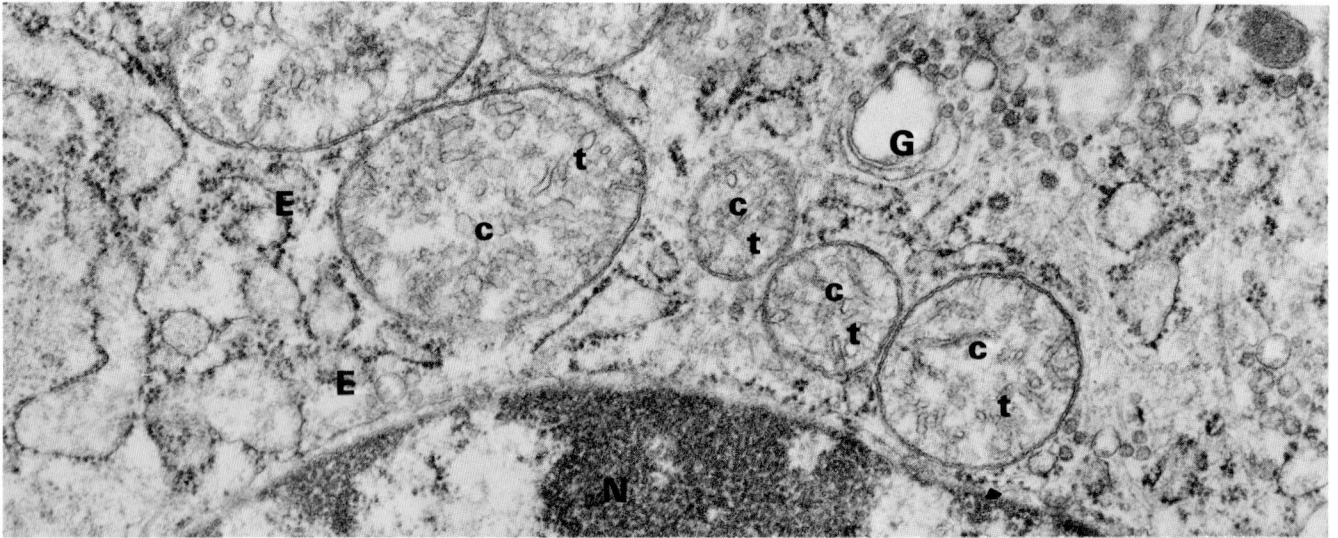

Figure 34.12. Gaucher cell.

(c) Characteristic cytoplasmic bodies (c) with branching tubules (t) are visible. Note also nucleus (N), Golgi body (G), ribosome-studded endoplasmic reticulum (E). (× 18,000)

References to Part Seven

1. Bessis M., *Living Blood Cells and Their Ultrastructure,* Springer-Verlag, New York, 1973.
2. Burke, J. S., Mackay, B., and Rappaport, H., "Hairy cell leukemia (leukemic reticuloendotheliosis). II. Ultrastructure of the spleen," *Cancer,* 37, 2267, 1976.
3. Daniel, M. Th. and Flandrin, G., "Fine structure of abnormal cells in hairy cell (tricho leukocytic) leukemia with special reference to their *in vitro* phagocytic capacity," *Lab. Invest.,* 30, 1, 1974.
4. Deegan, M. J., Cossman, J., Chosney, B. T., and Schnitzer, B., "Hairy cell leukemia – An immunologic and ultrastructural study," *Cancer,* 38, 1952, 1976.
5. Franklin, E. C. and Zucker-Franklin D., "Current concepts of amyloid," *Adv. Immunol.,* 15, 249, 1972.
6. Glenner, G. G., Terry, W., Harada, M., Isersky, C., and Page, D., "Amyloid fibril proteins: proof of homology with immunoglobulin light chains by sequence analysis," *Science,* 171, 1150, 1971.
7. Glick, A. D., "Acute leukemia: electron microscopic diagnosis," *Semin. Oncol.,* 3, 229, 1976.
8. Hibbs, R. G., Ferrans, V. J., Cipriano, P. R., and Tardiff, K. J., "A histochemical and electron microscopic study of Gaucher cells," *Archs Path.,* 89, 137, 1970.
9. Jacob, H. S., in W. J. Williams, E. Beutler, A. J. Erslev, and R. W. Rundles (eds.), *Hypersplenism in Hematology,* McGraw-Hill, New York, 1972, pp. 511–519.
10 Jordan, S. W., "Electron microscopy of Gaucher cell," *Exp. Mol. Pathol.,* 3, 76, 1964.
11. Katayama, I., Li, C. Y., and Yam, L. T., "Ultrastructural characteristics of the hairy cells of leukemic reticuloendotheliosis," *Am. J. Path.* 67, 361, 1972.
12. Lee, R. E., Balcerzak, S. P., and Westerman, M. P., "Gaucher's disease. A morphologic study and measurements of iron metabolism," *Am. J. Med.,* 42, 891, 1967.
13. Lukes, R. J. and Collins, R. D., "Immunologic characterization of human malignant lymphomas," *Cancer,* 34, 1488, 1974.
14. Miale, J. B., "Hemopoietic system," in W. A. D. Anderson (ed.), *Pathology,* vol. 2, C. V. Mosby, St. Louis, 1971, pp. 1297–1387.
15. Molnar, Z. and Rappaport, H., "Fine structure of the red pulp of the spleen in hereditary spherocytosis," *Blood,* 39, 81, 1972.
16. Mori, Y. and Lennert, K., *Electron Microscopic Atlas of Lymph Node Cytology and Pathology,* Springer-Verlag, New York, 1969.

495

17. Nelson, D. A., "Cytomorphological diagnosis of acute leukemias," *Semin. Oncol.,* **3**, 201–208, 1976.

18. Olah, I., Röhlich, P., and Törö, I., *Ultrastructure of Lymphoid Organs,* Lippincott, Philadelphia, 1975.

19. Osserman, E. F. and Pick, A. I., "Amyloidosis," in *Hematology,* W. J. Williams, E. Beutler, A. J. Erslev, and E. W. Rundles (eds.), McGraw-Hill, New York, 1972, pp. 950–984.

20. Rappaport, H., "Tumors of the hematopoietic system," *Atlas of Tumor Pathology,* Armed Forces Institute of Pathology, Washington, 1966.

21. Rhodin, J. A. G., *Histology,* Oxford University Press, London, 1974.

22. Rozenzajn, L. A., Gutman, A., Radnay, J., *et al.,* "A study of the nature of 'hairy' cells with emphasis on enzymatic markers," *Am. J. clin. Path.,* **66**, 432, 1976.

23. Schnitzer, B. and Kass, L., "Hairy cell leukemia," *Am. J. Path.,* **61**, 176, 1974.

24. Tanaka, Y. and Goodman, J. R., *Electron Microscopy of Human Blood Cells,* Harper and Row, New York, 1972.

25. Yam, L. T., Li, C. Y., and Lam, K. W., Tartrate-resistant acid phosphatase isoenzyme in the reticulum cells of leukemic reticuloendotheliosis," *New Engl. J. Med.,* **284**, 357, 1971.

Index

498

500